# Introduction to Nonprofit Organization Accounting

■ **FOURTH EDITION**

# Introduction to Nonprofit Organization Accounting

■ *EMERSON O. HENKE,* D.B.A., C.P.A.

Emeritus J.E. Bush Professor of Accounting and Master Teacher
*Hankamer School of Business*
*Baylor University*

COLLEGE DIVISION South-Western Publishing Co.

Cincinnati Ohio

AK61DA

This text was originally developed and produced by PWS–KENT Publishing Company. South-Western will market and sell this and future editions.


Sponsoring Editor: *Mark Hubble*
Production Editors: *Susan Krikorian, Monique Calello*
Manufacturing Coordinator: *Marcia Locke*
Marketing Manager: *Randy Haubner*
Interior Designer: *Susan Krikorian*
Cover Designer: *Nancy Lindgren*


ISBN: 0–538–82182–5


1  2  3  4  5  6  7  8  AB  95  94  93  92


Printed in the United States of America.

Material from the Uniform CPA Examination Questions for the years 1951–1990, copyrighted by the American Institute of Certified Public Accountants, Inc., is reprinted or adapted with permission.

 *This book is printed on recycled, acid-free paper.*

Library of Congress Cataloging-in-Publication Data

Henke, Emerson O.
    Introduction to nonprofit organization accounting / Emerson O.
Henke.— 4th ed.
        p.    cm.
    Includes bibliographical references and index.
    ISBN 0–538–82182–5
    1. Corporations, Nonprofit—Accounting.  2. Finance, Public–
—Accounting.    I. Title.
HF5686.N56H45
657'.98 —dc20                                      91–36278
                                                        CIP

*To my wife Beatrice and our family*

# Preface

*Introduction to Nonprofit Organization Accounting, Fourth Edition,* is for students interested in the accounting practices of the growing nonprofit segment of our economy. It presumes an accounting background equivalent to that provided in college-level introductory accounting courses. Both the text and the problem and exercise sections help the student to develop a logical framework for understanding and solving the accounting-related problems of nonprofit organizations. The conceptual foundation provided by this text will be especially beneficial to students who anticipate careers in the nonprofit sector. Professional accountants will find this text useful when they establish accounting systems or evaluate the accounting practices for those organizations. Laypersons, too, can benefit because most will at some time need to interpret the financial statements of nonprofit entities.

This book is designed to be used as a text in an undergraduate accounting curriculum or in a Master of Public Administration program. It should also be effective in a first course in nonprofit organization accounting for MBA students.

The book is divided into four parts. Part One, "Conceptual Foundation," helps students understand the need for accounting data and relates profit-oriented accounting practices to the accounting procedures followed in the nonprofit area. The chapters in Part One point out similarities and differences between the two types of organizations as they relate to the generation of useful financial data. All elements of Part One are developed within a conceptual framework that places minimal emphasis on recording techniques. In the process of developing and illustrating that framework, nonprofit enterprises are divided into pure and quasi-nonprofit categories. The accounting practices of those two types of organizations are then related to their respective operating practices.

Part Two, "Governmental Accounting," leads the student from the conceptual base developed in Part One to an understanding of the accounting practices followed by government units. Here, too, the reasons for the accounting practices are emphasized while detailed procedures are minimized. We describe and illustrate the dollar-accountability procedures typically used in accounting for governmental fund resources. In the Appendix to Chapter 9, we show how a "cross-over" worksheet can be used to convert dollar-accountability data to accrual-based financial statements. Chapter 10 describes the accounting practices followed in federal government accounting.

Part Three, "Accounting for Other Nonprofit Organizations," describes and illustrates the accounting practices followed by hospitals, colleges and universities, health and welfare agencies, and churches. Procedures to be followed in implementing the requirements of FASB 93 into college and university accounting systems are included in this edition of the text.

Part Four, "Using Nonprofit Organization Accounting Data," helps students learn to read and interpret effectively the financial reports of nonprofit organizations. In this part, we show how management can use the financial data for planning and controlling operations. We also explain how the financial data are used by creditors and how the constituency can use the data in judging operating effectiveness. Here, too, students are encouraged to use their understanding of the operations of these organizations to critically evaluate present accounting and reporting practices by relating those practices to the ways in which the financial data may be used. Part Four is introduced by a new chapter in this edition entitled, "Cost Accounting Procedures for Nonprofit Organizations."

The appendix entitled "Audits of Nonprofit Organizations" has been updated, and the section on the single audit has been expanded. Other special considerations associated with auditing the financial statements of nonprofit organizations are also explained in the appendix.

Another feature of the Fourth Edition is the inclusion of an ethical issues section in a large number of the chapters. Glossaries of new terms introduced in each chapter are included at the ends of chapters, and a Master Glossary is provided at the end of the book.

Questions and exercises enlarge on the text and demonstrate how the procedures developed in each chapter can be applied to specific situations. The exercises encourage students to think creatively and to develop skills in applying the practices described in the chapters. Problems, intended to be used as outside assignments, provide students with an opportunity to expand their capabilities to properly record, classify, accumulate, and present financial data associated with more complex and comprehensive situations. Four cases have been included in a separate section after Chapter 17 that can be used to promote class discussion relating to the use of financial and other data in managing nonprofit organizations.

I wish to express my appreciation to Dana Buckley and Cathy Talbert for their tireless efforts and excellent work in typing the manuscript. I am also grateful to those who have reviewed past editions of this text: Elizabeth Baer, Miami University, Ohio; Richard Brown, Kent State University; Robert Elton, University of Northern Colorado; Jeffrey Harkins, University of Idaho; and David Ziebart, University of Illinois. Finally, my thanks to those who reviewed this Fourth Edition: Ruth W. Epps, Virginia Commonwealth University; Joseph R. Razek, University of New Orleans; and Walter Robbins, University of Alabama, Tuscaloosa.

*Emerson O. Henke*

# Contents

**PART ONE**  NONPROFIT ORGANIZATION ACCOUNTING SYSTEMS  **1**

■ **CHAPTER 1**  **Accounting and Economic Activities**  **3**

Evolution of Accounting  **4**
  Nonprofit Organizations  **5**
  Categorizing Nonprofit Organizations  **6**
Financial Reporting Needs  **7**
  Constituents and the Special Needs of Nonprofit Reporting  **7**
  The Differences: Profit and Nonprofit Reporting  **9**
  Accounting Cycle for Businesses  **9**
Analysis of Enterprise Unit Universe  **12**
  Operating Statements  **14**
  Periodic Statements Disclosing Resources and Obligations  **15**
  Dollar-Accountability Reporting  **16**
*Summary*  **16**
*Glossary*  **17**
*Suggested Supplementary References*  **18**
*Questions for Class Discussion*  **18**
*Exercises*  **19**
*Problems*  **21**

■ **CHAPTER 2**  **Dollar-Accountability Accounting System**  **24**

Dollar-Accountability Accounting Equation  **25**
  Elements of Dollar-Accountability Accounting Equation  **26**
  Recording Budgetary Data  **26**
Dollar-Accountability Accounting System Illustrated  **28**
  Illustrative Transactions and Statements  **28**
  Closing Entries  **30**

Account Groups—A Necessary Part of a Dollar-
Accountability System     **31**
Dollar-Accountability and Fund Accounting     **33**
Conceptual Foundation Underlying Accounting Systems     **35**
Actions by Professional Organizations     **37**
Pronouncements of Official Bodies     **38**
Underlying Assumptions, Principles, and Conventions     **41**
Bases of Accounting     **46**
Bases of Accounting—Profit Enterprises     **46**
Bases of Accounting—Nonprofit Enterprises     **47**
*Summary*     **48**
*Glossary*     **48**
*Suggested Supplementary References*     **52**
*Questions for Class Discussion*     **52**
*Exercises*     **53**
*Problems*     **56**


PART TWO          GOVERNMENTAL ACCOUNTING     65


■ CHAPTER 3          **Introduction to Governmental Accounting Practices     67**
Primary Objectives of Governmental Accounting     **69**
Users of Governmental Accounting Information     **70**
Evaluating Managerial Performance     **70**
Financial Data for Decision-Making Purposes     **73**
Summary Statement of Principles     **75**
Application of Basic Principles and Conventions     **79**
Types of Accounting Entities     **82**
Dollar-Accountability (Governmental-Type) Funds     **82**
Self-Sustaining (Proprietary-Type) Funds     **83**
Hybrid-Type (Fiduciary-Type) Funds     **84**
Account Groups     **84**
Interpretations and Other Statements     **85**
Interpretations of Selected Elements of Statement 1     **85**
Other NCGA Statements     **88**
The Governmental Accounting Standards Board     **89**
Ethical Considerations Associated with Governmental
Fund Operations     **94**
*Summary*     **95**
*Glossary*     **95**
*Suggested Supplementary References*     **96**
*Questions for Class Discussion*     **97**
*Problems*     **98**

■ **CHAPTER 4**   **Development and Use of Budgetary Data   102**

Budgetary Practices for Proprietary Funds   **103**
  Projecting Resource Inflows   **103**
  Applying Formula Relationships   **104**
  Changes Due to Managerial Decisions   **105**
  Summarizing the Budgetary Data   **105**
Philosophy Underlying General (Operating) Fund Budgets   **108**
Budget Development Cycle   **110**
  General Fund Expenditures Budget   **112**
Using the Budget as a Control Device   **121**
  Budgetary Accounts   **121**
  Implementing Controls over Expenditures   **122**
  End-of-Period Closing Entries   **123**
Program Budgeting   **124**
  Program Budgeting Illustrated   **124**
  Development of Functional Unit Costs   **125**
  Controlling Costs Through Use of Functional Cost Data   **126**
Planning the Acquisitions and Uses of Other Governmental
  Fund Resources   **126**
  Capital Projects Funds   **127**
  Debt-Service Funds   **127**
Development and Use of Cost Data   **128**
Ethical Considerations Associated with the Budgetary Process   **129**
*Summary*   **129**
*Glossary*   **130**
*Suggested Supplementary References*   **132**
*Questions for Class Discussion*   **133**
*Exercises*   **134**
*Problems*   **137**

■ **CHAPTER 5**   **General Fund and Special Revenue Fund
Accounting Procedures—I   144**

Operational Characteristics   **145**
General Fund Accounts   **147**
  Account Subclassifications   **149**
Typical Activities Requiring Accounting Recognition   **152**
Transactions Involving Other Funds and Account Groups   **154**
Special Problems Associated with General Fund
  Accounting Procedures   **154**
  Practical Deviations   **156**
  Capital Items   **156**
  Supplies Inventories   **157**
  Short-Term Borrowing   **158**

Encumbrances at End of Period    **159**
Probable Losses in the Collection of Taxes Receivable    **160**
Ethical Considerations Associated with Use of Data Produced by Use of the
Modified Accrual Basis of Accounting    **161**
*Summary*    **161**
*Glossary*    **162**
*Suggested Supplementary References*    **164**
*Questions for Class Discussion*    **164**
*Exercises*    **165**
*Problems*    **167**

■ CHAPTER 6     **General Fund and Special Revenue Fund Accounting Procedures—II    172**

General Fund Accounting Procedures Illustrated    **173**
General Fund Transactions    **173**
Journal Entries to Record Transactions in Control Accounts    **175**
Posting the Transactions    **180**
Closing Entries    **181**
Subsidiary Ledgers    **183**
Financial Statements for the General Fund    **183**
Objectives of Financial Statements    **183**
Statement of Revenues, Expenditures and Transfers, and Changes in
Fund Balance    **183**
Interpreting the Operating Statements    **184**
The Balance Sheet    **186**
Interim Reporting for the General Fund    **186**
Reciprocal and Complementing Entries    **188**
The Transactions Worksheet    **188**
Ethical Considerations Associated with Interfund Transfers of
Spendable Resources    **190**
*Summary*    **190**
*Glossary*    **191**
*Questions for Class Discussion*    **192**
*Exercises*    **192**
*Problems*    **194**

■ CHAPTER 7     **Accounting for Other Governmental Funds    213**

Accounting for General Capital Improvements    **214**
Assumed Transactions    **215**
Journalizing the Transactions    **215**
Closing Entries    **217**
Posting the Transactions    **218**
Financial Statements    **219**

Accounting for the Servicing of General Long-Term Debt    **220**
  Establishment of a Debt-Service Fund    **220**
  Investment of Debt-Service Fund Assets    **221**
  Illustrative Transactions Journalized    **221**
  Closing Entries Journalized    **223**
  Posting the Transactions    **223**
  Financial Statements    **224**
  Disposal of Debt-Service Fund Resources    **224**
  Use of Fiscal Agent to Service Debt    **225**
Accounting for Capital Improvements Financed by
  Special Assessments    **226**
  Assumed Transactions    **226**
  Journalizing, Financing, and Construction Transactions    **227**
  Closing Entries    **229**
  Posting the Transactions    **229**
  Financial Statements    **230**
  Journalizing the Debt-Service–Related Transactions    **230**
  Closing Entry    **232**
  Posting the Transactions    **232**
  Financial Statements    **233**
Reciprocal and Complementing Entries    **233**
Ethical Considerations Associated with Awarding a Capital
  Projects Contract    **233**
*Summary*    **234**
*Glossary*    **235**
*Questions for Class Discussion*    **237**
*Exercises*    **237**
*Problems*    **239**


■  **CHAPTER 8**      **Accounting for Other Funds and Account Groups**    **252**
Accounting for Proprietary Funds    **253**
  Specialized Accounting Procedures    **253**
  Internal-Service-Fund Accounting Procedures    **253**
  Enterprise-Fund Accounting Procedures    **256**
Fiduciary Funds    **265**
Account Groups    **270**
  General Fixed-Asset Account Group    **270**
  General Long-Term Debt Account Group    **274**
  NCGA Statements Relating to Account Group Data    **276**
  Accounting and Financial Reporting for Lease Agreements    **279**
Interfund Relationships    **280**
Appendix: Worksheet Summary    **282**
Ethical Considerations Associated with Establishing Billing Prices for
  Enterprise Fund Services    **292**

*Summary*    **292**
*Glossary*    **292**
*Questions for Class Discussion*    **294**
*Exercises*    **295**
*Problems*    **297**

■ CHAPTER 9    **Annual Financial Reports    335**

Reporting Provisions of NCGA Statement 1    **336**
Illustrated Financial Statements for Model City    **347**
Ethical Considerations Associated with Publicizing a City's
    Financial Statements    **351**
Summary    **352**
Appendix    **353**
    Explanation of Entries on Consolidated Balance Sheet Working
        Paper (Exhibit 9–5)    **360**
    Explanation of Entries for Statement of Financial Performance Working
        Paper (Exhibit 9–6)    **362**
*Glossary*    **363**
*Suggested Supplementary References*    **364**
*Questions for Class Discussion*    **365**
*Exercises*    **366**
*Problems*    **368**

■ CHAPTER 10    **Federal Government Accounting    382**

Historical Background    **383**
Statutorily Assigned Responsibilities    **385**
    General Accounting Office    **385**
    Treasury Department    **387**
    Office Management and Budget    **387**
    Congressional Budget Office    **388**
    General Services Administration    **388**
Terminology    **388**
Fund Structure    **390**
    Resources Derived from General Taxation and Revenue Powers and from
        Business Operations    **390**
    Resources Held by the Government in the Capacity of Custodian
        or Trustee    **391**
Basis of Accounting    **391**
Federal Agency Accounting Illustrated    **392**
    Authorization Actions    **392**
    Realization of Revenues    **393**
    Expenditure Transactions    **393**
    Interfund Transactions    **393**
    Recognition of Encumbrances    **393**

Elimination of Encumbrances (Obligations)    **394**
Other Actions and Transactions    **394**
Closing Entries    **395**
Ethical Considerations Associated with Deficit Reduction Actions    **398**
*Summary*    **399**
*Glossary*    **400**
*Suggested Supplementary References*    **401**
*Questions for Class Discussion*    **402**
*Exercises*    **402**
*Problems*    **404**


**PART THREE**        **ACCOUNTING FOR OTHER NONPROFIT
ORGANIZATIONS    407**


■ **CHAPTER 11**    **Accounting for Hospitals    409**
Accounting Practices and the Operating Environment    **410**
Operating Environment    **411**
Basis of Accounting    **413**
Cost-Allocation Procedures    **414**
Budgetary Practices for Hospitals    **415**
Asset Valuation Practices    **417**
Malpractice Litigation    **418**
Fund Entities Used in Hospital Accounting Systems    **418**
Unrestricted Funds    **419**
Restricted Funds    **422**
Accounting Procedures Peculiar to Hospital Operations    **426**
Hospital Financial Statements    **427**
Ethical Considerations Associated with Hospital Accounting Procedures    **427**
*Summary*    **427**
*Glossary*    **429**
*Suggested Supplementary References*    **429**
*Questions for Class Discussion*    **430**
*Exercises*    **430**
*Problems*    **433**


■ **CHAPTER 12**    **Accounting for Colleges and Universities    450**
Operating Characteristics and Accounting Practices    **451**
College and University Statement of Accounting Principles    **452**
Observations    **457**
Legal Provisions    **457**
Budgetary Practices    **458**
Basis of Accounting    **458**

Accounting for Depreciation        **459**
Auxiliary Enterprises        **459**
Summary of Changes Suggested by AICPA Audit Guide        **460**
Fund Entities        **461**
Current Funds        **461**
Loan Funds        **462**
Endowment Funds        **462**
Annuity and Life Income Funds        **464**
Plant Funds        **465**
Agency Funds        **466**
Financial Statements        **466**
Typical Transactions Described and Recorded        **474**
Realization of Current Fund Revenues        **474**
Recognition of Current Fund Expenditures        **475**
Realization of Other Resource Inflows        **481**
Recognition of Nonoperating Expenditures        **482**
Transfers Between Funds        **482**
Auxiliary Activity Transactions        **483**
Provisions of FASB 93        **484**
Ethical Considerations Associated with College and University
Accounting Practices        **488**
*Summary*        **488**
*Glossary*        **494**
*Suggested Supplementary References*        **495**
*Questions for Class Discussion*        **495**
*Exercises*        **496**
*Problems*        **499**

■ **CHAPTER 13**        **Accounting for Health and Welfare Agencies, Churches, and Other Similar Organizations        514**

Accounting for Health and Welfare Organizations        **515**
Evolution of Accounting Practices        **516**
Financial Statements        **521**
Typical Transactions Illustrated        **524**
Accounting for Churches        **528**
Other Developments        **534**
Ethical Considerations Associated with Health and Welfare Organization
Cost-Allocation        **535**
*Summary*        **536**
*Glossary*        **536**
*Suggested Supplementary References*        **537**
*Questions for Class Discussion*        **537**
*Exercises*        **538**
*Problems*        **539**

**PART FOUR**  **USING NONPROFIT ORGANIZATION ACCOUNTING DATA 557**

■ **CHAPTER 14**   **Cost-Accounting Procedures for Nonprofit Organizations 559**

Basic Types of Aggregate Costs   **562**
Accumulation and Allocation of Costs   **562**
Cost-Accumulation and -Allocation Procedures for Hospitals   **564**
Cost-Accumulation and -Allocation Procedures for Colleges
   and Universities   **568**
Ethical Considerations Associated with College and University
   Cost-Allocation Procedures   **572**
*Summary*   **572**
*Glossary*   **573**
*Questions for Class Discussion*   **574**
*Exercises*   **574**
*Problems*   **576**

■ **CHAPTER 15**   **Internal Use of the Accounting System Data   580**

Effective Budgeting Procedures   **581**
   Planning-Programming-Budgeting Procedures   **582**
   Zero-Base Review   **582**
   Cost–Volume Considerations   **583**
   Program Budgets and Functional Unit Costs   **584**
Measuring Input–Output Relationships   **584**
Financial Performance Reports   **585**
   Responsibility Accounting System   **585**
   Interim Performance Reports   **586**
   Motivating Cost Center Managers   **587**
   Effective Controllership   **588**
   Functions of the Internal Auditor   **591**
   Use of the Accrual Basis of Accounting   **591**
   Overhead and Service-Implementation Costs   **592**
Coping with Politics and Bureaucracy   **592**
The Effectively Managed Nonprofit Organization   **593**
Ethical Considerations Associated with the Political Process   **594**
*Summary*   **594**
*Glossary*   **595**
*Suggested Supplementary References*   **596**
*Questions for Class Discussion*   **597**
*Exercises*   **598**
*Problems*   **599**

■ **CHAPTER 16**    **Use of Accounting Data by Externally Interested Parties**    **605**

Evaluating the Fiduciary Responsibility of Internal Managers    **606**
Analysis and Interpretation of Financial Data    **607**
    Basic Concerns    **607**
    Analysis of Profit Enterprise Financial Statements    **608**
    Analysis of Nonprofit Organization Statements    **610**
Application of Analytical Techniques    **613**
    Analysis of Governmental Financial Statements    **613**
    Analyzing Financial Statements of Colleges and Universities    **615**
    Analysis of Hospital Financial Statements    **619**
    Analysis of Financial Statements for Health and Welfare Agencies    **621**
    Analysis of Financial Statements for Churches    **623**
    Actions in Response to Financial Statements Analysis    **623**
Ethical Considerations Associated with the Operations of a Voluntary
    Health and Welfare Organization    **624**
*Summary*    **625**
*Glossary*    **625**
*Suggested Supplementary References*    **625**
*Questions for Class Discussion*    **626**
*Exercises*    **627**
*Problems*    **631**

■ **CHAPTER 17**    **Operational-Accountability Reporting for Nonprofit Organizations**    **637**

Operational Accountability Defined    **638**
Operational Accountability and Financial Analysis    **639**
Analysis of Model City Operating Data    **640**
    Analysis of Expenditure-Based Data    **641**
    Analysis of Expense-Based Data    **641**
    Interpretations of the Analytical Data    **642**
The Case for Operational-Accountability Reporting    **643**
    Implications of the Basis of Accounting Used    **644**
    The Need for Objectivity and Consistency    **645**
    Full-Cost Data and the Service Story    **646**
    Effective Use of Community Resources    **646**
    Operational-Accountability Reporting and Fund Accounting    **647**
    The Depreciation Question    **648**
Ethical Considerations Associated with Reporting on
    Operational Efficiency    **654**
*Summary*    **655**
*Glossary*    **655**
*Suggested Supplementary References*    **655**
*Questions for Class Discussion*    **656**
*Problems*    **657**

■ **Thought Projection Cases for Chapters 14, 15, 16, and 17    661**

    Case 1: Slippery Handle Mental Health Center, Treacherous
       Waters, USA    **661**

        Introduction    **661**

        Outpatient Services    **662**

        Statistics    **662**

        Fees, Discounts, and Uncollectibles    **664**

    Case 2: Break-Even Community Mental Health Center    **667**

    Case 3: Seek-a-Client (SAC) Community Mental Health Center    **668**

    Case 4: Albatross CMHC    **671**


■ **APPENDIX**    **Audits of Nonprofit Organizations    677**

    Generally Accepted Accounting Practices    **680**

        Appropriation Control    **680**

        Fund Accounting Practices    **681**

        Bases of Accounting    **681**

        Special Accounts    **682**

        Official Literature    **683**

    Internal Controls    **683**

    Special Audit Considerations    **685**

        The Evidence-Gathering Process    **686**

        Reporting Requirements    **689**

    The Single Audit    **690**

    *Summary*    **694**

    *Suggested Supplementary References*    **695**

    *Questions for Class Discussion*    **696**

    *Exercises*    **697**

    *Problems*    **698**


    **Master Glossary**    **704**

    **Bibliography**    **724**

    **Index**    **734**

# Introduction to Nonprofit Organization Accounting

# PART ONE

# Nonprofit Organization Accounting Systems

■ *CHAPTER 1*
**Accounting and Economic Activities**

■ *CHAPTER 2*
**Dollar-Accountability Accounting System**

# Accounting and Economic Activities

## ■ Learning Objectives

When you have finished your study of this chapter, you should

1. Understand how accounting has evolved as the language used to record and report the financial results of economic activities.
2. Know the meanings of the terms *enterprise unit* and *nonprofit organization.*
3. Be aware of the primary operating objectives of both profit and nonprofit organizations and understand how financial statements should logically relate to those objectives.
4. Know what constitutes an ideal operating statement for a nonprofit organization and why such a statement cannot be presented within the constraints of generally accepted accounting principles.
5. Recognize that some enterprise units do not have all the operating characteristics associated with either *pure* profit or *pure* nonprofit entities and therefore can be more appropriately described as quasi-profit or quasi-nonprofit entities.
6. Be able to reason from the operating characteristics of both quasi- and pure nonprofit entities the data that logically should be included in their operating statements.

$A$*ccounting is the language used to describe the results of economic activities.* Those activities include the conversion of resources into consumable goods and services. Accounting, therefore, is concerned with measuring and disclosing the results of those resource conversion activities. Effective management of such activities requires the establishment of operating objectives and periodic measurement of the extent to which those objectives have been achieved. We frequently describe that management technique as MBO, "Management by Objective." *To be most useful, accounting disclosures should be expressed in terms that show the extent to which the objectives of the activities have been achieved.* When we drive an automobile toward a given destination, we measure the results of our driving efforts by reading the odometer. Similarly, accountants are concerned with disclosing the extent to which the resource conversion efforts have succeeded in achieving an entity's operating objectives. Accountants are also concerned with showing the resources available to the resource conversion entity and the obligations that the entity has incurred. This allows the users of the financial statements to measure objective achievement data against efforts represented by net resources committed to the activity.

Just as we need knowledge of the English language to understand the message of a book written in that language, so we need a knowledge of accounting to understand reports relating to the financial activities of any organization engaged in converting economic resources into goods and/or services. *This book explains the nature and use of that language in recording and reporting the financial activities of nonprofit organizations.*

Historical background helps in understanding any discipline. Therefore, we begin by *describing how the language of accounting has evolved* in response to our need for financial information. Then, we *briefly examine the financial reporting needs of both profit and nonprofit entities*. In the last section of the chapter, *we analyze the enterprise unit universe* for the purpose of showing relationships between the operating objectives of various types of enterprise units and what should be presented in their operating statements.

## ◼ Evolution of Accounting

The importance of any language increases as the need for using it in communicating with others increases. Primitive people had no need for a language of accounting because each family unit was largely self-sufficient. There was little reason to maintain records of resources and obligations and resource conversion activities. *However, as people began to accumulate productive resources in the form of weapons and tools, they began to realize the advantages of specializing in different types of productive activities and trading with others for those goods they no longer produced.* With specialization and trading, productive efforts became more efficient, allowing people to satisfy more of their material wants with less working time. As this pattern of economic activities developed, buyers and sellers of both consumable and productive resources found it necessary to maintain records of their trading positions with each other. At that point, the need for accounting records first arose.

The constant growth of population and the concurrent increase in the demand for goods and services were accompanied by the need to improve productive capabilities. The tendency to specialize showed that people could be more productive if they pooled their resources into larger resource conversion units. Therefore, the next logical step in satisfying the increased demand was the creation of *enterprise units*. This involved bringing together the productive resources and talents of two or more people into one coordinated resource conversion unit. This step in economic development introduced the new complications of joint ownership and management. Those complications in turn necessitated more sophisticated accounting data.

These early enterprise units were the forerunners of present-day profit and non-profit organizations. Such units can be engaged in either producing goods or providing services. However, they all have one thing in common: *they bring together productive resources for the purpose of carrying out resource conversion activities.* Early enterprise units were primarily profit motivated and as they became more common were characterized as business enterprises. As with businesses today, their primary operating objective was to realize a profit from their resource conversion activities for their owners.

## Nonprofit Organizations

As the complexities of society and government increased, another type of enterprise unit emerged that was not profit motivated. The communal Christian Church of Late Antiquity and the state-supported university at Alexandria are early examples of such private and public enterprises, and the instances and variety of such organizations have proliferated as we have approached modern times.

The operating objective of such nonprofit organizations is to *provide socially desirable services without the intention of realizing a profit. Such organizations have no ownership shares that can be sold or traded by individuals and any excess of revenues over expenses or expenditures is used to enlarge the service capability of the organization. They are financed, at least partially, by taxes and/or contributions based on some measure of ability to pay, and some or all of their services are distributed on the basis of need rather than effective demand for them.* Within this definition, we can characterize governmental entities, colleges and universities, most hospitals, health and welfare agencies, churches, and foundations as nonprofit enterprise units.

The reasons for the development of nonprofit organizations are many and complex. It is not possible within the constraints of this chapter to identify and describe all of them. However, in the United States they have come into existence primarily to provide services that society, or some segment thereof, feels are needed but cannot be effectively provided by profit entities. Such services, for example, as the maintenance of order within the community and military protection against exploitation by external groups, can best be provided by some sort of community supported entity. Thus, we see the development of governmental enterprise units, charged by the community with converting resources realized from taxes into specific services for all members of the community.

Democratically controlled governmental entities are today, in fact, among the most important nonprofit organizations, and the services supplied by them far exceed the maintenance of public order and protection against the threats of external entities. As people improved their productivity and their standard of living, they were able to give more attention to the reasons for their existence and to the improvement of the society in which they lived. They came to recognize that the basic needs of less fortunate members of society should be provided even when those members do not have the productive capability to satisfy those needs through their own efforts. In response to this developing *sense of social consciousness,* an ever-increasing sphere of responsibility has been delegated by the people to the government to provide such services for the good of society.

The expansion of governmental activities has been accompanied by the development of private, voluntarily supported nonprofit enterprises. Again let us reiterate that governmental and other nonprofit organizations are similar to business enterprises in that they convert resources into goods and/or services. They are, however, significantly different in that their operating objective is to provide goods or services without concern for the profits that could be realized from their resource conversion activities.

## Categorizing Nonprofit Organizations

*Public nonprofit organizations* are created by formal community action for the purpose of providing community services. They have the sanction of law allowing them to levy taxes as a source of support and typically include such entities as federal, state, and municipal governing units. In a democratic society, these organizations are managed by elected representatives who are expected to act in the best interests of the people in the community. Such officials are therefore *operationally accountable* to their constituency. As our level of social consciousness has grown, the nature and volume of services provided by these organizations has expanded significantly. As a result, the accounting and reporting practices of these entities have become increasingly important to all parties associated with them.

*Private nonprofit enterprise units* are created by groups of people who are interested in seeing particular services, such as education or health care, provided on a nonprofit basis within the community. They are generally chartered by a governmental unit but have no power to levy taxes as a source of support. They depend on voluntary contributions for some or all of their resources. In many instances, user fees are charged to cover part of their operating costs. The volume of operations of these organizations has also expanded significantly over recent years. This expansion, in turn, has increased the importance of their accounting and reporting practices to the groups interested in their operations.

Nonprofit organizations can be categorized in a number of ways. We have noted that some (governmental entities) are involuntarily supported by taxes while others are voluntarily supported by contributions. They can also be divided into categories based on the nature or extent of support from their constituencies. For example, some organizations such as hospitals and private colleges are *often expected to be self-sustaining, insofar as normal operations are concerned,* after receiving an initial capital contribution. In another group are those organizations that *require full operating support indefinitely.* This group includes governmental units, most health and welfare agencies, churches, and some other organizations. These distinctions are developed further as we relate these operational characteristics to financial reporting needs later in this chapter.

As nonprofit enterprise units have increased, both in size and variety, the sphere of bookkeeping and accounting responsibilities associated with them has also increased and become more clearly defined. In addition to *disclosing the resources and obligations of such units,* we have come to recognize that the accounting *records should also provide operational accountability information showing the extent to which the operating objectives of the enterprise units have been achieved.* The accounting profession has, in recent years, placed much emphasis on the importance of operational-accountability reporting. In the case of a business enterprise, this requires disclosure of the extent to which the profit objective has been realized. For nonprofit organizations, the financial reports should disclose, insofar as is possible, the extent to which the service objectives of the enterprise have been achieved. As we shall explain later, this difference in reporting objectives is the basic conceptual justification for the differences in accounting procedures followed in the profit and nonprofit areas.

# ■ Financial Reporting Needs

Accounting reports provide a visual representation of what has happened to an enterprise as a result of its economic activities. We may think of them as windows through which interested parties may see the nature and values of the resources and obligations of an enterprise and the ways in which resources and obligations have changed during a reporting period. One can see the physical structures of an enterprise unit in the form of buildings, equipment, etc. *It is impossible, however, to understand fully the results of the economic activities of an enterprise without accounting data.*

The effective managers of enterprise units normally follow a *plan-execute-evaluate-plan cycle* (PEEP) as they make and implement decisions relating to entity operations. Accounting data constitute an essential element that should be used in the effective implementation of this cycle. Managers need to know the extent to which the objectives of the enterprise have been achieved, along with the nature and volume of net resources available to an enterprise unit, in order to evaluate past operations and to plan its future activities.

In the case of businesses, where the primary objective is to earn a net income, the operating (net resource inflow–outflow) reports must be organized to show the extent to which that objective has been achieved. The managers of nonprofit enterprises, on the other hand, should logically have an operating statement that tells them the extent to which the entity's particular service objectives have been achieved. The managers of both types of organizations of course are concerned with the nature and volume of net resources available to the enterprise unit. The accounting system therefore should be organized to accumulate and present those data to managers in a format that is most useful for decision-making purposes.

## Constituents and the Special Needs of Nonprofit Reporting

An enterprise unit is controlled by persons having a participative interest in its activities. Such persons are characterized as the *constituents* of an entity. They include the stockholders of profit entities, and those contributing resources to nonprofit organizations. Other interested groups include internal managers, creditors, potential constituents, oversight bodies including regulatory and accreditation agencies, and to some extent the users of the goods and/or services of the organization. The ways in which accounting data are used by these groups are explained more fully in Part Four of this text. At this point, however, it is important to observe that these groups use accounting data primarily for two purposes: *to evaluate managerial performance and to make various operating and financial commitment decisions.* The accounting system for any enterprise unit should be organized to satisfy the specific financial information needs of those groups.

Stockholders exercise control over corporate business entities. The number of votes available to each stockholder is determined by the number of ownership shares held. The operations of a nonprofit enterprise are also controlled by some segment of its constituency. The citizens, in the case of governmental units, and the contributors, in the case of voluntarily supported organizations, exercise control through representative boards. *In a nonprofit enterprise, however, each constituent has one vote regardless of the amount contributed to the entity.* It is important to note that, to the extent that the voice in the decision-making process fails to be related to amounts of resources contributed, the voting rights normally associated with property ownership in the free enterprise system are violated. The specific ways in which some nonprofit organization resources may be used, however, are also subject to the externally imposed constraints of constituents. This creates a need for accounting records that show the nature and value of those resources along with the rights of management in their utilization.

The constituents, within regulatory imposed constraints, control the activities of nonprofit entities as they make various support/nonsupport decisions relating to the enterprise unit. In evaluating managerial performance, they must judge the effectiveness and efficiency with which management has handled the organization's resource conversion activities. This means that they will want information showing the extent to which the objectives of the enterprise have been achieved (effectiveness), along with the extent to which the quantity of goods or services provided has been maximized in relationship to resources consumed in providing them (efficiency).

If effectiveness and efficiency are to be appropriately evaluated, the users of the financial statement data must also have information relating to the resource–obligation position of the enterprise unit. Resources include the assets (things of value) available to the entity for the purpose of paying its obligations and carrying out its service activities. Obligations reflect the amounts of resources owed to others. The difference between these two items can be thought of as the net resources available to the entity. Obviously, an entity with a greater volume of net resources available to it should provide, other things being equal, a larger volume of services than an enterprise unit with less resources available to it.

Creditors have, as will be shown in Part Four, financial information interests extending beyond those described earlier. However, for the purposes of our current analysis, we can conclude that the accounting system for a nonprofit enterprise should provide financial information relating to (1) operational accountability and (2) the resource–obligation position of the enterprise unit. In addition, because these organizations generally operate under externally imposed constraints regarding the ways in which resources may be used, it is also important to have financial statements disclose the extent to which those constraints have been met.

As we observed earlier in this chapter, the resources of a business enterprise unit are brought together for the purpose of earning a profit, which is defined as the excess of resource inflows over outflows as a result of operations. If resource outflows exceed inflows, the business is said to have suffered a loss from operations—a risk that the owners assume as part of their contribution to the production effort. *Because nonprofit enterprises have no profit objective, their financial reports should not emphasize profits earned or losses incurred.* But, even though the salaried manager of a nonprofit enterprise has no owners seeking a profit to answer to, he or she does assume the responsibility of marshalling and using entity resources efficiently and effectively and therefore still needs resource inflow–outflow data to be used in the decision-making process.

## The Differences: Profit and Nonprofit Reporting

Since students using this text will have a business-oriented accounting background, we shall begin our discussion of financial reporting by recalling how the accounting systems of those profit-motivated enterprise units meet their financial reporting needs. After describing business entity financial statements, we shall briefly explain how the statements of nonprofit organizations logically should differ from those for profit entities.

## Accounting Cycle for Businesses

You will recall from your introductory accounting courses that the accounting cycle for profit entities proceeds from the journalizing of transactions to the preparation of financial statements as shown in Figure 1–1.

This cycle reflects the use of the accrual basis of accounting that requires recognition of the following types of nontransaction changes in resources and obligations:

1. amortization of limited life assets
2. accrued expenses
3. accrued revenues

**FIGURE 1–1.** The Accounting Cycle for Profit Entities

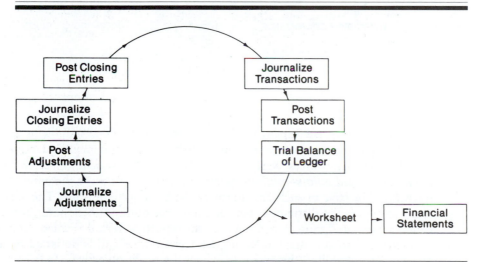

4.  prepaid expenses

5.  prepaid or unearned revenues

6.  provision for uncollectible accounts.

These are called *adjustments* and are recorded in the formal accounting records and in the worksheet from which financial statements are prepared.

**Business Enterprise Financial Statements.**   The cycle shown in Figure 1–1 is designed to produce the following financial statements:

1.  a *balance sheet* reflecting the resources and obligations of the enterprise

2.  an *income statement* that shows the inflows and outflows of resources from operations, measured on the basis of the points where resources were earned and used, respectively

3.  a *statement of cash flows,* designed to reflect the inflows and outflows of cash during the reporting period

4.  a *statement of retained earnings or changes in owners' equity,* designed to show what has caused the retained earnings balance to change from that shown at the beginning of the period to the amount shown at the end of the period.

Examples of these statements are shown in Exhibits 1–1, 1–2, and 1–3.

The balance sheet for Model Enterprise as of 12/31/19A is assumed to have reflected the following balances:

| Assets | | Liabilities | |
|---|---|---|---|
| Cash | $ 30,000 | Accounts payable | $ 40,000 |
| Accounts receivable | 65,000 | Taxes payable | 20,000 |
| Inventory | 60,000 | Bonds payable | 60,000 |
| Equipment | 70,000 | Capital stock | 100,000 |
| Accumulated depreciation | (25,000) | Retained earnings | 5,000 |
| Land | 25,000 | | |
| Total | $225,000 | Total | $225,000 |

**Nonprofit Enterprise Reporting Procedures.**   In financial statements for businesses, the principal inflow–outflow statement (the income statement) places emphasis on showing when resources were earned and used. We sometimes refer to this as an *expense-oriented inflow–outflow statement,* designed to show the extent to which the operating objective of such an enterprise has been accomplished. The accounting system focuses on the distinction between resource outflows benefiting future periods— called *assets*—and those benefiting only the reporting period—called *expenses*. We say that such a system is maintained on the *accrual basis* and is designed to reflect operational accountability (the extent to which the profit objective has been achieved). In

**EXHIBIT 1–1.** Model Enterprise Balance Sheet 12/31/19B

| Assets | | | Liabilities and Stockholders' Equity | | |
|---|---|---|---|---|---|
| Current assets | | | Current liabilities | | |
| Cash | | $ 50,000 | Accounts payable | | $ 60,000 |
| Accounts receivable | | 75,000 | Taxes payable | | 25,000 |
| Inventory | | 90,000 | | | |
| Total current assets | | $215,000 | Total current liabilities | | $ 85,000 |
| | | | | | |
| Noncurrent assets | | | Long-term liabilities | | |
| Equipment | $100,000 | | Bonds payable | | 100,000 |
| Less allowance for | | | Total liabilities | | $185,000 |
| depreciation | 30,000 | 70,000 | | | |
| Land | | 25,000 | Stockholders' equity | | |
| | | | Capital stock | | $100,000 |
| | | | Retained earnings | | 25,000 |
| | | | Total stockholders' equity | | $125,000 |
| | | | Total liabilities and | | |
| Total assets | | $310,000 | stockholders' equity | | $310,000 |

**EXHIBIT 1–2.** Model Enterprise Income Statement—for Year Ending 12/31/19B

| | | |
|---|---|---|
| Revenues from sales | | $500,000 |
| Cost of goods sold | | 350,000 |
| Gross margin | | $150,000 |
| Operating expenses | | |
| Selling expenses | $45,000 | |
| General expenses | 40,000 | 85,000 |
| Net operating income | | $ 65,000 |
| Tax expense | | 25,000 |
| Net income | | $ 40,000 |

reporting revenues and expenses, the emphasis is on an appropriate determination of the "bottom line" reflecting the net income or net loss from operations over a period of time.

Nonprofit enterprises, concerned with achieving their service objectives within the constraints of resources available to them, logically also require inflow–outflow statements that disclose the extent to which the organization's service objectives have been met. Ideally, such statements should show as revenues the values of services rendered. The expenses of providing the services should then be matched against those revenues to tell the "service story" of the organization. Both revenues and expenses logically should be accrual based to provide statement users with an objective measurement of periodic resource inflows and outflows.

**EXHIBIT 1–3.** Model Enterprises Statement of Cash Flows—for Year Ending 12/31/19B

| | | |
|---|---:|---:|
| Cash provided by operations | | |
|   Net income | | $ 40,000 |
|   Add depreciation | $ 5,000 | |
|     Increase in accounts payable | 20,000 | |
|     Increase in taxes payable | 5,000 | 30,000 |
| | | $ 70,000 |
| | | |
|   Less increase in accounts receivable | 10,000 | |
|   Increase in inventory | 30,000 | 40,000 |
| | | $ 30,000 |
| | | |
| Cash provided by financing activities | | |
|   Sale of bonds | $ 40,000 | |
|   Payment of dividends | (20,000) | 20,000 |
| Cash provided by investing activities | | |
|   Purchase of equipment | | (30,000) |
| | | |
| Increase in cash | | $ 20,000 |
| | | |
| Cash balance 12/31/19B | | $ 50,000 |
| Cash balance 12/31/19A | | 30,000 |
| Increase in cash balance | | $ 20,000 |

Because the ideal operating statement described above cannot be prepared within the constraints of generally accepted accounting principles (most specifically the principle of objectivity), the accounting profession has had to be satisfied with a less directly relevant statement. We can, however, reason our way to the next best alternative by dividing the enterprise unit universe into four categories as shown in Figure 1–2 and analyzing the operational characteristics of each of those types of entities. In doing that, we begin with the previously stated objective that the operating statement should be one that best shows the extent to which the operating objectives of an entity have been achieved.

## ◼ Analysis of Enterprise Unit Universe

When we seek to classify the elements of any universe into two significantly different subdivisions, we often find that many of the elements have some characteristics normally attributed to both categories. Such is the case when we seek to classify all enterprise units into profit and nonprofit categories. Since we have concluded that the organization and content of an entity's financial statements should be directly related to its operating objectives, it is important that we examine the elements of the enterprise unit universe more closely.

**FIGURE 1–2.** Elements of Enterprise Unit Universe

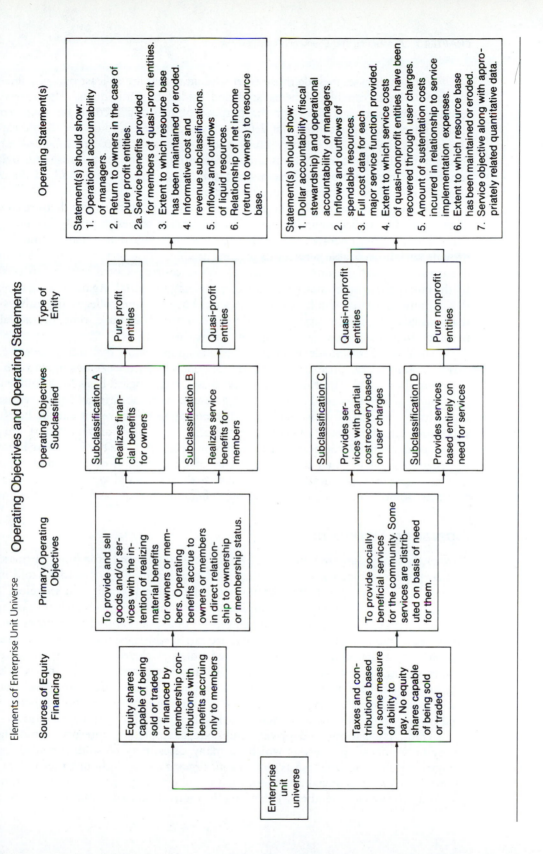

Profit enterprises include those enterprise units that are at least partially financed by equity shares capable of being sold and traded by individuals. They carry out resource conversion activities for the purpose of realizing income for those equity shareholders. Having accepted that definition, we may then ask how we should classify enterprise units such as country clubs and cooperatives that are financed largely through membership contributions and operate primarily for the purpose of providing services for those members. These organizations have many, but not all, of the operating characteristics of business (profit) entities.

Nonprofit enterprises, on the other hand, have no equity shares that are capable of being sold or traded by individuals. Their financing comes primarily from taxes or contributions. They operate for the purpose of receiving those funds and using them to provide socially desirable services to persons needing those services. They do not seek to earn a profit, and if profits are earned, the resources represented by them are retained by the enterprise unit to enlarge its service-providing potential. Again, having accepted this definition, we may ask how enterprises like hospitals and colleges and universities, that charge fees for their services, should be classified. They have some, but not all, of the operating characteristics of nonprofit enterprise units.

The observations made in the preceding paragraphs show that some types of enterprise units are neither pure profit nor nonprofit entities when evaluated against the definitions of those units. Therefore, as we seek to establish a logical basis for identifying the data that should be presented in the operating statements of the different types of enterprise units, based on relating those data to entity operating objectives, it can be helpful to subdivide each of the major categories of enterprise units (profit and nonprofit) into pure and quasi elements. We demonstrate that division in Figure 1–2. The term *pure* is used to describe those entities that meet all elements of the definition of profit and nonprofit entities. The term *quasi* means almost, or similar to, and is used to describe those entities that meet some, but not all, elements of the definitions of profit and nonprofit entities.

## Operating Statements

*Pure profit enterprises* are best exemplified by individual proprietorships, partnerships, and corporations that convert resources into goods and/or services to be sold in the marketplace. They operate for the purpose of earning a profit and therefore their operating statements should be organized to show the extent to which that objective has been achieved. In addition, many enterprise units, operating substantially as nonprofit organizations, have subentities that are expected to sustain themselves or realize a profit. For example, a municipally owned utility is clearly a marketplace-oriented subentity of the municipality. A municipal garage originated to maintain city vehicles is generally expected to operate so that it will sustain itself after an initial grant of equity capital from the city. Profit-oriented accounting procedures should therefore be used in accounting for the activities of such subentities of governmental units.

Trade associations and private clubs are examples of enterprise units having equity or membership interests which, in many cases, may be sold or traded. In our analysis, we characterize these as *quasi-profit organizations*. Although they do not seek to provide a direct financial return for their members, they operate for the purpose of providing services for members. Therefore, the motivation to commit resources to these enterprises is primarily the anticipated member-service benefits. As a result, we can conclude that their operating statements should logically be similar to those of profit enterprises with some modifications, as shown in Figure 1–2.

Many enterprises, generally classified as nonprofit organizations, have some of the operating characteristics of profit-motivated enterprise units. In Figure 1–2, we have characterized these as *quasi-nonprofit entities*. Colleges and universities and hospitals, for example, realize a considerable portion of their resource inflows from user charges that are directly related to services provided. They generally operate with the intention of recovering a specified portion or all of the costs of services rendered either from the service recipients or from third parties acting for those recipients. However, since they have no equity interests capable of being sold or traded and since they also receive resources in the form of contributions and/or grants not directly related to the services provided, they are generally classified as nonprofit organizations. Logically, however, the operating statements of these organizations should be organized to some extent along the lines of those normally presented for profit entities. For example, *the costs of providing user services should logically be matched against revenues received from users*. At the same time, however, those statements should also be organized to emphasize the costs of providing different types of services, rather than the "bottom line" net income or net loss. They should also disclose the extent of contributor support coming in the form of nonoperating inflows.

The fourth category of organization, characterized as *pure nonprofit enterprises*, includes such entities as governmental units, health and welfare agencies, and foundations that realize resource inflows exclusively on the basis of some measure of ability and/or willingness to pay and provide services on the basis of need. Operating statements for these entities should logically tell the *service story* by showing the sources from which resource inflows have been realized and by classifying resource outflows by functions. These statements should also disclose the amount of resources used to sustain the entity (sustentation costs). Such organizations also operate in a fiduciary capacity with specifically established constraints on the ways in which resources may be used. Therefore, at least one statement reflecting fiscal stewardship (dollar accountability) must be included in their financial statements.

## Periodic Statements Disclosing Resources and Obligations

Persons interested in the operations of any enterprise will also be concerned with its resource base. While they will especially want to know the amounts of assets and obligations, they will also be concerned with the *nature of those resources from the point of view of liquidity and the discretionary rights of management in their use*. The typical balance sheet of a profit enterprise, and to some extent the balance sheets of segments of some nonprofit enterprises, provides that information by classifying assets into current and noncurrent categories and by appropriately labeling the individual assets. The nature of creditors' claims is also disclosed by individual labeling and by current/noncurrent classifications. Parenthetical or footnote disclosures are used to indicate the assets that have been pledged against creditor claims. Equity claims of businesses are typically divided to show the amounts of originally contributed capital and the amounts realized from operations.

Balance sheets for pure nonprofit enterprises use meaningful labels for the various assets and liabilities, but do not generally carry current/noncurrent classifications. Resources available for discretionary use by managers are generally current. However, many of the resources of these entities can be used only for specified purposes. Therefore the emphasis in these statements is on distinguishing between *restricted* and *unrestricted resources*. Restricted resources may be used only for the purposes set out in the agreement under which they were realized. Long-term fixed assets, available for operations, are shown in a separate fund or account group. These limitations on the ways in which assets may be used also cause us to follow the fund accounting practices, described later in the text, for these organizations. Equity balances in nonprofit organization balance sheets are also typically divided into *reserved* and *unreserved* segments. The reserved portion represents the amount of assets contractually committed to be used for specified purposes.

## Dollar-Accountability Reporting

In actual practice, some nonprofit organizations (primarily governmental entities and colleges and universities) have settled for accounting systems that produce only dollar- rather than both dollar- and operational-accountability data as proposed by the preceding discussion. Such a system produces an operating statement that reflects spendable resource inflows and outflows rather than accrual-based revenues and expenses. It concentrates on disclosing where dollars have come from and how they were used; therefore, we have characterized it as a *dollar-accountability–oriented accounting system*. Since such a system is unique to the nonprofit area, we give further attention to the procedures associated with it in Chapter 2.

## ◼ Summary

We began this chapter by observing that accounting is the language used to record and report the financial results of economic activities. The evolution of the need for such data was then related to the specialization of production activities and trading which also fostered the use of enterprise units and the need for financial accountability among those units.

Next, we observed that an entity's accounting system should be designed to disclose its asset–obligation position at the end of each reporting period and the extent to which its primary operating objective was achieved during the reporting period. That was judged to require showing the extent to which the profit objective had been achieved for profit entities and disclosure of the service story for nonprofit entities.

The statement that would best reflect the service story for a nonprofit organization would include an imputed value for services rendered matched against the expenses of rendering those services. However, the revenue part of such a statement would not be objectively reliable enough to meet the requirements of generally accepted accounting principles. Therefore, nonprofit organizations have had to settle for something less than an ideal operating statement.

In the last part of the chapter, logically derived requirements for the next best type operating statement for both quasi-nonprofit and pure nonprofit organizations were developed. We then pointed out that some entities have settled for something less than those logically derived type statements by using dollar-accountability–oriented accounting systems.

# ◼ Glossary

**Accounting System.**   The total structure of records and procedures that discover, record, classify, summarize, and report information on the financial position and results of operations of any entity including a government or any of its funds, fund types, balanced account groups, or organizational components.

**Constituency.**   All those who directly support an organization; in the case of a nonprofit enterprise, this group includes those contributing time or resources without receiving equivalent tangible benefits in exchange for those contributions.

**Dollar-Accountability Reporting.**   A system of reporting that shows the flows of spendable resources into and out of the reporting entity. The emphasis in this type of reporting is on the sources from which dollars were realized and the ways in which those dollars were used.

**Enterprise Units.**   A pool of productive resources and talents contributed by two or more parties for the purpose of carrying out coordinated resource conversion activities.

**Nonprofit Entity.**   An organization created for the purpose of providing socially desirable services without the intention of realizing a profit and having no ownership shares that can be sold or traded. Any excess of revenues over expenses or expenditures realized by these organizations is used to enlarge the service capability of the organization. These organizations must be financed at least partially by taxes and/or contributions based on some measure of ability to pay, and some or all of the services must be distributed on the basis of need rather than effective demand for them.

**Operating Statement.**   The basic financial statement that discloses the financial results of operations of an entity during an accounting period in conformity with GAAP. Under NCGA Statement 1, operating statements and statements of changes in fund equity are combined into "all-inclusive" operating statement formats.

**Operational Accountability.**   The state of being held accountable for the efficiency and effectiveness of an entity's resource conversion activities when measured against its operating objectives.

**Operational-Accountability Reporting.**   A system of financial reporting that discloses the extent to which an organization has efficiently and effectively met its operating objectives.

**Pure Nonprofit Entity.**   An enterprise unit that provides socially beneficial services to the community based entirely on the need for services. Revenues for such an organization are realized from taxes and contributions based on some measure of ability to pay. Also, the organization has no equity shares that are capable of being sold or traded.

**Pure Profit Entity.**   An enterprise unit organized for the purpose of realizing financial benefits for its owners.

**Quasi-Nonprofit Entities.**   A nonprofit organization that provides services with partial cost recovery based on user charges.

**Quasi-Profit Entity.**   An enterprise unit that is financed by member contributions and provides service benefits for its members. A country club is an example of a quasi-profit entity.

**Statement of Revenues and Expenses.**   The basic financial statement which is the proprietary fund, nonexpendable trust fund, and pension trust fund GAAP operating statement. It presents increases (revenues) and decreases (expenses) in an entity's net total assets resulting from operations.

## ▪ Suggested Supplementary References

Anthony, Robert N. "What Nonbusiness Organization Accounting Information Do Users Need?" *Governmental Finance* (May 1978).

Gustafson, George A. "Depreciation in Governmental Accounting." *Federal Accountant,* 21 (1972): 47–59.

Gustafson, George A. "Needed: A Conceptual Framework for Federal Government Accounting." *Federal Accountant,* 20 (1971): 40–51.

## ▪ Questions for Class Discussion

**Q1-1.**   Trace the evolution of the need for accounting data.

**Q1-2.**   Relate accounting to the communication cycle.

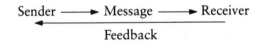

**Q1-3.**   Explain how accounting can be characterized as a language.

**Q1-4.**   Explain what is meant by the term *resource conversion activities.*

**Q1-5.**   How is the need for accounting data related to product specialization and trading?

**Q1-6.**   What is meant by the term *enterprise unit?* What purpose do they serve?

**Q1-7.**   Define a nonprofit enterprise unit.

**Q1-8.**   a.   What do profit enterprises have in common with governmental and other nonprofit organizations?

   b.   How are they different?

**Q1-9.**   Why do we need financial statements for nonprofit organizations? What messages should such statements convey?

**Q1-10.**   What types of financial statements should be prepared for profit enterprises? How are they different from those that should be prepared for nonprofit enterprises?

**Q1-11.**   How do accounting data fit into the plan-execute-evaluate-plan cycle?

Q1-12.   a.   What is meant by the term *operational accountability?*
         b.   Does this concept of reporting relate to both profit-seeking businesses and non-profit organizations? Explain.

Q1-13.   Why is it more difficult to measure management's operational efficiency in the non-profit area than in the profit area? Explain.

Q1-14.   How does the accounting data needed for managing a university differ from that required for managing a governmental entity? Explain fully.

Q1-15.   Contrast operational accountability with dollar accountability. Are the terms mutually exclusive? Explain.

Q1-16.   How do constituents express their approval or disapproval of the operating record of an organization?

Q1-17.   Differentiate between pure nonprofit and quasi-nonprofit enterprise units. How does that difference affect the financial data logically required for each of them?

Q1-18.   Describe the characteristics that distinguish a pure nonprofit entity from a quasi-nonprofit entity.


# ■ Exercises

E1-1.   A pure nonprofit organization that maintains its accounting records on the accrual basis shows the following end-of-the-period trial balance.

|  | Debit | Credit |
|---|---|---|
| Cash | $ 3,000 | |
| Revenues receivable | 4,000 | |
| Fixed assets | 40,000 | |
| Allowance for depreciation of fixed assets | | $ 15,000 |
| Vouchers payable | | 6,000 |
| Fund balance | | 20,000 |
| Revenues from constituency | | 65,000 |
| Revenues from restricted fund | | 1,000 |
| Expenses incurred in rendering service Number 1 | 9,000 | |
| Expenses incurred in rendering service Number 2 | 20,000 | |
| Expenses incurred in rendering service Number 3 | 25,000 | |
| Depreciation expense (to be allocated on the basis of relative direct expenses) | 5,400 | |
| Assets restricted to use as investments | 10,000 | |
| Accrued revenues | 2,000 | |
| Prepaid expenses | 800 | |
| Accrued expenses | | 1,000 |
| Restricted fund balance | | 10,000 |
| Prepaid revenues | | 1,200 |
| Total | $119,200 | $119,200 |

**Required:**
Prepare an operating statement, organized as suggested in Figure 1−2, for this pure nonprofit organization.

**E1-2.** A quasi-nonprofit organization shows the following end-of-the-period trial balance. User charges are expected to cover 80 percent of operating expenses.

| | Debit | Credit |
|---|---|---|
| Cash | $ 4,000 | |
| User fees receivable | 6,000 | |
| Fixed assets | 100,000 | |
| Allowance for depreciation of fixed assets | | $ 40,000 |
| Vouchers payable | | 8,000 |
| Revenue from user fees | | 90,000 |
| Direct expenses for service Number 1 | 18,000 | |
| Direct expenses for service Number 2 | 30,000 | |
| Direct expenses for service Number 3 | 62,000 | |
| Assets restricted to use as investments | 20,000 | |
| Depreciation expense to be allocated equally to services 2 and 3 | 6,000 | |
| Revenue from contributions | | 26,000 |
| Revenue from investments | | 2,000 |
| Contributions receivable, net of allowances for uncollectible amounts | 3,000 | |
| Fund balance | | 62,000 |
| Prepaid expenses | 1,000 | |
| Restricted fund balance | | 20,000 |
| Accrued expenses | | 2,000 |
| Total | $250,000 | $250,000 |

**Required:**
Prepare an operating statement, organized as suggested in Figure 1−2, for this quasi-nonprofit organization.

**E1-3.** Refer to Exercise E1-1. Assume now that the organization is a private club operated for the benefit of its members. As a result of that fact, the revenues from the constituency should be labeled "revenues from dues," and the total of the two fund balance accounts are distributed as follows:

| | |
|---|---|
| Member investments ($200 each) | $28,000 |
| Accumulated excess of dues revenue over expenses | $ 2,000 |

**Required:**
Prepare an operating statement, organized as suggested in Figure 1−2, for the club from the trial balance data. You are to treat the club as a quasi-profit organization.

**E1-4.** Refer to Exercise E1-2. Assume that the organization is a profit enterprise with the same trial balance data except for the following items:

1.  Fees for services rendered in the amount of $116,000 replaces the first two revenue accounts (revenue from user fees and revenues from contributions).
2.  The total of the two fund balance accounts is replaced by capital stock $100 par in the amount of $70,000 and retained earnings amounting to $12,000.

**Required:**
Prepare an operating statement, organized as suggested in Figure 1–2, for the profit enterprise.

E1-5.   Prepare balance sheets for each of the four enterprise units described in Exercises E1-1 through E1-4.

# ■ Problems

P1-1.   A quasi-nonprofit organization has been created and begins operations by receiving a contribution for the purchase of long-term assets in the amount of $500,000. The organization is to provide services in exchange for user fees that are expected to cover about 60 percent of the costs of providing the services. The following transactions occur during the first year of operations:
1.  A building appropriately furnished for the services to be provided is purchased at a cost of $300,000. The cost is allocated $200,000 to building, $100,000 to equipment. The building is expected to have a twenty-year life. The equipment should be depreciated over a ten-year period.
2.  Of the initial contribution, $150,000 is invested in securities.
3.  Additional contributions for operating purposes are received in the amount of $100,000. Fund-raising expenses in the amount of $20,000 are incurred in carrying out the solicitation effort.
4.  Operating expenses as follows are paid in cash:
    salaries, $70,000
    utilities, $5,000
    other expenses, $80,000
5.  Vouchers payable from fund-raising expenses in the amount of $8,000 are paid.
6.  User fees amounting to $98,000 are collected for services rendered.
7.  Interest in the amount of $10,000 is received from funds invested in securities.

**Required:**
A.   Record the preceding transactions, including the initial contribution and any implied adjustments in T-accounts, using an accrual (expense-oriented) accounting system.
B.   Prepare financial statements from the T-accounts developed in requirement A above.

P1-2.   The Ridgeview Country Club came into existence at the beginning of the current year when 1,000 persons agreed to purchase membership equity interests at $1,500 per person. It was agreed that monthly dues in the amount of $60 per member would be assessed for use of the club. Food, beverage, and entertainment services were to be paid for by the recipients of such services. During the first year the following transactions occurred:
1.  A club house was constructed at a cost of $600,000.
2.  A golf course was built at a cost of $500,000.

3. All members paid their dues over the entire year.
4. In addition to dues, members provided revenues as follows:
     beverages, $50,000
     food services, $460,000
     other services, $100,000
5. Operating expenses paid in cash were as follows:
     salaries, $1,050,000
     beverage costs, $100,000
     food costs, $250,000
     other expenses, $200,000

**Required:**
A. Record the transactions and depreciation adjustment for the first year of operation in T-accounts. You may assume that the building and equipment and golf course should be depreciated over a period of twenty-five years. You may assume a full year of operations for the purpose of calculating depreciation.
B. Prepare financial statements for the country club showing the results of operations for the year and the financial position of the club at the end of the year.
C. Comment on the operations of the club.

P1-3.  In 1950, a group of civic-minded merchants in Albury City organized the "Committee of 100" for the purpose of establishing the Community Sports Club, a nonprofit sports organization for local youth. Each of the Committee's 100 members contributed $1,000 toward the Club's capital, and in turn received a participation certificate. In addition, each participant agreed to pay dues of $200 a year for the Club's operations. All dues have been collected in full by the end of each fiscal year ending March 31. Members who have discontinued their participation have been replaced by an equal number of new members through transfer of the participation certificates from the former members to the new ones. Following is the Club's trial balance at April 1, 19X2:

| | Debit | Credit |
|---|---|---|
| Cash | $ 9,000 | |
| Investments (at market, equal to cost) | 58,000 | |
| Inventories | 5,000 | |
| Land | 10,000 | |
| Building | 164,000 | |
| Accumulated depreciation—building | | $130,000 |
| Furniture and equipment | 54,000 | |
| Accumulated depreciation—furniture and equipment | | 46,000 |
| Accounts payable | | 12,000 |
| Participation certificates (100 at $1,000 each) | | 100,000 |
| Cumulative excess of revenue over expenses | | 12,000 |
| | $300,000 | $300,000 |

Transactions for the year ended March 31, 19X3, were as follows:

| | | |
|---|---|---:|
| (1) | Collections from participants for dues | $20,000 |
| (2) | Snack bar and soda fountain sales | 28,000 |
| (3) | Interest and dividends received | 6,000 |
| (4) | Additions to voucher register: | |
| | House expenses | 17,000 |
| | Snack bar and soda fountain | 26,000 |
| | General and administrative | 11,000 |
| (5) | Vouchers paid | 55,000 |
| (6) | Assessments for capital improvements not yet incurred (assessed on March 20, 19X3; none collected by March 31, 19X3; deemed 100% collectible during year ending March 31, 19X4) | 10,000 |
| (7) | Unrestricted bequest received | 5,000 |

*Adjustment data:*

| | | |
|---|---|---:|
| (1) | Investments are valued at market, which amounted to $65,000 at March 31, 19X3. There were no investment transactions during the year. | |
| (2) | Depreciation for the year: | |
| | Building | $ 4,000 |
| | Furniture and equipment | 8,000 |
| (3) | Allocation of depreciation: | |
| | House expenses | 9,000 |
| | Snack bar and soda fountain | 2,000 |
| | General and administrative | 1,000 |
| (4) | Actual physical inventory at March 31, 19X3, was $1,000, and pertains to the snack bar and soda fountain. | |

**Required:**

On a functional basis,

A.  Record the transactions and adjustments in journal entry form for the year ended March 31, 19X3. Omit explanations.

B.  Prepare the appropriate all-inclusive activity statement for the year ended March 31, 19X3.

**—AICPA Adapted**

# CHAPTER 2

# Dollar-Accountability Accounting System

## ■ Learning Objectives

When you have finished your study of this chapter, you should

1. Know the meanings of the elements of the dollar-accountability accounting equation.
2. Be able to record simple actions and transactions typically associated with dollar-accountability–oriented accounting systems by reference to the dollar-accountability accounting equation and use of the rule of debit and credit implicit in the equation.
3. Be able to prepare dollar-accountability–oriented financial statements from an end of period trial balance.
4. Understand how account groups are incorporated into a dollar-accountability accounting system and the reasons for using them.
5. Know the meaning of the term *fund* and be able to relate the fund accounting technique to dollar-accountability accounting.
6. Have a general understanding of the elements of the conceptual foundation underlying accounting systems and be able to relate them to the dollar-accountability accounting system.
7. Understand how the transaction, realization, matching, going concern, and entity conventions relate to accounting decisions.
8. Know the meanings of the accrual and modified accrual bases of accounting and how they relate to the recognition of resource inflows and outflows in an entity's operating statement.

In Chapter 1, we observed that accounting is the language used to disclose the financial results of economic activities. The accounting profession has said that the data disclosed through the accounting system should meet the needs of parties interested in the operations of the enterprise unit. Following that line of reasoning, we concluded that the financial statements coming from the system should disclose, among other things, the resource–obligation position of the entity and information about the extent to which the primary operating objective of the entity has been achieved. To demonstrate that point, we presented illustrative financial statements for a business enterprise including an income statement showing the extent to which the profit objective of the entity had been achieved during the past reporting period.

Next, we turned our attention to determining the types of financial statements that should logically be prepared for nonprofit organizations to disclose the service stories of those organizations. At the end of the chapter, we recognized that, because of the practical difficulties of presenting the ideal operating statement for nonprofit entities, some types of entities (governmental organizations and colleges and universities) have settled for statements primarily disclosing dollar accountability. In this chapter, we give attention to the procedures for maintaining such a system and to the conceptual justifications for the system itself.

We begin our discussion by developing the *dollar-accountability accounting equation*. Next, we demonstrate *how a series of transactions should be recorded and summarized* when using a dollar-accountability–oriented accounting system. After that, we identify and describe *elements of the conceptual foundation underlying accounting systems* and relate them to the dollar-accountability–oriented accounting system. In the final section of the chapter, we briefly consider the *various bases of accounting* derived from the underlying conceptual foundation.

## ■ Dollar-Accountability Accounting Equation

The primary difference between the equation underlying the operational-accountability–oriented accounting system used by businesses and some nonprofit organizations and the dollar-accountability accounting equation centers on the points at which resource inflows and outflows from operations are recognized in the operating statement. In an operational-accountability statement, the accrual basis is used. That means that *resource inflows are recognized as revenues as they are earned* and *resource outflows are recognized as expenses as they are used in producing the inflows*. On the other hand, in a dollar-accountability–oriented accounting system, only spendable resource inflows and outflows are recognized in the operating statement. Furthermore, *inflows are recognized in the accounting period in which they become available and are measurable* without regard for when they are earned. *Outflows are recognized in the accounting period in which a fund liability is incurred and is measurable,* rather than at the point where resources are used. That difference in the points of recognizing resource inflows and outflows causes the dollar-accountability accounting system to use an accounting equation that is different from the operational-accountability equation, which is stated as follows:

$$\text{assets} + \text{expenses} = \text{liabilities} + \text{owners' equity} + \text{revenues}$$

In this section of the chapter, we begin by identifying the elements of the equation used to accumulate the actual financial information. After that, the equation is expanded to show how budgetary data are incorporated into the accounting records to facilitate the control of dollar inflows and dollar outflows within budgetary constraints. In the last part of this section, we extend the dollar accountability concept to the use of separate funds to account for the inflows and the outflows of resources whose uses are specifically restricted.

## Elements of Dollar-Accountability Accounting Equation

Dollar-accountability accounting systems emphasize inflows and outflows of *spendable resources*. Inflows are called *revenues* and the outflows are called *expenditures*. Therefore, the basic accounting equation for such a system can be stated as follows:

$$\text{assets} + \text{expenditures} = \text{liabilities} + \text{fund balance} + \text{revenues}$$

As you examine this equation, you will observe that the term *expenditures* has been substituted for expenses in the profit entity equation. Expenditures is used to describe all outflows of spendable resources regardless of whether they are for expenses, the acquisitions of assets, or in some instances, the retirement of debt. The Summary Statement of Principles for governmental entities states that these outflows of spendable resources should, with limited exceptions, be recognized as expenditures in the accounting period in which the fund liability is incurred and is measurable.

The term *revenues* in this equation is used to reflect all inflows of spendable resources regardless of whether they have been earned in the reporting period. The Summary Statement of Principles for governmental entities states that inflows of spendable resources should be recognized as revenues in the accounting period in which they become available and are measurable. As we shall demonstrate later, the amounts accumulated in all revenue- and expenditure-type accounts during the reporting period are reflected in an operating statement called a *statement of revenues and expenditures*.

The term *fund balance* is substituted for owners' equity and may be visualized as the basic equity account for a dollar-accountability system. The balances in all fund balance accounts are reflected in the balance sheet. These often include reserved and unreserved elements.

## Recording Budgetary Data

In addition to the special interpretations associated with the inflow and outflow classifications described above, the implementation of the concept of dollar accountability also requires that accounts be established to reflect budgetary data.

To properly incorporate the budgetary data into the accounts of these entities, we add account classifications for estimated revenues, encumbrances, appropriations, and reserve for encumbrances. The *estimated revenues* classification is used to reflect the amount of revenues expected to be realized during the reporting period. The *appropriations* classification shows the amounts that have been approved to be spent for various items of expenditures. Both of these accounts are originated prior to the beginning of the operating period when the budget for the entity has been approved by the governing board. Both are closed at the end of each fiscal period.

The term *encumbrances* is used to record commitments to incur expenditures for goods or services anytime that a significant period of time is expected to elapse between the time of the commitment and the time the expenditure is expected to be recognized. *Reserve for encumbrances* is the account used to segregate a portion of the fund balance for commitments to incur expenditures. The balances shown in these accounts will be equal to each other and will be closed against each other at the end of the fiscal period. As we explain later, that, in turn, calls for another entry to adjust the *fund balance reserved for encumbrances* account to the balance shown in the closing entry, by either debiting or crediting *unreserved fund balance* and crediting or debiting *fund balance reserved for encumbrances*.

As we add the two budgetary accounts and the encumbrance-related accounts to the basic equation, we find that it reads as follows:

assets + expenditures + estimated revenues + encumbrances = liabilities + fund balance + revenues + appropriations + reserve for encumbrances

The rule of debit and credit can then be related to the elements of this equation by stating that all items on the left side should be debited to reflect increases and credited to reflect decreases in them. Increases and decreases to the items on the right side of the equation would be recorded as credits and debits, respectively.

Figure 2–1 should help you understand the relationships between the terms *encumbrance, expenditure,* and *expense* as they relate to the acquisition and use of goods and services.

**Figure 2–1.** Phases of a Purchase Transaction

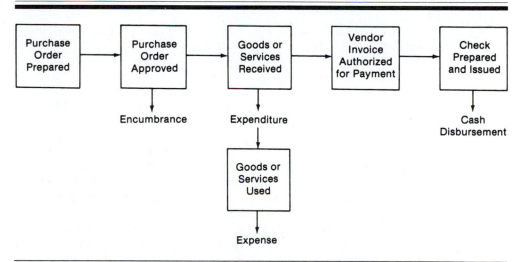

*Source:* Ernst and Young, *Introduction to Governmental Accounting,* p. 3-2. Used with permission.

## ▪ Dollar-Accountability Accounting System Illustrated

To more completely explain the procedures followed in accounting for the financial activities of an entity using a dollar-accountability system, we illustrate through the use of T-accounts the ways in which selected budgetary and transaction data should be recorded.

### Illustrative Transactions and Statements

We begin by assuming the following beginning balances, budgetary actions, resource commitments, and transactions for Model Pure Nonprofit Organization:

1. Beginning balances include cash $40,000; vouchers payable $25,000; and unreserved fund balance $15,000.

2. The approved budget calls for estimated revenues of $200,000 and appropriations for expenditures in the amount of $195,000.

3. Revenues realized in cash during the period amount to $198,000.

4. Expenditures incurred during the period amount to $174,000.

5. Vouchers amounting to $180,000 were paid.

6. Commitments were made for equipment purchases amounting to $15,000.

The preceding financial activities of Model Pure Nonprofit Organization would be recorded in T-accounts as illustrated below. The numbers shown beside the amounts in the T-accounts reflect the items of data being recorded.

| Cash | | | | | Vouchers Payable | | | | | Unreserved Fund Balance | | |
|---|---|---|---|---|---|---|---|---|---|---|---|---|
| (1) | 40,000 | (5) | 180,000 | | (5) | 180,000 | (1) | 25,000 | | | (1) | 15,000 |
| (3) | 198,000 | | | | | | (4) | 174,000 | | | (2) | 5,000 |

| Estimated Revenues | | | | Appropriations | | | | Revenue | | |
|---|---|---|---|---|---|---|---|---|---|---|
| (2) | 200,000 | | | | | (2) | 195,000 | | (3) | 198,000 |

| Expenditures | | | | Encumbrances | | | | Reserve for Encumbrances | | |
|---|---|---|---|---|---|---|---|---|---|---|
| (4) | 174,000 | | | (6) | 15,000 | | | | (6) | 15,000 |

The financial data reflected in the T-accounts should then be summarized in a trial balance (see Exhibit 2–1) to prove the mathematical accuracy of the recording process.

The data from the trial balance should be used to present a statement of revenues and expenditures, a balance sheet, and a statement of changes in fund balance, as shown in Exhibits 2–2, 2–3, and 2–4.

The accounting cycle for a dollar-accountability accounting system is shown in Figure 2–2. As you compare the steps in this cycle with the ones in an operational-accountability cycle (see Figure 1–1), observe that this one includes no end-of-period adjustments designed to recognize nontransaction-related revenues and expenses. Changes in resources and obligations in a dollar-accountability system are recognized only as transactions occur.

**EXHIBIT 2–1.** Model Pure Nonprofit Organization Trial Balance—End of Period

| | Debit | Credit |
|---|---|---|
| Cash | $ 58,000 | |
| Vouchers payable | | $ 19,000 |
| Fund balance | | 20,000 |
| Estimated revenues | 200,000 | |
| Appropriations | | 195,000 |
| Revenues | | 198,000 |
| Expenditures | 174,000 | |
| Encumbrances | 15,000 | |
| Reserve for encumbrances | | 15,000 |
| | $447,000 | $447,000 |

**EXHIBIT 2–2.** Model Pure Nonprofit Organization Statement of Revenues and Expenditures—for Period

| | Estimated | Actual | Difference |
|---|---|---|---|
| Revenues | $200,000 | $198,000 | $ –2,000 |
| Expenditures | 195,000 | 174,000 | –21,000 |
| Excess of revenues over expenditures | $ 5,000 | $ 24,000 | $+19,000 |

**EXHIBIT 2–3.** Model Pure Nonprofit Organization Balance Sheet—End of Period

| | | | |
|---|---|---|---|
| Cash | $58,000 | Vouchers payable | $19,000 |
| | | Fund balance reserved for encumbrances | 15,000 |
| | | Unreserved fund balance | 24,000 |
| Total | $58,000 | Total | $58,000 |

**EXHIBIT 2–4.** Model Pure Nonprofit Organization Statement of Changes in Fund Balance—for Period

| | |
|---|---|
| Unreserved fund balance—beginning of period | $ 15,000 |
| Revenues for period | 198,000 |
| Total | $213,000 |
| Expenditures for period | 174,000 |
| Total | $ 39,000 |
| Fund balance reserved for encumbrances | 15,000 |
| Unreserved fund balance—end of period | $ 24,000 |

**FIGURE 2–2.**   The Accounting Cycle for a Dollar-Accountability System

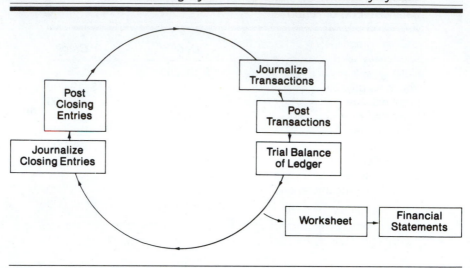

The actions and transactions that are unique to the dollar-accountability system can be classified according to the actions that give rise to them as follows:

1. authorization actions
2. realization of revenues transactions
3. expenditure transactions
4. interfund transactions
5. recognition of encumbrances
6. elimination of encumbrances.

Figure 2–2 demonstrates how items 1, 2, 3, and 5 should be recorded. We demonstrate interfund transactions later in this section as we consider the technique of fund accounting. We clear an encumbrance (item 6) when the commitment represented by the encumbrance becomes an expenditure. That is done by reversing the original encumbrance entry (item 5) and recording the expenditure (item 3).

## Closing Entries

At the end of each fiscal period, the inflow and outflow accounts, both budgetary and actual, should be closed into the fund balance accounts. These closing entries should be recorded in much the same manner as you would close the income and expense accounts of a profit enterprise into the capital or retained earnings account. We begin by reversing the budgetary entry (see C-1 below). After that, we close revenues against expenditures with the difference being debited or credited to an unreserved fund balance account (see C-2). We also need to reverse the reserve for encumbrances and encumbrance balances outstanding at the end of the year (see C-3) and transfer the amount of end-of-year encumbrances from the unreserved fund balance to fund balance reserved for encumbrances (see C-4). These entries for Model Pure Nonprofit Organization would be recorded as follows:

C-1

| | | |
|---|---|---|
| Appropriations | 195,000 | |
| Unreserved fund balance | 5,000 | |
|   Estimated revenues | | 200,000 |

C-2

| | | |
|---|---|---|
| Revenues | 198,000 | |
|   Unreserved fund balance | | 24,000 |
|   Expenditures | | 174,000 |

C-3

| | | |
|---|---|---|
| Reserve for encumbrances | 15,000 | |
|   Encumbrances | | 15,000 |

C-4

| | | |
|---|---|---|
| Unreserved fund balance | 15,000 | |
|   Fund balance reserved for encumbrances | | 15,000 |

## Account Groups—A Necessary Part of a Dollar-Accountability System

Because a dollar-accountability–oriented system recognizes all spendable resource inflows and outflows as revenues (or as a type of revenue item) and expenditures (or as a type of expenditure item), separate supplemental accounting records must be maintained to provide data about long-lived assets and long-term debt. These elements of the accounting system are characterized as account groups or plant funds. They are typically called:

1. general fixed-asset account group
2. general long-term debt account group
3. plant fund.

**General Fixed-Asset Account Group.**   The general fixed-asset account group is used to reflect the acquisition values of general fixed assets and the sources from which the spendable resources have come to acquire those assets. The entries in this accounting entity are directly related to fixed asset acquisition and disposal transactions. We record complementing entries in this account group each time an entity using a dollar-accountability accounting system acquires a long-lived asset or disposes of such an asset. An acquisition would be recognized as an expenditures transaction (see item 3 on page 29) while the proceeds from disposal would be recognized as a revenues transaction (see item 2 on page 29). To illustrate the complementing entries to be made in connection with these transactions, let's assume that Model Pure Nonprofit Organization purchases a long-lived asset for $50,000 and sells another such asset carried at a cost of $5,500 for $1,000. Those transactions would require the following complementing entries in the general fixed asset account group:

| | | |
|---|---|---|
| Equipment | 50,000 | |
|   Investment in equipment | | 50,000 |
| Investment in equipment | 5,500 | |
|   Equipment | | 5,500 |

**General Long-Term Debt Account Group.**   Data are recorded in a general long-term debt account group as a result of long-term debt transactions. In our illustration, we have assumed no incurrence of long-term debt. However, had the organization chosen to issue bonds in the amount of $500,000 for the purpose of constructing a building or some similar facility, the issuance of the bonds would have been recorded in the general long-term debt account group by use of the following complementing entry:

| | | |
|---|---|---|
| Amount to be provided for retirement of bonds | 500,000 | |
|   Bonds payable | | 500,000 |

Let's further assume that $50,000 is placed in a debt-service fund to be used in retiring the bonds. That fact would be recorded in the general long-term debt account group as follows:

| | | |
|---|---|---|
| Amount provided for retirement of bonds | 50,000 | |
|   Amount to be provided for retirement of bonds | | 50,000 |

Following that entry, the financial report of the long-term debt account group would show the following balances:

| | | | |
|---|---|---|---|
| Amount provided for retirement of bonds | $ 50,000 | Bonds payable | $500,000 |
| Amount to be provided for retirement of bonds | 450,000 | | |
| Total | $500,000 | Total | $500,000 |

**Plant Fund.**   A plant fund includes a combination of the financial data recorded in the two account groups plus accounts showing the resources earmarked for replacement and maintenance of plant or additions to plant. Since these funds are typically found in the accounting records of colleges, universities, and health and welfare agencies, we shall deal with their accounting procedures in the chapters covering the accounting practices for those organizations.

## Dollar-Accountability and Fund Accounting

In the preceding pages, we explained how the dollar amounts of spendable resource inflows and outflows are recorded and subsequently reported in the financial statements including an operating statement showing the sources of dollar inflows and the ways in which dollars were used. We also demonstrated how budgetary data are recorded in the accounts to facilitate the control of dollar outflows within formal budgetary constraints. Such controls over expenditures can be characterized as a form of *appropriation control* over spendable resources.

Nonprofit organizations often acquire resources that require an even stronger type control over the ways they are used. When that occurs, a separate self-balancing accounting entity, called a *fund,* is originated to account for the acquisitions and uses of such resources. In this way, the *technique of fund accounting* is incorporated into the dollar-accountability accounting system. That means that the system will include more than one set of self-balancing accounting entities. A *fund* is defined as

> a fiscal and accounting entity with a self-balancing set of accounts recording cash and other financial resources, together with all related liabilities and residual equities or balances, and changes therein, which are segregated for the purpose of carrying on specific activities or attaining certain objectives in accordance with special regulations, restrictions, or limitations.

The introduction of separate funds into the dollar-accountability accounting system also creates the possibility of having interfund transactions (see item 4 on page 29). These transactions occur as resources are transferred between funds or as a fund provides services for another fund creating a claim against that fund. Stated another way, individual funds within an organization can deal with each other as though they were separate business entities. Such transactions between funds fall into the following categories:

1. Spendable resources transferred from one fund to another with the expectation of them being repaid by the transferee. This transaction should be recorded as a receivable (due from) by the transferor and as a payable (due to) by the transferee.

2. Spendable resources transferred from one fund to another for use by that fund but with no anticipation of them being repaid. This transaction should be recorded as a transfer to (a type of expenditure account) by the transferor and as a transfer from (a type of revenue account) by the transferee.

3. Services performed by one fund for another. Such an interfund transaction should be recorded by the fund rendering the service as a debit to a due from account and a credit to revenues. The fund receiving the services should debit expenditures and credit a due to account. As settlement occurs the balances will be cleared from the due to and due from accounts.

Constraints requiring separate accounting entities may be either *legal, contributor,* or *management* imposed. The accounting system should be organized to disclose the extent of adherence to these constraints. The accounting records should show, for example, that resources realized from the sale of bonds issued for the construction of a municipal building were actually used for that purpose. Externally imposed restrictions often specifically require the accountant to divide the accounting records of nonprofit organizations into separate self-balancing accounting entities. Separate funds may also be used to account for resources when their uses are restricted by management (internally restricted resources).

If we analyze restricted and unrestricted resources, we find that both categories of resources can be subdivided into spendable and nonspendable categories. Spendable resources are those that, in the normal course of operations, will be exchanged for other resources or services. Some, such as the cash received from the issuance of bonds in the example cited above, carry restrictions as to how the spendable resources may be used. Other spendable resources are unrestricted as to use and are therefore available for use at the discretion of management. Such spendable resources are available for general operations and are therefore called *appropriable resources.*

*Nonspendable resources,* on the other hand, include assets that are not readily spendable because of their nature or because they must be retained by the organization for the purpose of producing revenues or services. Buildings and equipment are examples of the first type of nonspendable resource. Endowment funds and resources earmarked as capital for self-sustaining operating activities illustrate the second type.

Fund accounting techniques are used to disclose the extent to which constraints on the uses of resources have been met. Figure 2–3 shows how the accounting system is typically fragmented to meet fund-oriented dollar-accountability reporting requirements for those resources. For example, Accounting Entity A in our illustration would be the one reflecting data relating to spendable operating (unrestricted) resources. Entity B would then be used to account for the fixed (nonspendable) assets, such as the buildings and equipment that are available for general operating purposes. Entity C would be used, for example, to account for the spendable (restricted) resources received from the sale of bonds in our earlier construction example. Entity D would be used to account for certain assets, such as endowment (nonspendable restricted) resources required to be held for the production of revenue.

Most of us think of the term *fund* as being used to describe a reservoir of cash. As used here, however, it may be thought of as including both cash and near cash resources, as well as obligations and commitments against those resources. We should observe that the *fund concept calls for accounting segregation rather than physical segregation of resources.* Nevertheless, resources are often also physically segregated through the use of separate checking accounts for the cash portions of the different funds.

From an organizational viewpoint, the primary difference between the typical accounting records for a profit enterprise and those of a nonprofit enterprise using fund accounting techniques is that the records of a nonprofit organization will be fragmented into various self-balancing accounting entities. They will include a separate self-balancing set of accounts for each fund entity and account group rather than one self-balancing ledger for the organization as a unit. Also, the organization using fund

**FIGURE 2–3.**   Typical Fragments of a Fund Accounting System

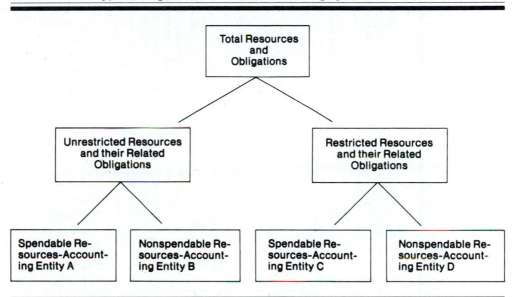

accounting techniques will often present separate financial statements for each fund and account group.

In summary, dollar accountability for the acquisitions and uses of spendable resources is achieved within a fund by using an accounting system built around the dollar-accountability accounting equation including budgetary accounts. We can characterize this as an *appropriation control* technique. However, we also use separate accounting entities called *funds* to account for resources that require a higher level of dollar accountability than can be provided through appropriation control. When such funds are incorporated into an accounting system, it is characterized as a *fund accounting system*. A dollar-accountability accounting system also requires the use of account groups or a plant fund to preserve financial information relating to long-term assets and long-term liabilities.

# ■ Conceptual Foundation Underlying Accounting Systems

An accounting system should be designed to produce and report financial data that are useful to parties who have an interest in the operations of the reporting entity. The flowchart in Figure 2–4 suggests that those financial data should be both *relevant* and *reliable* if they are to be useful. These two qualitative requirements may be thought of as requiring financial data that are judged to be the most relevant to the decision-making process within the limits of an appropriate level of reliability. Thus, any system operating within this conceptual framework will include some trade-offs between relevance and reliability.

**FIGURE 2–4.** A Conceptual Framework for Determining Generally Accepted Accounting Practices

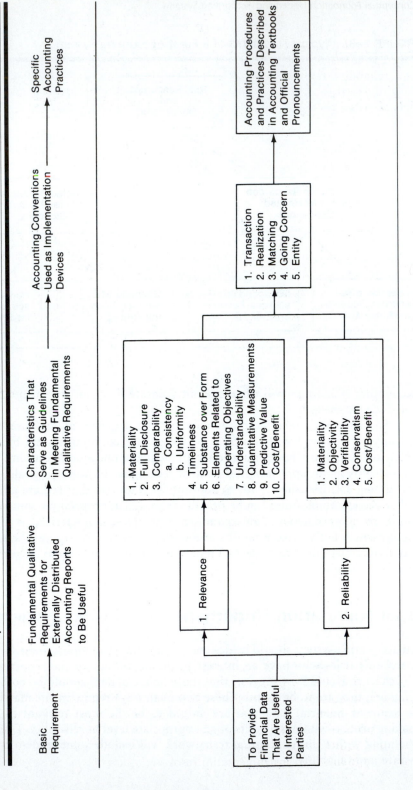

The third column of the flowchart reflects characteristics and concepts (sometimes called *principles*) that accountants have typically associated with meeting the relevance and reliability requirements. The fourth column lists five accounting conventions (sometimes also called *concepts*) which accountants have identified as implementing devices based on those basic requirements that can be used in deciding

1. when changes in assets and liabilities should be recognized (transaction convention)

2. when resource inflows from operations should be recognized as revenues in the operating statement (realization convention)

3. when resources outflows should be recognized as expenses rather than as creating assets or eliminating liabilities (matching convention)

4. what values should be assigned to assets and liabilities in the balance sheet (going concern convention)

5. which segments of net resources require the presentation of financial statements relating to them (entity convention).

Use of the implementation devices described in the preceding pages has produced the accounting procedures and practices reflected in accounting textbooks. Those procedures and practices have also been significantly influenced by study and research supplemented by

1. actions of professional organizations

2. specific statements and pronouncements of official bodies.

## Actions by Professional Organizations

When we examine the contributions made by professional accounting organizations, we immediately recognize the importance of the American Institute of Certified Public Accountants (AICPA) and its predecessor organization, the American Institute of Accountants, in promoting and developing sound accounting practices. Two very important groups, the Committee on Accounting Procedures and the Accounting Principles Board, were created and monitored by this organization for the purpose of developing and promoting better accounting practices. The AICPA has also funded and monitored many research projects that have been instrumental in shaping accounting thought over the years. Although this organization is generally recognized as the most important one serving accounting practitioners, its membership also includes many accountants from the teaching profession and from the general fields of business and governmental accounting. As an organization, it has probably had more effect on the development of accounting theory than any other professional body.

The American Accounting Association (AAA) is an organization more directly representing college and university accounting teachers. Although it includes many professional practitioners and private accountants, the general administration and operation of the organization historically have been carried out by accountants in the teaching profession. This organization, too, has sponsored a significant amount of research and has been instrumental in resolving a number of controversial issues that have faced the accounting profession. It has been especially valuable as a catalyst for new ideas and thoughts developed by academically oriented accountants.

## Pronouncements of Official Bodies

The Committee on Accounting Procedures was the first group charged by the AICPA with the responsibility of preparing and issuing statements concerning controversial accounting practices. The statements issued by that committee over the years were ultimately summarized in the Committee's Statement Number 43. Many recommendations of this committee, set out in this summarizing statement, are still elements of generally accepted practice.

The Accounting Principles Board, established as the successor to the Committee on Accounting Procedures, came into existence in 1959. It also operated under the direct supervision of the AICPA. From 1959 to 1972, this arm of the AICPA issued thirty-one pronouncements and four statements concerning controversial accounting issues. Except as specifically modified or superseded by Statements of the Financial Accounting Standards Board, the provisions of these pronouncements still apply to accounting practices.

The most recent professional body established for the purpose of developing and issuing general pronouncements relating to financial reporting is the Financial Accounting Standards Board (FASB), established in 1972. This Board is organizationally separate from the AICPA and includes seven full-time members plus a larger Financial Accounting Standards Advisory Council. The Advisory Council includes financial executives, representatives of governmental agencies, representatives of brokerage firms, accounting educators, lawyers, and certified public accountants. Only four of the seven members of the Financial Accounting Standards Board may be drawn from accountants engaged in public practice. The other three members must be well qualified in the field of accounting but need not be certified public accountants. The Financial Accounting Standards Board has issued a number of statements dealing with controversial accounting issues and has also been actively engaged in researching various areas of accounting.

In 1977, the Financial Accounting Standards Board embarked on a project designed to establish a conceptual framework from which sound, generally accepted accounting practices could be developed. The results of that project are reflected in six statements entitled *Statements of Financial Accounting Concepts* (SFAC), Numbers 1 through 6. These statements do not constitute standards of accounting. Rather, they describe concepts and relationships that should underlie accounting standards and practices and serve as a basis for evaluating existing standards and practices. Some of the terms and the reasoning process followed in the SFACs are incorporated into the data shown in Figure 2–4. For example, SFAC Number 2 identifies *relevance* and *reliability* as the two primary qualities that make accounting data useful.

SFAC Number 3 is entitled "Elements of Financial Statements of Business Enterprises." It identifies and defines various items that typically appear in financial statements. (This statement has now been superseded by SFAC Number 6.)

SFAC Number 4, entitled "Objectives of Financial Reporting by Nonbusiness Organizations," takes the position that it is not necessary to develop an independent conceptual framework for each individual category of enterprise unit. The FASB in this statement concludes that the objectives of general external financial reporting for non-business (nonprofit) entities, engaged in activities not unique to government, should be similar to those of business enterprises engaged in similar activities. This statement does, however, recognize that "the objectives of financial reporting are affected by the economic, legal, political, and social environment in which the financial reporting takes place." The emphasis throughout this statement is on the need for financial reports of nonbusiness (nonprofit) organizations to provide information that would be useful to present and potential constituents (in particular, resource providers). It defines "useful" to include information that helps constituents

1. assess the services provided and the ability of the entity to continue to provide those services
2. evaluate the effectiveness of management
3. know about the resources and obligations of the entity
4. evaluate the efforts and accomplishments of the entity
5. understand the nature of cash inflows and outflows.[1]

SFAC Number 6 is of particular importance to the nonprofit area. It is entitled "Elements of Financial Statements" and replaces previously issued SFAC Number 3. It includes definitions, concepts, and relationships that the FASB feels should underlie the preparation and presentation of the financial statements of nongovernmental, not-for-profit organizations. The thoughts presented in this publication, where they fail to support presently accepted practices, are mentioned at various points throughout this text. *You must remember, however, that the SFACs do not in themselves constitute generally accepted accounting practices,* but only a framework from which to develop those practices.

Governmental agencies also have contributed to the overall body of accounting practice. The Securities and Exchange Commission (SEC) has been active in its issuance of statements regarding specific practices that should be followed in presenting published financial reports. The Cost Accounting Standards Board (CASB), during its existence, was primarily concerned with achieving greater uniformity in accounting practices among companies holding government contracts. It tried to develop more consistency in the treatment of various types of costs incurred in connection with those contracts and had a significant influence on general cost allocation practices. The Internal Revenue Service (IRS), through enforcement of the Internal Revenue Code and the issuance of its interpretations of the Code, has also significantly affected the accounting practices followed by various tax-paying entities.

Many of the statements and pronouncements cited in the preceding paragraphs apply to both profit and nonprofit entities. However, various committees and organizations, primarily concerned with accounting practices in the nonprofit area, have issued statements more specifically defining the accounting practices for various types of non-

---

1. Financial Accounting Standards Board, *Statement of Financial Accounting Concepts No. 4* (December 1980), p. xiv.

profit organizations. The National Council on Governmental Accounting (NCGA), in cooperation with the Municipal Finance Officers' Association (MFOA, now the Government Finance Officers' Association—GFOA), has published *Governmental Accounting, Auditing, and Financial Reporting,* which sets out the accounting practices that should be followed in the governmental area. A new edition of this publication was published in 1988 and is quoted extensively in Chapters 3 and 9. The NCGA has also issued seven statements regarding various aspects of governmental accounting practices.

A new era for standard setting in governmental accounting began in 1984 when the GASB (Governmental Accounting Standards Board) met with the NCGA to transfer the standard-setting responsibilities to the GASB. With this transfer, the Government Finance Officers' Association (GFOA) took on a new supporting role in the governmental accounting standards-setting process. The relationship of the GASB to the overall accounting standards-setting structure can be visualized as shown in Figure 2–5. Within this arrangement, the GASB assumed responsibility for establishing the standards to be followed in accounting for the activities of state and local governments. The FASB establishes the standards to be followed by all other enterprises.

The National Association of College and University Business Officers has provided a publication entitled *College and University Business Administration,* which includes a section prescribing accounting practices for those institutions. The American Hospital Association in its publication *Chart of Accounts for Hospitals* describes the accounting practices recommended for hospitals. Both of these publications are quoted extensively in the chapters of this text covering accounting procedures for those institutions.

**FIGURE 2–5.**   Accounting Standard-Setting Structure

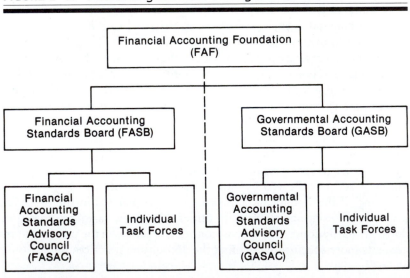

*Source:* Government Finance Officers' Association, *Governmental Finance* 13 (December 1984), p. 10. Used with permission.

The National Health Council, National Assembly of National Voluntary Health and Social Welfare Organizations, and United Way of America have jointly produced *Standards of Accounting and Financial Reporting for Voluntary Health and Welfare Organizations*. This publication outlines the recommended accounting practices for those organizations. The AICPA has also developed audit guides for each of the four major nonprofit areas that establish financial reporting standards for audited financial statements.

All of these publications have been important in defining the accounting practices currently followed by nonprofit organizations. Furthermore, the Financial Accounting Standards Board has carried out a research project designed to identify and explore the conceptual issues of financial accounting for nonbusiness organizations. The results of the study were published under the title *Financial Accounting in Nonbusiness Organizations*. The author is Robert N. Anthony. Two other research studies, one by William W. Holder and the other by Allan R. Drebin, James L. Chan, and Lorna C. Fergurson, have been sponsored by the NCGA. Holder's study, "A Study of Selected Concepts for Government Financial Accounting and Reporting," was published in 1980. The Drebin study was published in 1981. All of these research studies are listed in the bibliography.

## Underlying Assumptions, Principles, and Conventions

As we have observed, the accounting profession has not officially spelled out the specific principles and concepts that it uses as guidelines in recording, classifying, and summarizing accounting data. Nevertheless, as we analyze the qualitative factors described in the preceding section, as we observe the practices followed by accountants, and as we review textbook summaries and official pronouncements relating to those practices, we can, in effect, derive some of the guidelines underlying generally accepted accounting practices. They include at least one assumption, five principles, and five conventions, all of which are reflected in Figure 2–4.

**Basic Assumption.** We have emphasized the fact that data should be accumulated showing the amount of resources available to an entity along with its obligations and resource inflows and outflows. In communicating these data to the users of financial statements, the accountant has quite logically taken the position that they can best be expressed by using the monetary unit as the common unit of measure. The dollar, as the monetary unit of the United States, is therefore used to communicate both financial position and operating results data. Generally accepted practice implicitly views historical dollars as being the same measuring unit as current dollars. Therefore, in failing to adjust the dollar for price-level changes, the accountant is implicitly assuming it to be a stable measuring unit.

**Principles.** Financial data, to be most useful, must possess appropriate levels of *relevance* and *reliability*. In making judgments with regard to how these qualitative characteristics are to be met, the accounting profession has identified certain principles that should be followed in determining the trade-offs to be made between these two characteristics and, in general, how the financial data should be accumulated and presented.

A *principle* has been defined as "a general or fundamental law . . . underlying the working of an artificial device."[2] If we examine financial reports, official pronouncements, and textbook materials, we can logically conclude that the accountant follows at least five such laws or doctrines.

Underlying all of the accountant's activities is the *principle of materiality*. Realistically, the volume and complex nature of resource conversion activities make it imperative that the accountant follow this guideline. Within the provisions of this principle, only material matters relating to the financial data need be disclosed in the financial statements. This guideline also means that items that are insignificant in amount need not be treated in strict accordance with accounting definitions. As an illustration of this point, the distinction between an asset and an expense hinges primarily on the period(s) benefited by an expenditure. An economic entity may spend small amounts for such things as wastepaper baskets, which, based on the periods benefited concept, should be classified as assets. However, because it is often more economical and convenient to do so, such expenditures may be justifiably classified as expenses within this guideline.

Reliance on the *principle of conservatism* can also be observed in decisions by accountants, particularly in the areas of asset valuation and income determination. Fundamentally, the guideline of conservatism means that the accountant, in considering approximately equally acceptable alternatives, will use the one that tends to portray the less or least optimistic picture of the financial position and/or operating results of the entity. Thus, the smaller of two or more otherwise equally acceptable values for an asset would normally be the one recorded. At the same time, the larger of two acceptable values would be used for a liability.

The accountant also follows the guideline of conservatism in classifying assets and liabilities. If a question arises as to whether they should be placed in a more liquid (current) or a less liquid (noncurrent) classification, the issues are resolved toward a less liquid classification for assets and a more quickly to be paid (current) one for liabilities. Also, we often find the principle of conservatism guiding the accountant in his or her distinction between assets and expenses or losses. The accountant's attitude in these matters is more specifically reflected in the practice of *anticipating losses but never anticipating gains*. The desire to be conservative is a powerful influence on accountants as they seek to avoid the danger of overstating operating results or financial strength. However, the guideline of conservatism should not be distorted to the point of justifying a deliberate misrepresentation of the financial position or operating results of an enterprise unit.

Earlier in this chapter, we noted the need for neutrality in the presentation of financial data. The effort on the part of accountants to prevent subjective judgments from entering into the presentation of financial data has caused them to follow the *principle of objectivity*. This guideline requires that, insofar as is practicable, items and amounts recorded in financial statements should be those that are most clearly verifiable by supporting documents or other evidence originating outside the business. *The principle of objectivity is the basic reason for accepting the transaction as the primary*

---

2.  *Merriam-Webster Pocket Dictionary* (New York: Simon and Schuster, 1964), p. 394.

*point for recognizing changes in resources and obligations.* The accountant reasons that at the point where two parties, each having opposite interests—such as a buyer and a seller—agree upon a value, there is an objectively determined basis for assigning that value.

In using the principle of objectivity as a basic guideline for accounting practice, we must also be aware that estimates must be introduced at selected points, such as in the calculation of depreciation and bad debt expenses. In justifying these and other departures from specific principles and concepts, we must recognize that as accountants make decisions regarding accounting practices to be followed, they will frequently find various principles and concepts to be in conflict with each other as far as relevance and reliability of the data are concerned. In those cases, they must make choices (trade-offs) in deciding which principle or concept should prevail to best meet the needs of the users of the financial data. In some instances, one principle or concept will be allowed to prevail, and in other instances, another will prevail as the accountant judges the relative importance of each in meeting financial data user needs.

Comparison is important in the analysis and use of financial data. In recognition of that fact, accountants have adopted the *principle of consistency* to guide them in the accumulation and presentation of these data. This means that the same generally accepted accounting procedures should be followed in recording and reporting the financial data of a given enterprise in successive periods. The principle of consistency is considered so important that exceptions to it must be disclosed in the independent auditor's report.

*Consistency* should be carefully distinguished from *uniformity*. The latter is used by accountants to mean use of the same generally accepted accounting practices among different enterprise units engaged in similar activities. Uniformity *is not* a generally accepted principle at this time. However, pronouncements by the Accounting Principles Board and the Financial Accounting Standards Board suggest that the profession is moving in the direction of greater uniformity of accounting practices.

It is important for the users of financial data to have all significant financial facts relating to the economic entity being studied. The *principle of full disclosure* requires the accountant to accept the responsibility of seeing that all significant financial facts are appropriately disclosed, either within the body of the financial statements or in footnotes and parenthetical statements. The emphasis on the term *significant financial facts* also means that the principle of materiality is applied in determining which financial facts are to be disclosed. This principle should not, however, be taken as a license for excessive disclosures of events that are merely interesting, rather than essential, to a fair presentation.

**Accounting Conventions.** The term *convention* is defined as a general agreement regarding the way that basic principles should be applied in meeting a specific problem.[3] As accountants have used the principles described in the preceding portion of this section as guidelines, they appear to have adopted at least five conventions that they follow in assigning valuations, recognizing revenue, identifying the financial reporting unit, and measuring the operating achievements of profit enterprises.

---

3. *Merriam-Webster,* p. 108.

The *going-concern convention,* sometimes referred to as the *continuity concept,* has been adopted by the accounting profession as a basic guideline in assigning values to items in the financial statements. It causes the accountant to assign values to items in the financial statements that are consistent with the assumption that the enterprise unit will continue to operate during the foreseeable future. That means that assets should be valued according to what is expected to happen to them in the normal course of operations. An enterprise unit, as a going concern, will normally convert some assets to cash and will consume others in resource conversion activities. This convention suggests that the assets to be converted into cash, in the normal course of operations, should be valued at a conservative cash-realizable value. Amounts receivable from customers, taxpayers, and others are included in this group of assets. Therefore, we provide an allowance for anticipated uncollectible amounts, which is deducted from the total amount due to reflect the net valuations of such items.

The going-concern convention supported by the principle of objectivity also suggests that assets to be used in resource conversion activities should be valued at cost or cost amortized as they are presented in the balance sheet. The use of the cost and cost-amortized bases of valuation for inventory and depreciable fixed assets, respectively, illustrates applications of the going-concern concept of valuation to those assets.

We should also observe that there are times when the going-concern convention should not apply. As an example, evidence that an economic entity faces bankruptcy or plans to terminate its operations in the near future would make the going-concern concept of valuation inappropriate. When such a situation exists, valuations should be based on anticipated liquidation values rather than on the going-concern convention.

As a general rule, the occurrence of a *transaction* between the reporting entity and another party is the point at which changes in the elements of the accounting equation are recognized. For example, the passage of title (a transaction) signals when changes in assets and liabilities should be recognized in connection with the acquisitions and disposals of assets. In effect, the accounting profession has said that resource transfers between enterprise units should be recognized at the point where the title to the resource changes from one entity to the other. This point for recognizing the acquisitions and disposals of assets is used primarily because it is an *objectively verifiable* event. Thus, in answering the question as to *when* changes in elements of the accounting equation should be recorded, accountants have concluded that most such changes should be recognized when transactions occur. The nature of the transaction plus the amount spelled out in connection with it are then used in determining *what* is to be recorded.

There are, however, some exceptions to the transaction convention. For example, the amortization of fixed assets, the accrual of revenues and expenses related to the passage of time, and the recognition of prepaid portions of revenues and expenses are all changes in elements of the accounting equation that are recognized without the occurrence of a transaction. These deviations are justified in the interest of providing more relevant information. Because such changes are based on *systematic procedures,* they are judged to be reliable enough to meet the reliability requirement.

The *realization convention* identifies the criteria that are used in determining when resource inflows from operations should be recognized as revenues. It requires that such resource inflows be recognized as revenue at the point where *cash, a cash equivalent, or a legally enforceable claim to cash is received in exchange for goods and services, and the earning process has been completed.* It also relates to the transactions convention in that the earning process relating to the sale of merchandise is generally presumed to have been completed when title to such goods passes to the purchaser. In the case of revenue from services, the earning is presumed to have occurred when the services have been rendered and a legally enforceable claim to fees from those services has been established. This convention, in effect, helps accountants determine *when* to recognize increases to the revenues element of the accounting equation.

One notable exception to the application of the realization convention to the recognition of revenues occurs when accountants use the percentage of completion method for recognizing revenues from long-term construction contracts. That procedure calls for recognition of revenues equal to the percentage of total expected cost incurred up to the date of the financial statements, multiplied by the expected total net revenue from the contract. Again, this procedure is judged to present the data in a more relevant manner with a reasonable degree of reliability.

Accountants have also had to wrestle with the problem of identifying the economic entities requiring separate financial reports. In meeting that problem, the profession has adopted the *entity convention.* It suggests that accounting reports shall be presented for each individual economic unit. Such a unit is defined as *any body of resources being used toward the achievement of a common operating goal.* Reports of entity activities should be prepared for use by persons interested in the operations of each enterprise unit. Therefore, when two or more enterprise units combine their resources toward the achievement of a common economic goal, the accountant is obligated to prepare financial statements for the combined entity, as well as for the individual enterprise units included in the consolidated group.

In the nonprofit area, the application of the entity concept is particularly evident in the requirement that separate financial data be presented for each fund included within the accounting system of the organization. This concept also suggests that the fund entity statements should be combined or consolidated to show the financial position and operating results of the organization as a unit because many data users will be primarily interested in the operations of the organization as a unit.

Earlier, we emphasized the importance of matching efforts against achievements when such information would be useful in judging the success or failure of an economic entity in achieving its operating objectives. The *matching convention* has been adopted by accountants as a means of reflecting one element of that effort–achievement relationship for profit enterprises. Ideally, every economic entity, insofar as is practicable, should seek to assign values to its achievements. Those values, generally characterized as revenues, should then be matched against efforts in the form of expenses or expenditures in order to help in evaluating the effort–achievement relationship. As we noted, this is very difficult for pure nonprofit organizations to do because of problems encountered in assigning values to their service achievements. However, any economic entity that provides goods or services in exchange for buyer or user fees should, within this convention, match the resources consumed in earning revenue against the revenue in its operating statement. By so doing, the entity can determine a net operating result, generally labeled net income or net loss, from that part of its operations.

Although pure nonprofit entities will often find it impracticable to match the values of its achievements against the costs of rendering them, other devices can be used to relate efforts to achievements. Aggregate costs can be divided by the number of units of service performed to arrive at unit cost data. These data provide an effort–achievement measurement by relating the volume of services rendered to the total cost of rendering them. Other things being equal, a lower unit cost figure would indicate a better effort–achievement relationship than a higher one. It may also be beneficial for governmental units to match tax and other revenues realized during a period against *expenses* for the period to *show the extent to which the present generation is paying for the services that it is receiving.* We can think of this as a disclosure of "intergenerational equity," a concept that will be explored further later in the text.

The relationships between the various underlying qualitative factors, principles, and conventions discussed in the preceding pages may be visualized by displaying them in a flowchart such as the one shown in Figure 2–4. Most of these relationships are described and discussed in *Statements of Financial Accounting Concepts,* Nos. 2 and 6 (see Suggested Supplementary References).

This manner of presentation recognizes relevance and reliability as the two fundamental qualitative characteristics that appropriately developed accounting data should meet. Other qualitative characteristics and the principles described in the preceding pages help the accountant in determining what should be done to meet the relevance and reliability criteria. Actual accounting practices are then more specifically prescribed by the five conventions designed to best meet the guidelines set out by the qualitative factors and principles.

# ■ Bases of Accounting

The principles and concepts discussed in the preceding paragraphs serve as guidelines for recording changes in the resources and obligations of an economic entity. We now direct our attention more specifically to determining just when resource inflows and outflows should be recognized. Since cash is the most readily spendable resource of an enterprise, financial statement users ultimately need to know about cash flow information. The need for periodic reporting, however, prompts us to consider other points for recognizing resource inflows and outflows as revenues and expenses or expenditures. We use the term *basis of accounting* to describe the system used in establishing the points for recognizing these inflows and outflows as revenues and expenses or expenditures, respectively. We now examine those bases as they relate to the accounting practices for *profit enterprises* and *nonprofit enterprises.*

## Bases of Accounting–Profit Enterprises

Profit enterprises operate within an economic environment controlled by the forces of supply and demand. They require frequent periodic reports for planning and decision purposes. Periodic profit achievement is best measured by showing the *changes in the net resource position* resulting from the operations of the entity over the reporting period. The primary operating objective of profit enterprises is to earn a profit for their owners. The financial statements, therefore, emphasize the points *where resources are earned and used* in determining net income. This is characterized as the *accrual basis of accounting,* which is the generally accepted basis of accounting for profit enterprises.

It places emphasis on *earning* as a measure of achievements and on the net resources *consumed* in the earning process as the measure of efforts rather than on the inflows and outflows of any one type of resource. The accrual basis of accounting for profit enterprises means that inventories, prepaid items, accrued items, and appropriately depreciated assets, as well as receivables and payables, will be reflected in the balance sheet as resources and obligations at the end of each reporting period.

Profit enterprises that are primarily involved in providing services in exchange for fees often use the *cash basis of accounting* in developing their financial reports. It uses the points at which cash is received and disbursed to measure resource inflows and outflows rather than the points where resources are earned and used. That basis of accounting in some cases can be theoretically justified for profit entities within the *principle of materiality*. That means that the statements derived from using the cash basis do not differ materially from what they would be if the accrual basis was used.

The *modified accrual basis of accounting,* used in the profit area, is a compromise between the cash basis and the accrual basis. It generally provides for the recognition of such things as inventory, receivables, payables, and depreciation, but gives no recognition to accrued or prepaid items. Again, this basis of accounting may be appropriately used in the profit area only when the statements derived from using it do not differ materially from what they would be if the accrual basis were used.

In presenting a statement of cash flows, a profit enterprise in effect converts the accrual-based data reflected in its income statement to a cash basis by recognizing inflows and outflows at the points where cash was received and given up. Profit enterprises, therefore, realistically present both accrual and cash basis inflow–outflow statements when they include both an income statement and a statement of cash flows in their financial reports.

Some funds within nonprofit entities operate as proprietary, or self-sustaining, funds. That means that they operate like profit entities. As a result, these funds use the accrual basis of accounting to best reflect the extent to which their self-sustaining operating objective has been achieved during each reporting period.

## Bases of Accounting—Nonprofit Enterprises

Because many nonprofit enterprises operate primarily for the purpose of providing socially desirable services, some accountants have taken the position that the points of earning and using resources are not important in the accounting process for these organizations. They conclude that it is more important to show the inflows and outflows of spendable resources. As a result, we frequently find the *cash* or *modified accrual basis* of accounting used in this area. The operating statements prepared on these bases show the inflows and outflows of cash or spendable (net appropriable) resources rather than the total resources earned and used during the period. The balance sheet will then show only spendable resources and obligations against those resources.

Only hospitals and health and welfare agencies, among nonprofit organizations, require use of the *full accrual basis of accounting* (as defined for profit enterprises) in the statements defining their accounting practices. For hospitals the use of the accrual basis is logical because a hospital's operations are typically expected to show a relationship between revenues and expenses. That same logic would appear to call for use of the accrual basis by colleges and universities depending heavily on tuition and fees or appropriations based on services rendered. Although the official literature in this area calls for use of the accrual basis, the recommended accounting practices are fundamentally those required by the modified accrual basis and thus emphasize dollar- rather than operational-accountability reporting. Health and welfare agencies use the accrual basis to more appropriately disclose full cost data.

Governmental units, primarily involved in rendering services by using resources acquired through tax assessments, clearly use the *modified accrual basis* for most fund entities. This system does not distinguish between capital and revenue expenditures and does not recognize depreciation of fixed assets. It also does not recognize certain accrued and prepaid items. Their operating statements show inflows and outflows of appropriable resources so as to disclose dollar accountability. Little attention is given to the disclosure of operational accountability by these enterprise units. However, self-sustaining (proprietary) units of a governmental entity use the full accrual basis of accounting.

## ■ Summary

In this chapter, we first described the framework within which a dollar-accountability accounting system operates. We began by developing the basic accounting equation, which is used to account for spendable resource inflows and outflows. We then ex- plained how budgetary accounts are added to the equation to facilitate appropriation control over spendable resource outflows.

After having developed and explained the dollar-accountability accounting equa- tion, we demonstrated how the system operates by recording a series of transactions typically associated with the operations of entities using dollar-accountability account- ing systems. The data accumulated from those transactions were then summarized in the three statements (Statement of Revenues and Expenditures, Balance Sheet, and Statement of Changes in Fund Balance) typically used to display dollar-accountability– oriented financial information. In this part of the chapter, we also explained how multiple self-balancing accounting entities, called *funds* and *account groups,* are used in a dollar-accountability–oriented system.

In the last part of the chapter, we discussed the conceptual foundation underlying accounting systems and explained how the points for recognizing resource inflows and outflows as revenues and expenses or expenditures, respectively, are identified under both the accrual and modified accrual bases of accounting.

## ■ Glossary

**Adjusting Entries.**    Nontransaction changes in assets and liabilities and the offsetting changes in revenue and expense items required to meet the earning and use criteria established under the accrual basis of accounting.

**Appropriable Resources.** Spendable resources available for use in carrying out general operations.

**Appropriation.** A legal authorization granted by a legislative body to make expenditures and to incur obligations for specific purposes. An appropriation is usually limited in amount and as to the time when it may be expended.

**Cash Basis.** A basis of accounting under which transactions are recognized only when cash changes hands.

**Closing Entries.** Entries recorded at the end of each fiscal period to transfer the balances in the various revenue and expense or expenditure accounts to the permanent equity accounts of an accounting entity.

**Conservatism.** The interpretation of accounting valuations and classifications so as to reflect the less or least optimistic disclosure of equally acceptable alternatives.

**Consistency.** The use of the same generally accepted accounting practice for a particular reporting entity in each reporting period.

**Due from _____ Fund.** An asset account used to indicate amounts owed to a particular fund by another fund in the same governmental entity for goods sold or services rendered. This account includes only short-term obligations on open account and not noncurrent portions of long-term loans.

**Due to _____ Fund.** A liability account reflecting amounts owed by a particular fund to another fund in the same governmental entity for goods sold or services rendered. These amounts include only short-term obligations on open account and not noncurrent portions of long-term loans.

**Encumbrances.** Commitments related to unperformed (executory) contracts for goods or services.

**Entity.** The basic unit upon which accounting and/or financial reporting activities focus. The basic governmental legal and *accounting entity* is the individual fund and account group. Under NCGA Statement 1, governmental GAAP *reporting entities* include (1) the combined statements—overview (the "liftable" GPFS) and (2) financial statements of individual funds (which may be presented as columns on combining statements—by fund type, on physically separate individual fund statements, or both). The term *entity* is also sometimes used to describe the composition of "the government as a whole" (whether the library is part of the city or a separate government, whether the school system is part of the county or an independent special district, etc.).

**Entity Convention.** A practice followed by accountants that requires that accounting reports shall be presented for each individual economic unit, defined as any body of resources being used toward the achievement of a common operating goal.

**Estimated Revenues.** The amount of spendable resource inflows expected to be realized during a budgetary period.

**Expenditures.** Decreases in net spendable resources; these include current operating expenses that require current or future use of net current assets, payments toward the retirement of general long-term debt, and outlays for long-term assets.

**Full Disclosure.**  A principle followed by accountants that requires them to accept responsibility of seeing that all significant financial facts are appropriately disclosed either within the body of the financial statements or in the footnotes and parenthetical statements accompanying those statements.

**Fund.**  A fiscal and accounting entity with a self-balancing set of accounts recording cash and other financial resources, together with all related liabilities and residual equities or balances, and changes therein, which are segregated for the purpose of carrying on specific activities or attaining certain objectives in accordance with special regulations, restrictions, or limitations.

**Fund Balance.**  The fund equity of governmental funds and trust funds.

**Fund Balance Reserved for Encumbrances.**  The part of the total fund balance that has been reserved to cover encumbrances outstanding at the end of a reporting period.

**General Fixed Assets Account Group.**  A self-balancing group of accounts set up to account for the general fixed assets of a government.

**General Long-Term Debt Account Group.**  A self-balancing group of accounts set up to account for the unmatured general long-term debt of a government.

**Generally Accepted Accounting Principles (GAAP).**  Uniform minimum standards of and guidelines to financial accounting and reporting. They govern the form and content of the basic financial statements of an entity. GAAP encompass the conventions, rules, and procedures necessary to define accepted accounting practice at a particular time. They include not only broad guidelines of general application, but also detailed practices and procedures. GAAP provide a standard by which to measure financial presentations. The primary authoritative statement on the application of GAAP to state and local governments is NCGA Statement 1. Every government should prepare and publish financial statements in conformity with GAAP. The objectives of governmental GAAP financial reports are different from, and much broader than, the objectives of business enterprise GAAP financial reports.

**Going Concern Convention.**  An accounting practice that requires accountants to present financial data with the assumption that the enterprise unit will continue to operate during the foreseeable future unless there is reason to doubt the continuity of existence.

**Matching Convention.**  An accounting practice adopted by accountants that requires that expenses incurred in the realization of revenues should be matched against those revenues for financial reporting purposes.

**Materiality.**  A principle or concept followed by accountants that in effect says that, in making decisions relating to the accounting process, the accountant should be concerned only with those things and amounts that have a significant effect on the financial statement data.

**Modified Accrual Basis.**  The accrual basis of accounting adapted to the governmental fund type, spending measurement focus. Under it, revenues are recognized when they become both "measurable" and "available to finance expenditures of the current period." Expenditures are recognized when the related fund liability is incurred, except for: (1) inventories of materials and supplies that may be considered expenditures either when purchased or when used; (2) prepaid insurance and similar items that need not be reported; (3) accumulated unpaid vacation, sick pay, and other employee benefit amounts that need not be recognized in the current period, but for which larger-than-normal accumulations must be disclosed in the notes to the financial statements; (4) interest on special assessment indebtedness that may be recorded when due rather than accrued, if approximately offset by interest earnings on special assessment levies; and (5) principal and interest on long-term debt that are generally recognized when due. All governmental funds and expendable trust funds are accounted for using the modified accrual basis of accounting.

**Nonspendable Resources.** Assets that cannot be spent either because of their nature (for example buildings) or because they are restricted from being spent (for example endowment assets).

**Objectivity.** A principle or concept of accounting that requires that the items and amounts reported in the financial statements should, insofar as is practical, be those that are most clearly verifiable to supporting documents or other evidence originating outside the business.

**Realization Convention.** The primary guideline that the accountant uses in determining when inflows of resources should be recognized as revenues. The point of recognition under this convention is the point where the earning process has been completed and either cash or a legally enforceable claim to cash has been received in exchange for the goods delivered or services rendered.

**Relevance.** The financial information that is appropriate for its intended use.

**Reliability.** In accounting theory, the requirement that accounting information be verifiable and representationally faithful.

**Reserve for Encumbrances.** An account used to segregate a portion of fund balance for expenditure upon vendor performance.

**Revenues (dollar accountability).** Spendable resource inflows.

**Statement of Revenues and Expenditures.** The basic financial statement that is the governmental fund and expendable trust fund GAAP operating statement. It presents increases (revenue and other financing sources) and decreases (expenditures and other financing uses) in an entity's net spendable assets.

**Substance Over Form.** Used to express the fact that in presenting financial statement data, the economic substance of the transaction originating the data should be used in reflecting those data, even though it may be different from the legal form describing the transaction.

**Transaction Convention.** The primary guideline that accountants use in determining when changes in resources and obligations should be recognized.

**Trial Balance.** A list of the balances of the accounts in a ledger kept by double entry, with the debit and credit balances shown in separate columns. If the totals of the debit and credit columns are equal or their net balance agrees with a control account, the ledger from which the figures are taken is said to be "in balance."

# ■ Suggested Supplementary References

Anthony, Robert N. *Financial Accounting in Nonbusiness Organizations—An Exploratory Study of Conceptual Issues*. Stamford, Conn.: Financial Accounting Standards Board, 1978.

Henke, Emerson O. "Governmental Financial Statements—A Creative Response to User Needs." *Government Accountants Journal* (Summer 1986).

*Holder, William W. "Revenue Recognition in Not-for-Profit Organizations." *CPA Journal* (November 1976), New York State Society of Certified Public Accountants.

Financial Accounting Standards Board. *Statement of Financial Accounting Concepts No. 2 — Qualitative Characteristics of Accounting Information* (May 1980).

Financial Accounting Standards Board. *Statement of Financial Accounting Concepts No. 4 — Objectives of Financial Reporting by Nonbusiness Organizations* (December 1980).

Financial Accounting Standards Board. *Statement of Financial Accounting Concepts No. 6 — Elements of Financial Statements* (December 1985).

Ingram, Robert W., Walter A. Robbins, and Mary S. Stone. "Financial Reporting Practices of Local Governments: An Overview." *Government Finance Review* (April 1988).

Miller, Girard. "Providing Public Sector Financial Information." *Governmental Finance*, 11 (June 1982): 27–35.

Shwartz, Bill Neal. "Social Accounting Revisited." *Government Accountants Journal*, 28 (Winter 1980): 43–48.

# ■ Questions for Class Discussion

**Q2-1.**  List three sources from which nonprofit organizations may realize revenues.

**Q2-2.**  Contrast operational-accountability with dollar-accountability financial reporting. Why do some nonprofit organizations often follow dollar-accountability reporting practices?

**Q2-3.**  How are legal and/or contributor constraints on the uses of resources reflected within the accounting systems of nonprofit organizations?

**Q2-4.**  How are capital and revenue expenditures generally distinguished from each other in a dollar-accountability accounting system? Explain fully.

**Q2-5.**  Can a nonprofit organization follow a program of deficit financing? Explain.

**Q2-6.**  Contrast the term *fund* as used in nonprofit organization accounting with the traditional usage of that term in the profit area.

**Q2-7.**  How are fund accounting entities created within nonprofit organizations?

**Q2-8.**  Which fund will every nonprofit enterprise have within its accounting records? Explain.

**Q2-9.**  Are the terms *expense* and *expenditure* synonymous? Explain.

**Q2-10.**  Why should budgetary data be included in the accounting records of pure nonprofit entities? Explain fully.

**Q2-11.**  Distinguish between restricted and unrestricted resources.

*Also available in *Accounting in the Public Sector: A Changing Environment—A Book of Readings* by Robert W. Ingram. Salt Lake City: Brighton Publishing Company, 1980.

Q2-12.  Classify the following accounts into real or nominal categories:
>    fund balance
>    estimated revenues
>    encumbrances
>    reserve for encumbrances
>    appropriations
>    vouchers payable
>    expenditures
>    cash
>    revenues

Q2-13.  What is meant by *spendable resources?* How do pure nonprofit entities account for the inflows and outflows of those resources?

Q2-14.  How does inflation affect the data reflected in the financial statements of a business enterprise prepared in accordance with GAAP?

Q2-15.  What other accounting practices in addition to the failure to adjust for the effects of inflation may limit the usefulness of the financial statement data? Discuss.

Q2-16.  List the qualitative factors that should underlie financial statements. Relate each to the reasons for preparing those statements.

Q2-17.  State the accounting equation for a dollar-accountability accounting system. How does it relate to the rule of debit and credit followed in recording entity transactions?

Q2-18.  Which statement prepared for profit enterprises most closely resembles a statement of revenues and expenditures for a pure nonprofit entity? Discuss the similarities between the two statements.

Q2-19.  How are acquisitions and disposals of fixed assets accounted for in the records of a dollar-accountability accounting system? What is the justification for those procedures?


# ■ Exercises

E2-1.  Two enterprise units each have ten constituents. One of the units, a pure profit entity, is organized as a corporation with ten stockholders that we shall label A through J. The Stockholders A through E each own 100 shares of stock acquired at its par value of $100 per share. Stockholders F through J each own ten shares of stock also acquired at par value. In that way, the ten stockholders have provided the corporation with a total resource base of $55,000. The second enterprise unit is a governmental entity with ten taxpayers also labeled A through J. Taxpayers A through E each pay $10,000 in taxes while constituents F through J each pay $1,000 giving the governmental entity a total resource base of $55,000. A question of operating policy is to be settled by the constituents of both organizations. In both instances, Constituents A, B, and C favor implementation of the proposed policy while the other constituents vote against it.

**Required:**
Will the proposed operating policy be accepted by either of the two enterprise units? Discuss the general implications of the way this issue was resolved for each enterprise unit.

**E2-2.**   Record the following actions and transactions for a pure nonprofit organization accounting for inflows and outflows on the modified accrual (expenditure-oriented) basis in T-accounts.

1.   The controlling board approves a budget calling for estimated revenues in the amount of $100,000 and appropriations of $98,000.
2.   Revenue in the amount of $60,000 is received in cash.
3.   The organization incurs obligations for the following items:
        salaries, $10,000
        equipment purchases, $5,000
        supplies, $5,000
        payment on long-term debt, $10,000
        miscellaneous operating outlays, $5,000
4.   The organization places an order for equipment, expected to be received in approximately sixty days, amounting to $20,000.
5.   One piece of equipment ordered in transaction 4 and previously estimated to cost $5,000 is received. The billed price is $4,800.

**E2-3.**   Both a business and a municipality purchase five trucks at a cost of $8,000 each. The trucks are expected to have a useful life of five years after which they should have a salvage value of $1,000 each. The business enterprise uses the generally accepted full accrual basis of accounting while the municipality follows the modified accrual (expenditure-oriented) basis of accounting.

a.   Record the purchase of the trucks for each of the two enterprise units.
b.   Record straight-line depreciation (as required) at the end of each of the five years over which the trucks are used.
c.   Journalize the disposal of the trucks at the estimated salvage value for each enterprise unit at the end of the five-year period.
d.   Comment regarding the effects of the accounting practices followed by each of the enterprise units on its respective operating statements for the five years over which the trucks were used. Which reflects the more appropriate allocation of trucking costs to specific operating periods? Explain.

**E2-4.**   The following data are taken from the accounts of a dollar-accountability–oriented entity:

| | |
|---|---:|
| Estimated revenues | $100,000 |
| Revenues | 95,000 |
| Expenditures | 80,000 |
| Appropriations | 94,000 |
| Encumbrances | 8,000 |
| Reserve for encumbrances | 8,000 |
| Vouchers payable | 25,000 |
| Fund Balance (end of last period) | 15,000 |
| Cash | 55,000 |

**Required:**
Prepare appropriate financial statements for the fund.

**E2-5.** A nonprofit organization operating under appropriation control shows the following account balances for equipment acquisitions:

| Appropriation | $100,000 |
|---|---|
| Expenditures | 60,000 |
| Encumbrances | 12,000 |

**Required:**
What amount does the organization still have available to spend for acquisition of equipment?

**E2-6.** A business has purchased a three-year fire and casualty insurance policy at the beginning of the current calendar year at a premium cost of $6,000. At the end of the year, a question is raised regarding the value that should be assigned to the asset element of the insurance premium. The chief executive officer maintains that, because the liquidation value (cancellation value) of the policy has been determined to be $2,800, that value should be assigned to the asset—prepaid insurance—in the end-of-the-year balance sheet.

**Required:**
Evaluate the position of the chief executive officer regarding this matter. Relate your discussion to the pertinent principles and/or conventions discussed in this chapter.

**E2-7.** Opportunist, Inc., an enterprise unit typically carrying a significant amount of inventory, has for many years used the first-in, first-out method of assigning values to that inventory. Prices have risen significantly over the years since the firm was organized. The chief executive officer discovers that the inventory for end of the current period valued on the last-in, first-out basis would amount to $60,000. The first-in, first-out method produces a value of $90,000 for the same inventory. The officer is concerned about showing a large amount of inventory and suggests that it be valued at last-in, first-out ($60,000) at the end of the current year. He calls your attention to the fact that he has recently read an accounting publication that says that either of these two methods of valuing inventory is considered acceptable.

**Required:**
How should the accountant respond to the president's request? Discuss fully, including reference to any accounting principles and/or conventions involved in the valuation decision.

**E2-8.** Service Welfare Agency shows the following data relating to fixed assets in its balance sheet at the end of the current year:

| Fixed assets (at cost) | $625,000 | |
|---|---|---|
| Accumulated depreciation | 300,000 | $325,000 |

The chief executive officer is concerned because the balance sheet shows fixed assets valued at $325,000, which he is certain could be sold for $500,000. He asks you, as his accountant, why the balance sheet does not reflect the "true value" for fixed assets.

**Required:**
Draft a reply to the chief executive officer.

**E2-9.**  Select the best answer for each of the following items:

1.  The organization that has had the greatest impact on the development of accounting theory is the:
    a.  Financial Accounting Standards Board
    b.  Securities and Exchange Commission
    c.  American Accounting Association
    d.  American Institute of Certified Public Accountants.

2.  The valuation of accounts receivable is governed primarily by the:
    a.  matching convention
    b.  going-concern convention
    c.  verifiability concept
    d.  principle of full disclosure.

3.  The method of valuation that is most appropriate for fixed assets subject to amortization is:
    a.  cost
    b.  fair market value
    c.  liquidation value
    d.  cost amortized
    e.  lower of cost or market.

# ■ Problems

**P2-1.**  A nonprofit organization provides its services through a dollar-accountability operating fund showing the following account balances at the beginning of the period:

Cash, $25,000
Vouchers payable, $10,000
Fund balance, $15,000

The governing board of the organization approves an operating budget showing estimated revenues of $500,000 and appropriations of $495,000. The following transactions occur during the year:

1.  Revenues are realized in cash in the amount of $502,000.
2.  Expenditures in the amount of $465,000 are incurred during the year.
3.  The appropriations account includes an item in the amount of $25,000 to be used to establish a print shop to be *operated on a self-sustaining basis*. The print shop is expected to do work for the operating fund, as well as for the general public. The obligation to the print shop is recognized.
4.  Vouchers payable in the amount of $450,000 are paid.
5.  The amount due to the print shop is transferred to that enterprise unit.
6.  Equipment estimated to cost $4,000 is ordered by the operating fund. It is anticipated that the equipment will be delivered in approximately six months.
7.  The print shop purchases equipment costing $15,000 and supplies in the amount of $5,000. These items are paid in cash.
8.  The print shop incurs operating expenses in the amount of $3,000.
9.  The print shop completes a job for the operating fund that is billed at $500. It also realizes $4,000 of income from the public.

10. Half of the equipment ordered in transaction Number 6 of this problem is received at a billed cost of $1,900.
11. Supplies on hand (print shop) at end of period are valued at $4,800.

**Required:**
A. Record the preceding data in T-accounts for the operating fund and for the print
shop. You may assume that print shop equipment has a fifteen-year life with no
salvage value. Assume that the equipment has been used for 6 months.
B. Prepare financial statements from the T-accounts developed in A.

P2-2. A dollar-accountability–oriented fund begins the year with the following account balances:

| | |
|---|---|
| Cash | $40,000 |
| Revenues receivable | 10,000 |
| Vouchers payable | 20,000 |
| Reserve for encumbrances | 10,000 |
| Fund balance | 20,000 |

The fund's operations included the following actions and transactions during the
period:

1. Budget was approved calling for estimated revenues in the amount of $1,200,000
and appropriations amounting to $1,150,000.
2. Revenues receivable of $1,000,000 were recognized.
3. Revenues received in cash, $180,000.
4. Revenues receivable were collected in amount of $1,005,000.
5. Expenditures incurred, $1,120,000.
6. Agreed to purchase equipment estimated to cost $20,000.
7. Paid vouchers payable in amount of $1,130,000.
8. Received equipment relating to beginning-of-period reserve for encumbrances at a
billed cost of $10,000.

**Required:**
A. Record the preceding data in T-accounts.
B. Prepare end-of-period financial statements for the fund.

P2-3. A dollar-accountability fund has the following trial balance at the end of its fiscal
period:

| | | |
|---|---|---|
| Cash | $ 35,000 | |
| Accounts receivable | 40,000 | |
| Vouchers payable | | $ 30,000 |
| Reserve for encumbrances | | 10,000 |
| Fund balance (unreserved) | | 20,000 |
| Estimated revenues | 425,000 | |
| Appropriations | | 420,000 |
| Revenues | | 430,000 |
| Expenditures | 400,000 | |
| Encumbrances | 10,000 | |
| Totals | $910,000 | $910,000 |

**Required:**

A.   Journalize the closing entries required for the fund.

B.   Prepare appropriate dollar-accountability financial statements for the fund.

**P2-4.**   A self-sustaining (proprietary) fund ends its fiscal year with the following trial balance:

| | | |
|---|---:|---:|
| Cash | $ 5,000 | |
| Accounts receivable | 10,000 | |
| Fund balance | | $120,000 |
| Retained earnings | | 4,000 |
| Building | 80,000 | |
| Equipment | 60,000 | |
| Allowance for depreciation—building | | 8,000 |
| Allowance for depreciation—equipment | | 8,000 |
| Revenues from operations | | 125,000 |
| Operating expenses | 118,000 | |
| Vouchers payable | | 8,000 |
| Totals | $273,000 | $273,000 |

You ascertain that the following data have not been recognized in the accounts:

1.   Accrued revenue, $2,000.
2.   Accrued operating expenses, $1,500.
3.   Prepaid operating expenses, $800.
4.   Provision should be made for uncollectible accounts in the amount of one percent of customer accounts receivable.
5.   The building is being depreciated over a forty-year life.
6.   Equipment is being depreciated over a twenty-year life.
7.   No salvage value is anticipated for either asset. All fixed assets were owned for the entire year.

**Required:**

A.   Record the preceding data in T-accounts.

B.   Prepare financial statements for the fund.

**P2-5.**   The accounting records of a pure nonprofit organization include the following data:

| *End of Prior Year Account Balances* | | |
|---|---:|---:|
| Cash | $10,000 | |
| Receivables | 8,000 | |
| Vouchers payable | | $14,000 |
| Fund balance | | 4,000 |
| Totals | $18,000 | $18,000 |

*End of Current Year Account Balances*

| | |
|---|---:|
| Cash | $ 4,000 |
| Receivables | $12,000 |
| Vouchers payable | $13,000 |
| Fund balance | $ 7,000 |
| Estimated revenues | $80,000 |
| Appropriations for service Number 1 | $35,000 |
| Appropriations for service Number 2 | $20,000 |
| Appropriations for service Number 3 | $22,000 |
| Revenues | $78,000 |
| Expenditures for service Number 1 | $35,000 |
| Expenditures for service Number 2 | $21,000 |
| Expenditures for service Number 3 | $23,000 |

**Required:**

A. Prepare a statement of revenues and expenditures for the year.

B. Prepare a balance sheet as of the end of the year.

C. Comment on the service story as reflected in the financial statements.

**P2-6.** Select the best answer for each of the following items:

1. Which of the following is an accrued liability?
   a. cash dividends payable
   b. wages payable
   c. rent revenue collected one month in advance
   d. portion of long-term debt payable in current year

2. The premium on a three-year insurance policy that expires in 19X4 was paid in advance in 19X0. What is the effect of this transaction on the 19X0 financial statements for each of the following?

   | | *Prepaid assets* | *Expenses* |
   |---|---|---|
   | a. | Increase | No effect |
   | b. | Increase | Increase |
   | c. | No effect | Increase |
   | d. | No effect | No effect |

3. Rent received in advance by the lessor for an operating lease should be recognized as revenue:
   a. when received.
   b. at the lease's inception.
   c. over the period specified by the lease.
   d. at the lease's expiration.

4. One of the differences between accounting for a governmental (not-for-profit) unit and a commercial (for-profit) enterprise is that a governmental (not-for-profit) unit should:
   a. *not* record depreciation expense in any of its funds.
   b. always establish and maintain complete self-balancing accounts for each fund.
   c. use only the cash basis of accounting.
   d. use only the modified accrual basis of accounting.

5. When goods that have been previously approved for purchase are received by a governmental unit but *not* yet paid for, what account is credited?
   a. reserve for encumbrances
   b. vouchers payable
   c. expenditures
   d. appropriations

6. Which of the following accounts is closed out at the end of the fiscal year?
   a. fund balance
   b. expenditures
   c. vouchers payable
   d. revenues receivable

7. What journal entry should be made at the end of the fiscal year to close out encumbrances for which goods and services have *not* been received?
   a. debit reserve for the encumbrances and credit encumbrances
   b. debit reserve for encumbrances and credit fund balance
   c. debit fund balance and credit encumbrances
   d. debit encumbrances and credit reserve for encumbrances

—**AICPA Adapted**

P2-7. Select the best answer for each of the following items:

1. When reporting for governmental units, what type of costs should be presented in the financial statements?
   a. historical
   b. historical adjusted for price-level changes
   c. current appraisal
   d. historical and current presented in two separate columns

2. Revenue is generally recognized when the earning process is virtually complete and an exchange has taken place. What convention is described herein?
   a. consistency
   b. matching
   c. realization
   d. conservatism

3. Price-level adjusted financial statements (general purchasing power) have been a controversial issue in accounting. Which of the following arguments in favor of such financial statements is not valid?
   a. Price-level adjusted financial statements use historical cost.
   b. Price-level adjusted financial statements compare uniform purchasing power among various periods.
   c. Price-level adjusted financial statements measure current value.
   d. Price-level adjusted financial statements measure earnings in terms of a common dollar.

4. Determining periodic earnings and financial position depends on measuring economic resources and obligations and changes in them as these changes occur. This explanation pertains to:
   a. disclosure.
   b. accrual accounting.

    c.   materiality.

    d.   the matching concept.

5.  Lower-of-cost-or-market accounting is an example of which principle or convention?

    a.   consistency

    b.   conservatism

    c.   realization

    d.   matching

—**AICPA Adapted**

**P2-8.**  Select the best answer for each of the following items:

1.  The Financial Accounting Standards Board has stated that certain lease contracts, including provisions that cause most of the value of the asset plus normal financing charges to be paid over a period approximating the life of the asset, should be treated as a purchase and sale rather than as a lease. This statement illustrates the application of:

    a.   the principle of materiality.

    b.   the matching convention.

    c.   substance over form.

    d.   the realization convention.

2.  Recognizing a small expenditure for a long-term asset as an expense can be justified within:

    a.   the realization convention.

    b.   the matching convention.

    c.   the principle of objectivity.

    d.   the principle of materiality.

3.  The allocation of resource costs to expense in the period during which the revenue earned by their use is recognized illustrates the application of the:

    a.   matching convention.

    b.   principle of consistency.

    c.   principle of conservatism.

    d.   principle of full disclosure.

4.  The valuation of an asset at its cost less the amount of cost amortized rather than at its liquidation value on the balance sheet is an example of the application of the:

    a.   principle of objectivity.

    b.   matching convention.

    c.   principle of conservatism.

    d.   the going-concern convention.

5.  The requirement in governmental accounting that financial reports be presented for each fund is an example of the application of the:

    a.   principle of full disclosure.

    b.   entity convention.

    c.   principle of objectivity.

    d.   matching convention.

—**AICPA Adapted**

**P2-9.**   Select the best answer for each of the following items:

1.  The principle of objectivity includes the concept of:
    a.  summarization.
    b.  classification.
    c.  conservatism.
    d.  verifiability.

2.  Financial statements that are expressed assuming a stable monetary unit are:
    a.  general price-level financial statements.
    b.  historical-dollar financial statements.
    c.  current-value financial statements.
    d.  fair-value financial statements.

3.  What is the underlying concept that supports the immediate recognition of a loss?
    a.  conservatism
    b.  consistency
    c.  judgment
    d.  matching

4.  Objectivity is assumed to be achieved when an accounting transaction:
    a.  is recorded in a fixed amount of dollars.
    b.  involves the payment or receipt of cash.
    c.  involves an arm's-length transaction between two independent parties.
    d.  allocates revenues or expenses in a rational and systematic manner.

5.  Under *Statement of Financial Accounting Concepts,* No. 2, feedback value is an ingredient of the primary quality of:

|  | *Relevance* | *Reliability* |
|---|---|---|
| a. | No | No |
| b. | No | Yes |
| c. | Yes | Yes |
| d. | Yes | No |

6.  Under *Statement of Financial Accounting Concepts,* No. 2, which of the following interacts with both relevance and reliability to contribute to the usefulness of information?
    a.  comparability
    b.  timeliness
    c.  neutrality
    d.  predictive value

7.  The valuation of a promise to receive cash in the future at present value on the financial statements of a business entity is valid because of the accounting convention of:
    a.  entity.
    b.  materiality.
    c.  going concern.
    d.  neutrality.

8.  Which of the following is an example of the expense recognition principle of associating cause and effect?
    a.  allocation of insurance cost

    b.   sales commissions

    c.   depreciation of fixed assets

    d.   officer's salaries

9.   Accruing net losses on firm purchase commitments for inventory is an example of the accounting concept of:

    a.   conservatism.

    b.   realization.

    c.   consistency.

    d.   materiality.

10.   Which of the following accounting concepts states that an accounting transaction should be supported by sufficient evidence to allow two or more qualified individuals to arrive at essentially similar measures and conclusions?

    a.   matching

    b.   objectivity

    c.   periodicity

    d.   stable monetary unit

11.   Under *Statement of Financial Accounting Concepts*, No. 2, the ability through consensus among measures to ensure that information represents what it purports to represent is an example of the concept of:

    a.   relevance.

    b.   verifiability.

    c.   comparability.

    d.   feedback value.

12.   Under *Statement of Financial Accounting Concepts*, No. 2, which of the following is an ingredient only of the primary quality of relevance?

    a.   predictive value

    b.   materiality

    c.   understandability

    d.   verifiability

13.   Under *Statement of Financial Accounting Concepts*, No. 2, which of the following is an ingredient only of the primary quality of reliability?

    a.   understandability

    b.   verifiability

    c.   predictive value

    d.   materiality

14.   Uncertainty and risks inherent in business situations should be adequately considered in financial reporting. This statement is an example of the concept of:

    a.   conservatism.

    b.   completeness.

    c.   neutrality.

    d.   representational faithfulness.

—**AICPA** Adapted

# PART TWO

# Governmental Accounting

■ *CHAPTER 3*

**Introduction to Governmental Accounting Practices**

■ *CHAPTER 4*

**Development and Use of Budgetary Data**

■ *CHAPTER 5*

**General Fund and Special Revenue Fund Accounting Procedures—I**

■ *CHAPTER 6*

**General Fund and Special Revenue Fund Accounting Procedures—II**

■ *CHAPTER 7*

**Accounting for Other Governmental-Type Funds**

■ *CHAPTER 8*

## Accounting for Other Funds and Account Groups

■ *CHAPTER 9*

## Annual Financial Reports

■ *CHAPTER 10*

## Federal Government Accounting

# CHAPTER 3

# Introduction to Governmental Accounting Practices

## ■ Learning Objectives

When you have finished your study of this chapter, you should

1. Be aware of the generally accepted objectives of governmental accounting systems.
2. Know who are the users of governmental financial statements.
3. Be familiar with the contents of National Council on Governmental Accounting (NCGA) Statement 1.
4. Recognize the characteristics of the different types of funds and account groups used in governmental accounting systems.
5. Have a general understanding of the functions of the Governmental Accounting Standards Board (GASB) and the provisions of the statements it has issued.

In Part One, we observed that a nonprofit organization is an enterprise unit that has:

1. an operating objective of providing socially desirable services without the intention of realizing a profit from providing them
2. no ownership shares that are capable of being sold or traded.

We also briefly reviewed the conceptual foundation underlying general accounting practices and developed the framework within which a *dollar-accountability account-ing system* operates. That system is designed to give special attention to controlling dollar outflows through use of *appropriation controls* and *fund accounting* techniques.

In Part Two, we illustrate the adaptation of the dollar-accountability accounting system to governmental entities. Although these organizational units typically include some profit-oriented (self-sustaining) subentities, their overall operating objectives cause them to be characterized primarily as pure nonprofit enterprises. Most of their subentities have all the characteristics of a pure nonprofit-type activity. Others, however, operate as quasi-nonprofit or profit-oriented segments of the total organizational unit. This diversification of operational characteristics requires that the governmental accountant have an understanding of accounting practices ranging from those designed to disclose dollar accountability, through hybrid systems, to systems similar to those used for business enterprises. In this chapter, we shall *identify and explain the general principles underlying the accounting practices of the various types of subentities typically found within governmental units.*

Legal requirements force governmental entities to place a strong emphasis on dollar-accountability–oriented records. This is evidenced by the use of different funds, the presentation of expenditure- rather than expense-oriented financial data, and the incorporation of appropriation control accounts into the accounting records of operating funds. Over a period of many years, this has caused a major controversy within the public accounting profession. Governmental Accounting, Auditing, and Financial Reporting (GAAFR) has always taken the position that legal provisions should take precedence over generally accepted accounting practices whenever they are in conflict.[1] On the other hand, the accounting profession has conducted a number of studies and has concluded that the financial reports should be presented in accordance with generally accepted accounting principles (GAAP).[2]

NCGA Statement 1, published in 1979, compromised these two positions by stating that the accounting system should make it possible to meet both legal and GAAP requirements.[3] Obviously, public administrators must follow the laws governing financial reporting. The present situation is summarized by Freeman and Nuttall: "Legal compliance reporting of governments must conform to legal provisions, but the financial statements of governmental units should be prepared in conformity with generally accepted accounting principles."[4] If a governmental entity wants an unqualified opinion from its auditors, it should prepare its financial statements in conformity with GAAP as an extension beyond the legally required reports. Because of this controversy and the logic supporting full accrual basis reporting, we will show in Chapter 9 how the legal compliance (dollar-accountability) financial data developed in Chapters 5 through 8 can be converted to accrual-based statements.

As we work from the conceptual base developed in Part One toward the objective of more specifically identifying the accounting practices followed by governmental units, it will be helpful for us to

1. National Council on Governmental Accounting, *Governmental Accounting, Auditing, and Financial Reporting* (Chicago: Municipal Finance Officers Association—now Government Finance Officers Association, 1988), p. 10.
2. See, for example, *AICPA Industry Audit Guide on Audits of State and Local Governmental Units,* 5th ed. (New York: AICPA, 1989), p. 3.
3. National Council on Governmental Accounting, *NCGA Statement 1* (Chicago: Municipal Finance Officers Association, 1979), p. 2.
4. Robert J. Freeman and Donald M. Nuttall, "The GAAFR Restatement Principles: An Executive Summary," *Governmental Finance* (May 1978): 3.

1. review the generally accepted objectives of governmental accounting systems
2. identify more specifically the users of governmental accounting information
3. examine NCGA Statement 1 (*Summary Statement of Governmental Accounting Principles*)
4. relate the underlying principles and concepts described in Part One to governmental accounting practices
5. briefly describe the different types of funds and account groups included within the accounting systems of governmental units
6. summarize subsequently issued interpretations of NCGA Statement 1 and other statements issued by that body and by the Governmental Accounting Standards Board (GASB).

## ■ Primary Objectives of Governmental Accounting

We have observed that the financial statements for any enterprise unit should be designed to show the extent to which the operating objectives of the entity have been achieved and to disclose the nature and amounts of resources and obligations associated with entity operations. In addressing these general financial reporting objectives for governmental units, a committee of the American Accounting Association has recommended that the accounting practices of the public sector be designed to provide information

1. necessary for faithful, efficient, effective, and economical management of an operation and of resources entrusted to it (This objective relates to *management control*.)
2. to enable managers to report on the discharge of their responsibilities to administer faithfully, efficiently, and effectively the programs and uses of the resources under their direction; and to permit all public officials to report to the public on the results of government operations and uses of public funds (This objective relates to *accountability*.).[5]

If we accept these two objectives of management control and accountability, we can conclude that the accounting system for governmental entities should be designed to provide the type of fiscal control that will facilitate disclosure of the extent of compliance with legal requirements and at the same time allow meaningful and useful financial statements to be presented within the guidelines of generally accepted accounting principles (GAAP). The 1979 NCGA Statement 1 was designed to permit those objectives to be met. This statement was published by the Municipal Finance Officers Association in cooperation with the National Council on Governmental Accounting. Later in this chapter, we will present the Summary Statement of Principles

---

5. "Report of Committee on Not-for-Profit Organizations, 1972–73," *Accounting Review,* Supplement to Vol. XLIX, pp. 228–229.

from that publication and relate elements of it to the general framework and conceptual foundation developed in Part One. This Statement stresses that an important function of a governmental accounting system is to disclose whether those charged with administrative responsibilities have complied with pertinent legal provisions. If, for example, the law requires that particular resources be accounted for in a separate fund, the accounting system must be organized to provide that type of accountability. The appropriate revenue (inflow) and expenditure (outflow) accounts must also be included within the fund.

The accounting practices required to disclose legal accountability in some instances may conflict with those dictated by generally accepted accounting principles. *The Summary Statement of Principles clearly states that the system should be organized to allow the organization to meet both reporting requirements.*

## ■ Users of Governmental Accounting Information

We have described the different groups generally interested in the financial information of enterprise units. As we relate those groups to governmental enterprises, we find that *internal managers* primarily include chief administrators and departmental supervisors. The *external management group* can be thought of as including legislators, legislative committees, city councils, and other similar groups. The *constituency* includes the public as individuals, public interest groups, and the news media. The typical group of *creditors and creditor-associated parties* for governmental entities may include bondholders, investment bankers, bond-rating services, and short-term creditors. Other external groups interested in the financial data of governmental entities include grantors and revenue sharing agencies, regulatory agencies, research groups, and employee unions. These groups primarily use the data for two purposes: to evaluate managerial performance and to make various operating and financial-commitment decisions relating to the entity.

### Evaluating Managerial Performance

The management of any economic entity will always have an expressed or implied obligation to account to its constituency for the ways it has used the resources put at its disposal. The constituency generally provides those resources and is therefore the group ultimately concerned with evaluating management's performance. In the case of governmental units, the constituency includes the citizens who pay taxes or have a right to vote on officials and the activities of the entity.

When we seek to identify the financial data and the ways that the system should be organized and used to facilitate the evaluation of managerial performance, it seems that the constituent and potential constituent groups will be concerned with

1. evaluating the effectiveness of management in discharging its stewardship responsibility relating to resources at its disposal
2. evaluating the efficiency with which management has handled the resource conversion activities of the entity

3. evaluating the extent to which management has adhered to regulations governing entity activities

4. disclosing the rights of various parties as they relate to the uses of resources held by the entity.

**Stewardship of Resources.** As stewards of the resources put at their disposal, managers have a responsibility for disclosing through the accounting system that the resources have been properly used. Misuse is interpreted to include using resources for other than their intended purposes, the embezzlement or theft of resources, or the failure to use the resources within the legal constraints imposed by national, state, or local laws.

The constituency of an organization must depend primarily on the *system of internal control* for assurance that resources have not been embezzled or stolen. Most of the elements of such a system are the same for both profit and nonprofit entities. They include such things as an organization chart and a procedures manual that provide for a proper separation of responsibilities among entity employees and the assignment of specific responsibilities to specific individuals. To be effective, the accounting system must also include an appropriate set of procedures and forms to be used in authorizing and recording the various financial activities of the enterprise. The enterprise must also follow employment practices that assure the placement of properly qualified personnel in positions involving custodial and recordkeeping responsibilities.

Having established a system of control incorporating these elements, management must still make sure that employees are complying with the established procedures. In small enterprise units, this can be a direct responsibility of the owner-manager. In larger enterprises, it will often be necessary to delegate compliance enforcement to an internal auditing staff. As an illustration, the General Accounting Office of the United States government is the internal auditing arm of Congress charged with the responsibility of policing the activities of the various governmental agencies.

All enterprise units operate within legal constraints imposed by national, state, and local laws, as well as provisions embodied in corporate charters and partnership agreements. *Governmental units and many other nonprofit organizations operate within much stricter and more detailed constraints than those imposed upon businesses.* These additional constraints include specific regulations as to how resources may be acquired and used. Operating within those constraints is often characterized as *fiscal compliance.* Among these entities, therefore, there is a need for accounting records and financial reports that disclose the extent to which management has met legal and/or constituency-imposed constraints relating to the acquisitions and uses of resources. This is done through the use of separate funds and by controlling outflows within funds on an item-by-item basis. Evidence of compliance is shown in the statements of revenues and expenditures or in a combined statement of those inflows and outflows as shown later in the text (see page 350). Such a statement reflects the *dollar-accountability* stewardship story by showing where dollars came from, how they were used, and the extent of deviations from budgetary plans.

**Measurement of Entity Achievement.** In addition to the responsibilities for using resources appropriately within legal and constituency-imposed constraints, management also has an implied responsibility to *use the resources available to it in an effective and efficient manner*. Accounting records and financial reports should be organized to provide suitable measures of efficiency and effectiveness. This can be characterized as the disclosure of *operational accountability*. It is one of the more important features to be incorporated into any accounting system designed to help evaluate managerial performance.

Among business enterprises the disclosure of operational accountability is achieved through the preparation of an income statement and by showing relationships between net income and the resources available to the entity. As an example, earnings-per-share data, which disclose the amount of earnings for each share of common stock, are extremely important in the profit area because they represent key figures in the disclosure of operational accountability. Earnings-per-share data help measure the level of efficiency that management has achieved in pursuing the profit objective. Other things being equal, a higher ratio of earnings per share to market value per share reflects greater efficiency in the use of resources than does a lower ratio.

The emphasis on net income in operational-accountability reporting for profit enterprises is consistent with the primary operating objective of those entities. Beyond that, it is also important to recognize that long-term continuous failure of a firm to earn a profit will ultimately force such an entity out of existence. The constituents of these enterprises withdraw their support by selling ownership shares in less efficient entities and investing in more efficient ones. In this way, the capitalistic system forces less efficient profit-seeking entities out of existence and causes the more efficient ones to grow and prosper.

Because governmental units have no profit objective, we are unable to use the profit-accountability technique for measuring either managerial efficiency or entity performance. Logically, the ideal method of measuring operational accountability in this area would be to match the imputed value of the services rendered against the expenses associated with rendering those services. During the mid-1960s some attention was given to this concept in attempting to measure the operational effectiveness of certain federal governmental programs. Unfortunately, our present level of knowledge does not permit a reasonably objective and dependable determination of an imputed value for such services. We have no objective criteria against which to measure, for example, the value of police services to the citizens of a municipality.

Functional unit costs accompanied by nondollar quantitative data, however, can be used to partially evaluate operational efficiency. If such information is available, users can compare the functional cost data of one governmental unit with those data for other similar entities. The author has suggested, for example, that the development of *cost-per-capita* data for the various types of services rendered by a governmental entity would be helpful in evaluating the efficiency of operations.[6] He also suggests that such a figure might even be labeled "cost per share" to more directly relate it to the earnings-per-share data for profit enterprises.

6.  Emerson O. Henke, "Governmental Financial Reports: A Creative Response to User Needs," *Government Accountants Journal* (Summer 1986): 22–26.

## Financial Data for Decision-Making Purposes

In Chapter 1, we discussed how the managers of enterprise units go through a plan-execute-evaluate-plan cycle as they monitor and control the operations of an entity. Both the planning and evaluation elements of this operating cycle require the use of data provided by the accounting system. In the planning phase of the cycle, budgetary projections are used to quantify the anticipated operating plans. The budgetary data should be developed along lines paralleling the historical data accumulated and reported by the accounting system. As managers evaluate the operations of a past period, they analyze the historical operating and financial position data provided by the accounting records and compare those data with budgetary amounts developed during the planning phase of the cycle.

In addition to the managers of economic entities, the constituents, potential constituents, creditors, and regulatory agencies must make various decisions regarding their relationships with the entity. We shall now examine, more specifically, the financial information that these groups would logically want to use in making those decisions.

**Managerial Operating Decisions.**  Decisions relating to operating policies and practices are made by both external and internal managers of governmental units. The legislative bodies or councils of these entities concern themselves mostly with evaluating internal managers, with establishing operating policies, and with major decisions regarding internal operating practices. Because they are concerned with these types of decisions, they require data disclosing general operating results along with the resource-obligation position of the entity.

The *matching of efforts against achievements is one of the primary concerns of all external managers*. Governmental entities have no profit objective and provide most of their services on the basis of need. As we observed earlier, they are unable to match efforts in the form of resource outlays against achievements in the form of an objectively determined value for services rendered. Therefore, they have to be especially concerned with how well internal managers adhere to predetermined operating plans for realizing and spending resources. Nevertheless, judgments must be made as to whether the services provided by the organization are being provided with a reasonable degree of efficiency, and whether they are worth the cost of providing them. That creates a need for alternate evaluation data. Within the limits of our present level of knowledge, that seems to require the computation and presentation of functional unit costs, such as the costs per capita of providing various types of services to the citizens of the governmental entity. Since each citizen is, in effect, a shareholder in the governmental entity, we could call those amounts *cost per share* data, as suggested before.

**Constituency Decisions.**  The constituents of a governmental unit are frequently expected to make decisions as to whether they will support one course of action or another. Those decisions often involve choices between spending more or less and paying more or less in the way of taxes. *The constituency of a governmental entity expresses its will through the ballot box*. Their votes should be cast with as much useful information available to them as possible. They will certainly be influenced by whether or not they feel resources have been used efficiently. The system, then, should provide information for the constituency that will show how much it has cost the entity to support itself apart from its rendering of services to others. The financial statements should also include nondollar quantitative disclosures of the amounts of services provided and the functional unit costs of providing those services. In practice, however, the financial statements of governmental entities, prepared within the constraints of prescribed accounting practices for that area, generally do not disclose much of this desired information.

**Decisions by Creditors.**    Business creditors desire accounting information that will *help them determine whether they can expect to receive periodic interest payments on their loans and the return of principal upon maturity of the loan.* The creditors of governmental units logically expect to have the same questions answered as they decide whether they will grant credit to those organizations. Business creditors are interested in asset–liability relationships and the extent to which the earnings of the business entity are capable of meeting its obligations. In many instances, prospective long-term creditors are also concerned with the value and nature of the collateral that can be pledged to secure the loan. However, the single purpose nature of many longer-term assets of governmental entities makes them less attractive as loan collateral. Otherwise, the evaluation of a loan opportunity is similar for both types of entities.

Realistically, *all creditors are much more interested in revenue-producing capability than they are in the collateral that can be pledged as security for a loan.* This strong interest in revenue potential requires that the financial statement data be organized to provide as much information as possible about an entity's ability to generate resource inflows. In the case of local governmental entities, the ability to generate revenue is best reflected by either the anticipated taxing capabilities and/or the ability to realize subsidy support from the federal government. It is important, then, for the accounting reports of these organizations to disclose, insofar as is practicable, information that will help creditors evaluate the potential capability of increasing the inflows of liquid assets from one or both of the sources noted above. In the case of such an entity, it is important for the financial statement data to include supplementary quantitative information that will allow the potential creditor to judge whether taxes can be increased, or federal support can be secured that will assure the interest-paying and debt-redemption capabilities of the entity.

Bonds constitute the primary media through which nonprofit organizations secure long-term credit. Governmental entities, in particular, rely heavily on resources realized from the issuance of bonds. According to Hugh C. Sherwood, Standard & Poor's has always required that at least eight pieces of information, in addition to financial statement data, be considered in the process of evaluating municipal general-obligation bonds. They are

1. a statement of the issuer's overall debt outstanding: this statement should show when each issue will mature and the sources from which resources are expected to be realized for payment of principal and interest

2. a statement disclosing the total assessed valuations of property for each of the last four years

3. a statement of tax collections for each of the last four years

4.  a recent estimate of the population of the area

5.  a list of the ten largest taxpayers, including the valuations placed on their properties

6.  a brief description of the area's economy

7.  a statement of the borrowing plans for a reasonable period into the future

8.  a statement setting out capital improvement program plans for the next five years.[7]

As you can see from this list of supplementary data, potential long-term creditors are vitally interested in the probable resource inflows and outflows of the enterprise unit.

# ■ Summary Statement of Principles

The National Council on Governmental Accounting, in considering the objectives of governmental accounting and the needs of perceived users of financial information described earlier, has developed the following Summary Statement of Principles setting out the various elements of generally accepted accounting principles for governmental units. Although it is called a Statement of Principles, it is more realistically a statement defining accounting practices for governmental units.[8]

### Summary Statement of Principles[9]

**Accounting and Reporting Capabilities**

1.  A governmental accounting system must make it possible both: (a) to present fairly and with full disclosure the financial position and results of financial operations of the funds and account groups of the governmental unit in conformity with generally accepted accounting principles; and (b) to determine and demonstrate compliance with finance-related legal and contractual provisions.

**Fund Accounting Systems**

2.  Governmental accounting systems should be organized and operated on a fund basis. A fund is defined as a fiscal and accounting entity with a self-balancing set of accounts recording cash and other financial resources, together with all related liabilities and residual equities or balances, and changes therein, which are segregated for the purpose of carrying on specific activities or attaining certain objectives in accordance with special regulations, restrictions, or limitations.

7.  Hugh C. Sherwood, *How Corporate and Municipal Debt Is Rated* (New York: John Wiley & Sons, 1976), pp. 115–116.

8.  Reproduced with permission from National Council on Governmental Accounting, *NCGA Statement 1 — Governmental Accounting and Financial Reporting Principles* (Chicago: Municipal Finance Officers Association of the United States and Canada — now Government Finance Officers Association, 1979). Copyright © 1979 by the Municipal Finance Officers Association of the United States and Canada — now Government Finance Officers Association.

9.  Adapted to provisions of GASB 6 eliminating use of special assessment funds and GASB 9 requiring the presentation of cash flow statements for proprietary funds.

### Types of Funds

3.  The following types of funds should be used by state and local governments:

**Governmental Funds**

a.  *The General Fund*—to account for all financial resources except those required to be accounted for in another fund.

b.  *Special Revenue Funds*—to account for the proceeds of specific revenue sources (other than expendable trusts, or for major capital projects) that are legally restricted to expenditure for specified purposes.

c.  *Capital Projects Funds*—to account for financial resources to be used for the acquisition or construction of major capital facilities (other than those financed by proprietary funds, Special Assessment Funds, and Trust Funds).

d.  *Debt-Service Funds*—to account for the accumulation of resources for, and the payment of, general long-term debt principal and interest.

**Proprietary Funds**

e.  *Enterprise Funds*—to account for operations (a) that are financed and operated in a manner similar to private business enterprises—where the intent of the governing body is that the costs (expenses, including depreciation) of providing goods or services to the general public on a continuing basis be financed or recovered primarily through user charges; or (b) where the governing body has decided that periodic determination of revenues earned, expenses incurred, and/or net income is appropriate for capital maintenance, public policy, management control, accountability, or other purposes.

f.  *Internal Service Funds*—to account for the financing of goods or services provided by one department or agency to other departments or agencies of the governmental unit, or to other governmental units, on a cost-reimbursement basis.

**Fiduciary Funds**

g.  *Trust and Agency Funds*—to account for assets held by a governmental unit in a trustee capacity or as an agent for individuals, private organizations, other governmental units, and/or other funds. These include (a) Expendable Trust Funds, (b) Nonexpendable Trust Funds, (c) Pension Trust Funds, and (d) Agency Funds.

## Number of Funds

4.  Governmental units should establish and maintain those funds required by law and sound financial administration. Only the minimum number of funds consistent with legal and operating requirements should be established, however, since unnecessary funds result in inflexibility, undue complexity, and inefficient financial administration.

## Accounting for Fixed Assets and Long-Term Liabilities

5.  A clear distinction should be made between (a) fund fixed assets and general fixed assets and (b) fund long-term liabilities and general long-term debt.

a.  Fixed assets related to specific proprietary funds or Trust Funds should be accounted for through those funds. All other fixed assets of a governmental unit should be accounted for through the General Fixed Assets Account Group.

b. Long-term liabilities of proprietary funds and Trust Funds should be accounted for through those funds. All other unmatured general long-term liabilities of the governmental unit should be accounted for through the General Long-Term Debt Account Group.

## Valuation of Fixed Assets

6. Fixed assets should be accounted for at cost or, if the cost is not practicably determinable, at estimated cost. Donated fixed assets should be recorded at their estimated fair value at the time received.

## Depreciation of Fixed Assets

7. a. Depreciation of general fixed assets should not be recorded in the accounts of governmental funds. Depreciation of general fixed assets may be recorded in cost accounting systems or calculated for cost finding analyses; and accumulated depreciation may be recorded in the General Fixed Assets Account Group.

   b. Depreciation of fixed assets accounted for in a proprietary fund should be recorded in the accounts of that fund. Depreciation is also recognized in those Trust Funds where expenses, net income, and/or capital maintenance are measured.

## Accrual Basis in Governmental Accounting

8. The modified accrual or accrual basis of accounting, as appropriate, should be utilized in measuring financial position and operating results.

   a. *Governmental fund* revenues and expenditures should be recognized on the modified accrual basis. Revenues should be recognized in the accounting period in which they become available and measurable. Expenditures should be recognized in the accounting period in which the fund liability is incurred, if measurable, except for unmatured interest on general long-term debt and on special assessment indebtedness secured by interest-bearing special assessment levies, which should be recognized when due.

   b. *Proprietary fund* revenues and expenses should be recognized on the accrual basis. Revenues should be recognized in the accounting period in which they are earned and become measurable; expenses should be recognized in the period incurred, if measurable.

   c. *Fiduciary fund* revenues and expenses or expenditures (as appropriate) should be recognized on the basis consistent with the fund's accounting measurement objective. Nonexpendable Trust and Pension Trust Funds should be accounted for on the accrual basis; Expendable Trust Funds should be accounted for on the modified accrual basis. Agency Fund assets and liabilities should be accounted for on the modified accrual basis.

   d. *Transfers* should be recognized in the accounting period in which the interfund receivable and payable arise.

## Budgeting, Budgetary Control, and Budgetary Reporting

9. a. An annual budget(s) should be adopted by every governmental unit.

   b. The accounting system should provide the basis for appropriate budgetary control.

c.  Budgetary comparisons should be included in the appropriate financial statements and schedules for governmental funds for which an annual budget has
been adopted.

### Transfer, Revenue, Expenditure, and Expense Account Classification

10.  a.  Interfund transfers and proceeds of general long-term debt issues should be
classified separately from fund revenues and expenditures or expenses.

b.  Governmental fund revenues should be classified by fund and source. Expenditures should be classified by fund, function (or program), organization unit,
activity, character, and principal classes of objects.

c.  Proprietary fund revenues and expenses should be classified in essentially the
same manner as those of similar business organizations, functions, or activities.

### Common Terminology and Classification

11.  A common terminology and classification should be used consistently throughout
the budget, the accounts, and the financial reports of each fund.

### Interim and Annual Financial Reports

12.  a.  Appropriate interim financial statements and reports of financial position,
operating results, and other pertinent information should be prepared to
facilitate management control of financial operations, legislative oversight,
and, where necessary or desired, for external reporting purposes.

b.  A comprehensive annual financial report covering all funds and account
groups of the governmental unit—including appropriate combined, combining, and individual fund statements; notes to the financial statements; schedules; narrative explanations; and statistical tables—should be prepared and
published.

c.  General purpose financial statements may be issued separately from the comprehensive annual financial report. Such statements should include the basic
financial statements and notes to the financial statements that are essential to
fair presentation of financial position and operating results (and statements of
cash flow for proprietary funds and similar Trust Funds).

d.  A component unit financial report covering all funds and account groups of
a component unit—including introductory section; appropriate combined,
combining, and individual fund statements; notes to the financial statements;
required supplementary information; schedules; narrative explanations; and
statistical tables—may be prepared and published, as necessary.

e.  Component unit financial statements of a component unit may be issued
separately from the component unit financial report. Such statements should
include the basic financial statements and notes to the financial statements
that are essential to the fair presentation of financial position and results of
operations (and statements of cash flow for proprietary funds and similar trust
funds). Those statements may also be required to be accompanied by required
supplementary information, essential to financial reporting of certain entities.

Dollar-accountability accounting procedures are followed in accounting for governmental and expendable trust and agency funds. This means that the primary objective of their accounting systems is to show the sources of spendable resource inflows and

how those resources were used in rendering services. Figure 3–1 shows the typical sources from which such resource inflows are realized and how they are used for the various governmental and expendable trust and agency funds. In Chapters 4 through 9, we will demonstrate the procedures followed in recording those resource inflows and outflows.

## ■ Application of Basic Principles and Conventions

The qualitative factors, the monetary unit assumption, and the basic principles and concepts discussed in Chapter 2 underlie the basic statement of principles of governmental accounting just as they underlie commercial accounting practices. Statement 1 developed by the NCGA specifically emphasizes the importance of *consistency* and *full disclosure* as it spells out the accounting practices to be followed by governmental units. Adherence to the principle of objectivity causes changes in resources and obligations to be recognized at the points where transactions occur (*transaction convention*). The importance of comparability is recognized and, as a result, the statement requires that financial data be presented in a consistent manner from period to period. This means that the same form of presentation should be used, and that the same items should be included in the statements for succeeding periods. The emphasis on consistency indicates that the same accounting practices should be followed from period to period unless a change in them is disclosed.

The NCGA Statement 1 discussion of the elements of the Summary Statement frequently cites the need for fair and full disclosure of all significant financial facts. In referring to interim and annual financial reports, the statement also recognizes the need for adequate disclosure of financially related information by referring to other pertinent information schedules and statistical tables that should be included with the statements. Other discussion relating to the financial statements suggests that all information that might affect the conclusions of a reasonably informed reader should be included with the financial statements. More specifically, this is stated to require a summary of significant accounting policies and other notes to the financial statements necessary for adequate disclosure.[10] This can be interpreted to include information relating to the following items:

1. significant accounting policies
2. measurement bases
3. restrictions on assets
4. contingencies
5. important commitments not recognized in the bodies of the statements
6. changes in accounting principles
7. subsequent events.

In addition to these, governmental accounting reports should normally include explanatory disclosures relating to the nature, purpose, and legal bases of the various funds and account groups.

10. *NCGA Statement 1* (1979), p. 24.

**FIGURE 3–1.** Fund Resource Flows

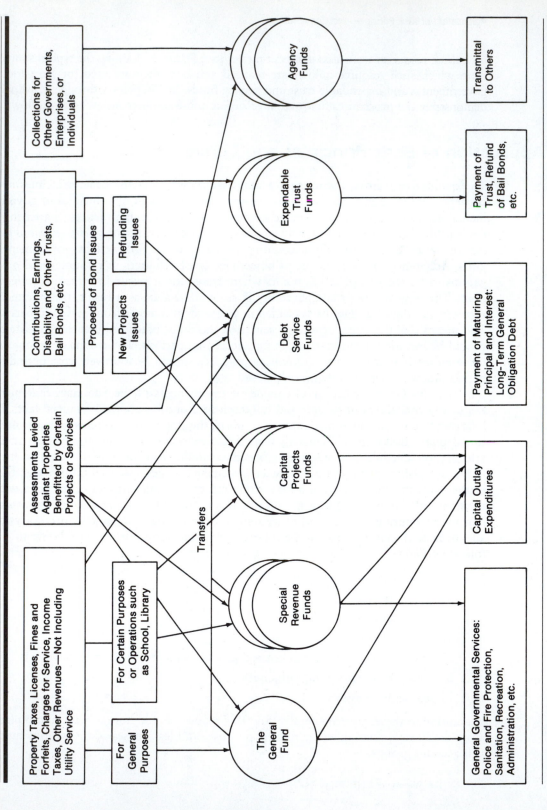

*Source:* Adapted from Ernst and Young, *Introduction to Governmental Accounting*, p. 1-16. Used with permission.

The *principle of materiality* focuses on the need for properly recognizing significant transactions and events. Since each fund or account group in a governmental accounting system constitutes a reporting entity, materiality must be evaluated in terms of the amounts reflected in the pertinent fund or account group, rather than in the combined data for the governmental unit. Any violations of legal, contractual, or regulatory provisions, regardless of amount, would be considered material in the accounting practices of these entities.

Although we find no direct reference to the *principle of conservatism* in the statement of principles itself, certain interpretations included in the GAAFR exposure draft suggest that, in applying judgment and approximation, possible errors in measurement should be in the direction of understatement of financial position or operating results rather than overstatement. Accountants are reminded that they should give "due regard to conservatism and practicality."[11]

By implication, at least, the valuation practices associated with accounting for the acquisitions of fixed assets clearly follow the *going-concern convention*. Those assets should ordinarily be recorded "at cost or if cost is not practicably determinable, at estimated cost."[12] Also, appropriable assets are valued at cash-realizable value. However, the failure to recognize accrued and prepaid items and the depreciation of general fixed assets represent deviations from the profit-oriented application of this convention. As will be noted later in this chapter, GASB Statement 11 will require the recognition of accrued and prepaid items when it becomes effective in 1994.

Although we have observed many similarities in the ways that these principles and concepts are applied in governmental and business accounting practices, we also find other principles that are not considered applicable to governmental units or are applied differently in the two areas. Except for proprietary (self-sustaining) funds, the *matching concept* is not considered applicable to governmental accounting practices because there are no *direct* cause-and-effect relationships between the inflows and outflows of resources for pure nonprofit accounting entities. We do find, however, that the matching concept is applied in accounting for self-sustaining funds (characterized as proprietary funds in the governmental area) in essentially the same manner as it is applied in the profit area.

In 1985, the GASB issued a research report entitled *The Needs of Users of Governmental Financial Reports*[13] which shows that users want a "bottom line" (outflows matched against inflows) in governmental operating statements. This suggests that the matching concept may also be important in governmental financial reporting because of the need to know the extent to which *intergenerational equity* is being maintained. In other words, have the current-year taxpayers paid for all of the services provided for the citizenry, have they shifted some of the burden to future-year taxpayers, or have they paid in advance for those future-year taxpayers?

The *realization convention* also applies to proprietary (self-sustaining) funds in much the same manner as it does in profit enterprise accounting. In the case of dollar-

---

11. *GAAFR Restatement Principles: Exposure Draft* (1978), p. 25.
12. National Council on Governmental Accounting, *NCGA Statement 1* (Chicago: Municipal Finance Officers Association, 1979), p. 3.
13. Governmental Accounting Standards Board, *The Needs of Users of Governmental Financial Reports* (Stamford, Conn.: Governmental Accounting Standards Board, 1985).

accountability funds (characterized as *governmental funds* in the governmental area), however, we find that revenues should be recognized in the accounting period in which they *"become both measurable and available."*[14] The term *available* is interpreted to mean resources in either spendable or near spendable form such as taxes receivable. Outflows, characterized as expenditures, should be recognized in the accounting period in which "the fund liability is incurred, if measurable."[15] It is important to note that these differences in interpretation of the realization concept are consistent with the strong emphasis on dollar-accountability reporting in the governmental area.

Probably the most significant difference in the way any accounting principle or convention is applied in the two areas is in the way that the *entity convention* is applied. In accounting for profit enterprises, the enterprise unit, in total, is recognized as the primary accounting entity for external reporting purposes. The governmental unit, however, is composed of numerous separate funds and other accounting entities, each of which requires separate financial reports. Therefore, within the accounting records of a governmental unit, each fund and account group will have its own self-balancing set of accounts and its own set of financial statements. The emphasis in financial reporting is on these entities rather than the organizational entity. This difference is also consistent with the emphasis on dollar accountability.

# ■ Types of Accounting Entities

One of the important features of dollar-accountability accounting procedures is the establishment of separate accounting records for each fund and account group. The funds typically found in the accounting records of governmental units can be divided into three categories:

1. dollar-accountability (governmental-type) funds
2. self-sustaining (proprietary-type) funds
3. hybrid (fiduciary-type) funds containing operating characteristics of both of the other two categories of funds.

General fixed assets and general long-term debts are accounted for through other separate accounting entities called "account groups."

## Dollar-Accountability (Governmental-Type) Funds

Funds that operate primarily as dollar-accountability–type entities are characterized in governmental accounting as *governmental funds*. This category includes the *general fund, special revenue funds, capital projects funds, and debt-service funds*. Each of these funds is described briefly in the Summary Statement, and the accounting procedures followed for each of them will be developed later in the text. At this point, however, we call attention to the fact that the Summary Statement refers to the general

14.  *NCGA Statement 1,* p. 11 (emphasis added).
15.  Ibid., p. 3.

fund in the singular, while all other fund classifications carry plural labels. That difference is noted to emphasize that every governmental unit will have one general fund through which it will account for the inflows and outflows of resources available for general operations. As a result, the general fund may be characterized as the operating fund for the governmental entity.

The plural designation of the other categories of governmental-type funds suggests that a particular governmental unit may have a number of each of them. On the other hand, it may not have any of those categories of funds. Special revenue, capital projects, and debt-service funds are originated only when the governmental unit acquires resources that are designated to be used for the specific purposes suggested by the fund names. In reviewing the purpose of accounting for a governmental-type fund, NCGA Statement 1 states that *the measurement focus should be on "determination of financial position and changes in financial position (sources, uses, and balances of financial resources) rather than upon income determination."*[16] The accounting practices followed in achieving those reporting objectives will be developed and illustrated in the chapters that follow.

Governmental funds can also be categorized according to their operating cycles. General and special revenue funds operate on an annual fiscal period basis. Their nominal accounts are closed at the end of each fiscal period and operations begin anew in the next fiscal period. Capital projects and debt-service funds, on the other hand, are *project-oriented*. A capital projects fund is originated when a project is authorized and operates on a continuing basis until the project is completed. A debt-service fund comes into existence as resources are required to be accumulated to pay interest and financial obligations relating to general long-term debt and continues to exist until the debt is retired. This type of *project* orientation, however, does not preclude the preparation of periodic financial statements showing the results of fund operations to date and the status of the fund resources and obligations at the end of each fiscal period.

NCGA Statement 1 originally required that special assessment projects be accounted for through the use of special assessment funds. GASB 6 (see page 91) ruled out future use of such a fund. The inflows and outflows of resources associated with special assessment projects should now be accounted for by using two funds—one labeled "special assessment capital projects fund" and another called a "special assessments debt-service fund." These funds will operate like capital projects and debt-service funds, respectively.

## Self-Sustaining (Proprietary-Type) Funds

In the governmental area, self-sustaining funds are included in the proprietary fund classification. As you will observe from the Summary Statement, proprietary funds are divided into two subcategories called *enterprise funds* and *internal service funds*. Enterprise funds are used to account for goods and services provided for the general public on a continuing basis in exchange for user fees. Their operating plans generally anticipate the recovery of all costs and in some instances the realization of a net income from operations. Internal service funds are used to account for the operations of fund entities

16. *NCGA Statement 1*, p. 3.

that provide goods and/or services for other units of the governmental entity on a cost recovery basis. The accounting practices for both types of proprietary funds are essentially the same as those followed by profit enterprises.

## Hybrid-Type (Fiduciary-Type) Funds

The Summary Statement of Principles also lists fiduciary-type funds, including trust and agency funds, as entities often found in governmental accounting records. These funds can be either dollar-accountability (governmental-type) funds, proprietary funds, or a mixture of those two types of funds. They are placed in a fiduciary category because their assets are held by the governmental unit as a trustee or agent for other individuals or entities.

Fiduciary-type funds may have characteristics of two or more of the types of accounting entities discussed in the preceding pages. Some trust and agency funds may include operational elements characterized as self-sustaining, others characterized as dollar-accountability, and still others characterized as account-group–type activities. Later, when we illustrate the accounting procedures for the various types of governmental subentities, we shall see how the overall accounting practices of fiduciary-type funds incorporate a mixture of accrual and modified accrual accounting practices.

## Account Groups

Because the accounting systems for dollar-accountability (governmental-type) funds do not distinguish between capital and revenue items in recognizing the inflows and outflows of spendable resources, governmental accounting records include *separate accounting entities* for *general fixed assets* and *general long-term debt*. These accounting entities are maintained to reflect accountability for and control of the governmental unit's general fixed assets and general long-term debt. The general fixed-asset account group includes all fixed assets except those reflected in proprietary or fiduciary-type funds. All general long-term liabilities will be reflected in the general long-term debt account group.

By establishing a separate accounting entity for general fixed assets we recognize that those assets belong to the governmental unit rather than to any specific fund. Assets recorded in this account group will include those purchased outright plus others acquired through noncancellable lease arrangements. Some "public domain" or "infrastructure" fixed assets such as roads, bridges, drainage systems, and other similar assets dedicated directly to the public sector rather than to use by the governmental unit in providing public service may or may not be included in the general fixed-asset account group.[17] The inclusion or exclusion of these assets, incidentally, is one element of the governmental unit's accounting policy that should be disclosed under the heading of significant accounting policies in a governmental unit's annual report.

Fixed assets should be recorded at cost just as they are in accounting for the fixed assets of a business enterprise. In the case of assets acquired by gift, fair market value at the time of receipt should be used.[18] In some instances, governmental units may have

17.  *NCGA Statement 1*, p. 9.
18.  Ibid., pp. 9–10.

to establish fixed-asset records when documents reflecting their cost have been destroyed or lost. In such cases, it will be necessary to use estimated original costs in accounting for those assets. Although depreciation is recognized as an element of expense resulting from the use of long-term assets by business entities, it is not recognized in the accounting records of governmental funds. The most recent NCGA publication permits the disclosure of accumulated depreciation in the general fixed-assets account group, but does not allow depreciation expense to be shown in the records of governmental-type funds.[19]

Long-term liabilities other than those associated with proprietary or special assessment projects are general obligations of the governmental entity and therefore should be included in the general long-term debt account group. The term *general long-term debt* can be interpreted to include not only debt instrument obligations but also such noncurrent liabilities as might be associated with pension plans, lease purchase agreements, and other similar commitments.[20] The basic requirement for inclusion of a debt in this account group is that the debt is supported by the general credit and revenue-raising power of the government rather than by the resources of any individual fund entity.[21] In the event that the governmental unit is contingently liable for proprietary fund or special assessment project indebtedness, the contingency should be included in the footnotes incorporated into the annual report.[22]

## ■ Interpretations and Other Statements

As observed earlier in the chapter, NCGA Statement 1 is the basic pronouncement defining generally accepted accounting principles for governmental entities. Since that statement was issued in 1979, the National Council on Governmental Accounting has clarified and expanded that body of principles by issuing

1.  a number of interpretations of NCGA Statement 1
2.  certain supplementing statements.

### Interpretations of Selected Elements of Statement 1

One of the problems that has troubled accountants since NCGA Statement 1 was issued centers on the point at which revenues from taxes should be recognized. In applying the "both measurable and available" criterion to these items, we logically recognize as revenue such things as sales taxes and income taxes when they are collected, because they are neither measurable nor available until that time. However, in the case of property taxes, we generally consider the "measurable and available" criterion to have been met when tax notices are sent out. Therefore, we record them by debiting taxes receivable and crediting revenues. This treatment raises questions as to how far in the future collection can be delayed and still meet the "available" test. Also, Statement 1

19.  Ibid., p. 10.
20.  Ibid., p. 9.
21.  Ibid., p. 9.
22.  Ibid., p. 9.

does not specifically deal with the question of property taxes collected in advance of the time they are expected to be used to provide services. As a result, the NCGA has issued an interpretation establishing the following criteria for recognizing revenues from these sources:

1.  In connection with property taxes, "available" is interpreted to mean taxes that are expected to be used to pay liabilities of the current period. Furthermore, they must be expected to be collected during the current fiscal period or within 60 days after the end of the period.

2.  If property taxes are collected in advance of the fiscal year, during which they are expected to be used, revenue recognition should be deferred to the fiscal year in which they are budgeted to be used.

The flowchart in Figure 3–2 shows how these interpretations should be implemented.

Another problem requiring clarification involved the accounting and financial reporting practices for public-employee retirement systems and pension funds. *Statement 1 states that pension trust funds are accounted for in essentially the same manner as proprietary funds.* A subsequent interpretation (Interpretation 4) provided guidelines for valuing assets in a pension fund that are essentially the same as those followed by business enterprises. This interpretation also required that information on the actuarial present value of accumulated planned benefits shall be accounted for in accordance

**FIGURE 3–2.**   NCGA Interpretation 3: Revenue Recognition—Property Taxes

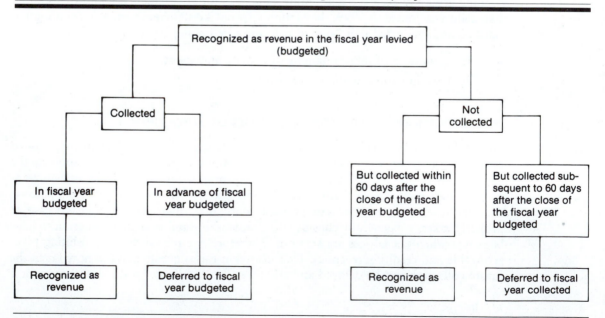

*Source:* National Council on Governmental Accounting, *NCGA Interpretation 3* (Chicago: National Council on Governmental Accounting, 1981). Used with permission.

with the provisions of FASB 35. It also required that the information disclosed in the footnotes to the financial statements should include

  a.  vested benefits of participants receiving payments
  b.  vested benefits of current employees
  c.  nonvested accumulated benefits of current employees.[23]

That interpretation was, however, superseded by NCGA Statement 6 (see page 89).

Interpretation 6 clarifies the data that should be disclosed in the notes to the financial statements. More specifically, it requires that the following items be disclosed:

> Statement 1 . . . states that notes to the financial statements essential to fair presentation at the GPFS level include
>
>   a.  summary of significant accounting policies
>   b.  significant contingent liabilities
>   c.  encumbrances outstanding
>   d.  significant effects of subsequent events
>   e.  pension plan obligations
>   f.  accumulated unpaid employee benefits, such as vacation and sick leave (amended by NCGA Statement 4)
>   g.  material violations of finance-related legal and contractual provisions
>   h.  debt-service requirements to maturity
>   i.  commitments under noncapitalized leases
>   j.  construction and other significant commitments
>   k.  changes in general fixed assets
>   l.  changes in general long-term debt
>   m.  any excess of expenditures over appropriations in individual funds
>   n.  deficit fund balance or retained earnings of individual funds
>   o.  interfund receivables and payables.
>
> *The above notes to the financial statements disclosures are not all-inclusive, and additional disclosures should be made if applicable.* For example, such additional disclosures may include the following:
>
> reporting entity [associated agencies] (see NCGA Statement 3)
>
> claims and judgments (see NCGA Statement 4)
>
> property taxes (see NCGA Interpretation 3)
>
> segment information for Enterprise Funds (see NCGA Interpretation 2)
>
> budget basis of accounting
>
> short-term debt instruments and liquidity
>
> related party transactions
>
> capital leases
>
> contingencies.[24]

23.  National Council on Governmental Accounting, *NCGA Interpretation 4* (Chicago: National Council on Governmental Accounting, 1981). Used with permission.
24.  National Council on Governmental Accounting, *NCGA Interpretation 6* (Chicago: National Council on Governmental Accounting, 1982). p. 1. Used with permission.

## Other NCGA Statements

Since the issuance of Statement 1, the National Council on Governmental Accounting has issued six additional statements covering various aspects of generally accepted accounting practices (GAAP) for governmental entities. These statements, like the statements issued by the FASB for nongovernmental entities, are designed to deal with specific issues that have created problems for governmental accountants.

NCGA Statement 2, entitled *Grant Entitlement and Shared Revenue Accounting and Reporting by State and Local Governments,* provides guidelines for recording and reporting such items. It is designed to incorporate pertinent aspects of *Audits of State and Local Governmental Units* (the 1947 Industry Audit Guide of the American Institute of Certified Public Accountants as amended) into the NCGA Statements. This Audit Guide was subsequently revised in 1986 and 1989.

This statement recognizes that resources received by governmental units from other governments are frequently accompanied by legal or contractual requirements that govern their use and often include special accounting and reporting requirements. When those accounting and reporting requirements are not consistent with GAAP, the recipient government must provide for the accomplishment of both

1. accounting and reporting in conformity with GAAP
2. accounting and reporting in accordance with the legal or contractual requirements of the grant provisions.[25]

This statement is also intended to clarify the application of GAAP to grants, entitlements, and shared revenues received by local governments. The basis of accounting used is determined by the fund type in which the grant entitlement or shared revenue transaction is recorded. That means that transactions accounted for in governmental funds should be recorded on the *modified accrual basis,* while those recorded in enterprise and internal service funds should be accounted for on the *accrual basis.*

The basis of accounting then fundamentally determines the point at which such revenues should be recognized. However, legal and contractual requirements should be carefully reviewed for guidance in recognizing such revenues. For example, some resources (usually entitlements or shared revenues) are restricted more in form than in substance. Only a failure on the part of the recipient to comply with prescribed regulations may cause a forfeiture of resources. On the other hand, some restrictions may be so stated that the resource inflows should be *recognized as revenues only when the qualifying expenditure has been made, rather than at the point where the grant or entitlement is tentatively committed to the governmental entity.*[26]

Grants, entitlements, or shared revenues received before the revenue-recognition criteria have been met should be reported as deferred revenue, a liability account, if a cash receipt or receivable is to be recognized in the balance sheet.[27] When such resources have not been received and the revenue-recognition criteria have not been met,

---

25.  National Council on Governmental Accounting, *NCGA Statement 2* (Chicago: National Council on Governmental Accounting, 1979), p. 2. Used with permission.
26.  Ibid., p. 2.
27.  Ibid., p. 2.

the receivable should not be reported on the balance sheet, but may be disclosed in the notes to the financial statements.[28]

Another problem that has troubled governmental accountants over the years has been defining the governmental reporting entity. In 1981, the NCGA issued Statement 3, which is intended to provide guidance in defining the governmental reporting entity. Because of its direct application in the preparation of combined financial reports, this statement will be discussed in Chapter 9.

In 1982, the NCGA issued Statement 4. This statement defines the procedures to be followed in accounting for claims and judgments and compensated absences. Basically, it explains how FASB 5 and AICPA Statement of Position 75-3 should be applied to the accounting practices of governmental units. Because Statement 4's provisions can best be understood after you have worked through our Model City illustration (Chapters 6–8), we discuss this statement more completely near the end of Chapter 8.

NCGA Statement 5 describes the accounting and financial reporting practices to be followed for capital lease agreements involving state and local governments. It explains how FASB 13 and other pronouncements relating to long-term leases should be applied to the accounting practices of governmental entities. Since the accounting and financial-reporting practices for proprietary funds will be essentially the same as those followed by business entities, the statement gives primary attention to the procedures that should be followed when a governmental-type fund is involved either as a lessor or lessee in a capital lease agreement. Because the provisions of this statement also can best be understood after you have worked through our Model City illustration, we discuss this statement more completely near the end of Chapter 8.

NCGA Statement 6 supersedes Interpretation 4 discussed earlier. It does that by more specifically describing the procedures that should be followed in actually establishing the amounts to be disclosed in the financial statements. It requires a separate financial report for pension funds similar to the requirement established by the FASB for business entities. It also describes the actuarial cost methods to be used and the financial statements to be presented in reporting on PERS (Public Employer Retirement Systems).[29] However, because of differences between the requirements of NCGA Statement 6 and those of FASB 35, the implementation of reporting requirements for PERS has been postponed indefinitely. This action is officially reflected in FASB 75.

Some of the provisions of the NCGA Statements have been modified and clarified by subsequent GASB Statements. These changes are described in the following section of the chapter.

## ■ The Governmental Accounting Standards Board

Since 1984, the GASB has issued thirteen statements, a number of exposure drafts, a research report entitled *The Needs of Users of Governmental Financial Reports*, a

---

28. Ibid., p. 2.
29. National Council on Governmental Accounting, *NCGA Statement 6* (Chicago: National Council on Governmental Accounting, 1983). Used with permission.

concepts statement, and a number of GASB Action Reports.[30] The provisions of the thirteen statements are summarized below.

As observed in Chapter 2, the Governmental Accounting Standards Board assumed the responsibility of setting the standards for governmental accounting in 1984. In its first official statement (Statement 1), issued in July 1984, the GASB stated its acceptance of all currently effective NCGA and AICPA pronouncements until they were revoked or suspended by subsequent GASB pronouncements. This statement is appropriately entitled *Authoritative Status of NCGA Pronouncements and AICPA Audit Guide*.

GASB Statement 2 is entitled *Financial Reporting of Deferred Compensation Plans Adopted Under the Provisions of Internal Revenue Code Section 457*. In summary, it provides that, for employees using governmental fund accounting, Internal Revenue Code Section 457 deferred compensation plan balances may "be displayed in an agency fund of the governmental employer that has legal access to the resources, whether the assets are held by the employer, a public employee/retirement system (PERS), a nongovernmental third party, or another governmental entity under a multiple jurisdiction plan. Governmental public utilities and public authorities should report the liability on the balance sheet with a corresponding designated asset."[31]

Deferred compensation plans in general offer employees the opportunity to defer the receipt of a portion of their salary, and also to defer the payment of taxes on the deferred portion. IRC Section 457 allows state and local governments to establish such plans for their employees. Under NCGA Statement 1, the assets of the plan, as well as the liability to the employee, should be shown in an agency fund.

GASB Statement 3 is entitled *Deposits with Financial Institutions, Investments (Including Repurchase Agreements), and Reverse Repurchase Agreements*. This statement requires certain footnote disclosures relating to these agreements and also provides guidance on accounting for them. In a repurchase agreement, the governmental entity transfers cash to a broker dealer or financial institution, and that party then transfers securities to the governmental entity along with a promise to repay the cash plus interest when the securities are returned. Reverse repurchase agreements occur when governmental entities wish to temporarily convert securities in their portfolio to cash. The securities are surrendered to the loaning entity in exchange for the cash, accompanied by an agreement that the governmental entity will repurchase them by paying the loaning party cash for the securities plus interest on the cash advanced. Later GASB Technical Bulletin No. 87-1 was issued to provide guidance in answering two questions raised in applying GASB 3.

1.  Should a financial institution or broker-dealer that purchases securities for a governmental entity be considered a counter-party in applying Paragraph 68 of the statement?

2.  What is the effect on required disclosure by risk category when a governmental entity uses the book-entry systems of the Federal Reserve and Depos-

---

30.  Governmental Accounting Standards Board, *The Needs of Users of Governmental Financial Reports* (Stamford, Conn.: Governmental Accounting Standards Board, 1985).
31.  American Institute of Certified Public Accountants, "Official Releases," *Journal of Accountancy* (July 1986), p. 145.

itory Trust Company to hold its securities in a custodian's account, rather than in its own name?

Statement 3 requires that liabilities resulting from reverse repurchase agreements be reported as fund liabilities called "obligations bonds reverse repurchase agreements" and that the underlying securities be reported separately as "investments." Interest for both types of agreements should be reported as interest revenue or interest expenditure (expense).

In 1986, the GASB issued Statement 4 entitled *Applicability of FASB Statement No. 87 "Employers Accounting for Pensions" to State and Local Governmental Employers.* This statement in effect provides that such employers should not change their accounting and financial reporting of pension activities as a result of FASB Statement 87. The GASB contemplated issuing one or more pronouncements on pension accounting; the first of these was in the form of GASB Statement 5.

GASB Statement 5, entitled *Disclosure of Pension Information by Public Employee Retirement Systems and State and Local Governmental Employers,* was issued in 1986. It requires that the pension benefit obligation of defined benefit pension plans, calculated using the actuarial present value of credited projected benefits, be disclosed along with a description of the plan, a summary of significant policies and actuarial assumptions, and contributions required and made during the reporting period. In addition, ten years of supplementary information is mandated. The schedule should include information about net assets available for benefits, accrued pension benefit obligations, and a comparison of revenues by source to expenses by type.

GASB Statement 6, entitled *Financial Reporting for Special Assessments,* requires that transactions of a service-type special assessment project should be reported in the fund type that best reflects the nature of the transactions. This would usually be the general fund, a special revenue fund or an enterprise fund. Service-type special assessment revenues should be treated as user fees. Assessment revenues and expenditures, or expenses for which the special assessments were levied, should be recognized on the same basis of accounting as that normally used for the fund type used to record the transactions. The provisions of this statement relating to special assessment projects are discussed in Chapter 7.

GASB Statement 7, entitled *Advance Refundings Resulting in Defeasance of Debt,* was issued in 1987 to provide guidance on accounting for refundings that result in the termination of debt recorded in the general long-term debt account group. It requires that the proceeds of the new debt be reported as "other financing sources— proceeds of refunding bonds" in the fund receiving the proceeds. Payments to the escrow agent from those funds should be reported as an "other financing use—payment to bond refund escrow agent." Any payments made with other resources should be labeled "debt-service expenditures." The Statement also requires certain disclosures such as the economic gain or loss on refunding (the difference between the present value of the old debt-service requirements and the present value of the new debt-service requirements, discounted at the effective interest rate plus additional cash paid).

GASB Statement 8 is entitled *Applicability of FASB Statement 93 "Recognition of Depreciation by Not-for-Profit Organizations" to Certain State and Local Governmental Entities.* In summary, it states that governmental entities (including colleges and universities) that use specialized industry accounting and reporting principles and practices should not change their accounting and reporting for depreciation of capital assets as a result of FASB 93. We shall refer to this Statement again in Chapter 11.

GASB Statement 9 is entitled *Reporting Cash Flows of Proprietary and Nonexpendable Trust Funds and Governmental Entities That Use Proprietary Fund Accounting*. It was issued in 1989 apparently as a complementing reaction to FASB 95 requiring the preparation of a statement of cash flows instead of a statement of changes in financial position for private entities. GASB 9 requires a statement of cash flows as part of the financial statements for all proprietary and nonexpendable trust funds. However, it exempts public employee retirement systems and pension trust funds from the requirement. The cash flow statement required by this statement is different from the one required by FASB 95 in that the former requires that cash flows be classified into four categories rather than three. These include operating, noncapital financing, capital, and related financing and investing categories.

Governmental enterprises are encouraged to report cash flows from operating activities by use of the "direct" method but this Statement also recognizes the "indirect" method as acceptable.

GASB Statement 10 is entitled *Accounting and Financial Reporting for Risk Financing and Related Insurance Issues*. It establishes accounting and financial reporting standards for those items. It lists the types of risks intended to be covered. In general, it requires public entity risk pools to follow the current accounting and financial reporting standards of business enterprises based primarily on FASB 60 (Accounting and Reporting by Insurance Enterprises). Pool premiums or required contributions are to be recognized as revenue over the contract period in proportion to the amount of risk protection provided. Claims costs relating to covered events should be recognized in the period in which the event that triggers coverage occurs. Costs that vary with and are primarily related to the acquisition of insurance or pool participation contracts should be capitalized and amortized as premium revenue is recognized.

State and local governmental entities, other than entity risk pools, are required to report an estimated loss as an expense and liability if both of the two following conditions are met:

1. Information available indicates that it is *probable* that an asset has been impaired or a liability has been incurred.

2. The amount of the loss can be reasonably estimated.

These requirements parallel those required for recognizing a loss contingency as a liability under FASB 5.

GASB Statement 11 is entitled *Measurement Focus and Basis of Accounting— Governmental Fund Operating Statements*. It will require use of the accrual (rather than the modified accrual) basis of accounting for recognizing governmental fund revenues and expenditures when implemented. Generally, revenues will be recognized when the underlying transaction or event occurs, and tax revenues will be recorded when payment is demanded. Expenditures will be recognized when claims against financial resources take place, regardless of when paid.

One objective of this Statement is to help financial statement users assess interperiod equity, that is, whether reporting period revenues have been sufficient to pay for services provided during the period. In judging the extent to which that evaluation may be facilitated by the provisions of this Statement, it is important to recognize that the so-called accrual basis in this Statement does not provide for a distinction between capital and revenue expenditures or the recognition of depreciation of long-term assets. The author contends that, unless accounting procedures include those requirements, the data that would be most useful in assessing interperiod equity is not available.[32]

This pronouncement becomes effective for reporting periods beginning after June 15, 1994. For that reason, our illustrations in later chapters of the text continue to follow the modified accrual basis for governmental funds.

GASB Statement 12 is entitled *Disclosure of Information on Post-Employment Benefits Other than Pension Benefits by State and Local Government Employers*. It requires such employers to make certain disclosures. However, except for the required disclosures, these employers are not required to change their accounting and financial reporting of those benefits until the GASB has completed its project relating to those items.

GASB Statement 13, entitled *Accounting for Operating Leases with Scheduled Rent Increases,* establishes standards of accounting and reporting for such leases that vary according to the reasons for the increases as follows:

1. When the increases are intended to cover the anticipated effects of cost increases or property value appreciation, the accounting would be based on the terms of the lease.

2. When the increases are intended to compensate for the effect of a rent reduction (rent holiday), the accounting would be measured either on a straight-line basis over the lease term or based on the estimated fair value of the rental.

In 1989, the AICPA published the fifth edition of *Audits of State and Local Governmental Units,*[33] which presents the recommendations of the AICPA State and Local Government Committee regarding the application of generally accepted auditing standards to audits of the financial statements of these entities. It also includes descriptions and recommendations relating to their accounting and reporting practices. More specifically, it identifies GAAP for state and local government units to include NCGA Statements 1 through 7 and Interpretations 1 through 11. It also refers to the Governmental Accounting Standards Board pronouncements as being applicable to the financial statements of governmental units.

Perhaps of even greater importance than the statements issued are the major conceptual projects that the Board has undertaken. These include consideration of the following issues:

1. *Financial reporting.* In working with this project, the GASB has conducted a user-needs study, the results of which were published in 1985. An objectives exposure draft has been issued in connection with this project.

2. *Measurement-focus—basis of accounting-governmental funds.* This project is important because it addressed the issues of whether the accrual basis of

32. Emerson O. Henke, "Governmental Financial Statements—Generational Equity Reporting," *Government Accountants Journal* (Spring 1987).
33. American Institute of Certified Public Accountants, *Audits of State and Local Governmental Units,* 5th ed. (New York: AICPA, 1989).

accounting should be followed in accounting for governmental funds, and the extent to which the financial reports should focus on the results of individual fund operations. GASB 11 has now been issued, based on this project.

3. *Infrastructure fixed assets.* This project is directed toward determining what should be reported for these assets and how they should be valued.

4. *Public authority enterprise funds.* Here the Board is giving attention to both the measurement focus and the reporting problems of these entities.

The GASB has had as one of its objectives the development of a conceptual framework that could be used to provide a logical basis to support future procedural pronouncements. In 1987, the first concepts statement, entitled *Objectives of Financial Reporting,* was issued. It sets out three broad objectives that should be achieved by all governmental financial reports. Such reports should

1. assist in filling a government's duty to be publicly accountable and enable users to assess that accountability

2. assist users in evaluating the operating results of the governmental entity

3. assist users in assessing the level of services that can be provided by the governmental entity and its ability to meet its obligations when they become due.

These broad objectives then more explicitly require the provision of information that will

1. show whether current-year revenues were sufficient to pay for current-year services

2. demonstrate whether revenues were obtained and used in accordance with the entity's legally adopted budget

3. assist users in evaluating the service efforts, costs, and accomplishments of the governmental entity

4. show the sources and uses of financial resources

5. show how the governmental entity financed its activities and met its cash requirements, and whether its financial position improved or deteriorated.

On examination of these more explicit requirements for financial reporting, we can see their relationship to the concepts of intergenerational equity (1), fiscal accountability (2, 4, and 5), and operational efficiency (3). In the author's judgment, it is likely that these relationships will be developed further in future concepts statements.

# ■ Ethical Considerations Associated with Governmental Fund Operations

Dollar-accountability accounting procedures are designed to hold managers accountable for the uses of spendable resources. However, management should also be concerned with the efficiency with which those resources are used. Consider the ethical issues that might be involved in simply using spendable resources in accordance with budgetary appropriations without regard for benefits to be realized from their use.

## ■ Summary

In this chapter, we have considered the objectives of governmental accounting procedures and have reviewed the Summary Statement of Accounting Principles for governmental entities developed to meet those objectives. The Summary Statement provides a system of accounting that can disclose the extent to which managers have complied with legal requirements and at the same time produce meaningful and useful financial statements presented in accordance with generally accepted accounting principles.

An important element of governmental accounting systems is the division of the accounts into a number of self-balancing accounting entities called *funds* and *account groups*. We have shown how fund entities can be classified operationally into governmental, proprietary, and fiduciary fund categories. We briefly described each of the three types of fund entities and noted the characteristics of specific funds included in each category.

Account groups are used to account for general fixed assets and general long-term debt. These account groups are required because the dollar-accountability reporting objective emphasizes inflows and outflows of appropriable resources rather than the determination of periodic income and expenses. As a result, we find no real distinction between current and long-term inflow and outflow items. Therefore, memo account group records must be originated to provide information about the costs of general long-term assets and the amounts owed on general long-term obligations.

In the last part of the chapter, the interpretations that have been issued regarding certain elements of NCGA Statement 1, the other NCGA statements that have been issued since 1979, and statements issued by the GASB were described.

## ■ Glossary

**Accrual Basis.**   The basis of accounting under which inflows of resources are recognized as revenues when the rights to them have been earned, and resource outflows are recognized as expenses when resources and services are used.

**Appropriation Control.**   The control placed on the incurrence of expenditures by virtue of legal authorizations granted by a legislative or other controlling body.

**Capital Projects Fund.**   A fund created to account for financial resources to be used for acquisition or construction of major capital facilities (other than those financed by proprietary funds, and trust funds).

**Depreciation.**   (1) Expiration in the service life of fixed assets other than wasting assets attributable to wear and tear, deterioration, action of the physical elements, inadequacy, and obsolescence. (2) The portion of the cost of a fixed asset other than a wasting asset that is charged as an expense during a particular period. In accounting for depreciation, the cost of a fixed asset, less any salvage value, is prorated over the estimated service life of such an asset, and each period is charged with a portion of such cost. Through this process, the entire difference between the cost and salvage value of the asset is ultimately charged off as an expense.

**Enterprise Fund.**    A fund established to account for operations (a) that are financed and operated in a manner similar to private business enterprises—where the intent of the governing body is that the costs (expenses, including depreciation) of providing goods or services to the general public on a continuing basis be financed or recovered primarily through user charges; or (b) where the governing body has decided that periodic determination of revenues earned, expenses incurred, and/or net income is appropriate for capital maintenance, public policy, management control, accountability, or other purposes. Examples of enterprise funds are those for water, gas, and electric utilities; swimming pools; airports; parking garages; and transit systems.

**General Fund.**    The fund used to account for all financial resources except those required to be accounted for in another fund.

**Intergenerational Equity.**    A measurement of the extent to which the taxpayers of a particular reporting period are paying for the services which the governmental entity is providing during that period.

**Internal Service Fund.**    A fund used to account for the financing of goods or services provided by one department or agency to other departments or agencies of a government, or to other governments, on a cost–reimbursement basis.

**Statement of Cash Flows.**    A statement showing the sources of cash inflows and how cash was used during a reporting period. The net difference between inflows and outflows is reconciled to the change in the cash balance during the period.

**Trust and Agency Fund.**    One of the eight generic fund types in governmental accounting.

# ■ Suggested Supplementary References

*Bellucomini, Frank S. "Local Governmental Units: The Going Concern Question." *Journal of Accounting* (June 1977).

Cooley, John W., and Michael E. Simon. "The Case for a Standard Government-Wide Chart of General Ledger Accounts." *Government Accountants Journal* (Summer 1987).

Donnelly, W. F., and Gary Miller. "Financial Officers' Opinions to GASB's Proposed Statement on Measurement Focus and Basis of Accounting-Government Funds." *Government Accountants Journal* (Fall 1989).

Engstrom, John H., John Simon, and Louis Karrison. "Property Tax Revenue Recognition Under NCGA Interpretation 3." *Government Accountants Journal* (Spring 1986).

Freeman, Robert J., and Donald M. Nuttall. "The GAAFR Restatement Principles: An Executive Summary." *Governmental Finance* (May 1978): 2–13.

Freeman, Robert J., and Craig D. Shoulders. "Evaluating the Revised GASB Measurement Focus and Basis of Accounting Proposals." *Government Accountant's Journal* (Fall 1989).

Jump, Bernard, Jr. "Evaluating the Financial Condition of Public Employee Pension Plans: Some Guidelines for the Unwary." *Governmental Finance* (February 1978).

*Also available in *Accounting in the Public Sector: A Changing Environment—A Book of Readings* by Robert W. Ingram. Salt Lake City: Brighton Publishing Company, 1980.

Kamnikar, Judith A., and Edward C. Kamnikar. "The Professional Recognition of Governmental Accounting and Auditing." *Government Accountants Journal* (Fall 1987).

McHugh, Joseph A. "The New Orleans Connection—The Workshop on Governmental Accounting and Auditing." *Government Accountants Journal*, 28 (Winter 1979–80): 32–88.

O'Keefe, Herbert A., and Pete Rose. "Overview of the Issues Involved in Measurement Focus and Basis of Accounting for Governmental Funds." *Government Accountants Journal* (Summer 1987).

Pumphrey, Lela D., and J. Dwight Hadley. "Measurement Focus and Basis of Accounting—Governmental Fund Operating Statement." *Government Accountants Journal* (Summer 1990).

Remis, James S. "An Historical Perspective on Setting Governmental Accounting Standards." *Governmental Finance*, 2 (June 1982): 3–9.

Sadowski, Thomas J. "AGA Testimony at GASB Hearing on Agenda and General Progress to Date." *Government Accountants Journal* (Fall 1988).

Schramm, John E. "Municipal Accounting and Reporting." From *Readings in Governmental and Nonprofit Accounting* by Richard J. Vargo. Belmont, Calif.: Wadsworth Publishing Company, 1977, pp. 64–69.

Shoulders, Craig, Walter L. Johnson, and W. T. Wrege. "The Rise and Near Demise of the Governmental Accounting Standards Board." *Government Accountants Journal* (Spring 1990).

Stroud, J. B. "Prioritization of Municipal Financial Statement Users." *Government Accountants Journal* (Fall 1988).

Weirich, Thomas R., and Alan Reinstein. "Implementing the Disclosure Requirements of GASB Statement No. 3." *Government Accountants Journal* (Fall 1990).

## ▪ Questions for Class Discussion

**Q3-1.** Explain how legal requirements have influenced presently accepted accounting practices for governmental entities.

**Q3-2.** Discuss the differences between the accounting practices described in GAAFR and those normally characterized as GAAP.

**Q3-3.** Identify the users of governmental accounting information. What questions do the various users seek to have answered through the financial statements?

**Q3-4.** Explain the difference between the procedures followed in accounting for general fixed assets and enterprise fund fixed assets.

**Q3-5.** Why should a proprietary fund use the accrual basis of accounting? Explain.

**Q3-6.** Both governmental units and businesses are resource conversion entities. Why do we place more emphasis on the matching convention in business accounting than in accounting for governmental units?

**Q3-7.** Compare and contrast the way the entity convention is applied in presenting business financial reports to the way it is applied in financial reporting for governmental units.

**Q3-8.** Explain the difference between a governmental dollar-accountability fund and a proprietary fund. Give an example of each.

**Q3-9.** What is a fiduciary-type fund? Give an example.

**Q3-10.** What is the purpose of an "account group"? Why is such an accounting entity used in governmental accounting systems?

Q3-11.  Give two examples of an account group.

Q3-12.  How many funds should a governmental unit have within its accounting system? Explain.

Q3-13.  Why are budgetary controls so important in governmental accounting? How do they relate to appropriation control?

Q3-14.  Would violation of a regulatory provision constitute a material deviation in operating practice? Explain.

Q3-15.  Does a governmental unit always have a general-fund accounting entity within its accounting system? Explain.

Q3-16.  What determines which funds will be included within a specific governmental accounting system?

Q3-17.  Explain the difference between a fund and an account group.

Q3-18.  What is the operating objective of the debt-service fund? How is a debt-service fund initiated?

Q3-19.  At what point should revenues from sales taxes be recognized? Justify your answer.

Q3-20.  At what point should revenues from property taxes be recognized? Justify your answer.

## ■ Problems

P3-1.  Select the best answer for each of the following items:

1. Accounting for a governmental unit tends to be somewhat different from that for a business, but accounting for a business is most like accounting for:
   a.  a special revenue fund.
   b.  a special assessment project.
   c.  an enterprise fund (utility fund).
   d.  a capital projects fund.

2. Fixed and current assets are not accounted for in the same fund, with the exception of the:
   a.  general fund.
   b.  internal service fund.
   c.  debt-service fund.
   d.  special revenue fund.

3. Depreciation on the fixed assets of a municipality should be recorded as an expense in the:
   a.  enterprise (utility) fund.
   b.  general fund.
   c.  debt-service fund.
   d.  special revenue fund.

4. Rogers City should record depreciation as an expense in its:
   a.  enterprise fund and internal service fund.
   b.  internal service fund and general fixed-assets group of accounts.
   c.  general fund and enterprise fund.
   d.  enterprise fund and capital projects fund.

5. In municipal accounting, the accrual basis is recommended for:
    a. only agency, debt-service, enterprise, general, and special revenue funds.
    b. only capital projects, enterprise, internal service, special assessment, and trust funds.
    c. only enterprise and internal service funds.
    d. none of the funds.

6. What financial statement is *not* specifically recommended for the general fund?
    a. analysis of changes in fund balance
    b. statement of cash receipts and disbursements
    c. statement of expenditures and encumbrances compared with authorizations
    d. statement of revenue—actual and estimated

7. Which of the following types of governmental revenue would be susceptible to accrual using the modified accrual method of accounting?
    a. state sales tax
    b. property tax
    c. income tax
    d. business licenses

—AICPA Adapted

**P3-2.** Select the best answer for each of the following items:

1. Which one of the following funds of a governmental unit is a governmental fund?
    a. enterprise funds
    b. internal service funds
    c. debt service funds
    d. nonexpendable trust funds

2. In a lease that is recorded as an operating lease by the lessee, the equal monthly rental payments should be:
    a. allocated between interest expenses and depreciation expense.
    b. allocated between a reduction in the liability for leased assets and interest expense.
    c. recorded as a reduction in the liability for leased assets.
    d. recorded as rental expense.

3. Which of the following funds of a governmental unit recognizes revenues in the accounting period in which they become available and measurable?
    a. capital projects funds
    b. nonexpendable trust funds
    c. enterprise funds
    d. internal service funds

4. Which of the following accounts of a governmental unit is (are) closed out at the end of the fiscal year?

| | Estimated revenues | Fund balance |
|---|---|---|
| a. | No | No |
| b. | No | Yes |
| c. | Yes | Yes |
| d. | Yes | No |

5. Which of the following funds of a governmental unit uses the modified accrual basis of accounting?
   a. general
   b. enterprise
   c. internal service
   d. nonexpendable trust

6. Which of the following requires the use of the encumbrance system?
   a. general fund
   b. debt-service fund
   c. general fixed-assets group of accounts
   d. enterprise fund

7. Which of the following funds of a governmental unit would account for depreciation in the accounts of the fund?
   a. general
   b. internal service
   c. capital projects
   d. special revenue

8. Revenues of a special revenue fund of a governmental unit should be recognized in the period in which the:
   a. revenues become available and measurable.
   b. revenues become available for appropriation.
   c. revenues are billable.
   d. cash is received.

9. Which of the following funds of a governmental unit recognizes revenues and expenditures under the same basis of accounting as the general fund?
   a. debt-service
   b. enterprise
   c. internal service
   d. nonexpendable pension trust

10. Which of the following funds of a governmental unit uses the same basis of accounting as the special revenue fund?
    a. internal service
    b. expendable trust
    c. nonexpendable trust
    d. enterprise

11. Which of the following funds of a governmental unit uses the same basis of accounting as an enterprise fund?
    a. special revenue
    b. internal service
    c. expendable trust
    d. capital projects

12. Which of the following funds should use the modified accrual basis of accounting?
    a. enterprise
    b. internal service
    c. special revenue
    d. trust

13. What is *not* a major concern of governmental units?
    a. budgets
    b. funds
    c. legal requirements
    d. consolidated statements

14. For state and local governmental units, the full accrual basis of accounting should be used for what type of fund?
    a. special revenue
    b. general
    c. debt-service
    d. internal service

15. A state governmental unit should use which basis of accounting for each of the following types of funds?

    |    | Governmental | Proprietary |
    |----|--------------|-------------|
    | a. | Cash | Modified accrual |
    | b. | Modified accrual | Modified accrual |
    | c. | Modified accrual | Accrual |
    | d. | Accrual | Accrual |

16. Revenues of a municipality should be recognized in the accounting period in which they become available and measurable for a:

    |    | Governmental fund | Proprietary fund |
    |----|-------------------|------------------|
    | a. | Yes | No |
    | b. | Yes | Yes |
    | c. | No | Yes |
    | d. | No | No |

—AICPA Adapted

# CHAPTER 4

# Development and Use of Budgetary Data

## ■ Learning Objectives

When you have finished your study of this chapter, you should

1. Be aware of the benefits that can be realized from the budgetary process in managing an enterprise unit.

2. Understand the basic differences between budgetary procedures for proprietary funds and procedures followed in developing budgetary data for governmental funds.

3. Know what is meant by *program budgeting*.

4. Have a general understanding of the steps followed in developing a budget for general fund operations.

5. Be able to develop budgetary data from a given set of assumptions.

6. Know how to account for general fund budgetary data from the time the budget is approved through the closing of the budgetary accounts at the end of the reporting period.

The budgeting process is part of the "plan" portion of the plan-execute-evaluate-plan cycle followed in managing an entity. We may think of it as the initial step in achieving financial and managerial control over the operations of an enterprise unit. In the governmental area, the budget approved by the appropriate legislative authority becomes the operating blueprint for acquiring and using operating (general and special revenue) fund resources during the next fiscal period. *It is the operating plan of the fund projected in the form of financial measurements.* Budgets are used by all types of enterprise units. However, the ones used in planning the sources and uses of general and special revenue-fund resources for governmental units become especially important because of the *legal implications associated with legislatively approved budgetary data.* These budgets are, in effect, the devices used in controlling the operations of these funds.

In this chapter, we describe the procedures normally followed in developing and using budgetary data for governmental entities. Since proprietary funds in the governmental area operate in much the same manner as business enterprises, we begin by briefly *describing the budgetary process for those funds*. Following that, we give attention to the *budgetary and financial control procedures normally associated with governmental fund operations*. In that part of the chapter, we shall

1. briefly develop the general philosophy of general (operating) fund budgeting
2. describe the budget development cycle
3. explain how the budgetary data are used in controlling expenditures
4. discuss briefly program budgeting procedures
5. relate the budgetary process to the operations of project-oriented governmental funds
6. explain how budget-related cost data can be used in controlling operations.

## ■ Budgetary Practices for Proprietary Funds

Proprietary funds operate in essentially the same manner as business enterprises, and the budgetary practices associated with the plan-execute-evaluate-plan cycle for these funds closely parallel those followed by businesses. This requires that the budgetary process begin with a projection of the estimated level of operations in the form of the amounts of sales, fees, or other primary sources of income expected to be realized. Operating outlays in the form of expenses are then projected on a *formula-related basis* to complete the operating budget. However, since the sale prices of goods and services of these funds are often based on the costs of providing them, the *anticipated level of operations is generally first projected in nondollar quantitative terms*. After that, they can be converted to dollars based on the projected relationship between the expected level of services and the costs of providing those services.

As we describe the budgetary practices for proprietary funds, we will be concerned with

1. procedures to be followed in projecting inflows of resources from operations
2. identifying formula relationships among the budgetary data
3. recognizing the points at which managerial decisions can be introduced to deliberately shape the budgetary plan
4. describing the budgetary summarization process.

### Projecting Resource Inflows

The budgetary process for profit-seeking entities generally begins with a projection of anticipated sales or other revenues because this is the primary factor constraining the overall level of operations. The revenue budget is developed by reference to the past period data, managerial plans for pricing and selling goods or services, and various forecasts relating to the probable future level of operations. Generally speaking, this procedure should also be followed by nonprofit enterprise funds. In developing revenue projections for such funds, historical data, pricing and promotion plans, and the anticipated change in the volume of customers should be considered in arriving at revenue projections. These projections can also be presented more informatively by first estimating the quantity of units of service to be sold and converting that figure into dollars by applying the projected sale price to it.

For funds supplying only internally used services, however, the projected level of operations will be determined largely from some *measurement of the goods and services provided in prior periods to the units being served, adjusted for planned changes in their general levels of operations.* As an illustration of such an internal customer-related activity, let's assume that a municipal entity operates a vehicle maintenance center on a self-sustaining basis. If the city plans a 25 percent increase in the number of city vehicles, the maintenance center would, assuming other things are expected to remain the same, project a 25 percent increase in its volume of services for the next period. Initially, this increase might be expressed in terms of service hours. Service hours could then be converted to dollars by pricing them on the basis of an agreed-upon relationship to operating costs.

## Applying Formula Relationships

The revenue projections developed in the preceding paragraphs constitute the basic measurement of the anticipated level of operations for the budgetary period. In a profit entity, concerned with producing and selling units of product, the number of units to be produced or purchased can be calculated by using the following formula:

$$\text{beginning inventory} + \text{units to be produced or purchased}$$
$$- \text{ units projected to be sold} = \text{ending inventory}$$

Historical data should provide the beginning inventory element of the equation and managerial projections should establish an ending inventory target. When the revenue budget has been established, projecting the anticipated number of units to be sold, the number of units to be purchased or produced can be calculated by entering the three known elements in the four-element equation.

Governmental proprietary funds are often involved in providing services rather than products. In that type of situation, the primary concern is with establishing formula relationships between the projected level of operations and the various operating expenses to be incurred in rendering the services. This involves the development and application of observed *cost–volume relationships* in projecting various operating expenses. In identifying cost–volume relationships, we classify all items of expense into fixed and variable categories. Fixed expenses include those operating outlays that, in the aggregate, are expected to remain constant regardless of the level of operations. Variable expenses, on the other hand, are those items that are expected to change in direct relationship to changes in the level of operations. As a practical matter, many expenses are neither completely fixed nor completely variable. When working with such expenses, we should try to identify and list separately the fixed and variable elements included in the mixed classification.

In addition to cost–volume relationships, it is also important to consider the effect that inflation and programmed increases in salaries and wages will have on the final budgeted amounts. In Exhibit 4–1, we demonstrate the procedures that should be followed in projecting selected operating expenses for the budget period. We have assumed that the proprietary fund in this illustration is projected to have a 25 percent increase in the volume of operations and that the inflation rate will be approximately 5 percent.

Exhibit 4–2 shows more specifically how the formula relationships are applied to prior period data to arrive at next-period projections. It also explains why projected operating expenses are $17,345 greater for the next period than they were in the last period.

## Changes Due to Managerial Decisions

Earlier in this section, we noted that, in budgeting for profit enterprises, managers can make decisions that directly affect the budget data. Pricing, sales promotion, inventory, and research and development decisions are examples of managerial actions that will specifically affect certain segments of the budgetary projections. Any or all of these can enter into the budgetary process for enterprise fund operations and some of them can enter into the budgetary process for internal service funds. The main point we want to make here is that, in addition to the formula-type projections discussed in the preceding paragraphs, the accountant may be required to inject the anticipated results of certain management decisions relating to revenue and/or expense activities of proprietary funds.

## Summarizing the Budgetary Data

Quite logically, much of the emphasis in the budgetary process for proprietary funds is on the projection of resource inflows and outflows in the forms of revenues and expenses. However, any enterprise unit charged with the responsibility of financing its own operations will also be concerned with its projected day-by-day cash position. This

**EXHIBIT 4–1.**  Proprietary Fund Budgeted Operating Expenses for Next Period

| | Prior Period Data | Programmed Increases | Other Adjustments | Budget for Next Period |
|---|---|---|---|---|
| Salaries (fixed) | $12,000 | $ 720 | $ 0 | $12,720 |
| Wages (variable) | 20,000 | 1,200 | 5,300 | 26,500 |
| Other operating expenses (fixed) | 15,000 | 0 | 750 | 15,750 |
| Other operating expenses (variable) | 30,000 | 0 | 9,375 | 39,375 |
| Depreciation (fixed) | 3,000 | 0 | 0 | 3,000 |
| Totals | $80,000 | $1,920 | $15,425 | $97,345 |

**EXHIBIT 4–2.**  Analysis of Projected Changes in Operating Expenses Between Current Period and Next Period

| Causes of Changes | | Amount |
|---|---|---|
| Programmed salary increases | | $ 1,920 |
| Increases caused by anticipated increase in level of operations | | |
| Variable wages ($21,200 × .25) | $5,300 | |
| Other operating expenses (variable) ($30,000 × .25) | 7,500 | 12,800 |
| Increases caused by anticipated inflation | | |
| Other operating expenses (fixed) ($15,000 × .05) | 750 | |
| Other operating expenses (variable) ($37,500 × .05) | 1,875 | 2,625 |
| Total increase | | $17,345 |

information can be provided through a cash-flow budget showing the beginning-of-period cash balance adjusted for anticipated cash inflows and outflows to arrive at a projected end-of-period cash balance.

After the accountant has completed his or her projection of operating activities in the form of projected revenues and expenses, a projected operating statement can be prepared. Those data can then be combined with the beginning-of-the-period balance sheet figures, the cash budget projecting inflows and outflows of cash, and the capital expenditures budget to present a pro forma balance sheet for the end of the period. These data can best be combined by use of a worksheet showing beginning-of-period balances adjusted for transactions projected by the budgetary plans and for nonbudgetary items such as depreciation in order to arrive at a budgeted end-of-period balance sheet.

In developing budgetary plans for internal service funds, a billing price per unit of service must be established. If services are to be billed at cost, the billing rate per unit of service (such as per hour of mechanical service) can be established by dividing total budgeted costs by the units of service that the entity expects to provide. To illustrate this point, let's assume that the fund, the operating expenses budget of which is shown in Exhibit 4–1, expects to provide 10,000 hours of service during the budget period. The billing rate would be $9.73 (rounded to the nearest cent). In such a situation, services might actually be billed at $10 per hour to provide greater assurance of recovering total costs of operations.

Enterprise funds may also establish billing rates based on projected operating expense for the period. Here again, the level of services to be provided must be estimated. In such situations, however, estimating the probable level of services involves more variables than is the case for internal service funds. The estimation process must consider such things as projected population change and any probable change in the level of business activity within the city during the next year. Nevertheless, when the probable level of activity has been determined, projected operating expenses, or projected operating expenses plus the desired excess of revenues over expenses, should be divided by the units of services anticipated to be provided, in order to arrive at the billing rate per unit of service.

The sequence of steps involved in developing a master budget for an enterprise fund is shown in Figure 4–1. By way of contrast, the budgetary process for an internal service fund would generally begin by estimating the number of hours of services expected to be provided to other governmental entities. The labor and operating expenses expected to be incurred for the estimated hours of services would then be formula projected to arrive at total expected expenses to be recovered from rendering the services. That amount would then be divided by the number of expected billing units (perhaps hours of service) to arrive at a basis for billings to other governmental entities.

**FIGURE 4–1.**   Master Budget for an Enterprise Fund

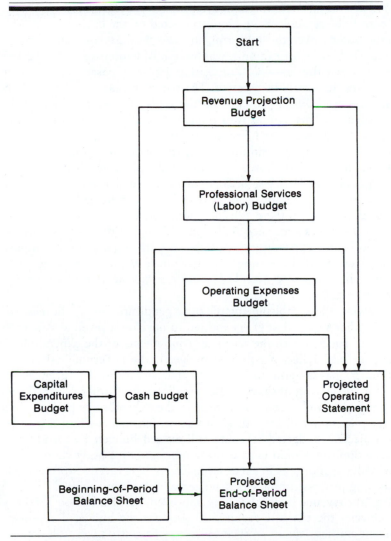

Emerson O. Henke and Charlene W. Spoede, *Cost Accounting: Managerial Use of Accounting Data* (Boston: PWS-KENT, 1991), p. 550. Used with permission.

# ■ Philosophy Underlying General (Operating) Fund Budgets

The general fund is the operating fund of a governmental entity. Budgeting the activities of this fund involves allocating limited financial resources to the various programs and activities of the governmental entity financed by the fund. Although the final decisions relating to these allocations will be made by an elected representative group such as a city council, much of the work associated with developing the budgetary data will be done by a budget committee. That group, working in cooperation with city department heads and financial officers, takes the primary responsibility for developing an expenditures budget. *That budget should reflect an expenditure plan that, within the constraints of available resources, the elected group feels will most appropriately meet the needs and desires of the voting citizens.*

Because the representative group is elected by the citizens, such an arrangement allows the voters, over the long run, to have the last voice in shaping expenditure programs. That voice, for example, was forcefully demonstrated by the 1978 California election in which the famous "Proposition 13" was passed, limiting the amount of property taxes that could be assessed. The voters in that election were saying that too many services were being provided on the basis of need for them at the expense of property owners. This should lead directly to reduced expenditure budgets for the governmental units supported by those taxes.

In developing an expenditures plan, the budget committee generally begins by considering changes that should be made to the prior year's program of services because of population changes, because of observed deficiencies in services provided during that year, and because new services have been judged to be beneficial to community welfare. Beyond these considerations, the changes in the costs of providing a given level of services because of inflation and salary adjustments must be considered. Furthermore, since expenditures must be met by levying taxes, Proposition 13 and other taxpayer revolts have shown us that much *attention must be given to the willingness of voters to accept a level of taxation sufficient to meet the projected program of expenditures.*

Following the establishment of an expenditures plan, the elected group (city council or other similar body) is expected to develop a revenue budget that is appropriately synchronized with the resource requirements of the expenditures budget. The revenue plan may reflect a balanced budget if the governmental entity proposes to operate on a "pay as you go" basis. In that situation, the revenues budget should provide for the levying of taxes and the realization of other revenues (excluding borrowing) approximately equal to the total of the expenditures budget. Or the proposed budgetary plan may call for either surplus or deficit financing. If a surplus-financing plan is projected, budgeted revenues will exceed budgeted expenditures (appropriations). The opposite would be true if the representative body chooses to operate temporarily with expenditures in excess of revenues. The revenues projected in this step of the budgeting process can be characterized as the *revenue goal.*

After the revenue budget has been approved, the elected body of the governmental unit establishes the tax rate required to produce the budgeted revenues. Most local government entities depend on such sources as property taxes, sales taxes, and income taxes, along with fines and fees to provide operating revenues. As a general rule, rates and allocation procedures for sales taxes and income taxes will have been established through other levels of management (generally the state) in the decision-making process. The local property tax rate, however, will normally be established by the representative board. The tax rate required to meet the revenue goal can be calculated by using the following formula:

$$\frac{\text{total budgeted revenues} - \text{anticipated revenues from other sources}}{\text{the assessed valuation of property within the governmental jurisdiction}}$$
$$= \text{the tax rate per dollar of assessed valuation}$$

In some instances, the calculation of the tax rate will also take into consideration a projected change in the unreserved fund balance account during the year. Because the tax rate for the next year will always have to be calculated before the end of the current year, it will then be necessary to project the estimated change in the fund balance account for the remainder of the year before setting the tax rate. To illustrate how this is done, let's assume the following data for a small city:

| | |
|---|---|
| Current balance in unreserved fund balance | $100,000 |
| Anticipated revenues for remainder of year | 60,000 |
| | $160,000 |
| Anticipated expenditures for remainder of year | 40,000 |
| Projected-end-of-year unreserved fund balance | $120,000 |

Let's assume further that the governing board of a city wishes to reduce the unreserved fund balance to $75,000 by the end of the next year and also expects to realize other revenues during the year of $80,000. If total projected expenditures for the next year is $3,000,000, the amount to be raised from property taxes would be $2,875,000, calculated as follows:

| | | |
|---|---|---|
| Projected expenditures | | $3,000,000 |
| Less: Anticipated decrease in fund balance | | |
| ($120,000 − $75,000) | $45,000 | |
| Projected other revenues | 80,000 | 125,000 |
| Revenues to be raised from property taxes | | $2,875,000 |

The $2,875,000 would then be divided by the assessed value of property to arrive at the property tax rate.

The tax rate calculated as described here must be approved by the city council or other elected body before tax assessment notices may be sent out to the citizens. The rate is generally expressed in terms of dollars per hundred or thousand dollars of assessed value. In other instances, it may be stated in terms of mills per dollar of assessed value. A tax rate of $5 per $1,000 of assessed value, for example, could also be stated as fifty cents per $100 or as five mills per dollar. We should also observe that assessed value often bears only a fractional relationship to market value. *The important consideration, as far as the taxpayer is concerned, is the relationship between property taxes assessed and fair market value of the property.* The amount of taxes assessed against a particular piece of property can be increased either by increasing the tax rate or by increasing the ratio of assessed value to market value or a combination of these two changes.

Many jurisdictions also have some exemptions, such as the homestead exemption, which must be considered in calculating the tax rates and the obligations of individual taxpayers. For instance, in a taxing entity having a $5,000 homestead exemption, houses occupied by their owners would be taxed on the assessed value less $5,000.

The property tax rate calculation process for an operating fund such as the one described above can be summarized in a flowchart like the one shown in Figure 4–2.

# ■ Budget Development Cycle

The general fund budgeting process is designed to allocate financial resources to various programs and activities with the objective of creating the best community environment

**FIGURE 4–2.**  Budgetary Process for Preparation of Operating Fund Budget

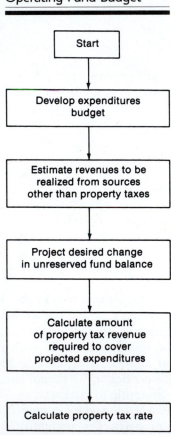

that the limited resources available to the governmental entity can provide. Much attention has been given to the development of procedures designed to more effectively achieve that goal. A planning-programming-budgeting system (PPBS) has been adopted by some segments of the federal government to implement the allocation process. These systems were initially heralded as the best approach to a rational budget and improved management of governmental resources. Unfortunately, however, the PPBS has failed to fully meet the expectations of its proponents. Ideally, it is intended to include

1. a classification of the cost of government by programs with common goals or objectives

2. the development of qualitative and quantitative measures of program outputs

3. a projection of anticipated program cost inputs and the related service outputs over a period of time generally covering several years

4. the identification of special problem areas and the use of analytical techniques to appraise various possible solutions for them

5. an integration of this information into the budgetary process so that it becomes a part of governmental financial management.[1]

One of the principal problems associated with the implementation of a PPBS is the difficulty of developing objective dollar values for the service outputs. Viewed realistically, the system may be seen as an ideal goal toward which managers of governmental entities may work in the development of budgetary allocations. However, it cannot be used for quantitatively relating the values of anticipated service outputs to anticipated expenditures. Nevertheless, the current emphasis on program budgeting (which is discussed later in this chapter) to some extent is an outgrowth of the PPBS concept of budgeting.

Another philosophical approach to the budgetary allocation process is called *zero-base budgeting*. It is designed to achieve a more complete review of ongoing governmental programs and, hopefully, as a result of that review, a more efficient allocation of resources. Conventional budgetary practices generally involve the development of new budgetary allocations on the basis of prior-period expenditures adjusted for increases or decreases projected for the next period. Such an arrangement can easily allow previously approved but currently unnecessary or inefficient activities to continue indefinitely.

The concept of zero-base budgeting was proposed by President Carter in 1977 for various federal agencies as a modification of the more conventional budgeting procedures then followed by those agencies. *It is designed to require every segment of the governmental unit to identify each function it performs and to project the personnel and other costs associated with performing those functions at various levels of service.* Thus, it is supposed to require a clear description of the results that can be expected from every dollar spent. It seems to have the advantages of requiring complete financial planning prior to the preparation of the budget, a more direct accountability on the part of segment managers for all of their activities, and increased involvement of

---

1. See Ernest L. Enke, "The Accounting Preconditions of PPB," *Readings in Governmental and Nonprofit Accounting* (Belmont, Calif.: Wadsworth Publishing Company, 1977), pp. 27–39.

lower-level supervisory personnel in the budgetary process. The one major disadvantage is the increased time and effort required in the development of the budget.

## General Fund Expenditures Budget

In the preceding section, we described the general philosophy underlying general fund budgetary procedures. In this section, we shall illustrate those procedures by identifying the specific steps that are followed in developing the general fund budget for Waco, Texas, a city of slightly more than 100,000 residents that follows zero-base budgeting procedures.[2]

The budgetary process described in the following pages is under the working supervision of the Finance Department but involves all department heads. Figure 4–3 shows the organization chart for the City of Waco. It outlines the relationships of city departments to each other, to the city manager, and to the city council.

The manual of budget instructions for Waco requires that the following steps (listed chronologically) be followed in the preparation of the city's annual general fund budget:

1. The annual budgetary process begins with a meeting between the city manager and the city council. The purpose of that meeting is to explain the budgeting process and obtain an expression of priorities from the city council.

2. The proposed use hearings for revenue-sharing funds are advertised and conducted.

3. The finance department, which is charged with the actual budget preparation, prepares budget expenditure projections based on five months of actual data and seven months of projected data.

4. The finance department passes out departmental folders to departmental managers and conducts training meetings with the heads of the various departments of the city.

5. The departmental managers are expected to return their completed budgets with activities ranked in order of priority to the finance department. The instructions to departmental managers as they are brought into the budgetary process include the following items:

   a. Read the budget manual.

   b. Verify budget-package projections prepared by the finance department with particular emphasis on verification of salaries and wages and the reasonableness of other projections.

   c. Divide the current operating projections into programs, if applicable (using Program Budget Request Forms—see Figure 4–4).

---

2. Materials in this section are taken from City of Waco Budget Instructions Manual. Used with permission of David Smith, City Manager, granted in 1982.

**FIGURE 4–3.** Organization Chart, City of Waco, Texas—January 1982

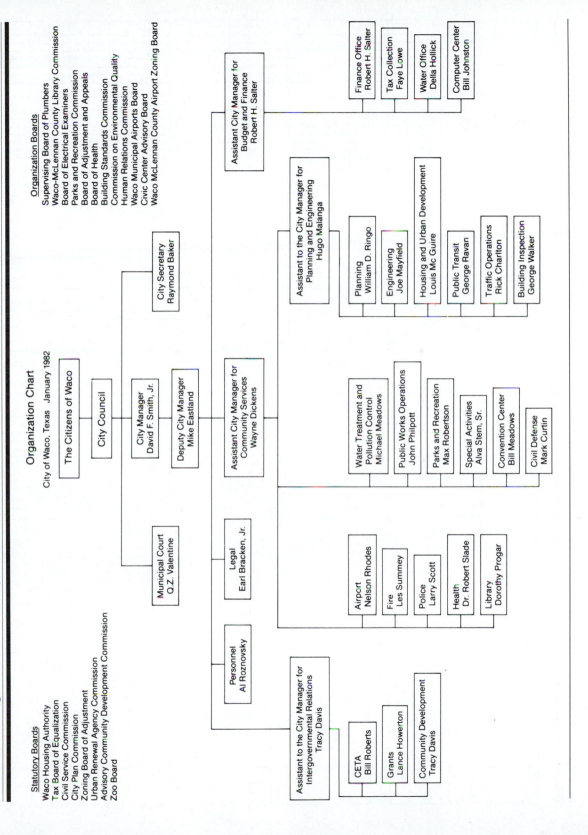

Organization Chart

City of Waco, Texas    January 1982

Statutory Boards
Waco Housing Authority
Tax Board of Equalization
Civil Service Commission
City Plan Commission
Zoning Board of Adjustment
Urban Renewal Agency Commission
Advisory Community Development Commission
Zoo Board

Organization Boards
Supervising Board of Plumbers
Waco-McLennan County Library Commission
Board of Electrical Examiners
Parks and Recreation Commission
Board of Adjustment and Appeals
Board of Health
Building Standards Commission
Commission on Environmental Quality
Human Relations Commission
Waco Municipal Airports Board
Civic Center Advisory Board
Waco McLennan County Airport Zoning Board

The Citizens of Waco

City Council

City Manager
David F. Smith, Jr.

City Secretary
Raymond Baker

Municipal Court
Q.Z. Valentine

Deputy City Manager
Mike Eastland

Legal
Earl Bracken, Jr.

Personnel
Al Roznovsky

Assistant City Manager for
Community Services
Wayne Dickens

Assistant to the City Manager for
Planning and Engineering
Hugo Malanga

Assistant City Manager for
Budget and Finance
Robert H. Salter

Assistant to the City Manager for
Intergovernmental Relations
Tracy Davis

Water Treatment and
Pollution Control
Michael Meadows

Public Works Operations
John Philpott

Parks and Recreation
Max Robertson

Special Activities
Alva Stem, Sr.

Convention Center
Bill Meadows

Civil Defense
Mark Curtin

Airport
Nelson Rhodes

Fire
Les Summey

Police
Larry Scott

Health
Dr. Robert Slade

Library
Dorothy Progar

Planning
William D. Ringo

Engineering
Joe Mayfield

Housing and Urban Development
Louis Mc Guire

Public Transit
George Ravan

Traffic Operations
Rick Charlton

Building Inspection
George Walker

Finance Office
Robert H. Salter

Tax Collection
Faye Lowe

Water Office
Della Hollick

Computer Center
Bill Johnston

CETA
Bill Roberts

Grants
Lance Howerton

Community Development
Tracy Davis

**FIGURE 4–4.** Program Budget Request

Department Code: _____     Year Ended: _____
Name: _____

## City of Waco, Texas
## Program Budget Request

| Code | Appropriation Class | Program Sub-Acct. | Amount | Program Sub-Acct. | Amount | Program Sub-Acct. | Amount | Program Sub-Acct. | Amount | Total Request | Recommended Budget |
|------|---------------------|-------------------|--------|-------------------|--------|-------------------|--------|-------------------|--------|---------------|--------------------|
|      |                     |                   |        |                   |        |                   |        |                   |        |               |                    |

    **d.** Divide current operating projections or programs into decision packages (using Program Budget Request Forms and the Decision Package Forms—see Figures 4–4, 4–5, 4–6, and 4–7).

    **e.** Determine alternative ways of performing activity.

    **f.** Determine various possible levels of service.

    **g.** Prepare measures of effectiveness or efficiency.

    **h.** Rank decision packages in order of priority.

    **i.** Turn completed budget into the finance department as soon as completed.

**6.** The finance department sends the checked budgets to appropriate upper-level supervisory personnel for priority rankings.

**7.** Upper-level managers return the departmental decision packages ranked in priority order to the finance department.

**8.** The city manager's office examines the rankings provided by assistants and department heads and changes any priorities desired. At this point, the city manager's office determines the funding level required to balance the expenditures proposed in the tentative budget.

**9.** The city manager's office discusses the proposed funding level including cuts or additions approved with department heads.

**10.** The budget summary is prepared for examination by the city council.

**11.** A seminar with the city council relating to recommended priority levels in the budget is conducted by the city manager's office.

**12.** The final budget is prepared.

Budget instructions, available to all persons involved in the budgetary process, specifically explain various elements included in the preceding list. The preceding steps in the budgeting process are carried out over a period of approximately six months in accordance with a prescribed budget calendar.

Figures 4–4, 4–5, 4–6, and 4–7 are copies of blank forms used in the budgetary process. A review of them should improve your understanding of some of the steps listed earlier for the preparation of the budget.

Step 5h of the budget instruction manual requires departmental managers to rank budgeted activities in order of priority. The finance department of the City of Waco has developed a weighted method of ranking these activities, which is intended to provide greater uniformity among departments in the ranking process. Those guidelines are shown in Figure 4–8. As you can see, each number is associated with a descriptive comment reflecting the perceived importance of various packages of activities. As proposed expenditures are listed on the Decision Package Ranking Form (Figure 4–6), they are assigned numbers representing the departmental manager's perceived importance of the item, based on the priority levels reflected in Figure 4–8.

**FIGURE 4–5.** Request for Equipment

City of Waco, Texas
Request for Equipment

Year Ending September 30, _____
Department Code: _____    Name: _____

Replacement Codes:

1. Scheduled Replacement
2. Replace Worn Out Equipment
3. Expanded Service
4. New Operation
5. Increased Safety
6. Present Equipment Obsolete
7. Cut Personnel Time
   (Explain how much)

| Number Requested | Description of Item Requested | Replacement Code | Estimated Cost | Number | Age | Make | Description | Prior Year Maintenance Cost | Trade In Value | Remarks |
|---|---|---|---|---|---|---|---|---|---|---|
| | | | | | | | | | | |
| | | | | | | | | | | |
| | | | | | | | | | | |
| | | | | | | | | | | |
| | | | | | | | | | | |
| | | | | | | | | | | |
| | | | | | | | | | | |
| | | | | | | | | | | |
| | | | | | | | | | | |
| | | | | | | | | | | |
| | | | | | | | | | | |
| | | | | | | | | | | |
| | | | | | | | | | | |
| | | | | | | | | | | |
| | | | | | | | | | | |

Equipment to be Replaced

Additional Remarks:

**FIGURE 4–6.** Decision Package Ranking Form

## City of Waco, Texas

## Decision Package Ranking Form

| Name and Short Description | Rank | Dept. No. | Level Of Effort | Estimated FY | | Budget FY | | Cumulative Level | |
|---|---|---|---|---|---|---|---|---|---|
| | | of | | People | Amount | People | Amount | Amount | % |
| | | | | | | | | | |
| | | | | | | | | | |
| | | | | | | | | | |
| | | | | | | | | | |
| | | | | | | | | | |
| | | | | | | | | | |
| | | | | | | | | | |
| | | | | | | | | | |
| | | | | | | | | | |
| | | | | | | | | | |
| | | | | | | | | | |
| | | | | | | | | | |
| | | | | | | | | | |
| | | | | | | | | | |
| | | | | | | | | | |
| | | | | | | | | | |
| | | | | | | | | | |
| | | | | | | | | | |
| | | | | | | | | | |
| | | | | | | | | | |
| | | | | | | | | | |
| | | | | | | | | | |
| | | | | | | | | | |
| | | | | | | | | | |
| | | | | | | | | | |
| | | | | | | | | | |
| | | | | | | | | | |

**FIGURE 4–7.** Decision Package Form

| City of Waco, Texas Decision Package Form | Year Ended | (1) Package Name | 1 of | (2) Department | (3) Program | (4) Activity New / Old | (5) Rank |
|---|---|---|---|---|---|---|---|

(6) Statement of Purpose

(7) Description of Actions (Operations)

| Expense Titles | FY. | FY. | FY. | FY. |
|---|---|---|---|---|
| A. Salaries and Wages | | | | |
| B. Supplies | | | | |
| C, D, E. Maintenance | | | | |
| F. Miscellaneous Service | | | | |
| G. Pension & FICA | | | | |
| H. Miscellaneous | | | | |
| I. Contributions | | | | |
| Total Operating | | | | |
| Capital Outlay | | | | |
| Totals | | | | |

Sources of Funds

| | | | | |
|---|---|---|---|---|
| City | | | | |
| Grants | | | | |
| Other | | | | |
| Totals | | | | |

Measures of Efficiency or Effectiveness

(8) Achievements from Actions

(9) Consequences of Not Approving Package

People–Positions–(Number)

Prepared by                                    Date                    Page 1 of

# City of Waco, Texas — Decision Package Form

| | | |
|---|---|---|
| City of Waco, Texas Decision Package Form | Year Ended | (1) Package Name ____ of |
| (2) Department | (3) Program | (4) Activity New ☐ Old ☐ | (5) Rank |

**(10) Alternatives (Different Levels of Service) and Cost**

| Alternate Levels of Service — Expense Titles | | | | |
|---|---|---|---|---|
| A. Salaries and Wages | | | | |
| B. Supplies | | | | |
| C, D, E. Maintenance | | | | |
| F. Miscellaneous Service | | | | |
| G. Pension & FICA | | | | |
| H. Miscellaneous | | | | |
| I. Contributions | | | | |
| Total Operating | | | | |
| Capital Outlay | | | | |
| Totals | | | | |

**Sources of Funds**

| | | | | |
|---|---|---|---|---|
| City | | | | |
| Grants | | | | |
| Other | | | | |
| Totals | | | | |

**Measures of Efficiency or Effectiveness**

| | | | | |
|---|---|---|---|---|
| | | | | |
| | | | | |
| | | | | |

People – Positions – (Number)

**(11) Alternatives**
(Different Ways of Performing the Same Function, Activity, or Operation)

Prepared by ____  Date ____  Page 2 of ____

**FIGURE 4–8.**   Weighted Method of Activity-Decision Package Ranking

| | |
|---|---|
| 8 | Basic level of service—should be funded. |
| 7 | First packages to fund above basic service. |
| 6 | Next packages to fund above basic service. |
| 5 | Packages have some muscle but these would be the first packages to cut if expenditure levels were reduced. |
| | Decision Point: Goal Expenditure Level |
| 4 | Packages have some muscle and these would be first packages to add if the goal expenditure level were increased. |
| 3 | Next package to fund if expenditures are increased. |
| 2 | Next package to fund if expenditures are increased. |
| 1 | Packages should not be seriously considered given the current expenditure goals. |

The budget calendar for the fiscal year ending September 30 begins on the preceding January 24. The events in the budgetary process are scheduled as follows:

| | |
|---|---|
| January 24 | Budgetary step No. 1 |
| February 2 to 27 | Budgetary step No. 2 |
| March 1 to April 1 | Budgetary step No. 3 |
| April 4 | Budgetary step No. 4 |
| April 13 to May 4 | Budgetary step No. 5 |
| May 4 to May 11 | Budgetary step No. 6 |
| May 13 to May 20 | Budgetary step No. 7 |
| May 23 to May 25 | Budgetary step No. 8 |
| May 30 to June 1 | Budgetary step No. 9 |
| June 1 to June 10 | Budgetary step No. 10 |
| June 13 | Budgetary step No. 11 |
| July | Budgetary step No. 12 |

Needless to say, the development of a budget generally will require a number of sets of projected data, incorporating different underlying assumptions, prior to its adoption. These projections can be most efficiently developed by use of a computer. When that is done, the alternatively considered assumptions, along with the basic quantitative data, are used as inputs to allow the computer to print out the budgetary data that would result from each of the assumptions.

# ■ Using the Budget as a Control Device

We have followed the development of a typical object-of-expenditure or line-item budget for the general fund of a municipality. The budget data developed would then be recorded in the budgetary accounts included in the general fund accounting records. Those records should be organized to provide a continuing comparison between budgeted and actual data as the operations of the period are carried out. We now develop the procedures for recording budgetary data and implementing actual-to-budgetary comparisons by

1. describing budgetary accounts
2. showing how budgetary data are recorded
3. explaining how expenditures are controlled within budgetary limits
4. illustrating how closing entries clear budgetary accounts at the end of each fiscal period.

## Budgetary Accounts

The estimated revenue and planned expenditure data for the general fund, developed during the budgetary process, are recorded in ledger accounts that appropriately describe them. Budgeted expenditures are recorded in *appropriation accounts,* while budgeted revenues are reflected in *estimated revenue accounts*. Control accounts are usually used to record these data. These control accounts are supported by subsidiary ledgers that show the amounts available to be used for each object of expenditure item and the relationships between estimated and actual amounts for each type of revenue listed in the budget. The subsidiary ledger forms for appropriations are generally designed to reflect, within the same form, appropriations, expenditures, and encumbrances on a line-item basis. Such an arrangement facilitates the comparison of budget and actual data on a continuing basis. The forms shown in Exhibit 4–3 illustrate how the control and subsidiary ledger data may be accumulated for appropriations, expenditures, and encumbrances.

The estimated revenues control account will also have a subsidiary ledger showing the amounts of revenues expected to be realized from each of the various sources reflected in the budget. Due to the fact that managers cannot be expected to control actual revenues within the limits of estimates in the same manner as they can expenditures, the subsidiary records for estimated and actual revenues may well be maintained separately. Each subsidiary ledger, however, is expected to balance against its respective control account.

**EXHIBIT 4–3.**  Control Accounts

| | Account No. 400 Expenditures | Account No. 500 Encumbrances | Account No. 600 Appropriations |
|---|---|---|---|
| | (1)  450,000 | (1)  40,000 | (1)  1,500,000 |

*Subsidiary Ledger Street Maintenance Services*

| | Account No. 410 Expenditures | | | Account No. 510 Encumbrances | | | Account No. 610 Appropriations | | |
|---|---|---|---|---|---|---|---|---|---|
| | Dr. | Cr. | Balance | Dr. | Cr. | Balance | Dr. | Cr. | Balance |
| | **Account No. 411 Salaries** | | | **Account No. 511 Salaries** | | | **Account No. 611 Salaries** | | |
| Budget entry | | | | | | | | 200,000 | 200,000 |
| Expenditure entry | $90,000 | | $90,000 | | | | $90,000 | | 110,000 |
| | **Account No. 412 Maintenance Supplies** | | | **Account No. 512 Maintenance Supplies** | | | **Account No. 612 Maintenance Supplies** | | |
| Budget entry | | | | | | | | 150,000 | 150,000 |
| Expenditure entry | 70,000 | | 70,000 | | | | 70,000 | | 80,000 |
| | **Account No. 413 Maintenance Equipment** | | | **Account No. 513 Maintenance Equipment** | | | **Account No. 613 Maintenance Equipment** | | |
| Budget entry | | | | | | | | 50,000 | 50,000 |
| Expenditure entry | 15,000 | | 15,000 | | | | 15,000 | | 35,000 |
| Encumbrance entry | | | | 20,000 | 20,000 | | 20,000 | | 15,000 |

(1) Control accounts include appropriations, expenditures and encumbrance items for Street Maintenance Services of $400,000, $175,000 and $20,000, respectively.

## Implementing Controls over Expenditures

After budgetary data have been given final approval they should be recorded in the respective control accounts of the general fund as follows:

     Dr. Estimated revenues
     Dr. or Cr. Budgetary fund balance for difference
        Cr. Appropriations

As budgetary data are posted to the accounts from the preceding entry, the amounts appropriated for each line item will be entered in their respective line-item subsidiary ledger accounts. They should be reflected in the appropriations column of the subsidiary ledger as is shown in Exhibit 4–3.

When expenditures are incurred, the control account for expenditures will be debited and the individual expenditure items will be recorded in the expenditures section of the subsidiary ledger. Since a subsidiary ledger account will be maintained for each line item of expenditures, that ledger provides a continuing record of the amount of appropriations and the expenditures against those appropriations for each item appearing in the budget. In that way, expenditures can be effectively controlled within the appropriation limits.

The budgetary account, *encumbrances,* is used to help prevent overspending an appropriation when a significant amount of time is expected to elapse between the commitment to spend resources and the time the actual expenditure occurs. For example, a commitment to buy equipment scheduled for delivery six months later should be recognized in the accounts by recording the following entry:

Encumbrances
   Reserve for encumbrances

The accumulation of data in these accounts can be facilitated by the use of account code numbers. To illustrate that point, let's assume that the control accounts for expenditures, encumbrances, and appropriations carry code numbers of 400, 500, and 600, respectively. Assume also that street maintenance services are coded as 1 in the second digit place from the left and that salaries, maintenance supplies, and maintenance equipment are coded 1, 2, and 3, respectively, in the third digit place from the left. This type of coding would allow us to identify expenditures for street maintenance equipment, for example, as Account No. 411. Coding the accounts in this way is helpful in identifying the specific items as they are recorded and in using a computer to maintain the accounting records. The assumed code numbers are shown with the account titles in Exhibit 4–3.

Encumbrances should also be recorded in a control account as is shown in Exhibit 4–3. When the individual encumbrance is recorded, it will be reflected in the line-item subsidiary ledger account to show that that part of the appropriation balance has been committed to be spent. The controller can then, by looking at the line-item subsidiary ledger account, recognize that the difference between the original appropriation and the sum of expenditures and encumbrances against the appropriation is the remaining amount available to be spent for that item.

## End-of-Period Closing Entries

At the end of each fiscal period, after the budgetary (estimated revenues and appropriations) data have served their usefulness as control devices, those account balances should be closed. This is done by reversing the entry originally made to record them. That allows the actual revenues and expenditures to be closed directly to the unreserved fund balance. The amount debited or credited to that account will then reflect the difference between actual revenues and expenditures for the period.

The balance shown in the encumbrance account at the end of a fiscal period should be closed against reserve for encumbrances. If, as is generally the case, encumbrances do not lapse, the fund balance reserved for encumbrances should then be adjusted to reflect a balance equal to the amount of encumbrances outstanding at the end of the period. The offsetting debit or credit in this entry will be to unreserved fund balance. If encumbrances lapse (government is not bound by them) at year end, they need not be reported. However, if a government in such a situation intends to honor the lapsed encumbrances, they should be disclosed as footnotes or as a reservation of fund balance. In illustrations throughout this text, we assume that encumbrances do not lapse.

# ■ Program Budgeting

Earlier in this chapter, we discussed briefly the concept of the PPBS and noted some of the problems involved in implementing such a budgeting system. Conceptually, it is designed to do what the budgetary system for a governmental unit should do, but the practical problems of implementing it have seriously limited its use. We then demonstrated how the object-of-expenditure or line-item budget can be used in planning and controlling the inflows and outflows of resources for the general fund of a governmental unit. Classifications under this system are item-of-expenditure– or input-oriented. They are designed to record the amounts to be spent for salaries, services, supplies, etc. by each department or subelement of the general fund.

Partially as a result of the conceptual desirability of PPBS, program-oriented budgets are often developed as a supplement to the more conventional line-item–type budget. *These budgets include output-oriented classifications based on programs, functions, or activities, and they relate spending to specific activity goals.* In our illustration of the City of Waco budgetary process, we saw the emphasis on this way of thinking in the requirement that requests be based on changes in services and activity levels. That requires consideration of the programs to be implemented. In this section, we further develop the concept of program budgeting by

1. illustrating the relationship between the line-item and program budgets for the general fund of the City of Waco

2. explaining how functional unit cost data may be developed from program budget data

3. showing how costs can be controlled through the use of program budgetary data.

## Program Budgeting Illustrated

Each department or agency in a governmental entity exists for the purpose of either producing a service or assisting other departments in providing such services. A review of the budgetary process for the City of Waco clearly demonstrates these underlying objectives. We may think of the departments engaged in providing these services as being similar to the productive departments of a manufacturing enterprise. Following that line of thought a bit further, we can then think of the support activities, such as the controller's office, as a service department.

The program budgeting process begins with the identification of the programs or activities provided by the city and the community needs met by those programs or activities. If the programs are to be operated effectively, the next step involves the assignment of priorities to the different activities. That process should include an examination of all programs to determine how well they are achieving their purposes. The final step in the budgetary process requires an estimation of the resources required to operate each program over a period of time.

The budgetary procedures for the City of Waco clearly include elements of program budgeting. Indeed, the city budgetary process develops a program budget as well as a line-item budget for its activities. In Exhibits 4–4 and 4–5, a condensed expenditures budget for the general fund is reflected on line-item and program bases, respectively. In the City of Waco illustration, budgetary data are first developed within the line-item format shown in Exhibit 4–4. An examination of these two illustrations shows that they represent the same total of projected expenditures classified in two different ways. The process of converting the information from one reporting format to the other is frequently referred to as *cross-walking*. By properly coding the items and establishing the allocation processes to be followed, the cross-walk procedure can be implemented by use of a computer.

## Development of Functional Unit Costs

The terms *program, activity,* and *function* are often used synonymously. Therefore, with the development of appropriate nondollar quantitative data relating to the activities being performed, functional unit costs can be developed. For example, the amount of crime and delinquency (police) service cost per unit of population can be determined by dividing the total police service cost by the population being served. Other unit functional costs can be developed in a similar manner. To illustrate the calculation of functional unit cost, let's assume that the population of the City of Waco is 100,000 and the total police service cost is $3,510,468. The direct functional unit cost of providing police protection would then be $35.10, calculated as follows:

$$\frac{\$3,510,468}{100,000} = \$35.10 \text{ per capita}$$

Observe that we have used the term *cost* to describe expenditures per capital. As we explain later, this is more appropriately labled *expenditure per capita*.

**EXHIBIT 4–4.**  City of Waco, Texas—Expenditures Budget (Line-Item Basis)

| | |
|---|---:|
| Salaries and wages | $13,675,241 |
| Supplies | 1,182,484 |
| Maintenance | 1,206,940 |
| Utilities, travel, and contractual services | 1,732,174 |
| Pensions and social security | 1,677,276 |
| Miscellaneous expense | 2,155,977 |
| Contributions | 114,910 |
| Capital outlays | 1,738,376 |
| Debt service | 2,738,474 |
| Total | $26,221,852 |

**EXHIBIT 4–5.**   City of Waco, Texas—Expenditures Budget
(Program Basis)

| | |
|---|---:|
| Administration | $ 4,683,272 |
| Crime and delinquency | 3,510,468 |
| Health | 1,452,942 |
| Manpower | 628,537 |
| Environmental protection and development | 8,967,777 |
| Housing | 217,783 |
| Transportation | 3,832,146 |
| Recreation and culture | 2,618,248 |
| Social service | 23,816 |
| Unallocated balance | 286,863 |
| Total | $26,221,852 |

## Controlling Costs Through Use of Functional Cost Data

Budgetary data and actual expenditure data should be classified in the same manner. If data are not projected on a program basis, both budget and actual expenditures can be cross-walked from the line-item–type classification into functional expenditure categories. We can then calculate actual functional unit costs by relating nondollar quantitative data to the functional classifications of actual expenditures. Those unit costs can then be compared with the budgetary projections of those costs and the costs incurred by other cities. Differences between budgeted functional unit costs and actual functional unit costs should then be analyzed so that control measures may be introduced to reduce the deviations between those figures in future periods.[3]

We have suggested that functional unit cost data can be used in projecting budgetary needs. This process places the primary emphasis on the program budget rather than on the line-item budget. Such an approach to the budgeting process often requires that cross-walk procedures be employed to reclassify the program-oriented budgetary data to the line-item classifications required for meeting legally imposed operating requirements. This could well be another step in improving the efficiency of the budgetary process and the resulting controls over expenditures.

## ◼ Planning the Acquisitions and Uses of Other Governmental Fund Resources

In the preceding portions of this chapter, we have dealt with budgetary procedures for proprietary funds and the general fund of governmental entities. Generally speaking, other governmental funds follow planning procedures that are similar in many respects

---

3.   See Emerson O. Henke, "Performance Evaluation for Not-for-Profit Organizations," *Journal of Accountancy* (June 1972), pp. 51–55.

to those described for the general fund. However, the sources of authority for acquiring and using certain types of resources and the period covered by the authorization are somewhat different. This is particularly true for capital projects funds and debt-service funds.

## Capital Projects Funds

Capital projects funds are created to account for resources designated to be used for the acquisition or construction of general capital facilities of a governmental unit. The budget for each capital projects fund is established on a *project basis rather than on a period basis,* as is the case for the general fund and special revenue funds. As a general rule, a separate capital projects fund will be established for each authorized project.

A capital projects fund tentatively comes into existence with the proposal of a capital improvement program and the development of projected costs of completing the program. Having developed the anticipated expenditures associated with the project, the next step normally involves the clearance of legal authorization to secure financing for the project. Although the revenue side of the budget will normally be provided by the sale of bonds, other types of debt instruments may be used. In other instances, financing may be realized from grants provided by other governmental agencies. If general obligation bonds are to be used, legal authorization must generally be secured by a referendum to the voters. A favorable vote would initiate the establishment of the capital projects fund with the proposed expenditure and financing arrangement approved by the voters. This action has essentially the same budgetary implications for the capital projects fund as does the approval of the general fund budget by the appropriate legislative body.

The origination of a capital projects fund to be financed through the issuance of bonds can be recorded as follows:

Estimated bond issue proceeds
    Appropriations or project authorization

These are budgetary accounts and therefore often are completely omitted from the records of capital projects funds. Nevertheless, the use of this type of entry clearly discloses the revenue and expenditure plans of the fund and facilitates later comparison of actual inflows and outflows with them.

## Debt-Service Funds

Debt-service funds are originated to account for the inflows and outflows of resources designated for the payment of principal and interest on long-term general obligation debt. This does not include debt incurred in financing special assessment projects or certain types of enterprise fund activities. Debt-service funds typically require annual contributions from general fund resources. As resources are received by the debt-service fund, some may be used to pay interest on long-term debt and the balance will be invested for the purpose of producing interest and dividend income. Again, just as with the capital projects fund, the debt-service fund is *project-oriented,* covering the period over which the general long-term debt is expected to be outstanding.

The bond indenture provision generally will require the establishment of a debt-service fund for the purpose of accumulating resources to be used in the payment of loan interest and principal. That constitutes the authorization to originate a debt-service fund. At the time of the authorization to issue bonds, budgetary action will have to be taken authorizing transfers from the general fund to the debt-service fund for the purpose of paying interest and ultimately retiring the principal of the bonds. Because this is an annual authorization, the budgetary entry for fund inflows can be recorded annually as follows:

Estimated revenues from investments
Required general fund contributions
   Budgetary fund balance

Again, because this is a budgetary entry, it may be completely excluded from the accounting records of the debt-service fund. In that case, the first entry in the debt-service fund would occur as funds are transferred from the general fund to the debt-service fund.

# ▪ Development and Use of Cost Data

We have discussed how unit cost data can be developed and used in accounting for proprietary fund activities. These data are derived from records maintained on the accrual basis that allows determination of the full costs of providing services, including depreciation and amortization charges. These costs are properly characterized as *full cost* or *expense per unit* of service performed.

    We have also dealt with the possibility of accumulating unit functional cost data for general fund activities to help evaluate the efficiency with which the services of the entity were being performed. However, most of those unit cost data are really *expenditures per unit* rather than *expense per unit*. The only way that an expense per functional unit of service performed can be developed for governmental fund operations is to divide expenditures between expense and asset categories, adjust expense items for accrued and prepaid amounts, and recognize depreciation as the expense associated with the usage of fixed assets. If such data are developed, budgetary projections can be based on an extension of the functional units of service needed multiplied by the anticipated full functional cost per unit. Such a budgeting arrangement would not only help provide more efficient control over the conversion of resources to services but, if generally accepted, would also provide an avenue for a meaningful intergovernmental entity comparison of unit functional costs. That type of comparison should help in evaluating the efficiency of operations of different governmental units. We sometimes refer to this type of budgeting process as *performance budgeting*.

    The development of full, accrual-based projected cost data is at this time an idealistic expectation. Present day governmental accounting practices cling tenaciously to the line-item budget because of the legal requirements associated with the uses of governmental fund resources. Within some jurisdictions, program budgeting, through which expenditures are based primarily on service categories and secondarily on objects of expenditure, is beginning to be used. This type of budget may be thought of as representing a step toward the performance budget described earlier. Future developments in budgetary and accounting procedures for governmental units will probably see greater use of the program budget and perhaps ultimately more use of the performance budget.

# ■ Ethical Considerations Associated with the Budgetary Process

General fund budgets are generally developed from prior period expenditures data adjusted for anticipated changes in operations for the budgetary period. Therefore, managers of these funds recognize that failure to spend the amounts appropriated in prior periods can trigger reductions in appropriations for future periods. Consider the ethical issues involved in managers concentrating their attention on spending all amounts appropriated without regard for the need for the services provided by those expenditures.

Also, in recognition of the probability that budget requests may be reduced as they go through the budgetary process, some managers may pad their requests, asking for larger appropriations than are really needed to carry out their service responsibilities. Consider the ethical issues involved in such actions.

# ■ Summary

We began this chapter by describing the budgetary process for proprietary funds and observing that it was similar to that followed by businesses. We saw how anticipated changes in the level of operations, programmed expenditure changes, and a provision for inflation can be incorporated into the operating budget.

The budgetary procedures normally followed in planning the inflow–outflow activities of governmental funds with primary emphasis on general fund budgetary procedures were next described. The basic philosophy underlying the establishment of budgetary allocations within these funds calls for planning the uses of available resources in such a way that the services provided by the governmental entity will be the ones desired by a majority of its citizens. In relating that to budgetary procedures, we have shown how the expenditures budget for the general fund is planned to provide the community services that the elected body perceives to be desired and needed by the citizens of the community. This requires a careful analysis of the services performed by various departments of the governmental entity, including some judgments regarding the priorities that should be assigned to the various services.

After the expenditures plan has been developed, the legislative body must turn its attention to establishing a plan for realizing sufficient revenues to cover the planned expenditures. Much of the revenue needed to meet expenditure plans must be acquired through the assessment of taxes. This requires the establishment and approval of tax rates, including a rather delicate balancing of the assessment rates acceptable to the citizens against the volume of services to be provided.

After expenditure and revenue plans have been established, the governmental entity is ready to move from the "plan" phase of the plan execute-evaluate-plan cycle to the "execute" phase. In that phase of the cycle, expenditures must be carefully controlled against budgetary appropriations on an item-by-item basis. The accounting records should be organized to provide the information required for this type of control. The financial managers must continuously review these data in deciding whether specific expenditures can be approved.

We also discussed briefly the procedures that should be followed in developing program and performance budgets, and showed how functional unit expenditure or unit expense data can be used in controlling the operations of governmental funds. We noted the possibility of using a crossover worksheet to convert line-item budgetary data to program-based data. We illustrated how general fund budgetary data might be presented both within the legally required object-of-expenditure format and a program format.

In the last part of the chapter, we described the authorization actions preceding the establishment of capital projects and debt-service funds, and showed how the authorization data should be recorded in the records of those funds.

## ■ Glossary

**Appropriation Account.**   A budgetary account set up to record specific authorizations to spend. The account is credited with original and any supplemental appropriations.

**Appropriation Ledger.**   A subsidiary ledger containing an account for each appropriation. Each account usually shows the amount originally appropriated, transfers to or from the appropriation, amounts charged against the appropriation, the net balance, and other related information.

**Budget.**   A plan of financial operation embodying an estimate of proposed expenditures for a given period and the proposed means of financing them. Used without any modifier, the term usually indicates a financial plan for a single fiscal year. The term *budget* is used in two senses in practice. Sometimes it designates the financial plan presented to the appropriating body for adoption and sometimes the plan finally approved by that body. It is usually necessary to specify whether the budget under consideration is preliminary and tentative or whether it has been approved by the appropriating body.

**Budgetary Accounts.**   Accounts used to enter the formally adopted annual operating budget into the general ledger as part of the management control technique of formal budgetary integration.

**Budgetary Comparisons.**   Governmental GAAP financial reports must include comparisons of approved budgeted amounts with actual results of operations. Such reports should be subjected to an independent audit, so that all parties involved in the annual operating budget/legal appropriation process are provided with assurances that government monies are spent in accordance with the mutually agreed-upon budgetary plan.

**Budgetary Control.** The control or management of a government or enterprise in accordance with an approved budget for the purpose of keeping expenditures within the limitations of available appropriations and available revenues.

**Cost–Volume Relationships.** The identifiable relationship between the aggregate amount of a cost and the volume of operations.

**Estimated Revenues.** The amount of revenues expected to be realized during a budgetary period as reflected in an adopted (approved) budget.

**Formula-Related Basis.** Used in this chapter to identify calculable relationships between budgetary items.

**Functional Classification.** Expenditure classification according to the principal purposes for which expenditures were made. Examples are public safety, public health, public welfare, etc.

**Functional Unit Cost.** The amount of expenditures or expenses incurred in providing one unit of service; the units of service may be identified in terms of units of activity or number of persons served.

**Master Budget.** A document that consolidates all budgets of an entity into an overall plan of operations for a budgetary period.

**Notes to the Financial Statements.** The summary of significant accounting policies and other disclosures required for a fair presentation of the basic financial statements of an entity in conformity with GAAP which are not included on the face of the basic financial statements themselves. The notes to the financial statements are an integral part of the basic financial statements.

**Performance Budget.** A budget emphasizing the relationships between outputs of services and the costs of providing those services.

**PPBS.** Acronym for planning-programming-budgeting systems. Such systems include procedures for evaluating the probable efficiency and effectiveness of new programs by relating the anticipated values of proposed services to the costs of providing those services.

**Program Budget.** A budget wherein expenditures are based primarily on programs of work and secondarily on character and object class. A program budget is a transitional type of budget between the traditional character and object class budget, on the one hand, and the performance budget, on the other.

**Proprietary Funds.** Funds, within a governmental accounting system, that operate like business entities. These funds are characterized as either enterprise or internal service funds.

**Revenue Goal.** The targeted amount of revenue needed to meet projected expenditures within the constraints of a planned change in the unreserved fund balance during the budgetary period.

**Subsidiary Account.** One of a group of related accounts that support in detail the debit and credit summaries recorded in a control account. An example is the individual property taxpayers' accounts for the taxes receivable control account in the general ledger. See *Subsidiary Ledger.*

**Subsidiary Ledger.**    A group of subsidiary accounts, the sum of the balances of which is equal to the balance of the related control account. See *Subsidiary Account*.

**Zero-Base Budgeting.**    A budgeting program that requires a complete review and annual justification on the basis of that review prior to the approval of budgeted expenditures for the accounting entity.

# ■ Suggested Supplementary References

*Barton, Marvin. "The Impact of Inflation—A Major Problem in Budgeting and Planning." *Federal Accountant* (December 1975).

Brown, Robert C., and C. Lowell Harriss. "The Impact of Inflation on Property Taxation." *Governmental Finance* (November 1977): 16–23.

Brownsher, Charles A. "Improvements to the Congressional Budget and Impoundment Control Act of 1974." *Government Accountants Journal* (Spring 1983): 13–22.

Caldwell, Kenneth S. "The Accounting Aspects of Budgetary Reform: Can We Have Meaningful Reform Without Significant Changes in Traditional Accounting Practices?" *Governmental Finance* (August 1978): 10–17.

Doczy, Edward F. "Linking a Strategic Plan to the Budgetary Process." *Government Finance Review* (December 1987).

Doost, Roger K. "The Importance of Budget Execution in Governments." *Government Accountants Journal* (Spring 1986).

Draper, Frank D., and Bernard T. Pitsvada. "Limitations in Federal Budget Execution." *Government Accountants Journal* (Fall 1981): 15–25.

Enke, Ernest L. "The Accounting Preconditions of PPB." *Management Accounting* 53 (1972): 33–37.

Fort, Debra B. "From Reactive to Proactive Fiscal Planning: The Results of Strategic Planning in McKinney, Texas." *Government Finance Review* (August 1989).

Frengen, James M. "Fixed Budgets in a Flexible World: The Dilemma of Government Management." *Government Accountants Journal* (Summer 1978): 62–68.

Hermanson, Roger H. "A New Era of Budget Philosophy on the Federal Scene—ZBB—How to Make it Work." *Government Accountants Journal* (Summer 1977).

*Holder, William W., and Robert W. Ingram. "Flexible Budgeting and Standard Costing: Keys to Effective Cost Control." *Government Accountants Journal* (Fall 1976).

Kerns, Dennis W., Vic Tomlinson, and Rodney E. Gordon. "Automating the Budget Process." *Government Finance Review* (April 1988).

Lazenby, Scott D., Donald E. Siggelkow, and Robert R. Drake. "Priority on Policies: How Glendale, Arizona, Streamlined the Budget Process." *Government Finance Review* (February 1990).

Letzkus, William C. "Zero-Base Budgeting: Some Implications of Measuring Accomplishments." *Government Accountants Journal* (Summer 1978): 34–42.

Minmier, George S., and Roger H. Hermanson. "A Look at Zero-Base Budgeting—The Georgia Experience." *Atlanta Economic Review* 26 (1976): 5–12.

O'Toole, Daniel E., and Marshall, James. "Budgeting Practices in Local Government: The State of the Art." *Government Finance Review* (October 1987).

*Also available in *Accounting in the Public Sector: A Changing Environment—A Book of Readings* by Robert W. Ingram (Salt Lake City: Brighton Publishing Company, 1980).

Pitsvada, Bernard T., and James A. Howard. "The Theory and Practice of Budget Execution." *Government Accountants Journal* (Summer 1986).

*Pyhor, Peter A. "The Zero-Base Approach to Government Budgeting." *Public Administration Review* (January/February 1977).

*Rehfuss, John. "Zero-Base Budgeting: The Experience to Date." *Public Personnel Management* (May/June 1977).

*Said, Kamal E. "A Goal-Oriented Budgetary Process." *Management Accounting* (January 1975).

Simpson, C. R. "Municipal Budgeting—A Case of Priorities." *Governmental Finance* 5 (1976): 12–19.

Stallings, Wayne. "Improving Budget Communications in Smaller Local Governments." *Governmental Finance* (August 1978): 18–25.

Steinberg, Harold I., and James D. Carney, "Program Budgeting for Towns and Villages." *Management Controls* 20 (1973): 121–124.

*Steinberg, Harold I., and James D. Carney. "Halting a Rise in a Town's Tax Structure Through PPBS." *Management Adviser* (January/February 1974).

Venketaraman, V. K., and Richard G. Stevens. "Capital Budgeting in the Federal Government." *Government Accountants Journal* (Winter 1981–1982): 45–50.

White, Michael J. "Budget Policy: Where Does it Begin and End?" *Governmental Finance* (August 1978): 2–9.

## ■ Questions for Class Discussion

**Q4-1.** Why do governmental units place such a strong emphasis on budgeting as an element of their accounting systems?

**Q4-2.** Compare and contrast governmental budgeting practices with those of businesses.

**Q4-3.** How are revenues generally projected for a proprietary fund?

**Q4-4.** Describe the procedures followed in budgeting expenses for a proprietary fund.

**Q4-5.** Explain the difference between surplus and deficit financing by governmental units.

**Q4-6.** What implications are associated with a projected deficit for a governmental unit during a particular period?

**Q4-7.** Relate deficit financing to the concept of "intergenerational equity."

**Q4-8.** Explain the relationships between appropriations and the property tax rate for a governmental fund.

**Q4-9.** Describe the procedures followed in a PPBS. What is the primary objective of a PPBS?

**Q4-10.** Explain what is meant by zero-base budgeting. What are the primary advantages and disadvantages of this budgetary process?

**Q4-11.** What meaning does a balance in an encumbrance account convey? When is such an account used?

**Q4-12.** What is a program budget? How does it relate to functional unit cost data?

---

*Also available in *Accounting in the Public Sector: A Changing Environment—A Book of Readings* by Robert W. Ingram (Salt Lake City: Brighton Publishing Company, 1980).

Q4-13.   What is meant by the term *cross-walking?* How does it relate to the use of program budgets?

Q4-14.   What is the purpose of a capital projects fund? How is its budgeting process different from that of the general fund?

Q4-15.   Describe the distinguishing features of a special assessment capital projects fund.

Q4-16.   What is the operating objective of a debt-service fund? How is it related to the general long-term debt account group?

Q4-17.   Compare a program budget with an object-of-expenditures budget. Can we have an object-of-expenditures budget for a particular program? Explain.


# ■ Exercises

E4-1.   The assessed value (equal to 70 percent of current market value) of all property in Denver City is $35,000,000. The city council adopts a budget calling for total expenditures in the amount of $775,000. They estimate that $75,000 of revenue will be realized from sources other than property taxes.

**Required:**
A.   Calculate the tax rate that should be assessed by Denver City.
B.   What percentage of current market value is currently being assessed as taxes?

E4-2.   The general fund of the city of Denby has, among others, the following account balances at the end of the fiscal period:

| | |
|---|---|
| Estimated revenues | $500,000 |
| Appropriations | 485,000 |
| Revenues | 508,000 |
| Expenditures | 460,000 |
| Encumbrances | 20,000 |
| Reserve for encumbrances | 20,000 |

**Required:**
Journalize the closing entries.

E4-3.   The subsidiary ledger for police department expenditures shows, among others, the following balances:

| | |
|---|---|
| Appropriation—supplies | $5,000 |
| Expenditures—supplies | 2,500 |
| Encumbrances for supplies | 500 |

**Required:**
What amount does the department still have available to spend for supplies? Explain.

E4-4.   The police department's budgeted expenditures for the current year are as follows:

| | Fixed Expenditures | Expenditures that Vary with the Level of Population | Total Expenditures |
|---|---|---|---|
| Salaries | $400,000 | | $400,000 |
| Equipment repairs | 21,000 | $24,000 | 45,000 |
| Vehicle services | 100,000 | 10,000 | 110,000 |
| Other expenditures | 14,000 | 16,000 | 30,000 |
| Totals | $535,000 | $50,000 | $585,000 |

Although salaries of police personnel are listed as a fixed expenditure, the city contemplates adding one new officer at a starting salary of $12,000 per year with each 5 percent growth in population. The city expects population to increase 8 percent next year over the current year. An inflation rate of 6 percent is anticipated. Presently employed personnel are scheduled to receive a salary increase amounting to 9 percent of their present salaries.

**Required:**
Prepare the police department budget for next year.

E4-5. The *Budgeted Expenditures* for the general fund of the City of Huntsburg for 19XX were:

| | |
|---|---|
| Police expenditures | $560,000 |
| Recreation expenditures | 120,000 |
| Sanitation expenditures | 410,000 |
| Fire protection expenditures | 595,000 |
| Unallocated expenditures | 75,000 |

Assume that unallocated expenditures are to be allocated to the various service programs on the basis of direct expenditure charges.

**Required:**
A. Prepare a budget that shows all expenditures allocated to specific service programs.
B. Calculate the percentages of total expenditures expected to be incurred in providing each type of service for the city.

E4-6. Refer to Exercise E4-5. Assume that the city being served by these programs has a population of 100,000.

**Required:**
Calculate the amount of expenditures per capita being used to provide each of the services.

E4-7. The general fund subsidiary ledger shows the following balances for selected accounts as of December 31, 19XX:

|                 | Budget    | Expenditures | Encumbrances |
|-----------------|-----------|--------------|--------------|
| Salaries        | $115,000  | $107,500     | $ 7,400      |
| Misc. equipment | 4,000     | 3,900        | 200          |
| Supplies        | 5,000     | 4,000        | 800          |
| Vehicles        | 36,000    | 18,000       | 17,500       |

**Required:**

Calculate the differences between the budgeted expenditures and those incurred and committed for each line item and in total. Comment on your findings.

**E4-8.** City Motor Pool provides maintenance and repair services for a city's fleet of 100 vehicles. This internal service fund operated with the following budget last year. That budget was based on the assumption that all vehicles would be driven an average of 1,000 miles per vehicle per month.

|                    | Total Expenses | Fixed Expenses | Variable Expenses |
|--------------------|----------------|----------------|-------------------|
| Salaries and wages | $125,000       | $100,000       | $25,000           |
| Auto parts         | 45,000         | 18,000         | 27,000            |
| Supplies           | 15,000         | 10,000         | 5,000             |
| Depreciation       | 25,000         | 25,000         |                   |

The anticipated rate of inflation for next year is 6 percent. Salaries and wages are expected to increase 8 percent.

**Required:**

A.  Prepare an expense budget for City Motor Pool on the assumption that vehicle mileage can be reduced to 800 miles per vehicle per month.

B.  Prepare the budget assuming that vehicle mileage is expected to increase to 1,200 miles per vehicle per month.

C.  Calculate the average cost per mile to maintain city vehicles under each assumption.

**E4-9.** The following program budgets have been prepared covering general fund activities for Home City:

| Fire Services |  |
|---|---|
| 1. Salaries | $540,000 |
| 2. Equipment | 80,000 |
| 3. Misc. | 58,000 |
| 4. Supplies | 22,000 |
| Police Services |  |
| 1. Salaries | $420,000 |
| 2. Equipment | 24,000 |

| | |
|---|---|
| 3. Misc. | 19,000 |
| 4. Supplies | 22,000 |
| Recreational Services | |
| 1. Salaries | $85,000 |
| 2. Equipment | 2,000 |
| 3. Misc. | 3,500 |
| 4. Supplies | 1,700 |

**Required:**
Develop an object-of-expenditures budget for Home City general fund.

# ■ Problems

P4-1. Select the best answer for each of the following items:
1. In preparing the general fund budget of Brockton City for the forthcoming fiscal year, the city council appropriated a sum greater than expected revenues. This action of the council will result in:
   a. a cash overdraft during that fiscal year.
   b. an increase in encumbrances by the end of that fiscal year.
   c. a decrease in the fund balance.
   d. a necessity for compensatory offsetting action in the debt-service fund.
2. The budget that relates input of resources to output of services is the:
   a. line-item budget.
   b. object-of-expenditure budget.
   c. performance budget.
   d. resource budget.
3. If a credit was made to the fund balance in the process of recording a budget for a governmental unit, it can be assumed that:
   a. estimated expenses exceed actual revenues.
   b. actual expenses exceed estimated expenses.
   c. estimated revenues exceed appropriations.
   d. appropriations exceed estimated revenues.
4. A performance budget relates a governmental unit's expenditures to:
   a. objects of expenditure.
   b. expenditures of the preceding fiscal year.
   c. individual months within the fiscal year.
   d. activities and programs.
5. A city's general fund budget for the forthcoming fiscal year shows estimated revenues in excess of appropriations. The initial effect of recording this will result in an increase in:
   a. taxes receivable.
   b. fund balance.
   c. reserve for encumbrances.
   d. encumbrances.

6. Which of the following accounts is a budgetary account in governmental accounting?
   a. reserve for inventory of supplies
   b. fund balance
   c. appropriations
   d. estimated uncollectible property taxes

7. When the budget of a governmental unit is adopted, and the estimated revenues exceed the appropriations, the excess is:
   a. debited to reserve for encumbrances.
   b. credited to reserve for encumbrances.
   c. debited to fund balance.
   d. credited to fund balance.

8. Which of the following accounts of a governmental unit is debited when a purchase order is approved?
   a. appropriations control
   b. vouchers payable
   c. fund balance reserved for encumbrances
   d. encumbrances control

9. The budget of a governmental unit, for which the appropriations exceed the estimated revenues, was adopted and recorded in the general ledger at the beginning of the year. During the year, expenditures and encumbrances were less than appropriations, whereas revenues equaled estimated revenues. The budgetary fund balance account is:
   a. credited at the beginning of the year and **not** changed at the end of the year.
   b. credited at the beginning of the year and debited at the end of the year.
   c. debited at the beginning of the year and **not** changed at the end of the year.
   d. debited at the beginning of the year and credited at the end of the year.

10. The appropriations control account of a governmental unit is credited when:
    a. supplies are purchased.
    b. expenditures are recorded.
    c. the budget is recorded.
    d. the budgetary accounts are closed.

11. The estimated revenues control account of a governmental unit is debited when:
    a. the budget is closed at the end of the year.
    b. the budget is recorded.
    c. actual revenues are recorded.
    d. actual revenues are collected.

—**AICPA Adapted**

**P4-2.** The comptroller of the city of Helmaville recently resigned. In his absence, the deputy comptroller attempted to calculate the amount of money required to be raised from property taxes for the general fund for the fiscal year ending June 30, 19B. The calculation is to be made as of January 1, 19A, to serve as a basis for setting the property tax rate for the following fiscal year. The mayor has requested you to review the deputy comptroller's calculations and obtain other necessary information to prepare a formal statement for the general fund that will disclose the amount of money required to be raised from property taxes for the fiscal year ending June 30, 19B. Following are the calculations prepared by the deputy comptroller:

City resources other than proposed tax levy:

| | |
|---|---|
| Estimated general fund working balance, January 1, 19A | $ 352,000 |
| Estimated receipts from property taxes (January 1, 19A—June 30, 19A) | 2,222,000 |
| Estimated revenue from investments (January 1, 19A—June 30, 19B) | 442,000 |
| Estimated proceeds from sale of general obligation bonds in August 19A | 3,000,000 |
| Total | $6,016,000 |

General fund requirements:

| | |
|---|---|
| Estimated expenditures (January 1, 19A—June 30, 19A) | $1,900,000 |
| Proposed appropriations (July 1, 19A—June 30, 19B) | 4,300,000 |
| Total | $6,200,000 |

Additional information:
1. The general fund working balance required by the city council for July 1, 19B, is $175,000.
2. Property tax collections are due in March and September of each year. Your review indicates that during the month of February 19A, estimated expenditures will exceed available funds by $200,000. Pending collection of property taxes in March 19A, this deficiency will have to be met by the issuance of thirty-day tax-anticipation notes of $200,000 at an estimated interest rate of 9 percent per annum.
3. The proposed general obligation bonds will be issued by the City Water Fund and will be used for the construction of a new water-pumping station.

**Required:**
Prepare a statement as of January 1, 19A, calculating the property tax levy required for the City of Helmaville general fund for the fiscal year ending June 30, 19B.

—AICPA Adapted

P4-3. A proprietary fund incurred the following expenses during the past year:

| | |
|---|---|
| Salaries | $ 64,000 |
| Other operating expenses | 90,000 |
| Depreciation | 6,000 |
| Total expenses | $160,000 |

Depreciation is a fixed expense. It is estimated that $40,000 of salaries and $50,000 of other operating expenses are also fixed. The remaining amount of each item is considered variable.

In preparing the expense budget for next year, the department anticipates a 10 percent increase in its level of operations. An 8 percent rate of inflation is expected for the year. Salaries are expected to be increased to compensate for inflation plus 3 percent (total 11 percent).

**Required:**
Prepare an expense budget for the self-sustaining fund for next year.

P4-4.   A city's general fund incurred the following expenditures during the past year:

| | |
|---|---:|
| Salaries | $140,000 |
| Supplies | 30,000 |
| Equipment | 50,000 |
| Other expenditures | 20,000 |
| Total | $240,000 |

This fund provides services that should vary directly with the level of population within the city. The city manager anticipates a 10 percent growth in population and an inflation rate for next year over the past year of approximately 8 percent. Property taxes are the only source of revenue and revenue was equal to expenditures last year. City property currently has an assessed value of $9,600,000. The population increase should provide a 6 percent increase in the assessed valuation of property. The city council is concerned about taxpayer reaction to any increase in the tax rate.

**Required:**
You have been engaged to assist the city manager in preparing a budget for the coming year. Within the constraint of not increasing the tax rate, what observations and suggestions can you make to help him in that task. Be specific, including the development of useful numerical data.

P4-5.   The following object-of-expenditure budget has been prepared for the general fund of a city:

| | |
|---|---:|
| Salaries and wages | $6,000,000 |
| Supplies | 500,000 |
| Maintenance | 600,000 |
| Employee benefits | 800,000 |
| Capital outlays | 900,000 |
| Other expenditures | 500,000 |
| Total | $9,300,000 |

Services provided by these expenditures include administration, police protection, recreation and culture, and sanitation services. The city desires to prepare a program budget as a first step in determining the amounts of different types of service expenditures per person to be provided for its citizens. Analysis of the various object-of-expenditure items discloses that they should be allocated to the various service functions as follows:

| | Administration | Police | Recreation & Culture | Sanitation |
|---|---|---|---|---|
| Salaries and wages | 40% | 30% | 10% | 20% |
| Supplies | 20% | 20% | 40% | 20% |
| Maintenance | 10% | 30% | 20% | 40% |
| Employee benefits | 40% | 30% | 10% | 20% |
| Capital outlays | 20% | 30% | 10% | 40% |
| Other expenditures | On basis of total allocated expenditures. | | | |

**Required:**

A.   Prepare a program budget for general fund operations.

B.   Assume the city has a population of 100,000. Calculate the budgeted expenditures per person for each service provided.

**P4-6.**   Last year's budget for the city of Panola is presented as follows:

| | |
|---|---:|
| Estimated revenues | |
| General property taxes | $ 7,500,000 |
| City sales taxes | 3,500,000 |
| Permits, licenses, and fees | 1,500,000 |
| User fees | 2,000,000 |
| Miscellaneous | 500,000 |
| Total estimated revenues | $15,000,000 |
| Budgeted expenditures | |
| Salaries and wages (including fringe benefits) | $ 7,000,000 |
| Supplies and services | 1,500,000 |
| Maintenance of facilities | 1,000,000 |
| Capital expenditures | 2,000,000 |
| Debt service | 2,000,000 |
| Miscellaneous expenditures | 1,300,000 |
| Total budgeted expenditures | $14,800,000 |

The city expects to have a 5 percent increase in population and in assessed value of property next year. The price level for all expenditures except debt service and salaries and wages is expected to increase 7 percent.

An analysis of expenditures shows that the following amounts from last year's budget are expected to vary directly with changes in population:

| | |
|---|---:|
| Supplies and services | $400,000 |
| Maintenance of facilities | 200,000 |
| Miscellaneous expenditures | 800,000 |

Other expenditures are fixed except as noted next. Salaries and wages will be increased by 8 percent. The volume of capital expenditures are to be budgeted at the same volume as last year.

Permits, licenses, and fees are expected to vary with the level of population but will not be adjusted for inflation. Individual user fees are being increased by 6 percent to partially compensate for inflationary changes. These fees are also expected to increase in direct relationship to any increase in population. City sales taxes are based on retail sales within the city. Miscellaneous revenues are expected to increase by 10 percent.

**Required:**

A.   Prepare a budget for the City of Panola for next year. The budget should provide for a $100,000 excess of revenues over expenditures. No new services will be added. The City Council has asked that last year's operating plan simply be adjusted for the anticipated changes cited previously. All budget amounts are to be rounded to the nearest thousand dollars. Property tax rates will be established at the level required to meet budgetary goals.

B.   Comment on the effect the budget will have on property tax rates.

P4-7.   Governmental accounting gives substantial recognition to budgets, with those budgets being recorded in the accounts of the governmental unit.

**Required:**
A.   What is the purpose of a governmental accounting system and why is the budget recorded in the accounts of a governmental unit? Include in your discussion the purpose and significance of appropriations.
B.   Describe when and how a governmental unit records its budget and closes it out.

—**AICPA Adapted**

P4-8.   **Thought Projection Problem.** The Board of Education of the Victoria School District is developing a budget for the school year ending June 30, 19X1. The budgeted expenditures follow:

**Victoria School District Budgeted Expenditures for the Year Ending June 30, 19X1**

| | | | |
|---|---|---|---|
| Current operating expenditures: | | | |
| Instruction: | | | |
| General | $1,401,600 | | |
| Vocational training | 112,000 | | |
| | | $1,513,600 | |
| Pupil Service: | | | |
| Bus transportation | 36,300 | | |
| School lunches | 51,700 | 88,000 | |
| Attendance and health service | | 14,000 | |
| Administration | | 46,000 | |
| Operation and maintenance of plant | | 208,000 | |
| Pensions, insurance, etc. | | 154,000 | |
| Total current operating expenditures | | | $2,023,600 |
| Other expenditures: | | | |
| Capital outlays from revenues | | 75,000 | |
| Debit service (annual installment and interest on long-term debt) | | 150,000 | |
| Total other expenditures | | | 225,000 |
| Total budgeted expenditures | | | $2,248,600 |

The following data are available:
1.   The estimated average daily school enrollment of the School District is 5,000 pupils including 200 pupils enrolled in a vocational training program.
2.   Estimated revenues include equalizing grants-in-aid of $150 per pupil from the state. The grants were established by state law under a plan intended to encourage raising the level of education.

3. The federal government matches 60 percent of state grants-in-aid for pupils enrolled in a vocational training program. In addition, the federal government contributes toward the cost of bus transportation and school lunches a maximum of $12 per pupil based on total enrollment within the school district but not to exceed 6⅔ percent of the state per-pupil equalization grants-in-aid.
4. Interest on temporary investment of school tax receipts and rents of school facilities are expected to be $75,000 and are earmarked for special equipment acquisitions listed as "capital outlays from revenues" in the budgeted expenditures. Cost of the special equipment acquisitions will be limited to the amount derived from these miscellaneous receipts.
5. The remaining funds needed to finance the budgeted expenditures of the School District are to be raised from local taxation. An allowance of 9 percent of the local tax levy is necessary for possible tax abatements and losses. The assessed valuation of the property located within the School District is $80,000,000.

**Required:**
A. Prepare a schedule computing the estimated total funds to be obtained from local taxation for the ensuing school year ending June 30, 19X1, for the Victoria School District.
B. Prepare a schedule computing the estimated current operating cost per regular pupil and per vocational pupil to be met by local tax funds. Assume that costs other than instructional costs are assignable on a per capita basis to regular and vocational students.
C. Without prejudice to your solution to requirement A, assume that the estimated total tax levy for the ensuing school year ending June 30, 19X1, is $1,092,000. Prepare a schedule computing the estimated tax rate per $100 of assessed valuation of the property within the Victoria School District.

**—AICPA Adapted**

# CHAPTER 5

# General Fund and Special Revenue Fund Accounting Procedures—I

---

## ■ Learning Objectives

When you have finished your study of this chapter, you should

1. Be familiar with the operating characteristics of the general fund and special revenue fund.

2. Know the meanings of the various accounts used to record transactions in the general fund and special revenue fund accounting records and understand how they relate to each other.

3. Understand the procedures followed in recording both complementing and reciprocal entries.

4. Be able to deal with the special problems associated with general fund accounting procedures discussed in the last part of the chapter.

---

In Chapter 4, we discussed the procedures followed in developing a budget for general fund operations. In this chapter, we turn our attention to the specialized *accounting procedures followed in accounting for general fund and special revenue fund activities.* Both are characterized as governmental funds in NCGA Statement 1 and in Governmental Accounting, Auditing, and Financial Reporting (GAAFR). Since the accounting procedures for these two funds are identical, you should recognize that, as we discuss and illustrate the accounting practices for the general fund, we are at the same time describing those followed in accounting for special revenue fund activities.

The procedures described and illustrated in this chapter and in Chapter 6 are basically those recommended in Governmental Accounting, Auditing, and Financial

Reporting Principles, and NCGA Statement 1.[1] The *interpretations of that statement* included in the 1988 edition of GAAFR, however, are the ones followed in our illustrated journal entries. With a few minor exceptions, those entries are also consistent with the recommendations of the AICPA industry audit guide for governmental units.[2] The differences include useful clarifications and alternate methods. Therefore, our procedures conform basically with those recommended by both publications.

Following the general format set out earlier in the text, we shall develop the logical framework supporting the procedures as they are illustrated. In this chapter, we do that for the general and special revenue funds by

1. examining briefly the operational characteristics of the general fund

2. reviewing the types of accounts used in accounting for the operations of the general fund

3. describing the typical activities requiring accounting recognition in the general fund

4. identifying general fund transactions that require accounting recognition in other funds and/or account groups

5. recognizing some of the special problems associated with general fund accounting procedures.

## ■ Operational Characteristics

In the Summary Statement of Principles discussed in Chapter 3, the general fund is described as an accounting entity used "to account for all *financial resources* except those required to be accounted for in another fund."[3] It will be helpful to think of the general fund as *an independent fiscal and accounting entity used to account for the acquisitions and uses of spendable resources available to the governmental entity for carrying out its general operations.* The accounting records for this fund include a self-balancing ledger with accounts to show the inflows and outflows of the entity's spendable resources plus the appropriable assets and the obligations against those assets at the end of each period. Although it is not completely correct to do so, when we talk about accounting for the operations of a governmental unit we are, for the most part, referring to activities recorded in the general fund accounting records. Also, when we refer to the budget for a governmental entity, we are usually referring to the general fund budget. To be more precise we should recognize that governmental operations involve the use of resources from other funds and that budgets may also be prepared for those funds. However, *the general fund is the primary vehicle through which the services of a governmental unit are provided.*

---

1. National Council on Governmental Accounting, *NCGA Statement 1* (Chicago: Municipal Finance Officers Association, 1979).
2. American Institute of Certified Public Accountants, *AICPA Industry Audit Guide on Audits of State and Local Governmental Units,* 5th ed. (New York: AICPA, 1989).
3. *GAAFR Statement 1,* p. 2.

It is important to recall that the general fund is characterized as a governmental fund in the Statement of Principles (see Chapter 3). In accounting for the resource conversion activities of this accounting entity, we therefore will be primarily concerned with reflecting the *inflows and outflows of appropriable (spendable) resources* available for general operations.

Taxes constitute the major source of resource inflows, labeled revenues, and are levied on the basis of some measure of ability to pay, such as the assessed valuations of property or amounts of net income. Outflows, described as expenditures, are incurred for the purpose of providing community services. Such things as police protection, fire protection, sanitation services, and recreation services are provided through use of general fund resources. Most of these services are distributed to individual citizens on the basis of need and desire for them. In theory at least, each voter in the governmental unit has the same voice in deciding the nature and amounts of services to be provided and how the resource inflows shall be realized to meet the costs of providing them.

Because the general fund is used to account for the resources available for the general operations of the governmental unit, all governmental units will have a general fund. Other funds may or may not be found within the accounting records of any specific governmental unit. Their existence depends on whether the unit has segments of resources designated for specified purposes other than general operations. Furthermore, because the general fund is an operating fund, the emphasis in accounting for its activities is on *periodic* reporting. As we have noted, some governmental funds are *project*-oriented rather than *period*-oriented.

In Chapter 4, we showed that budgetary procedures are particularly important in planning and controlling the operations of governmental funds. This is especially true for the general fund. The overall budgetary process may be thought of as including preparation, adoption, and execution phases. The initial step in the budgetary process calls for the preparation of an expenditures plan, generally by a financial officer or committee. That plan is then presented to a council or legislative body elected by the voters of the governmental unit. When a proposed expenditures plan is adopted by that legally authorized body of officers, the items included in it become appropriations that are legally available to be used for the various designated purposes.

The next step in the budgetary process involves the development of a plan for realizing the revenues required to meet the proposed expenditures. Generally, the major portion of revenues for the general fund must be provided by a tax levy. However, to ascertain the amount of revenues that must be realized from taxes it is first necessary to estimate the inflows of resources that will probably be realized from other sources such as licenses, traffic fines, and fees. If the managers plan to provide governmental services on a pay-as-you-go basis, taxes must then be levied to provide an amount equal to the difference between appropriations and other revenues. If the governmental unit is depending on property taxes for its tax revenue, the amount so calculated must then be divided by the total assessed valuation of all property within the governmental unit to calculate the tax rate. Again, the legally authorized body of officers must approve the tax rate before tax assessment notices can be sent out to property owners.

Specific practices regarding budget preparation and approval and the determination of tax rates are generally stipulated and controlled by the laws of the particular entity involved. Internal managers must always be prepared to show that they have adhered to these legal requirements. Also, as we noted in Chapter 4, the accounting records should be organized and maintained to show the extent of adherence to the approved budget plan. The system designed to provide those disclosures begins to unfold as the budgetary plan moves into the execute phase.

# ■ General Fund Accounts

In Chapter 2, we developed the accounting equation that includes the types of accounts typically found within the accounting records of governmental funds. That equation also establishes the basis for applying the rule of debit and credit as we record transactions in such funds. The general fund accounting entity, as a governmental fund, will contain at least *asset, liability, fund balance, revenue,* and *expenditure* accounts. The ledger for this fund will also generally include budgetary accounts for *estimated revenues, appropriations, encumbrances,* and *reserve for encumbrances.* In many instances, the ledger will also contain accounts for interfund transfers, and amounts due from and due to other funds.

Although the accounts in the accounting equation have been defined in general terms, it is important to recognize some of the specific implications associated with their uses as we develop the general fund accounting system. General fund assets are limited to appropriable (spendable) assets such as cash and near-cash items. This is interpreted to include such things as taxes receivable, which are considered appropriable because proceeds from them will be available to meet current period expenditures. Among the notable exclusions are such things as prepaid items and long-term assets available to be used in the normal operations of the governmental entity. Supplies on hand are sometimes reflected as assets, but are more typically disclosed with an offsetting reserve account equal to the on-hand balance. This has the effect of disclosing the existence of supplies without allowing a net asset balance for them to be included in the balance sheet total. The recordkeeping procedures for supplies are illustrated later in this chapter.

Insofar as liabilities are concerned, use of the modified accrual basis precludes the recognition of various accrued expense and prepaid revenue items. Also, general long-term debt is not included among the liabilities of the general fund. Therefore, the liability section of the general fund balance sheet will include only such things as vouchers payable, short-term notes payable, and amounts payable to other funds. In some instances, a liability for taxes collected in advance will also be reflected in the general fund balance sheet as deferred revenues.

The fund balance account is defined in GAAFR as the fund equity of governmental and trust funds.[4] Certain parts of it may be reserved for encumbrances or other purposes. We may think of the unreserved fund balance account as reflecting the net amount of spendable resources available for carrying out future general operations of the governmental unit.

The new edition of GAAFR actually uses four fund balance accounts in its illustrated entries for the general fund. One of these is labeled *budgetary fund balance* and

---

4. National Council on Governmental Accounting, *Governmental Accounting, Auditing and Financial Reporting* (Chicago: Municipal Finance Officers Association, 1988), p. 19.

reflects the difference between estimated revenues and appropriations. Fund balances associated with actual financial data may carry as many as three different labels. The term *reserved fund balance* is used to describe the portion of fund balance that is not available for appropriation or expenditure or is segregated legally for a specific future use. Part of an otherwise unreserved fund balance may be labeled as a *designated fund balance* to indicate tentative plans for use of current financial resources in the future. The balance of net assets is labeled *unreserved fund balance* to show that those resources are available to finance expenditures other than those already planned.[5]

Revenue and expenditure accounts, as defined earlier, are the principal nominal accounts for the general fund. They are used to accumulate the inflows (revenues) and outflows (expenditures) of fund resources. Because the emphasis in general fund accounting is on reflecting inflows and outflows of appropriable resources, the revenue and expenditure accounts used in the general fund accounting records must be carefully distinguished from the revenue and expense accounts used for business entities and for proprietary funds. Net appropriable resources can be described as the net liquid assets that, within the going-concern concept, are capable of being used to meet expenditures incurred during the current period.

In Chapter 4, we observed that budgetary accounts are used to record the budget plans in the accounting records. Estimated revenues are recorded to show the anticipated inflows of appropriable resources. Appropriation accounts show the budgeted outflows of such resources. The National Council on Governmental Accounting defines an appropriation as the "maximum expenditure authorization that cannot be exceeded legally."[6] Kohler defines an appropriation as

> . . . an expenditure authorization with specific limitations as to amount, purpose, and time; a formal advance approval of an expenditure or class of expenditures from designated resources available or estimated to be available. An appropriation may vary in binding force from an expression of intent by management of a business concern to a restrictive limitation by the legislature imposed on a governmental agency.[7]

Both of these budgetary accounts (estimated revenue and appropriations) are closed at the end of each fiscal period and are therefore classified as nominal accounts.

The legal constraints placed on the uses of general fund resources through the adoption and approval of the budget also make it desirable to use encumbrance and encumbrance reserve accounts in accounting for general fund operations. Kohler defines an encumbrance as "an anticipated expenditure evidenced by a contract or a purchase order or determined by administrative action."[8] The encumbrance account is another nominal account. It is closed against reserve for encumbrances at the end of each fiscal period. After the encumbrance and reserve for encumbrance accounts have been closed, the amount shown in the fund balance reserved for encumbrances will be increased or decreased to the amount shown as encumbrances at the end of the period. The offsetting debit or credit in this entry will be to unreserved fund balance.

As observed earlier, interfund accounts are used to reflect claims against and obligations to other fund entities. Although they may be thought of, respectively, as

5. Ibid., p. 19.
6. Ibid., p. 16.
7. *Kohler's Dictionary for Accountants* (Englewood Cliffs, N.J.: Prentice-Hall, Inc., 1983), p. 35.
8. Ibid., p. 194.

assets and liabilities of the general fund, they cannot be construed as assets and liabilities of the governmental unit because they are internal receivables and payables. They are typically labeled *due to* and *due from* other funds.

General fund nominal accounts are designed to account for the flows of appropriable resources into and out of the operating entity. The names of revenue accounts should disclose the *sources from which the inflows were realized*. Expenditure account subclassifications should be designed to *show how the resources have been used*. Thus, through the use of these accounts and the other related nominal accounts, dollar accountability is maintained for general fund resources. In accordance with this concept of control, capital and revenue items are accounted for in much the same manner. For example, except for the difference in account names, a purchase of equipment from general fund resources is recorded within the general fund exactly as is the payment of payroll. Each is treated as an expenditure or an outflow of appropriable resources for the reporting period.

Each type of nominal account described earlier will be used as a control account in the general fund ledger. By implication then, the general fund records must also contain appropriate subsidiary ledgers reflecting the various types of revenues, expenditures, and encumbrances. In our illustration in Chapter 6, this control–subsidiary account relationship is explained more completely. A portion of a subsidiary ledger is also included in the section of that chapter illustrating general fund accounting procedures.

## Account Subclassifications

We have noted that the elements of each major nominal account will generally be more completely explained through use of subsidiary ledgers. That practice provides more informative disclosure of the data and helps managers to maintain better control over the flows of resources. These subclassifications are organized to provide more specific information regarding the various types of revenues and expenditures.

Revenue accounts are subclassified primarily by source. Typical categories for the subsidiary revenues ledger of a general fund are

1. revenue from taxes
2. revenue from fines and forfeits
3. revenue from licenses and permits
4. other revenue.

These classifications may be further subdivided to explain more specifically the sources from which the revenues are realized. Revenue from taxes may be subdivided to show the amounts realized from different tax sources such as property taxes and sales taxes. Other categories may be similarly subdivided. This second level of subdivision can result in subsidiary control accounts such as shown in Figure 5–1. The division of revenues into these subcategories can be facilitated by the use of code numbers. For example, if a code number of 300 is assigned to revenues, we may use numbers from 1 through 9 as the second digit place from the left to identify the general category of revenue being recognized. The third digit place from the left can then be used to identify the specific type of revenue being recorded. To illustrate what we have just said, let's assume that we assign the number 1 to revenue from taxes and the number 2 to sales

**FIGURE 5–1.**    Control Account

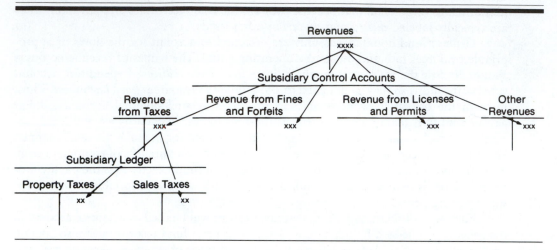

tax revenue. An inflow of resources from sales taxes would then be coded 312 to permit its inclusion in the subsidiary control account for revenue from taxes, and in the subsidiary ledger for sales taxes. Code numbers like the ones described above are especially useful when the accounting records are maintained on a computer.

Object-of-expenditure accounts are often subclassified by function and perhaps even by subfunction or by department to provide more information regarding the ways that resources have been used. Typical functional classifications might include

1. general government
2. public safety
3. highways and streets
4. sanitation services
5. culture and recreation services
6. health services
7. welfare services
8. education services
9. debt retirement
10. miscellaneous services
11. conservation of natural resources.

The specific functional classifications used within the general fund naturally will depend on the services provided by the governmental unit. The volume of such services has grown significantly over the last fifty years. The program budget for the City of Waco (see Exhibit 4–5, page 126) shows that city providing administrative (general government), health, manpower, environmental protection, housing, transportation, recreation, and social services in addition to the basic services of police and fire protection.

We will often find the major functional classifications further subdivided into subfunctions or departments. The general government function, for example, may be divided into executive, legislative, and judicial subfunctions or departments. Within each of these categories, subclassifications are again reflected by object of expenditure. The expenditures for the legislative function, for example, could be subdivided into categories for salaries, supplies, and other objects-of-expenditure items. Such an arrangement allows the financial manager of the general fund, through departmental or subfunction managers, to establish detailed item-by-item budgetary control over individual expenditures. The four levels of expenditure classifications that could be used are shown in Figure 5–2. It follows that the individual object-of-expenditure subclassification items can be accumulated to arrive at an object-of-expenditure statement for the fund similar to the object-of-expenditure budget shown in Chapter 4 (see Exhibit 4–4, page 125).

Again, account code numbers can be used to facilitate recording the various subdivisions of expenditures. We will, however, because of the use of eleven functional categories, need to use large code numbers to carry out the allocations. We may use a four-digit-plus decimal series of coding numbers. If, for example, we assign a code number of 4000 to expenditures, we can use numbers from 01 through 99 in the second and third digit places from the left to identify the functional classifications. Numbers 1 through 9 can then be used in the fourth digit place from the left to identify the department incurring

**FIGURE 5–2.**   Control Account

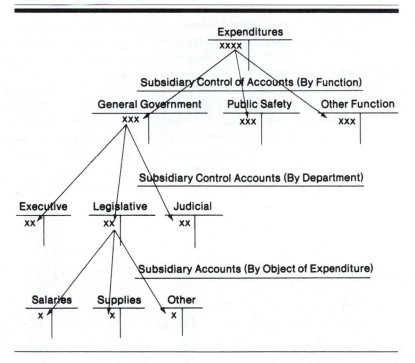

the expenditure. Decimal numbers 1 through 9 can then be used to identify the object-of-expenditure subsidiary account being charged with the expenditure. To illustrate such a use of code numbers, let's assume that general government expenditures are coded 01 and that the legislative department is assigned a code number of 2. Assume also that the code number for salaries is .1. Within those assumptions, general government salary expenditures for the legislative department would be coded 4012.1.

## ■ Typical Activities Requiring Accounting Recognition

In Chapter 2, we listed six types of activities requiring recognition in accounting for governmental fund operations. In applying this group of activities to the general fund, we find that *authorization action* (a type 1 activity) occurs as the budgetary plans for expenditures and revenues are approved by the appropriately authorized body. That action is recorded by the following entry:

> Estimated revenues
> Dr. or Cr. Budgetary fund balance
> Appropriations

The procedures for recognizing revenues and expenditures are controlled by the use of the modified accrual basis of accounting described in the Summary Statement of Principles (see Chapter 3, page 75). That requires that revenues be recognized when appropriable (spendable) resources flow into the general fund. They should be recognized in the accounting period in which "they become measurable and available."[9] With the exception of property taxes and intergovernmental inflows, this is judged to occur when cash is received. Revenues realized from such sources as fines and forfeits, licenses and permits, and miscellaneous other sources are recognized when cash is received. Revenues from property taxes are generally recognized when assessment notices are sent out. Sales tax revenues, on the other hand, are recognized when they are collected. An allowance for uncollectible taxes should be established to allow taxes receivable to be reflected at its anticipated cash-realizable value, and to cause revenue to be equal to the anticipated inflow of spendable resources. Intergovernmental revenue composed of amounts transferred between governmental accounting entities should be recognized when specific claims are established. All of these revenue recognition procedures are consistent with the emphasis on dollar-accountability reporting. The *realization* of revenues (a type 2 activity) should be recorded as follows:

> Cash
> Taxes Receivable
>   Revenues
>   Allowance for uncollectible taxes

The modified accrual basis also requires the recognition of expenditures at the time "the related liability is incurred."[10] For the most part, this has been interpreted to

---

9.  *GAAFR Statement 1*, p. 11.
10. Ibid., p. 12.

require the recognition of expenditures for salaries and similar items when cash is disbursed. However, expenditures evidenced by invoices from outside enterprise units should be recognized upon receipt of the invoice *provided the services or materials have also been received by the governmental entity.* Interfund outflows, like expenditures, should be recognized when they are objectively measurable. This generally occurs when the services have been performed or the materials have been delivered. All of these procedures are also consistent with the emphasis on dollar-accountability reporting in the governmental area. Expenditures (a type 3 activity) should be recorded as follows:

Expenditures
   Cash or vouchers payable

*Encumbrances* should be recognized any time we expect to have a significant lapse of time between the date a commitment to spend resources is made and the consummation of the expenditure transaction. As an example, an encumbrance should be recognized when an order is placed for delivery of equipment to be delivered at a later date. Under these circumstances, the encumbrance should be recognized at the time the order is placed by debiting an encumbrance account and crediting a reserve for an encumbrance account. That entry should be reversed upon receipt of the equipment and recognition of the expenditure. These actions (types 5 and 6 activities) should be recorded as follows:

**Encumbrance recognized**
Encumbrances
   Reserve for encumbrances
**Elimination of encumbrance**
Reserve for encumbrances
   Encumbrances
Expenditures
   Cash or vouchers payable

*Closing entries* occur at the end of each fiscal period. The nature of general fund operations and the legal constraints placed upon the uses of resources make it imperative that the accounting system for the general fund be organized to differentiate each period's operations from those of the immediately preceding and immediately following periods. This requires that all nominal accounts, including revenues, expenditures, and their related budgetary accounts, be closed at the end of each fiscal period.

The accounting equation for funds using the modified accrual basis of accounting was developed in Chapter 2 (see page 27). We repeat it here as we begin illustrating the journal entries that should be made to record a series of assumed general fund transactions for Model City (see Chapter 6). The equation is stated as follows:

assets + expenditures + estimated revenues + encumbrances = liabilities
+ fund balance + revenues + appropriations + reserve for encumbrances

Again, we remind you that all of the accounts fitting into the classifications on the left side of the equation are increased by debits and decreased by credits. Increases in the accounts in the classifications on the right side are reflected as credits, while decreases are reflected as debits.

# ■ Transactions Involving Other Funds and Account Groups

As we have observed, the accounting records of governmental entities can include a number of funds and account groups, each of which is treated as a separate fiscal and accounting entity. Each has a separate self-balancing ledger and operates as a separate entity. Funds are related to each other in much the same way as are business enterprises that trade with each other. Account groups are used to provide supplemental information about general fixed assets and general long-term debt. Therefore, some of the transactions carried out by the general fund will require *reciprocal* and/or *complementing* entries in other funds and account groups. These relationships will be identified and illustrated in Chapters 6, 7, and 8 as we present an integrated illustration of the accounting procedures for the various funds and account groups.

As we prepare to illustrate general fund accounting procedures, it is appropriate that we list the types of transactions occurring within that fund that typically require accounting recognition in other funds or account groups. When these transactions involve revenue- and expenditure-type activities, they should *generally* be reflected as *transfers* rather than as revenues and expenditures and should be shown separately from those items in the financial statements. This is true except for *quasi-external transactions,* which are defined as transactions that would be treated as revenues or expenditures if they involved organizations external to the governmental unit.[11] An internal service fund billing for services is an example of a quasi-external transaction.

The general fund transactions involving other funds and account groups and the entries required in those funds and account groups may be visualized as shown in Figure 5–3. The entries shown in the figure plus other entries are discussed further in the next section of the chapter.

In addition to the transactional relationships shown in Figure 5–3, we sometimes find reciprocal recognition of budgetary appropriations. For example, the *recognition of budgetary data* in the general fund may include provisions for planned transfers to other funds such as a debt-service fund, a special assessment capital projects fund, or a proprietary fund. In view of the fact that the debt-service and special assessment capital projects funds are governmental entities, the authorization to receive resources from the general fund should be recorded in the accounting records of those funds.

Reciprocal and complementing entries of the types just described are included in the integrated illustration in Chapters 6, 7, and 8.

# ■ Special Problems Associated with General Fund Accounting Procedures

Our discussion to this point has been concerned with general fund accounting procedures required to record routine, regularly occurring actions and transactions. Familiarity with that framework is basic to understanding the accounting procedures for all

---

11.  Ibid., p. 15.

**FIGURE 5–3.** Illustrative Reciprocal and Complementing Entries

## Reciprocal Relationships

| General Fund Entry | Other Fund Entry |
|---|---|
| 1. *Loans to another fund* | |
|   Due from other fund | Cash |
|     Cash |   Due to general fund |
| 2. *Services provided by another fund* | |
|   Expenditures | Due from general fund |
|     Due to other fund | Revenues |
| 3. *Resource transfers to another fund (no repayment expected)* | |
|   Transfers to other fund or other financing uses | Cash |
|     Cash | Transfers from general fund or other financing sources |

## Complementing Relationships

| General Fund Entry | Account Group Entry |
|---|---|
| 4. *Purchase of long-term asset with general fund resources* | |
|   Expenditures | *Fixed asset |
|     Vouchers payable or cash |   Investments in fixed assets— general fund |
| 5. *Long-term borrowing* | |
|   Cash | **Amount to be provided |
|     Proceeds from long-term loan |   Long-term debt payable |
| 6. *Sale of long-term asset* | |
|   Cash | *Investment in fixed assets |
|     Revenue |   Fixed asset |

*Recorded in general fixed-asset account group.
**Recorded in general long-term debt account group.

governmental funds. However, a number of problems can arise that demand special attention in the accounting records and reports of the general fund. These special problems include

1. practical deviations from the described ideal accounting practices
2. special accounting procedures required for recording capital items, including the acquisitions and disposals of fixed assets, the realization of revenues from long-term debt, and the retirement of that debt
3. achieving an appropriate disclosure of inventory data
4. transactions involving short-term borrowing
5. accounting procedures to be followed in disposing of encumbrances outstanding at the end of the fiscal period
6. recognition of probable losses in the collection of taxes receivable.

## Practical Deviations

We have described the procedures that *should* be followed in recording the financial activities, including budgetary data, in the formal accounting records of the general fund. As a practical matter, however, *budgetary data are not always formally recorded in the accounts.* In many instances, only actual revenues and expenditures will be reflected as nominal accounts in the general fund records. When this practice is followed, budgetary accountability can be shown by periodic supplementary comparisons of actual and budgeted amounts for each revenue and expenditure item. These reports are illustrated later in the text.

In other instances, accounting records for the general fund may be maintained strictly on the cash basis. When this practice is followed, revenues are recognized only when cash is received and expenditures are recorded when cash is disbursed for goods or services. Such an arrangement omits the recognition of taxes receivable and vouchers payable. When this method of accounting is followed, the general fund balance sheet will show only cash as an asset offset by an equal amount in the fund balance account. In such situations, the account balances should be adjusted to convert them to the modified accrual basis before financial statements are prepared. Cash basis financial statements are not in accordance with GAAP.

## Capital Items

The lack of distinction between capital and revenue items is one of the unique characteristics of governmental fund accounting. Because of this practice, the procedures followed in recording the acquisitions and disposals of fixed assets, the recognition of proceeds from the sale of bonds, and amounts transferred from the general fund for retirement of long-term debt are significantly different from those found in the profit area. We have observed that the purchase of long-term assets from general fund resources should be recorded by debiting expenditures and crediting vouchers payable or cash. That practice creates a need for a record of fixed assets to be maintained in the fixed-assets account group. When fixed assets are sold, the proceeds from the sale will generally come to the general fund and should be recorded in that fund as follows:

> Cash
>     Revenues from sale of assets
> To record the sale of fixed assets

The balance in the account for the fixed asset that was sold should then be eliminated from the general fixed-assets account group with the following *complementing* entry:

> Fixed assets provided from general fund resources
>     Fixed assets
> To record the removal of fixed assets sold from general fixed-assets account group

Cash made available for general fund use by the sale of bonds is recorded as a credit to a revenue account called *proceeds from the sale of bonds* or other financing sources in the general fund accounting records, much as is the collection of fines or the assessment of taxes. The obligation for the bonds will be reflected in the general long-term debt account group. The sale of such bonds would be recorded in that account group as follows:

> Amount to be provided for retirment of bonds
>   Bonds payable
> To record the sale of bonds

The retirement of long-term debt from general fund resources represents an outflow of appropriable resources and therefore is recorded as a debit to an expenditure account. In most instances, however, long-term debt will be retired from assets held in a debt-service fund. Such an arrangement requires annual general fund contributions to the debt-service fund (reflected in an expenditure-type account called transfers to debt-service fund) in the general fund as follows:

> Transfers to debt-service fund
>   Cash
> To record transfer of cash to debt-service fund

If the transfer is earmarked for the retirement of long-term debt (as opposed to interest payments), the transfer should be recorded in the long-term debt account group with the following *complementing* entry:

> Amount available for retirement of bonds
>   Amount to be provided for retirement of bonds
> To record the effect of the transfer of resources from general fund to debt-service fund

The elimination of the liability associated with the long-term debt from debt-service fund resources should be recorded in the general long-term debt account group with the following *complementing* entry:

> Bonds payable
>   Amount available for retirement of bonds
> To record the effect of the retirement of bonds in the general long-term debt account group

## Supplies Inventories

Another reporting problem centers on the need for disclosing the costs of supplies and other similar nonappropriable resources on hand. As we have observed, the balance sheet for the general fund is designed to show the values of appropriable (spendable) resources along with the claims against those resources. As supplies are purchased, their acquisition cost is generally charged to expenditures at the time of purchase, as shown below:

> Expenditures
>   Vouchers payable or cash

Within this arrangement, the inventory of supplies on hand is considered to be a nonappropriable resource and therefore excluded from the assets of the general fund.

On the other hand, in meeting the requirements of the principle of full disclosure, it is desirable to show the cost of supplies still on hand at the balance-sheet date if the amount is significant. This can be accomplished by recording the following memo entry:

    Supplies on hand
      Fund balance reserved for supplies on hand

When this procedure is followed, the memo accounts may be adjusted periodically to reflect increases and decreases in the balance of supplies on hand. When the amount of supplies on hand declines, the balances can be reduced by reversing the entry shown above for the amount of the change. If the balance becomes larger, the additional amount is recorded by another memo entry similar to the one illustrated.

Although the method just cited is generally used in accounting for supplies, the 1988 edition of GAAFR also permits use of the consumption method. Under this method, the acquisitions and uses of supplies are accounted for much as they are for profit entities. In other words, expenditures for supplies would be recognized when supplies are used rather than when they are purchased.

## Short-Term Borrowing

Although inflows of cash or other appropriable resources are generally recognized as revenues in the general fund, not every inflow of cash is so recorded. As an example, an inflow of cash resulting from borrowing on a short-term note does not increase the net appropriable (spendable) assets and therefore should not be recorded as revenue. That type of transaction is recorded as follows:

    Cash
      Notes payable

Similarly, *an obligation should be recognized when cash from taxes is received in advance*. In such a case, the liability account offsetting the debit to cash can be labeled as "advance payment of taxes," "deferred tax revenue," or some other similarly descriptive title.

As observed earlier, the general fund may also loan to or borrow from other funds within the governmental unit. If, for example, the general fund borrows cash from another fund, that fact should be recorded in the general fund as follows:

    Cash
      Due to other fund

If the general fund loans cash to another fund, that fact should be recorded as follows:

    Due from other fund
      Cash

What determines whether a revenue-type account or a fund liability account is to be credited when cash is received? In answering that question, we must determine *whether the amount must be repaid from appropriable resources already available or to become available to the general fund within the current fiscal period.* Long-term obligations will be paid from resources realized in subsequent years. Short-term payables will be paid from noncash resources such as taxes receivable already recorded as an appropriable asset in the general fund. When tax assessments are made, the liability for "advance payment of taxes" will be met as the period covered by the taxes passes. When such short-term obligations are incurred, a liability account rather than a revenue account should be credited when the cash is received.

Earlier discussions relating to interfund spendable resource transfers suggest that they may be classified into three categories, as follows:

1. resource transfers appropriately designated as expenditures, expenses, or revenues
2. resource transfers representing loans to be reimbursed
3. resource transfers that should be reflected as transfers to and from funds involved in the transaction.

Transactions that would be treated as expenditures, expenses, or revenues if they involved outside organizations (called *quasi-external transactions*) should be reflected as expenditures, expenses, or revenues when they occur between fund entities. As an example, amounts paid to a municipal garage fund by the general fund for maintenance of vehicles would be recognized as expenditures by the general fund and as revenues by the municipal garage fund.

Transactions involving the transfer of resources (generally cash) that are later to be repaid to the loaning fund should be treated as loans and reflected as "due from" and "due to" items in the accounts for the respective funds. This type of transaction also occurs when an obligation is paid by a fund that is properly chargeable to some other fund. A "due from" account should be debited in the loaning fund's accounts and a "due to" account should be credited in the borrowing fund's accounts.

All payments between funds that do not fall into either of the first two categories should be reflected in "transfers to" and "transfers from" accounts in the statements of the funds involved. These may be thought of as special types of expenditures and revenues for the respective funds. The uses of these accounts are illustrated in Chapters 6, 7, and 8.

## Encumbrances at End of Period

Encumbrances outstanding at the end of a fiscal period require a departure from the routine procedures described earlier in this chapter. Such encumbrances represent commitments to use appropriable (spendable) resources during the next period. However, because encumbrances are considered nominal accounts, they should be closed at the end of the fiscal period. This requires us to reverse them against reserve for encumbrances as follows:

```
Reserve for encumbrances
    Encumbrances
```

The preceding entry will also close out the reserve for encumbrances account. However, if encumbrances do not lapse, the financial statements must disclose the fact that resources equal to the amount of encumbrances outstanding at the end of the year are not available to be used in meeting new appropriations of the next year. We use a *fund balance reserved for encumbrances* account to disclose that fact. This is a balance sheet account that will already reflect a balance equal to the encumbrances outstanding at the end of the prior year. Therefore, it must now be adjusted to reflect a balance equal to the encumbrances outstanding at the end of the current year. If that amount is larger than the amount outstanding at the end of the previous year, the following entry will be made to disclose the reservation of resources.

> Unreserved fund balance
>     Fund balance reserved for encumbrances

If, on the other hand, the end of current period encumbrances balance is less than that of the previous year, the fund balance reserved for encumbrances will be reduced to the current year balance by the following entry:

> Fund balance reserved for encumbrances
>     Unreserved fund balance

## Probable Losses in the Collection of Taxes Receivable

The possibility of losses occurring in the collection of taxes receivable is another problem that requires special consideration. To provide for losses in collecting accounts receivable, a business charges an expense account for the anticipated losses. Because taxes receivable do not actually become resources available for meeting expenditures until collected, *they should be recorded in the appropriate revenue account at their cash-realizable value.* Such an arrangement means that the anticipated losses in collecting taxes are recorded as a reduction of revenue rather than as an expenditure. To illustrate this situation, let's assume that a governmental unit assesses taxes in the amount of $1,460,000. Past experience has shown that approximately $10,000 will probably not be collected. The entry to show the recognition of tax revenue within these assumptions would be recorded as follows:

> Taxes receivable                                  1,460,000
>     Allowance for uncollectible taxes                          10,000
>     Revenues from taxes                                      1,450,000

The account for taxes receivable reflects the amount receivable from the current tax levy. When taxes become delinquent, the amounts receivable should be so designated by using taxes receivable—delinquent and related allowance for uncollectible taxes—delinquent accounts as shown below:

> Taxes receivable—delinquent
> Allowance for uncollectible taxes
>     Taxes receivable
>     Allowance for uncollectible taxes—delinquent

As penalties are assessed on delinquencies, they should be recorded in a penalties receivable account with an offsetting credit to revenues from penalties.

When delinquent taxes are not paid within a prescribed time, they are converted to tax liens receivable in much the same manner as taxes receivable are converted to taxes receivable—delinquent taxes. Eventually, cash will be realized on such claims or they will cease to be an asset of the general fund. When this occurs, the tax liens receivable balance should be written off against the allowance for uncollectible tax liens account. These actions may be recorded as follows:

```
Tax liens receivable
Allowance for uncollectible taxes—delinquent
    Taxes receivable—delinquent
    Allowance for uncollectible tax liens
To record the transfer of delinquent taxes receivable to tax liens receivable


Cash
Allowance for uncollectible tax liens
    Tax liens receivable
    Revenues from tax liens
To record the receipt of cash from tax liens


Allowance for uncollectible tax liens
    Tax liens receivable
To record the failure to collect tax liens receivable
```

## ■ Ethical Considerations Associated with Use of Data Produced by Use of the Modified Accrual Basis of Accounting

Fantasy City faces a dilemma. The city council feels it needs to increase general fund expenditures approximately $150,000 to meet the projected service needs of the city. The council has followed a plan of operating with a balanced budget each year and feels it must do so again next year to meet the goal of preserving intergenerational equity. An increase in taxes to cover the additional costs is expected to be very unpopular politically. As the problem is being discussed, the controller notes that the city has been regularly spending approximately $200,000 per year to acquire fixed assets. He suggests that those expenditures be reduced by $150,000 during the next year to allow the proposed increase in service expenditures to be made within a balanced budget format. Consider the ethical issues that might be involved in the city council publicizing the fact that the additional services will be provided within a balanced budget plan calling for no increase in taxes.

## ■ Summary

In this chapter, we have developed the framework of procedures followed in accounting for the inflows and outflows of general fund and special revenue resources. It is important to recognize that even though our discussion has referred to procedures followed to record general fund activities, those same procedures should also be followed in accounting for the inflows and outflows of special revenue fund resources.

We began by observing that the general fund is used to account for all externally unrestricted resources except those required to be accounted for in another fund. The transactions clearing through the general fund are basically those associated with the general operations of a governmental unit. To meet the dollar-accountability reporting requirement, the accounting procedures are designed to disclose the sources of general fund resources and how they were used. Such an accounting system requires as a minimum asset, liability, fund balance, revenue, and expenditures accounts. Ideally, the budgetary accounts for estimated revenues, appropriations, and encumbrances should also be included in the system. Beyond that, there is often a need to recognize interfund transfers. These transfers may be recorded as revenues and expenditures, as amounts "due to" and "due from" other funds, or as "transfers to" and "transfers from" other funds. We also noted that control accounts will generally be used to record revenues and expenditures, with subsidiary ledgers providing the appropriate subclassifications for each of these nominal accounts.

Typical activities requiring accounting recognition in the general fund accounting records are authorization actions creating the initial budgetary account balances, realization of revenues, expenditure transactions, interfund transactions, and encumbrance transactions. At the end of each fiscal period, the nominal accounts, composed of the budgetary accounts along with actual revenues, expenditures, and transfers, should be closed. We also noted that a number of general fund transactions require accounting recognition in other funds or accounts groups.

In the last portion of the chapter, the special problems associated with general fund accounting practices were discussed. We noted that although it is desirable to include budgetary data in the formal accounting records, those data are not always so recorded. Procedures followed in recording capital items such as the acquisitions of long-term assets and the realization of revenue from long-term borrowing were described. We observed that supplies are generally recorded as expenditures when they are purchased, thus necessitating the use of special accounting procedures for the purpose of disclosing the cost of supplies on hand.

Although inflows of cash or other appropriable resources are generally recorded as revenues, we noted some exceptions to this practice particularly in connection with short-term borrowing and appropriable (spendable) resource transfers between funds.

We noted that encumbrances outstanding at the end of the year are closed against reserve for encumbrances. After that the account, fund balance reserved for encumbrances, is adjusted to reflect the amount of encumbrances outstanding at the end of the fiscal period.

We also observed that the provision for probable losses in the collection of taxes receivable should be offset against revenues from taxes, rather than charged to an expenditure account.

## ■ Glossary

**Appropriation.**   A legal authorization granted by a legislative body to make expenditures and to incur obligations for specific purposes. An appropriation is usually limited in amount and as to the time when it may be expended.

**Appropriation Ledger.** A subsidiary ledger containing an account for each appropriation. Each account usually shows the amount originally appropriated, transfers to or from the appropriation, amounts charged against the appropriation, the net balance, and other related information.

**Control Account.** An account in the general ledger in which are recorded the aggregate of debit and credit postings to a number of identical or related accounts called subsidiary accounts. For example, taxes receivable is a control account supported by the aggregate of individual balances in individual property taxpayers' subsidiary accounts. See *Subsidiary Account.*

**Delinquent Taxes.** Taxes remaining unpaid on and after the date on which a penalty for nonpayment is attached. Even though the penalty may be subsequently waived and a portion of the taxes may be abated or cancelled, the unpaid balances continue to be delinquent taxes until abated, cancelled, paid, or converted into tax liens.

**Due from _____ Fund.** An asset account used to indicate amounts owed to a particular fund by another fund in the same government for goods sold or services rendered. This account includes only short-term obligations on open account and not noncurrent portions of long-term loans.

**Due to _____ Fund.** A liability account reflecting amounts owed by a particular fund to another fund in the same government for goods sold or services rendered. These amounts include only short-term obligations on open account and not noncurrent portions of long-term loans.

**Encumbrances.** Commitments related to unperformed (executory) contracts for goods or services.

**General Fixed Assets.** Fixed assets used in operations accounted for in governmental funds. General fixed assets include all fixed assets not accounted for in proprietary funds or in trust and agency funds.

**General Fixed Assets Account Group.** A self-balancing group of accounts set up to account for the general fixed assets of a government.

**General Fund.** The fund used to account for all financial resources except those required to be accounted for in another fund.

**General Long-Term Debt.** Long-term debt (other than special assessment bonds) expected to be repaid from governmental funds.

**General Long-Term Debt Account Group.** A self-balancing group of accounts set up to account for the unmatured general long-term debt of a government.

**Quasi-External Transactions.** Interfund transactions that would be treated as revenues, expenditures, or expenses if they involved organizations *external* to the governmental unit—for example, payments in lieu of taxes from an enterprise fund to the general fund; internal service fund billings to departments; routine employer contributions from the general fund to a pension trust fund; and routine service charges for inspection engineering, utilities, or similar services provided by a department financed from one fund to a department financed from another fund—should be accounted for as revenues, expenditures, or expenses in the funds involved.

**Reserve for Encumbrances.** An account used to segregate a portion of fund balance for expenditure to be recognized upon vendor performance.

**Reserve for Inventory of Supplies.** An account used to segregate a portion of fund balance to indicate that, using the purchase method, inventories of supplies do not represent "available spendable resources" even though they are a component of net current assets.

**Subsidiary Account.** One of a group of related accounts that support in detail the debit and credit summaries recorded in a control account. An example is the individual property taxpayers' accounts for the taxes receivable control account in the general ledger. See *Control Account* and *Subsidiary Ledger*.

**Subsidiary Ledger.** A group of subsidiary accounts, the sum of the balances of which is equal to the balance of the related control account. See *Subsidiary Account*.

**Taxes Receivable—Current.** The uncollected portion of taxes that a government has levied, which are due within one year and which are not considered delinquent.

**Taxes Receivable—Delinquent.** Taxes remaining unpaid on and after the date on which a penalty for nonpayment attaches. Delinquent taxes receivable are classified as such until paid, abated, cancelled, or converted into tax liens.

**Vouchers Payable.** Liabilities for goods and services evidenced by vouchers that have been preaudited and approved for payment but that have not been paid.

# ■ Suggested Supplementary References

American Institute of Certified Public Accountants, *AICPA Industry Audit Guide on Audits of State and Local Governmental Units*. New York: AICPA, 1989.

National Council on Governmental Accounting, *GAAFR Statement 1*. Chicago: Municipal Finance Officers Association, 1979.

# ■ Questions for Class Discussion

**Q5-1.** For what purposes are the resources of the general fund used? Explain.

**Q5-2.** Would it be appropriate to label the general fund as an *operating fund*? Explain.

**Q5-3.** Describe three phases in the budgetary process for the general fund.

**Q5-4.** What accounts do we typically expect to find in the assets section of the general fund balance sheet? Are any of them long-term assets? Explain.

**Q5-5.** What is the purpose of the appropriations account in the general fund records?

**Q5-6.** What is the purpose of an encumbrance account? When is it used? How is an encumbrance different from an expenditure? Explain.

**Q5-7.** Why is the revenue account usually subclassified by sources? Explain.

**Q5-8.** How are general fund expenditures typically subclassified? How are the subclassifications shown in the accounting records? Explain fully.

**Q5-9.** When are general fund revenues realized? Explain.

**Q5-10.** What are quasi-external transactions? Give an example. How are they recorded in the general fund records?

Q5-11. Explain the differences between the "due to" and "transfers to" accounts found in general fund records.

Q5-12. Describe the sequence of events that typically occur as a tax receivable becomes a tax lien.

Q5-13. How is the short-term borrowing of cash reflected in the records of the general fund? How does that differ from the realization of resources from long-term obligations such as bonds? Explain.

Q5-14. What is the purpose of a special assessment capital projects fund? How is it different from and similar to a capital projects fund? Explain.

Q5-15. What is the purpose of recording supplies on hand in the general fund records if the supplies are treated as expenditures when purchased? What entry should be made to record supplies on hand in such a situation? Explain.

Q5-16. What does a fund balance reserved for encumbrances account appearing on an end-of-the-period balance sheet tell the reader of the statement? How will it ultimately be eliminated from the accounting records?

# ■ Exercises

The following information is to be used in Exercises E5-1 through E5-8. Pleasant City has approved an operating budget calling for appropriations of $3,225,000. The city expects to realize $20,000 from fines, $1,000,000 from user-based charges for sanitation and waste disposal services, and $225,000 from sales taxes. Property taxes are expected to provide the rest of the revenue to "balance" the budget. Market value of property within the city limits is $150,000,000. Property is assessed at 66⅔ percent of market value. Past experience has shown that 5 percent of all assessed taxes are likely to be uncollectable.

E5-1. Journalize the budget data for Pleasant City.

E5-2. Compute the tax rate required to provide the needed property tax revenue for Pleasant City.

E5-3. Prepare the journal entry to record the assessment of property taxes for Pleasant City.

E5-4. Assuming that 96 percent of the property taxes for Pleasant City are collected, journalize the collection of taxes. Other revenues amounting to $1,500,000 are received.

E5-5. Refer to Exercise E5-4. What journal entry should be used to transfer the uncollected taxes to a delinquent taxes account?

E5-6. Expenditures are incurred in the amount of $3,000,000. The city also signed a contract for a signal light system expected to cost $125,000. The installation of the signal light system will take several months.

**Required:**
A. Record the preceding transactions in the general fund accounts.
B. Post all entries from Exercises E5-1 through E5-6 to T-accounts.

E5-7. Prepare the entries required to close the general fund accounts of Pleasant City.

**E5-8.** Assume now that general fund expenditures for Pleasant City include $25,000 for office supplies of which $10,000 are still on hand.

**Required:**
How should these facts be recorded if (1) supplies are recognized as expenditures when purchased and (2) supplies are recognized as expenditures when used?

**E5-9.** A city borrows $75,000 on a short-term note to finance general fund activities over the period preceding the collection of taxes.

**Required:**
A. Journalize the borrowing transaction.
B. What entry should be made to record payment of the note?

**E5-10.** A contract to purchase street cleaning equipment expected to cost $100,000 was recorded in the general fund accounts as an encumbrance near the end of the year.

**Required:**
What entry or entries relating to this transaction should be recorded in the general fund accounts (1) at the end of the year and (2) during the next year when the equipment is received at a cost of $98,000?

**E5-11.** The City Council decided to sell a building that had been purchased ten years ago with general fund resources. The cost of the building was $100,000. It is sold for $40,000.

**Required:**
Record the sale of the building in the general fund.

**E5-12.** The City purchased a building to be used by the police department for $24,000. General fund resources in the amount of $25,000 had been appropriated for that purpose at the beginning of the year.

**Required:**
A. Journalize the purchase of the building.
B. What will happen to the difference between the appropriation and the purchase price of the building? Explain.

**E5-13.** Refer to Exercises E5-1 through E5-12.

**Required:**
Classify each journal entry into one of the following type of entries:
a. authorization entry
b. realization of revenue entry
c. expenditure entry
d. encumbrance entry
e. elimination of encumbrance entry
f. closing entry
g. other entries

# ■ Problems

**P5-1.**   Bend City Council has accumulated the following action and transaction data for the
city's general fund during its first year of operations:
1.   A budget was approved at the beginning of the year calling for estimated revenues
from taxes in the amount of $100,000 and from other sources in the amount of
$5,000. Appropriations for expenditures were approved amounting to $101,000.
2.   Tax notices amounting to $100,500 were sent out. It is estimated that $1,000 of
those taxes will be uncollectible.
3.   Expenditures amounting to $94,000 were incurred during the year. These expen-
ditures included equipment purchases amounting to $20,000.
4.   Purchase orders for various items of undelivered equipment totaling $6,500 were
outstanding at the end of the year.
5.   Taxes amounting to $98,000 were collected during the year.
6.   Other revenues amounting to $5,500 were realized in cash during the year.
7.   Payments were made on vouchers payable in the amount of $85,000.

**Required:**
The City Council has asked you to journalize the preceding data.

**P5-2.**   Select the best answer for each of the following items:
1.   The operations of a public library receiving the majority of its support from property taxes levied for that purpose should be accounted for in:
a.   the general fund.
b.   a special revenue fund.
c.   an enterprise fund.
d.   an internal service fund.
e.   none of the above.
2.   Of the following items, those most likely to have parallel accounting procedures,
account titles, and financial statements are:
a.   special revenue funds and special assessment capital projects funds.
b.   internal service funds and debt-service funds.
c.   the general fixed-assets group of accounts and the general long-term debt
group of accounts.
d.   the general fund and special revenue funds.
3.   The accounting for special revenue funds is most similar to which type of fund?
a.   capital projects
b.   enterprise
c.   general
d.   special assessment capital projects

—AICPA Adapted

**P5-3.**   The following information pertains to the operations of the general fund of X County.
Functions of this county government include operating the county jail and caring for
the county courts.

Funds to finance these operations are provided from a levy of county tax against the various towns of the county, from the state distribution of unincorporated business taxes, from jail prisoners' board assessed against the towns and the state, and from interest on savings accounts. The balances in the accounts of the fund on January 1, 19XX, were as follows:

| | |
|---|---:|
| Cash in savings accounts | $ 60,650 |
| Cash in checking accounts | 41,380 |
| Cash on hand (undeposited prisoners' board receipts) | 320 |
| Inventory of jail supplies | 3,070 |
| Due from towns and state for board of prisoners | 3,550 |
| Unreserved general fund balance | 108,970 |

The budget for the year 19XX, as adopted by the county commissioners, provided for the following items of revenues and expenditures:

| | |
|---|---:|
| (1)  Town and county taxes | $20,000 |
| (2)  Jail operating costs | 55,500 |
| (3)  Court operating costs | 7,500 |
| (4)  Unincorporated business tax | 18,000 |
| (5)  Board of prisoners (revenue) | 5,000 |
| (6)  Commissioners' salaries and expenses | 8,000 |
| (7)  Interest on savings | 1,000 |
| (8)  Miscellaneous expenses | 1,000 |

Unreserved general fund balance was appropriated in sufficient amount to balance the budget. On December 31, 19XX, the inventory of jail supplies amounted to $5,120; cash on hand amounted to $380; and $1,325 of prisoners' board bills were unpaid. The following items represent all of the transactions that occurred during the year, with all current bills vouchered and paid by December 31, 19XX:

| | |
|---|---:|
| Item (1) was transacted exactly as budgeted | |
| Item (2) cash expenditures amounted to | $55,230 |
| Item (3) amounted to | 7,110 |
| Item (4) amounted to | 18,070 |
| Item (5) billings amounted to | 4,550 |
| Item (6) amounted to | 6,670 |
| Item (7) amounted to | 1,050 |
| Item (8) amounted to | 2,310 |

During the year, $25,000 was transferred from the savings accounts to the checking accounts.

**Required:**

From the preceding information, prepare a worksheet providing columns to show:

A. the transactions for the year (journal entries not required)
B. differences between budgeted and actual revenues and expenditures for the year
C. the balance sheet of the general fund for December 31, 19XX.

—AICPA Adapted

**P5-4.** The Township of Hamlet finances its operations from revenues provided by property taxes, water distribution, fines levied by the municipal court, and interest on savings accounts.

Hamlet maintains only a general fund. You were engaged to conduct the audit for the year ended December 31, 19X1, and determined the following:

1. General fund account balances on January 1, 19X1, were

| | |
|---|---:|
| Cash in savings accounts | $ 62,030 |
| Cash in checking accounts | 38,450 |
| Cash on hand (undeposited water receipts) | 160 |
| Water works supplies | 3,640 |
| Due from water customers | 3,670 |
| Fund balance | 107,950 |

2. The budget for 19X1 adopted by the city commission and the transactions relating to the budget (with all current bills vouchered and paid on December 31, 19X1) for the year were

| | Budget | Transactions |
|---|---:|---:|
| Property taxes | $26,750 | $26,750 |
| Water works costs | 66,500 | 64,360* |
| City constable and court fees | 10,000 | 9,550 |
| Water revenues | 30,000 | 32,060** |
| Court fines | 12,500 | 11,025 |
| Commissioners' salaries and expenses | 6,000 | 5,470 |
| Interest on savings accounts | 2,000 | 2,240 |
| Miscellaneous expenses | 1,200 | 2,610 |

*Cash expenditures
**Billings

3. The commissioners appropriated sufficient fund balance resources to balance the revenues and appropriations that were budgeted. The difference was caused by anticipated repairs to water mains. It was also necessary to transfer $15,000 from a savings account to a checking account to pay for these repairs during 19X1.
4. Your count of cash on December 31, 19X1, determined that there was $250 on hand that was not deposited until January 2, 19X2.
5. All billings for water during 19X1 were paid with the exception of statements that totaled $2,230 which were mailed to customers during the last week of December.

6.  All water works supplies were consumed during the year on the repair of water mains. Hamlet's charter specifies that appropriation expenditures are to be based on purchases.

**Required:**

Prepare a worksheet for the Township of Hamlet for the year ended December 31, 19X1. Column headings should provide for: (1) a trial balance, (2) transactions for the year, (3) variances from budget, and (4) a balance sheet at December 31, 19X1. Formal statements and journal entries are not required.

**—AICPA Adapted**

P5-5.   **Thought Projection Problem.** The general fund trial balance of the city of Solna at December 31, 19X0, was as follows:

|  | Dr. | Cr. |
|---|---|---|
| Cash | $ 62,000 |  |
| Taxes receivable—delinquent | 46,000 |  |
| Estimated uncollectible taxes—delinquent |  | $  8,000 |
| Stores inventory—program operations | 18,000 |  |
| Vouchers payable |  | 28,000 |
| Fund balance reserved for stores inventory |  | 18,000 |
| Fund balance reserved for encumbrances |  | 12,000 |
| Unreserved undesignated fund balance |  | 60,000 |
|  | $126,000 | $126,000 |

Collectible delinquent taxes are expected to be collected within 60 days after the end of the year. Solna uses the "purchases" method to account for stores inventory. The following data pertain to 19X1 general fund operations:

1.  *Budget adopted:*

**Revenues and other financing sources**

| | |
|---|---|
| Taxes | $220,000 |
| Fines, forfeits, and penalties | 80,000 |
| Miscellaneous revenues | 100,000 |
| Share of bond issue proceeds | 200,000 |
| | $600,000 |

**Expenditures and other financing uses**

| | |
|---|---|
| Program operations | $300,000 |
| General administration | 120,000 |
| Stores—program operations | 60,000 |
| Capital outlay | 80,000 |
| Periodic transfer to special assessment capital projects fund | 20,000 |
| | $580,000 |

2. Taxes were assessed at an amount that would result in revenues of $220,800, after deduction of 4% of the tax levy as uncollectible.

3. *Orders placed but not received:*

| | |
|---|---:|
| Program operations | $176,000 |
| General administration | 80,000 |
| Capital outlay | 60,000 |
| | $316,000 |

4. The city council designated $20,000 of the unreserved undesignated fund balance for possible future appropriation for capital outlay.

5. *Cash collections and transfer:*

| | |
|---|---:|
| Delinquent taxes | $ 38,000 |
| Current taxes | 226,000 |
| Refund of overpayment of invoice for purchase of equipment | 4,000 |
| Fines, forfeits, and penalties | 88,000 |
| Miscellaneous revenues | 90,000 |
| Share of bond issue proceeds | 200,000 |
| Transfer of remaining fund balance of a discontinued fund | 18,000 |
| | $664,000 |

6. *Cancelled encumbrances:*

| | Estimated | Actual |
|---|---:|---:|
| Program operations | $156,000 | $166,000 |
| General administration | 84,000 | 80,000 |
| Capital outlay | 62,000 | 62,000 |
| | $302,000 | $308,000 |

7. *Additional vouchers:*

| | |
|---|---:|
| Program operations | $188,000 |
| General administration | 38,000 |
| Capital outlay | 18,000 |
| Transfer to special assessment fund | 20,000 |
| | $264,000 |

8. Albert, a taxpayer, overpaid his 19X1 taxes by $2,000. He applied for a $2,000 credit against his 19X2 taxes. The city council granted his request.

9. Vouchers paid amounted to $580,000.

10. Stores inventory on December 31, 19X1, amounted to $12,000.

**Required:**

Prepare journal entries to record the effects of the foregoing data. Omit explanations.

**—AICPA Adapted**

# General Fund and Special Revenue Fund Accounting Procedures—II

---

## ■ Learning Objectives

When you have finished your study of this chapter, you should

1. Be able to journalize and post the routine transactions of a general fund.
2. Know how to prepare general fund financial statements from data in the fund's ledger accounts.
3. Be able to recognize the general fund transactions that require reciprocal and/or complementing entries in other funds and/or account groups.
4. Be capable of adapting the journalizing, posting, and statement preparation procedures for the general fund to a transactions worksheet format.

---

In Chapter 5, we developed the logical framework of general fund accounting and described the procedures followed in recording typical general fund transactions. In this chapter, we *demonstrate how typical general fund transactions should be recorded and show how the financial data are accumulated in the accounts and summarized in the financial statements*. To do this, we use an assumed series of transactions for the general fund of Model City. This is the first part of an integrated illustration that continues through Chapters 7, 8, and 9. In this first part of the Model City illustration, we shall

1. illustrate the journalizing and posting procedures that should be followed in recording a series of assumed financial activities for the general fund of Model City

2. summarize the financial data from the general fund ledger accounts in end-of-the-period financial statements

3. explain and illustrate how interim financial reports for the general fund would normally be presented

4. list the general fund transactions requiring reciprocal and/or complementing entries

5. demonstrate how a transactions worksheet can be used to record the transactions of the general fund.

# ■ General Fund Accounting Procedures Illustrated

In the pages that follow, we illustrate the various steps of the accounting cycle for a general fund. We begin by describing a series of actions and transactions assumed to have occurred within the general fund of Model City during a fiscal period. These actions and transactions are then journalized and posted to T-accounts to illustrate those steps in the accounting cycle. After that, we accumulate the financial data in the general fund T-accounts and develop financial statements from them. We begin our illustration by assuming the following beginning-of-the-period balance sheet for the general fund of Model City.

| Assets | | Liabilities and Fund Balance | |
|---|---|---|---|
| Cash | $20,000 | Vouchers payable | $10,000 |
| | | Unreserved fund balance | 10,000 |
| | $20,000 | | $20,000 |

## General Fund Transactions

During the year, the following actions and transactions are assumed to have occurred:

1. The city council adopted and approved the following budget for the next fiscal year:

| Estimated Revenues Classified by Sources | |
|---|---|
| Property taxes | $1,450,000 |
| Sales taxes | 300,000 |
| Municipal court fines | 50,000 |
| Traffic fines | 50,000 |
| Retail store permits | 100,000 |
| Fees for special services | 25,000 |
| Other revenues | 25,000 |
| Total estimated revenue | $2,000,000 |

Appropriations Classified by Functions

| | |
|---|---:|
| General government | $  350,000 |
| Police services | 250,000 |
| Street maintenance services | 400,000 |
| Acquisition of water utility plant | 100,000 |
| Recreation services | 100,000 |
| Sanitation services | 165,000 |
| Payment into debt-service fund | 50,000 |
| School services | 400,000 |
| Payment toward special assessment project | 25,000 |
| Establishment of municipal garage | 85,000 |
| Miscellaneous | 25,000 |
| Total appropriations | $1,950,000 |

(With this budget, the city council is planning to receive $50,000 more revenue than it plans to spend during the fiscal period.)

2. The property tax rate is determined by dividing the estimated revenue needed from this source by the assessed valuation, which is assumed to be $36,250,000. The tax rate is calculated as follows:

$$\frac{1,450,000}{36,250,000} = .04 \text{ per dollar}$$

This rate is commonly expressed as $4.00 per hundred dollars of assessed valuation.

After certain adjustments are made, tax bills in the amount of $1,460,000 are sent out. (At this point, a subsidiary ledger showing taxes receivable from individual taxpayers is prepared to support the debit to the control account for taxes receivable. The revenue control account and the subsidiary ledger account for revenue from property taxes are credited.)

3. Other revenues in the amount of $545,000 are received during the year. The entry to record this transaction is actually a summary of many entries recorded during the year as the individual revenue receipts occur.

Revenues Classified by Sources

| | |
|---|---:|
| Sales taxes | $320,000 |
| Municipal court fines | 60,000 |
| Traffic fines | 35,000 |
| Retail store permits | 90,000 |
| Fees for special services | 20,000 |
| Revenue from water department | 20,000 |
| Total | $545,000 |

4. Property taxes in the amount of $1,445,000 are collected. Individual accounts in the taxes receivable subsidiary ledger are credited as the entry is made to the control account.

5. During the year, expenditures and transfers in the amount of $1,739,000 are made against the following appropriations (these are a summation of numerous transactions that occurred as salaries were paid, as equipment was purchased, and so forth).

### Expenditures Classified by Functions

| | Debits |
|---|---|
| General government | $ 348,000 |
| Police services | 249,000 |
| Street maintenance services | 248,000 |
| Acquisition of water utility company | 100,000 |
| Recreation services | 75,000 |
| Sanitation services | 160,000 |
| Payment into debt-service fund | 50,000 |
| School services | 375,000 |
| Payment toward special assessment project | 25,000 |
| Establishment of municipal garage | 85,000 |
| Miscellaneous expenditures | 24,000 |
| Total | $1,739,000 |

6. Contracts are signed for the purchase of equipment estimated to cost $200,000. The equipment includes street maintenance units estimated at $150,000, recreational equipment estimated at $25,000, and school equipment estimated at $25,000.

### Encumbrances Classified by Functions

| | Debits |
|---|---|
| Street maintenance services | $150,000 |
| Recreational services | 25,000 |
| School services | 25,000 |
| Total | $200,000 |

7. The street maintenance equipment is received. Its actual cost is $145,000.
8. Vouchers and amounts due to other funds in the amount of $1,800,000 are paid during the year.
9. Old street maintenance equipment originally costing $60,000 is sold as scrap for $5,000.

## Journal Entries to Record Transactions in Control Accounts

We now present the journal entries that are used to record the Model City general fund transactions. Each entry shows the number of the corresponding transaction described in the preceding list.

**Transaction (1)**

| | | |
|---|---|---|
| Estimated revenue | 2,000,000 | |
| Appropriations | | 1,950,000 |
| Budgetary fund balance | | 50,000 |

**Estimated Revenues Subsidiary Ledger (Debits)**

| | |
|---|---|
| Property taxes | $1,450,000 |
| Sales taxes | 300,000 |
| Municipal court fines | 50,000 |
| Traffic fines | 50,000 |
| Retail store permits | 100,000 |
| Fees for special services | 25,000 |
| Other revenues | 25,000 |
| Total | $2,000,000 |

**Appropriations Subsidiary Ledger (Credits)**

| | |
|---|---|
| General government | $ 350,000 |
| Police services | 250,000 |
| Street maintenance services | 400,000 |
| Acquisition of water utility plant | 100,000 |
| Recreation services | 100,000 |
| Sanitation services | 165,000 |
| Transfer to debt-service fund | 50,000 |
| School services | 400,000 |
| Transfer to special assessment capital projects fund | 25,000 |
| Transfer to municipal garage fund | 85,000 |
| Miscellaneous expenditures | 25,000 |
| Total | $1,950,000 |

This entry records in the formal accounting records the amounts of revenues that Model City expects to realize and the amounts appropriated for proposed expenditures. The description of transaction (1) on page 174 shows that $400,000 is appropriated for the city's street maintenance services. The subsidiary ledger (Exhibit 6–1) shows further limitations placed on the use of these funds. It shows that $200,000 is earmarked for salaries, $50,000 for maintenance, and $150,000 for equipment purchases. In this way, the dollar accountability for the street maintenance services appropriation is maintained on an item-by-item basis.

Estimated revenues, subclassified by sources, are also recorded in this entry. A subsidiary ledger for revenues is normally used to show the relationship between revenues budgeted by sources and actual revenues realized from each source.

**Transaction (2)**

| | | |
|---|---|---|
| Taxes receivable | 1,460,000 | |
| Revenue | | 1,460,000 |

**Revenues Subsidiary Ledger (Credit)**

| | |
|---|---|
| Property taxes | $1,460,000 |

**Transaction (3)**

| | | |
|---|---|---|
| Cash | 545,000 | |
| Revenue | | 545,000 |

**EXHIBIT 6–1.** Subsidiary Appropriations Ledger, Street Maintenance Services

**Salaries Expenditures**

| | Encumbrances | | | Salaries Expenditures | | | Appropriations | | |
|---|---|---|---|---|---|---|---|---|---|
| | Dr. | Cr. | Balance | Dr. | Cr. | Balance | Dr. | Cr. | Balance |
| (1) | | | | | | | | $200,000 | $200,000 |
| (5) | | | | $200,000 | | $200,000 | $200,000 | | 0 |
| (C-2) | | | | | $200,000 | 0 | | | 0 |

**Maintenance Expenditures**

| | Encumbrances | | | Maintenance Expenditures | | | Appropriations | | |
|---|---|---|---|---|---|---|---|---|---|
| | Dr. | Cr. | Balance | Dr. | Cr. | Balance | Dr. | Cr. | Balance |
| (1) | | | | | | | | 50,000 | 50,000 |
| (5) | | | | 48,000 | | 48,000 | 48,000 | | 2,000 |
| (C-2)(C-1) | | | | | 48,000 | 0 | 2,000 | | 0 |

**Equipment Expenditures**

| | Encumbrances | | | Equipment Expenditures | | | Appropriations | | |
|---|---|---|---|---|---|---|---|---|---|
| | Dr. | Cr. | Balance | Dr. | Cr. | Balance | Dr. | Cr. | Balance |
| (1) | | | | | | | | 150,000 | 150,000 |
| (6) | $150,000 | | $150,000 | | | | 150,000 | | 0 |
| (7b) | | $150,000 | 0 | | | | | 150,000 | 150,000 |
| (7a) | | | | 145,000 | | 145,000 | 145,000 | | 5,000 |
| (C-2)(C-1) | | | | | 145,000 | 0 | 5,000 | | 0 |

**Revenues Subsidiary Ledger (Credits)**

| | |
|---|---:|
| Sales taxes | $ 320,000 |
| Municipal court fines | 60,000 |
| Traffic fines | 35,000 |
| Retail store permits | 90,000 |
| Fees for special services | 20,000 |
| Other revenues | 20,000 |
| Total | $ 545,000 |

**Transaction (4)**

| | | |
|---|---:|---:|
| Cash | 1,445,000 | |
|    Taxes receivable | | 1,445,000 |

The journal entry to record transaction (2) shows the result of billing individual taxpayers for their respective obligations. Credits are entered in the control account for revenues and in the revenues subsidiary ledger. Other revenues are recorded as they are realized. Journal entry (3) shows the summation of transaction (3) entries for the fiscal period. Entry (4) records the collection of taxes recorded as receivables in transaction (2).

It is important to note that the amounts credited to revenues should reflect only resource inflows that are used or are available to be used to meet expenditures incurred during the reporting period. For example, resources are sometimes received by a fund to be used only for specified purposes, such as services for senior citizens. When spendable resource inflows are restricted in that way, only the amount actually spent for that purpose during the reporting period should be recognized as revenues during that period. The unexpended amounts should be reflected in a *deferred revenues* account until they are used for the specified purpose.

**Transaction (5)**

| | | |
|---|---:|---:|
| Transfer to water utility fund | $ 100,000 | |
| Transfer to debt service fund | 50,000 | |
| Transfer to special assessment capital projects fund | 25,000 | |
| Transfer to municipal garage fund | 85,000 | |
| Expenditures | 1,479,000 | |
|    Vouchers payable | | $1,444,000 |
|    Due to debt-service fund | | 50,000 |
|    Due to municipal garage fund | | 120,000* |
|    Due to special assessment capital projects fund | | 25,000 |
|    Due to water utility fund | | 100,000 |

**Expenditures and Transfers Subsidiary Ledger (Debits)**

| | |
|---|---:|
| General government | $ 348,000 |
| Police services | 249,000 |
| Street maintenance services | 248,000 |
| Recreation services | 75,000 |
| Sanitation services | 160,000 |
| School services | 375,000 |
| Miscellaneous expenditures | 24,000 |
| Total expenditures | $1,479,000 |
| | |
| Transfer to water utility fund | $ 100,000 |
| Transfer to debt-service fund | 50,000 |

| | |
|---|---:|
| Transfer to special assessment capital projects fund | 25,000 |
| Transfer to municipal garage fund | 85,000 |
| Total transfers | $260,000 |
| Total expenditures and transfers | $1,739,000 |

*This includes $85,000 of transfers plus $35,000 for services rendered in maintaining city vehicles (included in expenditures account).

In the journal entry for transaction (5), $1,739,000 of expenditures and transfers are recorded. Supporting details show that $248,000 of this amount is for street maintenance services, which includes $200,000 for salaries and $48,000 for maintenance. After entering these amounts in the subsidiary ledger (Exhibit 6–1), we see that the entire appropriation for salaries has been used and that $2,000 remains for maintenance. Of the total outlays, $295,000 represents a recognition of interfund obligations. This fact is recorded by crediting accounts showing the amounts due to the debt-service fund, municipal garage fund, special assessment capital projects fund, and water utility fund. The balance, amounting to $1,444,000, is credited to vouchers payable.

**Transaction (6)**

| | | |
|---|---:|---:|
| Encumbrances | 200,000 | |
| Reserve for encumbrances | | 200,000 |

**Encumbrances Subsidiary Ledger (Debits)**

| | |
|---|---:|
| Street maintenance services | $150,000 |
| Recreational services | 25,000 |
| School services | 25,000 |
| Total | $200,000 |

The entry for transaction (6) records an encumbrance against appropriations for equipment purchases. In the subsidiary ledger (Exhibit 6–1), the effect on the balance available for street maintenance equipment is shown by extending the effect of the encumbrance in the appropriations balance column. This column shows that the city has no more resources to spend for street maintenance equipment during the fiscal period. The reserve for encumbrances is credited to show the extent to which appropriable resources are committed.

**Transaction (7a)**

| | | |
|---|---:|---:|
| Expenditures | 145,000 | |
| Vouchers payable | | 145,000 |

**Expenditures Subsidiary Ledger (Debit)**

| | |
|---|---:|
| Street maintenance services | $145,000 |

**Transaction (7b)**

| | | |
|---|---:|---:|
| Reserve for encumbrances | 150,000 | |
| Encumbrances | | 150,000 |

**Encumbrances Subsidiary Ledger (Credit)**

| | |
|---|---:|
| Street maintenance services | $150,000 |

Transaction (7a) entry shows the actual cost of equipment purchases, and transaction (7b) entry reverses the previously recorded encumbrance. These amounts are also recorded in the equipment section of the street maintenance services subsidiary ledger. The net effect of these two entries is to leave $5,000 available for equipment purchases (see Exhibit 6–1). Not all expenditures are encumbered before they are incurred, as shown in transaction (5). Encumbrance accounts are used only when a significant period of time is expected to elapse between the dates of commitment to spend and expenditure recognition.

**Transaction (8)**

| | | |
|---|---:|---:|
| Due to water utility fund | 100,000 | |
| Due to municipal garage fund | 120,000 | |
| Vouchers payable | 1,505,000 | |
| Due to special assessment capital projects fund | 25,000 | |
| Due to debt-service fund | 50,000 | |
|    Cash | | 1,800,000 |

The entry for transaction (8) records payment of $1,505,000 in vouchers payable plus amounts due to the water utility fund, debt-service fund, special assessment capital projects fund, and municipal garage fund of $100,000, $50,000, $25,000, and $120,000, respectively.

**Transaction (9)**

| | | |
|---|---:|---:|
| Cash | 5,000 | |
|    Revenue | | 5,000 |

Revenue in the amount of $5,000 from the sale of old street-cleaning equipment is recorded in the entry for transaction (9). Cash is debited and revenue is credited. Because the equipment was charged to expenditures when it was purchased, the only record of its original cost will be found in the general fixed-assets accounting records discussed in Chapter 8.

## Posting the Transactions

The preceding journal entries are posted to general fund accounts, as shown in the following T-accounts. Each posting is keyed to the transaction giving rise to it.

T-Accounts for Model City
(Numbers in parentheses represent transaction numbers used in the text.)

| Estimated Revenue | | Appropriations | |
|---|---|---|---|
| (1)   2,000,000 | (C-1)   2,000,000 | (C-1)   1,950,000 | (1)   1,950,000 |

| Revenues | | Expenditures | |
|---|---|---|---|
| (C-2)   2,010,000 | (2)   1,460,000 | (5)   1,479,000 | (C-2)   1,624,000 |
| | (3)     545,000 | (7a)    145,000 | |
| | (9)       5,000 | | |

| Transfers to Debt-Service Fund | |
|---|---|
| (5) 50,000 | (C-2) 50,000 |

| Transfers to Special Assessment Capital Projects Fund | |
|---|---|
| (5) 25,000 | (C-2) 25,000 |

| Budgetary Fund Balance | |
|---|---|
| (C-1) 50,000 | (1) 50,000 |

| Transfers to Municipal Garage Fund | |
|---|---|
| (5) 85,000 | (C-2) 85,000 |

| Unreserved Fund Balance | |
|---|---|
| (C-4) 50,000 | Bal. 10,000 |
| | (C-2) 126,000 |

| Encumbrances | |
|---|---|
| (6) 200,000 | (7b) 150,000 |
| | (C-3) 50,000 |

| Taxes Receivable | |
|---|---|
| (2) 1,460,000 | (4) 1,445,000 |

| Reserve for Encumbrances | |
|---|---|
| (7b) 150,000 | (6) 200,000 |
| (C-3) 50,000 | |

| Cash | |
|---|---|
| Bal. 20,000 | (8) 1,800,000 |
| (3) 545,000 | |
| (4) 1,445,000 | |
| (9) 5,000 | |

| Vouchers Payable | |
|---|---|
| (8) 1,505,000 | Bal. 10,000 |
| | (5) 1,444,000 |
| | (7a) 145,000 |

| Due to Special Assessment Capital Projects Fund | |
|---|---|
| (8) 25,000 | (5) 25,000 |

| Due to Municipal Garage Fund | |
|---|---|
| (8) 120,000 | (5) 120,000 |

| Fund Balance Reserved for Encumbrances | |
|---|---|
| | (C-4) 50,000 |

| Due to Debt-Service Fund | |
|---|---|
| (8) 50,000 | (5) 50,000 |

| Transfer to Water Utility Fund | |
|---|---|
| (5) 100,000 | (C-2) 100,000 |

| Due to Water Utility Fund | |
|---|---|
| (8) 100,000 | (5) 100,000 |

## Closing Entries

At the end of the fiscal period, the following "C" entries (posted in the T-accounts illustrated) are recorded to close the nominal accounts of the general fund:

```
(C-1)
Appropriations                1,950,000
Budgetary fund balance           50,000
   Estimated revenues                      2,000,000
```

(C-2)

| | | |
|---|---|---|
| Revenues | 2,010,000 | |
| Expenditures | | 1,624,000 |
| Transfers to debt-service fund | | 50,000 |
| Transfers to special assessment capital projects fund | | 25,000 |
| Transfers to municipal garage fund | | 85,000 |
| Transfers to water utility fund | | 100,000 |
| Unreserved fund balance | | 126,000 |

(C-3)

| | | |
|---|---|---|
| Reserve for encumbrances | 50,000 | |
| Encumbrances | | 50,000 |

(C-4)

| | | |
|---|---|---|
| Unreserved fund balance | 50,000 | |
| Fund balance reserved for encumbrances | | 50,000 |

Entry (C-1), recorded at the end of the fiscal period, reverses the original budgetary entry (1). Entry (C-2) is used to close the revenue, expenditure, and transfer accounts to the unreserved fund balance account. Subsidiary records for all those items are also closed at this time. Entry (C-3) reverses the balances shown in the encumbrance and reserve for encumbrances accounts. Entry (C-4) adjusts the unreserved fund balance to show the amount of that balance that should be reserved for encumbrances.

As a result of these entries, we can see that the budgetary plan contemplated an unreserved fund balance of $60,000 ($10,000 beginning balance plus a $50,000 budgeted increase). The fund actually ended up with an unreserved fund balance of $86,000: $10,000 beginning balance plus $126,000 from entry (C-2) minus $50,000 from entry (C-4).

During the next year, when the encumbrance-related expenditure is recognized, it will be recorded as a normal expenditure but will be labeled to show that it relates to the prior fiscal period. At the end of the next year, the balance in the fund balance reserved for encumbrances should again be adjusted to reflect the amount of year-end encumbrances outstanding. To illustrate how that should be done, let's assume that the encumbrances outstanding at the end of the next year amount to $40,000. That would require the fund balance reserved for encumbrances to be adjusted as follows:

| | | |
|---|---|---|
| Fund balance reserved for encumbrances | 10,000 | |
| Unreserved fund balance | | 10,000 |

In the subsidiary ledger (Exhibit 6–1), credits of $200,000, $48,000, and $145,000 to expenditures for salaries, maintenance, and equipment, respectively, are parts of the credit to expenditures of $1,624,000 shown in entry (C-2). As explained earlier, all debits to the appropriations sections of this subsidiary ledger are part of the $1,950,000 debit to appropriations (see C-1).

## Subsidiary Ledgers

Detailed subsidiary ledgers should be maintained for each control account used in the preceding illustrations. This helps management to exercise item-by-item control, which is particularly important in accounting for expenditures. Appropriations are made for the budget period, and authorization to spend against them usually expires at the end of that period.

Control of expenditures requires item-by-item coordination of appropriations, expenditures, and encumbrances. This control is generally achieved by combining the subsidiary records of these accounts as they relate to each specific type of expenditure. Exhibit 6–1 shows the street maintenance services section of the subsidiary appropriations, expenditures, and encumbrances ledger with the assumed transactions recorded in it.

# ■ Financial Statements for the General Fund

Accountants for governmental units prepare separate financial statements for each fund. In this section, we consider the financial statements that should be prepared for the general fund of Model City at the end of the fiscal period. More specifically, we will

1. identify the objectives of general fund financial statements
2. illustrate the preparation of an operating statement (statement of revenues, expenditures, and changes in fund balance)
3. note observations that can be made from reading the revenues and expenditures parts of the operating statement
4. present an illustrated balance sheet.

## Objectives of Financial Statements

Adherence to the concept of dollar accountability for reporting financial data for the general fund requires that the statements show

1. the sources and uses of appropriable (spendable) resources
2. the extent to which the budgetary plan for revenues and expenditures has been achieved
3. the financial position of the fund at the end of the period with respect to appropriable resources.

## Statement of Revenues, Expenditures and Transfers, and Changes in Fund Balance

The first two of these objectives are accomplished by the preparation of a statement showing both budgeted and actual revenues and expenditures and transfers. This information should generally be combined in one statement, with expenditures and transfers offset against revenues. Governmental entities, however, may present these data for internal use in two statements—one for revenues and another for expenditures and transfers. The relationships between actual and budgeted amounts are emphasized in each statement. Exhibit 6–2 is prepared using this plan of reporting, to show general fund revenues, expenditures and transfers, and changes in fund balance for the fiscal period. Generally accepted accounting practice (GAAP), as spelled out in NCGA Statement 1, requires that these statement data be combined with those of other funds, as illustrated in Chapter 9 for external reporting purposes.

In reporting for business enterprises, a statement showing changes in retained earnings is prepared to show a connecting-link history of the business. Similar information showing the changes in the fund balance account should also be included among the general fund financial statements. The lower part of Exhibit 6–2 shows changes in the general fund balance of Model City during the fiscal period. This is the statement format recommended in NCGA Statement 1.

## Interpreting the Operating Statements

Financial statements are prepared to be read and interpreted. In the following paragraphs, some important facts that can be observed from the statement of revenues, expenditures and transfers, and changes in fund balances are discussed as are their implications for the users of these statements.

The statement in Exhibit 6–2 shows that Model City has realized actual revenues amounting to $10,000 more than was budgeted. The realization of excess amounts from property taxes, sales taxes, and municipal court fines more than offsets deficiencies in amounts realized from other budgeted sources of revenue. Also, the unanticipated sale of assets accounted for $5,000 of the excess revenues. Because the amount of taxes collected is a function of governmental taxing power, the excess amount realized from these sources cannot be said to be either good or bad; it simply shows the extent to which the budget plan for revenues has been achieved. As an example, the deficiency in revenues from traffic fines could be caused by inadequate traffic control or by a general tendency toward fewer traffic violations.

The expenditures part of the statement discloses the extent to which the actual outflows of appropriable resources have coincided with the original plan for the uses of these resources. It is important, however, to understand the significance of the differences between appropriations and actual amounts expended. For example, the failure of sanitation services to spend $5,000 of its appropriation could mean that less service was provided than was planned. Because each appropriation anticipates a certain level of service, a saving can always be achieved by refusing to provide the full amount of service planned. On the other hand, actual expenditures can exceed appropriated amounts because of inefficiencies in rendering the planned level of services. The conventional statement of revenues and expenditures does not provide sufficient information to determine exactly what has caused the differences between budgeted and actual expenditures.

The presently accepted practice of emphasizing spendable resource inflows and outflows, rather than income and expense data, in the operating reports of governmental funds often leads to the use of funds without adequate regard for the benefits

**EXHIBIT 6–2.** Model City General Fund: Statement of Revenues, Expenditures and Transfers, and Changes in Fund Balances for Fiscal Period

| | Budget | Actual | Variances Favorable/ (Unfavorable) |
|---|---|---|---|
| Revenues | | | |
| Property taxes | $1,450,000 | $1,460,000 | $ 10,000 |
| Sales taxes | 300,000 | 320,000 | 20,000 |
| Municipal court fines | 50,000 | 60,000 | 10,000 |
| Traffic fines | 50,000 | 35,000 | (15,000) |
| Retail store permits | 100,000 | 90,000 | (10,000) |
| Fees for special services | 25,000 | 20,000 | (5,000) |
| Revenue from water department | 25,000 | 20,000 | (5,000) |
| Revenue from sale of assets | 0 | 5,000 | 5,000 |
| Total | $2,000,000 | $2,010,000 | $ 10,000 |
| Expenditures | | | |
| General government | $ 350,000 | $ 348,000 | $ 2,000 |
| Police services | 250,000 | 249,000 | 1,000 |
| Sanitation services | 165,000 | 160,000 | 5,000 |
| Recreation services | 100,000 | 75,000 | 25,000[a] |
| Street maintenance services | 400,000 | 393,000 | 7,000 |
| School services | 400,000 | 375,000 | 25,000[b] |
| Miscellaneous | 25,000 | 24,000 | 1,000 |
| Total | $1,690,000 | $1,624,000 | 66,000 |
| Excess (deficiency) of revenues over expenditures | $ 310,000 | $ 386,000 | $ 76,000 |
| Transfers | | | |
| To water utility fund | 100,000 | 100,000 | 0 |
| To debt-service fund | 50,000 | 50,000 | 0 |
| To special assessment capital projects fund | 25,000 | 25,000 | 0 |
| To municipal garage fund | 85,000 | 85,000 | 0 |
| Total | $ 260,000 | $ 260,000 | 0 |
| Excess (deficiency) of revenues over expenditures and transfers | $ 50,000 | $ 126,000 | $ 76,000 |
| Fund balance at beginning of period | $ 10,000 | 10,000 | |
| Fund balances at end of period | $ 60,000 | $ 136,000 | $ 76,000 |
| | | | |
| Fund balance reserved for encumbrances | | $ 50,000 | |
| Unreserved fund balance | | 86,000 | |
| Total fund balances | | $ 136,000 | |

[a]Recreation services has been encumbered for $25,000 covering equipment ordered but not received at the end of the fiscal period.
[b]School services has been encumbered for $25,000 covering equipment ordered but not received at the end of the fiscal period.

realized from their use. For example, this practice may occur when management decides to spend resources simply because they have been appropriated rather than because of a real need for providing more or better services.

The revenues and expenditures statement is generally characterized as a statement of operations. We must be careful to recognize that such statements of operations disclose information that is significantly different from that contained in the operating statements of profit enterprises. Those operating statements show periodic revenues and expenses offset against each other to determine net income for the period, whereas revenue and expenditure statements show inflows and outflows of appropriable resources for the period. Because revenue and expenditure statements include such things as the sales of assets and expenditures for capital items, they are more appropriately described as *statements of sources and uses of appropriable resources*.

## The Balance Sheet

The balance sheet shows the financial position of the general fund, with primary emphasis on the appropriable resources available to the fund. The general fund balance sheet for Model City (Exhibit 6–3) shows $230,000 of appropriable resources. Commitments against those resources amount to $144,000, leaving an unreserved fund balance of $86,000 available for use in future periods.

# ■ Interim Reporting for the General Fund

Internal managers of governmental entities need financial information on a current basis to properly control the activities under their jurisdiction. This requires monthly financial statements showing comparisons between actual and estimated revenues and actual and estimated expenditures for general and special revenue funds. These statements are usually prepared on a monthly and year-to-date basis within the format shown in Exhibit 6–2.

Since the management of cash is particularly important in the administration of general fund and special revenue fund resources, the interim financial reports can advantageously include a statement of cash receipts and disbursements along with a projection of anticipated future cash flows. These statements can be prepared within the formats shown in Exhibits 6–4 and 6–5.

**EXHIBIT 6–3.**   Model City General Fund Balance Sheet, End of Fiscal Period

| Assets | | Liabilities and Fund Balance | |
|---|---|---|---|
| Cash | $215,000 | Vouchers payable | $ 94,000 |
| Taxes receivable | 15,000 | Fund balance reserved for encumbrances | 50,000 |
| | | Unreserved fund balance | 86,000 |
| Total | $230,000 | Total | $230,000 |

**EXHIBIT 6–4.** Model City General Fund Interim Statement of Cash Receipts and Disbursements

| | | |
|---|---:|---:|
| Cash balance—beginning of period | | xxxx |
| Receipts | | |
|   Collection of property taxes | xxxx | |
|   Sales taxes received | xxxx | |
|   Fines collected | xxx | |
|   Retail store permits sold | xxx | |
|   Fees for special services | xxx | |
|   Receipts from water department | xxx | xxxx |
| Total cash available | | xxxx |
| Disbursements | | |
|   Vouchers paid | xxxx | |
|   Payments to municipal garage fund | xxx | |
|   Payment to special assessment capital projects fund | xxx | |
|   Payment to debt-service fund | xxx | xxxx |
| Cash balance—end of period | | xxxx |

**EXHIBIT 6–5.** Model City General Fund Forecast of Cash Flows

| | | |
|---|---:|---:|
| Cash balance—beginning of period | | xxxx |
| Anticipated receipts during period | | |
|   From property taxes | xxxx | |
|   From sales taxes | xxxx | |
|   From fines | xxx | |
|   From store permits | xxx | |
|   From special services | xxx | |
|   From water department | xxx | xxxx |
| Estimated cash available during period | | xxxx |
| Anticipated disbursements during period | | |
|   Payment of expenditures | xxxx | |
|   Payments to other funds | xxxx | xxxx |
| Estimated cash balance—end of period | | xxxx |
| Estimated amount to be borrowed or repaid | | xxxx |

In addition to the more formal interim and annual financial presentations illustrated in this chapter, many local governments prepare and distribute to the citizens, often through local newspapers, summaries of the major elements of operations. These are always highly condensed, nontechnical reports and are often accompanied by graphic illustrations and explanatory materials.

Interim statements of revenues, expenditures, and changes in fund balances are also very important to the budgeting process. Because the operating budget for the next fiscal year will have to be completed and approved before the end of the current year, the interim data for the current year will provide the most recent historical operating data that can be used in projecting the next year's operating budget. Observe, for example, that the City of Waco's final budget for the next fiscal year, ending September 30, is scheduled to be prepared in July (see page 120). That type of schedule makes the interim operating data through June 30 very important to the budgetary process.

# ■ Reciprocal and Complementing Entries

A number of the assumed transactions for the general fund of Model City require reciprocal and/or complementing entries in other funds and account groups. These entries will be illustrated in later chapters. However, it seems appropriate at this time to call attention to the other funds and account groups in which information relating to these transactions should be recorded. We do that in Exhibit 6−6.

# ■ The Transactions Worksheet

In actual practice, the transactions illustrated in this chapter would most likely be recorded by use of a computer. Nevertheless, we have illustrated the recording process by using manually maintained journals and ledger accounts to facilitate your understanding of the relationships among the transactions data. For problem-solving purposes, however, a transactions worksheet, similar to that shown in Exhibit 6−7, may serve as a better summarizing device. It can save a significant amount of time without

**EXHIBIT 6−6.**  Other Funds and Account Groups in Which Reciprocal and Complementing Entries Must Be Recorded

| General Fund Transaction Number | Requires Reciprocal Entries | Requires Complementing Entries |
|---|---|---|
| Transaction 1 | Debt-Service Fund Special Assessment Capital Projects Fund | |
| Transaction 5 | Water Utility Fund Debt-Service Fund Special Assessment Capital Projects Fund Municipal Garage Fund | |
| Transaction 7 | | General Fixed-Assets Account Group |
| Transaction 8 | Water Utility Fund Municipal Garage Fund Special Assessment Capital Projects Fund Debt-Service Fund | General Long-Term Debt Account Group |
| Transaction 9 | | General Fixed-Assets Account Group |

**EXHIBIT 6–7.   Model City Transactions Worksheet**

| Account | Balances Beginning of Period | Transactions[a] (left) | Transactions[a] (right) | Revenues, Expenditures, and Transfers | End-of-Period Balance Sheet |
|---|---|---|---|---|---|
| Cash | 20,000 | (3)(4)(9) 545,000 / 1,445,000 / 5,000 | (8) 1,800,000 | | 215,000 |
| Taxes receivable | 10,000 | | | | 15,000 |
| Vouchers payable | | (2)(8) 1,460,000 / 1,505,000 | (4)(5)(7a) 1,445,000 / 1,444,000 / 145,000 | | 94,000 |
| Due to debt-service fund | | (8) 50,000 | (5) 50,000 | | |
| Due to special assessment fund | | (8) 25,000 | (5) 25,000 | | |
| Due to municipal garage fund | | (8) 120,000 | (5) 120,000 | | |
| Due to water utility fund | | (8) 100,000 | (5) 100,000 | | 40,000 |
| Unreserved fund balance | 10,000 | (C-4) 50,000 | (1) 50,000 | | |
| Budgetary fund balance | | | | 50,000 | |
| Fund balance reserved for encumbrances | | | | | 50,000 |
| Reserve for encumbrances | | (7b)(C-3) 150,000 / 50,000 | (C-4)(6) 50,000 / 200,000 | | |
| Estimated revenues | | (1) 2,000,000 | (1) 1,950,000 | 2,000,000 | |
| Appropriations | | | (2) 1,460,000 | 1,950,000 | |
| Revenues | | | (3)(9) 545,000 / 5,000 | 2,010,000 | |
| Transfers to water utility fund | | (5) 100,000 | | 100,000 | |
| Transfers to debt-service fund | | (5) 50,000 | | 50,000 | |
| Transfers to special assessment capital projects fund | | (5) 25,000 | | 25,000 | |
| Transfers to municipal garage fund | | (5) 85,000 | | 85,000 | |
| Expenditures | | (5)(7a) 1,479,000 / 145,000 | | 1,624,000 | |
| Encumbrances | | (6) 200,000 | (7b)(C-3) 150,000 / 50,000 | | |
| **Totals** | **20,000** | **9,589,000** | **9,589,000** | **3,884,000** | **270,000 / 144,000** |
| Balance to unreserved fund balance | | | | 126,000 | 126,000 |
| **Totals** | **20,000** | **9,589,000** | **9,589,000** | **4,010,000** | **270,000** |

[a]Transaction numbers keyed to journal entries illustrated in this chapter.

sacrificing any of the technical understanding expected from problem solving. The worksheet simply combines on one page of columnar paper the essential elements of the transactions and statements previously illustrated and discussed in this chapter.

## ■ Ethical Considerations Associated with Interfund Transfers of Spendable Resources

The city of Crafty is having problems finding the spendable general fund resources required to meet the city council's perceived service needs within a "no tax increase" political environment. The city also has a special revenue fund through which its library services are financed. Recently, a wealthy citizen contributed a nonspendable trust fund, from which the income is to be used to enlarge the city's library services. The general fund has provided accounting and other administrative services for the library fund for many years without charging the fund for those services.

In discussing the problem of acquiring additional general-fund spendable resources, the city controller observes that the additional revenue expected to be earned by the library fund will amount to approximately $15,000 and suggests that the general fund could charge the library fund that amount for services rendered without reducing spendable resources currently available for library operations. Such action would provide the general fund with $15,000 additional spendable resources to use in providing city services. Consider the ethical issues that might be involved in such action.

## ■ Summary

In this chapter, we have illustrated the procedures that should be followed in carrying out the accounting cycle for a general (operating) fund. We began by demonstrating how a series of assumed actions and transactions for the general fund of Model City should be journalized and posted and how subsidiary ledgers may be used in support of both revenue-and-expenditure control accounts. We then showed how the financial results of the assumed transactions are summarized in T-accounts and presented in end-of-the-period financial statements.

We also explained and illustrated how interim financial reports may be presented showing general fund operations for a portion of a fiscal period. Designed to show the extent to which revenue and expenditure activities are being carried out in relationship to the budgetary plans for those activities, these statements are especially important to internal managers. They are helpful in identifying failure to realize revenues as anticipated and in showing tendencies toward overspending individual budgetary allocations in time to allow these situations to be remedied within the fiscal period.

The use of a transactions worksheet for recording and summarizing the transactions of a general fund was also illustrated. We noted that the financial data reflected in the revenues, expenditures and transfers, and balance sheet columns of the transactions worksheet were the same as the data developed from journalizing and posting the transactions to ledger accounts. The transactions worksheet is especially useful to students in solving problems involving a series of transactions to be recorded and summarized in financial statements.

## ■ Glossary

**Appropriation Expenditure.** An expenditure chargeable to an appropriation. Since virtually all expenditures of governments are chargeable to appropriations, the term *expenditures* by itself is widely and properly used.

**Assess.** To value property officially for the purpose of taxation.

**Assessed Valuation.** A valuation set upon real estate or other property by a government as a basis for levying taxes.

**Assessment.** (1) The process of making the official valuation of property for purposes of taxation. (2) The valuation placed upon property as a result of this process.

**Control Account.** An account in the general ledger in which are recorded the aggregate of debit and credit postings to a number of identical or related accounts called subsidiary accounts. For example, taxes receivable is a control account supported by the aggregate of individual balances in individual property taxpayers' subsidiary accounts.

**Cost.** The amount of money or other consideration exchanged for property or services. Costs may be incurred even before money is paid; that is, as soon as a liability is incurred. Ultimately, however, money or other consideration must be given in exchange. Again, the cost of some property or service may, in turn, become a part of the cost of another property or service. For example, the cost of part or all of the materials purchased at a certain time will be reflected in the cost of articles made from such materials or in the cost of those services in the rendering of which the materials were used.

**Delinquent Taxes.** Taxes remaining unpaid on and after the date on which a penalty for nonpayment is attached. Even though the penalty may be subsequently waived and a portion of the taxes may be abated or cancelled, the unpaid balances continue to be delinquent taxes until abated, cancelled, paid, or converted into tax liens.

**Fiscal Period.** The period of time lapsing between the dates on which the accounting records of a reporting entity are closed.

**Interfund Accounts.** Accounts in which transactions between funds are reflected.

**Interim Financial Statement.** Financial statements prepared for a reporting entity covering less than a full fiscal period.

**Statement of Changes in Fund Balance.** The basic financial statement that reconciles the equity balances of an entity at the beginning and end of an accounting period in conformity with GAAP. It explains the relationship between the operating statement and the balance sheet. Under NCGA Statement 1, statements of changes in fund equity are combined with operating statements into "all-inclusive" operating statement formats.

Taxes Receivable—Current.    The uncollected portion of taxes that a government has levied, which are due within one year and which are not considered delinquent.

Taxes Receivable—Delinquent.    Taxes remaining unpaid on and after the date on which a penalty for nonpayment attaches. Delinquent taxes receivable are classified as such until paid, abated, cancelled, or converted into tax liens.

## ■ Questions for Class Discussion

**Q6-1.**    What does the amount in the unreserved fund balance account for the general fund reflect? Explain.

**Q6-2.**    An encumbrance account is used to earmark appropriations that have been committed to be spent. What function is performed by the fund balance reserved for encumbrances account?

**Q6-3.**    Explain the difference between a transfer and an expenditure in accounting for interfund flows of resources.

**Q6-4.**    What is the purpose of maintaining detailed subsidiary ledgers for revenues and expenditures? Explain fully.

**Q6-5.**    What part of the "operating story" does the general-fund revenues part of the statement of revenues, expenditures and transfers, and changes in fund balance disclose?

**Q6-6.**    What part of the "operating story" does the general-fund expenditures part of the statement of revenues, expenditures and transfers, and changes in fund balance disclose?

**Q6-7.**    What significant financial information is disclosed in the changes in the general-fund balance part of the statement of revenues, expenditures and transfers, and changes in fund balance?

**Q6-8.**    What is the justification for preparing general-fund financial statements on a periodic basis? Explain fully.

**Q6-9.**    What do we mean when we refer to appropriations lapsing? Explain.

**Q6-10.**    Explain what is meant by interim financial statements for the general fund. How are they useful?

**Q6-11.**    Explain how a transactions worksheet can be used to accumulate and summarize the financial data for the general fund.

## ■ Exercises

**E6-1.**    The balance sheet for the general fund of Texas City shows the following balances at the beginning of the year:

| Cash | $25,000 | Vouchers payable | $15,000 |
|------|---------|------------------|---------|
|      |         | Unreserved fund balance | 10,000 |

The following actions and transactions occur during the year:
1.  The city council estimates general fund revenues to be $1,350,000 and has approved a budget authorizing expenditures of $1,490,000.
2.  Property tax notices in the amount of $1,000,000 are mailed.
3.  Property taxes in the amount of $900,000 are collected.
4.  The city realizes $250,000 in sales taxes and collects fines amounting to $70,000.
5.  Expenditures in the amount of $900,000 are incurred.
6.  Checks in the amount of $500,000 are issued in payment of vouchers payable.
7.  A contract to construct a storage building at an anticipated cost of $100,000 is signed.
8.  Budgeted expenditures include $150,000 to be paid to a special assessment capital projects fund, $70,000 to be paid to the debt-service fund, and $100,000 to be used to establish a municipal garage fund. These obligations are recognized.
9.  The amount due to the special assessment capital projects fund is paid.
10. Nominal accounts are closed.

**Required:**
Record the preceding data on a transactions worksheet. Be sure to code each action and transaction to the number listed beside it.

E6-2.  Refer to Exercise E6-1.

**Required:**
Prepare financial statements for the general fund of Texas City.

E6-3.  Queen City shows the following estimates in its general-fund revenues subsidiary ledger:

> property tax revenue, $1,400,000
>
> revenue from traffic fines, $45,000
>
> revenue from water department, $48,000
>
> revenue from building permits, $14,000

Amounts actually realized were as follows:

> property taxes, $1,295,250
>
> traffic fines, $55,000
>
> revenue from water department, $51,000
>
> revenue from building permits, $12,000

**Required:**
Prepare a statement showing general fund revenues for the fiscal period.

E6-4.  Queen City also shows the following appropriations in its general-fund expenditures subsidiary ledger:

> general government, $339,000
>
> police services, $214,000

transfer to debt-service fund, $37,000

transfer to municipal garage fund, $72,000

miscellaneous, $22,000

school services, $335,000

Expenditures actually incurred as follows:

general government, $337,000

police services, $210,000

transfers to debt-service fund, $37,000

transfers to municipal garage fund, $72,000

miscellaneous, $21,000

school services, $334,000

**Required:**
Prepare a statement showing general fund expenditures for the fiscal period.

E6-5.   Queen City (see Exercises E6-3 and E6-4) showed an unreserved fund balance in its general fund of $55,000 at the beginning of the fiscal period.

**Required:**
Using the revenue and expenditure data in Exercises E6-3 and E6-4, prepare a statement of changes in fund balance.

## ■ Problems

P6-1.   The balance sheet for the general fund of Bloomville included the following balances at the beginning of the year:

| | |
|---|---|
| Cash | $40,000 |
| Vouchers payable | 20,000 |
| Unreserved fund balance | 20,000 |

The following actions and transactions relating to general fund operations occurred during the year:

1.   The city council approved the following budget for the year:

| | |
|---|---|
| Estimated revenues | |
| Property taxes | $2,900,000 |
| Other revenues | 1,100,000 |
| Total | $4,000,000 |
| | |
| Appropriations | |
| General government | $  700,000 |
| Police services | 500,000 |

| Street maintenance | 800,000 |
|---|---|
| Recreation services | 200,000 |
| Sanitation services | 330,000 |
| Payment to debt-service fund | 100,000 |
| School services | 800,000 |
| Payment to special assessment capital projects fund | 50,000 |
| Establishment of municipal service center | 170,000 |
| Other expenditures | 250,000 |
| Total | $3,900,000 |

2. The property tax rate is determined by dividing estimated revenue from this source by the assessed valuation, which is assumed to be $145,000,000. After the tax rate has been determined, property with an assessed valuation of $1,000,000 was added to the tax rolls. Tax bills were then sent out based on the total assessed valuation of properties.
3. Other revenues in the amount of $1,090,000 were received during the year.
4. Property taxes in the amount of $2,890,000 were collected.
5. The following expenditures and transfers were incurred during the year:

| General government | $ 696,000 |
|---|---|
| Police services | 498,000 |
| Street maintenance | 496,000 |
| Recreation services | 150,000 |
| Sanitation services | 320,000 |
| Payment to debt-service fund | 100,000 |
| School services | 750,000 |
| Payment to special assessment capital projects fund | 50,000 |
| Payment to establish Municipal Services Center | 170,000 |
| Other expenditures | 248,000 |
| Total | $3,478,000 |

6. Contracts are signed for the purchase of equipment at a cost of $400,000. This includes street maintenance equipment expected to cost $300,000, recreational equipment estimated at $50,000, and school equipment expected to cost $50,000.
7. The street maintenance equipment is received. Its billed price is $290,000.
8. Old street maintenance equipment costing $120,000 is sold for $10,000.
9. All amounts due to other funds and vouchers payable, amounting to $3,110,000, were paid.

**Required:**
A. Enter the beginning-of-year balance sheet items in the first two columns of a worksheet and record the actions and transactions listed previously in a general fund transactions worksheet similar to the one shown in Exhibit 6–7.
B. Prepare end-of-year financial statements for the general fund of Bloomville.
C. Determine the amounts of unused appropriations for each of the items listed in the approved budget (see item 1) as of the end of the year.

P6-2.    You were engaged to examine the financial statements of the Mayfair School District for the year ended June 30, 19A, and were furnished the general fund trial balance. Your examination disclosed the following information:

1.    The recorded estimate of losses for the current year taxes receivable was considered to be sufficient.

2.    The local government unit gave the school district twenty acres of land to be used for a new grade school and a community playground. The unrecorded estimated value of the land donated was $50,000. In addition, a state grant of $300,000 was received and the full amount was used in payment of contracts pertaining to the construction of the grade school. Purchases of classroom and playground equipment costing $22,000 were paid from general funds.

3.    Five years ago a 4 percent, 10-year, sinking-fund bond issue in the amount of $1,000,000 for constructing school buildings was made and is outstanding. Interest on the issue is payable at maturity. Budgetary requirements of an annual contribution of $90,000 and accumulated earnings to date aggregating $15,000 were accounted for in separate debt-service fund accounts.

4.    Outstanding purchase orders for operating expenses not recorded in the accounts at year end were as follows:

| | |
|---|---:|
| Administration | $1,000 |
| Instruction | 1,200 |
| Other | 600 |
| Total | $2,800 |

5.    The school district operated a central machine shop. Billings amounting to $950 were properly recorded in the accounts of the general fund but not in the internal service fund.

**Required:**

A.    Prepare the formal adjusting and closing entries for the general fund.

B.    Prepare general fund financial statements as of June 30, 19A.

### Mayfair School District General Fund Trial Balance, June 30, 19A

| | Debit | Credit |
|---|---:|---:|
| Cash | $    47,250 | |
| Taxes receivable—current year | 31,800 | |
| Estimated losses—current year taxes | | $    1,800 |
| Temporary investments | 11,300 | |
| Inventory of supplies | 11,450 | |
| Buildings | 1,300,000 | |
| Estimated revenues | 1,007,000 | |
| Appropriations—operating expenses | | 850,000 |
| Appropriations—other expenditures | | 150,000 |
| State grant revenue | | 300,000 |
| Bonds payable | | 1,000,000 |

|                                                                 | Debit | Credit |
|-----------------------------------------------------------------|------:|-------:|
| Vouchers payable                                                |       | 10,200 |
| Due to internal service fund                                    |       | 950    |
| Operating expenses                                              |       |        |
|   Administration                                      | 24,950 | |
|   Instruction                                         | 601,800 | . |
|   Other                                               | 221,450 | |
| Debt service from current funds (principal and interest)        | 130,000 | |
| Capital outlays (equipment)                                     | 22,000 | |
| Revenues from tax levy, licenses, and fines                     |       | 1,008,200 |
| Unreserved fund balance                                         |       | 87,850 |
|   Totals                                              | $3,409,000 | $3,409,000 |

—AICPA Adapted

**P6-3.** Select the best answer for each of the following items:

1. Which of the following accounts of a governmental unit is credited when a purchase order is approved?
   a. reserve for encumbrances
   b. encumbrances
   c. vouchers payable
   d. appropriations

2. Which of the following accounts of a governmental unit is credited to close it out at the end of the fiscal year?
   a. appropriations
   b. revenues
   c. reserve for encumbrances
   d. encumbrances

3. Repairs that have been made for a governmental unit, and for which a bill has been received, should be recorded in the general fund as a debit to an:
   a. expenditure.
   b. encumbrance.
   c. expense.
   d. appropriation.

4. Which of the following accounts of a governmental unit is credited when taxpayers are billed for property taxes?
   a. estimated revenues
   b. revenues
   c. appropriations
   d. reserve for encumbrances

5. Which of the following types of revenue would generally be recorded directly in the general fund of a governmental unit?
   a. receipts from a city-owned parking structure
   b. interest earned on investments held for retirement of employees
   c. revenues from internal service funds
   d. property taxes

6. The encumbrance account of a governmental unit is debited when:
   a. a purchase order is approved.
   b. goods are received.
   c. a voucher payable is recorded.
   d. the budget is recorded.

7. When fixed assets purchased from general fund revenues are received, the appropriate journal entry is made in the general fixed assets group of accounts. What account, if any, should be debited in the general fund?
   a. No journal entry should be made in the general fund.
   b. expenditures
   c. fixed assets
   d. due from general fixed-assets group of accounts

—**AICPA Adapted**

**P6-4.** Select the best answer for each of the following items:

1. The following items were among Kew Township's expenditures from the general fund during the year ended July 31, 19X1:

| | |
|---|---|
| Minicomputer for tax collector's office | $22,000 |
| Furniture for Township Hall | 40,000 |

How much should be classified as fixed assets in Kew's general fund balance sheet at July 31, 19X1?
   a. $0
   b. $22,000
   c. $40,000
   d. $62,000

2. The following balances are included in the subsidiary records of Burwood Village's Parks and Recreation Department at March 31, 19X2:

| | |
|---|---|
| Appropriations—supplies | $7,500 |
| Expenditures—supplies | 4,500 |
| Encumbrances—supply orders | 750 |

How much does the department have available for additional purchases of supplies?
   a. $0
   b. $2,250
   c. $3,000
   d. $6,750

3. Kingsford City incurred $100,000 of salaries and wages for the month ended March 31, 19X2. How should this be recorded at that date?

| | | Dr. | Cr. |
|---|---|---|---|
| a. | Expenditures—salaries and wages | $100,000 | |
| | Vouchers payable | | $100,000 |
| b. | Salaries and wages expense | $100,000 | |
| | Vouchers payable | | $100,000 |

|  |  | Dr. | Cr. |
|---|---|---|---|
| c. | Encumbrances—salaries and wages | $100,000 | |
|  | Vouchers payable | | $100,000 |
| d. | Fund balance | $100,000 | |
|  | Vouchers payable | | $100,000 |

4. The Board of Commissioners of the City of Rockton adopted its budget for the year ending July 31, 19X2, which indicated revenues of $1,000,000 and appropriations of $900,000. If the budget is formally integrated into the accounting records, what is the required journal entry?

|  |  | Dr. | Cr. |
|---|---|---|---|
| a. | Memorandum entry only | | |
| b. | Appropriations | $ 900,000 | |
|  | General fund | 100,000 | |
|  | Estimated revenues | | $1,000,000 |
| c. | Estimated revenues | $1,000,000 | |
|  | Appropriations | | $ 900,000 |
|  | Fund balance | | 100,000 |
| d. | Revenues receivable | $1,000,000 | |
|  | Expenditures payable | | $ 900,000 |
|  | General fund balance | | 100,000 |

Item 5 is based on the following information:

The following balances appeared in the City of Reedsbury's general fund at June 30, 19X1:

| Account | Balance Dr. (Cr.) | |
|---|---|---|
| Encumbrances—current year | $ 200,000 | |
| Expenditures | | |
| Current year | 3,000,000 | |
| Prior year | 100,000 | |
| Fund balance reserved for encumbrances | | |
| Current year | (200,000) | |
| Prior year | None | |

Reedsbury maintains its general fund books on a legal budgetary basis, requiring revenues and expenditures to be accounted for on a modified accrual basis. In addition, the sum of current year expenditures and encumbrances cannot exceed current year appropriations.

5. What total amount of expenditures (and encumbrances, if appropriate) should Reedsbury report in the general fund column of its combined statement of revenues, expenditures, and changes in fund balance for the year ended June 30, 19X1?

a. $3,000,000

b. $3,100,000

        c.  $3,200,000
        d.  $3,300,000

**—AICPA Adapted**

**P6-5.**  Select the best answer for each of the following items:

1. For state and local governmental units, generally accepted accounting principles require that encumbrances outstanding at year-end be reported as:
   a. expenditures.
   b. reservations of fund balance.
   c. deferred liabilities.
   d. current liabilities.

2. Revenues that are legally restricted to expenditures for specified purposes should be accounted for in special revenue funds, including:
   a. accumulation of resources for payment of general long-term debt principal and interest.
   b. pension trust fund revenues.
   c. gasoline taxes to finance road repairs.
   d. proprietary fund revenues.

3. The appropriations control account of a governmental unit is debited when:

   | | The budgetary accounts are closed | Expenditures are recorded |
   | --- | --- | --- |
   | a. | No | Yes |
   | b. | No | No |
   | c. | Yes | No |
   | d. | Yes | Yes |

4. The reserve for encumbrances account of a governmental fund type is increased when:
   a. a purchase order is approved
   b. supplies previously ordered are received
   c. appropriations are recorded
   d. the budget is recorded.

5. The encumbrances control account of a governmental unit is increased when:

   | | A voucher payable is recorded | The budgetary accounts are closed |
   | --- | --- | --- |
   | a. | No | No |
   | b. | No | Yes |
   | c. | Yes | Yes |
   | d. | Yes | No |

6. The expenditures control account of a governmental unit is increased when:

   | | A purchase order is approved | The budget is recorded |
   | --- | --- | --- |
   | a. | No | No |
   | b. | No | Yes |
   | c. | Yes | Yes |
   | d. | Yes | No |

7. The estimated revenues control account balance of a governmental fund type is eliminated when:
   a. the budgetary accounts are closed.
   b. the budget is recorded.
   c. property taxes are recorded.
   d. appropriations are closed.

8. The expenditures control account of a governmental unit is credited when:
   a. the nominal accounts are closed.
   b. the budget is recorded.
   c. supplies are purchased.
   d. supplies previously encumbered are received.

9. The reserve for encumbrances account of a governmental unit is decreased when:
   a. supplies previously ordered are received.
   b. a purchase order is approved.
   c. the vouchers are paid.
   d. appropriations are recorded.

10. The revenues control account of a governmental unit is increased when:
    a. the budget is recorded.
    b. property taxes are recorded.
    c. appropriations are recorded.
    d. the budgetary accounts are closed.

    —AICPA Adapted

P6-6. Select the best answer for each of the following items:

1. The following items were among Wood Township's expenditures from the general fund during the year ended June 30, 19X7:

   | | |
   |---|---|
   | Furniture for Township Hall | $10,000 |
   | Minicomputer for tax collector's office | 15,000 |

   The amount that should be classified as fixed assets in Wood's general fund balance sheet at June 30, 19X7 is:
   a. $25,000.
   b. $15,000.
   c. $10,000.
   d. $0.

2. Lake City incurred $300,000 of salaries and wages expense in its general fund for the month ended May 31, 19X9. For this $300,000 expense, Lake should debit
   a. fund balance—unreserved, undesignated.
   b. encumbrances control.
   c. appropriations control.
   d. expenditures control.

3. The following proceeds were received by Kew City from specific revenue sources that are legally restricted to expenditure for specified purposes:

| | |
|---|---|
| Gasoline taxes to finance road repairs | $400,000 |
| Levies on affected property owners to finance sidewalk repairs | 300,000 |

The amount that should be accounted for in Kew's special revenue funds is:
a.  $0.
b.  $300,000.
c.  $400,000.
d.  $700,000.

Items 4 through 9 are based on the following information:

Cliff Township's fiscal year ends on July 31. Cliff uses encumbrance accounting. On October 2, 19X1, an approved $5,000 purchase order was issued for supplies. Cliff received these supplies on November 2, 19X1, and the $5,000 invoice was approved for payment by the general fund.

During the year ended July 31, 19X2, Cliff received a state grant of $150,000 to finance the purchase of a senior citizens recreation bus, and an additional $15,000 grant to be used for bus operations during the year ended July 31, 19X2. Only $125,000 of the capital grant was used during the year ended July 31, 19X2, for the bus purchase, but the entire operating grant of $15,000 was disbursed during the year.

Cliff's governing body adopted its general fund budget for the year ending July 31, 19X3, comprising estimated revenues of $50,000,000 and appropriations of $40,000,000. Cliff formally integrates its budget into the accounting records.

4. What accounts should Cliff debit and credit on October 2, 19X1, to record the approved $5,000 purchase order?

| | *Debit* | *Credit* |
|---|---|---|
| a. | Encumbrances control | Appropriations control |
| b. | Appropriations control | Encumbrances control |
| c. | Encumbrances control | Reserve for encumbrances |
| d. | Budgetary fund balance—reserve for encumbrances | Encumbrances control |

5. What accounts should Cliff debit and credit on November 2, 19X1, upon receipt of the supplies and approval of the $5,000 invoice?

| | *Debit* | *Credit* |
|---|---|---|
| a. | Reserve for encumbrances | Encumbrances control |
| | Expenditures control | Vouchers payable |
| b. | Appropriations control | Vouchers payable |
| c. | Appropriations control | Encumbrances control |
| | Supplies inventory | Vouchers payable |
| d. | Encumbrances control | Appropriations control |
| | Expenditures control | Vouchers payable |

6. The senior citizens recreation bus program is accounted for as part of Cliff's general fund. What amount should Cliff report as grant revenues for the year ended July 31, 19X2, in connection with the state grants?
   a. $165,000
   b. $150,000
   c. $140,000
   d. $125,000

7. When Cliff records budgeted revenues, estimated revenues control should be:
   a. debited for $10,000,000.
   b. credited for $10,000,000.
   c. debited for $50,000,000.
   d. credited for $50,000,000.

8. To record the $40,000,000 of budgeted appropriations, Cliff should:
   a. debit estimated expenditures control.
   b. credit estimated expenditures control.
   c. debit appropriations control.
   d. credit appropriations control.

9. The $10,000,000 budgeted excess of revenues over appropriations should be:
   a. debited to budgetary fund balance—unreserved.
   b. credited to budgetary fund balance—unreserved.
   c. debited to estimated excess revenues control.
   d. credited to estimated excess revenues control.

Items 10 through 16 are based on the following information:

Maple Township uses encumbrance accounting, and formally integrates its budget into the accounting records for its general fund. For the year ending June 30, 19X1, the Township Council adopted a budget comprising estimated revenues of $10,000,000, appropriations of $9,000,000, and an estimated transfer of $300,000 to the debt-service fund. The following additional information is provided:

1. For the month of April 19X1, salaries and wages expense of $200,000 was incurred.
2. On April 10, 19X1, an approved $1,500 purchase order was issued for supplies. These supplies were received on May 1, 19X1, and the $1,500 invoice was approved for payment.
3. In November 19X0, an unexpected state grant of $100,000 was received to finance the purchase of school buses, and an additional grant of $5,000 was received for bus maintenance and operations. Only $60,000 of the capital grant was used in the current year for the purchase of buses, but the entire operating grant of $5,000 was disbursed in the current year. The remaining $40,000 of the capital grant is expected to be expended during the year ending June 30, 19X2. Maple's school bus system is appropriately accounted for in the general fund.

10. On adoption of the budget, the journal entry to record the budgetary fund balance should include a:
    a. debit of $700,000.
    b. credit of $700,000.

   c.  debit of $1,000,000.

   d.  credit of $1,000,000.

11.  Budgeted revenues would be recorded by a:

   a.  debit to estimated revenues control, $10,000,000.

   b.  debit to estimated revenues receivable, $10,000,000.

   c.  credit to estimated revenues, $10,000,000.

   d.  credit to other financing sources control, $10,000,000.

12.  Budgeted appropriations would be recorded by a:

   a.  debit to estimated expenditures, $9,300,000.

   b.  credit to appropriations control, $9,300,000.

   c.  debit to estimated expenditures, $9,000,000.

   d.  credit to appropriations control, $9,000,000.

13.  What journal entry should be made on April 10, 19X1, to record the approved purchase order?

|  | Debit | Credit |
|---|---|---|
| a. Expenditures control | $1,500 | |
|    Encumbrances control | | $1,500 |
| b. Encumbrances control | 1,500 | |
|    Expenditures control | | 1,500 |
| c. Encumbrances control | 1,500 | |
|    Reserve for encumbrances | | 1,500 |
| d. Encumbrances control | 1,500 | |
|    Appropriations control | | 1,500 |

14.  What journal entries should be made on May 1, 19X1, upon receipt of the supplies and approval of the invoice?

|  | Debit | Credit |
|---|---|---|
| a. Encumbrances control | $1,500 | |
|    Appropriations control | | $1,500 |
|    Supplies expense | 1,500 | |
|    Vouchers payable | | 1,500 |
| b. Reserve for encumbrances | 1,500 | |
|    Encumbrances control | | 1,500 |
|    Expenditures control | 1,500 | |
|    Vouchers payable | | 1,500 |
| c. Appropriations control | 1,500 | |
|    Encumbrances control | | 1,500 |
|    Expenditures control | 1,500 | |
|    Vouchers payable | | 1,500 |
| d. Expenditures control | 1,500 | |
|    Encumbrances control | | 1,500 |
|    Supplies expense | 1,500 | |
|    Vouchers payable | | 1,500 |

15.  In connection with the grants for the purchase of school buses and bus maintenance and operations, what amount should be reported as grant revenues for the year ending June 30, 19X1?

a.  $5,000
b.  $60,000
c.  $65,000
d.  $100,000

16.  What journal entry should be made to record the salaries and wages expense incurred for April?

|  | Debit | Credit |
|---|---|---|
| a. Salaries and wages expense | $200,000 |  |
| Vouchers payable |  | $200,000 |
| b. Appropriations control | 200,000 |  |
| Vouchers payable |  | 200,000 |
| c. Encumbrances control | 200,000 |  |
| Vouchers payable |  | 200,000 |
| d. Expenditures control | 200,000 |  |
| Vouchers payable |  | 200,000 |

—AICPA Adapted

P6-7.  The accounts of the City of Daltonville were kept by an inexperienced bookkeeper during the year ended December 31, 19B. The following trial balance of the general fund was available when you began your examination:

City of Daltonville General Fund Trial Balance, December 31, 19B

|  | Debit | Credit |
|---|---|---|
| Cash | $ 75,600 |  |
| Taxes receivable—current year | 29,000 |  |
| Estimated losses—current year taxes receivable |  | $  9,000 |
| Taxes receivable—prior year | 4,000 |  |
| Estimated losses—prior year taxes receivable |  | 5,100 |
| Appropriations |  | 174,000 |
| Estimated revenues | 180,000 |  |
| Building addition constructed | 25,000 |  |
| Serial bonds paid | 8,000 |  |
| Expenditures | 140,000 |  |
| Special assessment bonds payable |  | 50,000 |
| Revenues |  | 177,000 |
| Accounts payable |  | 13,000 |
| Unreserved fund balance |  | 33,500 |
|  | $461,600 | $461,600 |

Your examination disclosed the following:
1.  The estimate of losses of $9,000 for current-year taxes receivable was found to be a reasonable estimate.

2.  The building addition constructed account balance is the cost of an addition to the municipal building. The addition was constructed during 19B and payment was made from the general fund as authorized.

3.  The serial bonds paid account reports the annual retirement of general obligation bonds issued to finance the construction of the municipal building. Interest payments amounting to $3,800 for this bond issue are included in expenditures.

4.  A physical count of the current operating supplies at December 31, 19B, revealed an inventory of $6,500. The decision was made to record the inventory in the accounts; expenditures are to be recorded on the basis of usage rather than purchases.

5.  Operating supplies ordered in 19A and chargeable to 19A appropriations were received, recorded, and consumed in January 19B. The outstanding purchase orders for these supplies, which were not recorded in the accounts at year end, amounted to $4,400. The vendors' invoices for these supplies totaled $4,700. Appropriations lapse one year after the end of the fiscal year for which they are made.

6.  Outstanding purchase orders at December 31, 19B, for operating supplies totaled $5,300. These purchase orders were not recorded on the books.

7.  The special assessment bonds were sold in December 19B to finance a street-paving project. No contracts have been signed for this project and no expenditures have been made.

8.  The balance in the revenues account includes credits for $10,000 for a note issued to a bank to obtain cash in anticipation of tax collections to pay current expenses and for $900 for the sale of scrap iron from the city's water plant. The note was still outstanding at year end. The operations of the water plant are accounted for by a separate fund.

**Required:**

Prepare the formal correcting and closing journal entries for the general fund.

—AICPA Adapted

P6-8.   The following summary of transactions was taken from the accounts of the Annaville School District general fund *before* the books had been closed for the fiscal year ended June 30, 19X2.

|  | Post-Closing Balances | Pre-Closing Balances |
|---|---|---|
|  | June 30, 19X1 | June 30, 19X2 |
| Cash | $400,000 | $  700,000 |
| Taxes receivable | 150,000 | 170,000 |
| Estimated uncollectible taxes | (40,000) | (70,000) |
| Estimated revenues | — | 3,000,000 |
| Expenditures | — | 2,842,000 |
| Expenditures—prior year | — | — |
| Encumbrances | — | 91,000 |
|  | $510,000 | $6,733,000 |

|  | Post-Closing Balances | Pre-Closing Balances |
|---|---|---|
|  | June 30, 19X1 | June 30, 19X2 |
| Vouchers payable | $ 80,000 | $ 408,000 |
| Due to other funds | 210,000 | 142,000 |
| Fund balance reserved for encumbrances | 60,000 | 91,000 |
| Unreserved fund balance | 160,000 | 182,000 |
| Revenues from taxes | — | 2,800,000 |
| Miscellaneous revenues | — | 130,000 |
| Appropriations | — | 2,980,000 |
|  | $510,000 | $6,733,000 |

*Additional information:*
1. The taxes receivable for the year ended June 30, 19X2, were $2,870,000, and taxes collected during the year totaled $2,810,000.
2. An analysis of the transactions in the vouchers payable account for the year ended June 30, 19X2, follows:

|  | Debit (Credit) |
|---|---|
| Current expenditures | $(2,700,000) |
| Expenditures for prior year | (58,000) |
| Vouchers for payment to other funds | (210,000) |
| Cash payments during year | 2,640,000 |
| Net change | $ (328,000) |

3. During the year the general fund was billed $142,000 for services performed on its behalf by other city funds.
4. On May 2, 19X2, commitment documents were issued for the purchase of new textbooks at a cost of $91,000.

**Required:**
Based on the preceding data, reconstruct the *original detailed journal entries* that were required to record all transactions for the fiscal year ended June 30, 19X2, including the recording of the current year's budget. Do *not* prepare closing entries at June 30, 19X2.

—**AICPA Adapted**

**P6-9.** Information concerning the accounting records for the city of Bruceville on December 31, 19X1, is presented in the following table:

## Balances in Selected Accounts

|  | Debit | Credit |
|---|---|---|
| Supplies inventory (physical inventory 12/31/X1) | $10,000 |  |
| Estimated revenue—miscellaneous | 20,000 |  |
| Estimated revenue—taxes | 95,000 |  |
| Appropriations |  | $112,000 |
| Revenue—miscellaneous |  | 19,900 |
| Revenue—taxes |  | 95,500 |
| Encumbrances | 20,000 |  |
| Expenditures | 80,000 |  |
| Expenditures chargeable against prior years' encumbrances | 7,100 |  |
| Reserve for encumbrances (balance, 1/1/X1, $7,000) |  | 27,000 |
| Reserve for supplies inventory (balance at 1/1/X1) |  | 12,000 |
| Unreserved fund balance |  | 3,300 |

*Additional information:*

1. The unencumbered balance of the fire department's appropriation of December 31, 19X1, was $10,025. As legally authorized, the city council voted to carry over this balance, in the rounded amount of $10,000, to 19X2. This action has not been recorded in the accounts.
2. On December 31, 19X1, unfilled purchase orders for the general fund totaled $20,000.

**Required:**

A. Prepare the correcting journal entry or entries for general fund accounts for December 31, 19X1.
B. Prepare the closing journal entry or entries for general fund accounts for December 31, 19X1.
C. Prepare in columnar form an analysis of changes in fund balance for the year 19X1. Use the following column headings: "Estimated," "Actual," and "Excess or deficiency of actual compared with estimate."

**—AICPA Adapted**

P6-10. The following financial activities affecting Judbury City's general fund took place during the year ended June 30, 19X1;

1. The following budget was adopted:

| Estimated revenues | |
|---|---|
| Property taxes | $4,500,000 |
| Licenses and permits | 300,000 |
| Fines | 200,000 |
| Total | $5,000,000 |

Appropriations
| | |
|---|---:|
| General government | $1,500,000 |
| Police services | 1,200,000 |
| Fire department services | 900,000 |
| Public works services | 800,000 |
| Acquisition of fire engines | 400,000 |
| Total | $4,800,000 |

2.  Property tax bills totaling $4,650,000 were mailed. It is estimated that $300,000 of this amount will be delinquent, and $150,000 of this amount will be uncollectible.

3.  Property taxes totaling $3,900,000 were collected. The $150,000 previously estimated to be uncollectible remained unchanged, but $630,000 was reclassified as delinquent. It is estimated that delinquent taxes will be collected soon enough after June 30, 19X1, to make these taxes available to finance obligations incurred during the year ended June 30, 19X1. There was no balance of uncollected taxes at July 1, 19X0.

4.  Tax anticipation notes in the face amount of $300,000 were issued.

5.  Other cash collections were as follow:

| | |
|---|---:|
| Licenses and permits | $270,000 |
| Fines | 200,000 |
| Sale of public works equipment (original cost, $75,000) | 15,000 |
| Total | $485,000 |

6.  The following purchase orders were executed:

| | Total | Outstanding at 6/30/X1 |
|---|---:|---:|
| General government | $1,050,000 | $ 60,000 |
| Police services | 300,000 | 30,000 |
| Fire department services | 150,000 | 15,000 |
| Public works services | 250,000 | 10,000 |
| Fire engines | 400,000 | — |
| Totals | $2,150,000 | $115,000 |

No encumbrances were outstanding at June 30, 19X0.

7.  The following vouchers were approved:

| | |
|---|---:|
| General government | $1,440,000 |
| Police services | 1,155,000 |
| Fire department services | 870,000 |
| Public works services | 700,000 |
| Fire engines | 400,000 |
| Total | $4,565,000 |

8.  Vouchers totaling $4,600,000 were paid.

**Required:**
Prepare journal entries to record the foregoing financial activities in the general fund. Omit explanations. Ignore interest accruals.

**—AICPA Adapted**

P6-11.  The following information was abstracted from the accounts of the general fund of the City of Rom after the books had been closed for the fiscal year ended June 30, 19X1:

| | Post-Closing Trial Balance June 30, 19X0 | Transactions July 1, 19X0 to June 30, 19X1 | | Post-Closing Trial Balance June 30, 19X1 |
|---|---|---|---|---|
| | | Debit | Credit | |
| Cash | $700,000 | $1,820,000 | $1,852,000 | $668,000 |
| Taxes receivable | 40,000 | 1,870,000 | 1,828,000 | 82,000 |
| | $740,000 | | | $750,000 |
| | | | | |
| Allowance for uncollectible taxes | $ 8,000 | 8,000 | 10,000 | $ 10,000 |
| Vouchers payable | 132,000 | 1,852,000 | 1,840,000 | 120,000 |
| Fund balance | | | | |
| Reserved for encumbrances | — | 1,000,000 | 1,070,000 | 70,000 |
| Unreserved | 600,000 | 140,000 | 60,000 | 550,000 |
| | | | 30,000 | |
| Totals | $740,000 | | | $750,000 |

*Additional information:*
1.  The budget for the fiscal year ended June 30, 19X1, provided for estimated revenues of $2,000,000 and appropriations of $1,940,000.

**Required:**
Prepare journal entries to record the budgeted and actual transactions for the fiscal year ended June 30, 19X1.

**—AICPA Adapted**

P6-12.  **Thought Projection Problem.** The Crescent City Council has employed you to examine the general fund. The following information is made available to you directly or as the result of your examination.
1.  The account balances of the general fund at the *end* of the fiscal year are as follows:

| Debits | |
|---|---|
| Cash | $    600,000 |
| Taxes receivable—current | 500,000 |
| Appropriation expenditures | 9,300,000 |
| | $10,400,000 |
| | |
| **Credits** | |
| Revenues received | $ 9,900,000 |
| Deferred tax collections | 500,000 |
| | $10,400,000 |

2. At the beginning of the year, the council formally approved the budget for the fiscal year. The budget is presented with the cash receipts and disbursements information in 3 below.
3. Cash receipts and disbursements, together with budgeting information, are presented next.

| | Estimated Revenues | Actual Receipts |
|---|---|---|
| Taxes | | |
| Current year | $ 9,700,000 | $9,500,000 |
| Collected in advance | 0 | 20,000 |
| Licenses and permits | 200,000 | 250,000 |
| Fines and forfeits | 70,000 | 78,000 |
| Rentals from use of properties | 30,000 | 32,000 |
| Miscellaneous | | |
| Refunds and rebates of current service charges by other agencies | | |
| Utility fund | 0 | 6,000 |
| Internal service fund | 0 | 4,000 |
| Unused (excess) cash from capital projects fund | 0 | 10,000 |
| Total | $10,000,000 | $9,900,000 |

| | Planned Expenditures | Actual Disbursements |
|---|---|---|
| Departmental expenses* | $7,100,000 | $6,894,000 |
| Contribution to retirement pension fund | 150,000 | 140,000 |
| Creation of a petty cash fund | 0 | 5,000 |
| City's share of cost of special assessments | 150,000 | 150,000 |
| Establishment of internal service fund | 50,000 | 50,000 |
| Equipment—general office | 420,000 | 421,000 |
| Land for building site | 500,000 | 500,000 |
| Debt-service fund contribution | 1,000,000 | 1,000,000 |
| Matured serial general obligation bonds | 100,000 | 100,000 |
| Interest on bonds | | |
| Sinking fund bonds | 20,000 | 20,000 |
| Serial bonds | 10,000 | 10,000 |
| Temporary loan to internal service fund | 0 | 10,000 |
| Total | $9,500,000 | $9,300,000 |
| *Include the following | | |
| Billed by utility fund | $ 70,000 | $ 80,000 |
| Billed by internal service fund | 0 | $ 39,000 |

4. City taxes receivable, per tax roll, amounted to $10,000,000.
5. All unpaid city taxes become delinquent at the end of the year in which levied.

6. Unrecorded amounts at the close of the fiscal year consisted of:

| | | |
|---|---:|---:|
| Accrued salaries | $60,000 | |
| Invoices for materials and supplies | 19,000 | $79,000 |
| Orders placed by the city but not filled | | 30,000 |

7. Services billed by the internal service fund, not recorded on the books of general fund, amounted to $1,000.
8. The general fund stores inventory amounted to $35,000 at end of period and is to be recorded. The city's charter provides that expenditures are based on purchases.
9. The city's charter specifies that purchase orders unfilled at the end of the year do not lapse.

**Required:**

Prepare a worksheet for the general fund with columns for "Balances per Books," "Corrections and Adjustments," and "Corrected Balances." Key the corrections and adjustments to the related transaction numbers. Formal general journal entries are not required.

—**AICPA Adapted**

# CHAPTER 7

# Accounting for Other Governmental Funds

## ■ Learning Objectives

When you have finished your study of this chapter, you should

1. Know when a capital projects fund should be originated as part of a governmental entity's accounting records.

2. Be able to record the typical transactions associated with a capital projects fund.

3. Be able to close the accounts of a capital projects fund and prepare end-of-period financial statements for the fund.

4. Recognize the typical transactions that should be recorded in a debt-service fund and be able to record those transactions.

5. Be able to close the accounts of a debt-service fund and prepare end-of-period financial statements for the fund.

6. Know how to account for typical special assessment project transactions in a special assessments capital projects fund and a special assessment agency fund.

7. Recognize the reciprocal and complementing entries required for transactions recorded in the capital projects, debt-service, and special assessment project funds.

$\mathbf{A}$s we have observed, governmental fund accounting techniques are used in recording the resource inflows and outflows of any fund entity that is primarily concerned with acquiring and using resources in accordance with a specified, predetermined plan. A separate, self-balancing accounting entity is established for each segment of resources required to be used only for specified purposes. The accounting systems for these funds are designed primarily to reflect *dollar accountability* in the form of inflows and outflows of spendable resources. They are organized to show the sources from which those resources were realized and how they were used.

Although a governmental unit could conceivably receive and use only general fund resources and thus require records for only one accounting entity, this is not the typical situation. Most government entities will have some resources that must be used in accordance with externally imposed restrictions. Separate fund accounting records must therefore be established within the overall accounting system to account for the acquisitions and uses of such resources. Most of these separate self-balancing accounting entities will be governmental funds.

In the preceding chapter, we demonstrated the procedures that should be followed in accounting for general fund and special revenue fund resources. In this chapter, we describe and illustrate the procedures that should be followed in accounting for

1.  general capital improvements
2.  accumulation of resources to be used in servicing general long-term debt
3.  capital improvements financed by special assessments.

The illustrations include assumed transactions for each of the funds used to account for resources acquired and used to carry out those actions.

# ◼ Accounting for General Capital Improvements

The inflows and outflows of resources for the acquisition or improvement of general capital facilities, not financed through the use of general fund or enterprise fund resources, are accounted for in a *capital projects fund*. This fund is *project oriented;* it continues to function as an accounting entity only until the capital project is finished. Authorization actions are for the project rather than for a specified period of time. This type of fund frequently comes into being when the voters authorize a governmental unit to issue general bonds for the purpose of acquiring long-term (capital) assets. Resources designated to be used for this purpose may also come from the federal government or from other sources, but most of them will be realized from the sale of general obligation bonds. General obligation bonds are defined as bonds issued and to be retired by the total governmental unit rather than by a segment of that unit.

As we discuss and illustrate capital projects fund accounting procedures, it is important to recognize that not all major capital projects are accounted for in such funds. The general or special revenue fund may be used to account for such projects if they do not need additional financing. However, if the project requires financing beyond the amount available from the revenues of such funds, a capital projects fund should be used. As a general rule, a separate fund should be used for each project.

Prudent managers of governmental entities will typically develop a plan for capital expenditures to be incurred each year over a number of years to focus attention on future capital needs. When data are reflected in the form of a definite time frame for individual capital projects, we characterize it as a *capital program*.

The primary objective in accounting for a capital projects fund is to show the *acquisitions and disposals of resources realized from the sale of general obligation bonds and/or other sources that are earmarked for the acquisitions of long-term assets.* Even though the fund is project oriented, financial statements should be prepared to reflect the results of its operations and its financial position at the end of each fiscal period during which the project is being implemented. It is important to recognize that this accounting entity is designed to account for the inflows and outflows of resources designated for the use specified in the origination of the fund. *The liability for the bonds sold through this fund is recorded in the accounts of the general long-term debt account group* as illustrated in Chapter 8. The accumulation of funds to be used to retire the bonds will be accounted for in the records of a debt-service fund as shown later in this chapter.

The capitalization of interest, required by FASB 34, is of concern in accounting for capital outlays. Although interest capitalization is permissible under GAAP for governmental entities, it is usually not required for governmental fund accounting because it would not, in most instances, have a material effect on governmental fund statements.

We now describe and illustrate the recordkeeping practices used in recording the activities of a capital projects fund for Model City. The assumed transactions will be

1.  journalized
2.  posted to the ledger
3.  summarized in financial statements for the fund.

## Assumed Transactions

Let's assume that a capital projects fund for Model City has the following transactions during the fiscal period:

CP-1.   A general bond issue of $500,000 is authorized for financing street improvements.

CP-2.   The bonds are sold for $502,000.

CP-3.   Expenditures of $350,000 are made for part of the street-improvement program. Of this amount, $5,000 is for services performed by the municipal garage.

CP-4.   Contracts amounting to $140,000 are signed for the balance of the improvements.

CP-5.   A contract (see transaction CP-4) amounting to $50,000 is completed, and a voucher is prepared to cover it. Because of changes in certain specifications, the amount to be paid is agreed upon as $52,000. The contract stipulates that, pending satisfactory performance of the improvements, the city may retain 10 percent of the original contract price.

CP-6.   Vouchers amounting to $387,000 and $5,000 due to the municipal garage are paid.

## Journalizing the Transactions

The following journal entries should be made to record the preceding transactions:

Transaction (CP-1)
Estimated bond-issue proceeds                    500,000
    Appropriations                                                    500,000

The authorization of a bond issue is to the capital projects fund what the approval of the budget is to the general fund. Entry (CP-1) records this authorization in the accounts. This entry, a type (1) transaction (see page 30), reflects the plan for the operation of the capital projects fund. Because resources are not actually being received or disbursed, these data are sometimes omitted from the formal accounting records, in which case transaction (CP-2) would be the first one recorded. The authorization of a general bond issue to finance a project, however, is normally the signal for formally establishing a capital projects fund accounting entity.

Transaction (CP-2)

| | | |
|---|---|---|
| Cash | 502,000 | |
| Premium on bonds | | 2,000 |
| Proceeds from sale of bonds | | 500,000 |

We have used the term *proceeds from the sale of bonds* to describe the inflow of resources from the sale of bonds. The illustration in the 1988 edition of GAAFR (see page 50) credits such inflows to an account labeled *other financing sources control*. When that account title is used, a subsidiary ledger is maintained to more specifically describe those sources. With only one inflow item in our illustration, it is more appropriate to label it as we have in the preceding entry.

This entry, a type (2) transaction (see page 30), records the sale of the bonds at a premium of $2,000. The fact that the amount appropriated for this project is equal to the face value of the bonds raises a question as to how the premium may be used. Legal provisions can govern the use of the premium. It may be made available as additional financing for the project. In this case, the appropriations account should be credited for an amount equal to the premium. When there are no legal provisions, any premium received from the sale of bonds should logically be paid to the debt-service fund so that it may be used in liquidating the bond issue. When this procedure is followed, an interfund obligation account entitled "due to debt-service fund" is credited for the amount of the premium. Because the bonds carry a contractual rate of interest that is higher than market, causing them to be sold at a premium, it is theoretically sound to require that any premium be paid to the debt-service fund.

If the bonds are sold at a discount, the disposition of the discount also depends on legal requirements. Thus, the appropriation balance might be reduced, or the amount of the discount might be transferred from the debt-service fund or general fund to the capital projects fund. In our illustration, the transfer of the premium is recorded as follows:

Transaction (CP-2a)

| | | |
|---|---|---|
| Premium on bonds | 2,000 | |
| Due to debt-service fund | | 2,000 |

Transaction (CP-2b)

| | | |
|---|---|---|
| Due to debt-service fund | 2,000 | |
| Cash | | 2,000 |

The assumed expenditure and encumbrance entries are as follows:

**Transaction (CP-3)**

| | | |
|---|---|---|
| Expenditures | 350,000 | |
| Vouchers payable | | 345,000 |
| Due to municipal garage fund | | 5,000 |

**Transaction (CP-4)**

| | | |
|---|---|---|
| Encumbrances | 140,000 | |
| Reserve for encumbrances | | 140,000 |

**Transaction (CP-5a)**

| | | |
|---|---|---|
| Reserve for encumbrances | 50,000 | |
| Encumbrances | | 50,000 |

**Transaction (CP-5b)**

| | | |
|---|---|---|
| Expenditures | 52,000 | |
| Vouchers payable | | 47,000 |
| Contract payable—retained percentage | | 5,000 |

Encumbrance and expenditure entries, reflecting type (3), (4), and (5) transactions (see page 30), involve little that is different from similar entries illustrated for the general fund except for use of the account "contract payable—retained percentage" in entry (CP-5b). This account represents the amount designated for delayed payment pending satisfactory performance of the streets improved by the contractor. When the city has had an opportunity to check this performance, the obligation will be paid in the normal manner. If the street improvement does not function satisfactorily, the contractor will be required to make the necessary corrections before this amount will be paid.

**Transaction (CP-6)**

| | | |
|---|---|---|
| Due to municipal garage fund | 5,000 | |
| Vouchers payable | 387,000 | |
| Cash | | 392,000 |

This entry records an ordinary voucher payment.

The issuance of general obligation bonds to finance a capital project requires a complementing entry in the general long-term debt account group debiting an amount-to-be-provided account and crediting bonds payable. When the project has been completed, a complementing entry should be recorded in the general fixed-asset account group reflecting a debit to the appropriate fixed-asset account and a credit to an investment in fixed assets from capital projects fund. These entries are discussed further in Chapter 8.

## Closing Entries

Either at the end of the fiscal period or when the project is completed, the nominal accounts will be closed. When all proceeds from the sale of bonds have been properly used, the capital projects fund accounts will be closed and eliminated from the accounting records of the city. If the books of the capital projects fund are closed after the illustrated transactions have been completed, the following closing entries should be recorded. Behind these entries is the assumption that outstanding encumbrances can be met at their recorded value and that resources unused and uncommitted will be held in a fund balance account pending their ultimate disposal.

| | | |
|---|---:|---:|
| **(C-1)** | | |
| Dr. Appropriations | 500,000 | |
|    Cr. Estimated bond-issue proceeds | | 500,000 |
| **(C-2)** | | |
| Dr. Proceeds from the sale of bonds | 500,000 | |
|    Cr. Unreserved fund balance | | 98,000 |
|    Cr. Expenditures | | 402,000 |
| **(C-3)** | | |
| Dr. Reserve for encumbrances | 90,000 | |
|    Cr. Encumbrances | | 90,000 |
| **(C-4)** | | |
| Dr. Unreserved fund balance | 90,000 | |
|    Cr. Fund balance reserved for encumbrances | | 90,000 |

In the preceding illustration, we assume that no action has been taken regarding disposition of unused resources—that is, the resources represented by the balance reflected in the account entitled "unreserved fund balance." If this amount is to be transferred to the debt-service fund, an entry will be made debiting transfer to debt-service fund and crediting an account entitled "due to debt-service fund."

In our illustration, we assume that this capital project is financed entirely from the proceeds of a bond issue. If revenues are realized from other sources, they should be recorded with an entry similar to that shown for transaction (CP-2), except that the credit will specify the sources of the revenues.

If a capital projects fund experiences a cost overrun in carrying out an authorized construction project, the additional funds required to meet the overrun may be acquired through the incurrence of additional long-term debt or from general fund resources. If an overrun is small, the additional resources will probably come from the general fund. However, a large overrun would almost certainly have to be met by incurring additional long-term debt.

## Posting the Transactions

The preceding entries are posted to the capital projects fund ledger accounts as illustrated in the following T-accounts. Each amount is keyed to its respective transaction by the transaction number listed in parentheses beside it.

| Estimated Bond Issue Proceeds | | Appropriations | |
|---|---|---|---|
| (CP-1) 500,000 | (C-1) 500,000 | (C-1) 500,000 | (CP-1) 500,000 |

| Proceeds from Sale of Bonds | |
|---|---|
| (C-2) 500,000 | (CP-2) 500,000 |

| Expenditures | |
|---|---|
| (CP-3) 350,000 | (C-2) 402,000 |
| (CP-5b) 52,000 | |

| Cash | |
|---|---|
| (CP-2) 502,000 | (CP-6) 392,000 |
| | (CP-2b) 2,000 |

| Encumbrances | |
|---|---|
| (CP-4) 140,000 | (CP-5a) 50,000 |
| | (C-3) 90,000 |

| Vouchers Payable | |
|---|---|
| (CP-6) 387,000 | (CP-3) 345,000 |
| | (CP-5b) 47,000 |

| Reserve for Encumbrances | |
|---|---|
| (CP-5a) 50,000 | (CP-4) 140,000 |
| (C-3) 90,000 | |

| Contract Payable—Retained Percentage | |
|---|---|
| | (CP-5b) 5,000 |

| Due to Debt-Service Fund | |
|---|---|
| (CP-2b) 2,000 | (CP-2a) 2,000 |

| Premium on Bonds | |
|---|---|
| (CP-2a) 2,000 | (CP-2) 2,000 |

| Due to Municipal Garage Fund | |
|---|---|
| (CP-6) 5,000 | (CP-3) 5,000 |

| Unreserved Fund Balance | |
|---|---|
| (C-4) 90,000 | (C-2) 98,000 |

| Fund Balance Reserved for Encumbrances | |
|---|---|
| | (C-4) 90,000 |

## Financial Statements

Financial statements for the capital projects fund are prepared to show financial position, and revenues, other financing sources, expenditures and transactions, and changes in the fund balance. Statements for the capital projects fund of Model City are shown in Exhibits 7–1 and 7–2.

**EXHIBIT 7–1.** Model City Capital Projects Fund Balance Sheet—End of Period

| Assets | | Liabilities and Fund Balances | |
|---|---|---|---|
| Cash | $108,000 | Vouchers payable | $ 5,000 |
| | | Contract payable—retained percentage | 5,000 |
| | | Total liabilities | $ 10,000 |
| | | Fund balance | |
| | | Fund balance reserved for encumbrances | $ 90,000 |
| | | Unreserved fund balance | 8,000 |
| | | | $ 98,000 |
| Total assets | $108,000 | Total liabilities, reserves, and fund balance | $108,000 |

**EXHIBIT 7-2.**  Model City Capital Projects Fund—Statement of Revenues, Other Financing Sources, Expenditures, and Changes in Fund Balance for Period

|  | Budget | Actual | Variances Favorable/ (Unfavorable) |
|---|---|---|---|
| Revenues |  |  |  |
| Proceeds from sale of bonds | $500,000 | $500,000 | $        0 |
| Expenditures | 500,000 | 402,000 | 98,000 |
| Excess of revenues over expenditures | $        0 | $  98,000 | $98,000 |
| Fund balance at beginning of period | $        0 | $        0 | $        0 |
| Fund balance at end of period | $        0 | $  98,000 | $98,000 |
| Fund balance reserved for encumbrances |  | 90,000 |  |
| Unreserved fund balance |  | 8,000 |  |
| Total |  | $  98,000 |  |

## ■ Accounting for the Servicing of General Long-Term Debt

A debt-service fund is used to account for resources that are accumulated to pay interest on general long-term debt and to retire those obligations when they come due. The primary accounting objective is to show the sources of such funds and how they were used. This fund, like the capital projects fund, is *project oriented* and will remain in existence until the debt to be paid from its resources has been retired. Even though it is a project-oriented fund, a balance sheet disclosing the resources and obligations of the fund should be prepared at the end of each fiscal period to show the extent to which the debt retirement objective is being met.

In many respects, the debt-service fund is similar to a sinking fund used by a business to accumulate resources to retire bonded debt. It is different, however, in that it provides a level of resource segregation that is not normally found in sinking funds for profit enterprises. The debt-service fund goes beyond a simple earmarking of assets to the creation of a separate self-balancing accounting entity. In this section, we illustrate and explain the

1. establishment of a debt-service fund for Model City
2. investment of debt-service fund assets
3. journalizing of illustrative transactions
4. posting of transactions
5. preparation of debt-service fund financial statements
6. disposal of debt-service fund resources.

### Establishment of a Debt-Service Fund

A general bond issue may have a specified term or it may mature in series over a number of years. Bonds included in an issue that matures in total at a specified date are called *term bonds*. Those that mature in series (parts of the issue mature each year over a period of time) are called *serial bonds*. Regardless of which kind of issue is involved, resources realized from taxes must be set aside each year to be used for payment of interest and retirement of the bonds. Therefore, when general bonds are sold, a debt-service fund is generally established to accumulate and temporarily invest the earmarked resources. Those resources not used for the payment of interest generally are held in the debt-service fund until the bonds mature. When serial bonds are issued, resources will flow through the debt-service fund more rapidly because of the periodic payments made in retiring such bonds. This significantly reduces the investing responsibilities associated with operation of the debt-service fund.

Also, in situations where the debt-service fund is created for the purpose of accumulating funds to retire term bonds, some of its resources may be used to reacquire bonds from the issue to be retired on the open market rather than for investment in other securities. The resources of the fund should be invested to maximize return on them. Within the limits of safety and with certain price fluctuations, reacquisition of the entity's own bonds may be the best way to invest the fund's resources.

The establishment of a debt-service fund is often required by provisions of the bond indenture originated when bonds are issued. The first evidence of the debt-service fund as a separate accounting entity occurs when the amount of required contributions from the general fund or other sources is determined. At this time, the budget or authorization entry is made to establish the fund.

## Investment of Debt-Service Fund Assets

As resources are accumulated in the fund, they are invested to produce income until they are needed for the payment of interest and/or to retire the bonds. Operationally, this practice creates a need for recording interest or dividend income in the fund in much the same manner as such income is recorded in the sinking fund of a profit enterprise.

As observed before, the most efficient investment action in some instances may involve the reacquisition of some of the governmental entity's own outstanding bonds.

## Illustrative Transactions Journalized

Let's assume that Model City establishes a debt-service fund to retire the bonds whose proceeds were accounted for in the preceding portion of this chapter. Furthermore, we assume that the bonds have an 8-year life and that the required annual contribution from the general fund [see general fund transaction (1), page 176] is $50,000. The following typical transactions illustrate the recordkeeping practices followed in accounting for the acquisitions and uses of debt-service fund resources.

DS-1.    The bond indenture (see capital project fund, pages 214–220) includes a provision requiring the general fund to pay $50,000 per year into a debt-service fund [see appropriation in general fund transaction (1), p. 176]. It is estimated that the investment earnings will amount to $2,000 for the first year.

DS-2. The obligation of the general fund to contribute the appropriate amount to the debt-service fund is recognized [see general fund, transaction (5), pages 178–179].

DS-3. Payment is received from the general fund [see general fund, transaction (8), page 185].

DS-4. Debt-service fund resources of $49,000 are invested in securities.

DS-5. Interest income of $1,950 is received by the debt-service fund.

DS-6. Premium in the amount of $2,000 realized from the sale of bonds (see capital project fund, page 216) is acquired by the debt-service fund.

The following entries record the transactions of the debt-service fund:

**Transaction (DS-1)**

| | | |
|---|---|---|
| Estimated revenues from investments | 2,000 | |
| Required general fund contributions | 50,000 | |
| Budgetary fund balance | | 52,000 |

The bond-indenture provision, requiring the establishment of a debt-service fund to which the general fund will contribute $50,000 per year, is to the debt-service fund what the approval of the budget is to the general fund. Entry (DS-1) records this requirement in the debt-service fund records. When the budget for the general fund was approved, the required amount was appropriated and recorded in the general fund accounts [see general fund, transaction (1), page 176].

It is desirable to show the items included in entry (DS-1) in the debt-service fund records; however, because of the nature of budgetary accounts, this action may be left unrecorded.

**Transaction (DS-2)**

| | | |
|---|---|---|
| Due from general fund | 50,000 | |
| Transfers from general fund | | 50,000 |

**Transaction (DS-3)**

| | | |
|---|---|---|
| Cash | 50,000 | |
| Due from general fund | | 50,000 |

Entry (DS-2) records the amount receivable from the general fund. It is the first transaction involving actual financial data. "Transfers from general fund" shows the resources acquired from the general fund. The debit to "due from general fund" is an interfund account that constitutes an asset to the debt-service fund. The collection of this claim against the general fund is shown in entry (DS-3).

**Transaction (DS-4)**

| | | |
|---|---|---|
| Investments | 49,000 | |
| Cash | | 49,000 |

This entry records the investment of debt-service fund cash.

Transaction (DS-5)
| | | |
|---|---|---|
| Cash | 1,950 | |
|    Revenue from investments | | 1,950 |

The fact that interest amounting to $1,950 has been earned from debt-service fund investments is recorded in entry (DS-5).

Transaction (DS-6a)
| | | |
|---|---|---|
| Due from capital projects fund | 2,000 | |
|    Bond issue premium | | 2,000 |

Transaction (DS-6b)
| | | |
|---|---|---|
| Cash | 2,000 | |
|    Due from capital projects fund | | 2,000 |

This entry records the receipt of $2,000 from the capital projects fund.

## Closing Entries Journalized

The T-accounts illustrated next show that sources of actual revenues are as follows:

| | |
|---|---|
| Transfers from general fund | $50,000 |
| Interest earned on investments | 1,950 |
| Bond issue premium from capital project fund | 2,000 |

The budgetary accounts show that these figures are in line with the estimates, except for a difference of $50 in income from investments and $2,000 realized from the capital projects fund. The following closing entries facilitate this disclosure:

(C-1)
| | | |
|---|---|---|
| Dr. Budgetary fund balance | 52,000 | |
|    Cr. Estimated revenues from investment | | 2,000 |
|    Cr. Required general fund contributions | | 50,000 |

(C-2)
| | | |
|---|---|---|
| Dr. Transfers from general fund | 50,000 | |
| Dr. Revenue from investments | 1,950 | |
| Dr. Bond issue premium | 2,000 | |
|    Cr. Fund balance | | 53,950 |

## Posting the Transactions

The preceding entries are posted to the debt-service fund ledger accounts as illustrated in the following T-accounts. Each amount is keyed to its respective transaction by the transaction number listed in parentheses beside it.

Required General Fund Contributions

| | |
|---|---|
| (DS-1)  50,000 | (C-1)  50,000 |

Bond Issue Premium

| | |
|---|---|
| (C-2)  2,000 | (DS-6a)  2,000 |

Estimated Revenue from Investments

| | |
|---|---|
| (DS-1)  2,000 | (C-1)  2,000 |

Transfers from General Fund

| | |
|---|---|
| (C-2)  50,000 | (DS-2)  50,000 |

Due from Capital Projects Fund

| | |
|---|---|
| (DS-6a)  2,000 | (DS-6b)  2,000 |

Budgetary Fund Balance

| | |
|---|---|
| (C-1)  52,000 | (DS-1)  52,000 |

Due from General Fund

| | |
|---|---|
| (DS-2)  50,000 | (DS-3)  50,000 |

Cash

| | |
|---|---|
| (DS-3)  50,000 | (DS-4)  49,000 |
| (DS-5)  1,950 | |
| (DS-6b)  2,000 | |

Investments

| | |
|---|---|
| (DS-4)  49,000 | |

Revenue from Investments

| | |
|---|---|
| (C-2)  1,950 | (DS-5)  1,950 |

Fund Balance

| | |
|---|---|
| | (C-2)  53,950 |

## Financial Statements

Statements are prepared for the debt-service fund at the end of each fiscal period. They should disclose essentially the same information about the debt-service fund that previously illustrated statements for the general fund and capital projects fund show for those accounting entities. Statements prepared from the debt-service fund T-accounts are shown in Exhibits 7–3 and 7–4.

## Disposal of Debt-Service Fund Resources

No expenditures are included among the transactions for the debt-service fund illustrated in the preceding paragraphs. If interest had been paid from debt-service fund resources, the entry to record the obligation for interest would be reflected as follows:

| | | |
|---|---|---|
| Expenditures | xxxxx | |
|    Interest payable | | xxxxx |

The payment of the interest obligation would be recorded as follows:

| | | |
|---|---|---|
| Interest payable | xxxx | |
|    Cash | | xxxx |

**EXHIBIT 7–3.** Model City Debt-Service Fund Balance Sheet—End of Period

| | | | |
|---|---|---|---|
| Cash | $ 4,950 | Fund balance | $53,950 |
| Investments | 49,000 | | |
| Total assets | $53,950 | Total fund balance | $53,950 |

**EXHIBIT 7–4.** Model City Debt-Service Fund—Statement of Revenues, Other Financial Sources, Expenditures, and Changes in Fund Balance, End of Period

| | Requirements and Estimates | Actual Revenues and Expenditures | Variances Favorable/ (Unfavorable) |
|---|---|---|---|
| Transfer from general fund | $50,000 | $50,000 | $    0 |
| Revenues from investments | 2,000 | 1,950 | (50) |
| Bond issue premium from capital projects fund | 0 | 2,000 | 2,000 |
| Total | $52,000 | $53,950 | $1,950 |
| Fund balance at beginning of period | $    0 | $    0 | $    0 |
| Fund balance at end of period | $52,000 | $53,950 | $1,950 |

Expenditures to reflect the retirement of bonds could also be recorded by debiting expenditures and crediting cash. In the illustration for Model City, the fund will probably show only resource acquisitions and interest payments during the first seven years of its existence. By the end of the eighth year, assets amounting to approximately $500,000 should have accumulated in the debt-service fund for the purpose of retiring the bonds and they will be used to do that. If a balance remains in the debt-service fund after all requirements of the bond issue have been met, it will generally be turned back to the general fund to be used as needed for the general operations of the city.

It is important to note that, as funds are accumulated in a debt-service fund for the retirement of long-term debt, complementing entries are required in the general long-term debt account group to show that funds have been provided for that purpose. This involves debiting an amount-provided account and crediting the amount-to-be-provided account. When bonds are retired by use of debt-service fund resources, the debt payable account will be debited and the amount-provided account will be credited. These complementing entries are discussed further in Chapter 8.

## Use of Fiscal Agent to Service Debt

In some instances, a city may choose or be required by bond indenture to use a fiscal agent to receive and invest resources set aside for the retirement of debt. With such an arrangement, the debt-service fund would show "deposits with trustee" as its only asset. That asset, and the balancing fund balance account, would be adjusted as payments are made to the trustee. Expenditures would be recognized as the bonds are reported redeemed by the trustee.

# ■ Accounting for Capital Improvements Financed by Special Assessments

Prior to the issuance of GASB 6 (see summary on page 91), capital improvements, primarily benefiting a particular group of property owners and paid for largely from special assessments against those properties, were accounted for by use of a special assessment fund. With the issuance of GASB 6, however, that type fund has been eliminated from use for financial reporting purposes. This pronouncement recognizes that special assessments have two distinct phases:

1.  an initial phase that involves financing and constructing the project
2.  a second phase involving the collection of assessments, along with interest on them, and the repayment of obligations associated with financing the project.

Each of these elements of the special assessment project should be recorded in a separate fund maintained on the modified accrual basis.

Transactions relating to the construction phase of the project should be accounted for in a capital projects-type fund. The activities of that fund will typically include budget or authorization actions, the receipts of cash to be used in the construction, and the recognition of expenditures as the construction activities are carried out.

Transactions relating to the incurrence of long-term obligations against the project *involving no general liability of the governmental unit* and the servicing of that debt should be accounted for in an agency-type fund. This shows that the governmental entity's responsibilities are limited to acting as agent for the specially assessed property owners.

We now demonstrate how a typical set of assumed special assessment projects transactions for Model City should be recorded, summarized in T-accounts, and ultimately presented in financial statements. As you will see, we use two separate accounting entities like the ones described above. Also, we label all transactions with the letters "SA" to identify them as special assessment project-related transactions.

## Assumed Transactions

A typical set of transactions for a special assessment project for Model City follows. Some of these can be related to some of the general fund entries illustrated in Chapter 6, whereas others are more directly related to some of the special funds discussed in this chapter. To illustrate these entries, let's assume that the special assessment project has the following transactions:

SA-1.    A special assessment project is authorized that calls for the construction of streets in a new residential area. The general fund portion of these expenditures has been approved as part of the general fund appropriations [see transaction (1), page 176] for $25,000. This approval contemplated the assessment of a special tax levy of $225,000 against property owners in the area. The total authorized improvement is $250,000. The special tax levy is to be paid over a period of ten years.

SA-2.      The general fund contribution is received [see general fund transactions (5) and (8), pages 178–179 and 180].

SA-3.      Special assessment bonds, with a face value of $225,000, are issued at par to provide funds for construction.

SA-4.      Construction expenditures amounting to $200,000 are incurred. Of this amount, $10,000 is for services performed by the municipal garage.

SA-5.      Contracts amounting to $45,000 for completion of the street improvements are signed.

SA-6.      The contracts in transaction (SA-5) are completed, and obligations relating to them are recognized. It is agreed that 10 percent of the contract price will be retained pending satisfactory use of the streets for three months.

SA-7.      The first installment of the special tax levy ($22,500) is received.

SA-8.      Interest amounting to $6,075 is received on deferred assessments receivable.

SA-9.      Vouchers amounting to $230,000 are paid.

SA-10.      Interest amounting to $4,050 is paid to bondholders.

SA-11.      Interest amounting to $2,000 is due to be paid on bonds payable.

SA-12.      Interest amounting to $900 is due to be received on deferred assessments receivable.

## Journalizing, Financing, and Construction Transactions

The initial financing and construction transactions should be recorded in a *special assessment capital projects fund* as follows:

**Transaction (SA-1a)**

| | | |
|---|---|---|
| Estimated financing sources | 250,000 | |
|    Appropriations | | 250,000 |

**Transaction (SA-1b)**

| | | |
|---|---|---|
| Due from general fund | 25,000 | |
|    Transfers from general fund | | 25,000 |

Upon authorization of the street-improvement project, entry SA-1a is made to establish the special assessment capital projects fund. Because it is a type (1) transaction (see page 30), comparable to the budget entry for the general fund, it may in some instances be omitted from the fund accounting records.

Entry SA-1b, a type (2) transaction (see page 30), is recorded as the general fund recognizes its obligation to the special assessment capital project.

**Transaction (SA-2)**

| | | |
|---|---|---|
| Cash | 25,000 | |
| Due from general fund | | 25,000 |

**Transaction (SA-3a)**

| | | |
|---|---|---|
| Cash | 225,000 | |
| Contributions from property owners | | 225,000 |

Entry (SA-2) shows the receipt of cash from the general fund. Entry (SA-3a) shows the realization of cash from the sale of special assessment bonds. As you will see later, the obligation for the bonds is recorded in the special assessment agency fund (see transaction SA-3b).

**Transaction (SA-4)**

| | | |
|---|---|---|
| Expenditures | 200,000 | |
| Vouchers payable | | 190,000 |
| Due to municipal garage fund | | 10,000 |

**Transaction (SA-5)**

| | | |
|---|---|---|
| Encumbrances | 45,000 | |
| Reserve for encumbrances | | 45,000 |

**Transaction (SA-6a)**

| | | |
|---|---|---|
| Reserve for encumbrances | 45,000 | |
| Encumbrances | | 45,000 |

**Transaction (SA-6b)**

| | | |
|---|---|---|
| Expenditures | 45,000 | |
| Vouchers payable | | 40,500 |
| Contracts payable—retained percentage | | 4,500 |

Entries (SA-4), (SA-5), and (SA-6) are similar to those used to record the transactions illustrated for other funds of Model City. They are type (3), (4), and (5) transactions (see page 30), respectively.

**Transaction (SA-9)**

| | | |
|---|---|---|
| Vouchers payable | 230,000 | |
| Cash | | 230,000 |

When the special assessment project has been completed, a complementing entry should be recorded in the general fixed-asset account group debiting the appropriate fixed-asset account and crediting an investment in fixed assets from special assessments project. This entry is discussed further in Chapter 8.

## Closing Entries

We assume that the special assessment project was completed during the period. When that occurred, the nominal accounts of this fund would have been closed with the following entries:

| | | |
|---|---|---|
| **(C-1)** | | |
| Appropriations | 250,000 | |
|    Estimated financing sources | | 250,000 |
| | | |
| **(C-2a)** | | |
| Transfers from general fund | 25,000 | |
| Contributions from property owners | 225,000 | |
|    Expenditures | | 245,000 |
|    Fund balance | | 5,000 |

## Posting the Transactions

The journal entries recorded in the special assessment capital projects fund would be posted to the accounts in that fund, as shown in the following T-accounts. Each amount is keyed to its respective transaction by the number listed in parentheses beside it.

| Estimated Financing Sources | | | | Expenditures | | |
|---|---|---|---|---|---|---|
| (SA-1a) | 250,000 | (C-1)  250,000 | | (SA-4) | 200,000 | (C-2a)  245,000 |
| | | | | (SA-6b) | 45,000 | |

| Appropriations | | | | Vouchers Payable | | |
|---|---|---|---|---|---|---|
| (C-1) | 250,000 | (SA-1a)  250,000 | | (SA-9)  230,000 | (SA-4) | 190,000 |
| | | | | | (SA-6b) | 40,500 |

| Due from General Fund | | | | Due to Municipal Garage | |
|---|---|---|---|---|---|
| (SA-1b)  25,000 | (SA-2)  25,000 | | | | (SA-4)  10,000 |

| Transfers from General Fund | | | | Reserve for Encumbrances | |
|---|---|---|---|---|---|
| (C-2a)  25,000 | (SA-1b)  25,000 | | | (SA-6a)  45,000 | (SA-5)  45,000 |

| Cash | | | | Contract Payable—Retained Percentage | |
|---|---|---|---|---|---|
| (SA-2) | 25,000 | (SA-9)  230,000 | | | (SA-6b)  4,500 |
| (SA-3a) | 225,000 | | | | |

| Contributions from Property Owners | | | | Fund Balance | |
|---|---|---|---|---|---|
| (C-2a)  225,000 | (SA-3a)  225,000 | | | | (C-2a)  5,000 |

| Encumbrances | |
|---|---|
| (SA-5)  45,000 | (SA-6a)  45,000 |

## Financial Statements

The financial statements for the special assessment capital projects fund, drawn from the data in the T-accounts, would be similar to those shown earlier in the chapter for a capital projects fund used to account for general capital improvements. We present those statements in Exhibits 7–5 and 7–6.

## Journalizing the Debt-Service–Related Transactions

Transactions related to the special assessments, the incurrence of long-term obligations against the project, and the servicing of those obligations should be recorded in a *special assessment agency fund* as follows. Observe that this fund includes both spendable resources and general long-term debt-type accounts.

| Transaction (SA-1c) | | |
|---|---|---|
| Special assessments receivable—current | 22,500 | |
| Special assessments receivable—deferred | 202,500 | |
|   Revenues | | 22,500 |
|   Deferred revenues | | 202,500 |
| | | |
| Transaction (SA-3b) | | |
| Amounts to be provided from special assessments | 225,000 | |
|   Bonds payable from special assessments | | 225,000 |
| | | |
| Transaction (SA-7a) | | |
| Cash | 22,500 | |
|   Special assessments receivable—current | | 22,500 |
| | | |
| Transaction (SA-7b) | | |
| Amounts provided from special assessments | 22,500 | |
|   Amounts to be provided from special assessments | | 22,500 |

Entry (SA-1c) is a type (2) transaction (see page 30). It reflects the special tax levy originated to cover the portion of the cost to be borne by the primarily benefited property owners. Because $202,500 of the special assessment will not be available for use until after the end of the current period, that amount has been credited to deferred revenues.

**EXHIBIT 7–5.**  Model City Special Assessment Capital Projects Fund Balance Sheet— End of Period

| Assets | | Liabilities and Fund Balances | |
|---|---|---|---|
| Cash | $20,000 | Vouchers payable | $ 500 |
| | | Due to municipal garage fund | 10,000 |
| | | Contract payable—retained percentage | 4,500 |
| | | Fund balance | 5,000 |
| Total assets | $20,000 | Total liabilities and fund balance | $20,000 |

**EXHIBIT 7–6.** Model City Special Assessment Capital Projects Fund—Statement of Revenues, Expenditures, Transfers, and Changes in Fund Balance for Period

| | |
|---|---:|
| Revenues | |
| Contributions from property owners | $225,000 |
| Expenditures | |
| Construction | 245,000 |
| Excess (deficiency) of revenues over expenditures | ($ 20,000) |
| Transfers from general fund | 25,000 |
| Excess (deficiency) of revenues and transfers over | |
| expenditures | $   5,000 |
| Fund balance at beginning of period | 0 |
| Fund balance at end of period | $   5,000 |

Entry (SA-3b) is used to record the special assessment bonds payable and to show the amount that must be provided by property owners to meet those obligations. Entry (SA-7a) reflects the collection of the current special assessment and entry (SA-7b) is the complementing entry showing that $22,500 of the total amount to be provided by property owners has now been provided.

In our illustration, we assume that the bonds relating to the special assessment project must be paid from the assessments against the primarily benefited property owners. In some instances, the general credit of the city will be extended as a secondary source of funds in the event that the specially assessed property owners default on their obligations. The 1988 edition of GAAFR requires that special assessment debts for which the government is "obligated in some manner" be included in the general long-term debt account group.[1]

| | | |
|---|---:|---:|
| **Transaction (SA-8)** | | |
| Cash | 6,075 | |
| Revenues from interest | | 6,075 |
| | | |
| **Transaction (SA-10)** | | |
| Expenditures for interest | 4,050 | |
| Cash | | 4,050 |
| | | |
| **Transaction (SA-11)** | | |
| Expenditures for interest | 2,000 | |
| Interest payable | | 2,000 |
| | | |
| **Transaction (SA-12)** | | |
| Interest receivable | 900 | |
| Revenues from interest | | 900 |

1.  Government Finance Officers Association, *Government Accounting, Auditing, and Financial Reporting* (Chicago: Government Finance Officers Association, 1988), p. 57.

The collection of interest on deferred tax assessments receivable is recorded in entry (SA-8). Entry (SA-10) reflects the payment of interest on bonds payable. Observe that under the modified accrual basis the amount of the payment is debited to expenditures rather than to expense. Entries (SA-11) and (SA-12) are made to record the interest payable and receivable respectively at the end of the reporting period.

## Closing Entry

The nominal accounts of the special assessment agency fund should be closed with the following entry:

```
(C-2b)
Revenues                           22,500
Revenues from interest              6,975
    Expenditures for interest                  6,050
    Fund balance                              23,425
```

## Posting the Transactions

The journal entries recorded in the special assessment agency fund would be posted to the accounts in the fund as shown in the following T-accounts. Each amount is keyed to its respective transaction by the number listed in parentheses beside it.

| Special Assessments Receivable—Current | | Cash | |
|---|---|---|---|
| (SA-1c)  22,500 | (SA-7a)  22,500 | (SA-7a)  22,500 | (SA-10)  4,050 |
| | | (SA-8)     6,075 | |

| Special Assessments Receivable—Deferred | | Amount Provided by Property Owners | |
|---|---|---|---|
| (SA-1c)  202,500 | | | (SA-7b)  22,500 |

| Revenues | | Revenues from Interest | |
|---|---|---|---|
| (C-2b)  22,500 | (SA-1c)  22,500 | (C-2b)  6,975 | (SA-8)   6,075 |
| | | | (SA-12)    900 |

| Deferred Revenues | | Expenditures for Interest | |
|---|---|---|---|
| | (SA-1c)  202,500 | (SA-10)  4,050 | (C-2b)  6,050 |
| | | (SA-11)  2,000 | |

| Amounts to Be Provided from Special Assessments | | Interest Payable | |
|---|---|---|---|
| (SA-3b)  225,000 | (SA-7b)  22,500 | | (SA-11)  2,000 |

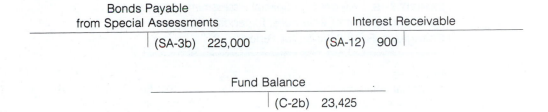

## Financial Statements

Financial statements for the special assessment agency fund are presented in Exhibits 7–7 and 7–8.

# ■ Reciprocal and Complementing Entries

As observed earlier, a number of the assumed transactions initiated in the four funds discussed in this chapter require reciprocal and/or complementing entries in other funds and account groups. These entries have been or will be illustrated in other chapters. However, it seems appropriate at this time to call attention to the other funds and account groups in which those entries are recorded. We do that in Exhibit 7–9.

# ■ Ethical Considerations Associated with Awarding a Capital Projects Contract

A city is initiating a capital project involving the expansion and improvement of its sewer system. A bond issue has been approved to provide financing for the project and the construction contract is about to be awarded to one of two contractors, both of whom are considered equally reliable. One contracting firm is local, and the other is located in a neighboring city. The low bid has been submitted by the nonlocal firm. The

---

**EXHIBIT 7–7.** Model City Special Assessment Agency Fund Balance Sheet—End of Period

| *Assets* | | *Liabilities and Fund Balances* | |
|---|---|---|---|
| Cash | $ 24,525 | Deferred revenues | $202,500 |
| Special assessment receivable—deferred | 202,500 | Interest payable | 2,000 |
| Interest receivable | 900 | Fund balance | 23,425 |
| Total | $227,925 | Total | $227,925 |
| *Bond Debt-Related Items* | | | |
| Amounts to be provided from special assessments | $202,500 | Bonds payable | $225,000 |
| Amounts provided from special assessments | 22,500 | | |
| Total | $452,925 | Total | $452,925 |

**EXHIBIT 7–8.** Model City Special Assessment Agency Fund—Statement of Revenues, Expenditures, and Changes in Fund Balance for Period

| | |
|---|---:|
| Revenues | |
| Special assessments | $22,500 |
| Revenues from interest | 6,975 |
| Total | $29,475 |
| Expenditures | |
| Expenditures for interest | 6,050 |
| Excess of revenues over expenditures | $23,425 |
| Fund balance at beginning of period | 0 |
| Fund balance at end of period | $23,425 |

**EXHIBIT 7–9.** Other Funds and Account Groups in Which Reciprocal and Complementing Entries Must Be Recorded

| Transactions Originating in Connection with General Capital Projects, Debt-Service, and Special Assessment Projects | Requires Reciprocal Entries In | Requires Complementing Entries In |
|---|---|---|
| CP-2 | | General long-term debt account group |
| CP-2a and 2b | Debt-service fund | General long-term debt account group |
| CP-3 | Municipal garage fund | General fixed-asset account group |
| CP-5b | | General fixed-asset account group |
| CP-6 | Municipal garage fund | |
| D5-5 | | General long-term debt account group |
| SA-4 and SA-6b | | General fixed-asset account group |

president of the local firm suggests that his firm should receive the contract anyway because it is a local taxpayer. Consider the ethical issues that might be involved in awarding the contract under these circumstances.

# ■ Summary

In this chapter, we have discussed and illustrated the elements of the accounting cycles for governmental funds other than the general fund. This included journalizing and posting transactions relating to general capital projects, debt service, and special assessment projects for Model City, plus the preparation of illustrative financial statements from the summarized financial data.

We explained the characteristics of each of the funds used in connection with those activities, and the stipulations associated with resources flowing through them, as we illustrated their accounting procedures. We observed that a capital projects fund is a project-oriented fund originated to account for the inflows and outflows of resources designated to be used in the acquisition of capital facilities that are not financed from general fund, special assessment, or enterprise fund resources. Although proceeds from the sale of bonds is the most frequent source of capital projects fund resources, they may also come from federal government grants or from other sources.

Debt-service funds are used to account for the inflows and outflows of resources designated to be used for the payment of interest and principal of general long-term debt. Inflows of resources are typically realized from general fund transfers and from the investment of resources held by the fund. We observed that these are also project-oriented funds that remain in existence until the general long-term debt has been retired.

Two funds are used to account for special assessment projects. A special assessment capital projects fund is used to account for the inflows and outflows of resources that are acquired and used in carrying out the project. A special assessment agency fund is used to account for the collections of special assessments, special assessment long-term debt, and the servicing of that debt.

# ■ Glossary

**Bond.** A written promise to pay a specified sum of money, called *the face value* or *principal amount,* at a specified date or dates in the future, called the *maturity date(s),* together with periodic interest at a specified rate. The difference between a note and a bond is that the latter runs for a longer period of time and requires greater legal formality.

**Bond Discount.** The excess of the face value of a bond over the price for which it is acquired or sold. The price does not include accrued interest at the date of acquisition or sale.

**Bond Fund.** A fund formerly used to account for the proceeds of general obligation bond issues. Such proceeds are now accounted for in a capital projects fund.

**Bond Ordinance or Resolution.** An ordinance or resolution authorizing a bond issue.

**Bond Premium.** The excess of the price at which a bond is acquired or sold over its face value. The price does not include accrued interest at the date of acquisition or sale.

**Bonds Authorized and Unissued.** Bonds that have been legally authorized but not issued and that can be issued and sold without further authorization. This term must not be confused with the term *margin of borrowing power* or *legal debt margin,* either one of which represents the difference between the legal debt limit of a government and the debt outstanding against it.

**Bonds Issued.** Bonds sold.

**Bonds Payable.** The face value of bonds issued and unpaid.

**Capital Outlays.** Expenditures that result in the acquisition of or addition to fixed assets.

**Capital Program.** A plan for capital expenditures to be incurred each year over a fixed period of years to meet capital need. It sets forth each project or other contemplated expenditure in which the government is to have a part and specifies the full resources estimated to be available to finance the projected expenditures.

**Capital Projects Fund.** A fund created to account for financial resources to be used for acquisition or construction of major capital facilities (other than those financed by proprietary funds, special assessment projects, and trust funds).

**Contracts Payable—Retained Percentage.** A liability account reflecting amounts due on construction contracts that have been completed but on which part of the liability has not been paid pending final inspection or the lapse of a specified time period, or both. The unpaid amount is usually a stated percentage of the contract price.

**Current Special Assessments.** Special assessments levied and becoming due within one year.

**Debt-Service Fund.** A fund established to account for the accumulation of resources for, and the payment of, general long-term debt principal and interest. Formerly called a *sinking fund*.

**General Obligation Bonds.** Bonds for the payment of which the full faith and credit of the issuing government are pledged.

**Matured Bonds Payable.** A liability account reflecting unpaid bonds that have reached or passed their maturity date.

**Other Financing Sources.** Governmental fund spendable resource inflows from long-term debt, transfers, and material amounts received from fixed-asset dispositions. A revenue-type account.

**Registered Bond.** A bond whose owner is registered with the issuing government and which cannot be sold or exchanged without a change of registration. Such a bond may be registered as to principal and interest or as to principal only.

**Serial Bonds.** Bonds included in an issue that mature in series (parts of the issue mature each year over a period of time).

**Special Assessment.** A compulsory levy made against certain properties to defray part or all of the cost of a specific improvement or service deemed to primarily benefit those properties.

**Special Assessment Bonds.** Bonds payable from the proceeds of special assessments. If the bonds are payable only from the collections of special assessments, they are known as special assessment bonds. If, in addition to the assessments, the full faith and credit of the government are pledged, they are known as general obligation special assessment bonds.

**Special Assessments Receivable—Current.** Uncollected special assessments that a government has levied and are due within one year.

**Special Assessments Receivable—Deferred.** Uncollected special assessments that a government has levied but that are not due within one year.

**Term Bonds.** Bonds included in an issue that mature in total on a specified date.

# ■ Questions for Class Discussion

**Q7-1.** What are the distinguishing operating characteristics of a governmental fund? Discuss fully.

**Q7-2.** How does a city determine how many governmental funds it should have within its accounting system? Explain.

**Q7-3.** Relate the definition of a fund to the type of resources accounted for in a capital projects fund. What is the accounting objective of such a fund?

**Q7-4.** Explain the difference between a project-oriented and a period-oriented fund. Give examples of each.

**Q7-5.** Are the bonds associated with a capital project reflected in the capital projects fund? Explain.

**Q7-6.** How should the resources realized as a premium on the sale of bonds associated with a capital project be used? Explain fully, including the logic associated with your answer.

**Q7-7.** Do we use encumbrance and expenditure accounts in the accounting records of a capital projects fund? Explain.

**Q7-8.** Under what circumstances would a city establish a debt-service fund? What are the operating objectives of such a fund?

**Q7-9.** Is the debt-service fund a project- or period-oriented fund? Explain.

**Q7-10.** How does a city account for bonds issued to finance a special assessment project? How are those accounting procedures different from those followed in recording bonds issued to finance a capital project?

**Q7-11.** What relationships exist between the following funds and/or account groups?
1. capital projects fund and general fixed-asset account group
2. debt-service fund and general long-term debt account group
3. general fund and debt-service fund
4. special assessment capital projects fund and general fixed-asset account group
5. general fund and special assessment capital projects fund
6. general fund and capital projects fund
7. capital projects fund and general long-term debt account group

# ■ Exercises

**E7-1.** The citizens of Home City have voted to issue bonds in the amount of $1,000,000 for the construction of a new municipal building. Record the following actions and transactions in the capital projects fund originated to account for proceeds from the sale of the bond issue.
1. A bond issue in the amount of $1,000,000 is authorized to finance the construction of the new municipal building.
2. The bonds are sold for $1,010,000.
3. The contract for constructing the new building is negotiated at a cost of $950,000.
4. Construction of the building is completed at a cost of $965,000, and the building is accepted by the city.

5. The obligation associated with the construction of the building is paid.
6. The accounts in the capital projects fund are closed, and unused resources are transferred to the debt-service fund.

**Required:**
Journalize the preceding actions and transactions in the capital projects fund.

**E7-2.** Refer to Exercise E7-1.

**Required:**
Indicate which of the transactions recorded in Exercise E7-1 would also require journal entries in other fund(s) and/or account group(s). Describe the journal entry required in each instance.

**E7-3.** Bonds having a face value of $2,000,000 are sold by a capital projects fund for $2,010,000.

**Required:**
A. What amount of resources would normally be available for the completion of the capital project? Explain.
B. Assume now that the bond issue has been sold for $1,990,000. What amount of resources would normally be available to be used on the project? Explain.

**E7-4.** A city establishes a debt-service fund to account for resources earmarked for the retirement of a general bond issue in the amount of $700,000. The following actions and transactions are carried out relating to that fund:
1. The debt-service fund is established in accordance with requirements of the bond indenture. That indenture requires the general fund to transfer $70,000 to the debt-service fund each year. It is anticipated that $5,000 can be earned from investing these funds during the next year.
2. The general fund recognizes its obligation to transfer $70,000 to the debt-service fund.
3. Payment is received by the debt-service fund from the general fund.
4. Debt-service fund resources are invested in interest-bearing securities.
5. Interest amounting to $4,500 is received.

**Required:**
Journalize the preceding transactions in the records of the debt-service fund.

**E7-5.** Refer to Exercise E7-4.

**Required:**
Indicate which of the entries in Exercise E7-4 require entries in other fund(s) and/or account group(s). List the fund(s) and/or account group(s) and the journal entries that should be made in each case.

**E7-6.** Assume now that a debt-service fund has the following balance sheet after meeting all obligations associated with a bond issue:

Cash        $5,000       Fund balance        $5,000

**Required:**

A. What journal entry is required to terminate the debt-service fund?

B. What other fund and/or account group would be affected by the termination of the debt-service fund? Journalize the entry in each case.

E7-7. A city enters into a special assessment project involving the use of resources contributed jointly by the city and property owners for the purpose of improving the streets and sidewalks in a residential section of the city. The operating arrangement calls for property owners to pay 75 percent of the improvement cost with the balance being paid from general fund resources. The following transactions relating to this project occur during the period:

1. A special assessment capital projects fund is authorized under an arrangement calling for property owner assessments of $75,000 and general fund contributions of $25,000 for the project.

2. The general fund contribution to the project is received.

3. Assessment notices are sent out to property owners calling for payment of the $75,000 over a period of five years.

4. The first annual payment of property owner assessments is received.

5. The city negotiates a long-term loan in the amount of $60,000 to be paid from property owner assessments as they are collected. The city has no liability for this loan.

6. The contract for the improvement project is signed. The total cost reflected on the contract is $95,000.

7. The contract is completed and the work is accepted by the city at the originally agreed-upon price.

**Required:**

A. Record the preceding transactions in the funds used for the special assessment project.

B. Identify the transactions requiring entries in the records of other fund(s) and/or account group(s). Journalize the entries in those fund(s) and/or account group(s).

E7-8. A city has just completed a street improvement project costing $300,000 that was financed and accounted for through a special assessment capital projects fund.

**Required:**

Journalize the entry that should be recorded in the fixed-asset account group upon completion of this project.

## ■ Problems

P7-1. The City of Bloomville (see Problem P6-1) adds a capital projects fund, a debt-service fund, and a special assessment project to its accounting system. These funds carry out the following actions and transactions during the year:

*Capital Projects Fund*
1. A general bond issue of $1,000,000 was authorized for the construction of a new municipal building.
2. The bonds (see item 1) were sold for $1,004,000.
3. Construction expenditures of $700,000 were incurred. Of this amount, $10,000 was for services performed by the Municipal Services Center.
4. Contracts amounting to $280,000 were signed for completion of the work on the building.
5. Part of the contract (see item 4) amounting to $100,000 was completed and a voucher was prepared to cover it. The actual amount to be paid, due to certain changes after the contract was signed, amounts to $104,000.
6. Vouchers amounting to $774,000 and the $10,000 due to the Municipal Services Center were paid.
7. The premium received on the sale of bonds is transferred to the debt-service fund.

*Debt-Service Fund*
1. The bond indenture for the capital projects fund bonds includes a provision requiring the general fund to pay $100,000 per year into a debt-service fund. The estimated earnings from investments is expected to amount to $4,000 for the current year. These data are to be recorded in the debt-service fund records.
2. The payment of $100,000 is received from the general fund.
3. Debt-service fund cash in the amount of $98,000 is invested in securities.
4. Interest income in the amount of $3,900 is received by the fund.
5. Premium in the amount of $4,000 realized from the sale of capital-projects-fund bonds is received from the capital projects fund.

*Special Assessment Project*
1. A special assessment project is authorized for the construction of streets in a new subdivision. The general fund portion of these expenditures was approved as part of general fund appropriations (see Problem P6-1) in the amount of $50,000. This approval was part of an agreement by the primarily benefited property owners to pay an assessment of $450,000. The total authorized improvement amounts to $500,000. The special tax levy is to be paid over a period of ten years.
2. The agreed-upon general fund contribution is received.
3. Special assessment bonds valued at $450,000 are issued at that price to provide funds for construction.
4. Construction expenditures amounting to $400,000 are incurred. Of this amount, $20,000 was for services performed by the Municipal Services Center.
5. Contracts amounting to $90,000 for completion of the street project are signed.
6. The contracted work in item 5 is completed and the obligation is recognized. It is agreed that 10 percent of the contract price will be retained pending satisfactory use of the streets for four months.
7. The first installment of the special tax levy amounting to $45,000 is received.
8. Interest amounting to $12,150 is received on the deferred assessments receivable.
9. Vouchers amounting to $460,000 are paid.

10. Interest amounting to $8,100 is paid to bondholders.
11. Interest amounting to $4,000 is due to be paid on the bonds.
12. Interest in the amount of $1,800 is due to be received on the deferred assessments receivable.

**Required:**
A. Record the preceding actions and transactions of the three funds in transactions worksheets for the funds. Observe that there are no beginning balances; therefore the first pair of columns in each case will be for transaction data.
B. Prepare end-of-year financial statements for each of the funds.

**P7-2.** Select the best answer for each of the following items:
1. The activities of a street improvement project that is being financed by requiring each owner of property facing the street to pay a proportionate share of the total cost should be accounted for in the:
   a. capital projects (bond) fund.
   b. general fund.
   c. special assessment capital projects fund.
   d. special revenue fund.
2. In order to provide for the retirement of general obligation bonds, the City of Osborn invests a portion of its receipts from general property taxes in marketable securities. This investment activity should be accounted for in:
   a. a capital projects fund.
   b. a debt-service fund.
   c. a trust fund.
   d. the general fund.
3. The City of Paden should use a capital projects fund to account for:
   a. structures and improvements constructed with the proceeds of a special assessment.
   b. proceeds of a bond issue to be used to acquire land for city parks.
   c. construction in progress on the city-owned electric utility plant, financed by an issue of revenue bonds.
   d. assets to be used to retire bonds issued to finance an addition to the city hall.
4. The liability for special assessment bonds that carry a secondary pledge of a municipality's general credit should be recorded in:
   a. an enterprise fund.
   b. a special revenue fund and general long-term debt group.
   c. a footnote in the statement of a general long-term debt.
   d. none of the above.
5. The proceeds of a federal grant made to assist in financing the future construction of an adult training center should be recorded in:
   a. the general fund.
   b. a special revenue fund.
   c. a capital projects fund.
   d. a special assessment capital projects fund.
   e. none of the above.

6. The receipts from a special tax levy to retire and pay interest on general obligation bonds issued to finance the construction of a new city hall should be recorded in:
   a. a debt-service fund.
   b. a capital projects fund.
   c. a revolving interest fund.
   d. a special revenue fund.
   e. none of the above.

7. A transaction in which a municipality issued general obligation serial bonds to finance the construction of a fire station requires accounting recognition in:
   a. the general fund.
   b. the capital projects and general fund.
   c. the capital projects fund and the general long-term debt group of accounts.
   d. the general fund and the general long-term debt group of accounts.
   e. none of the above.

8. Expenditures of $200,000 were made during the year on the fire station in item 7. This transaction requires accounting recognition in:
   a. the general fund.
   b. the capital projects fund and the general fixed-assets group of accounts.
   c. the capital projects fund and the general long-term debt group of accounts.
   d. the general fund and the general fixed-assets group of accounts.
   e. none of the above.

9. When Brockton City realized $1,020,000 from the sale of a $1,000,000 bond issue, the entry in its capital projects fund was:

| | | |
|---|---|---|
| Cash | $1,020,000 | |
|   Proceeds from bond issue | | $1,000,000 |
|   Bond premium | | 20,000 |

Recording the transaction in this manner indicates that:
   a. the $20,000 cannot be used for the designated purpose of the fund but must be transferred to another fund.
   b. the full $1,020,000 can be used by the capital projects fund to accomplish its purpose.
   c. the nominal rate of interest on the bonds is below the market rate for bonds of such term and risk.

                                                   **—AICPA Adapted**

**P7-3.** Select the best answer for each of the following items:
   1. A debt-service fund of a municipality is an example of which of the following types of fund?
      a. fiduciary
      b. governmental
      c. proprietary
      d. internal service
   2. A capital projects fund of a municipality is an example of what type of fund?

a. internal service (intragovernmental service)
b. proprietary
c. fiduciary
d. governmental

3. When a capital project is financed entirely from a single bond issue, and the proceeds of the bond issue equal the par value of the bonds, the capital projects fund would record this transaction by debiting cash and crediting:
a. bond issue proceeds.
b. fund balance.
c. appropriations.
d. bonds payable.

4. The debt-service fund of a governmental unit is used to account for the accumulation of resources to pay, and the payment of, general long-term debt:

|  | Principal | Interest |
|---|---|---|
| a. | Yes | Yes |
| b. | Yes | No |
| c. | No | No |
| d. | No | Yes |

—AICPA Adapted

**P7-4.** Select the best answer for each of the following items. Items 1 and 2 are based on the following information:

The following events relating to the City of Albury's debt-service funds occurred during the year ended December 31, 19X1:

| | |
|---|---:|
| Debt principal matured | $2,000,000 |
| Unmatured (accrued) interest on outstanding debt at Jan. 1, 19X1 | 50,000 |
| Interest on matured debt | 900,000 |
| Unmatured (accrued) interest on outstanding debt at Dec. 31, 19X1 | 100,000 |
| Interest revenue from investments | 600,000 |
| Cash transferred from general fund for retirement of debt principal | 1,000,000 |
| Cash transferred from general fund for payment of matured interest | 900,000 |

All principal and interest due in 19X1 were paid on time.

1. What is the total amount of expenditures that Albury's debt-service funds should record for the year ended December 31, 19X1?
a. $900,000
b. $950,000
c. $2,900,000
d. $2,950,000

2. How much revenue should Albury's debt-service funds record for the year ended December 31, 19X1?
a. $600,000
b. $1,600,000
c. $1,900,000
d. $2,500,000

Items 3 and 4 are based on the following information:

On December 31, 19X1, Madrid Township paid a contractor $2,000,000 for the total cost of a new firehouse built in 19X1 on Township-owned land. Financing was by means of a $1,500,000 general obligation bond issue sold at face amount on December 31, 19X1, with the remaining $500,000 transferred from the general fund.

3. What should be reported on Madrid's 19X1 financial statements for the capital projects fund?
   a. revenues, $1,500,000; expenditures, $1,500,000
   b. revenues, $1,500,000; other financing sources, $500,000; expenditures, $2,000,000
   c. revenues, $2,000,000; expenditures, $2,000,000
   d. other financing sources, $2,000,000; expenditures, $2,000,000

4. What should be reported on Madrid's 19X1 financial statements for the general fund?
   a. expenditures, $500,000
   b. other financing uses, $500,000
   c. revenues, $1,500,000; expenditures, $2,000,000
   d. revenues, $1,500,000; other financing uses, $2,000,000

—**AICPA Adapted**

**P7-5.** Select the best answer for each of the following items:
1. Grove Township issued $50,000 of bond anticipation notes at face amount in 19X9 and placed the proceeds into its capital projects fund. All legal steps were taken to refinance the notes, but Grove was unable to consummate refinancing. In the capital projects fund, what account should be credited to record the $50,000 proceeds?
   a. other financing sources control
   b. revenues control
   c. deferred revenues
   d. bond anticipation notes payable

2. On December 31, 19X8, Park Township paid a contractor $4,000,000 for the total cost of a new police building built in 19X8. Financing was by means of a $3,000,000 general obligation bond issue sold at face amount on December 31, 19X8, with the remaining $1,000,000 transferred from the general fund. What amount should Park record as resource inflows in the capital projects fund in connection with the bond issue proceeds and the transfer?
   a. $0
   b. $1,000,000
   c. $3,000,000
   d. $4,000,000

3. In 19X6, Menton City received $5,000,000 of bond proceeds to be used for capital projects. Of this amount, $1,000,000 was expended in 19X6. Expenditures for the $4,000,000 balance were expected to be incurred in 19X7. These bond proceeds should be recorded in capital projects funds for:
   a. $5,000,000 in 19X6.
   b. $5,000,000 in 19X7.
   c. $1,000,000 in 19X6 and $4,000,000 in 19X7.
   d. $1,000,000 in 19X6 and in the general fund for $4,000,000 in 19X6.

4. Burr City has approved a special assessment project providing for total assessments of $300,000, to be collected from affected property owners in five equal annual installments starting in 19X7. The entry to be made to record the levy of assessments in 19X7 is:

|  |  | Debit | Credit |
|---|---|---|---|
| a. | Special assessments receivable—current | $ 60,000 | |
|  | Special assessments receivable—deferred | 240,000 | |
|  | Revenues control | | $ 60,000 |
|  | Deferred revenues | | 240,000 |
| b. | Special assessments receivable—current | $ 60,000 | |
|  | Revenues control | | $ 60,000 |
| c. | Special assessments receivable | $300,000 | |
|  | Revenues control | | $300,000 |
| d. | Special assessments receivable | $300,000 | |
|  | Deferred revenues | | $300,000 |

5. In 19X8, Beech City issued $400,000 of bonds, the proceeds of which were restricted to the financing of a capital project. The bonds will be paid wholly from special assessments against benefited property owners. However, Beech is obligated to provide a secondary source of funds for repayment of the bonds in the event of default by the assessed property owners. In Beech's general purpose financial statements, this $400,000 special assessment debt should:
   a. not be reported.
   b. be reported in the special assessment fund.
   c. be reported in the general long-term debt account group.
   d. be reported in an agency fund.

Items 6 and 7 are based on the following information:
   On December 31, 19X7, Vane City paid a contractor $3,000,000 for the total cost of a new municipal annex built in 19X7 on city-owned land. Financing was provided by a $2,000,000 general obligation bond issue sold at face amount on December 31, 19X7, with the remaining $1,000,000 transferred from the general fund.

6. What account and amount should be reported in Vane's 19X7 financial statements for the general fund?
   a. other financing uses control, $1,000,000
   b. other financing sources control, $2,000,000
   c. expenditures control, $3,000,000
   d. other financing sources control, $3,000,000

7. What accounts and amounts should be reported in Vane's 19X7 financial statements for the capital projects fund?
   a. other financing sources control, $2,000,000; general long-term debt, $2,000,000
   b. revenues control, $2,000,000; expenditures control, $2,000,000
   c. other financing sources control, $3,000,000; expenditures control, $3,000,000
   d. revenues control, $3,000,000; expenditures control, $3,000,000

8.  During its fiscal year ended June 30, 19X8, Lake County financed the following projects by special assessments:

    | | |
    |---|---|
    | Capital improvements | $2,000,000 |
    | Service-type projects | 800,000 |

    For financial reporting purposes, what amount should appear in special assessment funds?
    a.  $2,800,000
    b.  $2,000,000
    c.  $800,000
    d.  $0

9.  In connection with Albury Township's long-term debt, the following cash accumulations are available to cover payment of principal and interest on:

    | | |
    |---|---|
    | Bonds for financing of water treatment plant construction | $1,000,000 |
    | General long-term obligations | 400,000 |

    The amount of these cash accumulations that should be accounted for in Albury's debt-service funds is:
    a.  $0.
    b.  $400,000.
    c.  $1,000,000.
    d.  $1,400,000.

10.  The following information pertains to Wood Township's long-term debt. Cash accumulations to cover payment of principal and interest on:

     | | |
     |---|---|
     | General long-term obligations | $350,000 |
     | Proprietary fund obligations | 100,000 |

     How much of these cash accumulations should be accounted for in Wood's debt-service funds?
     a.  $0
     b.  $100,000
     c.  $350,000
     d.  $450,000

     —**AICPA Adapted**

**P7-6.**  The Village of Hope, by referendum on November 30, 19X1, was authorized to sell bonds, the proceeds of which were to be used for constructing a municipal building to provide adequate facilities for the offices and departments of the Village. The cost of the building was estimated to be $90,000, and the ordinance provided for the issuance of general obligation bonds in that amount, at an interest rate of 8 percent per annum. Bonds were to be dated January 1, 19X2, and were to become due and payable in equal annual installments on January 1 of each of the nine years beginning in 19X4. Interest was to be due semiannually on January 1 and July 1, except that the first coupon was to be due on July 1, 19X3. Bonds were to be payable out of the proceeds of a direct annual tax sufficient to pay the principal and interest when due. Funds for payment of interest and retirement of bonds are to be accumulated in and paid from the general fund.

The Village advertised for bids on the bonds, and on January 15, 19X2, the bids were opened and the bonds awarded to Municipal Bond Company. The following transactions occurred:

1. November 30, 19X1 — Bonds were authorized in accordance with the referendum.
2. February 1, 19X2 — Bonds were sold to Municipal Bond Company and a certified check was received in the amount of $93,636, including premium and accrued interest at 8 percent to date of sale.
3. February 10, 19X2 — Initial architectural fees of $2,000 were paid to the firm which prepared the plans and specifications and was to have construction supervision. The fee for their services was to be 6 percent of the building cost.
4. April 15, 19X2 — The general contractor had bid $81,400 to construct the building. The first contractor's invoice in the amount of $30,000 was received from the architect, properly approved. The invoice was paid, less 10 percent retained until the building was accepted by the Village.
5. July 30, 19X2 (entry as of September 1, 19X2) — The appropriation ordinance of the Village for the fiscal year ending August 31, 19X3, was adopted. The ordinance contained provision for the retirement of the bonds due on January 1, 19X4, and interest due through that date. It has been the experience of the Village that the tax levy should provide an additional 3 percent to provide for losses and costs on collection.
6. September 20, 19X2 — The final contractor's invoice was received in the amount of $54,500, including approved extras totaling $3,100. The invoice was paid less a 10 percent retention. At the same time, an invoice in the amount of $2,000 was paid to the architects.
7. December 21, 19X2 — Final approval of the building was given by the architect and the Board of Trustees and final payments were made to the general contractor and architect.

**Required:**
Journalize the preceding transactions in the capital projects fund. *Key* the entries to the transaction number indicated.

—AICPA Adapted

P7-7. The City Hall capital projects fund was established on July 1, 19A, to account for the construction of a new City Hall financed by the sale of bonds. The building was to be constructed on a site owned by the City.

The building construction was to be financed by the issuance of 10-year $2,000,000 general obligation bonds bearing interest at 8 percent. Through prior arrangement $1,000,000 of these bonds were sold on July 1, 19A. The remaining bonds are to be sold on July 1, 19B.

The only funds in which transactions pertaining to the new City Hall were recorded were the City Hall capital projects fund and the general fund. The capital projects fund's trial balance follows:

### City of Larnaca City Hall Capital Project Fund June 30, 19B

|  | Debit | Credit |
|---|---|---|
| Cash | $ 893,000 | |
| Appropriation expenditures | 180,500 | |
| Encumbrances | 715,500 | |
| Accounts payable to general fund | | $ 11,000 |
| Reserve for encumbrances | | 723,000 |
| Appropriations | | 1,055,000 |
| | $1,789,000 | $1,789,000 |

An analysis of the appropriation expenditures account follows:

|  | Debit |
|---|---|
| 1. A progress billing invoice from General Construction Company (with which the City contracted for the construction of the new City Hall for $750,000—other contracts will be let for heating, air conditioning, etc.) showing 10 percent of the work completed | $ 75,000 |
| 2. A charge from the general fund for work done in clearing the building site | 11,000 |
| 3. Payments to suppliers for building materials and supplies purchased | 14,500 |
| 4. Payment of interest on bonds outstanding | 80,000 |
| | $180,500 |

An analysis of the reserve for encumbrances account follows:

|  | Debit (Credit) |
|---|---|
| 1. To record contract with General Construction Company | $(750,000) |
| 2. Purchase orders placed for materials and supplies | (55,000) |
| 3. Receipt of materials and supplies and payment therefor | 14,500 |
| 4. Payment of General Construction Company invoice less 10 percent retention | 67,500 |
| | $(723,000) |

An analysis of the appropriations account follows:

|  |  | Debit (Credit) |
| --- | --- | --- |
| 1. | Face value of bonds sold | $(1,000,000) |
| 2. | Premium realized on sale of bonds | (55,000) |
|  |  | $(1,055,000) |

**Required:**
Prepare a worksheet for the City Hall capital projects fund at June 30, 19B, showing:
A.  preliminary trial balance
B.  adjustments (formal journal entries are not required)
C.  adjusted trial balance.

—**AICPA Adapted**

**P7-8.**  The city of Bergen entered the following transactions during 19XX:
1.  A bond issue is authorized by vote to provide funds for the construction of a new municipal building, estimated to cost $500,000. The bonds are to be paid in ten equal installments from a debt-service fund, payments being due March 1 of each year. Any balance of the bond fund is to be transferred directly to the debt-service fund.
2.  An advance of $40,000 is received from the general fund to underwrite a deposit of $60,000 on the land contract. The deposit is made.
3.  Bonds with a face value of $450,000 are sold for cash at 102. A decision is made to sell only a portion of the bonds, because the cost of the land was less than expected.
4.  Contracts amounting to $390,000 are let to Michela and Company, the lowest bidder, for construction of the municipal building.
5.  The temporary advance from the general fund is repaid, and the balance on the land contract is paid.
6.  Based on the architect's certificate, warrants are issued for $320,000 for the work completed to date.
7.  Warrants paid in cash by the treasurer amount to $310,000.
8.  Because of changes in the plans, the amount of the contract with Michela and Company is revised to $440,000. The remainder of the bonds are sold at 101.
9.  The building is finished before the end of the year, and additional warrants amounting to $115,000 are issued to the contractor in final payment for the work. All warrants are paid by the treasurer.

**Required:**
A.  Record the preceding transactions and closing entries in T-accounts for the capital projects fund. Key the entries in the T-accounts by number to the preceding data.
B.  Prepare an applicable fund balance sheet for the capital projects fund as of December 31, 19XX.

—**AICPA Adapted**

**P7-9.**   The city of Jarrell authorized a sewer project, estimated to cost $500,000, and a bond issue of $350,000 to permit deferral of assessment payments. According to the terms of the project, property owners were to be assessed 80 percent of the estimated cost of construction and the balance was to be made available by the city. The following transactions occurred relating to the project during the year:

1. Bonds with a face value of $300,000 were sold for $301,000. Any premium on sale is to be earmarked for payment of interest.
2. The first of five equal annual assessments from property owners was collected. From each assessment $30,000 is to be set aside to be used in retiring the bonds.
3. The general fund contribution is received.
4. Payment is made on construction in the amount of $185,000.
5. Interest expense in the amount of $5,000 is paid.
6. Interest received on deferred assessments in the amount of $8,000.
7. Remainder of bond issue is sold for $50,500.
8. Payment is made on construction in the amount of $170,000.
9. Accrued interest expense in the amount of $5,000 is recognized.
10. Interest receivable in the amount of $6,000 is recognized.

**Required:**

A. Prepare a special assessment capital projects fund worksheet in which you record the transactions relating to the sewer project. The project was not completed at the end of the year.

B. Prepare a special assessment agency fund worksheet in which you record the appropriate transactions relating to the special assessment project.

**P7-10.**   The City of Westgate's fiscal year ends on June 30. During the fiscal year ended June 30, 19X0, the City authorized the construction of a new library and sale of general-obligation term bonds to finance the construction of the library. The authorization imposed the following restrictions:

> Construction cost was not to exceed $5,000,000.
>
> Annual interest rate was not to exceed 8½ percent.

The City does not record project authorizations, but other budgetary accounts are maintained. The following transactions relating to the financing and construction of the library occurred during the fiscal year ended June 30, 19X1:

1. On July 1, 19X0, the City issued $5,000,000 of 30-year 8 percent general obligation bonds for $5,100,000. The semiannual interest dates are December 31 and June 30. The premium of $100,000 was transferred to the library debt-service fund.
2. On July 3, 19X0, the library capital projects fund invested $4,900,000 in short-term commercial paper. These purchases were at face value with no accrued interest. Interest on cash invested by the library capital projects fund must be transferred to the library debt-service fund. During the fiscal year ending June 30, 19X0, estimated interest to be earned is $140,000.
3. On July 5, 19X0, the City signed a contract with F&A Construction Company to build the library for $4,980,000.

4. On January 15, 19X1, the library capital projects fund received $3,040,000, from the maturity of short-term notes purchased on July 3. The cost of these notes was $3,000,000. The interest of $40,000 was transferred to the library debt-service fund.

5. On January 20, 19X1, F&A Construction Company properly billed the City $3,000,000 for work performed on the new library. The contract calls for 10 percent retention until final inspection and acceptance of the building. The library capital projects fund paid F&A $2,700,000.

6. On June 30, 19X1, the library capital projects fund made the proper adjusting entries (including accrued interest receivable of $103,000) and closing entries.

### Required:

A. Prepare in good form journal entries to record the six preceding sets of facts in the library capital projects fund. List the transaction numbers (1 to 6) and give the necessary entry or entries. Do not record journal entries in any other fund or group of accounts.

B. Prepare in good form a balance sheet for the City of Westgate—library capital projects fund as of June 30, 19X1.

—AICPA Adapted

# CHAPTER 8

# Accounting for Other Funds and Account Groups

## ■ Learning Objectives

When you have finished your study of this chapter, you should

1. Be capable of recording and posting the transactions of a proprietary fund.
2. Understand the operating characteristics of fiduciary funds and know how to record transactions in those funds.
3. Be able to recognize the transactions requiring complementing entries in account groups and be able to record them.
4. Know how to prepare financial statements for internal service, enterprise, and fiduciary funds.
5. Be able to prepare statements for both the general long-term debt and general fixed-asset account groups.

Having described the accounting procedures for the various governmental funds in the preceding chapters, we are now ready to turn our attention to the other types of accounting entities described in the GAAFR Statement of Principles. As we have observed, these accounting entities can be classified into three general categories:

1. proprietary funds
2. fiduciary funds
3. account groups.

After we have described and illustrated the procedures to be followed in accounting for these funds and account groups, we shall summarize our observations regarding *interfund relationships*.

# ■ Accounting for Proprietary Funds

Proprietary are reservoirs of resources established to carry on specified activities on a self-sustaining basis. They fall into two principal categories characterized as internal service funds and enterprise funds. *Internal service funds* are established to account for resources set apart to provide services or commodities for other departments of the same governmental unit.[1] *Enterprise funds,* on the other hand, are used to account for resources committed to self-supporting activities of governmental units that render services to the general public on a user-charge basis.[2] Although we use the term *self-sustaining* to describe proprietary funds, some of them may not be completely self-sustaining. *Any fund receiving a majority of its revenues from user fees should be accounted for as a proprietary fund.* Accounting procedures for two proprietary funds for Model City are described and illustrated in the pages that follow. Our illustrations will be concerned with

1. describing briefly the special accounting practices followed in accounting for proprietary fund activities
2. illustrating internal-service-fund accounting procedures
3. illustrating enterprise-fund accounting procedures.

## Specialized Accounting Procedures

The accounting procedures for all funds discussed thus far have been designed primarily to disclose accountability for the acquisitions and disposals of spendable resources. Revenues realized by these funds are not judged to be dependent on the earning power of assets held by the fund. The revenue realization potential is determined either directly or indirectly by the power to tax. Consistent with that line of reasoning, the accountant's primary responsibility in governmental fund accounting is to show dollar accountability by reflecting information regarding the flows of spendable resources through the fund.

Proprietary funds, like profit enterprises, are expected to sustain themselves through their operations. *Their accounting systems, therefore, should be organized like those of profit enterprises.* As a result, the accounting procedures for these funds use the full accrual basis of accounting, including a distinction between capital and revenue items and the recognition of depreciation of fixed assets.

## Internal-Service-Fund Accounting Procedures

The governmental activities most frequently carried on through internal service funds are maintenance and supply functions. We now illustrate the procedures followed in accounting for such funds by assuming that Model City has established a municipal

1. National Council on Governmental Accounting, *NCGA Statement 1* (Chicago: Municipal Finance Officers Association, 1979), p. 7.
2. Ibid.

garage to maintain city vehicles. The following transactions relating to this fund are assumed to have occurred during the fiscal period. After the assumed transactions have been journalized and posted, we will illustrate the financial statements that should be prepared for the fund. (The code letters "SS" are used to designate the fund as a self-sustaining fund.)

SS-1.   A contribution of $85,000 is received from the general fund to establish a vehicles maintenance center [see general fund transactions (1), (5), and (8), pages 176, 178, and 180].

SS-2.   Equipment costing $35,000 and supplies costing $10,000 are purchased.

SS-3.   Expenses of $40,000 are incurred during the period and $4,000 worth of supplies are used.

SS-4.   Services and parts are billed to other funds as follows:

| | |
|---|---:|
| General fund | $35,000 |
| Special assessment capital projects fund | 10,000 |
| Capital projects fund | 5,000 |

SS-5.   Cash is received from billings to the general fund and capital projects fund.

SS-6.   Vouchers amounting to $75,000 are paid.

SS-7.   Equipment is depreciated over a ten-year life with no salvage value.

The following journal entries record these transactions:

**Transaction (SS-1)**

| | | |
|---|---:|---:|
| Cash | 85,000 | |
| Capital contribution from general fund | | 85,000 |

**Transaction (SS-2)**

| | | |
|---|---:|---:|
| Equipment | 35,000 | |
| Supplies | 10,000 | |
| Vouchers payable | | 45,000 |

**Transaction (SS-3)**

| | | |
|---|---:|---:|
| Expenses | 44,000 | |
| Supplies | | 4,000 |
| Vouchers payable | | 40,000 |

**Transaction (SS-4)**

| | | |
|---|---:|---:|
| Due from general fund | 35,000 | |
| Due from special assessment capital projects fund | 10,000 | |
| Due from capital projects fund | 5,000 | |
| Revenue from services | | 50,000 |

**Transaction (SS-5)**

| | | |
|---|---:|---:|
| Cash | 40,000 | |
| Due from general fund | | 35,000 |
| Due from capital projects fund | | 5,000 |

**Transaction (SS-6)**

| | | |
|---|---|---|
| Vouchers payable | 75,000 | |
| Cash | | 75,000 |

**Transaction (SS-7)**

| | | |
|---|---|---|
| Expenses | 3,500 | |
| Accumulated depreciation | | 3,500 |

The accounts of the municipal garage fund are closed with the following entry:

**(C-1)**

| | | |
|---|---|---|
| Revenue from services | 50,000 | |
| Expenses | | 47,500 |
| Unreserved retained earnings | | 2,500 |

The preceding journal entries are posted to the self-sustaining fund accounts, as illustrated in the following T-accounts. Items are keyed to their transactions by the numbers in parentheses beside them.

| Cash | | Capital Contribution from General Fund | |
|---|---|---|---|
| (SS-1) 85,000 | (SS-6) 75,000 | | (SS-1) 85,000 |
| (SS-5) 40,000 | | | |

| Equipment | | Vouchers Payable | |
|---|---|---|---|
| (SS-2) 35,000 | | (SS-6) 75,000 | (SS-2) 45,000 |
| | | | (SS-3) 40,000 |

| Supplies | | Expenses | |
|---|---|---|---|
| (SS-2) 10,000 | (SS-3) 4,000 | (SS-3) 44,000 | (C-1) 47,500 |
| | | (SS-7) 3,500 | |

| Due from General Fund | | Revenue from Services | |
|---|---|---|---|
| (SS-4) 35,000 | (SS-5) 35,000 | (C-1) 50,000 | (SS-4) 50,000 |

| Due from Special Assessment Capital Projects Fund | | Accumulated Depreciation | |
|---|---|---|---|
| (SS-4) 10,000 | | | (SS-7) 3,500 |

| Due from Capital Projects Fund | | Unreserved Retained Earnings | |
|---|---|---|---|
| (SS-4) 5,000 | (SS-5) 5,000 | | (C-1) 2,500 |

The financial statements for this fund are similar to those for a profit enterprise. A statement of operations shows the revenues earned and expenses incurred for the period, and a balance sheet reflects residual balances. Statements should also be prepared to show the changes in the retained earnings account and cash flows. The first three of these statements, prepared from the T-accounts for the Model City Municipal Garage Fund, are shown in Exhibits 8–1, 8–2, and 8–3. The statement of cash flows is prepared from comparative balance sheets and other supplemental data. It is shown in Exhibit 8–4.

## Enterprise-Fund Accounting Procedures

Governmental units often own and operate their own utilities or other service enterprises that cover most or all of their operating costs through user charges. If these enterprises produce excess revenues over expenses, the net revenues can be used to finance part of the city's operating costs. These entities are characterized as *enterprise funds*. Generally, they are expected to operate on much the same basis as do profit entities furnishing similar services. They are, in effect, treated as individual business enterprises, and business accounting practices are followed in maintaining records of their activities. Periodical financial statements are prepared to show the results of operations and financial position.

**EXHIBIT 8–1.** Model City Municipal Garage Fund Statement of Operations for Period

| | | |
|---|---:|---:|
| Revenues from services | | $50,000 |
| Expenses | | |
| General expense | $40,000 | |
| Supplies expense | 4,000 | |
| Depreciation expense | 3,500 | $47,500 |
| Excess of revenues over expenses | | $ 2,500 |

**EXHIBIT 8–2.** Model City Municipal Garage Fund Balance Sheet—End of Period

| Assets | | | Liabilities and Fund Balance | |
|---|---:|---:|---|---:|
| Current assets | | | Current liabilities | |
| Cash | | $50,000 | Vouchers payable | $10,000 |
| Due from special assessment fund | | 10,000 | | |
| Supplies | | 6,000 | Contribution from general fund | 85,000 |
| | | $66,000 | | |
| Fixed assets | | | | |
| Equipment | $35,000 | | Unreserved retained earnings | 2,500 |
| Less accumulated depreciation | 3,500 | 31,500 | | |
| | | | Total Liabilities and Fund | |
| Total Assets | | $97,500 | Balance | $97,500 |

**EXHIBIT 8–3.**  Model City Municipal Garage Fund Statement of Retained Earnings

| | |
|---|---:|
| Balance of unreserved retained earnings—beginning of period | $ 0 |
| Add: excess of revenues over expenses for period | 2,500 |
| Balance of unreserved retained earnings—end of period | $2,500 |

**EXHIBIT 8–4.**  Model City Municipal Garage Fund Statement of Cash Flows

| | | | |
|---|---:|---:|---:|
| Cash provided by | | | |
|   Operations | | | |
|     Net income | | $ 2,500 | |
|     Add depreciation | | 3,500 | |
|     Increase to vouchers payable | | 10,000 | |
|     Total | | $16,000 | |
|     Less increase in due from accounts | $10,000 | | |
|       Increase to supplies | 6,000 | 16,000 | $ 0 |
|   Capital and related financing activities | | | |
|     Contribution from general fund | | | $ 85,000 |
|   Investing activities | | | |
|     Purchase of equipment | | | (35,000) |
|   Increase in cash | | | $ 50,000 |

The initial "equity" capital, similar to the contributed capital for a business, generally comes from the resources of the governmental unit. Accounts labeled to show the sources of the capital contributions then become the "equity" accounts of the enterprise fund. Long-term financing can also be acquired through the issuance of bonds secured by assets and/or anticipated income. These bonds are generally obligations of the fund rather than of the city; consequently, they are retired from revenues earned by the fund rather than from tax revenues. A retained earnings account is used to account for accumulated earnings.

An enterprise fund comes into existence when a governmental unit decides that it will provide some basic utility service, such as water, electricity, or natural gas, to its citizens on a user-fee basis. Other services may be provided in response to public demand or because of an unwillingness of private enterprises to provide them. Resources committed to the operations of hospitals, airports, swimming pools, and golf courses, within an arrangement calling for *patient or customer fees to be collected for services rendered,* are other examples of enterprise funds. The significant characteristic that is common to all of these activities is that they are financed primarily by fees charged to people using them based on some measure of usage.

The GASB's Codification of Governmental Accounting and Financial Reporting Standards (1987 Codification) states that enterprise funds should be used to account for operations:

a. "that are financed and operated in a manner similar to private business enterprises—where the intent of the governing body is that costs (expenses, including depreciation) of providing goods or services to the general public on a continuing basis be financed or recovered primarily through user charges; or

b. where the governing body has decided that periodic determination of revenues earned, expenses incurred, and/or net income is appropriate for capital maintenance, public policy, management control, accountability, or other purposes."[3]

It is important to recognize the difference between user fees and taxes as sources of financing for services provided to citizens. Services provided on a user-fee basis are paid for on the basis of the amount of services received by each citizen. On the other hand, services provided by tax revenues are paid for on the basis of some measure of ability to pay but are distributed to citizens on the basis of their needs. When a city is considering how various services should be financed, this becomes an important political and sociological consideration. In our present political environment, the resistance to additional taxes has caused governmental units to move toward the use of more user fee arrangements in providing services.

Although an enterprise fund may not be required by law to adopt a budget of the type illustrated for governmental funds, sound financial administration requires budgetary planning similar to that used for business enterprises. Budgeted expenses should be tied to the anticipated level of demand for service rather than appropriated in specific amounts as is done in budgeting governmental-type fund operations.

*In general, the accounting practices for enterprise funds should be essentially the same as those followed for businesses.* The accrual basis of accounting should be used, including a distinction between capital and revenue items and the recognition of depreciation. The actual assets and liabilities resulting from the issuance of bonds are also reflected in the enterprise-fund balance sheet rather than in separate account groups. Separate account designations may be used within the enterprise fund to account for the proceeds of bond issues and other specifically restricted monies such as those set aside for the retirement and servicing of debt. In these respects, the asset classifications may be more specifically described than would typically be the case for assets similarly originated within a profit enterprise unit.

To illustrate the procedures followed in accounting for enterprise fund activities, let's assume that Model City acquires a water utility company and establishes an enterprise fund to account for its operations. The company provides water service for the citizens of Model City. We further assume that the company was acquired by using $100,000 of general fund resources (see page 178) and by selling $700,000 of revenue bonds. The balance sheet for Model City Water Fund immediately after acquisition is shown in Exhibit 8–5. (The code letter "E" is used to designate the fund as an enterprise fund.)

---

3. Government Finance Officers Association, *Governmental Accounting, Auditing and Financial Reporting* (Chicago: Government Finance Officers Association, 1988), p. 61.

**EXHIBIT 8–5.** Model City Water Utility Fund Balance Sheet—Beginning of Period

*Assets*

| Current assets | | |
|---|---|---|
| Cash | | $120,000 |
| Accounts receivable | | 20,000 |
| Supplies | | 5,000 |
| Total current assets | | $145,000 |
| Utility plant | | |
| Land | | $100,000 |
| Buildings | $300,000 | |
| Accumulated depreciation | 100,000 | 200,000 |
| Equipment | $600,000 | |
| Allowance for depreciation | 150,000 | 450,000 |
| Total assets | | $895,000 |

*Liabilities and Equity Balance*

| Current liabilities | |
|---|---|
| Vouchers payable | $ 65,000 |
| Revenue bonds payable | 10,000 |
| Customer deposits | 30,000 |
| Total current liabilities | $105,000 |
| Other liabilities | |
| Revenue bonds payable | 690,000 |
| Fund balance | |
| Contribution from city | 100,000 |
| Total liabilities and equity balance | $895,000 |

During the reporting period, the following transactions occur:

E-1.    Customers are billed for services in the amount of $600,000.

E-2.    Collections on account amount to $575,000.

E-3.    Meter deposits amounting to $7,000 are received from new customers.

E-4.    Meter deposits amounting to $900 are refunded to customers.

E-5.    General operating expenses amounting to $375,000 are incurred.

E-6.    Materials and supplies costing $35,000 are purchased on account.

E-7.    The inventory of materials and supplies at the end of the period amounts to $12,000.

E-8.    It is estimated that $450 of customer accounts receivable will be uncollectible.

E-9.    Depreciation amounting to $20,000 on buildings and $60,000 on equipment is recorded.

E-10.   Prepaid operating expenses at the end of the period amount to $2,000.

E-11.   Matured revenue bonds payable amounting to $10,000 plus current year interest on all bonds amounting to $30,000 are paid.

E-12.   Revenue bonds amounting to $10,000 due to be paid within one year are transferred to a current liability classification.

E-13.   Cash in the amount of $36,000 is transferred to a bond debt-service fund.

E-14.   General nonoperating expenses amounting to $5,000 are incurred.

E-15.   Cash in the amount of $30,000 held in the bond debt-service fund is invested in securities.

E-16.   Operating expenses amounting to $3,000 are accrued at the end of the period.

E-17.   Cash amounting to $1,800 is received as income from bond debt-service fund investments.

E-18.   Accounts judged to be uncollectible in the amount of $300 are written off.

E-19.   Vouchers payable in the amount of $410,000 are paid.

After the transactions listed above have been recorded, the accounts of the enterprise fund are closed as of the end of the fiscal period, and financial statements are prepared.

The following journal entries record the transactions:

Transaction (E-1)

| | | |
|---|---|---|
| Accounts receivable | 600,000 | |
| Water sales | | 600,000 |

Transaction (E-2)

| | | |
|---|---|---|
| Cash | 575,000 | |
| Accounts receivable | | 575,000 |

**Transaction (E-3)**

| | | |
|---|---|---|
| Cash | 7,000 | |
| Customer deposits | | 7,000 |

**Transaction (E-4)**

| | | |
|---|---|---|
| Customer deposits | 900 | |
| Cash | | 900 |

**Transaction (E-5)**

| | | |
|---|---|---|
| General operating expenses | 375,000 | |
| Vouchers payable | | 375,000 |

**Transaction (E-6)**

| | | |
|---|---|---|
| Supplies | 35,000 | |
| Vouchers payable | | 35,000 |

**Transaction (E-7)**

| | | |
|---|---|---|
| Supplies expense | 28,000 | |
| Supplies | | 28,000 |

**Transaction (E-8)**

| | | |
|---|---|---|
| Bad debt expense | 450 | |
| Allowance for bad debts | | 450 |

**Transaction (E-9)**

| | | |
|---|---|---|
| Depreciation expense | 80,000 | |
| Accumulated depreciation buildings | | 20,000 |
| Accumulated depreciation equipment | | 60,000 |

**Transaction (E-10)**

| | | |
|---|---|---|
| Prepaid operating expense | 2,000 | |
| General operating expenses | | 2,000 |

**Transaction (E-11)**

| | | |
|---|---|---|
| Revenue bonds payable | 10,000 | |
| Interest expense | 30,000 | |
| Cash | | 40,000 |

**Transaction (E-12)**
No entry required

**Transaction (E-13)**

| | | |
|---|---|---|
| Bond debt-service fund cash | 36,000 | |
| Cash | | 36,000 |

**Transaction (E-14)**

| | | |
|---|---|---|
| General nonoperating expenses | 5,000 | |
| Vouchers payable | | 5,000 |

**Transaction (E-15)**

| | | |
|---|---|---|
| Bond debt-service fund investments | 30,000 | |
| Bond debt-service fund cash | | 30,000 |

**Transaction (E-16)**

| | | |
|---|---|---|
| Operating expenses | 3,000 | |
| Accrued operating expenses | | 3,000 |

Transaction (E-17)
| | | |
|---|---|---|
| Bond debt-service fund cash | 1,800 | |
| Income from bond debt-service fund | | 1,800 |

Transaction (E-18)
| | | |
|---|---|---|
| Allowance for bad debts | 300 | |
| Accounts receivable | | 300 |

Transaction (E-19)
| | | |
|---|---|---|
| Vouchers payable | 410,000 | |
| Cash | | 410,000 |

The following entries are made at the end of the period to close the accounts:

(C-1)
| | | |
|---|---|---|
| Income summary | 519,450 | |
| Operating expenses | | 376,000 |
| Supplies expense | | 28,000 |
| Bad debt expense | | 450 |
| Depreciation expense | | 80,000 |
| Interest expense | | 30,000 |
| Nonoperating expense | | 5,000 |

(C-2)
| | | |
|---|---|---|
| Water sales | 600,000 | |
| Income from bond debt-service fund | 1,800 | |
| Income summary | | 601,800 |

(C-3)
| | | |
|---|---|---|
| Income summary | 82,350 | |
| Retained earnings | | 82,350 |

The preceding transactions and closing entries are posted to T-accounts, as illustrated next:

| Cash | | | Equipment | | Retained Earnings | |
|---|---|---|---|---|---|---|
| Bal 120,000 | 900 (E-4) | | Bal 600,000 | | | 82,350 (C-3) |
| (E-2) 575,000 | 40,000 (E-11) | | | | | |
| (E-3) 7,000 | 36,000 (E-13) | | | | | |
| | 410,000 (E-19) | | | | | |

| Accounts Receivable | | Accumulated Depreciation—Equipment | | Water Sales | |
|---|---|---|---|---|---|
| Bal 20,000 | 575,000 (E-2) | | 150,000 Bal | (C-2) 600,000 | 600,000 (E-1) |
| (E-1) 600,000 | 300 (E-18) | | 60,000 (E-9) | | |

| Supplies | | | | Vouchers Payable | | | | General Operating Expense | | | |
|---|---|---|---|---|---|---|---|---|---|---|---|
| Bal | 5,000 | 28,000 | (E-7) | (E-19) | 410,000 | 65,000 | Bal | (E-5) | 375,000 | 2,000 | (E-10) |
| (E-6) | 35,000 | | | | | 375,000 | (E-5) | (E-16) | 3,000 | 376,000 | (C-1) |
| | | | | | | 35,000 | (E-6) | | | | |
| | | | | | | 5,000 | (E-14) | | | | |

| Land | | | Revenue Bonds Payable | | | | Supplies Expense | | | |
|---|---|---|---|---|---|---|---|---|---|---|
| Bal | 100,000 | | (E-11) | 10,000 | 700,000 | Bal | (E-7) | 28,000 | 28,000 | (C-1) |

| Building | | | Customer Deposits | | | | Bad Debt Expense | | | |
|---|---|---|---|---|---|---|---|---|---|---|
| Bal | 300,000 | | (E-4) | 900 | 30,000 | Bal | (E-8) | 450 | 450 | (C-1) |
| | | | | | 7,000 | (E-3) | | | | |

| Accumulated Depreciation—Buildings | | | Contribution from City | | | Allowance for Bad Debts | | | |
|---|---|---|---|---|---|---|---|---|---|
| | 100,000 | Bal | | 100,000 | Bal | (E-18) | 300 | 450 | (E-8) |
| | 20,000 | (E-9) | | | | | | | |

| Depreciation Expense | | | | Prepaid Operating Expense | | Interest Expense | | | |
|---|---|---|---|---|---|---|---|---|---|
| (E-9) | 80,000 | 80,000 | (C-1) | (E-10) | 2,000 | (E-11) | 30,000 | 30,000 | (C-1) |

| Bond Debt-Service Fund Cash | | | | General Nonoperating Expenses | | | | Bond Debt-Service-Fund Investments | |
|---|---|---|---|---|---|---|---|---|---|
| (E-13) | 36,000 | 30,000 | (E-15) | (E-14) | 5,000 | 5,000 | (C-1) | (E-15) | 30,000 |
| (E-17) | 1,800 | | | | | | | | |

| Accrued Operating Expenses | | | Income from Bond Debt-Service Fund | | | | Income Summary | | | |
|---|---|---|---|---|---|---|---|---|---|---|
| | 3,000 | (E-16) | (C-2) | 1,800 | 1,800 | (E-17) | (C-1) | 519,450 | 601,800 | (C-2) |
| | | | | | | | (C-3) | 82,350 | | |

At the end of the fiscal period a balance sheet, statement of revenues and expenses, and statement of retained earnings would be prepared as shown in Exhibits 8–6, 8–7, and 8–8. A statement of cash flows is also prepared from comparative balance sheets and other supplementary data as shown in Exhibit 8–9.

**EXHIBIT 8–6.**   Model City Water Utility Fund Balance Sheet—End of Period

| Assets | | | Liabilities and Equity Balances | |
|---|---|---|---|---|
| Current assets | | | Current liabilities | |
| Cash | | $215,100 | Vouchers payable | $ 70,000 |
| Accounts receivable | $ 44,700 | | Revenue bonds payable | 10,000 |
| Allowance for bad debts | 150 | 44,550 | Customer deposits | 36,100 |
| Supplies | | 12,000 | Accrued operating expense | 3,000 |
| Prepaid operating expense | | 2,000 | | |
| Total current assets | | $273,650 | Total current liabilities | $119,100 |
| Bond debt-service fund | | | Other liabilities | |
| Cash | $ 7,800 | | | |
| Investments | 30,000 | 37,800 | Revenue bonds payable | 680,000 |
| Utility plant | | | Total liabilities | $799,100 |
| Land | | $100,000 | Contribution from city | 100,000 |
| Building | $300,000 | | | |
| Accumulated depreciation | 120,000 | 180,000 | Retained earnings | 82,350 |
| | $600,000 | | | |
| Equipment | | | | |
| Accumulated depreciation | 210,000 | 390,000 | | |
| | | 670,000 | | |
| Total assets | | $981,450 | Total liabilities and equity balance | $981,450 |

**EXHIBIT 8–7.** Model City Water Utility Fund Statement of Revenues and Expenses for Period

| | | |
|---|---:|---:|
| Operating revenues | | |
| Water sales | | $600,000 |
| Operating expenses | | |
| General operating expenses | $376,000 | |
| Supplies expense | 28,000 | |
| Depreciation expense | 80,000 | 484,000 |
| Net operating income | | $116,000 |
| Nonoperating revenue | | |
| Income from bond debt-service fund | | 1,800 |
| Total income | | $117,800 |
| Nonoperating expenses | | |
| Bad debt expense | $    450 | |
| Interest expense | 30,000 | |
| General | 5,000 | 35,450 |
| Net income to retained earnings | | $  82,350 |

**EXHIBIT 8–8.** Model City Water Utility Fund Analysis of Changes in Retained Earnings for Period

| | |
|---|---:|
| Balance of retained earnings—beginning of period | $        0 |
| Net income for period | 82,350 |
| Balance of retained earnings—end of period | $82,350 |

# ■ Fiduciary Funds

As we have observed, some resource units operate in such a way that they fail to fit neatly into either a governmental or proprietary fund category. Such units contain some resources that should be accounted for on a dollar-accountability basis and others for which proprietary fund accounting practices are appropriate. Trust and agency funds fit into this category. *These funds are used to account for resources received and held by the government in the capacity of trustee, custodian, or agent.* As the name implies, this group of funds can include trust funds whose resources may be held over a long period as well as certain agency funds held only for a brief period of time. All of these funds, however, have one characteristic in common: the fact that the governmental unit has a *fiduciary responsibility* for the fund's resources, which it holds subject to specific contractual commitments.

Trust and agency funds may be expendable, nonexpendable, or a combination of partially expendable and partially nonexpendable. Perhaps the most frequently encountered type of *expendable trust fund* is the one used to account for the resources of

**EXHIBIT 8–9.**  Model City Water Utility Fund Statement of Cash Flows

| | | |
|---|---:|---:|
| Cash provided by | | |
| Operations | | |
| Net income | | $ 82,350 |
| Add Depreciation | $ 80,000 | |
| Increase to vouchers payable | 5,000 | |
| Increase to customer deposits | 6,100 | |
| Increase to accrued operating expense | 3,000 | 94,100 |
| | | $176,450 |
| Less Increase to accounts receivable | 24,550 | |
| Increase to supplies | 7,000 | |
| Increase to prepaid expense | 2,000 | 33,550 |
| | | $142,900 |
| Capital and related financing activities | | |
| Payment of bonds | $(10,000) | |
| Establishment of debt-service fund | (37,800) | 47,800 |
| Increase to cash balance | | $ 95,100 |
| Cash balance—end of period | | $215,100 |
| Cash balance—beginning of period | | 120,000 |
| Increase in cash | | $ 95,100 |

pension and retirement systems. Resources made available to the city for the purpose of providing loans that must be repaid to maintain the original fund balance is an example of a *nonexpendable trust fund.* The combination expendable/nonexpendable-type of trust and agency fund arises when the city receives resources that are to be invested with the income to be used for specified purposes. Within this arrangement, the principal of the fund must be kept intact and only the income it produces is available to be used for designated purposes. This type of fund requires a careful distinction between expendable and nonexpendable resources and therefore involves some elements of accounting procedures normally found in accounting for governmental funds and others that require governmental fund type procedures.

When a governmental unit receives resources under an arrangement like the one just described, a separate accounting entity is established to reflect accountability in accordance with the agreement under which the assets are received. The accounting records for the nonexpendable part of these funds are ordinarily maintained on the accrual basis, which requires revenues to be recognized as they are earned. The governmental entity must account for the acquisitions and uses of resources to show that fund operations and investments have complied with the trust and agency agreement.

To illustrate the accounting procedures for a *hybrid-type trust fund,* we assume that Model City receives resources for such a fund and has the following transactions relating to those resources. (The code letters "TA" are used to designate the fund as a trust and agency fund.)

TA-1.  The city receives $100,000 from a wealthy citizen under the stipulated terms that the contribution is to be invested with revenues from the investment to be used to provide band concerts in the city parks.

TA-2.  The cash is invested.

TA-3.  Interest income amounting to $2,500 is earned and received.

TA-4.  Expenditures of $2,000 are made for band concerts.

The following journal entries record these transactions:

**Transaction (TA-1)**

| | | |
|---|---|---|
| Principal cash | 100,000 | |
| Fund balance reserved for endowment | | 100,000 |

**Transaction (TA-2)**

| | | |
|---|---|---|
| Investments | 100,000 | |
| Principal cash | | 100,000 |

**Transaction (TA-3)**

| | | |
|---|---|---|
| Income cash | 2,500 | |
| Income | | 2,500 |

**Transaction (TA-4)**

| | | |
|---|---|---|
| Expenditures against income | 2,000 | |
| Income cash | | 2,000 |

The following entry is used at the end of the period to close the nominal accounts:

**(C-1)**

| | | |
|---|---|---|
| Income | 2,500 | |
| Expenditures against income | | 2,000 |
| Unreserved fund balance | | 500 |

These entries involve only one significant departure from other entries illustrated in this chapter. This difference consists of the distinction made between principal and income resources, which is required by the trust indenture. We could make this distinction by using separate fund entities for income assets and principal assets. Generally, however, we use a lower level of restriction involving a designation of assets according to their sources complemented by separate fund balance accounts. This type of accountability is similar to that formerly used in accounting for special assessment fund resources.

The preceding journal entries are posted to the trust and agency fund accounts as illustrated in the following T-accounts. Postings are keyed to transactions by the numbers in parentheses beside them.

| Principal Cash | | | Fund Balance Reserved for Endowment | |
|---|---|---|---|---|
| (TA-1) 100,000 | (TA-2) 100,000 | | | (TA-1) 100,000 |

| Investments | | | Unreserved Fund Balance | |
|---|---|---|---|---|
| (TA-2) 100,000 | | | | (C-1) 500 |

| Income Cash | | | | Income | |
| --- | --- | --- | --- | --- | --- |
| (TA-3)  2,500 | (TA-4)  2,000 | | (C-1)  2,500 | (TA-3)  2,500 |

| Expenditures Against Income | |
| --- | --- |
| (TA-4)  2,000 | (C-1)  2,000 |

Trust and agency funds generally require three statements: a balance sheet, a statement of cash receipts and disbursements, and a statement of changes in fund balances. Since these statements are relatively simple to prepare from the ledger accounts shown above, and the format is the same as previously presented for other funds, we omit them here.

As we noted in Chapter 3, GASB 9 now requires the preparation of a statement of cash flows for all *proprietary and nonexpendable* trust funds. However, instead of the three categories of cash flows required by FASB 95, this pronouncement requires that cash flows be classified into the following categories:

1. operating
2. noncapital financing
3. capital and related financing
4. investing.

As we observed in Chapter 3, a trust and agency fund is also used to account for contributions to public employer retirement systems (PERS). Generally accepted accounting principles for such funds were originally set out in NCGA Statement 1 and the subsequent interpretation (Interpretation 4) of that statement and of NCGA Statement 6. NCGA Statement 6 fundamentally required that information on the actuarial present values of accumulated plan benefits be computed and presented somewhat in accordance with the provisions of FASB 35. It required disclosure of the following information in footnotes to the financial statements:

1. vested benefits of participants receiving payments
2. vested benefits of current employees
3. vested accumulated benefits of current employees.

However, as observed in Chapter 3, neither FASB 35 nor NCGA Statement 6 is now *required* to be followed by governmental entities in reporting on defined benefits pension plans. The GASB has been expected to issue a statement spelling out the reporting requirements that should be met, but, as of the date that this book is being written, has only issued the following "stop gap" statements.

GASB Statement 2, entitled *Financial Reporting of Deferred Compensation Plans Adopted under the Provisions of Internal Revenue Code Section 457*, states that such plan balances may be displayed in an agency fund of the governmental employer that has legal access to the resources regardless of whether those resources are held by the employer or some other party. Governmental public utilities and public authorities (self-sustaining entities) should also report a liability in their balance sheets with a corresponding designated asset.

GASB Statement 4, entitled *Applicability of FASB Statement 87, Employers' Accounting for Pensions to State and Local Governmental Employees,* requires that governmental employers not change their accounting and financial reporting of pension activities as a result of FASB Statement 87.

GASB Statement 5, entitled *Disclosure of Pension Information by Public Employee Retirement Systems and State and Local Governmental Employers,* was also issued in 1986. It requires that the pension benefit obligation of defined benefit pension plans, calculated using the actuarial present value of credited projected benefits, be disclosed along with a description of the plan, a summary of significant policies and actuarial assumptions, and the contributions required and made during the reporting period. In addition, ten years of supplementary information is mandated. That schedule should include information about net assets available for benefits, accrued pension benefit obligations, and a comparison of revenues by source to expenses by type. However, the 1988 edition of GAAFR points out that these statements do *provide specific guidance* on pension trust fund accounting. If these guidelines are followed, contributions to a pension trust fund by a governmental fund will be recognized as expenditures in that fund's accounting records. Their receipt by the pension trust fund will be recorded as revenues (part of the amount shown as contributions in Exhibit 8–10) in that fund. Furthermore, the employer's contribution expressed as percentages of annual covered payroll should be disclosed to the extent available for a *minimum of three years.*

The most recent edition of *Governmental Accounting, Auditing, and Financial Reporting,* published in 1988, shows a model operating statement and balance sheet for a pension trust fund similar to those reflected in Exhibits 8–10 and 8–11 for Illustration Pension Trust Fund. These statements would, of course, have to be supplemented by the data required by GASB 5.

As we noted in Chapter 3, GASB 12 requires certain disclosures relating to postemployment benefits other than pension benefits by state and local government employers. However, no changes in accounting and financial reporting practices should be made until the GASB has completed its project relating to these items.

**EXHIBIT 8–10.** Illustration Pension Trust Fund—Statement of Revenues, Expenses, and Changes in Fund Balances, Year Ending 12/31/X1

| | | |
|---|---:|---:|
| Operating revenues | | |
| Interest | | $ 30,000 |
| Contributions (employer's $85,000; employees' $85,000) | | $ 170,000 |
| Total operating revenues | | $ 200,000 |
| Operating expenses | | |
| Benefit payments | $25,000 | |
| Refunds to terminated employees | 10,000 | |
| Administration | 5,000 | 40,000 |
| Net income to fund | | $ 160,000 |
| Fund balance at beginning of year | | 1,400,000 |
| Fund balance at end of year | | $1,560,000 |

**EXHIBIT 8–11.** Illustration Pension Trust Fund—Balance Sheet, 12/31/X1

| Assets | |
|---|---|
| Cash | $ 60,000 |
| Investments | 1,488,000 |
| Interest receivable | 1,000 |
| Fixed assets net of depreciation | 5,000 |
| Due from other funds | 10,000 |
| Total assets | $1,564,000 |

| Liabilities and Fund Balance | |
|---|---|
| Accounts payable | $ 4,000 |
| Fund balance reserved for employees' retirement | 1,560,000 |
| Total liabilities and fund balance | $1,564,000 |

# ▪ Account Groups

Governmental units also use accounting entities whose primary objectives are to provide data relating to the acquisition values of fixed assets and the status of general long-term debt. No spendable resources are associated with these accounting entities. The general fixed-asset and general long-term debt account groups are examples of accounting entities included in this category.

An account group is different from a fund in that it is not a reservoir for appropriable resources. It is designed to disclose financial facts not normally provided by governmental fund records that reflect no ultimate distinction between capital and revenue items. Because of their position in the overall framework of fund accounting, they are sometimes referred to as "memo" account groups. Since they are expected to meet a disclosure weakness of governmental fund accounting, there are typically two of these account groups—one for *general fixed assets* and another for *general long-term debt*.

After we have described and illustrated the general accounting procedures for these account groups, we shall examine two NCGA statements that directly relate to account group accounting procedures.

## General Fixed-Asset Account Group

This account group discloses the acquisition values of the fixed assets of a governmental unit that are not accounted for in proprietary funds or trust funds and discloses the sources of funds used to acquire those assets. It is established as general fixed assets are acquired from the resources of various governmental-type funds. Entries for asset acquisitions in this accounting entity are directly related to expenditure entries of the general, special revenue, capital projects, and special assessment capital projects fund records. Assets associated with proprietary funds and trust funds, are reflected in the accounts of those funds.

We now illustrate how the records of the general fixed-asset account group are maintained. To help clarify the need for this accounting entity, we first compare entries used by a business with those used by a governmental unit to record the acquisitions of fixed assets by use of general fund resources.

Entry for business entity
Asset                                                            xxx
   Vouchers payable or cash                                                xxx

Entries for a governmental unit
  General fund
Expenditures                                                     xxx
   Vouchers payable or cash                                                xxx

  General fixed-asset account group
Asset                                                            xxx
   Investment in fixed assets—from general fund                            xxx

If we eliminate the debit to "expenditures" and the credit to "investment in fixed assets—from general fund," we leave the same account balances open for the city as are shown in the records of the business entity. Therefore, the fragmentation of accounting data into separate fund entities with no distinction between capital and revenue items within governmental fund records makes the use of this account group necessary to provide records relating to fixed assets.

The accounting equation for the fixed-asset account group accounting equity may be stated as follows:

$$\text{assets} = \text{investments in fixed assets}$$

Assets, on the left side of the equation, are debited to reflect increases and credited to recognize decreases. Investments in fixed assets are credited to show increases and debited to reflect decreases.

**Illustrative Transactions.**   Because each transaction in the general fixed-asset account group is associated with some governmental fund entry, *each entry listed for this accounting entity is keyed to the fund entry giving rise to it.* Assume that the following balances existed in the accounts before the current fiscal period began:

| | |
|---|---|
| Equipment | $450,000 |
| Structures and improvements | 900,000 |
| Investment in general fixed assets—from general fund | 750,000 |
| Investment in general fixed assets—from capital projects fund | 400,000 |
| Investment in general fixed assets—from special assessment capital projects fund | 200,000 |

Observe that we have included structures and improvements in the general fixed-asset account group. Both the AICPA Industry Audit Guide and the 1988 edition of GAAFR (see page 53 of that publication) make the inclusion of such "infrastructure" assets optional. From the point of view of the principle of full disclosure, however, it is preferable to include them.

Transactions from the various fund entities requiring complementing entries in the fixed-asset account group are as follows (the code letters "FA" are used to designate a fixed-asset account group):

FA-1.    New street maintenance equipment costing $145,000 is acquired (from general fund entry 7, page 179).

FA-2.    Old street maintenance equipment originally costing $60,000 is sold for $5,000 (from general fund entry 9, p. 180).

FA-3.    Street improvements amounting to $350,000 are completed (from capital projects fund entry CP-3, page 217).

FA-4.    Another unit of street improvements costing $52,000 is completed (from capital projects fund entry CP-5b, page 217).

FA-5.    Street improvements costing $245,000 are completed (from special assessment capital projects fund entries SA-4 and SA-6b, page 228).

The following journal entries record the preceding transactions in the records of the general fixed-assets account group:

Transaction (FA-1)
| | | |
|---|---|---|
| Equipment | 145,000 | |
|    Investment in general fixed assets—from | | |
|       general fund | | 145,000 |

Transaction (FA-2)
| | | |
|---|---|---|
| Investment in general fixed-assets—from | | |
|       general fund | 60,000 | |
|    Equipment | | 60,000 |

Transaction (FA-3)
| | | |
|---|---|---|
| Structures and improvements | 350,000 | |
|    Investment in general fixed assets—from | | |
|       capital projects fund | | 350,000 |

Transaction (FA-4)
| | | |
|---|---|---|
| Structures and improvements | 52,000 | |
|    Investment in general fixed assets—from | | |
|       capital projects fund | | 52,000 |

Transaction (FA-5)
| | | |
|---|---|---|
| Structures and improvements | 245,000 | |
|    Investment in general fixed assets—from special | | |
|       assessment project | | 245,000 |

The entries to record asset acquisitions in this accounting entity are designed to show the original costs of fixed assets and the sources of the funds used to acquire them. Entries (FA-1), (FA-3), (FA-4), and (FA-5) illustrate this feature of fixed-asset accounting.

When assets are retired, the entry originally made to reflect the acquisition is reversed. Entry (FA-2) illustrates this removal procedure. Revenue from the disposal of this asset is recorded in the general fund. The fund authorized to receive cash realized from the disposal of a fixed asset is determined by laws and policies. In the absence of any legal or established policy requirements, these proceeds are credited either to the fund that originally financed the asset or to the general fund.

The preceding journal entries are posted to the accounts of the general fixed-asset account group as illustrated in the following T-accounts:

| Equipment | | | | Investment in General Fixed Assets— from General Fund | | |
|---|---|---|---|---|---|---|
| Balance | 450,000 | (FA-2) | 60,000 | (FA-2) 60,000 | Balance | 750,000 |
| (FA-1) | 145,000 | | | | (FA-1) | 145,000 |

| Structures and Improvements | | Investment in General Fixed Assets— from Capital Projects Fund | | |
|---|---|---|---|---|
| Balance | 900,000 | | Balance | 400,000 |
| (FA-3) | 350,000 | | (FA-3) | 350,000 |
| (FA-4) | 52,000 | | (FA-4) | 52,000 |
| (FA-5) | 245,000 | | | |

| Investment in General Fixed Assets— from Special Assessment Project | | |
|---|---|---|
| | Balance | 200,000 |
| | (FA-5) | 245,000 |

**Statements.**   Since the fixed-asset account group is a memo record and is not involved with the flows of appropriable resources, it does not require a statement showing the sources and uses of resources. Exhibit 8–12 illustrates the kind of statement that is generally appropriate for this account group.

The statement of general fixed assets may be supplemented by other schedules for more complete disclosure of fixed-asset data. For example, statements may be prepared to show general fixed assets by functions or to disclose changes in general fixed assets over a period of time.

**EXHIBIT 8–12.**   Model City Statement of General Fixed Assets—End of Period

| Assets Held | | Sources of Funds Used to Acquire Assets | |
|---|---|---|---|
| Equipment | $ 535,000 | Investment in general fixed assets | |
| Structures and improvements | 1,547,000 | From general fund | $ 835,000 |
| | | From capital projects fund | 802,000 |
| | | From special assessment fund | 445,000 |
| Total | $2,082,000 | Total | $2,082,000 |

## General Long-Term Debt Account Group

This account group shows the status of a governmental entity's general long-term debt. Although most long-term debt is likely to be in the form of general obligation bonds, this accounting entity should also reflect the amounts of other general long-term debt, such as *obligations on capital lease agreements* and *long-term notes*. Obligations on capital lease agreements should be reflected at an amount equal to the discounted present value of future payments.

The amounts of the general long-term liabilities are shown as credits and the status of accumulations toward their retirement is reflected as debits. General long-term obligations may be incurred to finance operations or for the acquisition of long-term assets. General obligation debt may also be incurred to acquire fixed assets for a proprietary fund. Under NCGA Statement 1, if such general long-term debt is intended to be repaid from proprietary fund operations, these obligations should be shown only in the proprietary fund balance sheet. However, if they are to be retired by use of general fund resources, or if the city may become "obligated in some manner" they should be reflected in the records of the general long-term debt account group.

To illustrate how this accounting entity is used, we compare the entry for the sale of a bond issue on the books of a business entity with those for the sale of a general bond issue by a city.

| | | |
|---|---|---|
| **Entry for business entity** | | |
| Cash | xxx | |
|     Bonds payable | | xxx |
| **Entries for city** | | |
|     Capital projects fund | | |
| Estimated bond issue proceeds | xxx | |
|     Appropriations | | xxx |
| Cash | xxx | |
|     Proceeds from sale of bonds (other financing sources) | | xxx |
|     General long-term debt account group | | |
| Amount to be provided for retirement of bonds | xxx | |
|     Bonds payable | | xxx |

If we eliminate the budgetary entry, the credit to "proceeds from sale of bonds" in the capital project fund and the debit to "amount to be provided for the retirement of bonds" in the general long-term debt account group, we have the same account balances for the city as are shown on the books of the business entity. Therefore, we again see that fragmentation of accounting data into separate fund entities, with no distinction between capital and revenue items within governmental-fund records, makes this account group necessary to provide a record of general long-term liabilities.

The accounting equation for the long-term debt account group accounting entity may be stated as follows:

amount to be provided for the retirement of debt
+ amount provided for retirement of debt = long-term debt

The items on the left side of the equation are debited to reflect increases in them and credited when they are decreased. The opposite arrangement is followed for recording increases and decreases in the long-term debt accounts.

**Illustrative Transactions.**   Because each transaction in the general long-term debt account group is associated with some fund entry, each entry listed for this accounting entity is keyed to the fund entry giving rise to it. Transactions from the various fund entities affecting the general long-term debt account group are as follows (the code letters "LTD" indicate a long-term debt account group):

LTD-1.   Proceeds from sale of $500,000 of 8 percent bonds are received (from capital projects fund entry CP-2, page 216).

LTD-2.   General fund contribution of $50,000 is paid to debt-service fund (from debt-service fund entry DS-3, page 222).

LTD-3.   Revenue on debt-service fund investments in the amount of $1,950 is earned (from debt-service fund entry DS-5, page 223).

LTD-4.   Premium realized from the sale of bonds is transferred from the capital projects fund to the debt-service fund (from debt-service fund entry DS-6b, page 223).

The following journal entries record the preceding transactions:

**Transaction (LTD-1)**

| | | |
|---|---:|---:|
| Amount to be provided for retirement of bonds | 500,000 | |
| Bonds payable | | 500,000 |

**Transaction (LTD-2)**

| | | |
|---|---:|---:|
| Amount provided for retirement of bonds | 50,000 | |
| Amount to be provided for retirement of bonds | | 50,000 |

**Transaction (LTD-3)**

| | | |
|---|---:|---:|
| Amount provided for retirement of bonds | 1,950 | |
| Amount to be provided for retirement of bonds | | 1,950 |

**Transaction (LTD-4)**

| | | |
|---|---:|---:|
| Amount provided for retirement of bonds | 2,000 | |
| Amount to be provided for retirement of bonds | | 2,000 |

The originating entry for this accounting entity shows the general long-term obligations assumed by the city. Subsequent entries show the extent to which resources have been accumulated for the retirement of those obligations. Entries (LTD-1), (LTD-2), (LTD-3), and (LTD-4) illustrate these data. When the bonds are eventually paid, the related account balances will be reversed and all accounts in the account group will be closed.

The posting of the preceding entries is illustrated in the following T-accounts for the general long-term debt account group:

| Amount to Be Provided for Retirement of Bonds | | Bonds Payable | |
|---|---|---|---|
| (LTD-1)  500,000 | (LTD-2)  50,000 | | (LTD-1)  500,000 |
| | (LTD-3)   1,950 | | |
| | (LTD-4)   2,000 | | |

| Amount Provided for Retirement of Bonds | |
|---|---|
| (LTD-2)  50,000 | |
| (LTD-3)   1,950 | |
| (LTD-4)   2,000 | |

**Statements.**   Since the general long-term debt account group is a memo record and is not involved with the flow of appropriable resources, it does not require a statement showing the flows of resources. Exhibit 8–13 illustrates the kind of statement that is generally appropriate for this account group.

## NCGA Statements Relating to Account Group Data

In Chapter 3, we discussed the provisions of NCGA Statement 4, dealing with the problems of accounting for claims and judgments and compensated absences. A key element of the accounting procedures set out in that statement relates to the *accrual of long-term liabilities* for such items. The following quotations from it describe those accounting practices:

> 3) NCGA Statement 1 requires that "contingent liabilities not requiring accrual should be disclosed in the notes to the financial statements." The note reference in this quotation reads: "See FASB Statement 5, 'Accounting for Contingencies.'" Statement 1 provides no additional guidance, however, as to how contingent liabilities (claims and judgments) should be treated when accrual is required.
>
> 4) For accounting and financial reporting for compensated absences, Statement 1 adopted the position of the American Institute of Certified Public Accountants (AICPA) Statement of Position (SOP) 75-3, *Accrual of Revenues and Expenditures by State and Local Governmental Units*. SOP 75-3 states that for accumulated unused vacation and sick leave in governmental funds ". . . it is appropriate to disclose the estimated amount of such commitments in a footnote, if material, and not record the costs as expenditures at the time leave is accumulated. If accumulated unused vacation and sick pay at the end of a fiscal year does not exceed a normal year's accumulation, footnote disclosure is not required."

**EXHIBIT 8–13.**   Model City Statement of General Long-Term Debt—End of Period

| Amount Available and to Be Provided for Payment of General Long-Term Debt | | Obligations | |
|---|---|---|---|
| Amount to be provided for retirement of bonds | $446,050 | Bonds payable | $500,000 |
| Amount provided for retirement of bonds | 53,950 | | |
| Total | $500,000 | Total | $500,000 |

5) In determining the accounting and financial reporting treatment of claims and judgments and compensated absences for state and local governments, consideration must be given to the *distinctions between the governmental fund and proprietary fund models* with respect to: a) fund long-term liabilities and general long-term liabilities; and b) current liabilities and noncurrent liabilities. Accounting and financial reporting will differ depending on whether the liability is accounted for in a proprietary fund or a governmental fund. In addition, accounting and financial reporting will differ within a governmental fund depending on whether the liability is normally to be liquidated by using expendable available financial resources.

6) Statement 1 distinguishes between fund long-term liabilities and general long-term debt. It provides that "bonds, notes and other long-term liabilities (e.g., for capital leases, pensions, judgments and similar commitments) directly related to and expected to be paid from proprietary funds, Special Assessment Funds [now special assessment projects] and Trust Funds should be included in the accounts of such funds. These are *specific* fund liabilities. . . . All other unmatured long-term indebtedness of the government is *general long-term debt* and should be accounted for in the General Long-Term Debt Account Group" (GLTDAG).

7) Statement 1 distinguishes between current and noncurrent liabilities. Further, it recognizes that general long-term debt is not limited to liabilities arising from debt issuances *per se,* but it may also include noncurrent liabilities for other commitments that are not current liabilities properly recorded in governmental funds. Statement 1 notes that "just as general fixed assets do not represent financial resources available for appropriation and expenditure, the unmatured principal of general long-term debt does not require current appropriation and expenditure of governmental fund financial resources. To include it as a governmental fund liability would be misleading and dysfunctional to the current period management control (e.g., budgeting) and accountability functions." Therefore, in governmental funds, liabilities usually are not considered current until they are normally expected to be liquidated with expendable available financial resources. . . .

12) The claim cycle has various stages. These are, in reverse order: when paid, when vouchered for payment, when adjudicated or settled, when a loss is estimable and when a loss contingency occurs. The latter two stages, when a loss is estimable and when a loss contingency occurs, relate to incidents that occurred prior to the balance sheet date. If a claim is asserted and the probable loss is reasonably estimable, SFAS 5 requires that the liability be recognized in the financial statements. There also may be situations where incidents occurred before the balance sheet date, but claims are not asserted when the financial statements are prepared; nevertheless, if the loss can be reasonably estimated and it is probable that a claim will be asserted, SFAS 5 requires the recognition of a liability.

13) Because of the lapse between an incident creating a claim and the claim's ultimate settlement, claims frequently take on the nature of long-term liabilities. Proprietary fund liabilities can be accounted for in the fund. Governmental funds, however, reflect current operations with general long-term liabilities accounted for in the GLTDAG. Therefore, claims should be recognized as governmental fund liabilities when they normally would be liquidated with expendable available financial resources; otherwise, they should be reported in the GLTDAG. . . .

17) Since governmental fund balance sheets reflect current liabilities, only the current portion of the liability should be reported in the fund. The current portion is the amount left unpaid at the end of the reporting period that normally would be liquidated with expendable available financial resources. The remainder of the liability should be reported in the GLTDAG.[4]

4. National Council on Governmental Accounting, *NCGA Statement 4* (Chicago: National Council on Governmental Accounting, 1982). Used with permission.

Within the provisions of this pronouncement, both the current and long-term liabilities for claims and judgments and compensated absences will be recorded in the accounts of self-sustaining (proprietary) funds. This is consistent with profit entity accounting practices. In a governmental fund, any liability to be liquidated by using available expendable resources would be shown as liability of the fund. However, a long-term liability associated with the operations of such a fund would be reflected in the general long-term debt account group. *Therefore, we can have recognition of a general long-term debt in the general long-term debt account group without a transaction entry being recorded in a governmental fund.*

The following entry should be used to record such a long-term obligation in the general long-term debt account group:

Amount to be provided for claims and judgments
   Liability for claims and judgments

NCGA Statement 5 describes the accounting and financial reporting principles for lease agreements of state and local governments. This pronouncement reflects an interpretation of the application of FASB 13 and other pronouncements relating to long-term leases to accounting for such transactions in the records of governmental units. Because the accounting and financial reporting practices for proprietary funds will be essentially the same as those for business entities, the statement concentrates on the accounting and reporting practices that should be followed when governmental funds are involved either as a lessor or lessee in FASB 13 type lease agreements. The more important provisions of this statement are summarized as follows:

5) In determining the accounting and financial reporting treatment for lease agreements of state and local governments, consideration must be given to the distinctions between the governmental fund and proprietary fund models with respect to fund long-term liabilities and general long-term liabilities. Accounting and financial reporting will differ depending on whether the liability is accounted for in a governmental fund or a proprietary fund.

6) Statement 1 distinguishes between fund long-term liabilities and general long-term debt:

Bonds, notes and other long-term liabilities (e.g., for capital leases, pensions, judgments, and similar commitments) directly related to and expected to be paid from proprietary funds, Special Assessment Funds [now special assessment projects] and Trust Funds should be included in the accounts of such funds. These are *specific* fund liabilities. . . . All other unmatured long-term indebtedness of the government is *general long-term debt* and should be accounted for in the General Long-Term Debt Account Group.

7) Statement 1 also provides that general long-term debt can include noncurrent liabilities from capital lease agreements:

General long-term debt is not limited to liabilities arising from debt issuances per se, but may also include noncurrent liabilities on lease-purchase agreements and other commitments that are not current liabilities properly recorded in governmental funds.

9) Statement 1 requires that fixed assets, except those related to specific proprietary funds and Nonexpendable Trust and Pension Trust Funds, be accounted for in the General

Fixed Assets Account Group. Statement 1 notes that general fixed assets and long-term liabilities include fixed assets acquired and obligations arising from noncancelable leases. . . . [5]

## Accounting and Financial Reporting for Lease Agreements

11) The council concludes, subject to the accounting and financial reporting distinctions of governmental funds and Expendable Trust Funds, that the criteria of FASB Statement 13 (as amended and interpreted) should be the guidelines for accounting and financial reporting for lease agreements. SFAS (FASB) 13 (as amended and interpreted) should be consulted for specific guidance concerning detailed criteria referenced in this statement.

12) If a lease agreement is a capital lease following the criteria of this statement and SFAS (FASB) 13, the lease agreement should be capitalized.

13) In governmental funds, the primary emphasis is on the flow of financial resources, and expenditures are recognized on the modified accrual basis. Accordingly, if a lease agreement is to be financed from general government resources, it must be accounted for and reported on a basis consistent with governmental fund accounting principles.

14) General fixed assets acquired via lease agreements should be capitalized in the General Fixed Assets Account Group at the inception of the agreement in an amount determined by the criteria of SFAS (FASB) 13. A liability in the same amount should be recorded simultaneously in the General Long-Term Debt Account Group. When a capital lease represents the acquisition or construction of a general fixed asset, the acquisition or construction of the general fixed asset should be reflected as an expenditure and other financing source, consistent with the accounting and financial reporting for general obligation bonded debt. Subsequent governmental fund lease payments should be accounted for consistently with Statement 1 principles for general obligation debts. A Debt Service or Capital Projects Fund is not necessary unless required by NCGA Statement 1, principle 4.

15) In governmental funds, lease receivables and deferred revenues should be used to account for leases receivable when a state or local government is the lessor in a lease situation. Only the portion of lease receivables which represent revenue/other financing sources that are measurable and available should be recognized as revenue/other financing sources in governmental funds. The remainder of the receivable should be deferred.

16) Proprietary funds should follow SFAS (FASB) 13 without modification. All assets and liabilities of proprietary funds are accounted for and reported in the respective funds. Therefore, transactions for proprietary fund capital leases are accounted for and reported entirely within the individual proprietary fund.[6]

Adherence to the provisions of FASB 13 requires that long-term noncancelable leases, meeting any one of four requirements, be treated as capital leases. That means that they should be accounted for as installment purchases in which the assets acquired would be capitalized at their fair value, generally an amount equal to the present value of total lease payments. At the same time, a long-term liability should be recognized in an amount equal to the present value of unpaid lease payments. This requires the following entry in a governmental fund when that fund is the lessee party in a capital lease transaction:

5. National Council on Governmental Accounting, *NCGA Statement 5* (Chicago: National Council on Governmental Accounting, 1982). Used with permission.
6. Ibid. Used with permission.

Expenditures
Other financing source—capital leases

The following complementing entries should then be recorded in the general fixed-asset and general long-term debt account groups:

**General fixed-asset account group**
Asset
Investment in fixed assets

**General long-term debt account group**
Amount to be provided for lease payments
Amount payable on capital lease

If a governmental-type fund is the lessor in a capital lease transaction, that fact should be recorded in the fund accounting records as follows:

Receivable from capital lease
Other financing source (amount that is measurable and available)
Deferred revenues

If a governmental-type fund is the lessor in a capital lease transaction the long-term part of the receivable should be recorded in the governmental fund records rather than in the general fixed-assets account group as stated in the following paragraph of Statement 5:

> The noncurrent receivable created when a government is the lessor in a capital lease agreement is not considered a fixed asset and, therefore, is not accounted for in the general fixed assets account group under NCGA Statement 1.[7]

The offsetting credit should be to deferred revenue in the governmental fund.

## ■ Interfund Relationships

The various funds and account groups are related to each other in much the same way as are business entities trading with each other. These relationships can best be understood by analyzing the transactions included in our Model City illustration that require entries in more than one fund and/or account group.

These related entries can be described as *reciprocal entries and complementing entries*. Transactions involving the transfer of resources between funds or the recognition of claims and obligations of one fund against another require reciprocal entries in the accounting records of the fund entities involved in the transactions. Transactions of governmental funds that relate to the acquisition of fixed assets, disposal of fixed assets,

7.   Ibid. Used with permission.

the incurrence of long-term debt, the retirement of long-term debt, the accumulation of funds for the retirement of long-term debt, or the use of funds for the retirement of long-term debt require complementing entries in the appropriate account group.

To help you develop a more complete understanding of these relationships, code numbers for Model City transactions requiring related reciprocal and/or complementing entries in another fund or account group are shown in Exhibit 8–14. In that exhibit, the funds and account groups are listed across the top. Under these headings you will find the code numbers of related entries listed in compartments across the page.

In an appendix to this chapter (pages 282–291), we have also included a summary of all actions and transactions recorded in Chapters 6, 7, and 8 for Model City (excluding the enterprise fund), grouped to show the related entries. All entries shown between pairs of dark lines in the appendix are related to each other. Appendix footnotes also explain entries that include segments of reciprocal entries.

**EXHIBIT 8–14.** Relationships Among Funds and Account Groups

| General Fund | Capital Projects Fund | Debt-Service Fund | Special Assessment Capital Projects Fund | Special Assessment Agency Fund | Municipal Garage Fund | Federal Fixed Assets | General Long-Term Debt |
|---|---|---|---|---|---|---|---|
| GF-1 | | DS-1 | | | | | |
| GF-5 | | DS-2 | SA-1b | | | | |
| GF-7a | | | | | | FA-1 | |
| GF-8 | | DS-3 | SA-2 | | SS-1 | | LTD-2 |
| GF-9 | | | | | | FA-2 | |
| | CP-2 CP-2a CP-2b | DS-6a DS-6b | | | | | LTD-1 LTD-4 |
| | CP-3 | | | | | FA-3 | |
| | CP-5a CP-5b | | | | | FA-4 | |
| | | DS-5 | | | | | LTD-3 |
| | | | SA-3a | SA-3b | | | |
| | | | SA-4 SA-6b | | | FA-5 | |
| | CP-6 | | SA-4 | | SS-4 | | |

# ■ Appendix: Worksheet Summary

Worksheet Summary of Actions and Transactions for Model City (Excluding Enterprise Fund)

| | | Entries | | | Funds and Account Groups | | | |
|---|---|---|---|---|---|---|---|---|
| | | | General Fund | | Capital Projects Fund | | Debt-Service Fund | |
| Code No. | Accounts | | Dr. | Cr. | Dr. | Cr. | Dr. | Cr. |
| GF-1 | Estimated revenues | | 2,000,000 | | | | | |
| | Appropriations | | | 1,950,000 | | | | |
| | Budgetary fund balance | | | 50,000 | | | | |
| DS-1 | Estimated revenues from investments | | | | | | 2,000 | |
| | Required general fund contributions | | | | | | 50,000 | |
| | Budgetary fund balance | | | | | | | 52,000 |
| GF-2 | Taxes receivable | | 1,460,000 | | | | | |
| | Revenues | | | 1,460,000 | | | | |
| GF-3 | Cash | | 545,000 | | | | | |
| | Revenues | | | 545,000 | | | | |
| GF-4 | Cash | | 1,445,000 | | | | | |
| | Taxes receivable | | | 1,445,000 | | | | |
| GF-5 | Transfer to water utility fund | | 100,000 | | | | | |
| | Transfer to debt-service fund | | 50,000 | | | | | |
| | Transfer to special assessment capital projects fund | | 25,000 | | | | | |
| | Transfer to municipal garage fund | | 85,000 | | | | | |
| | Expenditures | | 1,479,000 | | | | | |
| | Vouchers payable | | | 1,444,000 | | | | |
| | Due to debt-service fund | | | 50,000 | | | | |
| | Due to municipal garage fund | | | 120,000[1] | | | | |
| | Due to special assessment capital projects fund | | | 25,000 | | | | |
| | Due to water utility fund | | | 100,000 | | | | |
| DS-2 | Due from general fund | | | | | | 50,000 | |
| | Transfers from general fund | | | | | | | 50,000 |
| SA-1b | Due from general fund | | | | | | | |
| | Transfers from general fund | | | | | | | |
| GF-6 | Encumbrances | | 200,000 | | | | | |
| | Reserve for encumbrances | | | 200,000 | | | | |
| GF-7a | Expenditures | | 145,000 | | | | | |
| | Vouchers payable | | | 145,000 | | | | |
| GF-7b | Reserve for encumbrances | | 150,000 | | | | | |
| | Encumbrances | | | 150,000 | | | | |

| | | | | Funds and Account Groups | | | | | | | |
| | | | | | | | | | | | |
| Special Assessment Capital Projects Fund | | Special Assessment Agency Fund | | Municipal Garage Fund | | Trust and Agency Fund | | General Fixed-Assets Account Group | | General Long-Term Debt Account Group | |
| Dr. | Cr. | Dr. | Cr. | Dr. | Cr. | Dr. | Cr. | Dr. | Cr. | Dr. | Cr. |
| 25,000 | | | | | | | | | | | |
| | 25,000 | | | | | | | | | | |

| Code No. | Accounts | General Fund Dr. | General Fund Cr. | Capital Projects Fund Dr. | Capital Projects Fund Cr. | Debt-Service Fund Dr. | Debt-Service Fund Cr. |
|---|---|---|---|---|---|---|---|
| FA-1 | Equipment | | | | | | |
| | Investment in general fixed assets from general fund | | | | | | |
| GF-8 | Due to water utility fund | 100,000 | | | | | |
| | Due to municipal garage fund | 120,000[1a] | | | | | |
| | Vouchers payable | 1,505,000 | | | | | |
| | Due to special assessment capital projects fund | 25,000 | | | | | |
| | Due to debt-service fund | 50,000 | | | | | |
| | Cash | | 1,800,000 | | | | |
| DS-3 | Cash | | | | | 50,000 | |
| | Due from general fund | | | | | | 50,000 |
| SA-2 | Cash | | | | | | |
| | Due from general fund | | | | | | |
| SS-1 | Cash | | | | | | |
| | Capital contribution from general fund | | | | | | |
| LTD-1 | Amount provided for retirement of bonds | | | | | | |
| | Amount to be provided for retirement of bonds | | | | | | |
| GF-9 | Cash | 5,000 | | | | | |
| | Revenues | | 5,000 | | | | |
| FA-2 | Investment in fixed assets from general fund | | | | | | |
| | Equipment | | | | | | |
| CP-1 | Estimated bond issue proceeds | | | 500,000 | | | |
| | Appropriations | | | | 500,000 | | |
| CP-2 | Cash | | | 502,000 | | | |
| | Premium on bonds | | | | 2,000 | | |
| | Proceeds from sale of bonds | | | | 500,000 | | |
| CP-2a | Premium on bonds | | | 2,000 | | | |
| | Due to debt-service fund | | | | 2,000 | | |
| CP-2b | Due to debt-service fund | | | 2,000 | | | |
| | Cash | | | | 2,000 | | |
| DS-6a | Due from capital projects fund | | | | | 2,000 | |
| | Bond issue premium | | | | | | 2,000 |
| DS-6b | Cash | | | | | 2,000 | |
| | Due from capital projects fund | | | | | | 2,000 |

| Special Assessment Capital Projects Fund | | Special Assessment Agency Fund | | Municipal Garage Fund | | Trust and Agency Fund | | General Fixed-Assets Account Group | | General Long-Term Debt Account Group | |
|---|---|---|---|---|---|---|---|---|---|---|---|
| Dr. | Cr. | Dr. | Cr. | Dr. | Cr. | Dr. | Cr. | Dr. | Cr. | Dr. | Cr. |
| | | | | | | | | 145,000 | | | |
| | | | | | | | | | 145,000 | | |
| 25,000 | | | | | | | | | | | |
| | 25,000 | | | | | | | | | | |
| | | | | 85,000 | | | | | | | |
| | | | | | 85,000 | | | | | | |
| | | | | | | | | | | 50,000 | |
| | | | | | | | | | | | 50,000 |
| | | | | | | | | 60,000 | | | |
| | | | | | | | | | 60,000 | | |

| Code No. | Accounts | General Fund Dr. | General Fund Cr. | Capital Projects Fund Dr. | Capital Projects Fund Cr. | Debt-Service Fund Dr. | Debt-Service Fund Cr. |
|---|---|---|---|---|---|---|---|
| LTD-4 | Amount provided for retirement of bonds | | | | | | |
| | Amount to be provided for retirement of bonds | | | | | | |
| LTD-1 | Amount to be provided for retirement of bonds | | | | | | |
| | Bonds payable | | | | | | |
| CP-3 | Expenditures | | | 350,000 | | | |
| | Vouchers payable | | | | 345,000 | | |
| | Due to municipal garage fund | | | | 5,000 | | |
| FA-3 | Structures and improvements | | | | | | |
| | Investment in general fixed assets from capital projects fund | | | | | | |
| SS-4 | Due from general fund | | | | | | |
| | Due from special assessment capital projects fund | | | | | | |
| | Due from capital projects fund | | | | | | |
| | Revenues | | | | | | |
| CP-4 | Encumbrances | | | 140,000 | | | |
| | Reserve for encumbrances | | | | 140,000 | | |
| CP-5a | Reserve for encumbrances | | | 50,000 | | | |
| | Encumbrances | | | | 50,000 | | |
| CP-5b | Expenditures | | | 52,000 | | | |
| | Vouchers payable | | | | 47,000 | | |
| | Contracts payable—retained percentages | | | | 5,000 | | |
| FA-4 | Structures and improvements | | | | | | |
| | Investment in general fixed assets from capital projects fund | | | | | | |
| CP-6 | Due to municipal garage fund | | | 5,000[3] | | | |
| | Vouchers payable | | | 387,000 | | | |
| | Cash | | | | 392,000 | | |
| DS-4 | Investments | | | | | 49,000 | |
| | Cash | | | | | | 49,000 |
| DS-5 | Cash | | | | | 1,950 | |
| | Revenues from investments | | | | | | 1,950 |
| LTD-3 | Amount provided for retirement of bonds | | | | | | |
| | Amount to be provided for retirement of bonds | | | | | | |
| SA-1a | Estimated financing sources | | | | | | |
| | Appropriations | | | | | | |

| | | | | | | | | | | | |
|---|---|---|---|---|---|---|---|---|---|---|---|
| | | | | | | | | | | | |

<table>

| Special Assessment Capital Projects Fund | | Special Assessment Agency Fund | | Municipal Garage Fund | | Trust and Agency Fund | | General Fixed-Assets Account Group | | General Long-Term Debt Account Group | |
|---|---|---|---|---|---|---|---|---|---|---|---|
| Dr. | Cr. | Dr. | Cr. | Dr. | Cr. | Dr. | Cr. | Dr. | Cr. | Dr. | Cr. |
| | | | | | | | | | | 2,000 | |
| | | | | | | | | | | | 2,000 |
| | | | | | | | | | | 500,000 | |
| | | | | | | | | | | | 500,000 |
| | | | | | | | | | 350,000 | | |
| | | | | | | | | | | 350,000 | |
| | | | | 35,000 | | | | | | | |
| | | | | 10,000 | | | | | | | |
| | | | | 5,000 | | | | | | | |
| | | | | | 50,000[2] | | | | | | |
| | | | | | | | | 52,000 | | | |
| | | | | | | | | | 52,000 | | |
| | | | | | | | | | | 1,950 | |
| | | | | | | | | | | | 1,950 |
| 250,000 | | | | | | | | | | | |
| | 250,000 | | | | | | | | | | |

| Code No. | Accounts | General Fund Dr. | General Fund Cr. | Capital Projects Fund Dr. | Capital Projects Fund Cr. | Debt-Service Fund Dr. | Debt-Service Fund Cr. |
|---|---|---|---|---|---|---|---|
| SA-1c | Special assessment receivable—current | | | | | | |
| | Special assessment receivable—deferred | | | | | | |
| | Revenues | | | | | | |
| | Deferred revenues | | | | | | |
| SA-3a | Cash | | | | | | |
| | Contributions from property owners | | | | | | |
| SA-3b | Amount to be provided from special assessments | | | | | | |
| | Bonds payable | | | | | | |
| SA-4 | Expenditures | | | | | | |
| | Vouchers payable | | | | | | |
| | Due to municipal garage fund | | | | | | |
| SA-5 | Encumbrances | | | | | | |
| | Reserve for encumbrances | | | | | | |
| SA-6a | Reserve for encumbrances | | | | | | |
| | Encumbrances | | | | | | |
| SA-6b | Expenditures | | | | | | |
| | Vouchers payable | | | | | | |
| | Contracts payable—retained percentage | | | | | | |
| FA-5 | Structures and improvements | | | | | | |
| | Investment in fixed assets from special assessment capital projects fund | | | | | | |
| SA-7a | Cash | | | | | | |
| | Special assessments receivable—current | | | | | | |
| SA-7b | Amount provided from special assessments | | | | | | |
| | Amount to be provided from special assessments | | | | | | |
| SA-6 | Cash | | | | | | |
| | Revenues from interest | | | | | | |
| SA-9 | Vouchers payable | | | | | | |
| | Cash | | | | | | |
| SA-10 | Expenditures for interest | | | | | | |
| | Cash | | | | | | |
| SA-11 | Expenditures for interest | | | | | | |
| | Interest payable | | | | | | |

| Special Assessment Capital Projects Fund | | Special Assessment Agency Fund | | Municipal Garage Fund | | Trust and Agency Fund | | General Fixed-Assets Account Group | | General Long-Term Debt Account Group | |
|---|---|---|---|---|---|---|---|---|---|---|---|
| Dr. | Cr. | Dr. | Cr. | Dr. | Cr. | Dr. | Cr. | Dr. | Cr. | Dr. | Cr. |
| | | 22,500 | | | | | | | | | |
| | | 202,500 | | | | | | | | | |
| | | | 22,500 | | | | | | | | |
| | | | 202,500 | | | | | | | | |
| 225,000 | | | | | | | | | | | |
| | 225,000 | | | | | | | | | | |
| | | 225,000 | | | | | | | | | |
| | | | 225,000 | | | | | | | | |
| 200,000 | | | | | | | | | | | |
| | 190,000 | | | | | | | | | | |
| | 10,000[4] | | | | | | | | | | |
| 45,000 | | | | | | | | | | | |
| | 45,000 | | | | | | | | | | |
| 45,000 | | | | | | | | | | | |
| | 45,000 | | | | | | | | | | |
| 45,000 | | | | | | | | | | | |
| | 40,500 | | | | | | | | | | |
| | 4,500 | | | | | | | | | | |
| | | | | | | | | 245,000 | | | |
| | | | | | | | | | 245,000 | | |
| | | 22,500 | | | | | | | | | |
| | | | 22,500 | | | | | | | | |
| | | 22,500 | | | | | | | | | |
| | | | 22,500 | | | | | | | | |
| | | 6,075 | | | | | | | | | |
| | | | 6,075 | | | | | | | | |
| 230,000 | | | | | | | | | | | |
| | 230,000 | | | | | | | | | | |
| | | 4,050 | | | | | | | | | |
| | | | 4,050 | | | | | | | | |
| | | 2,000 | | | | | | | | | |
| | | | 2,000 | | | | | | | | |

| | | | Entries | | | Funds and Account Groups | | | |
|---|---|---|---|---|---|---|---|---|---|

| | | General Fund | | Capital Projects Fund | | Debt-Service Fund | |
|---|---|---|---|---|---|---|---|
| Code No. | Accounts | Dr. | Cr. | Dr. | Cr. | Dr. | Cr. |
| SA-12 | Interest receivable | | | | | | |
| | Revenue from interest | | | | | | |
| SS-2 | Equipment | | | | | | |
| | Supplies | | | | | | |
| | Vouchers payable | | | | | | |
| SS-3 | Expenses | | | | | | |
| | Supplies | | | | | | |
| | Vouchers payable | | | | | | |
| SS-5 | Cash | | | | | | |
| | Due from general fund | | | | | | |
| | Due from capital projects fund | | | | | | |
| SS-6 | Vouchers payable | | | | | | |
| | Cash | | | | | | |
| SS-7 | Expenses | | | | | | |
| | Allowance for depreciation | | | | | | |
| TA-1 | Principal cash | | | | | | |
| | Fund balance reserved for endowment | | | | | | |
| TA-2 | Investments | | | | | | |
| | Principal cash | | | | | | |
| TA-3 | Income cash | | | | | | |
| | Income | | | | | | |
| TA-4 | Expenditures against income | | | | | | |
| | Income cash | | | | | | |

[1]No reciprocal entry for the transfer part of this item ($85,000) is recorded in the municipal garage fund because the capital contribution was not recognized in that fund until the cash was received (see SS-1). The expenditure part ($35,000) is recognized in entry SS-4 (see footnote 2).

[1a]This part of the entry contains a payment of $35,000 that is reciprocal to part of entry SS-5.

[2]The three accounts debited in this entry are reciprocals to elements of entries GF-5, SA-4, and CP-3. Because this entry relates to three other entries it is shown separately here.

[3]This part of the entry is reciprocal to part of entry SS-5.

[4]See footnote (2).

[5]See footnotes (3) and (1a).

*Funds and Account Groups*

| Special Assessment Capital Projects Fund | | Special Assessment Agency Fund | | Municipal Garage Fund | | Trust and Agency Fund | | General Fixed- Assets Account Group | | General Long- Term Dept Account Group | |
|---|---|---|---|---|---|---|---|---|---|---|---|
| Dr. | Cr. | Dr. | Cr. | Dr. | Cr. | Dr. | Cr. | Dr. | Cr. | Dr. | Cr. |
| | | 900 | 900 | | | | | | | | |
| | | | | 35,000 10,000 | 45,000 | | | | | | |
| | | | | 44,000 | 4,000 40,000 | | | | | | |
| | | | | 40,000[5] | 35,000 5,000 | | | | | | |
| | | | | 75,000 | 75,000 | | | | | | |
| | | | | 3,500 | 3,500 | | | | | | |
| | | | | | | 100,000 | 100,000 | | | | |
| | | | | | | 100,000 | 100,000 | | | | |
| | | | | | | 2,500 | 2,500 | | | | |
| | | | | | | 2,000 | 2,000 | | | | |

# ■ Ethical Considerations Associated with Establishing Billing Prices for Enterprise Fund Services

The city of Opportunity City Council has for years solicited firms to locate in the city by publicizing the fact that the city's property taxes are lower than those of competing cities. Part of the reason for these low taxes is that the city's water utility fund— operated as a proprietary fund—regularly produces a significant excess of revenues over expenses which has been used for city operating expenses. However, citizens are now demanding more and better services from the city. To meet this need, the council is considering an increase in water rates and the creation of another enterprise fund to provide trash collection services on a self-sustaining basis. Charges for the service would be established at a fixed amount per month for each household. Consider the ethical issues associated with such action by the council as an alternative to a proposed increase in property taxes.

# ■ Summary

This chapter has described and illustrated the procedures to be followed in accounting for the operations of proprietary funds, fiduciary funds, and account groups. We demonstrated how a series of assumed transactions for two of Model City's proprietary funds (internal service and enterprise funds) should be recorded and summarized in financial statements. Profit-oriented accounting procedures were followed in recording the assumed transactions.

Next, fiduciary fund accounting procedures, including elements from governmental as well as from proprietary fund practices, were illustrated through a series of assumed transactions for a Model City trust and agency fund.

In the last portion of the chapter, we showed how transactions involving general fixed assets and general long-term debt should be recorded and reported through the medium of account groups for general fixed assets and general long-term debt. The relationships between the various funds and account groups illustrated in Chapters 6, 7, and 8 were then demonstrated by showing the various assumed transactions that require entries in more than one of the illustrated funds and/or account groups.

# ■ Glossary

**Agency Fund.**   A fund used to account for assets held by a government as an agent for individuals, private organizations, other governments, and/or other funds; for example, taxes collected and held by a municipality for a school district.

**Amount Available in Debt-Service Funds.**   An "other debit" account in the general long-term debt account group that shows the amount of assets available in debt-service funds for the retirement of general obligation debt.

**Amount to Be Provided.**   An "other debit" account in the general long-term debt account group that shows the amount to be provided from taxes or other general revenues to retire outstanding general long-term debt.

**Customer Deposits.**   A liability account used in an enterprise fund to reflect deposits made by customers as a prerequisite to receiving services and/or goods provided by the fund.

**Deficit.**   (1) The excess of the liabilities of a fund over its assets. (2) The excess of expenditures over revenues during an accounting period; or, in the case of proprietary funds, the excess of expense over income during an accounting period.

**Enterprise Fund.**   A fund established to account for operations (a) that are financed and operated in a manner similar to private business enterprises—where the intent of the governing body is that the costs (expenses, including depreciation) of providing goods or services to the general public on a continuing basis be financed or recovered primarily through user charges, or (b) where the governing body has decided that periodic determination of revenues earned, expenses incurred, and/or net income is appropriate for capital maintenance, public policy, management control, accountability, or other purposes. Examples of enterprise funds are those for water, gas, and electric utilities; swimming pools; airports; parking garages; and transit systems.

**Expendable Trust Fund.**   A trust fund whose resources, including both principal and earnings, may be expended. Expendable trust funds are accounted for in essentially the same manner as governmental funds.

**General Fixed Assets.**   Fixed assets used in the general operations of a governmental entity. General fixed assets include all fixed assets not accounted for in proprietary funds or in trust and agency funds.

**General Fixed-Assets Account Group.**   A self-balancing group of accounts set up to account for the general fixed assets of a government.

**General Long-Term Debt.**   Long-term debt (other than special assessment bonds) expected to be repaid from governmental funds.

**General Long-Term Debt Account Group.**   A self-balancing group of accounts set up to account for the unmatured general long-term debt of a government.

**Internal Service Fund.**   A fund used to account for the financing of goods or services provided by one department or agency to other departments or agencies of a government, or to other governments, on a cost-reimbursement basis.

**Investment in General Fixed Assets.**   An account in the general fixed assets account group that represents the government's equity in general fixed assets. The balance of this account is generally subdivided according to the source of the monies that financed the asset acquisition, such as general fund revenues, special assessments, etc.

**Lease–Purchase Agreements.**   Contractual agreements that are termed "leases" but which in substance amount to purchase contracts.

**Nonexpendable Trust Fund.**   A trust fund, the principal of which may not be expended. Nonexpendable trust funds are accounted for in essentially the same manner as proprietary funds.

**Operating Expenses.** Proprietary fund expenses that are directly related to the fund's primary service activities.

**Operating Income.** The excess of proprietary fund operating revenues over operating expenses.

**Operating Revenues.** Proprietary fund revenues that are directly related to the fund's primary service activities. They consist primarily of user charges for services.

**Retained Earnings.** An equity account reflecting the accumulated earnings of an enterprise or internal service fund.

## ■ Questions for Class Discussion

**Q8-1.** Explain the difference between an internal service fund and an enterprise fund.

**Q8-2.** What is the logical justification for using the full accrual basis in accounting for the transactions of proprietary funds?

**Q8-3.** Do the accounting procedures for an internal service fund require an adjustment for anticipated uncollectible accounts? Explain.

**Q8-4.** Does an enterprise fund normally require an adjusting entry to provide for probable uncollectible accounts? Explain.

**Q8-5.** What financial statements should be prepared at the end of each fiscal period for an internal service fund? For an enterprise fund?

**Q8-6.** A business enterprise secures equity capital through the sale of shares of stock. From what source does an internal service fund secure its "equity capital"?

**Q8-7.** How are the operations of an enterprise fund typically financed?

**Q8-8.** From what sources may an enterprise fund typically secure debt capital?

**Q8-9.** What is a fiduciary fund?

**Q8-10.** Explain the difference between the expendable and nonexpendable portions of a trust and agency fund.

**Q8-11.** Why is it necessary to have a general fixed-asset account group within the accounting records of a governmental entity?

**Q8-12.** Describe the accounts normally included in the general fixed-assets account group.

**Q8-13.** What is the accounting objective of the general long-term debt account group?

**Q8-14.** Describe the accounts included in the general long-term debt account group.

**Q8-15.** Identify two transactions associated with each of the following funds that require a related journal entry in another fund or account group. Indicate which fund(s) and/or account group(s) would require the additional entries. What entry would be required in each case?
a. general fund
b. capital projects fund
c. debt-service fund
d. special assessment capital projects fund
e. internal service fund

**Q8-16.** How should a noncancellable lease agreement executed by a governmental fund as the lessee that meets the capital lease requirements of FASB 13 be recorded in the accounting records? Justify your answer.

**Q8-17.** Suppose that the governmental fund is the lessor in Question 8-16. How should the transaction be recorded? Justify your answer.

**Q8-18.** What type of fund entities should be used to account for employee pension funds being accumulated by a city for its employees?


# ■ Exercises

**E8-1.** Piney Ridge, a city with approximately 100,000 population, creates an Internal Service Center charged with the responsibility of providing printing services for the various operating departments of the city. During the current month the Service Center completed the following transactions:

1. Received a contribution from the general fund in the amount of $50,000 to be used in the initial financing of its operations.
2. Equipment costing $30,000 and supplies costing $5,000 were purchased for cash.
3. A building was rented from a real estate company at a cost of $3,600 per year. The full amount was paid at the time the lease was negotiated.
4. Other expenses amounting to $6,000 were incurred during the month.
5. Services were billed to the general fund in the amount of $9,000.
6. Equipment is estimated to have a five-year life with no salvage value at the end of that time.
7. An inventory discloses supplies on hand valued at $3,000 at the end of the month.

**Required:**
Journalize the preceding transactions in Service Center accounting records including any adjusting entries implied by them.

**E8-2.** Refer to Exercise E8-1.

**Required:**
Prepare financial statements (income statement, balance sheet, and statement of cash flows) for the Internal Service Center of Piney Ridge covering its first month of operations.

**E8-3.** The end-of-year trial balance for an internal service fund includes among others the following items:

1. equipment, $10,000
2. supplies inventory, $6,000
3. insurance expense, $3,000.

You, as the accountant, discover the following additional data relating to the financial position of the fund at the end of its fiscal year. Equipment is expected to have an estimated useful life of ten years with a $2,000 salvage value at the end of that period. Supplies on hand amount to $1,200. The amount in the insurance expense account represents the premium on a policy purchased at the beginning of the year and covering a three-year period. You also discover that the fund is obligated on a note on which interest in the amount of $75 is accrued at the end of the period.

**Required:**
Prepare the adjusting entries suggested by the preceding data.

**E8-4.**  The city of Bend operates an electric power plant that provides electric service for its citizens. The utility is expected to charge fees for electric services that will produce a net income from operations equal to approximately 5 percent of its service revenue. The utility has the following transactions during the period:
1.  Customers are billed for services in the amount of $100,000. The accounts receivable balance at the beginning of the period amounted to $20,000.
2.  Collections on account during the period were $95,000.
3.  Meter deposits of $500 were received from new customers.
4.  General operating expenses amounting to $50,000 were incurred during the period.
5.  Materials and supplies costing $10,000 were purchased on account.

**Required:**
Journalize the preceding transactions on the books of the utility fund.

**E8-5.**  Refer to Exercise E8-4. Assume the following information relating to end-of-the-period adjustments:
1.  Supplies on hand are inventoried at $2,000.
2.  Depreciation on plant and equipment amounts to $10,000.
3.  Operating expenses of $3,000 have accrued.
4.  Accrued interest expense amounting to $5,000 on bonds payable is recognized.
5.  It is estimated that approximately 1 percent of customer accounts receivable will be uncollectible.

**Required:**
Journalize the adjusting entries required by the preceding information.

**E8-6.**  A public utility operated by a city is required to accumulate funds to be used in the retirement of revenue bonds in a separate bond debt-service fund. At the end of the fiscal period, this fund shows a balance of $40,000 made up of $5,000 cash and $35,000 worth of investments.

**Required:**
How should the preceding data be reflected in the financial statements of the utility fund?

**E8-7.**  A city receives a contribution of $200,000 from a wealthy citizen with the stipulation that it is to be invested, with the earnings from the investment being used to provide college scholarships to worthy high school graduates living within the city. The city accepts the contribution and creates an agency fund to account for transactions relating to the contributed resources. During its first year of operation, the agency fund had the following transactions:
1.  Cash is received from the contributor.
2.  The cash is invested in securities.
3.  Investment income amounting to $12,000 is received.
4.  Scholarships amounting to $2,000 each are awarded to five worthy high school seniors.

**Required:**

A. Record the preceding transactions in the agency fund records.

B. Prepare a balance sheet for the fund at the end of the period.

E8-8. A municipality completes the following transactions during the current accounting period:

1. General fund transactions:
   a. Purchased automobiles for police use at a cost of $30,000.
   b. Sold an obsolete piece of equipment originally purchased with general fund resources at a cost of $25,000 for $3,000.
2. Capital projects fund transaction:
   a. Accepted completed municipal building costing $750,000, which was constructed from the proceeds of a bond issue.
3. Special assessment related transactions
   a. Completed a street improvement program financed jointly by the city and citizens with property adjacent to the street at a cost of $240,000.

**Required:**

Prepare the journal entries that should be reflected in the fixed-asset account group records as a result of the preceding transactions.

E8-9. A city has the following transactions relating to long-term debt during the current period:

1. Capital projects fund transactions:
   a. Issued bonds in the amount of $1,000,000 in exchange for cash in the amount of $1,010,000.
   b. $1,000,000 of the proceeds from the sale of bonds was spent in constructing a sewage processing plant.
2. Debt-service fund transactions:
   a. $100,000 received by the debt-service fund from the general fund to be invested and ultimately used in the retirement of general long-term debt.
   b. Interest earned from investing available funds amounts to $8,000.
3. Special assessment related transaction:
   a. Special assessment bonds amounting to $250,000 are issued for the purpose of financing a special assessment project.

**Required:**

Journalize the entries that should be recorded in the general long-term debt account group as a result of the preceding transactions.

# ■ Problems

P8-1. The Municipal Services Center for the City of Bloomville completed the following transactions for the year:

1. A contribution of $170,000 was received from the general fund to establish the Services Center.

2. Equipment costing $70,000 and supplies costing to $20,000 were purchased on account.
3. Expenses of $80,000 were incurred during the year.
4. Services were billed to other funds as follows:

| | |
|---|---:|
| General fund | $70,000 |
| Special assessments capital projects fund | 20,000 |
| Capital projects fund | 10,000 |

5. Cash was received to cover billings to the general fund and capital projects fund.
6. Vouchers amounting to $150,000 were paid.
7. Equipment is estimated to have a ten-year life with no salvage value.
8. Supplies valued at $12,000 are on hand at the end of the period.

**Required:**

A. Record the preceding transactions in a transactions worksheet. Note that there are no beginning balances. Therefore, the first pair of columns should be used for recording the transactions data. Additional columns should be provided for operating statement and balance sheet items.

B. Prepare the end-of-year financial statement for the Municipal Services Center.

**P8-2.** The general fixed-assets account group for Bloomville shows the following account balances at the beginning of the year:

| | |
|---|---:|
| Equipment | $ 900,000 |
| Structures and improvements | 1,800,000 |
| Investment in general fixed assets—from general fund | 1,500,000 |
| Investment in general fixed assets—from capital projects fund | 800,000 |
| Investment in general fixed assets—from special assessment capital projects fund | 400,000 |

During the year, the following transactions affecting the fixed-assets account group occurred:

1. New street maintenance equipment costing $290,000 was acquired through general fund expenditures.
2. Used street maintenance equipment originally purchased with general fund resources and costing $120,000 is sold for $10,000.
3. A municipal building costing $804,000 was completed by using capital projects fund resources.
4. Street improvements costing $490,000 were completed by using special assessment resources.

**Required:**

A. Enter the beginning-of-period balances for the general fixed-assets account group in the first two columns of a worksheet. Record the effects of the preceding transactions on the worksheet and complete the worksheet.

B. Prepare the appropriate end-of-year financial statement(s) for the general fixed-assets account group.

**P8-3.** The following transactions occurring during the year affect the Bloomville general long-term debt account group:
1. General obligation bonds of $1,000,000 were issued by the capital projects fund.
2. The general fund contributed $100,000 to the debt-service fund to be used for the retirement of bonds.
3. The debt-service fund realized revenues from investments in the amount of $3,900.
4. Premium from the sale of the capital project's fund bonds in the amount of $4,000 was transferred to the debt-service fund.

**Required:**
A. Journalize the effects of the preceding transactions in the general long-term debt account group accounting records.
B. Prepare the appropriate end-of-year financial statement(s) for the general long-term debt account group.

**P8-4.** Select the best answer for each of the following items:
1. Activities of a central print shop offering printing services at cost to various city departments should be accounted for in:
   a. the general fund.
   b. an internal service fund.
   c. a special revenue fund.
   d. a special assessment capital projects fund.
2. Sanders County collects property taxes for the benefit of the state government and the local school districts and periodically remits collections to these units. These activities should be accounted for in:
   a. an agency fund.
   b. the general fund.
   c. an internal service fund.
   d. a special assessment agency fund.
3. The general fixed-assets group of accounts for a municipality can best be described as:
   a. a fiscal entity.
   b. an accounting entity.
   c. an integral part of the general fund.
   d. the only fund in which to properly account for fixed assets.
4. The activities of a municipal employees' retirement and pension system should be recorded in:
   a. a general fund.
   b. a special assessment agency fund.
   c. an internal service fund.
   d. a trust fund.
5. Recreational facilities run by a governmental unit and financed on a user-charge basis would be accounted for in which fund?
   a. general
   b. trust
   c. enterprise
   d. capital projects

6. Which of the following funds frequently does not have a fund balance?
   a. general fund
   b. agency fund
   c. special revenue fund
   d. capital projects fund

7. "Excess of net billings to departments over costs" would appear in the financial statement of which fund?
   a. internal service
   b. enterprise
   c. capital projects
   d. special revenue

8. Which of the following governmental funds uses the accrual method of accounting?
   a. general
   b. internal service
   c. special service
   d. debt service

9. In which of the following funds would it be appropriate to record depreciation of fixed assets?
   a. capital projects
   b. general
   c. internal service
   d. special assessment capital projects

10. Which governmental fund would account for fixed assets in a manner similar to a "for-profit" organization?
   a. enterprise
   b. capital projects
   c. general fixed-asset group of accounts
   d. general

11. If a governmental unit established a data processing center to service all agencies within the unit, the data processing center should be accounted for as:
   a. a capital projects fund.
   b. an internal service fund.
   c. an agency fund.
   d. a trust fund.

12. The activities of a municipal golf course that receives three-fourths of its total revenue from a special tax levy should be accounted for in:
   a. an enterprise fund.
   b. the general fund.
   c. a special assessment agency fund.
   d. a special revenue fund.

13. Fixed assets used by a governmental unit should be accounted for in the:

| | Capital projects fund | General fund |
|---|---|---|
| a. | Yes | Yes |
| b. | Yes | No |
| c. | No | No |
| d. | No | Yes |

14. Unmatured general obligation bonds payable of a governmental unit should be reported in the liability section of the:
    a. general fund.
    b. capital projects fund.
    c. general long-term debt account group.
    d. debt-service fund.

15. Which of the following funds of a governmental unit uses the same basis of accounting as the enterprise fund?
    a. nonexpendable trust funds
    b. expendable trust funds
    c. special revenue funds
    d. capital projects funds

16. Fixed assets should be accounted for in the general fixed-assets account group for the:

    |  | *Enterprise fund* | *Special revenue fund* |
    |---|---|---|
    | a. | Yes | No |
    | b. | Yes | Yes |
    | c. | No | Yes |
    | d. | No | No |

17. Fixed assets of an enterprise fund should be accounted for in:
    a. the enterprise fund but no depreciation on the fixed assets should be recorded.
    b. the enterprise fund and depreciation on the fixed assets should be recorded.
    c. the general fixed-asset account group but no depreciation on the fixed assets should be recorded.
    d. the general fixed-asset account group and depreciation on the fixed assets should be recorded.

18. Customers' security deposits that cannot be spent for normal operating purposes were collected by a governmental unit and accounted for in the enterprise fund. A portion of the amount collected was invested in marketable debt securities and a portion in marketable equity securities. How would each portion be classified in the balance sheet?

    |  | *Portion in marketable debt securities* | *Portion in marketable equity securities* |
    |---|---|---|
    | a. | Unrestricted asset | Restricted asset |
    | b. | Unrestricted asset | Unrestricted asset |
    | c. | Restricted asset | Unrestricted asset |
    | d. | Restricted asset | Restricted asset |

19. Which of the following is an appropriate basis of accounting for a proprietary fund of a governmental unit?

    |  | *Cash basis* | *Modified accrual basis* |
    |---|---|---|
    | a. | Yes | Yes |
    | b. | Yes | No |
    | c. | No | No |
    | d. | No | Yes |

20. Which of the following funds of a governmental unit would include retained earnings in its balance sheet?
    a. expendable pension trust
    b. internal service
    c. special revenue
    d. capital projects

21. Fixed assets should be accounted for in the general fixed-assets account group for the

    |     | Internal service fund | Special revenue fund |
    | --- | --- | --- |
    | a. | No | Yes |
    | b. | No | No |
    | c. | Yes | No |
    | d. | Yes | Yes |

22. Which of the following funds of a governmental unit uses the same basis of accounting as an enterprise fund?
    a. special revenue
    b. expendable trust
    c. capital projects
    d. internal service

23. The amount available in debt-service funds is an account of a governmental unit that would be included in:
    a. the liability section of the general long-term debt account group.
    b. the liability section of the debt-service fund.
    c. the asset section of the general long-term debt account group.
    d. the asset section of the debt-service fund.

24. Which of the following funds of a governmental unit uses the same basis of accounting as the special revenue fund?
    a. expendable trust funds
    b. nonexpendable trust funds
    c. enterprise funds
    d. internal service funds

25. Customers' security deposits that cannot be spent for normal operating purposes were collected by a governmental unit and accounted for in the enterprise fund. A portion of the amount collected was invested in marketable securities. How would the portion in cash and the portion in marketable securities be classified in the balance sheet of the enterprise fund?

    |     | Portion in cash | Portion in marketable securities |
    | --- | --- | --- |
    | a. | Restricted asset | Restricted asset |
    | b. | Restricted asset | Unrestricted asset |
    | c. | Unrestricted asset | Unrestricted asset |
    | d. | Unrestricted asset | Restricted asset |

    —**AICPA Adapted**

**P8-5.** Select the best answer for each of the following items:
1. What would be the effect on the general fund balance in the current fiscal year of recording a $15,000 purchase of a new fire truck out of general fund resources,

for which a $14,600 encumbrance had been recorded in the general fund in the previous fiscal year?

   a.  Reduce the unreserved general fund balance $15,000.

   b.  Reduce the unreserved general fund balance $14,600.

   c.  Reduce the unreserved general fund balance $400.

   d.  Have no effect on the unreserved general fund balance.

2.  Brockton City's debt-service fund (for term bonds) recorded required additions and required earnings for the current fiscal year of $15,000 and $7,000, respectively. The actual additions and interest earnings were $16,000 and $6,500, respectively. What are the necessary entries to record the year's actual additions and earnings in the debt-service fund and in the general long-term debt group, respectively?

   a.  $22,500 and $22,000

   b.  $22,000 and $22,000

   c.  $22,500 and $22,500

   d.  $22,500 and no entry

3.  Brockton City's water utility, which is an enterprise fund, submits a bill for $9,000 to the general fund for water service supplied to city departments and agencies. Submission of this bill would result in:

   a.  creation of balances that will be eliminated on the city's combined balance sheet.

   b.  recognition of revenue by the water utility fund and of an expenditure by the general fund.

   c.  recognition of an encumbrance by both the water utility fund and the general fund.

   d.  creation of a balance that will be eliminated on the city's combined statement of changes in fund balances.

4.  Brockton City's water utility, which is an enterprise fund, transferred land and a building to the general city administration for public use at *no* charge to the city. The land was carried on the water utility books at $4,000 and the building at a cost of $30,000 on which $23,000 depreciation had been recorded. In the year of the transfer, what would be the effect of the transaction?

   a.  Reduce retained earnings of the water utility by $11,000 and increase the fund balance of the general fund by $11,000.

   b.  Reduce retained earnings of the water utility by $11,000 and increase the total assets in the general fixed-assets group by $11,000.

   c.  Reduce retained earnings of the water utility by $11,000 and increase the total assets in the general fixed-assets group by $34,000.

   d.  Have no effect on a combined balance sheet for the city.

5.  A city collects property taxes for the benefit of the local sanitary, park, and school districts and periodically remits collections to these units. This activity should be accounted for in:

   a.  an agency fund.

   b.  the general fund.

   c.  an internal service fund.

   d.  a special assessment agency fund.

   e.  none of the above.

6.  The activities of a central motor pool that provides and services vehicles for the use of municipal employees on official business should be accounted for in:
    a.  an agency fund.
    b.  the general fund.
    c.  an internal service fund.
    d.  a special revenue fund.
    e.  none of the above.

7.  Brockton City serves as collecting agency for the local independent school district and for a local water district. For this purpose, Brockton has created a single agency fund and charges the other entities a fee of 1 percent of the gross amounts collected. (The service fee is treated as general fund revenue.) During the latest fiscal year, a gross amount of $268,000 was collected for the independent school district and $80,000 for the water district. As a consequence of the foregoing, Brockton's general fund should:
    a.  recognize receipts of $348,000.
    b.  recognize receipts of $344,520.
    c.  record revenue of $3,480.
    d.  record encumbrances of $344,520.

8.  A transaction in which a municipal electric utility paid $150,000 out of its earnings for new equipment requires accounting recognition in:
    a.  an enterprise fund.
    b.  the general fund.
    c.  the general fund and the general fixed-assets group of accounts.
    d.  an enterprise fund and the general fixed-assets group of accounts.
    e.  none of the above.

9.  The liability for general obligation bonds issued for the benefit of a municipal electric company and serviced by its earnings should be recorded in:
    a.  an enterprise fund.
    b.  the general fund.
    c.  an enterprise fund and the general long-term debt group.
    d.  an enterprise fund and disclosed in a footnote in the statement of general long-term debt.
    e.  none of the above.

10. The operations of a municipal swimming pool receiving the majority of its support from charges to users should be accounted for in:
    a.  a special revenue fund.
    b.  the general fund.
    c.  an internal service fund.
    d.  an enterprise fund.
    e.  none of the above.

11. The fixed assets of a central purchasing and stores department organized to serve all municipal departments should be recorded in:
    a.  an enterprise fund and the general fixed-assets group.
    b.  an enterprise fund.
    c.  the general fixed-assets group.

    d.  the general fund.

    e.  none of the above.

12.  The monthly remittance to an insurance company of the lump sum of hospital-surgical insurance premiums collected as payroll deductions from employees should be recorded in:

    a.  the general fund.

    b.  an agency fund.

    c.  a special revenue fund.

    d.  an internal service fund.

    e.  none of the above.

13.  Several years ago, a city provided for the establishment of a debt-service fund to retire an issue of general obligation bonds. This year the city made a $50,000 contribution to the debt-service fund from general revenues and realized $15,000 in revenue from securities in the debt-service fund. The bonds due this year were retired. These transactions require accounting recognition in:

    a.  the general fund.

    b.  a debt-service fund and the general long-term debt group of accounts.

    c.  a debt-service fund, the general fund, and the general long-term debt group of accounts.

    d.  a capital projects fund, a debt-service fund, the general fund, and the general long-term debt group of accounts.

    e.  none of the above.

14.  What will be the balance sheet effect of recording $50,000 of depreciation in the accounts of a utility, an enterprise fund, owned by Brockton City?

    a.  Reduce total assets of the utility fund and the general fixed-assets group by $50,000.

    b.  Reduce total assets of the utility fund by $50,000 but have no effect on the general fixed-assets group.

    c.  Reduce total assets of the general fixed-assets group by $50,000 but have no effect on assets of the utility fund.

    d.  Have no effect on total assets of either the utility fund or the general fixed-assets group.

15.  The activities of a central data processing department that offers data processing services at a discount to other municipal departments should be accounted for in:

    a.  an enterprise fund.

    b.  an internal service fund.

    c.  a special revenue fund.

    d.  the general fund.

                                            **—AICPA Adapted**

**P8-6.**  Select the best answer for each of the following items.

    1.  What type of account is used to earmark the *fund balance* to liquidate the contingent obligations of goods ordered but not yet received?

        a.  appropriations

        b.  encumbrances

     c.  obligations

     d.  fund balance reserved for encumbrances

2. Premiums received on general obligation bonds are generally transferred to what fund or group of accounts?

     a.  debt service

     b.  general long-term debt

     c.  general

     d.  special revenue

3. Self-supporting activities that are provided to the public on a user-charge basis are accounted for in what fund?

     a.  agency

     b.  enterprise

     c.  internal service

     d.  special revenue

4. A statement of cash flows is prepared for which fund?

     a.  enterprise

     b.  capital projects

     c.  special assessment capital projects fund

     d.  trust

5. A city should record depreciation as an expense in its:

     a.  general fund and enterprise fund.

     b.  internal service fund and general fixed-assets group of accounts.

     c.  enterprise fund and internal service fund.

     d.  enterprise fund and capital projects fund.

6. Authority granted by a legislative body to make expenditures and to incur obligations during a fiscal year is the definition of:

     a.  an appropriation.

     b.  an authorization.

     c.  an encumbrance.

     d.  an expenditure.

7. An account for expenditures does *not* appear in which fund?

     a.  capital projects

     b.  enterprise

     c.  special assessment capital projects fund

     d.  special revenue

8. Part of the general-obligation bond proceeds from a new issuance was used to pay for the cost of a new city hall as soon as construction was completed. The remainder of the proceeds was transferred to repay the debt. Entries are needed to record these transactions in:

     a.  the general fund and general long-term debt group of accounts.

     b.  the general fund, general long-term debt group of accounts, and debt-service fund.

     c.  the trust fund, debt-service fund, and general fixed-assets group of accounts.

     d.  the general long-term debt group of accounts, debt-service fund, general fixed-assets group of accounts, and capital projects fund.

9. Cash secured from property tax revenue was transferred for the eventual payment of principal and interest on general obligation bonds. The bonds had been issued when land had been acquired several years ago for a city park. Upon the transfer, an entry would *not* be made in which of the following?
   a. debt-service fund
   b. general fixed-assets group of accounts
   c. general long-term debt group of accounts
   d. general fund

10. Equipment in general governmental service that had been constructed ten years before by a capital projects fund was sold. The receipts were accounted for as unrestricted revenue. Entries are necessary in:
   a. the general fund and capital projects fund.
   b. the general fund and general fixed-assets groups of accounts.
   c. the general fund, capital projects fund, and enterprise fund.
   d. the general fund, capital projects fund, and general fixed-assets group of accounts.

   —AICPA Adapted

**P8-7.** Select the best answer for each of the following items:
   1. Dodd Village received a gift of a new fire engine from a local resident. The fair market value of this fire engine was $200,000. The entry to be made in the general fixed assets account group for this gift is:

|   |   | Debit | Credit |
|---|---|---|---|
| a. | Machinery and equipment | $200,000 | |
|   | Investment in general fixed assets from private gifts | | $200,000 |
| b. | Investment in general fixed assets | $200,000 | |
|   | Gift revenue | | $200,000 |
| c. | General fund assets | $200,000 | |
|   | Private gifts | | $200,000 |
| d. | Memorandum entry only | — | — |

   2. Wells Township issued the following long-term obligations:

| | |
|---|---|
| Revenue bonds to be repaid from admission fees collected by the township swimming pool | $500,000 |
| General obligation bonds issued for the township water and sewer fund which will service the debt | 900,000 |

   Although the above-mentioned bonds are expected to be paid from enterprise funds, the full faith and credit of Wells Township has been pledged as further assurance that the liabilities will be paid. What amount of these bonds should be accounted for in the general long-term debt account group?

a. $1,400,000
b. $900,000
c. $500,000
d. $0

3. Lake City operates a centralized data processing center through an internal service fund, to provide data processing services to Lake's other governmental units. In 19X6, this internal service fund billed Lake's water and sewer fund $100,000 for data processing services. How should the internal service fund record this billing?

| | | Debit | Credit |
|---|---|---|---|
| a. | Memorandum entry only | — | — |
| b. | Due from water and sewer fund | $100,000 | |
| | Data processing department expenses | | $100,000 |
| c. | Intergovernmental transfers | $100,000 | |
| | Interfund exchanges | | $100,000 |
| d. | Due from water and sewer fund | $100,000 | |
| | Operating revenues control | | $100,000 |

4. Grove County collects property taxes levied within its boundaries and receives a 1 percent fee for administering these collections on behalf of the municipalities located in the county. In 19X7, Grove collected $1,000,000 for its municipalities and remitted $990,000 to them after deducting fees of $10,000. In the initial recording of the 1 percent fee, Grove's agency fund should credit:
a. fund balance—agency fund, $10,000.
b. fees earned—agency fund, $10,000.
c. due to Grove County general fund, $10,000.
d. revenues control, $10,000.

5. During 19X7, Pine City recorded the following receipts from self-sustaining activities paid for by users of the services rendered:

| | |
|---|---|
| Municipal bus system | $1,000,000 |
| Operation of water supply and sewage plant | 1,800,000 |

What amount should be accounted for in Pine's enterprise funds?
a. $2,800,000
b. $1,800,000
c. $1,000,000
d. $0

6. Ridge City issued the following bonds during the year ended July 31, 19X8:

| | |
|---|---|
| General obligation bonds issued for the Ridge water and sewer enterprise fund that are expected to service the debt (city secondarily liable) | $700,000 |
| Revenue bonds to be repaid from admission fees collected by the Ridge municipal swimming pool enterprise fund | 290,000 |

The amount of these bonds that should be accounted for in Ridge's general long-term debt account group is:

a. $990,000.
b. $700,000.
c. $290,000.
d. $0.

7. Kew City issued the following long-term obligations:

| | |
|---|---:|
| Revenue bonds to be repaid from admission fees collected from users of the city swimming pool | $1,000,000 |
| General obligation bonds issued for the city water and sewer fund which will service the debt | 1,800,000 |

Although the above mentioned bonds are expected to be paid from enterprise funds, the full faith and credit of the city has been pledged as further assurance that the obligations will be paid. What amount of these bonds should be accounted for in the general long-term debt account group?

a. $0
b. $1,000,000
c. $1,800,000
d. $2,800,000

8. Hull City has established a separate internal service (self-insurance) fund to pay claims and judgments of all of Hull's funds. In 19X7, payments to the insurer fund amounted to $500,000, while the actuarially determined amount was $400,000. The payments to the insurer fund should be accounted for as:

| | An operating transfer of | A residual equity transfer of |
|---|---|---|
| a. | $0 | $0 |
| b. | $100,000 | $400,000 |
| c. | $400,000 | $100,000 |
| d. | $500,000 | $0 |

9. The following proceeds received by Grove City in 19X7 are legally restricted to expenditure for specified purposes:

| | |
|---|---:|
| Donation by a benefactor mandated to an expendable trust fund to provide meals for the needy | $300,000 |
| Sales taxes to finance the maintenance of tourist facilities in the shopping district | 900,000 |

What amount should be accounted for in Grove's special revenue funds?

a. $0
b. $300,000
c. $900,000
d. $1,200,000

10. The following information for the year ended June 30, 19X8, pertains to a proprietary fund established by Burwood Village in connection with Burwood's public parking facilities:

| | |
|---|---|
| Receipts from users of parking facilities | $400,000 |
| Expenditures | |
|    Parking meters | 210,000 |
|    Salaries and other cash expenses | 90,000 |
| Depreciation of parking meters | 70,000 |

For the year ended June 30, 19X8, this proprietary fund should report net income of:
a. $0.
b. $30,000.
c. $100,000.
d. $240,000.

11. The following fund types used by Green Township had total assets at June 30, 19X9 as follows:

| | |
|---|---|
| Agency funds | $ 300,000 |
| Debt-service funds | 1,000,000 |

Total fiduciary fund assets amount to:
a. $0.
b. $300,000.
c. $1,000,000.
d. $1,300,000.

12. The following fund types used by Cliff City had total assets at December 31, 19X7, as follows:

| | |
|---|---|
| Special revenue funds | $100,000 |
| Agency funds | 150,000 |
| Trust funds | 200,000 |

Total fiduciary fund assets amounted to:
a. $200,000.
b. $300,000.
c. $350,000.
d. $450,000.

13. The following information pertains to a computer that Pine Township leased from Karl Supply Co. on July 1, 19X8, for general township use:

| | |
|---|---|
| Karl's cost | $5,000 |
| Fair value at July 1, 19X8 | $5,000 |
| Estimated economic life | 5 years |
| Fixed noncancelable term | 30 months |

| | |
|---|---|
| Rental at beginning of each month | $ 135 |
| Guaranteed residual value | $2,000 |
| Present value of minimum lease payments at July 1, 19X8, | |
| using Pine's incremental borrowing rate of 10.5% | $5,120 |
| Karl's implicit interest rate of 12.04% | $5,000 |

This lease is treated as a capital lease. On July 1, 19X8, what amount should Pine capitalize in its general fixed assets account group for this leased computer?

a. $0
b. $3,000
c. $5,000
d. $5,120

—AICPA Adapted

**P8-8.** Select the best answer for each of the following items. Items 1 through 6 are based on the following information:

Rock County has acquired equipment through a noncancelable lease–purchase agreement dated December 31, 19X9. This agreement requires no down payment and the following minimum lease payments:

| December 31 | Principal | Interest | Total |
|---|---|---|---|
| 1990 | $50,000 | $15,000 | $65,000 |
| 1991 | 50,000 | 10,000 | 60,000 |
| 1992 | 50,000 | 5,000 | 55,000 |

1. What account should be debited for $150,000 in the general fund at inception of the lease if the equipment is a general fixed asset and Rock does *not* use a capital projects fund?
   a. other financing uses control
   b. equipment
   c. expenditures control
   d. memorandum entry only

2. What account should be credited for $150,000 in the general fixed assets account group at inception of the lease if the equipment is a general fixed asset?
   a. fund balance from capital lease transactions
   b. other financing sources control—capital leases
   c. expenditures control—capital leases
   d. investment in general fixed assets—capital leases

3. What journal entry is required for $150,000 in the general long-term debt account group at inception of the lease if the lease payments are to be financed with general government resources?

|  | Debit | Credit |
|---|---|---|
| a. | Expenditures control | Other financing sources control |
| b. | Other financing uses control | Expenditures control |
| c. | Amount to be provided for lease payments | Capital lease payable |
| d. | Capital lease payable | Amount to be provided for lease payments |

4. If the lease payments are required to be made from a debt-service fund, what account or accounts should be debited in the debt-service fund for the December 31, 19X1, lease payment of $65,000?

| a. | Expenditures control | $65,000 |
|---|---|---|
| b. | Other financing sources control | $50,000 |
|  | Expenditures control | 15,000 |
| c. | Amount to be provided for lease payments | $50,000 |
|  | Expenditures control | 15,000 |
| d. | Expenditures control | $50,000 |
|  | Amount to be provided for lease payments | 15,000 |

5. If the equipment is used in enterprise fund operations and the lease payments are to be financed with enterprise fund revenues, what account should be debited for $150,000 in the enterprise fund at inception of the lease?
   a. expenses control
   b. expenditures control
   c. other financing sources control
   d. equipment

6. If the equipment is used in internal service fund operations and the lease payments are financed with internal service fund revenues, what account or accounts should be debited in the internal service fund for the December 31, 19X1, lease payment of $65,000?

| a. | Expenditures control | $65,000 |
|---|---|---|
| b. | Expenses control | $65,000 |
| c. | Capital lease payable | $50,000 |
|  | Expenses control | 15,000 |
| d. | Expenditures control | $50,000 |
|  | Expenses control | 15,000 |

Items 7 through 9 are based on the following information:

Elm City contributes to and administers a single-employer–defined benefit pension plan on behalf of its covered employees. The plan is accounted for in a pension trust fund. Actuarially determined employer contribution requirements and contributions actually made for the past three years, along with the percentage of annual covered payroll, were as follows:

|  | Contribution Made | | Actuarial Requirement | |
|  | Amount | Percent | Amount | Percent |
| --- | --- | --- | --- | --- |
| 19X9 | $ 11,000 | 26 | $ 11,000 | 26 |
| 19X8 | 5,000 | 12 | 10,000 | 24 |
| 19X7 | None | None | 8,000 | 20 |

7. What account should be credited in the pension trust fund to record the 19X9 employer contribution of $11,000?
   a. revenues control
   b. other financing sources control
   c. due from special revenue fund
   d. pension benefit obligation

8. To record the 19X9 pension contribution of $11,000, what debit is required in the governmental-type fund used in connection with employer pension contributions?
   a. other financing uses control
   b. expenditures control
   c. expenses control
   d. due to pension trust fund

9. In the notes to Elm's 19X9 financial statements, employer contributions expressed as percentages of annual covered payroll should be shown to the extent available for a minimum of:
   a. 1 year.
   b. 2 years.
   c. 3 years.
   d. 12 years.

—AICPA Adapted

P8-9. Select the best answer for each of the following items:
Items 1 through 5 are based on the following information:

Todd City formally integrates budgetary accounts into its general fund. Todd uses an internal service fund to account for the operations of its data processing center, which provides services to Todd's other governmental units.

During the year ended December 31, 19X9, Todd received a state grant to buy a bus and an additional grant for bus operation in 19X9. In 19X9, only 90 percent of the capital grant was used for the bus purchase, but 100 percent of the operating grant was disbursed.

Todd has incurred the following long-term obligations:

General obligation bonds issued for the water and sewer fund which will service the debt.

Revenue bonds to be repaid from admission fees collected from users of the municipal recreation center.

These bonds are expected to be paid from enterprise funds but are secured by Todd's full faith, credit, and taxing power as further assurance that the obligations will be paid.

Todd's 19X9 expenditures from the general fund include payments for structural alterations to a firehouse and furniture for the mayor's office.

1. To record the billing for data processing services provided to Todd's other governmental units, the internal service fund should credit:
   a. operating revenues.
   b. data processing departmental expenses.
   c. intergovernmental transfers.
   d. interfund exchanges.

2. In reporting the state grants for the bus purchase and operation, what should Todd include as grant revenues for the year ended December 31, 19X9?

| | 90% of the capital grant | 100% of the capital grant | Operating grant |
|---|---|---|---|
| a. | Yes | No | No |
| b. | No | Yes | No |
| c. | No | Yes | Yes |
| d. | Yes | No | Yes |

3. Which of Todd's long-term obligations should be accounted for in the general long-term debt account group?

| | General obligation bonds | Revenue bonds |
|---|---|---|
| a. | Yes | Yes |
| b. | Yes | No |
| c. | No | Yes |
| d. | No | No |

4. When Todd records its annual budget, which of the following control accounts indicates the amount of the authorized spending limitation for the year ending December 31, 19X9?
   a. reserved for appropriations
   b. appropriations

    c.   reserved for encumbrances

    d.   encumbrances

5.  In Todd's general fund balance sheet presentation at December 31, 19X9, which of the following expenditures should be classified as fixed assets?

| | Structural alterations to firehouse | Mayor's office furniture |
|---|---|---|
| a. | No | No |
| b. | No | Yes |
| c. | Yes | No |
| d. | Yes | Yes |

—**AICPA Adapted**

**P8-10.** The following accounts frequently appear in municipal accounting records. On a separate answer sheet, list the letter(s) next to the account indicating the municipal funds in which these accounts appear. An account might appear in more than one fund.

| | Accounts | | Municipal Accounting Funds |
|---|---|---|---|
| 1. | Bonds payable | a. | General |
| 2. | Reserve for encumbrances | b. | Special revenue |
| 3. | Proceeds from sale of bonds | c. | Capital projects |
| 4. | Estimated bond issue proceeds | d. | Special assessment capital projects |
| 5. | Equipment | e. | Debt service |
| 6. | Appropriation | f. | Internal service |
| 7. | Estimated revenues | g. | Trust and agency |
| 8. | Taxes receivable—current | h. | Utility or other enterprises |
| 9. | Amount provided for retirement of bonds | i. | General fixed assets |
| 10. | Contracts payable—retained percentage | j. | General long-term debt |

—**AICPA Adapted**

**P8-11.** Your examination of the financial statements of the Town of Ecalpon for the year ended June 30, 19X3, disclosed that the town's inexperienced bookkeeper was uninformed regarding governmental accounting and recorded all transactions in the general fund. The following general fund trial balance was prepared by the book-keeper:

## Town of Ecalpon General Fund Trial Balance June 30, 19X3

| | | |
|---|---:|---:|
| Cash | $ 12,900 | |
| Accounts receivable | 1,200 | |
| Taxes receivable, current year | 8,000 | |
| Tax anticipation notes payable | | $ 15,000 |
| Appropriations | | 350,000 |
| Expenditures | 344,000 | |
| Estimated revenues | 290,000 | |
| Revenues | | 320,000 |
| Town property | 16,100 | |
| Bonds payable retired | 36,000 | |
| Unreserved fund balance | | 23,200 |
| Totals | $708,200 | $708,200 |

Your audit disclosed the following:

1. The accounts receivable balance was due from the town's water utility for the sale of scrap iron. Accounts for the municipal water utility operated by the town are maintained in a separate fund.

2. The total tax levy for the year was $280,000, of which $10,000 was abated during the year. The town's tax collection experience in recent years indicates an average loss of 5 percent of the net tax levy for uncollectible taxes.

3. On June 30, 19X3, the town retired at face value 4 percent General Obligation Serial Bonds totaling $30,000. The bonds were issued on July 1, 19X1, in the total amount of $150,000. Interest paid during the year was also recorded in the bonds payable retired account.

4. At the beginning of the year, the Town Council authorized to service various departments a supply room with an inventory not to exceed $10,000. During the year, supplies totaling $12,300 were purchased and charged to expenditures. The physical inventory taken at June 30 disclosed that supplies totaling $8,400 were used.

5. Expenditures for 19X3 included $2,600 applicable to purchase orders issued in the prior year. Outstanding purchase orders at June 30, 19X3 not recorded in the accounts amounted to $4,100.

6. The amount of $8,200, due from the state for the town's share of state gasoline taxes, was not recorded in the accounts.

7. Equipment costing $7,500 was removed from service and sold for $900 during the year and new equipment costing $17,000 purchased. These transactions were recorded in the town property account.

**Required:**

A. Prepare the formal correcting and closing journal entries for the general fund.

B. Prepare the formal correcting journal entries for any other funds or groups of accounts. (The bookkeeper has recorded all transactions in the general fund.)

—**AICPA** Adapted

**P8-12.** The City of Larkspur provides electric energy for its citizens through an operating department. All transactions of the Electric Department are recorded in a self-sustaining fund supported by revenue from the sales of energy. Plant expansion is financed by the issuance of bonds that are repaid out of revenues.

All cash of the Electric Department is held by the City Treasurer. Receipts from customers and others are deposited in the treasurer's account. Disbursements are made by drawing warrants on the treasurer.

The following is the post-closing trial balance of the department as of June 30, 19A:

| | | |
|---|---:|---:|
| Cash on deposit with City Treasurer | $ 2,250,000 | |
| Due from customers | 2,120,000 | |
| Other current assets | 130,000 | |
| Construction in progress | 500,000 | |
| Land | 5,000,000 | |
| Electric plant | 50,000,000* | |
| Accumulated depreciation—electric plant | | $10,000,000 |
| Accounts payable and accrued liabilities | | 3,270,000 |
| 5 percent electric revenue bonds | | 20,000,000 |
| Accumulated earnings | | 26,730,000 |
| | $60,000,000 | $60,000,000 |

*The plant is being depreciated on the basis of a fifty-year composite life.

During the year ending June 30, 19B, the department had the following transactions:

1. Sales of electric energy, $10,700,000.
2. Purchases of fuel and operating supplies on account, $2,950,000.
3. Construction of miscellaneous system improvements (financed from operations), $750,000 paid in cash.
4. Fuel consumed, $2,790,000.
5. Miscellaneous plant additions and improvements placed in service, $1,000,000.
6. Wages and salaries paid, $4,280,000.
7. Sale on December 31, 19A, of twenty-year 5 percent Electric Revenue bonds, with interest payable semiannually, $5,000,000.
8. Expenditures out of bond proceeds for construction of Larkspur Steam Plant Unit No. 1 and control house, $2,800,000.
9. Operating materials and supplies consumed, $150,000.
10. Payments received from customers, $10,500,000.
11. Expenditures out of bond proceeds for construction of Larkspur Steam Plant Unit No. 2, $2,200,000.
12. Warrants drawn on City Treasurer in settlement of accounts payable, $3,045,000.
13. Larkspur Steam Plant placed in service June 30, 19B; depreciation on plant additions is $10,000.
14. Interest in the amount of $1,125,000 is paid.

**Required:**
Prepare a transactions worksheet for the Electric Department.

—AICPA Adapted

P8-13.   The City of New Arnheim has engaged you to examine the following balance sheet that was prepared by the city's bookkeeper:

### City of New Arnheim Balance Sheet June 30, 19B

#### Assets

| | |
|---|---:|
| Cash | $ 159,000 |
| Taxes receivable—current | 32,000 |
| Supplies on hand | 9,000 |
| Marketable securities | 250,000 |
| Land | 1,000,000 |
| Fixed assets | 7,000,000 |
| Total | $8,450,000 |

#### Liabilities

| | |
|---|---:|
| Vouchers payable | $  42,000 |
| Reserve for supplies inventory | 8,000 |
| Bonds payable | 3,000,000 |
| Fund balance | 5,400,000 |
| Total | $8,450,000 |

Your audit disclosed the following information:
1.   An analysis of the fund balance account:

| | | |
|---|---:|---:|
| Balance, June 30, 19A | | $2,100,000 |
| Add: | | |
| Donated land | $  800,000 | |
| Federal grant-in-aid | 2,200,000 | |
| Creation of endowment fund | 250,000 | |
| Excess of actual tax revenue over estimated revenue | 24,000 | |
| Excess of appropriations closed out over expenditures | 20,000 | |
| Net income from endowment funds | 10,000 | 3,304,000 |
| | | 5,404,000 |
| Deduct: | | |
| Excess of Cultural Center operating expenses over income | | 4,000 |
| Balance, June 30, 19B | | $5,400,000 |

2.  In July 19A, land appraised at a fair market value of $800,000 was donated to the City for a Cultural Center that was opened on April 15, 19B. Building construction expenditures for the project were financed from a federal grant-in-aid of $2,200,000 and from an authorized ten-year $3,000,000 issue of 8 percent general obligation bonds sold at par on July 1, 19A. Interest is payable on December 31 and June 30. The fair market value of the land and the cost of the building, respectively, are included in the land and fixed-assets accounts.

3.  The Cultural Center receives no direct state or city subsidy for current operating expenses. A Cultural Center endowment fund was established by a gift of marketable securities having a fair market value of $250,000 at date of receipt. The endowment principal is to be kept intact. Income is to be applied to any operating deficit of the center.

4.  Other data:
    a.  It is anticipated that $7,000 of the 19A–B tax levy is uncollectible.
    b.  The physical inventory of supplies on hand at June 30, 19B amounted to $12,500.
    c.  Unfilled purchase orders for the general fund at June 30, 19B, totaled $5,000.
    d.  On July 1, 19A, an all-purpose building was purchased for $2,000,000. Of the purchase price, $200,000 was allotted to the land. The purchase had been authorized under the budget for the year ended June 30, 19B.

**Required:**

Prepare a worksheet showing adjustments and distributions to the proper funds or groups of accounts. The worksheet should be in the form of the City of New Arnheim's balance sheet and have the following column headings:

A.  Balance per books
B.  Adjustments—debit
C.  Adjustments—credit
D.  General fund
E.  City Cultural Center endowment fund:
    Principal
    Income
F.  General fixed assets
G.  General long-term debt

(Number all adjusting entries. Formal journal entries are not required. Supporting computations should be in good form.)

—AICPA Adapted

**P8-14.**  From the following information concerning the City of Langdon, you are to prepare as of December 31, 19A:
    a.  a worksheet reflecting the transactions, closing entries and balance sheet for its general fund
    b.  a statement of operations for its internal service fund
    c.  a balance sheet for its internal service fund.

The accounts of the general fund as of January 1, 19A, were as follows:

| | |
|---|---:|
| Cash | $1,000 |
| Taxes receivable—delinquent | 8,000 |
| Accounts payable | 7,000 |
| Fund balance reserve for encumbrances | 1,500 |
| Unreserved fund balance | 500 |

The following transactions for the current year are to be considered:

1. The budget that was adopted for 19A provided for taxes of $375,000, fees of $15,000, and license revenues of $10,000. Appropriations were $290,000 for general fund operations, and $100,000 for the purpose of establishing an internal service fund.
2. All taxes became receivable.
3. Cash receipts for the general fund included:

| | |
|---|---:|
| Taxes from 19A | $360,000 |
| Fees | 16,000 |
| Licenses | 9,500 |
| Taxes receivable—delinquent plus interest of $500. Tax liens were obtained on the remainder of the delinquent taxes | 5,500 |

4. Contracts amounting to $75,000 were let by the general fund.
5. Services rendered by the internal service fund to other departments included: general fund, $40,000; utility fund, $20,000, of which $5,000 remained uncollected at the end of the year.
6. The following cash disbursements were made by the general fund:

| | |
|---|---:|
| Internal service fund | $100,000 |
| Accounts payable of the preceding year | 7,000 |
| Outstanding orders at beginning of year were all received and paid for | 2,000 |
| Expenses of fund incurred during year | 145,000 |
| Stores purchased for central storeroom established during year | 5,000 |
| Contracts let during year | 30,000 |
| Permanent advance to newly created petty cash fund | 1,000 |
| Services performed by internal service fund | 35,000 |
| Salaries paid during year | 30,000 |

7. The following cash disbursements were made by the internal service fund:

| | |
|---|---:|
| Purchase of equipment (estimated useful life 10 years) | $60,000 |
| Purchase of materials and supplies of which 1/5 remained at end of year | 40,000 |

Salaries and wages as follows:

| | |
|---|---|
| Direct labor | 9,000 |
| Office salaries | 2,000 |
| Superintendent's salary | 4,000 |
| Heat, light, and power | 2,000 |
| Office expenses | 500 |

8. All unpaid taxes become delinquent.
9. Stores inventory in general fund amounted to $2,000 on December 31, 19A.

— AICPA Adapted

P8-15. You have been engaged to examine the financial statements of the town of Workville for the year ended June 30, 19X6. Your examination disclosed that due to the inexperience of the town's bookkeeper all transactions were recorded in the general fund. The following general fund trial balance as of June 30, 19X6, was furnished to you:

### Town of Workville General Fund Trial Balance June 30, 19X6

| | Debit | Credit |
|---|---|---|
| Cash | $ 16,800 | |
| Short-term investments | 40,000 | |
| Accounts receivable | 11,500 | |
| Taxes receivable—current year | 30,000 | |
| Tax anticipation notes payable | | $ 50,000 |
| Appropriations | | 400,000 |
| Expenditures | 382,000 | |
| Estimated revenue | 320,000 | |
| Revenues | | 360,000 |
| General property | 85,400 | |
| Bonds payable | 52,000 | |
| Unreserved fund balance | | 127,700 |
| | $937,700 | $937,700 |

Your audit disclosed the following additional information:

1. The accounts receivable of $11,500 includes $1,500 due from the town's water utility for the sale of scrap. Accounts for the municipal water utility operated by the town are maintained in a separate fund.
2. The balance in taxes receivable—current year is now considered delinquent, and the town estimates that $24,000 will be uncollectible.
3. On June 30, 19X6, the town retired, at face value, 6 percent general obligation serial bonds totaling $40,000. The bonds were issued on July 1, 19X1, at face value of $200,000. Interest paid during the year ended June 30, 19X6, was charged to bonds payable.

4.  In order to service other municipal departments, the town at the beginning of the year authorized the establishment of a central supplies warehouse. During the year, supplies totaling $128,000 were purchased and charged to expenditures. The town chose to conduct a physical inventory of supplies on hand at June 30, 19X6, and this physical count disclosed that supplies totaling $84,000 were used.

5.  Expenditures for the year ended June 30, 19X6, included $11,200 applicable to purchase orders issued in the prior year. Outstanding purchase orders at June 30, 19X6, not recorded in the accounts amounted to $17,500.

6.  One June 28, 19X6, the State Revenue Department informed the town that its share of a state-collected, locally shared tax would be $34,000.

7.  During the year, equipment with a book value of $7,900 was removed from service and sold for $4,600. In addition, new equipment costing $90,000 was purchased. The transactions were recorded in general property.

8.  During the year, 100 acres of land were donated to the town for use as an industrial park. The land had a value of $125,000. No recording of this donation has been made.

**Required:**

A.  Prepare the formal reclassification, adjusting, and closing journal entries for the general fund as of June 30, 19X6.

B.  Prepare the formal adjusting journal entries for any other funds or groups of accounts as of June 30, 19X6.

—**AICPA Adapted**

**P8-16.**  The following transactions represent practical situations frequently encountered in accounting for municipal governments. Each transaction is independent of the others.

1.  The city council of Bernardville adopted a budget for the general operations of the government during the new fiscal year. Revenues were estimated at $695,000. Legal authorizations for budgeted expenditures were $650,000.

2.  Taxes of $160,000 were levied for the special revenue fund of Millstown. One percent was estimated to be uncollectible.

3.  a.  On July 25, 19X1, office supplies estimated to cost $2,390 were ordered for the city manager's office of Bullersville. Bullersville, which operates on the calendar year, does not maintain an inventory of such supplies.

    b.  The supplies ordered July 25 were received on August 9, 19X1, accompanied by an invoice for $2,500.

4.  On October 10, 19X1, the general fund of Washingtonville repaid to the utility fund a loan of $1,000 plus $40 interest. The loan had been made earlier in the fiscal year.

5.  A prominent citizen died and left ten acres of undeveloped land to Harper City for a future school site. The donor's cost of the land was $55,000. The fair value of the land was $85,000.

6.  a.  On March 6, 19X1, Dahlstrom City issued 8 percent special assessment bonds payable March 6, 19X6, at face value of $90,000. Interest is payable annually. Dahlstrom City, which operates on the calendar year, will use the proceeds to finance a curbing project.

    b.  On October 29, 19X1, the full $84,000 cost of the completed curbing project was accrued. Also, appropriate closing entries were made with regard to the project.

7.  a.  Conrad Thamm, a citizen of Basking Knoll, donated common stock valued at $22,000 to the city under a trust agreement. Under the terms of the agreement,

the principal amount is to be kept intact; use of revenue from the stock is restricted to financing academic college scholarships for needy students.

b. On December 14, 19X1, dividends of $1,100 were received on the stock donated by Mr. Thamm.

8. a. On February 23, 19X1, the town of Lincoln, which operates on the calendar year, issued 8 percent general obligation bonds with a face value of $300,000, payable Feb. 23, 19X1 + 10, to finance the construction of an addition to the city hall. Total proceeds were $308,000.

b. On December 31, 19X1, the addition to the city hall was officially approved, the full cost of $297,000 was paid to the contractor, and appropriate closing entries were made with regard to the project. (Assume that no entries have been made with regard to the project since February 23, 19X1.)

**Required:**

For each transaction, prepare the necessary journal entries for all of the funds and groups of accounts involved. No explanation of the journal entries is required. Use the following headings for your workpaper:

| Transaction Number | Journal Entries | Dr. | Cr. | Fund or Group of Accounts |
| --- | --- | --- | --- | --- |

In the far right column, indicate in which fund or group of accounts each entry is to be made, using the following coding:

Funds
  General                                                                                     G
  Special revenue                                                                          SR
  Capital projects                                                                          CP
  Debt-service                                                                               DS
  Special assessments capital projects                                      SA
  Enterprise                                                                                   E
  Internal service                                                                          IS
  Trust and agency                                                                       TA
Groups of accounts
  General fixed assets                                                                  GFA
  General long-term debt                                                            LTD

—**AICPA Adapted**

P8-17. In compliance with a newly enacted state law, Dial County assumed the responsibility of collecting all property taxes levied within its boundaries as of July 1, 19X1. A composite property tax rate per $100 of net assessed valuation was developed for the fiscal year ending June 30, 19X2, and is presented below:

| | |
| --- | --- |
| Dial County general fund | $ 6.00 |
| Eton City general fund | 3.00 |
| Bart Township general fund | 1.00 |
| | $10.00 |

All property taxes are due in quarterly installments and when collected are then distributed to the governmental units represented in the composite rate.

In order to administer collection and distribution of such taxes, the county has established a tax agency fund.

*Additional information:*
1.  In order to reimburse the county for estimated administrative expenses of operating the tax agency fund, the tax agency is to deduct 2 percent from the tax collections each quarter for Eton City and Bart Township. The total amount deducted is to be remitted to the Dial County general fund.
2.  Current year tax levies to be collected by the tax agency fund are as follows:

|  | Gross Levy | Estimated Amount to Be collected |
| --- | --- | --- |
| Dial County | $3,600,000 | $3,500,000 |
| Eton City | 1,800,000 | 1,740,000 |
| Bart Township | 600,000 | 560,000 |
|  | $6,000,000 | $5,800,000 |

3.  Because of an error in the original computation of its current gross tax levy and the estimated amount to be collected, $10,000 was charged back to Bart Township.
4.  As of September 30, 19X1, the tax agency fund has received $1,440,000 in first quarter payments. On October 1, this fund made a distribution to the three governmental units. Taxes are allocated on a pro rata basis based on the tax rates.

**Required:**
For the period July 1, 19X1, through October 1, 19X1, prepare journal entries to record the preceding transactions for the following funds:

Dial County tax agency fund
Dial County general fund
Eton City general fund
Bart Township general fund

Your answer sheet should be organized as follows:

| Accounts | Dial County Tax Agency Fund | | Dial County General Fund | | Eton City General Fund | | Bart Township General Fund | |
| --- | --- | --- | --- | --- | --- | --- | --- | --- |
|  | Debit | Credit | Debit | Credit | Debit | Credit | Debit | Credit |

—**AICPA** Adapted

P8-18. The following budget was proposed for 19X2 for the Mohawk Valley School District general fund:

| | |
|---|---:|
| Fund balance, January 1, 19X2 | $128,000 |
| Revenues | |
|   Taxes | 112,000 |
|   Investment income | 4,000 |
|     Total | $244,000 |
| Expenditures | |
|   Operating | $120,000 |
|   County treasurer's fees (1% of taxes collected) | 1,120 |
|   Bond interest | 50,000 |
|   Fund balance, December 31, 19X2 | 72,880 |
|     Total | $244,000 |

A general-obligation bond issue of the school district was proposed in 19X1. The proceeds are to be used for a new school. There are no other outstanding bond issues. Information about the bond issue follows:

| | |
|---|---|
| Face | $1,000,000 |
| Interest rate | 10 percent |
| Bonds dated | January 1, 19X2 |
| Coupons mature | January 1 and July 1 beginning July 1, 19X2 |

Bonds mature serially at $100,000 per year starting January 1, 19X4.

The school district uses a separate bank account for each fund. The general fund trial balance at December 31, 19X1 follows:

| | Debit | Credit |
|---|---:|---:|
| Cash | $ 28,000 | |
| Temporary investments—U.S. 8 percent bonds, | | |
|     interest payable May 1 and November 1 | 100,000 | |
| Unreserved fund balance | | $128,000 |
| | $128,000 | $128,000 |

The county treasurer will collect the taxes and charge a standard fee of 1 percent on all collections. The transactions for 19X2 were as follows:

January 1 — The proposed budget was adopted, the general-obligation bond issue was authorized, and the taxes were levied.

February 28 — Tax receipts from county treasurer ($49,500) were deposited.

April 1 — Bond issue was sold at 101 plus accrued interest. It was directed that the premium be used for payment of interest by general fund.

April 2 — The school district disbursed $47,000 for new school site.

April 3 — A contract for $950,000 for the new school was approved.

May 1 — Interest was received on temporary investments.

July 1 — Interest was paid on bonds.

August 31 — Tax receipts from County Treasurer, $59,400, were deposited.

November 1 — Payment on new school construction contract, $200,000, was made.

December 31 — Operating expenses paid during year were $115,000.

**Required:**

Prepare the formal journal entries to record the foregoing 19X2 transactions in the following funds or groups of accounts:

1. general fund
2. capital projects fund
3. general fixed assets
4. general long-term debt.

Each journal entry should be dated the same as its related transaction, as shown previously.

**—AICPA Adapted**

**P8-19.**    At the start of your examination of the accounts of the City of Waterford, you discovered that the bookkeeper failed to keep the accounts by funds. The following trial balance of the general fund for the year ended December 31, 19A, was available:

### City of Waterford General Fund Trial Balance December 31, 19A

|  | Debit | Credit |
|---|---|---|
| Cash | $ 207,500 |  |
| Taxes receivable—current | 148,500 |  |
| Allowance for uncollectible taxes—current |  | $ 6,000 |
| Appropriation expenditures | 760,000 |  |
| Revenues |  | 992,500 |
| Donated land | 190,000 |  |
| River Bridge bonds authorized—unissued | 100,000 |  |
| Work in process—River Bridge | 130,000 |  |
| River Bridge bonds payable |  | 200,000 |
| Contracts payable—River Bridge |  | 25,000 |
| Retained percentage—River Bridge contracts |  | 5,000 |
| Vouchers payable |  | 7,500 |
| Unreserved fund balance |  | 300,000 |
| Total | $1,536,000 | $1,536,000 |

Your examination disclosed the following:

1. The budget for the year 19A, not recorded on the books, estimated revenues and expenditures as follows: revenues $815,000, expenditures $775,000.

2. Outstanding purchase orders at December 31, 19A, for operating expenses not recorded on the books, totaled $2,500.
3. Included in the revenues account is a credit of $190,000 representing the value of land donated by the state as a grant-in-aid for construction of the River Bridge.
4. River Bridge bonds were sold at par for $200,000. $100,000 of the proceeds was paid on capital project.
5. Examination of the subledger containing the details of the appropriation expenditures account revealed the following items included therein:

| | |
|---|---:|
| Current operating expenses | $472,000 |
| Additions to structures and improvements | 210,000 |
| Equipment purchases | 10,000 |
| General obligation bonds paid | 50,000 |
| Interest paid on general obligation bonds | 18,000 |

**Required:**

Prepare a worksheet showing the given general fund trial balance, adjusting entries, and distributions to the proper funds or groups of accounts. The following column headings are recommended:

General fund trial balance — debit

General fund trial balance — credit

Adjustments — debit

Adjustments — credit

General fund — debit

General fund — credit

Capital projects fund

General fixed assets

General long-term debt

Number all adjusting and transaction entries. Formal journal entries are not required.

**— AICPA Adapted**

**P8-20.** On January 1, 19X1, Medium City established an internal service fund for operating a central motor vehicle pool. It transferred $100,000 from the general fund.

Immediately upon establishment, a fleet of trucks was purchased as follows:

| Type | Number | Cost per Truck |
|---|:---:|:---:|
| 4-ton GMC | 4 | $3,500 |
| 3-ton Ford | 4 | 2,500 |
| 3-ton Mack | 4 | 2,200 |
| 1-ton Dodge | 5 | 1,500 |

Operating each of the three- and four-ton trucks requires a driver and a helper who are paid standard wage rates of $4.00 and $3.00 per hour, respectively. The one-ton trucks do not require a helper.

All trucks are depreciated on a straight-line basis over a five-year period with 5 percent residual salvage value.

Trucks are rented to the general fund on an hourly basis and the following usage and gasoline costs were reported for the year ended December 31, 19X1:

| Type | Rental Rate per Hour | Total Number of Hours Used | Cost of Gasoline Used |
|------|------|------|------|
| 4-ton GMC | $10.50 | 6,000 | $2,400 |
| 3-ton Ford | 8.00 | 8,000 | 2,400 |
| 3-ton Mack | 8.00 | 8,000 | 2,800 |
| 1-ton Dodge | 5.00 | 15,000 | 3,000 |

The following additional costs were incurred in operation of the fleet:
1. Drivers' and helpers' wages were paid for exactly the hours the trucks were used. There was no unpaid payroll at the end of the year.
2. Unpaid gasoline invoices at December 31, 19X1, aggregated $1,500.
3. Other indirect costs incurred were as follows:

| | |
|---|---|
| Supervision | $15,000 |
| Repairs | 10,000 |
| Tires and tubes purchased | 1,600 |

There were no unpaid bills at December 31, 19X1, pertaining to the preceding items; however, at the end of the year, the fund had on hand an inventory of new tires costing $500.

During the year, the general fund paid the vehicle pool $195,000 on its account for services rendered.

**Required:**
A. You are to prepare the journal entries to open the fund, to record the transactions in it for 19X1, and to close the fund at December 31st.
B. Prepare a balance sheet in good form for the fund as of December 31, 19X1.

—AICPA Adapted

**P8-21.** The Village of Dexter was recently incorporated and began financial operations on July 1, 19X0, the beginning of its fiscal year.

The following transactions occurred during this first fiscal year, July 1, 19X0, to June 30, 19X1:

1. The village council adopted a budget for general operations during the fiscal year ending June 30, 19X1. Revenues were estimated at $400,000. Legal authorizations for budgeted expenditures were $394,000.

2. Property taxes were levied in the amount of $390,000; it was estimated that 2 percent of this amount would prove to be uncollectible. These taxes are available as of the date of levy to finance current expenditures.

3. During the year, a resident of the village donated marketable securities valued at $50,000 to the village under the terms of a trust agreement. The terms of the trust agreement stipulated that the principal amount is to be kept intact; use of revenue generated by the securities is restricted to financing college scholarships for needy students. Revenue earned and received on these marketable securities amounted to $5,500 through June 30, 19X1.

4. A general fund transfer of $5,000 was made to establish an internal service fund to provide for a permanent investment in inventory.

5. The village decided to install lighting in the village park and a special assessment project was authorized to install the lighting at a cost of $75,000. The appropriation was formally recorded.

6. The assessments were levied for $72,000 with the village contributing $3,000 out of the general fund. All assessments were collected during the year, including the village's contribution.

7. A contract for $75,000 was let for the installation of the lighting. At June 30, 19X1, the contract was completed but not approved. The contractor was paid all but 5 percent, which was retained to ensure compliance with the terms of the contract. Encumbrances and other budgetary accounts are maintained.

8. During the year, the internal service fund purchased various supplies at a cost of $1,900.

9. Cash collections recorded by the general fund during the year were as follows:

| | |
|---|---|
| Property taxes | $386,000 |
| Licenses and permits | 7,000 |

10. The village council decided to build a village hall at an estimated cost of $500,000 to replace space occupied in rented facilities. The village does not record project authorizations. It was decided that general obligation bonds bearing interest at 6 percent would be issued. On June 30, 19X1, the bonds were issued at their face value of $500,000, payable June 30, 19Z1.

    No contracts have been signed for this project and no expenditures have been made.

11. A fire truck was purchased for $15,000 and the voucher approved and paid by the general fund. This expenditure was previously encumbered for $15,000.

**Required:**
Prepare journal entries to properly record each of the preceding transactions in the appropriate fund(s) or group of accounts of Dexter Village for the fiscal year ended June 30, 19X1. Use the following funds and groups of accounts:

general fund

capital projects fund

special-assessment-related funds

internal service fund

trust fund

general long-term debt group of accounts

general fixed-assets group of accounts

Each journal entry should be numbered to correspond with the transactions described previously. Do *not* prepare closing entries for any fund.

Your answer sheet should be organized as follows:

| Transaction No. | Fund or Group of Accounts | Account Title and Explanation | Amounts Debit Credit |
|---|---|---|---|
| | | | |

—**AICPA Adapted**

**P8-22.**    Select the best answer for each of the following items:

1. Fixed assets utilized in a city-owned utility are accounted for in which of the following?

|  | Enterprise fund | General fixed-assets group of accounts |
|---|---|---|
| a. | No | No |
| b. | No | Yes |
| c. | Yes | No |
| d. | Yes | Yes |

2. Which of the following funds of a governmental unit would use the general long-term debt account group to account for unmatured general long-term liabilities?
   a. special assessment agency fund
   b. trust
   c. internal service
   d. capital projects

3. Encumbrances would *not* appear in which fund?
   a. general
   b. enterprise
   c. capital projects
   d. special revenue

4. The general fixed-assets group of accounts would be used for the fixed assets of:
   a. the special assessment capital projects fund.
   b. the enterprise fund.
   c. the trust fund.
   d. the internal service fund.

5. Taxes collected and held by a municipality for a school district would be accounted for in:
   a. an enterprise fund.
   b. an internal service fund.
   c. an agency fund.
   d. a special revenue fund.

6. Which of the following funds of a governmental unit would use the general long-term debt account group to account for unmatured general long-term liabilities?
   a. special assessment capital projects fund
   b. capital projects
   c. trust
   d. internal service

7. Which of the following accounts could be included in the balance sheet of an enterprise fund?

   |    | Reserve for encumbrances | Revenue bonds payable | Retained earnings |
   |----|----|----|----|
   | a. | No | No | Yes |
   | b. | No | Yes | Yes |
   | c. | Yes | Yes | No |
   | d. | No | No | No |

8. Which of the following funds of a governmental unit would include retained earnings in its balance sheet?
   a. expendable pension trust
   b. internal service
   c. special revenue
   d. capital projects

9. Customers' meter deposits that cannot be spent for normal operating purposes would be classified as restricted cash in the balance sheet of which fund?
   a. internal service (intragovernmental service)
   b. trust
   c. agency
   d. enterprise

10. Which of the following funds should account for the payment of interest and principal on revenue bond debt?
    a. capital projects
    b. enterprise
    c. trust
    d. debt-service

    —AICPA Adapted

P8-23. Select the best answer to each of the following items:
   1. Ariel Village issued the following bonds during the year ended June 30, 19X1:

| Revenue bonds to be repaid from admission fees collected by the Ariel Zoo enterprise fund | $200,000 |
| General obligation bonds issued for the Ariel water and sewer enterprise fund that will service the debt (city secondarily liable) | 300,000 |

How much of these bonds should be accounted for in Ariel's general long-term debt account group?

a. $0
b. $200,000
c. $300,000
d. $500,000

2. The following assets are among those owned by the City of Foster:

| Apartment building (part of the principal of a nonexpendable trust fund) | $ 200,000 |
| City Hall | 800,000 |
| Three fire stations | 1,000,000 |
| City streets and sidewalks | 5,000,000 |

How much should be included in Foster's general fixed-assets account group?

a. $1,800,000 or $6,800,000
b. $2,000,000 or $7,000,000
c. $6,800,000, without election of $1,800,000
d. $7,000,000, without election of $2,000,000

Items 3 and 4 are based on the following information:

During the year ended December 31, 19X1, Leyland City received a state grant of $500,000 to finance the purchase of buses, and an additional grant of $100,000 to aid in the financing of bus operations in 19X1. Only $300,000 of the capital grant was used in 19X1 for the purchase of buses, but the entire operating grant of $100,000 was spent in 19X1.

3. If Leyland's bus transportation system is accounted for as part of the city's general fund, how much should Leyland report as grant revenues for the year ended December 31, 19X1?

a. $100,000
b. $300,000
c. $400,000
d. $500,000

4. If Leyland's bus transportation system is accounted for as an enterprise fund, how much should Leyland report as grant revenues for the year ended December 31, 19X1?

a. $100,000
b. $300,000
c. $400,000
d. $500,000

—AICPA Adapted

**P8-24.** Select the best answer for each of the following items:

1. The "fund balance reserved for encumbrances" account represents amounts recorded by a governmental unit for:
   a. anticipated expenditures in the next year.
   b. expenditures for which purchase orders were made in the prior year but disbursement will be in the current year.
   c. excess expenditures in the prior year that will be offset against the current year budgeted amounts.
   d. unanticipated expenditures of the prior year that become evident in the current year.

2. Which of the following types of revenue would generally be recorded directly in the general fund of a governmental unit?
   a. receipts from a city-owned parking structure
   b. property taxes
   c. interest earned on investments held for retirement of employees
   d. revenues from internal service funds

3. The reserve for encumbrances account is properly considered to be:
   a. a current liability if payable within a year; otherwise, a long-term debt.
   b. a fixed liability.
   c. a floating debt.
   d. a reservation of the fund's equity.

4. The initial transfer of cash from the general fund in order to establish an internal service fund would require the general fund to credit cash and debit:
   a. accounts receivable—internal service fund.
   b. a "transfer to" account.
   c. reserve for encumbrances.
   d. appropriations.

5. The Town of Newbold general fund issued purchase orders to vendors and suppliers of $630,000. Which of the following entries should be made to record this transaction?

|   |   | Debit | Credit |
|---|---|---|---|
| a. | Encumbrances | $630,000 | |
|   | Reserve for encumbrances | | $630,000 |
| b. | Expenditures | 630,000 | |
|   | Vouchers payable | | 630,000 |
| c. | Expenses | 630,000 | |
|   | Accounts payable | | 630,000 |
| d. | Reserve for encumbrances | 630,000 | |
|   | Encumbrances | | 630,000 |

6. The sequence of entries listed below indicates which of the following?
   a. An adverse event was foreseen and a reserve of $12,000 was created; later the reserve was cancelled and a liability for the item was acknowledged.

b.   An order was placed for goods or services estimated to cost $12,000; the actual cost was $12,350 for which a liability was acknowledged upon receipt.

c.   Encumbrances were anticipated but later failed to materialize and were reversed. A liability of $12,350 was incurred.

d.   The first entry was erroneous and was reversed; a liability of $12,350 was acknowledged.

| | | |
|---|---|---|
| Encumbrances | $12,000 | |
|    Reserve for encumbrances | | $12,000 |
| Reserve for encumbrances | 12,000 | |
|    Encumbrances | | 12,000 |
| Expenditures | 12,350 | |
|    Vouchers payable | | 12,350 |

7.   Assuming appropriate governmental accounting principles were followed, the entries:

a.   occurred in the same fiscal period.

b.   did not occur in the same fiscal period.

c.   could have occurred in the same fiscal period, but it is impossible to be sure of this.

d.   reflect the equivalent of a "prior-period adjustment," had the entity concerned been one operated for profit.

8.   Immediately after the first entry was recorded, the municipality had a balanced general-fund budget for all transactions. What would be the effect of recording the second and third entries?

a.   No change in the balanced condition of the budget.

b.   The municipality would show a surplus.

c.   The municipality would show a deficit.

d.   No effect on the current budget, but the budget of the following fiscal period would be affected.

9.   Entries similar to those for the general fund may also appear on the books of the municipality's:

a.   general fixed-assets group.

b.   general long-term debt group.

c.   trust fund.

d.   special revenue fund.

**—AICPA Adapted**

# Annual Financial Reports

## ■ Learning Objectives

When you have finished your study of this chapter, you should

1. Have a general understanding of the provisions of NCGA Statement 1 relating to the presentation of both general purpose financial statements (GPFS) and comprehensive annual financial reports (CAFR) for a governmental entity.

2. Be able to prepare the appropriate combined financial statements for a governmental entity from fund and account group statements for the entity.

3. Be aware of the changes that would have to be made in modified accrual based financial statements to convert them to the full accrual basis.

In Chapters 6, 7, and 8, we have shown how a series of assumed transactions for Model City should be journalized, posted, and summarized in the financial statements for each of the various accounting entities included in the city's accounting records. In this chapter, we turn our attention to the preparation and presentation of the data to be included in the *annual financial report for the governmental unit as a reporting entity*.

The form and content of the annual financial report for a governmental entity is a subject that has been debated strenuously by governmental accountants over many years. The nature and extent of that debate is to some extent evidenced by the extensive list of Suggested Supplementary References provided at the end of this chapter. The controversies surrounding this topic can be summarized as follows:

1. Should individual-fund and account-group financial data be combined in any way, or should the statements for the individual funds and account groups be the sole governmental financial reporting entity focus?

2. If the financial data for the individual accounting entities are to be combined to reflect summarized accounting data for a governmental unit as a whole, should the combination be brought about by simply *combining* the individual-fund and

account-group data or should these data be *consolidated* into an overall financial report for the city as a unit?

3. If the financial data are to be combined, should they be presented on the accrual basis?

In answer to the first question, the profession historically has said that governmental financial reporting should focus on statements for the individual-fund and account-group accounting entities. Over the years, however, many accountants and financial statement users have contended that such financial reports were not adequate to *present fairly* a governmental unit's financial position and operating results in published financial reports. The feeling has evolved that the data should be summarized in some way to reflect the financial position and operating results for the overall reporting entity.

In regard to the controversy relating to the preparation of *combined* versus *consolidated* financial reports, you should recognize that the preparation of combined financial reports simply involves adding together the various similar items in the individual-fund and account-group financial statements. Consolidated financial statements, however, would eliminate interfund reciprocal items such as "due to" and "due from" account balances so as to show only the relationships of the governmental unit to outside enterprise units.

Against this background of controversy, the National Council of Governmental Accountants issued the reporting section of NCGA Statement 1. As we shall see, this pronouncement calls for *combined financial statements*.

In answer to the third question, up to this point, combined financial statement data for governmental and expendable trust funds have been presented on the modified accrual basis. With the issuance of GASB 11, it appears that some version of the accrual basis will be used for fiscal periods beginning after June 15, 1994. However, this statement still does not provide for the capitalization of expenditures for long-term assets and the recognition of depreciation on those assets.

We begin our discussion of annual financial reporting by *summarizing the reporting requirements of NCGA Statement 1*. After that, we illustrate how the provisions of NCGA Statement 1 would apply in *summarizing the financial data for Model City*. We also provide an appendix to this chapter *showing how the combined financial statements for Model City could be converted to consolidated statements presented on the accrual basis*.

## ■ Reporting Provisions of NCGA Statement 1

NCGA Statement 1 summarizes the reporting requirements for governmental entities by introducing the financial reporting pyramid shown in Figure 9–1. This figure identifies the data to be included in general purpose financial statements (GPFS) and comprehensive annual financial reports (CAFR). As you can see from Figure 9–1, GPFS consist of combined financial statements. CAFR [see items (1), (2), (3), and (4) in the figure] then include the combined statements plus combining statements by fund-type and individual-fund and account-group statements and, in some situations, supporting schedules.

**FIGURE 9–1.**    The Financial Reporting "Pyramid"

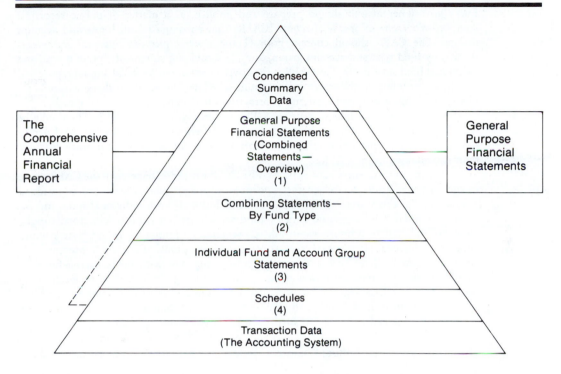

—Required
-- May be necessary
() Refers to "The Financial Section 'Pyramid'" discussion of Statement 1

National Council on Governmental Accounting, *NCGA Statement 1* (Chicago: Municipal Finance Officers Association—now Government Finance Officers Association, 1979), p. 20. Used with permission.

*GPFS are thus designed to provide a summary overview* of the financial position of all funds and account groups, plus a summary of the operating results of all funds. Since some fund statements are prepared on the modified accrual basis and others are presented on the accrual basis, the combined balance sheet reflects a mixture of these two bases. However, operating results are summarized in two combined statements— one for governmental-type funds and another for proprietary funds.

The condensed summary data shown at the peak of the pyramid refer to the data that might be presented to the public in condensed form, such as that reported through the news media. This type of data is not included in either the GPFS or the CAFR.

The specific provisions of NCGA Statement 1 regarding the presentation of financial statements and schedules are as follow:

## Annual Financial Reporting

Every governmental unit should prepare and publish, as a matter of public record, a *comprehensive annual financial report* (CAFR) that encompasses all funds and account groups. The CAFR should contain both (1) the *general purpose financial statements* (GPFS) by fund type and account group, and (2) combining statements by fund type and individual fund statements. The CAFR is the governmental unit's official annual report and should also contain introductory information, schedules necessary to demonstrate compliance with finance-related legal and contractual provisions, and statistical data.

Governmental units may issue the GPFS separately from the CAFR. These may be issued for inclusion in official statements for bond offerings and for widespread distribution to users requiring less detailed information about the governmental unit's finances than is contained in the CAFR.

The major differences between the GPFS and the other statements in the CAFR relate to the reporting entity focus and the reporting on finance-related legal and contractual provisions that differ from GAAP. The CAFR includes (1) both individual fund and account group data and aggregate data by fund types, together with introductory, supplementary, and statistical information; and (2) schedules essential to demonstrate compliance with finance-related legal and contractual provisions. The GPFS present only aggregate data by fund type and account group, together with notes to the financial statements that are essential to fair presentation, including disclosures of material violations of finance-related legal and contractual provisions and other important matters that are not apparent from the face of the financial statements. Standards for both the CAFR and separately issued GPFS are set forth below.

### The Comprehensive Annual Financial Report

The *comprehensive annual financial report* (CAFR) of a governmental unit should contain the statements indicated below, including notes thereto, and appropriate schedules, narrative explanations, and statistical tables. It should be prepared and published promptly after the close of the fiscal year and should contain the report of the independent auditor, if an audit has been performed, together with a letter(s) of transmittal and such other information as management deems appropriate.

The general outline and minimum content of the CAFR of a governmental unit (with references to examples in the appendixes) are as follows:

1. **Introductory Section**
   (Table of contents, letter(s) of transmittal, and other material deemed appropriate by management.)

2. **Financial Section**
   a. Auditor's Report
   b. General Purpose Financial Statements (Combined Statements—Overview)
      1. Combined Balance Sheet—All Fund Types and Account Groups
      2. Combined Statement of Revenues, Expenditures, and Changes in Fund Balances—All Governmental Fund Types
      3. Combined Statement of Revenues, Expenditures, and Changes in Fund Balances—Budget and Actual—General and Special Revenue Fund Types (and similar governmental fund types for which annual budgets have been legally adopted)
      4. Combined Statement of Revenues, Expenses, and Changes in Retained Earnings (or Equity)—All Proprietary Fund Types

       5. Combined Statement of Changes in Financial Position—All Proprietary Fund Types*

       6. Notes to the financial statements

       (Trust Fund operations may be reported in (2), (4), and (5) above, as appropriate, or separately.)

  c. Combining and Individual Fund and Account Group Statements and Schedules

       1. Combining Statements—By Fund Type—where a governmental unit has more than one fund of a given fund type

       2. Individual fund and account group statements—where a governmental unit has only one fund of a given type and for account groups and/or where necessary to present prior year and budgetary comparisons

       3. Schedules

          a. Schedules necessary to demonstrate compliance with finance-related legal and contractual provisions.

          b. Schedules to present information spread throughout the statements that can be brought together and shown in greater detail (e.g., taxes receivable, including delinquent taxes; long-term debt; investments; and cash receipts, disbursements, and balances).

          c. Schedules to present greater detail for information reported in the statements (e.g., additional revenue sources detail and object of expenditure data by departments).

       (Narrative explanations useful in understanding combining and individual fund and account group statements and schedules that are not included in the notes to the financial statements should be presented on divider pages, directly on the statements and schedules, or in a separate section.)

  3. **Statistical Tables**

## The Financial Section "Pyramid"

The financial section of the CAFR may be viewed as a "reporting pyramid" [see Figure 9–1]. The governmental unit need go only as far down the reporting pyramid—in terms of increasing levels of detail—as necessary to report the financial position and operating results of its individual funds and account groups, to demonstrate compliance with finance-related legal and contractual requirements, and to assure adequate disclosure at the individual fund entity level. Those statements and schedules necessary for these purposes are *required;* others are *optional.*

    The levels of the pyramid are:

  1. *General Purpose Financial Statements (Combined Statements—Overview).* These basic financial statements provide a summary overview of the financial position of all funds and account groups and of the operating results of all funds. They also serve as an introduction to the more detailed statements and schedules that follow. Separate columns should be used for each fund type and account group.

  2. *Combining Statements—By Fund Type.* Where a governmental unit has more than one fund of a given type (e.g., Special Revenue Funds), combining statements for all funds of that type should be presented in a columnar format. The total columns of these combining statements should agree with the amounts presented in the GPFS. (In some instances, disclosure sufficient to meet CAFR reporting objectives may be

*This has now been changed to "Combined Statement of Cash Flows."

achieved at this level; in other cases, these statements "link" the GPFS and the individual fund statements.)

3. *Individual Fund and Account Group Statements.* These statements present information on the individual funds and account groups where (a) a governmental unit has only one fund of a specific type, or (b) detail to assure disclosure sufficient to meet CAFR reporting objectives is not presented in the combining statements. These statements may also be used to present budgetary data and prior year comparative data.

4. *Schedules.* Data presented in schedules are not necessary for fair presentation in conformity with GAAP unless referenced in the notes to the financial statements. Schedules are used: (a) to demonstrate finance-related legal and contractual compliance (e.g., where bond indentures require specific data to be presented); (b) to present other information deemed useful (e.g., combined and combining schedules that encompass more than one fund or account group, such as a Combined Schedule of Cash Receipts, Disbursements, and Balances—All Funds); and (c) to provide details of data summarized in the financial statements (e.g., schedules of revenues, expenditures, transfers).

*All four pyramid levels of detail may be required in some circumstances. On the other hand, adequate disclosure may require only one or two levels.* Determination of the appropriate level of detail—and the distinction as to what is presented in a statement as opposed to a schedule—is a matter of professional judgment.[1]

Accountants have also raised the question as to whether budgetary data should be presented in the annual financial reports for a governmental unit. That question, as well as those relating to the presentation of statements of changes in financial position* and notes to the financial statements, are answered as follows by Statement 1:

*Budgetary Comparison Statements and Schedules.* The Combined Statement of Revenues, Expenditures, and Changes in Fund Balances—Budget and Actual—General and Special Revenue Fund Types, as the name implies, presents budget and actual data for the General Fund and all Special Revenue Funds. This statement should also include budget and actual data for other governmental fund types for which annual budgets have been adopted. Only the total budget and total actual data for all Special Revenue Funds (and for every other budgeted governmental fund type) are required.

If the budget is prepared on a basis consistent with GAAP, the actual data in this budgetary comparison statement is the same as in the Combined Statement of Revenues, Expenditures, and Changes in Fund Balances—All Governmental Fund Types. However, if the legally prescribed budgetary basis differs materially from GAAP, budgetary data should not be compared with GAAP-based operating data since these comparisons would not be meaningful. Rather, the Combined Statement of Revenues, Expenditures, and Changes in Fund Balances—Budget and Actual—General and Special Revenue Fund Types should present *comparisons of the legally adopted budget with actual data on the budgetary basis* (which may include encumbrances). In such cases, this "actual" data would be different from the GAAP presentations in the Combined Statement of Revenues, Expenditures, and Changes in Fund Balances—All Governmental Fund Types. The difference between the budgetary basis and GAAP should be explained in the notes to the financial statements.

---

1. National Council on Governmental Accounting, *NCGA Statement 1* (Chicago: Municipal Finance Officers Association—now Government Finance Officers Association, 1979), pp. 19–21. Used with permission.
* Now "Combined Statement of Cash Flows."

The CAFR should include budgetary comparisons for individual governmental funds for which an annual budget has been adopted. Budgetary comparisons are presented in the fund statement of revenues, expenditures, and other changes in fund balance when the budget is adopted on the modified accrual basis. If the legal budgetary basis differs from GAAP, budgeting data should not be presented in this fund statement. Rather, a schedule comparing the legally adopted budget with actual data on the budgetary basis should be presented. For example, if the legal budgetary basis requires the comparison of fund current year appropriations with the sum of current year expenditures and encumbrances outstanding at year end, this schedule would present this comparison.

*Statements of Changes in Financial Position.* Statements of changes in financial position are required for proprietary funds. As described above for the other statements at the GPFS (Combined Statements—Overview) level, the Combined Statement of Changes in Financial Position*—All Proprietary Fund Types should present the separate data for each major fund type in a columnar format and may contain a total column, with or without interfund eliminations. Total columns of combining statements of changes in financial position by fund type should agree with the column for that fund type in the Combined Statement of Changes in Financial Position*—All Proprietary Fund Types. Any interfund and similar eliminations made should be apparent from the headings or disclosed in the notes to the financial statements.

*Notes to the Financial Statements and Narrative Explanations.* Two types of disclosure are necessary in the CAFR: (1) notes to the financial statements that are essential for fair presentation at the GPFS (Combined Statements—Overview) level, and (2) narrative explanations useful in providing an understanding of combining and individual fund and account group statements and schedules.

Notes to the financial statements essential to fair presentation at the GPFS level include the Summary of Significant Accounting Policies and summary disclosure of such matters as significant contingent liabilities, encumbrances outstanding, significant effects of subsequent events, pension plan obligations, accumulated unpaid employee benefits (such as vacation and sick leave), material violations of finance-related legal and contractual provisions, debt service requirements to maturity, commitments under noncapitalized leases, construction and other significant commitments, changes in general fixed assets and general long-term debt, any excess of expenditures over appropriations in individual funds, deficit balances of individual funds, and interfund receivables and payables. Any other disclosures necessary in the circumstances should also be included.

Narrative explanations of combining and individual fund and account group statements and schedules should provide information *not* included in the financial statements, notes to the financial statements, and schedules that is necessary: (1) to assure an understanding of the combining and individual fund and account group statements and schedules, and (2) to demonstrate compliance with finance-related legal and contractual provisions. (In extreme cases, it may be necessary to prepare a separate legal-basis special report.) The narrative explanations, including a description of the nature and purpose of the various funds, should be presented on divider pages, directly on the statements and schedules, or in a separate section.[2]

The annual CAFR may also include certain statistical data to help users understand more completely the implications of the financial data. These data are described as follows in Statement 1:

---

*  Now "Combined Statement for Cash Flows."
2.  Ibid., pp. 23–24. Used with permission.

Statistical tables differ from financial statements because they usually cover more than two fiscal years and may present nonaccounting data. Statistical tables reflect social and economic data, financial trends, and the fiscal capacity of the government.

The following statistical tables should be included in the CAFR unless clearly inapplicable in the circumstances.

1.  General Governmental Expenditures by Function—Last Ten Fiscal Years.
2.  General Revenues by Source—Last Ten Fiscal Years.
3.  Property Tax Levies and Collections—Last Ten Fiscal Years.
4.  Assessed and Estimated Actual Value of Taxable Property—Last Ten Fiscal Years.
5.  Property Tax Rates—All Overlapping Governments—Last Ten Fiscal Years.
6.  Special Assessment Collections—Last Ten Fiscal Years.
7.  Ratio of Net General Bonded Debt to Assessed Value and Net Bonded Debt Per Capita—Last Ten Fiscal Years.
8.  Computation of Legal Debt Margin (if not presented in the GPFS).
9.  Computation of Overlapping Debt (if not presented in the GPFS).
10. Ratio of Annual Debt Service for General Bonded Debt to Total General Expenditures—Last Ten Fiscal Years.
11. Revenue Bond Coverage—Last Ten Fiscal Years.
12. Demographic Statistics.
13. Property Value, Construction, and Bank Deposits—Last Ten Fiscal Years.
14. Principal Taxpayers.
15. Miscellaneous Statistics.

Some of the statistical tables may be clearly inapplicable under certain circumstances. For example, a governmental unit with no bonded debt obviously would not need to present the statistical tables related to bonded debt. Similarly, a unit which does not levy special assessments would not present the table specified for special assessments. The Council encourages presentation of other appropriate statistical tables that give report users a better historical perspective and assist in assessing current financial status and trends of the governmental unit.[3]

The general objectives of Statement 1, as well as the ways in which the condensed summary (see Figure 9–1) may be used, are stated as follows:

The accounting principles and illustrative procedures in this volume are designed to enhance fiscal control, facilitate compliance with generally accepted accounting principles and finance-related legal and contractual requirements, and result in financial statements and reports that fulfill many user information needs. As such, they constitute the *minimum standards* of financial reporting for state and local governments.

The finance officer should assume responsibility for preparing supplemental fiscal data needed in reaching essential management decisions, formulating fiscal policy, informing the general and investing public, and submitting financial data to central compiling agencies such as national statistics bureaus. The finance officer should not assume that properly preparing a comprehensive annual financial report (CAFR), separately issuing general purpose financial statements (GPFS), and demonstrating finance-related legal and contractual compliance preclude additional reporting of fiscal data in total and/or on other than by fund types and funds. Neither generally accepted accounting principles nor

---

3.  Ibid., pp. 24–25. Used with permission.

finance-related legal and contractual requirements should be construed as establishing *maximum* reporting requirements. Supplementary information may be equally valuable in meeting other information needs and in providing a better understanding of the finances of the governmental unit.

Managers, legislators, and others may want to know the *total* revenues and other financing sources, and the amounts obtained from the various sources, as well as what is accounted for in each fund, fund type, or fund category. Further, a comparison by one governmental unit with another of particular taxes or expenditures, if based solely on data of a single fund, can be misleading.

Some governmental units have for many years published highly *condensed summary* financial data, usually as "popular" reports directed primarily to citizens. Often the data in such reports are represented in charts or graphs rather than in financial statements. More recently, several professional association committees and individuals have undertaken research and experimentation directed toward the design of highly condensed summary financial statements for governmental units. The Council encourages such research and experimentation, but believes that at the present time such statements should supplement, rather than supplant, the CAFR and the separately issued GPFS. Further, the Council believes that the data in such highly condensed summary statements should be reconcilable with the combined, combining, and individual fund and account group statements, and that the reader of such statements should be referred to the CAFR and/or the separately issued GPFS of the governmental unit. The Council will continue to monitor experimentation with highly condensed summary statements and will consider such reporting in its subsequent research.

The framework for providing much of the supplemental or special purpose financial and statistical data commonly needed is presented in this Statement. Where additional data are needed—for internal or external, routine or special purpose uses—the finance officer should take the initiative to assure that the accounting system of the governmental unit is sufficiently flexible not only to meet the fundamental requirements of fiscal and legal accountability, but also to facilitate provision of relevant supplemental and special purpose financial and statistical information on a timely basis.[4]

Since NCGA Statement 1 was issued, questions have been raised regarding the specific sub-entity reports that should be included in the GPFS of a governmental unit. In 1981, the NCGA issued NCGA Statement 3 to provide criteria for identifying those sub-entities. The major elements of that statement are included in the following pages:

4) The NCGA believes that the criteria for defining the reporting entity of a governmental unit should be established to clarify the organizations, functions and activities of government which should be included in the general purpose financial statements (GPFS) of that governmental unit. In particular, there is a need for criteria for inclusion in the financial statements of a reporting entity with a separately elected legislative body of financial data on separate agencies of government, such as public authorities, whose officials are appointed rather than elected.

5) The NCGA believes that criteria for defining the reporting entity should be developed for several reasons. Among these are:

a. **Comparability.** Users of financial reports may wish to make comparisons among units of government or between time periods for a given government. Criteria for the inclusion or exclusion of units of government would assist users in making such comparisons.

---

4. Ibid., p. 26. Used with permission.

b.  **Comprehensiveness.** Criteria for defining the reporting entity would help the users of the financial reports by reducing the possibility of arbitrary exclusions or inclusions of various organizations.

c.  **Responsibility and control.** Users interested in evaluating the performance of governmental entities need to be able to identify the operations for which their officials are responsible. Specific criteria for the reporting entity inclusion or exclusion can help fulfill that need.

### Entity Definition Criteria

6) Several different sets of criteria for defining the reporting entity have been proposed. The NCGA believes that specific criteria should be established since a concept without specific criteria may be impractical for use in implementing a definition.

7) The NCGA believes that the definition criteria should be broad enough to include all governmental activities, organizations and functions necessary to achieve the desired objectives of comparability, comprehensiveness and responsibility and control. A broad definition may cause inclusion of some separate agencies that have not been previously included by all reporting entities. However, the NCGA believes that a broad definition is necessary to provide users with all necessary information.

8) In developing the reporting entity definition criteria, the NCGA assumed that all functions of government are considered to be responsible to elected officials at the federal, state or local level. Therefore, all functions of government must be a part of either federal, state or local government and should be reported at the lowest level of legislative authority that is consistent with the criteria of this statement. There may be instances, other than joint ventures, where it is difficult to determine whether the statements of a specific separate agency should be included in the financial statements of a state or a particular local government of the state. State and local government fiscal officials should confer to resolve such problems; a possible solution might be to include the agency in the financial statements of one reporting entity and disclose it in the notes to the financial statements of the other entity.

9) The NCGA concludes that the basic—but not the only—criterion for including a governmental department, agency, institution, commission, public authority or other governmental organization in a governmental unit's reporting entity for general purpose financial reports is the exercise of oversight responsibility over such agencies by the governmental unit's elected officials. Oversight responsibility is derived from the governmental unit's power and includes, but is not limited to, financial interdependency, selection of governing authority, designation of management, ability to significantly influence operations and accountability for fiscal matters. Oversight responsibility implies that a governmental unit is dependent on another and the dependent unit should be reported as part of the other. The manifestations of oversight responsibility are described in paragraphs 10 and 13, below.

10) The most significant manifestation of oversight—which ordinarily is accompanied by other aspects of oversight as described in paragraph 13—is financial interdependency. To the extent that a separate agency produces a financial benefit or imposes a financial burden on a unit of government, users of financial statements need to know the magnitude of such activity and its present and prospective impact on the reporting entity. Manifestations of financial interdependency include responsibility for financing deficits, entitlements to surpluses and guarantees of or "moral responsibility" for debt.

11) There may be circumstances where factors other than oversight are so significant in the relationship between a particular agency and a reporting entity that exclusion of the agency from the reporting entity's financial statements would be misleading. These other factors include: a) scope of public service (defined in paragraph 14), where there may be only partial oversight; and b) special financing relationships, where there is no oversight. There may

also be circumstances where the degree of oversight is so remote (as in the case of certain industrial development corporations) that the relationship of the agency to the entity is best described in a note to the financial statements rather than in the financial statements.

## Applying the Criteria

12) The NCGA believes that a positive response to the foregoing criteria indicates that the agency should be included in the reporting entity. The NCGA recognizes that professional judgment is necessary in individual fact situations to determine whether a particular organization should be included in the reporting entity. The Appendix includes several illustrations intended to assist in the application of these criteria.

13) **Manifestations of oversight.** The following further guidance is provided concerning the various manifestations of oversight set forth in paragraph 9.

a.  **Selection of governing authority.** The governing authority is that person or persons, board, commission or other body which possesses final decision-making authority and is held primarily accountable for decisions. When the governing authority is appointed by elected officials, a determination must be made as to whether the appointment is authoritative. One made by an elected official principally because he or she is in an official position, where the position the person is appointed to has little continuing linkage to the elected official (e.g., appointment of a chairman for a charitable activity), is not authoritative. An authoritative appointment is one where the elected official maintains a significant continuing relationship with the appointed official with respect to carrying out important public functions.

b.  **Designation of management.** The management of an agency consists of those individuals responsible for the day-to-day operations of the governmental agency. When management is appointed by and held accountable to a governing authority that is included in the entity, the activity being managed will fall within the entity. A governing authority may be ceremonial in nature and not possess the powers of appointment over management. In this case, the organizational relationship must be examined, and the terms and conditions of an employer-employee relationship should be used as an indication of whether the activity should be included in the entity.

c.  **Ability to significantly influence operations.** The ability to significantly influence operations should include, but is not limited to, the authority to review and approve budgetary requests and budgetary adjustments and amendments, sign contracts as the contracting authority, approve the hiring or retention of key managerial personnel, exercise control over facilities and properties and determine the outcome or disposition of matters affecting the recipients of the services being provided.

d.  **Accountability for fiscal matters.** When absolute authority over all funds is vested within the jurisdiction of either a constitutional officer, a management official or a governing authority that is within the entity, the activity should be included in the entity. When responsibility for the fiscal condition of an agency is outside the direct purview of a governing authority or management deemed within the entity, judgment is required to determine the line of fiscal accountability and its applicability to including the activity within the entity. Likewise, judgment is necessary when the governing authority or management of an agency may not be clearly within the entity, but fiscal activities, or the results thereof, are directly related to it. When the lines of fiscal responsibility are not clear, the following specific areas of fiscal responsibilities should be reviewed in determining the classification of an agency for purposes of defining the reporting entity:

1. Budgetary authority. Who possesses the authority for final approval over the authorizations of budgetary appropriations? Who may authorize revisions to the approved budget?
2. Surplus/deficits. Who is responsible for funding deficits and operating deficiencies? Is this responsibility a legal or a moral one? Who governs or controls the use of surplus funds? How are surplus funds disposed of?
3. Fiscal management. Who governs the process controlling the collection and disbursement of funds? (Trust and Agency type funds would be included.) Who holds title to assets? (Ownership of assets would indicate inclusion.) Who possesses the right to require audits? (This may show ability to control.)
4. Revenue characteristics. Where revenues are derived by means of a public levy or charge, in contrast to being grant receipts, there should be the presumption to include the agency's revenues or expenditures within the reporting entity. For purposes of this criterion the following definitions apply:
   a. "Public." The origin of authority for making the levy or charge lies with elected officials of the entity, or persons appointed by the elected officials, or there exists a delegation, but not an abrogation, of the power to levy or charge; the authority or power would include the ability to determine the nature and type of tax imposed or fee collected.
   b. "Levy or charge." The imposition of a monetary payment, the proceeds of which are applicable to and for the benefit of the citizens served by the level of government imposing the levy or charge. The power to levy would include the determination of the terms of levy and establishment of the method of administration.

14) **Scope of public service.** This criterion for determining whether the statements of a specific agency should be included in the financial statements of a reporting entity embraces the following aspects:

a.   Whether the activity is for the benefit of the reporting entity and/or its residents.
b.   Whether the activity is conducted within the geographic boundaries of the reporting entity and is generally available to the citizens of that entity.[5]

The NCGA, in its last pronouncement before formation of the GASB, issued Statement 7. That statement describes the procedures that should be followed in reporting the financial data for component units identified as includable in the annual financial report by Statement 3. NCGA Statement 5 also was issued in 1982 to clarify the disclosure requirements of Statement 1 regarding long-term leases. The concluding paragraph of that statement reads as follows:

> The council concludes that the disclosure requirements of SFAS 13 be followed for financial reporting purposes. The disclosures are required for capital and operating leases and must be made by state and local governments in accordance with NCGA Statement 1 and NCGA Interpretation 6, *Notes to the Financial Statements Disclosure.*[6]

In 1986, the AICPA Industry Audit Guide, entitled *Audits of State and Local Governmental Units,* was revised to incorporate the provisions of NCGA Statements 1

---

5.  National Council on Governmental Accounting, *NCGA Statement 3* (Chicago: Municipal Finance Officers Association—now Government Finance Officers Association, 1981), pp. 1–3. Used with permission.
6.  National Council on Governmental Accounting, *NCGA Statement 5* (Chicago: Municipal Finance Officers Association—now Government Finance Officers Association, 1982), p. 3. Used with permission.

(also further revised in 1989), 3, and 7 relating to governmental financial reports. Because oversight is an important consideration in determining the component units that should be included in a governmental entity's annual financial report, it identifies the following criteria (extracted from NCGA statements) as important in determining whether the financial results of a unit should be reported separately or included in the general purpose financial statements of another level of government:

1. financial interdependency
2. selection of governing authority
3. designation of management
4. ability to significantly influence operations
5. accountability for fiscal matters
   a. budgetary authority
   b. surpluses and deficits
   c. fiscal management
   d. revenue characteristics
6. scope of public service
7. financing relationships.[7]

The 1988 edition of GAAFR enlarges upon the last criterion by observing that when a potential component unit has a funding relationship because of the issuance of bonds by the oversight unit, or the oversight unit is a significant user of the potential component unit's services, a special financing relationship may exist. Some of these possible relationships are identified in the 1987 GASB Codification.[8]

These criteria are expected to provide significant guidance in determining whether specific components relating to a government's operations should be included in the general purpose financial statements of the governmental entity. However, each of the criteria listed above requires extensive use of judgment by both management and the accountant.

# ■ Illustrated Financial Statements for Model City

Having reviewed the provisions of NCGA Statement 1 in the preceding portion of this chapter, we now present the combined financial statements that should be included in the CAFR for Model City. These statements reflect a combination of the individual-fund and account-group financial data accumulated in Chapters 6, 7, and 8. In Exhibit 9–1, we show a combined balance sheet for all funds and account groups required as part of GPFS [see Figure 9–1 and narrative requirement 2.b.(1) on page 338].

---

7. American Institute of Certified Public Accountants, *Audits of State and Local Governmental Units,* Revised Edition (New York: AICPA, 1986), p. 12.
8. Government Finance Officers Association, *Governmental Accounting, Auditing, and Financial Reporting* (Chicago: Government Finance Officers Association, 1988), p. 21.

| | General Fund | Capital Projects Fund | Debt-Service Fund |
|---|---|---|---|
| **Assets and interfund receivables** | | | |
| Cash | $215,000 | $108,000 | $ 4,950 |
| Taxes receivable | 15,000 | | |
| Investments | | | 49,000 |
| Special assessments receivable—deferred | | | |
| Interest receivable | | | |
| Due from special assessment fund | | | |
| Supplies | | | |
| Equipment | | | |
| Allowance for depreciation—equipment | | | |
| Accounts receivable | | | |
| Allowance for bad debts | | | |
| Prepaid operating expense | | | |
| Bond debt service fund | | | |
| Land | | | |
| Building | | | |
| Allowance for depreciation—building | | | |
| Structures and improvements | | | |
| Amount to be provided for retirement of bonds | | | |
| Amount provided for retirement of bonds | | | |
| Amounts to be provided by special assessments | | | |
| Amounts provided by special assessments | | | |
| Totals | $230,000 | $108,000 | $53,950 |
| **Liabilities and interfund payables** | | | |
| Vouchers payable | $ 94,000 | $  5,000 | |
| Contracts payable—retained percentage | | 5,000 | |
| Due to municipal garage fund | | | |
| Interest payable | | | |
| Deferred revenues | | | |
| Bonds payable | | | |
| Revenue bonds payable | | | |
| Customer deposits | | | |
| Accrued operating expense | | | |
| Special assessment bonds payable | | | |
| **Fund balances and retained earnings** | | | |
| Fund balances | | | |
| Reserved for encumbrances | 50,000 | 90,000 | |
| Unreserved | 86,000 | 8,000 | |
| Debt service | | | $53,950 |
| Reserved for endowment | | | |
| Investment in general fixed assets | | | |
| Contributed capital | | | |
| Unreserved retained earnings | | | |
| Totals | $230,000 | $108,000 | $53,950 |

| Special Assessment Capital Projects Fund | Special Assessment Agency Fund | Trust Fund | Municipal Garage Fund | Water Utility Fund | General Fixed Asset Account Group | General Long-Term Debt Account Group | Total—Memo Only |
|---|---|---|---|---|---|---|---|
| $20,000 | $ 24,525 | $ 500 | $50,000 | $ 215,100 | | | $ 638,075 |
| | | | | | | | 15,000 |
| | | 100,000 | | | | | 149,000 |
| | 202,500 | | | | | | 202,500 |
| | 900 | | | | | | 900 |
| | | | 10,000 | | | | 10,000 |
| | | | 6,000 | 12,000 | | | 18,000 |
| | | | 35,000 | 600,000 | $ 535,000 | | 1,170,000 |
| | | | (3,500) | (210,000) | | | (213,500) |
| | | | | 44,700 | | | 44,700 |
| | | | | (150) | | | (150) |
| | | | | 2,000 | | | 2,000 |
| | | | | 37,800 | | | 37,800 |
| | | | | 100,000 | | | 100,000 |
| | | | | 300,000 | | | 300,000 |
| | | | | (120,000) | | | (120,000) |
| | | | | | 1,547,000 | | 1,547,000 |
| | | | | | | $446,050 | 446,050 |
| | | | | | | 53,950 | 53,950 |
| | 202,500 | | | | | | 202,500 |
| | 22,500 | | | | | | 22,500 |
| $20,000 | $452,925 | $100,500 | $97,500 | $ 981,450 | $2,082,000 | $500,000 | $4,626,325 |
| $ 500 | | | $10,000 | $ 70,000 | | | $ 179,500 |
| 4,500 | | | | | | | 9,500 |
| 10,000 | | | | | | | 10,000 |
| | 2,000 | | | | | | 2,000 |
| | 202,500 | | | | | | 202,500 |
| | | | | | | $500,000 | 500,000 |
| | | | | 690,000 | | | 690,000 |
| | | | | 36,100 | | | 36,100 |
| | | | | 3,000 | | | 3,000 |
| | 225,000 | | | | | | 225,000 |
| | | | | | | | 140,000 |
| 5,000 | | $ 500 | | | | | 99,500 |
| | 23,425 | | | | | | 77,375 |
| | | 100,000 | | | | | 100,000 |
| | | | | | $2,082,000 | | 2,082,000 |
| | | | 85,000 | 100,000 | | | 185,000 |
| | | | 2,500 | 82,350 | | | 84,850 |
| $20,000 | $452,925 | $100,500 | $97,500 | $ 981,450 | $2,082,000 | $500,000 | $4,626,325 |

**EXHIBIT 9–2.** Model City Combined Statement of Revenues, Expenditures, and Other Changes in Fund Balances for All Governmental Funds for the Period

| Items | General Fund | Capital Projects Fund | Debt-Service Fund | Special Assessment Capital Projects Fund | Special Assessment Agency Fund | Trust Fund | Totals—Memo Only |
|---|---|---|---|---|---|---|---|
| Revenues | $2,010,000 | | | $225,000 | $22,500 | | $2,257,500 |
| Proceeds from sale of bonds | | $500,000 | | | | | 500,000 |
| Transfers from general fund | | | $50,000 | $ 25,000 | | | 75,000 |
| Bond premium from capital projects fund | | | 2,000 | | | | 2,000 |
| Interest earned on investments | | | 1,950 | | 6,975 | | 8,925 |
| Trust fund revenues | | | | | | $2,500 | 2,500 |
| Total | $2,010,000 | $500,000 | $53,950 | $250,000 | $29,475 | $2,500 | $2,845,925 |
| Expenditures | $1,624,000 | $402,000 | | $245,000 | | $2,000 | $2,273,000 |
| Transfers to utility fund | 100,000 | | | | | | 100,000 |
| Transfers to municipal garage fund | 85,000 | | | | | | 85,000 |
| Transfers to debt-service fund | 50,000 | | | | | | 50,000 |
| Transfers to special assessment capital projects fund | 25,000 | | | | | | 25,000 |
| Expenditures for interest | | | | | 6,050 | | 6,050 |
| Total | $1,884,000 | $402,000 | $53,950 | $245,000 | $ 6,050 | $2,000 | $2,539,050 |
| Excess (deficiency) of revenues and other inflows over expenditures and other outflows | $ 126,000 | $ 98,000 | $ 0 | $ 5,000 | $23,425 | $ 500 | $ 306,875 |
| Beginning fund balances | 10,000 | 0 | 0 | 0 | 0 | 0 | 10,000 |
| End-of-period fund balances | $ 136,000 | $ 98,000 | $53,950 | $ 5,000 | $23,425 | $ 500 | $ 316,875 |

350

The combined statement of revenues, expenditures, and changes in fund balances is reflected in Exhibit 9–2 [see narrative requirement 2.b.(2) on page 338].

In order to comply with requirement 2.b.(3), Model City would include the General Fund Statement of Revenues, Expenditures, and Changes in Fund Balances shown in Exhibit 6–2 on page 185. In our illustration, this is the only type of governmental fund for which an annual budget has been legally adopted.

In Exhibit 9–3, we present a combined statement of revenues, expenses, and changes in retained earnings for the period for the two proprietary funds. This exhibit is presented to meet requirement 2.b.(4) on page 338. Exhibit 9–4 reflects the combined statement of cash flows [see requirement 2.b.(5) on page 339]. Because the foregoing statements (Exhibits 9–1, 9–2, 9–3, and 9–4) are from assumed data that do not include information regarding many of the items listed on page 341, we have omitted all footnotes from them.

# ■ Ethical Considerations Associated with Publicizing a City's Financial Statements

The city council of the city of Hush is considering whether to publish a condensed version of the city's financial statements for the past year. Several members of the

**EXHIBIT 9–3.** Model City Combined Statement of Revenues, Expenses, and Changes in Retained Earnings for the Period

| | Internal Service | Enterprise | Totals— Memo Only |
|---|---|---|---|
| Revenues | | | |
| Revenues from services | $50,000 | | $ 50,000 |
| Water sales | | $600,000 | 600,000 |
| Total revenues | $50,000 | $600,000 | $650,000 |
| Operating expenses | | | |
| General expenses | $40,000 | $376,000 | $416,000 |
| Supplies expense | 4,000 | 28,000 | 32,000 |
| Depreciation expense | 3,500 | 80,000 | 83,500 |
| Total operating expenses | $47,500 | $484,000 | $531,500 |
| Operating income | $ 2,500 | $116,000 | $118,500 |
| Nonoperating revenues | | | |
| Income from bond debt-service fund | | 1,800 | 1,800 |
| Nonoperating expenses | | | |
| Bad debt expense | | 450 | 450 |
| Interest expense | | 30,000 | 30,000 |
| General | | 5,000 | 5,000 |
| Net income | $ 2,500 | $ 82,350 | $ 84,850 |
| Retained earnings—beginning of year | 0 | 0 | 0 |
| Retained earnings—end of year | $ 2,500 | $ 82,350 | $ 84,850 |

**EXHIBIT 9-4.**   Combined Statement of Cash Flows for the Period

| | Internal Service Fund | Water Utility Fund | Totals— Memo Only |
|---|---|---|---|
| Cash provided by operations | | | |
| Operations | | | |
| Net income | $ 2,500 | $ 82,350 | $ 84,850 |
| Add depreciation | 3,500 | 80,000 | 83,500 |
| Increase to vouchers payable | 10,000 | 5,000 | 15,000 |
| Increase to customer deposits | | 6,100 | 6,100 |
| Increase to operating expenses | | 3,000 | 3,000 |
| Less increase in receivables | (10,000) | (24,550) | (34,550) |
| Increase in supplies | (6,000) | (7,000) | (13,000) |
| Increase to prepaid expense | | (2,000) | (2,000) |
| Totals | $      0 | $142,900 | $142,900 |
| Financing activities | | | |
| Contribution from general fund | 85,000 | | 85,000 |
| Payment of bonds | | (10,000) | (10,000) |
| Establishment of debt-service fund | | (37,800) | (37,800) |
| Totals | $ 85,000 | $ (47,800) | $ 37,200 |
| Investing activities | | | |
| Purchase of equipment | (35,000) | | (35,000) |
| Totals | $(35,000) | | $ (35,000) |
| Increase in cash balances | $ 50,000 | $ 95,100 | $145,100 |
| Cash balance—end of period | $ 50,000 | $215,100 | $265,100 |
| Cash balance—beginning of period | 0 | 120,000 | 120,000 |
| Increases | $ 50,000 | $ 95,100 | $145,100 |

council are opposed to such action because of the controversies that might arise if citizens give serious attention to the statement data. These council members would rather not have to answer questions that might be raised if the statements data were publicized. Consider the ethical issues associated with the decision to publicize or not to publicize the financial statements.

# ■ Summary

In this chapter, we have described and illustrated the annual financial reporting procedures for governmental units. We began by discussing the general background against which present-day governmental financial reporting practices have been developed. Then we presented the most significant financial reporting provisions of NCGA Statement 1, along with clarifications provided in Statements 3, 5, and 7.

In the last part of the chapter, we presented the GPFS for Model City using the illustrative data accumulated in Chapters 6, 7, and 8. These statements were presented in accordance with the requirements of NCGA Statement 1.

# ■ Appendix

The combined financial statements illustrated earlier in this chapter include governmental fund data presented on the modified accrual basis. As we have observed, many arguments may be advanced for use of the full accrual basis, including the recognition of depreciation as the various transactions of a governmental entity are recorded. However, the legal constraints associated with the appropriation control practices followed in managing governmental funds are judged to require first priority in reflecting the financial data for those entities. As a result, the accounting practices for those funds, designed primarily to disclose the inflows and outflows of appropriable resources, follow the modified accrual basis as illustrated in Chapters 6, 7, and 8.

Even though the constraints imposed by legal requirements may cause the formal accounting records to be organized to reflect dollar rather than operational accountability, accrual-basis statements can be prepared by using *cross-over worksheets* similar to those shown in Exhibits 9−5 and 9−6. Actually, we may think of the conversion of the modified accrual basis inflow−outflow-oriented data to accrual-based data as being similar to the conversion of profit enterprise accrual-based data to the data included in a statement reflecting inflows and outflows of net working capital or cash. Such a statement is in many ways similar to a statement of revenues and expenditures prepared for the general fund. The adjustments in the cross-over worksheets simply run in the *opposite direction* from those made in converting the accrual-based data to reflect funds-flow information. In the cross-over worksheets, we convert financial statement data from the modified accrual basis, normally required to reflect the inflows and outflows of appropriable resources, to accrual-based financial position and operating statements. In our illustration, we also use these worksheets to *consolidate* the data from the various funds into operating and financial position statements for the governmental unit as one operating entity.

In the pages that follow, we demonstrate how to consolidate and adjust the combined financial statements for Model City to the accrual basis by using cross-over worksheets (see Exhibits 9−5 and 9−6). We shall make certain assumptions regarding accrued items, prepaid items, and the length of life for depreciable assets for the purpose of making some of the adjustments. After we have completed the worksheet, we prepare an accrual-based balance sheet (see Exhibit 9−7) and a statement of financial performance (see Exhibit 9−8) from the worksheet data.

It is important to recognize that the *illustrated accrual-basis statements are not required within presently accepted accounting practices for governmental entities.* They are presented here because they can provide useful financial information for constituents and other externally interested groups. For example, by placing the emphasis on the points of earning and using resources rather than on the points of acquiring and disbursing them, the accrual-basis statements more appropriately disclose the extent to

**EXHIBIT 9–5.** Model City Worksheet to Convert End-of-Period Combined Balance Sheet to Consolidated Accrual Basis Statement

| | Combined Statement Balances | Adjustments* | | Consolidated Balance Sheet |
|---|---|---|---|---|
| Cash | 638,075 | | (6) 157,975 | 480,100 |
| Taxes receivable | 15,000 | | | 15,000 |
| Investments | 149,000 | | | 149,000 |
| Special assessments receivable | 202,500 | | | 202,500 |
| Interest receivable | 900 | | | 900 |
| Equipment | 1,170,000 | | (13) 635,000 | 535,000 |
| Supplies | 18,000 | (7) 8,000 | | 26,000 |
| Due from special assessment capital projects fund | 10,000 | | (8) 10,000 | |
| Allowance for depreciation—equipment | 213,500 | (13) 213,500 | | |
| Structures and improvements | 1,547,000 | | | 1,547,000 |
| Amount to be provided for retirement of bonds | 446,050 | | (5) 446,050 | |
| Amount provided for retirement of bonds | 53,950 | | (5) 53,950 | |
| Accounts receivable | 44,700 | | | 44,700 |
| Allowance for bad debts | 150 | | | 150 |
| Prepaid operating expense | 2,000 | (11) 6,000 | | 8,000 |
| Bond debt-service fund | 37,800 | | | 37,800 |
| Land | 100,000 | | | 100,000 |
| Buildings | 300,000 | | | 300,000 |
| Allowance for depreciation—buildings | 120,000 | | | 120,000 |
| Vouchers payable | 179,500 | (16) 5,500 | | 174,000 |
| Contracts payable—retained percentage | 9,500 | | | 9,500 |
| Bonds payable | 1,415,000 | (14) 915,000<br>(19) 52,150 | | 447,850 |
| Interest payable | | | | 2,000 |
| Due to municipal garage fund | 10,000 | (8) 10,000 | | |
| Accrued operating expense | 3,000 | | | 3,000 |
| Customer deposits | 36,100 | | | 36,100 |
| Fund balance reserved for encumbrances | 140,000 | (2) 90,000 | | 50,000 |

| Account | | | | | | | |
|---|---|---|---|---|---|---|---|
| Fund balance reserved for endowment | 100,000 | | | | | | 100,000 |
| Fund balance—trust fund income | | | 500 | (1) | 500 | | 500 |
| Retained earnings | 84,850 | (3) | 84,850 | | | | |
| Investment in general fixed assets | 2,082,000 | (4) | 2,082,000 | | | | |
| Deferred revenues | 202,500 | (20) | 202,500 | | | | |
| Amount to be provided by special assessments | 202,500 | | 202,500 | (5a) | 202,500 | | |
| Amount provided by special assessments | 22,500 | | 22,500 | (5a) | 22,500 | | |
| Fund balance for debt service | 77,375 | (1) | 77,375 | | | | |
| Unreserved fund balance | 99,500 | (1) | 99,500 | | | | |
| Fund balance contributed by city—municipal garage fund | 85,000 | | | | | | 85,000 |
| Fund balance contributed by city—water utility fund | 100,000 | | | | | | 100,000 |
| Fund balance—general operations | 500,000 (5); 220,850 (9); 4,000 (12) | | | (1) 86,000; (4) 2,082,000; (7) 8,000; (11) 6,000; (15) 1,000; (18) 55,000; (11) 52,150; (1) 53,950 | | | 1,565,300 |
| Fund balance—general debt service | 1,800 (17); 52,150 (19) | | | | | | |
| Fund balance—special assessment project | 225,000 (5a) | | | (1) 28,425 | | 196,575 | |
| Fund balance—reserved for capital project encumbrances | 90,000 (2) | | | (2) 90,000 | | | 90,000 |
| Retained earnings—internal service fund | 2,500 (3) | | | (3) 2,500 | | | 2,500 |
| Retained earnings—water utility fund | 82,350 (3) | | | (3) 82,350 | | | 82,350 |
| Cash restricted to use on capital project | 108,000 (6) | | 108,000 | | | 108,000 | |
| Cash restricted to use in servicing debt | 4,950 (6) | | 4,950 | | | 4,950 | |
| Cash restricted to use for special assessment project | 44,525 (6) | | | | | | |

continues

**EXHIBIT 9–5.** *continued*

| | Combined Statement Balances | | Adjustments* | | | | Consolidated Balance Sheet | |
|---|---|---|---|---|---|---|---|---|
| | | | | | | | | |
| Cash restricted to use for trust fund project | | | (6) | 500 | | | 500 | |
| Allowance for depreciation—general fixed assets | | | (18) | 55,000 | (9) | 220,850 | | 165,850 |
| Fund balance—capital projects | | | | | (1) | 8,000 | | 8,000 |
| Accrued general operating expense | | | | | (12) | 4,000 | | 4,000 |
| Water utility equipment | | | (13) | 600,000 | | | 600,000 | |
| Allowance for depreciation of equipment | | | | | (13) | 210,000 | | 210,000 |
| Water utility bonds payable | | | | | (14) | 690,000 | | 690,000 |
| Special assessment bonds payable | | | | | (14) | 225,000 | | 225,000 |
| Accrued revenue | | | (15) | 1,000 | | | 1,000 | |
| Equipment— municipal garage | | | (13) | 35,000 | | | 35,000 | |
| Vouchers payable on capital project | | | | | (16) | 5,000 | | 5,000 |
| Vouchers payable on special assessment project | | | | | (16) | 500 | | 500 |
| Due from restricted funds | | | (10) | 10,000 | | | 10,000 | |
| Due to unrestricted funds | | | | | (10) | 10,000 | | 10,000 |
| Unamortized bond premium | | | | | (17) | 1,800 | | 1,800 |
| Allowance depreciation—municipal garage equipment | | | | | (13) | 3,500 | | 3,500 |
| Bonds payable from debt-service fund assets | | | | | (19) | 52,150 | | 52,150 |
| Special assessments restricted to use in retirement of special assessment bonds | | | | | (20) | 202,500 | | 202,500 |
| Totals | 4,959,975 | 4,959,975 | | 5,709,150 | | 5,709,150 | 4,446,550 | 4,446,550 |

*Adjustments explained on pages 360–362.

**EXHIBIT 9–6.** Model City Worksheet to Convert Combined Statement of Revenues, Expenditures, and Transfers to Accrual Basis Operating Statement

| | Combined Statement Balances | Adjustments* (Dr.) | Adjustments* (Cr.) | Consolidated Operating Statement |
|---|---|---|---|---|
| Revenues | 2,235,000 | (18) 225,000<br>(14) 5,000 | (6) 1,000 | 2,006,000 |
| Proceeds from sale of bonds | 500,000 | (7) 500,000 | | |
| Transfers from general fund | 75,000 | (8) 75,000 | | |
| Bond premium from capital projects fund | 2,000 | (7) 2,000 | | |
| Interest earned | 8,925 | (13) 9,125 | (15) 200 | |
| Revenues from special assessments | 22,500 | (8) 22,500 | | |
| Income from trust fund investments | 2,500 | (16) 2,000 | | 500 |
| Net income from municipal garage fund | | (11) 2,500 | (10) 2,500 | |
| Net income from water utility fund | | | (12) 82,350 | 82,350 |
| | | | (1) 792,000 | |
| | | | (2) 8,000 | |
| Expenditures (converted to expenses) | 2,273,000 | (5) 4,000 | (4) 6,000 | 1,466,500 |
| | | | (11) 2,500 | |
| | | | (16) 2,000 | |
| Transfer to utility fund | 100,000 | | (17) 100,000 | |
| Transfer to municipal garage fund | 85,000 | | (9) 85,000 | |
| Transfer to debt-service fund | 50,000 | | (8) 50,000 | |
| Transfer to special assessment capital projects fund | 25,000 | | (8) 25,000 | |
| Interest expenditures | 6,050 | | | 6,050 |
| Depreciation expense | | (3) 130,850 | | 130,850 |
| Interest earned by debt-service fund | | (13) 2,150 | (13) 2,150 | 2,150 |
| Interest earned by special assessment agency fund | | (6) 6,975 | (13) 6,975 | 6,975 |
| Excess of revenues over expenditures and transfers (converted to excess of revenues over expenses) | 306,875 | (8) 22,500<br>(14) 5,000<br>(18) 225,000 | (7) 502,000 | 494,575 |
| **Totals** | **2,845,925**  **2,845,925** | **2,055,025** | **2,055,025** | **2,097,975**  **2,097,975** |

*Adjustments explained on pages 362–363.

**EXHIBIT 9–7.** Model City Consolidated Balance Sheet—End of Period

### Unrestricted Resources and Related Obligations

#### Assets

| | | | |
|---|---:|---:|---:|
| Uncommitted assets | | | |
| Cash | | $ 215,000 | |
| Taxes receivable | | 15,000 | |
| Accrued revenue | | 1,000 | $ 231,000 |
| Assets committed to specified uses | | | |
| Municipal garage fund cash | | $ 50,000 | |
| Water utility fund cash | | 215,100 | |
| Due from restricted funds | | 10,000 | |
| Supplies | | 26,000 | |
| Prepaid operating expenses | | 8,000 | |
| Bond debt-service fund—utility bonds | | 37,800 | |
| Accounts receivable—utility fund | $ 44,700 | | |
| Allowance for bad debts | 150 | 44,550 | |
| Buildings—utility fund | $ 300,000 | | |
| Allowance for depreciation | 120,000 | 180,000 | |
| Equipment— utility fund | $ 600,000 | | |
| Allowance for depreciation | 210,000 | 390,000 | |
| Equipment— municipal garage | $ 35,000 | | |
| Allowance for depreciation | 3,500 | 31,500 | |
| Land—public utility | | 100,000 | |
| Structures and improvements | $1,547,000 | | |
| Equipment | 535,000 | | |
| | $2,082,000 | | |
| Allowance for depreciation | 165,850 | 1,916,150 | 3,009,100 |
| Total | | | $3,240,100 |

### Externally Restricted Resources and Related Obligations

#### Assets

| | | | |
|---|---:|---:|---:|
| Cash | | | |
| Reserved for capital project | | $ 108,000 | |
| Reserved for debt service | | 4,950 | |
| Reserved for special assessment project | | 44,525 | |
| Reserved for trust fund use | | 500 | $ 157,975 |
| Investments | | | |
| Held by debt-service fund | | $ 49,000 | |
| Held by trust fund | | 100,000 | 149,000 |
| Special assessments receivable | | | 202,500 |
| Interest receivable—special assessment agency fund | | | 900 |
| Total | | | $ 510,375 |
| Grand Total | | | $3,750,475 |

## Liabilities and Fund Balances

| | | | |
|---|---|---|---|
| Liabilities to be paid from uncommitted assets | | | |
| Vouchers payable | | $ 94,000 | |
| Accrued operating expense | | 4,000 | $ 98,000 |
| Other liabilities | | | |
| Vouchers payable—municipal garage | | $ 10,000 | |
| Vouchers payable—water utility | | 70,000 | |
| Customer deposits—water utility | | 36,100 | |
| Accrued expenses—water utility | | 3,000 | |
| Bond payable—general | | 447,850 | |
| Water utility bonds payable | | 690,000 | 1,256,950 |
| Total liabilities | | | $1,354,950 |
| Fund balances | | | |
| Fund balance—general | | | |
| Unreserved balance | $ 86,000 | | |
| Reserved for encumbrances | 50,000 | | |
| Committed balance | 1,479,300 | $1,615,300 | |
| Contributed to water utility | | 100,000 | |
| Contributed to municipal garage | | 85,000 | 1,800,300 |
| Retained earnings | | | |
| Municipal garage | | $ 2,500 | |
| Water utility | | 82,350 | 84,850 |
| Total | | | $3,240,100 |


## Liabilities and Fund Balances

| | | | |
|---|---|---|---|
| Liabilities | | | |
| Vouchers payable—capital project | | $ 5,000 | |
| Vouchers payable—special assessment | | 500 | $ 5,500 |
| Contract payable—retained percentage | | | 9,500 |
| Interest payable—special assessment | | | 2,000 |
| Special assessment bonds payable | | | 225,000 |
| Due to unrestricted funds from special | | | |
| assessment capital projects fund | | | 10,000 |
| General bonds payable from debt-service fund | | $ 52,150 | |
| Unamortized bond premium | | 1,800 | 53,950 |
| Total liabilities | | | $ 305,950 |
| Fund balances | | | |
| Capital project | | | |
| Available for use | $ 8,000 | | |
| Encumbered | 90,000 | $ 98,000 | |
| Special assessment | | | |
| Assessments restricted to use in retirement | | | |
| of bonds | $ 202,500 | | |
| Less fund balance | (196,575) | 5,925 | |
| Trust fund | | | |
| Principal balance | $ 100,000 | | |
| Expendable balance | 500 | 100,500 | 204,425 |
| Total | | | $ 510,375 |
| Grand total | | | $3,750,475 |

**EXHIBIT 9–8.**   Model City Statement of Financial Performance for Period

*General Operations*

| | | |
|---|---:|---:|
| Revenues | | |
| General revenues | | $2,006,000 |
| Net income from water utility operations | | 82,350 |
| | | $2,088,350 |
| Expenses | | |
| General operating expenses | $1,466,500 | |
| Depreciation expense | 130,850 | 1,597,350 |
| Excess of general operating revenues over expenses | | $ 491,000 |

*Restricted Operations*

| | | |
|---|---:|---:|
| Interest earned by debt-service fund | | 2,150 |
| Interest earned by special assessment agency fund | $    6,975 | |
| Interest expense—special assessment agency fund | 6,050 | 925 |
| Income from trust fund investments | | 500 |
| Excess of restricted revenues over expenses | | $    3,575 |
| Total excess of revenues over expenses | | $  494,575 |

which taxpayers have paid for all services received during the year. This is characterized as the disclosure of "intergenerational equity." Because such accrual-based data place emphasis on the points where resources are earned and used, rather than on where spendable resources are received and disbursed, they provide much more meaningful functional unit cost data that can be used in evaluating the efficiency and effectiveness of operations. We give more attention to the ways in which those data can be used by externally interested groups in Part Four of this text.

## Explanation of Entries on Consolidated Balance Sheet Working Paper (Exhibit 9–5)

1. The combined statement fund balance of $94,500 is made up of fund balances that are related to various separate activities of Model City. This entry allocates that balance back to those various separate activities.

2. The combined statement fund balance reserved for encumbrances includes $90,000 related to capital projects fund operations. This entry reestablishes that amount as fund balance reserved for capital projects encumbrances.

3. The combined balance for retained earnings includes amounts associated with the municipal garage fund and the water utility fund. This entry divides that total into those elements.

4.  In this entry, we transfer the balance in investment in fixed assets to fund balance—general operations. This entry, in effect, eliminates the general fixed-assets account group as a separate accounting entity.

5.  In this entry, we transfer balances shown in the general long-term debt account group and special assessment agency fund for amounts provided and to be provided for the retirement of long-term debt to the fund balance—general operations and fund balance—special assessment project, respectively. These entries, in effect, eliminate the general long-term debt account group as a separate accounting entity and remove the memo portion of the special assessment agency fund.

6.  Parts of the cash shown in the combined statement cash balance can only be used for specific purposes. This entry allocates the restricted portions of that balance to reflect those restrictions.

7.  This entry increases the asset supplies on hand to an assumed balance of $26,000. The cost of these supplies has been debited to expenditures at the time of purchase. Those expenditures were subsequently closed to fund balance.

8.  This entry eliminates interfund receivable and payable.

9.  This entry records depreciation of general fixed assets in the amount of $220,850. This includes adjustment for depreciation associated with prior years in the amount of $90,000.

10. This entry recognizes obligations and claims between restricted and unrestricted resources.

11. This entry recognizes *assumed* prepaid general operating expenses in the amount of $6,000.

12. This entry records *assumed* accrual of general operating expenses in the amount of $4,000.

13. Because the water utility and the internal service funds operate apart from the general operations of the city, this entry is introduced to transfer the fixed assets and the related accumulated depreciation account balances associated with those operations to separate accounts.

14. Special assessment bonds payable and revenue bonds payable are not general obligations of the city. Therefore, this entry is introduced to allow them to be shown as separate obligations on the consolidated balance sheet.

15. This entry recognizes *assumed* accrued revenue in the amount of $1,000.

16. This entry removes vouchers payable of restricted funds from general vouchers payable accounts.

17. This entry records unamortized premium on general bonds payable. *Assumed* life of bonds is ten years.

18. This entry eliminates accumulated depreciation on general fixed assets *assumed* to have been sold at book value (see transaction 9 for general fund).

19. This entry transfers amount equal to debt-service fund balance from general bonds payable to bonds payable from debt-service fund assets. Another

entry is used to close out the debt-service fund balance to fund balance — general operations.

20. The deferred revenues balance in the combined balance sheet is more appropriately reflected as special assessments restricted to use in retirement of special assessment bonds. This entry makes that change.

## Explanation of Entries for Statement of Financial Performance Working Paper (Exhibit 9–6)

1. This entry eliminates capital expenditures as follows:

| | |
|---|---:|
| General fund | $145,000 |
| Capital project fund | 402,000 |
| Special assessment capital projects fund | 245,000 |
| | $792,000 |

The entry is part of the process of converting expenditures to expenses. It removes expenditures from the account.

2. This entry records inventory of supplies on hand (see balance sheet entry 7). The entry is part of the process of converting expenditures to expenses. It removes expenditures for supplies still on hand from the expenditures account.

3. This entry records depreciation of fixed assets (see balance sheet entry 9) $220,850 − $90,000.

4. This entry records prepaid general operating expense (see balance sheet entry 11).

5. This entry records accrued general operating expense (see balance sheet entry 12).

6. This entry records accrued revenue (see balance sheet entry 15).

7. This entry removes bond fund items from operating statement data.

8. To make this statement a consolidated *operating statement* for the city as an entity, we must remove transfers between funds and collections of special assessments from the accounts. This entry eliminates those items relating to the special assessment agency fund and debt-service fund.

9. This entry removes transfer to municipal garage fund from operating statement data.

10. This entry recognizes excess of revenues over expenses of municipal garage fund.

11. This entry eliminates interfund net income of municipal garage fund.

12. This entry recognizes net income earned by operation of water utility service.

13. This entry provides needed disclosures of the sources from which interest was earned.

14. This entry removes proceeds from sale of asset from revenue (see general fund entry 9). Sale assumed to have been made at book value thus requiring no recognition of gain or loss on sale.

15. This entry records amortization of premium on bond payable—assumed life ten years.

16. These expenses are associated with trust fund activities rather than general operations.

17. This entry removes an interfund transfer.

18. This entry removes proceeds from sale of special assessment bonds from revenues.

# ■ Glossary

**Basic Financial Statements.**   Those financial statements, including notes thereto, that are necessary for a fair presentation of the financial position and results of operations of an entity in conformity with GAAP. Under Statement 1, basic financial statements include a balance sheet, an "all inclusive" operating statement, and (for proprietary funds, pension trust funds and nonexpendable trust funds) a statement of cash flows. See *Financial Reporting Pyramid; Combined Statements—Overview; Combining Statements—By Fund Type; General Purpose Financial Statements (GPFS); and Generally Accepted Accounting Principles.*

**CAFR.**   See *Comprehensive Annual Financial Report.*

**Combined Statements—Overview.**   The five basic financial statements comprising the first of the financial reporting pyramid's three reporting levels containing GAAP basic financial statements. They include: (1) combined balance sheet—all fund types and account groups; (2) combined statement of revenues, expenditures, and changes in fund balances—all governmental fund types; (3) combined statement of revenues, expenditures, and changes in fund balances—budget and actual—general and special revenue fund types (and similar governmental fund types for which annual budgets have been legally adopted); (4) combined statement of revenues, expenses, and changes in retained earnings (or equity)—all proprietary fund types; (5) combined statement of cash flows—all proprietary fund types; and (6) notes to the financial statements. Trust fund operations may be reported in (2), (4), and (5) above, as appropriate, or separately. The combined statements—overview are also referred to as the "liftable" general purpose financial statements (GPFS).

**Combining Statements—By Fund Type.**   The second of the financial reporting pyramid's three reporting levels containing GAAP basic financial statements. Such statements are presented for each fund type for which the government maintains more than one fund. They include GAAP basic financial statements for each fund of a particular fund type in separate adjacent columns and a total column that duplicates the column for that fund type in the combined statements—overview.

**Comprehensive Annual Financial Report (CAFR).**   The official annual report of a government. It includes five combined statements—overview (the "liftable" GPFS) and basic financial statements for each individual fund and account group prepared in conformity with GAAP and organized into a financial reporting pyramid. It also includes supporting schedules necessary to demonstrate compliance with finance-related legal and contractual provisions, extensive introductory material, and a detailed statistical section. Every government should prepare and publish a CAFR as a matter of public record.

**Financial Reporting Pyramid.**    NCGA Statement 1 organization plan for the Financial Section of the CAFR. The pyramid presents GAAP basic financial statements on three distinct and progressively more detailed reporting levels: (1) combined statements—overview (the "liftable" GPFS); (2) combining statements—by fund type; and (3) where necessary or appropriate, individual fund statements.

**General Purpose Financial Statements (GPFS).**    Those basic financial statements that comprise the minimum acceptable fair presentation in conformity with GAAP. As such, they constitute the minimum acceptable scope of independent annual GAAP audits. Under 1968 GAAFR, the GPFS included financial statements for each individual fund and account group maintained by a government. In Statement 1, the NCGA redefined governmental GPFS to consist of financial statements for each of the eight fund types in use and for both account groups presented in separate adjacent columns on the financial reporting pyramid's five Combined Statements—Overview. See *Basic Financial Statements, Combined Statements—Overview,* and *Financial Reporting Pyramid.*

**Trust Funds.**    Funds used to account for assets held by a government in a trustee capacity for individuals, private organizations, other governments, and/or other funds.

# ■ Suggested Supplementary References

Bowsher, Charles A. "Wanted: Commitment and Leadership. The Challenges of the 80's." *Government Accountants Journal* (Fall 1982): 1–7.

*Brodner, Howard W. "Consolidated Financial Statements for the Federal Government." *Government Accountants Journal* (Spring 1977).

Brodner, Howard W. "Improving Financial Reporting by Local Government." *Government Accountants Journal* (Fall 1981): 23–36.

Brodner, Howard W. "Improving Financial Reporting by Local Government." *Government Accountants Journal* (Spring 1982): 10–15.

Caldwell, Kenneth S. "The Accounting Aspects of Budgetary Reform: Can We Have Meaningful Reform without Significant Changes in Traditional Accounting Practices?" *Governmental Finance* (August 1978): 10–17.

Douglas, Patricia P. "GASB's Proposed Statement on Objectives of Financial Reporting." *Government Accountants Journal* (Summer 1986).

Freeman, Robert J., and Craig Shoulders. "Mastering the Interfund Maze." *Government Accountants Journal* (Spring 1983): 32–44.

*Also available in *Accounting in the Public Sector: A Changing Environment—A Book of Readings* by Robert W. Ingram (Salt Lake City: Brighton Publishing Company, 1980).

Henke, Emerson O. "Government Financial Reports: A Creative Response to User Needs." *Government Accountants Journal* (Summer 1986).

Hepp, Gerald W. "Governmental Financial Statements—A New Look." *Journal of Accountancy* (December 1976).

King, Randle R., and C. David Baron. "An Integrated Account Structure for Governmental Accounting and Financial Reporting." *Accounting Review,* 49 (1974): 76–87.

*Patitucci, Frank M. "Government Accounting and Financial Reporting: Some Urgent Problems." *Public Affairs Report,* 18 (June 1977), Berkeley Institute of Governmental Studies, University of California.

Points, Ronald J., and Bruce Michelson. "Improving Accounting and Financial Reporting in the Federal Government." *Government Accountants Journal* (Winter 1979–80): 39–42.

*Weinstein, Edward A. "Disclosure: Too Much or Too Little." *CPA Journal,* New York State Society of Certified Public Accountants (April 1977).

Wesberry, James P., Jr. "Avoiding Future Financial Ruin—How to Meet the Challenge." *Government Accountants Journal* (Spring 1982): 38–44.

Wesberry, James P., Jr. "Government Financial Statements: A Challenge Which Must Be Met." *Government Accountants Journal* (Winter 1981–1982): 37–43.

# ■ Questions for Class Discussion

Q9-1.   Explain the difference between the data logically required for external general purpose financial statements and those logically needed for internal management purposes.

Q9-2.   What is the conceptual difference between combined financial statements and consolidated financial statements for governmental entities?

Q9-3.   How does the interpretation of the entity concept enter into the determination of data to be included in the annual financial report for a city? Explain.

Q9-4.   Explain the relationship between the accrual basis of accounting and the concept of "intergenerational equity" (see appendix of this chapter).

Q9-5.   Does use of the accrual basis in accounting for the financial activities of a governmental entity provide more appropriate disclosure of the extent to which the current generation is paying for its own services than does use of the modified accrual basis? Support your position (see appendix of this chapter).

Q9-6.   Describe the adjustments that would typically have to be made to convert the conventional modified accrual-based financial data, reflected in combined governmental financial statements, to consolidated full accrual-basis statements (see appendix of the chapter).

Q9-7.   Compare and contrast the inflow and outflow elements of a modified accrual-basis operating statement with those same elements in an accrual-basis statement (see appendix of this chapter).

Q9-8.   Explain the difference between "presenting fairly in conformity with generally accepted accounting principles" the operating results of a governmental entity and presenting those results in such a way as to demonstrate the extent of compliance with legal provisions.

*Also available in *Accounting in the Public Sector: A Changing Environment—A Book of Readings* by Robert W. Ingram (Salt Lake City: Brighton Publishing Company, 1980).

Q9-9.    Why is it important to separate unrestricted resources and their related obligations from externally restricted resources and their related obligations? Explain.

Q9-10.    What significance should be attached to the difference between revenues and expenses in an accrual-basis statement of financial performance for a governmental entity? Explain fully (see appendix of this chapter).

Q9-11.    Explain the difference between CAFR and GPFS.

Q9-12.    How should the data relating to long-term leases be disclosed in the CAFR?

Q9-13.    Should GPFS contain footnotes? Explain.

Q9-14.    What criteria should a governmental entity use in determining which subentity financial reports should be included in GPFS? Discuss.

# ■ Exercises

E9-1.    The accounting records for Pleasant City show the following items in the balance sheets for the general fund and debt-service fund:

|  | General Fund | | Debt-Service Fund | |
|---|---|---|---|---|
| Cash | $ 40,000 | | $ 3,000 | |
| Investments | 10,000 | | 105,000 | |
| Taxes receivable | 50,000 | | | |
| Due to debt-service fund | | $ 30,000 | | |
| Fund balance | | 60,000 | | $138,000 |
| Vouchers payable | | 10,000 | | |
| Due from general fund | | | 30,000 | |
| Totals | $100,000 | $100,000 | $138,000 | $138,000 |

**Required:**

A.   Prepare a combined balance sheet for the two funds.

B.   Prepare a consolidated balance sheet for the two funds (see appendix of this chapter).

C.   Explain the conceptual difference between the two combining statements insofar as the entity concept is concerned.

E9-2.    In the process of converting the conventional combined financial statements for a city to full accrual-based consolidated financial statements at the end of the current year, you are given the following supplementary data:

1.   The city has fixed assets acquired four years ago at a cost of $1,000,000 that were expected to have a service life of ten years with no salvage value.

2.   Expenditures include fixed assets purchased at a cost of $30,000. These assets also have a ten-year life. They were acquired at the midpoint in the year.

3.  Supplies were inventoried at $12,000 and $8,000 at the beginning and end of the year, respectively. Supplies are conventionally included in expenditures when purchased.
4.  Expenses accrued but not paid at the beginning and end of the year were $0 and $3,000, respectively.

**Required:**
A.  Journalize the entries that should be recorded in a worksheet used to convert the conventional financial statements to full accrual-basis statements (see appendix of this chapter).
B.  How much are current-period operating outflows changed by conversion to the full accrual basis?

E9-3.   The following items appear on the combined balance sheet for a city:

> General fund
>> Cash
>> Investments
>> Taxes receivable
>
> Capital projects fund
>> Cash
>
> Debt-service fund
>> Cash
>> Investments
>
> Special assessment agency fund
>> Cash
>> Special assessments receivable
>
> Municipal garage fund
>> Cash
>> Equipment
>> Supplies
>
> General fixed-assets account group
>> Equipment
>> Land

**Required:**
Classify each item as restricted or unrestricted. Justify your position in each case.

E9-4.   A conventional statement of revenues and expenditures shows revenues of $500,000 and expenditures of $495,000. When these data are adjusted to the full accrual basis, the statement of operating performance shows revenues of $502,000 and expenses of $540,000.

**Required:**
A.  Evaluate the operations from the point of view of "intergenerational equity" as they are disclosed by each of the two statements. Discuss fully.
B.  List some of the things that could account for the differences in inflows and outflows reflected in the two statements.

# ■ Problems

**P9-1.**  This is a comprehensive problem requiring application of accounting procedures discussed and illustrated in Chapters 5 through 9. (A computer software package is available for solving this problem.)

New City begins its current year's operations with the following account balances:

| | |
|---|---:|
| Cash | $   20,000 |
| Vouchers payable | 10,000 |
| Unreserved fund balance | 10,000 |
| Equipment | 900,000 |
| Structure and improvements | 1,800,000 |
| Investment in general fixed assets from general fund | 1,500,000 |
| Investment in general fixed assets from special assessment<br>      projects | 400,000 |
| Investment in general fixed assets from capital project fund | 800,000 |

During the year, the following transactions and other financial activities occur:

1.  The City Council approved a budget calling for total estimated revenues of $4,000,000 and appropriations of $3,900,000.
2.  Tax notices in the amount of $2,920,000 were sent out.
3.  Other revenues in the amount of $1,090,000 were received during the year.
4.  Property taxes amounting to $2,890,000 were collected.
5.  During the year, expenditures and transfers in the amount of $3,478,000 were incurred by the general fund. These included $200,000 for the acquisition of a water utility company, $100,000 payment into a debt-service fund, $50,000 payment toward a special assessment project, and $170,000 payment into a municipal garage fund for the purpose of establishing a vehicle maintenance center.
6.  Contracts were signed for the purchase of equipment by the general fund estimated to cost $400,000.
7.  Part of the equipment ordered in item 6 above, estimated to cost $300,000, was received. Its actual cost was $290,000.
8.  Vouchers including all amounts due to other funds in the amount of $3,600,000 were paid during the year.
9.  Obsolete equipment originally costing $120,000 is sold as scrap for $10,000.
10.  A capital projects fund was originated with a general bond issue in the amount of $1,000,000 being authorized for financing the project.
11.  The general bond issue (see item 10) was sold for $1,004,000.
12.  Expenditures in the amount of $700,000 were incurred on the capital project. Of this amount, $10,000 was for services performed by the municipal garage fund.
13.  Contracts amounting to $280,000 were signed covering the remainder of the capital project.
14.  A contract (see item 13) amounting to $100,000 is completed and a voucher is prepared to cover it. Because of changes in certain specifications, the amount to be paid is agreed upon as $104,000. The contract also stipulates that, pending

satisfactory performance of the improvements, the city may retain 10 percent of the original contract price.

15. Vouchers amounting to $774,000 plus the $10,000 due to the municipal garage fund are paid by the capital projects fund.

16. The general bond indenture (see capital projects fund) includes a provision requiring the general fund to pay $100,000 per year into a debt-service fund (see appropriation transaction in general fund). It is estimated that the investment earnings will amount to $4,000 during the first year.

17. The obligation of the general fund to contribute the appropriate amount to the debt-service fund is recognized in that fund (see transaction 5).

18. The general fund pays its obligation to the debt-service fund (see transaction 8). The cash was invested in securities.

19. Interest income amounting to $3,900 was received by the debt-service fund.

20. The premium on the sale of general bonds in the amount of $4,000 (see capital projects fund transaction) is transferred to the debt-service fund.

21. A special assessment project was authorized for the construction of streets and sidewalks in a new residential area. The general fund portion of these expenditures was approved as part of the general fund appropriations in the amount of $50,000. This approval was contingent on the assessment of a special tax levy in the amount of $450,000 against property owners in the benefited area. The total authorized improvement is $500,000. A special tax levy scheduled to be paid over a period of ten years was authorized and recorded.

22. Special assessment project bonds amounting to $450,000 were issued at face value to provide funds for the project.

23. Construction expenditures amounting to $400,000 were incurred by the special assessment capital projects fund. Of this amount, $20,000 was for services performed by the municipal garage.

24. A contract amounting to $90,000, covering the completion of the special assessment improvement project, was signed.

25. The contract (see item 24) was completed and the obligation relating to it was recognized. It was agreed that 10 percent of the contract price would be retained pending satisfactory use of the streets for six months.

26. The first installment of the special tax levy amounting to $45,000 was received.

27. Interest amounting to $12,150 was received on the deferred assessments receivable.

28. Special assessment capital projects fund vouchers amounting to $460,000 were paid.

29. Interest amounting to $8,100 was paid to special assessment capital projects fund bond holders.

30. Interest amounting to $4,000 has accrued on special assessment capital projects fund bonds payable.

31. Interest amounting to $1,800 has accrued on deferred assessments receivable.

32. The municipal garage fund, after receiving its contribution from the general fund, purchased equipment costing $70,000 and supplies costing $20,000 on account.

33. Expenses in the amount of $80,000 were incurred by the municipal garage during the period.

34. Supplies valued at $8,000 were used in garage operations during the period.
35. Services of the municipal garage were billed to other funds as follows:

    General fund, $70,000
    Special assessment capital projects fund, $20,000 (see transaction 23)
    Capital projects fund, $10,000 (see transaction 12)

36. Vouchers amounting to $150,000 were paid by the municipal garage fund.
37. Equipment in the municipal garage fund was depreciated over a ten-year life.
38. The water utility fund purchased by use of general fund resources (see transaction 5) had the following assets and liabilities at the time of acquisition:

Assets

| | |
|---|---:|
| Cash | $    40,000 |
| Accounts receivable | 40,000 |
| Materials and supplies | 10,000 |
| Land | 200,000 |
| Building | 600,000 |
| Allowance for depreciation of buildings | 200,000 |
| Equipment | 1,200,000 |
| Allowance for depreciation of equipment | 300,000 |

Liabilities

| | |
|---|---:|
| Vouchers payable | 130,000 |
| Revenue bonds payable (including $20,000 due during the current year) | 1,400,000 |
| Customer deposits | 60,000 |

39. The water utility had the following transactions during the period:
    a. Customers were billed for services in the amount of $1,200,000.
    b. Collections on account amounted to $1,150,000.
    c. Meter deposits amounting to $14,000 were received from new customers.
    d. Meter deposits amounting to $1,800 were refunded to customers.
    e. General operating expenses amounting to $750,000 were incurred.
    f. Materials and supplies costing $70,000 were purchased on account.
    g. The inventory of material and supplies at the end of the period amounted to $24,000.
    h. It is estimated that $1,900 of customers' accounts receivable will be uncollectible.
    i. Depreciation amounting to $40,000 on the building and $120,000 on equipment was recorded.
    j. Operating expenses prepaid at the end of the period amount to $4,000.
    k. Matured revenue bonds payable amounting to $20,000 plus current year interest on all bonds amounting to $60,000 were paid. The next installment of the revenue bond in the amount of $20,000, due to be paid during the next year, should be transferred to a current liability classification.
    l. Cash in the amount of $72,000 was transferred to a bond debt-service fund.
    m. General nonoperating expenses amounting to $10,000 are incurred.

n. Cash in the amount of $60,000 held in the bond debt-service fund was invested in securities.

o. Operating expenses amounting to $60,000 were accrued at the end of the period.

p. Cash amounting to $3,600 is received as income from bond debt-service fund investments.

q. Accounts judged to be uncollectible in the amount of $600 were written off.

r. Vouchers payable in the amount of $820,000 were paid.

40. The city received $200,000 from a wealthy citizen under terms that required the contribution be invested and the revenues be used to finance cultural events in the city.

41. The cash received (see item 40) was invested.

42. Interest income amounting to $5,000 was received from the investment (see item 41).

43. Expenditures for cultural events paid from the revenues relating to this contribution amount to $4,000.

**Required:**

A. Prepare a transactions worksheet for each of the funds and account groups that should be used by New City in accounting for the year's actions and transactions. The worksheets should be organized to reflect beginning balances, actions and transactions, operating statement (where appropriate), and end-of-period balance sheet.

B. Prepare the combined financial statements required by the GAAFR Statement of Principles (see Chapters 3 and 9).

**P9-2.** Select the best answer for each of the following items:

1. In the comprehensive annual financial report (CAFR) of a governmental unit, the account groups are included in:
   a. both the combined balance sheet and the combined statement of revenues, expenditures, and changes in fund balances.
   b. the combined statement of revenues, expenditures, and changes in fund balances, but not the combined balance sheet.
   c. the combined balance sheet but not the combined statement of revenues, expenditures, and changes in fund balances.
   d. neither the combined balance sheet nor the combined statement of revenues, expenditures, and changes in fund balances.

2. The comprehensive annual financial report (CAFR) of a governmental unit should contain a combined statement of revenues, expenses, and changes in retained earnings for:

   | | Account groups | Proprietary funds |
   |---|---|---|
   | a. | Yes | Yes |
   | b. | Yes | No |
   | c. | No | No |
   | d. | No | Yes |

3. The comprehensive annual financial report (CAFR) of a governmental unit should contain a combined statement of revenues, expenditures, and changes in fund balances for:

| | Governmental funds | Proprietary funds |
|---|---|---|
| a. | Yes | No |
| b. | Yes | Yes |
| c. | No | Yes |
| d. | No | No |

4. Which of the following accounts would be included in the fund equity section of the combined balance sheet of a governmental unit for the general fixed-asset account group?

| | Investment in general fixed assets | Fund balance reserved for encumbrances |
|---|---|---|
| a. | Yes | Yes |
| b. | Yes | No |
| c. | No | No |
| d. | No | Yes |

5. The comprehensive annual financial report (CAFR) of a governmental unit should contain a combined statement of revenues, expenses, and changes in retained earnings for:

| | Account groups | Governmental funds |
|---|---|---|
| a. | Yes | Yes |
| b. | Yes | No |
| c. | No | No |
| d. | No | Yes |

6. The comprehensive annual financial report (CAFR) of a governmental unit should contain a combined statement of revenue, expenditures, and changes in fund balances for:

| | Account groups | Proprietary funds |
|---|---|---|
| a. | Yes | No |
| b. | Yes | Yes |
| c. | No | Yes |
| d. | No | No |

**—AICPA Adapted**

**P9-3.**   Select the best answer for each of the following items:

1. Which of the following accounts would be included in the asset section of the combined balance sheet of a governmental unit for the general long-term debt account group?

| | Amount available in debt-service funds | Amount to be provided for retirement of general long-term debt |
|---|---|---|
| a. | Yes | Yes |
| b. | Yes | No |
| c. | No | Yes |
| d. | No | No |

2. Which of the following accounts would be included in the combined balance sheet for the long-term debt account group?
   a. amount to be provided for retirement of general long-term debt
   b. unreserved fund balance

    c.   reserve for encumbrances

    d.   cash

3.   The balance sheet in the financial report of a municipality may be prepared:

    a.   on a consolidated basis after eliminating the effects of interfund transactions.

    b.   on a combined basis showing the assets and equities of each fund with a total column indicating the aggregate balance for each identical account in all of the funds.

    c.   on a combined basis showing the assets and equities of each fund but without a total column indicating the aggregate balance for each identical account in all of the funds.

    d.   for each fund in a separate statement but never presenting all funds together in the same statement.

4.   The comprehensive annual financial report (CAFR) of a governmental unit should contain a combined statement of cash flows for:

|  | Governmental funds | Proprietary funds |
|---|---|---|
| a. | No | No |
| b. | No | Yes |
| c. | Yes | No |
| d. | Yes | Yes |

—AICPA Adapted

**P9-4.**   The accounting records of Small City include a general fund and a fixed-asset account group. The trial balances for these two accounting entities at the end of the period are reflected in the following tables:

### General Fund

|  | Dr. | Cr. |
|---|---|---|
| Cash | $ 5,000 | |
| Revenues | | $105,000 |
| Expenditures | 102,000 | |
| Taxes receivable | 12,000 | |
| Vouchers payable | | 10,000 |
| Fund balance at beginning of period | | 4,000 |
| Totals | $119,000 | $119,000 |

### General Fixed Assets

|  | Dr. | Cr. |
|---|---|---|
| Equipment | $500,000 | |
| Land | 100,000 | |
| Investment in fixed assets | | $600,000 |
| Totals | $600,000 | $600,000 |

    The accountant has prepared the financial statements recommended by GAAFR but would also like to prepare accrual-based consolidated financial statements for distribution to the constituency. The following supplemental information is to be used in converting the conventional combined financial statements to the accrual basis:

1. Expenditures include an equipment purchase in the amount of $25,000 acquired on the last day of the year.
2. All other equipment was purchased three years ago and has an estimated service life of ten years with no salvage value.
3. Supplies inventories at the beginning and end of the year were $10,000 and $6,000, respectively. Supplies are conventionally recorded as expenditures when purchased.

**Required:**

A. Prepare conventional combined financial statements for the city.
B. Prepare a worksheet to convert the conventional statements to accrual-basis statements (see appendix to this chapter).
C. What observations can be made regarding the "operating story" disclosed by each of the two sets of statements?

P9-5.   Rearrange the elements included in the following balance sheet of Town of W into fund and account-group statements:

### Balance Sheet—June 30, 19A

| Assets | | |
| --- | ---: | ---: |
| Current | | |
| Cash | $ 50,000 | |
| Taxes receivable (including special assessments $80,000) | 100,000 | |
| Supply inventories | 10,000 | |
| Investments of trust funds | 30,000 | $ 190,000 |
| Fixed | | |
| Land | 100,000 | |
| Buildings | 800,000 | |
| Equipment | 50,000 | 950,000 |
| | | $1,140,000 |

| Liabilities | | |
| --- | ---: | ---: |
| Current | | |
| Accounts payable | | $ 10,000 |
| Fixed | | |
| General obligation bonds payable | $350,000 | |
| Special assessment bonds payable | 75,000 | 425,000 |
| Fund Equities: | | |
| General fund | $ 35,000 | |
| Trust funds | 40,000 | |
| Capital projects fund | 25,000 | |
| Special assessment capital projects fund | 5,000 | |
| Account groups balance | 600,000 | 705,000 |
| | | $1,140,000 |

—**AICPA** Adapted

P9-6. The Cobleskill City Council passed a resolution requiring a yearly cash budget by fund for the city beginning with its fiscal year ending September 30, 19X3. The city's financial director has prepared a list of expected cash receipts and disbursements, but is having difficulty subdividing them by fund. The list follows:

| | | |
|---|---|---:|
| Cash receipts | | |
| Taxes | | |
| | General property | $ 685,000 |
| | School | 421,000 |
| | Franchise | 223,000 |
| | | 1,329,000 |
| Licenses and permits | | |
| | Business licenses | 41,000 |
| | Automobile inspection permits | 24,000 |
| | Building permits | 18,000 |
| | | 83,000 |
| Intergovernmental revenue | | |
| | Sales tax | 1,012,000 |
| | Federal grants | 128,000 |
| | State motor vehicle tax | 83,500 |
| | State gasoline tax | 52,000 |
| | State alcoholic beverage licenses | 16,000 |
| | | 1,291,500 |
| Charges for services | | |
| | Sanitation fees | $ 121,000 |
| | Sewer connection fees | 71,000 |
| | Library revenues | 13,000 |
| | Park revenues | 2,500 |
| | | 207,500 |
| Bond issues | | |
| | Civic center | 347,000 |
| | General obligation | 200,000 |
| | Sewer | 153,000 |
| | Library | 120,000 |
| | | 820,000 |
| Other | | |
| | Proceeds from the sale of investments | 312,000 |
| | Sewer assessments | 50,000 |
| | Rental revenue | 48,000 |
| | Interest revenue | 15,000 |
| | | 425,000 |
| | | $4,156,000 |
| Cash disbursements | | |
| | General government | $ 671,000 |
| | Public safety | 516,000 |
| | Schools | 458,000 |
| | Sanitation | 131,000 |
| | Library | 28,000 |
| | Rental property | 17,500 |
| | Parks | 17,000 |
| | | 1,838,500 |

| | |
|---|---:|
| Debt service | |
| General obligation bonds | 618,000 |
| Street construction bonds | 327,000 |
| School bonds | 119,000 |
| Sewage disposal plant bonds | 37,200 |
| | 1,101,200 |
| Investments (capital projects fund) | 358,000 |
| State portion of sales tax | 860,200 |
| Capital expenditures | |
| Sewer construction (assessed area) | 114,100 |
| Civic center construction | 73,000 |
| Library construction | 36,000 |
| | 223,100 |
| | $4,381,000 |

The financial director provides you with the following additional information:

1. A bond issue was authorized in 19X2 for the construction of a civic center. The debt is to be paid from future civic center revenues and general property taxes.
2. A bond issue was authorized in 19X2 for additions to the library. The debt is to be paid from general property taxes.
3. General obligation bonds are paid from general property taxes collected by the general fund.
4. Ten percent of the total annual school taxes represents an individually voted tax for payment of bonds, the proceeds of which were used for school construction.
5. In 19X0, a wealthy citizen donated rental property to the city. Net income from the property is to be used to assist in operating the library. The net cash increase attributable to the property is transferred to the library on September 30 of each year.
6. All sales taxes are collected by the city; the state receives 85 percent of these taxes. The state's portion is remitted at the end of each month.
7. Payment of the street construction bonds is to be made from assessments previously collected from the respective property owners. The proceeds from the assessments were invested and the principal of $312,000 will earn $15,000 interest during the coming year.
8. In 19X2, a special assessment in the amount of $203,000 was made on certain property owners for sewer construction. During fiscal 19X3, $50,000 of this assessment is expected to be collected. The remainder of the sewer cost is to be paid from a $153,000 bond issue to be sold in fiscal 19X3. Future special assessment collections will be used to pay principal and interest on the bonds.
9. All sewer and sanitation services are provided by a separate enterprise fund.
10. The federal grant is for fiscal 19X3 school operations.
11. The proceeds remaining at the end of the year from the sale of civic center and library bonds are to be invested.

**Required:**

Prepare a budget of cash receipts and disbursements by fund for the year ending September 30, 19X3. All interfund transfers of cash are to be included.

—AICPA Adapted

**P9-7.** Your examination of the accounts of your new client, the City of Delmas, as of June 30, 19X2, revealed the following:

1. On December 31, 19X1, the city paid $115,000 out of general fund revenues for a central garage to service its vehicles, with $67,500 being applicable to the building, which has an estimated life of 25 years; $14,500 to land; and $33,000 to machinery and equipment, which has an estimated life of 15 years. A $12,200 cash contribution was received by the garage from the general fund on the same date.

2. The garage maintains no records, but a review of deposit slips and canceled checks revealed the following:

| | |
|---|---:|
| Collections for services to city departments financed from the general fund | $30,000 |
| Office salaries | 6,000 |
| Utilities | 700 |
| Mechanics' wages | 11,000 |
| Materials and supplies | 9,000 |

3. The garage had uncollected billings of $2,000, accounts payable for materials and supplies of $500, and an inventory of materials and supplies of $1,500 at June 30, 19X2.

4. On June 30, 19X2, the city issued $200,000 in special assessment bonds at par to finance a street improvement project estimated to cost $225,000. The project is to be paid by a $15,000 levy against the city (payable in fiscal year 19X2–X3) and $210,000 against property owners (payable in five equal annual installments beginning October 1, 19X2). The levy was made on June 30. A $215,000 contract was let for the project on July 2, 19X2, but work has not begun.

5. On July 1, 19X0, the city issued $400,000 in thirty-year, 6 percent general-obligation term bonds of the same date at par to finance the construction of a public health center. Construction was completed and the contractors fully paid a total of $397,500 in fiscal year 19X1–X2.

6. For the health center bonds, the city sets aside general fund revenues sufficient to cover interest (payable semiannually on July 1 and January 1 of each year) and $5,060 to provide for the retirement of bond principal, the latter transfer being made at the end of each fiscal year and invested at the beginning of the next. Your investigation reveals that such investments earned $304 during fiscal year 19X1–X2, the exact amount budgeted. This $304 was received in cash and will be invested at the beginning of the next year.

**Required:**
The preceding information disclosed by your examination was recorded only in the general fund. Prepare the formal entries as of June 30, 19X2, to adjust the funds other than the general fund. Entries should be classified into clearly labeled groups for each fund, and fund titles should be selected from the following list:

special revenue fund

capital projects fund (bond fund)

debt-service fund (sinking fund)

trust fund (endowment fund)

agency fund

internal service fund (working capital fund)

special assessment agency fund

special assessment capital projects fund

enterprise fund (utility fund)

general fixed-assets group of accounts (general fixed assets)

general long-term debt group of accounts (general bonded debt and interest)

—**AICPA Adapted**

**P9-8.**   The town of Sargentville uses budgetary accounts and maintains accounts for each of the following kinds of funds and account groups:

| Symbol | Funds and Account Groups |
|--------|--------------------------|
| A | Capital projects funds |
| B | General long-term debt |
| C | General fund |
| D | General fixed assets |
| E | Debt-service funds |
| F | Special assessment capital projects funds |
| G | Special revenue funds |
| H | Trust and agency funds |
| S | Utility funds |
| T | Internal service funds |

The chart of accounts for the general fund follows:

| Symbol | Account |
|--------|---------|
| 1 | Appropriations |
| 2 | Cash |
| 3 | Due from other funds |
| 4 | Due to other funds |
| 5 | Encumbrances |
| 6 | Expenditures |
| 7 | Reserve for encumbrances |
| 8 | Revenues |
| 9 | Revenues (estimated) |
| 10 | Fund balance |
| 11 | 19X4 taxes receivable |
| 12 | Vouchers payable |
| 13 | Transfers to other funds |

The following transactions are among those that occur during 19X4:

1.  The 19X4 budget, providing for $520,000 of general fund revenue and $205,000 of school fund revenue, is approved.
2.  The budgeted appropriations for the general fund amount to $516,000.

3. An advance of $10,000 from the general fund is made to a fund for the operation of a central printing service used by all departments of the municipal government. (This has not been budgeted and is expected to be repaid.)

4. Taxes totaling $490,000 for general fund revenues are levied.

5. Contractors are paid $200,000 for constructing an office building. This payment comes from proceeds of a general bond issue of 19X3.

6. Bonds of a general issue, previously authorized, are sold at par for $60,000 cash.

7. Orders are placed for supplies, estimated at $7,500, to be used by the Health Department (general fund).

8. Vouchers are approved for payment of salaries amounting to $11,200 for town officers. (No encumbrances are recorded for wages and salaries.)

9. The supplies ordered in item 7 are received and vouchers are approved for the invoice price of $7,480.

10. Fire equipment ordered 6 months ago was delivered at a cost of $21,500, and the voucher is approved.

11. A payment of $5,000 is made by the general fund to a fund for eventual redemption of general obligation bonds.

12. Of the taxes levied in item 4, $210,000 is collected.

13. Taxes amounting to $1,240, written off as uncollectible in 19X1, are collected. (These collections have not been budgeted.)

14. One thousand dollars of the advance made in item 3 is returned because it is not needed.

15. Supplies for general administrative use are requisitioned from the store's fund. A charge of $1,220 is made for the supplies.

16. The general fund advances $30,000 to provide temporary working capital for a fund out of which payment will be made for a new sewage installation. Eventual financing will be accomplished by assessments on property holders based on benefits received.

17. Equipment from the Highway Department is sold for $7,000 cash. (This sale is not included in the budget, and depreciation is not funded.)

18. The town receives a cash bequest of $75,000 for the establishment of a scholarship fund.

19. Previously approved and entered vouchers for payment of $6,200 for Police Department salaries and for the transfer of $500 to the police pension fund are paid.

20. Receipts from licenses and fees amount to $16,000.

**Required:**

Using an answer sheet organized as shown below, show the account debited and the account credited in the general fund for each transaction. If a transaction requires an entry in any fund(s) other than the general fund, indicate the fund(s) affected by printing the appropriate letter symbol(s) in the column headed "Other Funds Affected." If there is nothing to be entered for a transaction, leave the space blank:

| | General Fund | | Other Funds |
| Transaction | Debit | Credit | Affected |
| --- | --- | --- | --- |

—**AICPA Adapted**

**P9-9.** The City of Happy Hollow has engaged you to examine its financial statements for the year ended December 31, 19X1. The City was incorporated as a municipality and began operations on January 1, 19X1. You find that a budget was approved by the City Council and was recorded, but that all transactions have been recorded on the cash basis. The bookkeeper has provided an operating fund trial balance. Additional information is given next.

1. Examination of the appropriation-expenditure ledger revealed the following information:

|  | Budgeted | Actual |
|---|---|---|
| Personal services | $ 45,000 | $38,500 |
| Supplies | 19,000 | 11,000 |
| Equipment | 38,000 | 23,000 |
| Totals | $102,000 | $72,500 |

2. Supplies and equipment in the amounts of $4,000 and $10,000, respectively, had been received, but the vouchers had not been paid at December 31.
3. At December 31, outstanding purchase orders for supplies and equipment not yet received were $1,200 and $3,800, respectively.
4. The inventory of supplies on December 31 was $1,700 by physical count. The decision was made to record the inventory of supplies. A city ordinance requires that expenditures are to be based on purchases, not on the basis of usage.
5. Examination of the revenue subsidiary ledger revealed the following information:

|  | Budgeted | Actual |
|---|---|---|
| Property taxes | $102,600 | $ 96,000 |
| Licenses | 7,400 | 7,900 |
| Fines | 4,100 | 4,500 |
| Totals | $114,100 | $108,400 |

It was estimated that 5 percent of the property taxes would not be collected. Accordingly, property taxes were levied in an amount so that collections would yield the budgeted amount of $102,600.

6. On November 1, 19X1, Happy Hollow issued 8 percent general-obligation term bonds with $200,000 face value for a premium of $3,000. Interest is payable each May 1 and November 1 until the maturity date 14 years later. The City Council ordered that the cash from the bond premium be set aside and restricted for the eventual retirement of the debt principal. The bonds were issued to finance the construction of a city hall, but no contracts had been let as of December 31.

**Required:**

A. Complete a worksheet similar to the one on page 381 showing adjustments and distributions to the proper funds or groups of accounts in conformity with generally accepted accounting principles applicable to governmental entities. (Formal adjusting entries are not required.)

B.   Identify the financial statements that should be prepared for the general fund. (You are not required to prepare these statements.)

C.   Draft formal closing entries for the general fund.

## City of Happy Hollow Worksheet to Correct Trial Balance December 31, 19X1

| | Operating Fund Trial Balance | Adjustments | | General Fund | Debt-Service Fund | Capital Projects Fund | General Fixed Assets | General Long-Term Debt |
|---|---|---|---|---|---|---|---|---|
| | | Debit | Credit | | | | | |
| | | | *Debits* | | | | | |
| Cash | $238,900 | | | | | | | |
| Expenditures | 72,500 | | | | | | | |
| Estimated revenues | 114,100 | | | | | | | |
| Equipment | | | | | | | | |
| Encumbrances | | | | | | | | |
| Inventory of supplies | | | | | | | | |
| Taxes receivable— current | | | | | | | | |
| Amount to be provided for the payment of term bonds | | | | | | | | |
| Amount available in debt-service fund—term bonds | | | | | | | | |
| | $425,500 | | | | | | | |
| | | | *Credits* | | | | | |
| Appropriations | $102,000 | | | | | | | |
| Revenues | 108,400 | | | | | | | |
| Bonds payable | 200,000 | | | | | | | |
| Premium on bonds payable | 3,000 | | | | | | | |
| Fund balance | 12,100 | | | | | | | |
| Vouchers payable | | | | | | | | |
| Investment in general fixed assets— general fund revenue | | | | | | | | |
| Reserve for encum- brances | | | | | | | | |
| Reserve for inventory of supplies | | | | | | | | |
| Estimated uncollectible current taxes | | | | | | | | |
| | $425,500 | | | | | | | |

**—AICPA Adapted**

# Federal Government Accounting

## ■ Learning Objectives

When you have finished your study of this chapter, you should

1. Have a general understanding of the historical background from which present-day federal government accounting practices have developed.
2. Be aware of the general accounting system responsibilities assigned to the General Accounting Office, Treasury Department, Office of Management and Budget, Congressional Budget Office, and General Services Administration.
3. Know the meanings of terms peculiar to federal governmental accounting.
4. Be aware of the unique elements of the fund structure associated with federal government accounting.
5. Know how to record the routine transactions of a federal agency and be able to prepare statements from the data produced by recording those transactions.

Conceptually, the accounting practices of the federal government would be expected to be essentially the same as those we described in Chapters 3 through 9 for state and local governments. There are, however, significant differences caused by the operational structure of the federal government and the ways in which the federal government financial reports are used. As we develop the elements of the federal government accounting system in this chapter, our attention will be primarily focused on identifying the differences between these elements and those described in the preceding seven chapters of this book. Our analysis and discussion cover the following topics:

1. the historical background out of which the present federal government accounting system has developed

Note: Much of the material included in this chapter has been taken from *GAO Policy and Procedures Manual for Guidance of Federal Agencies Title 2-Accounting.* Used with permission.

2. statutory assignment of responsibilities for establishing and maintaining our federal government accounting system

3. new terminology associated with the system

4. the fund structure associated with a federal governmental accounting system

5. basis of accounting

6. illustrated transactions and financial statements for a federal agency.

# ■ Historical Background

The first statute requiring an accounting system for the federal government came into existence in 1789. In spite of that fact, there was no significant progress in formalizing such a system until the Budget and Accounting Act of 1921 was put into effect. That act provided, for the first time, a statutory basis for two fundamental elements of federal government operations:

1. a systematic annual national budgeting procedure

2. the exercise of jurisdiction over governmental finances by both the executive and legislative branches of the federal government.

This act required the president to submit each year an annual budget for the federal government to Congress for its approval. It also created the Bureau of the Budget (BOB) in the Department of the Treasury and removed the comptroller general from the Treasury Department to supervise a newly established General Accounting Office.

In 1949, the General Services Administration was created by the Federal Property and Administrative Services Act. This agency was charged with the responsibility of handling all federal housekeeping functions. It was also assigned the task of improving property accounting and record management policies.

As a result of the work of the Hoover Commission, the Budgeting and Accounting Procedures Act of 1950 came into existence. Some of the more relevant features of this act were as follow:

1. It required that the federal budget be prepared on a performance basis.

2. It made the General Accounting Office (GAO) responsible for developing principles, standards, and related requirements for federal government accounting.

3. It made the heads of executive agencies responsible for establishing systems of accounting and internal control for their respective agencies in conformity with the standards prescribed by the GAO.

4. It made the GAO responsible for periodically reviewing agency accounting systems and reporting on their adequacy.[1]

In 1970, the Office of Management and Budget (OMB) was created in the Executive Office of the President. This office was charged with a number of management responsibilities including:

1. Gerald Murphy, "Federal Financial Management—Will We Get Our Act Together?" *Government Accountants Journal* (Spring 1985): p. 13.

1.  improvement of government organization, information, and management systems

2.  development of new information systems to provide the president with needed performance and other data

3.  planning and promotion of a continuous program for improving governmental accounting and financial reporting

4.  improvement of governmental budgeting and accounting methods and procedures.[2]

Federal governmental operations are carried out through various departments and agencies. Under 31 U.S.C. 3511 (the Federal Financial Managers' Act), the comptroller general, after consulting with the secretary of the treasury and the president, has the responsibility of prescribing the principles, standards, and related requirements for accounting to be followed by each executive agency. Also, under 31 U.S.C. 3512, the head of each agency is held responsible for establishing and maintaining the systems of accounting and internal control for his or her agency in accordance with the principles and standards established by the comptroller general.

The comptroller general, acting within the provisions of 31 U.S.C. 3511, has issued *GAO Policy and Procedures Manual for Guidance of Federal Agencies Title 2-Accounting* for the purpose of establishing accounting principles and standards for the various agencies of the federal government. This document was first issued in 1978 and was later revised in 1984. Much of the material in this chapter is drawn from the revised edition of the Title 2 document.

Also in 1984, OMB issued Circular A-127. This document for the first time established formal criteria and standards for agency managers to follow in developing, operating, and evaluating financial management systems. Prior to that time, the development of those systems had been left largely to the discretion of agency management.

During the time that Title 2 was being revised, the Treasury Department began formulating the conceptual design of its new Central Financial Management System (CFMS). This document is expected to augment the treasury's reporting capability so as to better meet OMB and treasury needs for financial information used in exercising supervision over agency operations. This action may lead to remedies for three often-observed weaknesses in federal government accounting and reporting practices. These weaknesses can be stated as follows:

1.  The executive branch does not seem to have a single focus in its financial management activities.

2.  Program agencies seem to delegate financial management responsibility to widely varying, inconsistent levels of authority within their organizational structures.

3.  Agencies seem to have developed accounting and information systems to meet their special needs and purposes with little regard for government-wide reporting requirements.[3]

---

2.  Ibid., p. 13.
3.  Ibid., p. 14.

In March 1986, the Office of the Auditor General of Canada and the United States General Accounting Office completed a jointly conducted Federal Government Reporting Study (FGRS), which was directed at identifying the financial information about federal governments that users need. The most significant overall finding of the two-year study was that virtually *every user consulted required a comprehensive but succinct annual financial report.* An illustration of what such a document might look like, together with the *Detailed Report* of the study's findings, were issued late in March 1986.[4]

The volume of operations of the federal government, measured in dollars passing through the U.S. Treasury, has expanded astronomically since our nation was founded. The rate of expansion of federal government activities has accelerated in recent years to the point where the federal budget exceeded one trillion dollars for the first time during the fiscal year ending September 30, 1986. The volume of spending alone makes the accounting practices followed by the federal government very important to all of us as citizens paying taxes.

# ■ Statutorily Assigned Responsibilities

As we have seen in the preceding pages, the management of the financial affairs of the federal government primarily involves the following departments and agencies:

1. General Accounting Office
2. Treasury Department
3. Office of Management and Budget
4. Congressional Budget Office
5. General Services Administration.

In the preceding section of this chapter, we observed the actions taken to originate these agencies over the years. In this section, we further examine their statutorily assigned responsibilities relating to the establishment and maintenance of federal government accounting and reporting practices. The relationships of these departments and agencies to each other, and to the executive and legislative branches of the federal government, are reflected in Figure 10–1.

## General Accounting Office

As you can observe from Figure 10–1, the General Accounting Office operates under the supervision of the Congress of the United States. We can also see that it is responsible for establishing accounting policies, including the principles and standards within which those policies will be implemented. This office is also charged with the development of accounting and information systems, and periodically reviewing the perfor-

---

4. *Federal Government Reporting Study—Detailed Report,* Joint Study by the Office of the Auditor General of Canada and the United States General Accounting Office, 1986.

**FIGURE 10–1.** Federal Government Central Financial Management Functions Organization Chart—Current

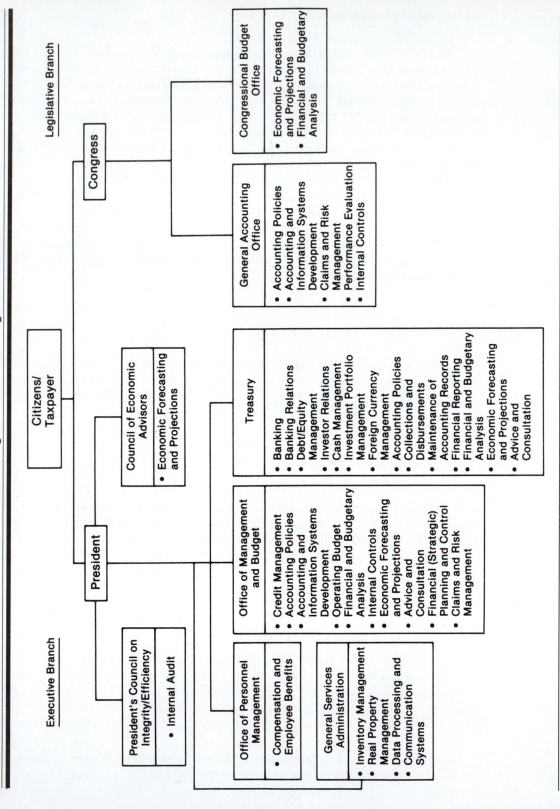

mance of those systems in terms of the usefulness and reliability of the information provided by them.

As we noted earlier, these responsibilities are carried out after consultation with the Treasury Department and the president of the United States regarding the information needed from the various agency and departmental accounting systems.

## Treasury Department

The secretary of the treasury heads the Treasury Department and, in that capacity, acts as the chief financial custodial officer of the federal government. This department is also charged with the responsibility of maintaining a system of accounts that will permit the preparation of statements to consolidate the accounts of individual departments and agencies with those of the Treasury Department. The revised edition of Title 2 requires that the following consolidated financial statements be prepared to reflect overall federal government financial affairs:

1. Statement of Financial Position
2. Statement of Operations
3. Statement of Changes in Financial Position
4. Statement of Reconciliation to the Budget.

These statements are expected to fulfill a responsibility assigned to the Treasury Department for informing interested parties about the financial operations of the federal government.

As we have noted, the General Accounting Office is also expected to consult with the Treasury Department regarding any pronouncements relating to the principles and standards established for federal government accounting.

## Office of Management and Budget

The director of the Office of Management and Budget (OMB) supervises the OMB and is appointed by the president. This department is charged with the responsibility of controlling the size and nature of appropriations requested by Congress. That, in turn, requires a projection of probable revenues and receipts, which is expected to be developed in coordination with the Council of Economic Advisors. This department is also expected to relate budget expenditures to planned activities in a meaningful manner. This has been interpreted to include the application of cost-accounting procedures to various agency operations.

As noted earlier, the OMB issued Circular A-127 late in 1984, providing for the first time established formal criteria and standards for developing, operating, and evaluating financial management systems. This circular prescribes standards for usefulness, timeliness, reliability, and comparability for information produced by the systems. It also prescribes certain standards of economy and efficiency for systems operations and requires that reasonable controls be built into the system.[5]

---

5. Gerald Murphy, "Federal Financial Management—Will We Get Our Act Together?" *Government Accountants Journal* (Spring 1985): 11.

## Congressional Budget Office

The director of the Congressional Budget Office is appointed jointly by the Speaker of the House and the president (*pro tempore*) of the Senate. This office participates in the development of the annual budget for the federal government, which is the most important act carried out in planning and controlling federal government expenditures. This budgetary process begins when the president, with advice and consultation from the OMB, submits a proposed budget to Congress. Congress, relying on information provided by the Congressional Budget Office (see Figure 10–1), then gives consideration to the budget and ultimately approves it or modifies it in the light of the legislative interpretation of what the financial operating plan of the federal government should be. Ultimately, a budget must be approved by Congress before resources may be committed to be used by the various governmental departments and agencies.

As you can see in Figure 10–1, the Congressional Budget Office, as a consulting and advising arm of the United States Congress, is responsible for economic forecasting and projections, and for developing the implications of those data for the budget. This office is also responsible for financial and budgetary analysis throughout the year.

## General Services Administration

As we have observed earlier, the General Services Administration (GSA) was created in 1949 as a result of the Federal Property and Administrative Services Act. The primary responsibility of the GSA is to provide an effective system for the management of governmental properties and the records associated with those properties. Part of that responsibility includes the annual provision of an inventory of all real property owned or leased by the federal government. As you can see in Figure 10–1, the GSA is also responsible for the data processing and communication systems of the federal government.

# ■ Terminology

Because of the nature of federal governmental operations, we find a number of unique terms used in connection with its financial activities and in agency financial reports. In this section, some of the more important of those terms are defined.

All payments of the federal government are made by the Treasury Department. That department is, in effect, the *banker for the federal government*. Therefore, an agency balance sheet, instead of reflecting cash as its chief spendable resource, will show an account entitled *Fund Balances with U.S. Treasury*. This account reflects the amount of cash that the treasury has available for use in meeting the agency's expenditures. As a result, the payment of an account payable, for example, will involve a debit to accounts payable and a credit to fund balances with U.S. Treasury.

The *governmental equity section* of an agency balance sheet, roughly equivalent to the fund balance section for the general fund of a municipality, will generally include at least three separate items:

1. invested capital
2. cumulative results of operations
3. unexpended appropriations.

These items are designed to show the status of the net assets of an agency as of a particular date insofar as their availability for spending is concerned.

*Invested Capital* reflects the amount invested in fixed assets used in agency operations. This account is increased for additions to fixed assets acquired through expenditures of agency spendable resources, or those provided by other agencies without a requirement to reimburse those agencies for them. It is decreased as a result of depreciation or amortization of fixed assets, and for any transfers to other agencies without the requirement that those agencies be reimbursed for them.

Another element of governmental equity is labeled *Cumulative Results of Operations*. This account reflects the accumulated difference between total expenses and losses of an agency and the total financing sources and gains of the agency from its inception. We may think of this account as being similar to the retained earnings account of a business. In fact, the cumulative results of operations are sometimes referred to as retained earnings when accounting for revolving funds or other businesslike activities of the federal government.

The third element of the governmental equity section of an agency balance sheet, entitled *Unexpended Appropriations*, reflects the amount of authority to spend that is either:

1. unobligated
2. obligated, but not yet expended.

Unexpended appropriations shows the remaining existing budgetary authority to spend for the agency, as of the date of the statement of financial position. Unobligated appropriations reflects the budget allocation that has been neither obligated nor spent. Obligations-not-yet-expended reflects the amounts committed on undelivered orders or uncompleted contracts. This account is reduced when an appropriation lapses, is withdrawn, or is rescinded, or when the undelivered orders are received and accepted. Amounts are transferred to this account from the unobligated account when orders are placed or contracts are signed.

Another element sometimes included in the governmental equity section is entitled *Donations and Other Items*. These reflect the values of assets or services transferred from state, local, or foreign governments, individuals, or others not considered a party related to the agency.

As observed above, the term *obligation* is used to reflect the expected costs of orders placed, contracts awarded, services ordered, and other similar items associated with bona fide needs existing during a given period that will require payments during the same or a future period and that comply with applicable laws and regulations. These may be thought of as being similar to encumbrances in municipal accounting.

The term *allocation* is used to reflect the distribution of an amount between periods, or to different segments of a fiscal period. Interperiod allocation is necessary in federal government accounting because some assets may be acquired by an entity over more than one reporting period. For example, the cost of acquiring a building or equipment may be allocated to an agency over two or more accounting periods.

The term *entitlements* is used to describe legally established payments of benefits to any person or unit of government meeting prescribed eligibility requirements. Authorizations for entitlements constitute a binding obligation of the federal government. However, such authorization may not necessarily include a corresponding appropriation of funds. As a result, a separate action providing the appropriation of funds necessary to meet entitlement claims may be required.

# ◼ Fund Structure

Fund accounting is a fundamental requirement for federal agencies to demonstrate compliance with legislation. Two types of funds are used to do that, namely:

1. funds to account for resources derived from general taxation and revenue powers and from business operations

2. funds to account for resources held by the government in the capacity of custodian or trustee.

## Resources Derived from General Taxation and Revenue Powers and from Business Operations

Resources derived from general taxation and revenue powers and from business operations are accounted for by use of the following funds:

1. general fund accounts
2. special fund accounts
3. revolving fund accounts
4. management fund accounts.

*General fund accounts* consist of receipt or inflow accounts for all collections of resources not dedicated to specific purposes, and expenditure (outflow) accounts to record financial transactions arising under congressional appropriations or other authorizations to spend resources. The balance sheet of such a fund will include asset, liability, and governmental equity accounts. The accounts, included in this statement, that are unique to federal governmental accounting have already been discussed briefly in the section on terminology (see page 388).

*Special fund accounts* include receipt and expenditure accounts for inflows and outflows of resources earmarked by law for a specific purpose but not generated by a cycle of operations for which there is continuing authority to reuse such receipts. The balance sheet accounts will be much the same as those found in the general fund accounts balance sheet.

*Revolving fund accounts* include receipt and expenditure accounts established by law to facilitate accounting for a continuing cycle of operations with the receipts from such operations usually available in their entirety for use by the fund without further action by Congress. Again, the balance sheet accounts will be similar to those found in general funds and special funds balance sheets.

*Management fund accounts* include receipt and expenditure accounts established by law to facilitate accounting for and administration of the *intragovernmental operations of an agency.* Working funds, for example, which are a type of management fund, may be established in connection with each of the previously described fund account types to account for advances from other segments of the governmental entity.

## Resources Held by the Government in the Capacity of Custodian or Trustee

Resources held by the government in the capacity of custodian or trustee are accounted for in:

1. trust fund accounts
2. deposit fund accounts.

*Trust fund accounts* are established to account for receipts that are held in trust for use in carrying out specific programs in accordance with an agreement or statute. The assets of trust funds are frequently held over a period of time and may involve such transactions as investments in revenue producing assets and the collection and use of resources realized as revenue from those assets.

*Deposit fund accounts* are used to account for resources that are: (1) held in suspense temporarily and later refunded or paid into some other fund of the government or other entity, or (2) held by the government as banker or agent for others and paid out at the direction of the owners of the funds. Expenditures are often offset by receipts within these funds.

## ■ Basis of Accounting

The overall goal of accounting and financial reporting in the federal government is to provide financial information that is useful. As a result, *Title 2 requires use of the accrual basis of accounting as prescribed by 31 U.S.C. 3512 (d).* That law states that the head of each executive agency shall cause the accounts of that agency to be maintained on the accrual basis, while at the same time, providing for suitable integration of that agency's accounting data with central accounting and reporting requirements of the secretary of the treasury. Although the accrual basis of accounting is prescribed, we should note that when differences between the results of cash and accrual accounting are insignificant, the cash basis of accounting may be followed.

The accrual basis prescribed for federal agencies is essentially the same as the one followed by businesses. It recognizes the accounting aspects of financial transactions, events, or allocations as they occur. This is interpreted to include the recognition of depreciation on fixed assets.

It is important to recognize that budgetary data should also be included in the accounting records of federal agencies. This involves, as a first step, the recognition of funds available from the U.S. Treasury when Congress approves the federal budget. These are typically labeled as unapportioned appropriations. The next step in the budgetary process recognizes allocations of budgeted funds as amounts are authorized to be used over a specific period of time, such as one quarter of the fiscal period. Such allocations are called unobligated allotments. When orders are placed, allocations become obligated, and that fact should be recorded by reducing the appropriations allocated and increasing the appropriations obligated. The procedures for recording these steps in the appropriation and obligation phases of an agency's operations are illustrated in the following section of this chapter.

The accounting equation for a federal agency may be stated as follows:

assets + operating costs = liabilities + government equity + financing sources

The accounts on the left side of the equation are debited to reflect increases in them and therefore normally reflect debit balances. We credit the accounts on the right side of the equation to reflect increases in them and they therefore normally have credit balances. Operating costs and financing sources are nominal accounts that are closed into a government equity account called *cumulative results of operations* at the end of each fiscal period. The account category financing sources will typically include two subclassifications called *expended appropriations* and *other financing sources* (depreciation). Government equity will typically include the following subcategories:

1. invested capital
2. cumulative results of operations
3. unexpended appropriations.

# ■ Federal Agency Accounting Illustrated

In Chapter 2 (see page 30), we identified six types of actions and transactions that are unique to governmental fund accounting. In this section, we identify and illustrate the accounting procedures followed in recording such actions and transactions in the accounts of a federal agency.

## Authorization Actions

In reflecting the data relating to authorization actions for state and local governmental entities to receive and spend resources, we recorded the budgetary data with a debit to estimated revenues and a credit to appropriations. Federal agencies record those actions in three steps. The first of these occurs *when the federal budget is approved*. Assuming that a federal agency receives an appropriation of $1,000,000, that action would be recorded as follows:

| | | |
|---|---|---|
| Fund balance available with U.S. Treasury 19X1 | 1,000,000 | |
| Unapportioned appropriation 19X1 | | 1,000,000 |

When the OMB approves quarterly apportionments in the amount of $250,000 per quarter, that fact should be recorded as follows:

| | | |
|---|---|---|
| Unapportioned appropriations 19X1 | 1,000,000 | |
| Unallocated appropriations 19X1 | | 1,000,000 |

When the agency head allocates the first quarter apportionment, the following entry should be made to record that fact:

| | | |
|---|---|---|
| Unallocated appropriations 19X1 | 250,000 | |
| Unobligated allotments 19X1 | | 250,000 |

The last of these entries, in effect, shows that the agency now has authority to spend $250,000 in carrying out agency activities during the next quarter of its fiscal year.

## Realization of Revenues

The inflow of resources from budgetary appropriations has been recorded in our original debt to "fund balance available with U.S. Treasury." Therefore, we have no typical transaction to record revenues as we do in accounting for state and local governmental activities.

## Expenditure Transactions

As expenditures are made by federal agencies, it is necessary to distinguish between capital and revenue items. Also, it is necessary to recognize expended appropriations. Therefore, the purchase of fixed assets for $50,000 and the incurrence of operating costs in the amount of $25,000 would be recorded as follows:

| | | |
|---|---|---|
| Unobligated allotments 19X1 | 75,000 | |
| Expended appropriations 19X1 | | 75,000 |
| Operating costs | 25,000 | |
| Fixed assets | 50,000 | |
| Accounts payable | | 75,000 |
| Expended appropriations 19X1 | 50,000 | |
| Invested capital | | 50,000 |

## Interfund Transactions

Interagency transactions in federal governmental operations are accounted for in much the same way as are interfund transactions for state and local governments.

## Recognition of Encumbrances

Federal agencies use the term *obligations,* rather than *encumbrances,* to reflect commitments to spend resources. Therefore, when goods are ordered or contracts are signed, we transfer an amount equal to the expected obligation from "unobligated allotments" to "unliquidated obligations." To illustrate the journal entry required to do that, let's assume that a federal agency issues purchase orders for inventory items costing $25,000, contracts to purchase fixed assets for $50,000, and obligates itself for $80,000 of payroll. Those actions would be recorded in the allotments and obligations accounts as follows:

| | | |
|---|---|---|
| Unobligated allotments 19X1 | 155,000 | |
|     Unliquidated obligations 19X1 | | 155,000 |

## Elimination of Encumbrances (Obligations)

Let's assume now that the goods ordered for inventory are received and that the payroll is met when employee services have been used. The following entries would be used to record those facts:

| | | |
|---|---|---|
| Unliquidated obligations 19X1 | 105,000 | |
|     Expended appropriation 19X1 | | 105,000 |
| Inventory | 25,000 | |
| Operating costs | 80,000 | |
|     Fund balance with U.S. Treasury 19X1 | | 80,000 |
|     Accounts payable | | 25,000 |

## Other Actions and Transactions

Federal agencies should also record depreciation of fixed assets and the use of inventory items. These actions are not generally recognized in state and local governmental accounting. To illustrate the entries used to record those items, let's assume that $10,000 worth of goods are used from inventory and that depreciation of fixed assets amounts to $8,000. The following entries would be used to record those facts:

| | | |
|---|---|---|
| Operating costs | 18,000 | |
|     Inventory | | 10,000 |
|     Accumulated depreciation | | 8,000 |
| Invested capital | 8,000 | |
|     Financing sources (depreciation) | | 8,000 |

To make our illustration more complete, let's also assume that accounts payable in the amount of $60,000, including $5,000 owed on 19X0 obligations, are paid. That fact would be recorded as follows:

| | | |
|---|---|---|
| Accounts payable | 60,000 | |
|     Fund balance with U.S. Treasury 19X1 | | 55,000 |
|     Fund balance with U.S. Treasury 19X0 | | 5,000 |

## Closing Entries

Because we use a transactions worksheet (see Exhibit 10–1) to show how the preceding transactions should be recorded working from assumed data for the end of 19X0 statement of financial position, we show no closing entries in that exhibit. However, we would use the following entries to close the nominal accounts into the governmental equity account entitled "Cumulative results of operations" in the formal accounting records:

| | | |
|---|---:|---:|
| Financing sources (depreciation) | 8,000 | |
| Expended appropriations 19X1 | 130,000 | |
|    Cumulative results of operations | | 15,000 |
|    Operating costs | | 123,000 |

In Exhibits 10–2 and 10–3, we show the statement of financial position and operating statement, respectively, for our federal agency. As you can see, the statement of financial position reflects the assets of the agency divided into current and fixed categories. Also, observe that fixed assets are reduced by the amount of accumulated depreciation. The liability and equity part of that statement shows current liabilities and governmental equity subcategories. Governmental equity, in turn, includes account categories for invested capital, cumulative results of operations, and unexpended appropriations.

It is interesting to observe the following relationships between the account balances in the governmental equity section of the statement of financial position and the net assets in that statement:

| | | |
|---|---:|---:|
| Invested capital balance | | $122,000 |
| Fixed assets | $150,000 | |
| Accumulated depreciation | 28,000 | $122,000 |
| Cumulative results of operations | | $ 35,000 |
| Cumulative results of operations at the end of period 19X0 | 20,000 | |
| Excess of financing sources over operating costs— first quarter 19X1 | 15,000 | $ 35,000 |
| Unexpended appropriations 19X1 | | |
|    Unallocated appropriations 19X1 | | $750,000 |
|    Unallocated allotments 19X1 | | 20,000 |
|    Unliquidated obligations 19X1 | | 50,000 |
| Total | | $820,000 |
| Fund balance with U.S. Treasury 19X1 | $865,000 | |
| Less accounts payable | 45,000 | $820,000 |

The agency operating statement shows revenues and gains offset by expenses and losses to arrive at the results of operations for the period. That amount is, in turn, closed to cumulative results of operations, an account shown on the statement of financial position.

**EXHIBIT 10–1.** Federal Agency Transactions Worksheet

| | Balances—End of Period 19X0 | | Actions and Transactions—First Quarter 19X1 | | Statement of Operations—First Quarter | | Statement of Financial Position—End of First Quarter | |
|---|---|---|---|---|---|---|---|---|
| | Dr | Cr | Dr | Cr | Dr | Cr | Dr | Cr |
| Fund balance with U.S. Treasury 19X0 | $ 5,000 | | | (12) $ 5,000 | | | | |
| Fund balance with U.S. Treasury 19X1 | | | (1) $1,000,000 | (12) 55,000 | | | $ 865,000 | |
| Inventory | 20,000 | | (9) 25,000 | (9) 80,000 | | | 35,000 | |
| Fixed assets | 100,000 | | (5) 50,000 | (10) 10,000 | | | $ 150,000 | |
| Accumulated depreciation | | $ 20,000 | | (10) 8,000 | | | | $ 28,000 |
| Accounts payable | | 5,000 | (12) 60,000 | (5) 75,000 (9) 25,000 | | | | 45,000 |
| Invested capital | | 80,000 | (11) 8,000 | (6) 50,000 | | | | 122,000 |
| Cumulative results of operations | | 20,000 | | | | | | 20,000 |
| Unapportioned appropriations 19X1 | | | (2) 1,000,000 | (1) 1,000,000 | | | | |
| Unallocated appropriations 19X1 | | | (3) 250,000 | (2) 1,000,000 | | | | 750,000 |
| Unobligated allotments 19X1 | | | (4) 75,000 (7) 155,000 | (3) 250,000 | | | | 20,000 |
| Expended appropriations 19X1 | | | (6) 50,000 | (4) 75,000 (8) 105,000 | | $130,000 | | |
| Operating costs | | | (5) 25,000 (9) 80,000 (10) 18,000 | | $123,000 | | | |
| Unliquidated obligations 19X1 | | | (8) 105,000 | (7) 155,000 | | | | 50,000 |
| Financing sources (depreciation) | | | | (11) 8,000 | | 8,000 | | |
| | | | | | | 15,000 | | 15,000 |
| Totals | 125,000 | 125,000 | | | 123,000 138,000 | 138,000 | 1,035,000 1,050,000 | 1,050,000 |
| Totals | $125,000 | $125,000 | | | $138,000 | $138,000 | $1,050,000 | $1,050,000 |

**EXHIBIT 10–2.**    Federal Agency Statement of Financial Position—End of First Quarter 19X1

*Assets*

| | | |
|---|---:|---:|
| Current assets | | |
| Fund balance with U.S. Treasury | $865,000 | |
| Inventory | 35,000 | $ 900,000 |
| Fixed assets | | |
| Fixed assets | 150,000 | |
| Accumulated depreciation | 28,000 | 122,000 |
| Total assets | | $1,022,000 |

*Liability and Equity Accounts*

| | | | |
|---|---:|---:|---:|
| Current liabilities | | | |
| Accounts payable | | | $ 45,000 |
| Government equity | | | |
| Invested capital | | $122,000 | |
| Cumulative results of operations | | 35,000 | |
| Unexpended appropriations 19X1 | | | |
| Unallocated appropriations | $750,000 | | |
| Unobligated allotments | 20,000 | | |
| Unliquidated obligations | 50,000 | 820,000 | 977,000 |
| Total liabilities and government equity | | | $1,022,000 |

**EXHIBIT 10–3.**    Federal Agency Statement of Operations—First Quarter 19X1

| | |
|---|---:|
| Financing sources | |
| Expended appropriations 19X1 | $130,000 |
| Financing source (depreciation) | 8,000 |
| Total | $138,000 |
| Operating costs | 123,000 |
| Excess of financing sources over operating costs | $ 15,000 |

Our federal agency's statement of changes in governmental equity for the first quarter of 19X1 is shown in Exhibit 10–4.

The statement of changes in financial position for our example federal agency is shown in Exhibit 10–5. Observe that the statement interprets funds as the fund balance with the U.S. Treasury. As a result, it is equivalent to a statement of cash flows.

**EXHIBIT 10-4.**  Federal Agency Statement of Changes in Governmental Equity—
First Quarter 19X1

| | Invested Capital | Cumulative Results of Operations | Unexpended Appropriations | Totals |
|---|---|---|---|---|
| Balance at end of period 19X0 | $ 80,000 | $20,000 | | $ 100,000 |
| Appropriations | | | $1,000,000 | 1,000,000 |
| Purchases of fixed assets | 50,000 | | (50,000) | |
| Transfers to financing sources | (8,000) | | | (8,000) |
| Appropriations expended for operations | | | (130,000) | (130,000) |
| Excess of financing sources over operating costs | | 15,000 | | 15,000 |
| Balances at end of first quarter 19X1 | $122,000 | $35,000 | $ 820,000 | $ 977,000 |

**EXHIBIT 10-5.**  Federal Agency Statement of Changes in Financial Position—First Quarter of 19X1

| | | | |
|---|---|---|---|
| Funds provided by appropriations | | | $1,000,000 |
|   Increase in accounts payable | | | 40,000 |
| | | | $1,040,000 |
| Funds applied to operating costs | $123,000 | | |
|   Less depreciation expense | 8,000 | $115,000 | |
|   Increase to inventory | | 15,000 | |
|   Purchase of fixed assets | | 50,000 | 180,000 |
| Increase in funds with U.S. Treasury | | | $ 860,000 |
| Fund balance with U.S. Treasury at end of period 19X0 | | | $ 5,000 |
| Increase during first quarter 19X1 | | | 860,000 |
| Fund with U.S. Treasury at end of first quarter 19X1 | | | $ 865,000 |

## ◾ Ethical Considerations Associated with Deficit Reduction Actions

For several years, the federal government has been operating with large and increasing deficits. Both the president and Congress have been reluctant to increase taxes because of the political backlash expected from such actions. Congress also has been reluctant to reduce expenditures because of expected voter reaction. Nevertheless, both parties have felt political pressure to reduce the deficit. As a result, the president and Congress agreed to the following "smoke and mirrors" actions:

1. The inflows from a governmental retirement insurance program, originally intended to be operated on an actuarially sound basis, are included in general governmental revenues under a new arrangement that expects currently employed people to pay the benefits due to retirees on a cash inflow–outflow basis.

2. Selected long-term federal government assets are projected to be sold with the proceeds to be recognized as revenues when sold.

3. Highly optimistic projections of gross national product are used in projecting tax revenues.

By taking these actions, the president and Congress were able to announce that the projected deficit of 200 billion dollars would be reduced to 140 billion dollars. Consider the ethical issues associated with this "smoke and mirrors" approach to the deficit problem. Give particular attention to the intergenerational equity implications of such actions.

## ■ Summary

In this chapter, we described the basic procedures followed in federal government accounting with particular attention being given to those procedures that differ from the ones described in Chapters 3 through 9. We began by describing the historical background against which present federal government accounting principles and standards have been developed.

As we considered the accounting practices themselves, we first gave attention to identifying the departments and agencies of the government that are involved in establishing and maintaining principles and standards of federal government accounting. We observed that the major responsibility rests on the shoulders of the comptroller general and the General Accounting Office. We also noted that the GAO prepares official pronouncements in consultation with the Treasury Department and Office of Management and Budget (OMB).

Next, some of the terms that are unique to federal government accounting and to the fund structure used in those accounting records were identified and defined. We noted that the records are divided into two types of funds, further subdivided into six separate categories of funds, for the purpose of allowing the accounting records to reflect compliance with legislative requirements.

Federal government agencies are supposed to use the full accrual basis of accounting including the recognition of depreciation on fixed assets. This is essentially the same basis of accounting as is used by profit entities. In accounting for federal agencies, we also noted that budgetary accounts should be introduced for the purpose of more effectively disclosing compliance with legislative authorizations. In the last part of the chapter, we demonstrated how a series of typical transactions for a federal agency would be recorded and how the results of those transactions are presented in the agency financial statements.

# ◼ Glossary

**Allocated Appropriation.** Previously appropriated amount distributed between periods or to different segments of a fiscal period.

**Bureau of the Budget (BOB).** A department of the executive branch of the U.S. government charged with assembling the budgeting data submitted by the various departments of the government and presenting the composite budget to Congress.

**Central Financial Management System (CFMS).** A system designed by the Treasury Department to augment its reporting capability and to facilitate its supervision over agency operations.

**Comptroller General.** The head of the General Accounting Office.

**Congressional Budget Office.** Office, operating under supervision of Congress, responsible for development and analysis of the federal budget.

**Council of Economic Advisors.** A group of economists, operating under the supervision of the president, responsible for economic forecasting and projections.

**Cumulative Results of Operations.** An account used to reflect the accumulated difference between total expenses and losses of an agency and the total financing sources and gains of the agency since its inception (comparable to *retained earnings* for a business entity).

**Department of Treasury.** A department of the executive branch of the federal government responsible for handling government finances. As the chief custodial office of the federal government, it can be thought of as the bank for the federal government.

**Entitlement.** A payment which an individual or other entity is entitled to receive under some statute, such as social security.

**Expended Appropriation.** An appropriation that has been used to cover the costs of goods or services.

**Financing Sources.** In this chapter, a nominal account to reflect the inflow of spendable resources equal to depreciation.

**Fund Balance with U.S. Treasury.** An account used by federal governmental agencies to reflect the amount of cash appropriated for agency operations.

**Funds Appropriated.** In this chapter, the amount of resources earmarked for use by a federal agency in the approved federal budget.

**General Accounting Office.** An arm of the legislative branch of the federal government that reports to Congress on the financial position, operating results, and accounting systems of government agencies. It functions mainly as an internal auditor of the federal government.

**General Fund Accounts.** Accounts used by federal agencies to record the financial transactions associated with congressional appropriations and other authorizations to spend those resources.

**General Services Administration (GSA).** A department of the executive branch of the federal government responsible for providing an effective system for the management of governmental properties and records associated with those properties, including data processing and communications systems.

**Government Equity.**   The owners' equity section of a federal agency balance sheet, including subcategories for invested capital, cumulative results of operations and unexpended appropriations.

**Invested Capital.**   The part of a federal agency's governmental equity represented by the book value of fixed assets.

**Management Fund Accounts.**   Federal agency receipt and expenditure accounts established by law to facilitate accounting for and administration of the intragovernmental operations of a federal agency.

**Office of Management and Budget (OMB).**   Office, operating under the supervision of the president, charged with various responsibilities relating to the continued improvement of governmental organization, information, management systems, governmental budgeting, and accounting procedures.

**Revolving Fund Accounts.**   Receipt and expenditure accounts established by law to facilitate accounting for a continuing cycle of operations with receipts from such operations usually available for use by the fund without further action by Congress.

**Special Fund Accounts.**   Receipt and expenditure accounts for receipts that are earmarked by law for a specific purpose but not generated by a cycle of operations for which there is continuing authority to reuse the receipts.

**Unallocated Appropriation.**   Appropriation that has not been apportioned to specific periods within the fiscal year.

**Unapportioned Appropriation.**   The amount appropriated for an agency's operation in the approved federal budget.

**Unexpended Appropriation.**   The amount of an agency's appropriation that has not been used at the end of a reporting period; the part of governmental equity that may include unallocated appropriations, unobligated allotments, and unliquidated obligations.

**Unobligated Allotment.**   The part of an unexpended appropriation that has been apportioned to a period of time but has not yet been committed to use.

## ■ Suggested Supplementary References

Brown, Ray L. "The Line Item Veto: How Well Does It Work?" *Government Accountants Journal* (Winter 1987–88).

Calvelli, Alfred M. "The Junkyard Dogs Versus the Federal Deficit." *Government Accountants Journal* (Fall 1987).

Cary, Thurman, and G. Stevenson Smith. "The U.S. Government Standard General Ledger: What It Means for Equity and Budgetary Accounting in the Federal Government." *Government Accountants Journal* (Fall 1988).

Kendig, William L. "Solving Federal Accounting System Problems." *Government Accountants Journal* (Fall 1988).

Short, Thomas W. "Financial Reporting—Treasury's Report on Operations." *Government Accountants Journal* (Spring 1986).

Stout, Larry D. "A Vision of Federal Financial Management: Can We Create a Bottom Line?" *Government Accountants Journal* (Summer 1987).

Sunner, Michael W. "Financing and Managing Our Public Debt." *Government Accountants Journal* (Fall 1990).

Tierney, Cornelius E., and Chuck Hamilton. "Strengthening Controllership in the Federal Government—A Proposal Revisited." *Government Accountants Journal* (Fall 1987).

Young, Ronald S. "GAO's Efforts to Establish Federal Government Accounting Standards." *Government Accountants Journal* (Fall 1989).

## ■ Questions for Class Discussion

Q10-1.    What were the major provisions of the Budget and Accounting Act of 1921?

Q10-2.    When was the General Services Administration (GSA) established? What are its primary responsibilities?

Q10-3.    Briefly discuss the more relevant features of the Budgeting and Accounting Procedures Act of 1950.

Q10-4.    What are the primary responsibilities of the Office of Management and Budget (OMB)? In which branch of the government does it operate?

Q10-5.    What are the primary responsibilities of the comptroller general?

Q10-6.    What department is primarily responsible for establishing accounting principles and procedures for the federal government? Discuss.

Q10-7.    In general, how does the Treasury Department relate to the financial reporting practices of the federal government?

Q10-8.    What are the primary responsibilities of the OMB? Discuss.

Q10-9.    What are the primary responsibilities of the Congressional Budget Office? Discuss.

Q10-10.   What are the primary responsibilities of the GSA? Discuss.

Q10-11.   Define the following terms used in accounting for federal agency activities:
a.   fund balance with U.S. Treasury
b.   invested capital
c.   cumulative results of operations
d.   unexpended appropriations.

Q10-12.   What funds are used in accounting for federal agency activities?

Q10-13.   What basis of accounting is used in accounting for federal agency activities? Discuss.

Q10-14.   What document has the GAO used to prescribe accounting principles and procedures for federal agency accounting?

Q10-15.   What consolidated financial statements are prepared to reflect overall federal government financial affairs?

## ■ Exercises

E10-1.    An agency of the federal government has been notified that an appropriation in the amount of $2,000,000 for the agency has been included in the recently adopted federal budget.

**Required:**

A. What journal entry should the agency use to record that action?

B. What is the meaning of the accounts used in the journal entry?

C. Where will those accounts appear in the agency's financial statements?

**E10-2.** Shortly after the federal budgetary item in E10-1 was approved, the OMB approved an apportionment of $500,000 per quarter for the agency.

**Required:**

A. Record the approval of the apportionment.

B. How does the preceding entry change the meaning of the balance in the governmental equity account?

**E10-3.** Later, the agency head allocated $400,000 of the appropriation recognized in E10-2 to first quarter operations.

**Required:**

A. Record the allocation.

B. Interpret the elements of governmental equity after the allocation has been recognized.

**E10-4.** A governmental agency spends $300,000 of its allotments to acquire fixed assets costing $100,000 and to pay salaries in the amount of $200,000.

**Required:**

A. Record the expenditures.

B. What journal entries should be recorded to reflect the effects of these expenditures on the governmental equity section of the agency's balance sheet?

**E10-5.** A federal agency issues purchase orders for fixed assets in the amount of $20,000 and obligates itself for payroll in the amount of $40,000.

**Required:**

A. Journalize these entries.

B. What entries should be made when the fixed assets are received and the payroll is paid?

**E10-6.** The following items are reflected in the end of period trial balance for a federal agency:

| | | |
|---|---:|---:|
| Fund balance with U.S. Treasury | $1,730,000 | |
| Inventory | 70,000 | |
| Fixed assets | 300,000 | |
| Accumulated depreciation | | $ 56,000 |
| Accounts payable | | 90,000 |
| Invested capital | | 244,000 |
| Cumulative results of operations | | 40,000 |
| Unallocated appropriations | | 1,500,000 |
| Unobligated allotments | | 40,000 |
| Expended appropriations | | 260,000 |
| Operating costs | 246,000 | |
| Unliquidated obligations | | 100,000 |
| Financing sources (depreciation) | | 16,000 |
| Totals | $2,346,000 | $2,346,000 |

**Required:**

A.   Prepare financial statements for the agency.

B.   Discuss the relationships among the items in the financial statements.


# ■ Problems

**P10-1.**   The Beta Agency was authorized by Congress to start operations on October 1, 19X1.

**Required:**

A.   Record the results of the following actions and transactions on a transactions worksheet for the agency:

   1.   The Beta Agency was notified that Congress had approved a one-year appropriation for the agency amounting to $4,000,000.

   2.   The OMB notified the agency that the appropriation had been approved to be spent equally over each quarter of the fiscal year beginning on October 1, 19X1.

   3.   The agency head allotted $1,000,000 to be spent during the first quarter.

   4.   Obligations approved for the first quarter are as follows:

| | |
|---|---:|
| Salaries and wages | $ 600,000 |
| Equipment | 250,000 |
| Other operating expenses | 150,000 |
| Total | $1,000,000 |

   5.   The payroll for October amounting to $200,000 is paid.

   6.   Invoices in the amount of $150,000, covering the purchase of equipment at a cost of $100,000 and other operating expenses amounting to $50,000, were approved.

   7.   Invoices in the amount of $150,000 were paid.

   8.   The following accruals was recorded at the end of October:

| | |
|---|---|
| Other operating expenses | $30,000 |

   9.   Supplies valued at $20,000, previously charged to other operating expenses, are found to be still on hand at the end of October.

   10.   Depreciation for the month of October amounted to $2,000.

B.   Prepare financial statements for the Beta Agency for the month of October.

C.   Journalize the closing entries for Beta Agency at the end of October.


**P10-2.**   The accounting records of an agency of the federal government show the following account balances at the end of a reporting period:

| | |
|---|---:|
| Financing sources (depreciation) | $ 24,000 |
| Accumulated depreciation | 84,000 |
| Fund balance with U.S. Treasury | 2,595,000 |
| Fixed assets | 450,000 |
| Accounts payable | 135,000 |
| Inventory | 105,000 |
| Expended appropriations | 390,000 |
| Unliquidated obligations | 150,000 |
| Operating costs | 369,000 |
| Unobligated allotments | 60,000 |
| Unallocated appropriations | 2,250,000 |
| Cumulative results of operations | 60,000 |
| Invested capital | 366,000 |

**Required:**

A. Prepare a trial balance of the accounts listed above.

B. Prepare financial statements for the agency.

# PART THREE

# Accounting for Other Nonprofit Organizations

■ *CHAPTER 11*

**Accounting for Hospitals**

■ *CHAPTER 12*

**Accounting for Colleges and Universities**

■ *CHAPTER 13*

**Accounting for Health and Welfare Agencies, Churches, and Other Similar Organizations**

# Accounting for Hospitals

## ■ Learning Objectives

When you have finished your study of this chapter, you should

1.  Have a general understanding of the relationship of hospital accounting practices to their operating environment.
2.  Know that hospital accounting practices call for use of the full accrual basis of accounting within the framework of a fund accounting system.
3.  Be aware of the fund entities used by hospitals and the relationships among those entities.
4.  Be able to record the routinely encountered transactions of a hospital and prepare financial statements from the data accumulated from those transactions.

**A**lthough some hospitals are privately owned and operate as profit enterprises, most are operated and supported by either other nonprofit organizations, such as religious groups, or by governmental units. Our attention in this chapter is focused on those institutions in the second category. Hospitals included in this group have many characteristics in common with colleges and universities, which are discussed in the next chapter. Both types of institutions exist for the purpose of providing a socially desirable service, and a significant portion of the costs of their services is paid by recipients of the service or by an organization obligated to them, such as the state, Medicare, Blue Cross, or some other insurance carrier. Both, therefore, can be described as quasi-nonprofit organizations. They are partially supported by contributions from constituents. Both require a large investment in plant per unit of service performed, and both have a similar combination of groups interested in their financial reports. However, with the adoption of cost-based formulas for payment of hospital costs by obligated third parties, *information regarding properly supported cost data has become very important* *in the hospital area.* As a result, hospital accounting procedures place a strong emphasis on development of appropriate cost data for the various services provided by these institutions.

Recommended accounting practices for hospitals were originally codified in the form of a statement of principles in *Chart of Accounts for Hospitals.*[1] The procedures set out in that publication are basically the same as those for business entities except for a requirement that a fund accounting system be used. Those procedures have been reaffirmed and elaborated upon by the American Institute of Certified Public Accountants in *Audits of Providers of Health Care Service.*[2]

In this chapter, we begin our discussion of hospital accounting procedures by relating them to the ones followed by business enterprises and those previously described for governmental units. We give particular attention to

1. the ways in which accounting practices for hospitals have been shaped to meet the needs of their operating environment

2. the fund entities used in hospital accounting systems.

After that, we shall summarize some of the accounting procedures that are peculiar to hospital accounting practices and present examples of financial statements for a typical hospital.

## ■ Accounting Practices and the Operating Environment

We have observed several times that accounting practices are always influenced by the environment within which an entity operates. This influence is especially evident in the accounting practices followed by hospitals. *They bear a much closer resemblance to those followed by profit enterprises because hospitals operate more like businesses than do most other nonprofit organizations.* However, they cannot be classified as profit enterprises because they have no ownership interests capable of being sold or traded and generally depend on contributions or taxes for part of their financing. Therefore, we can appropriately classify them as *quasi-nonprofit organizations* requiring some accounting procedures similar to those of governmental units. This is one segment of the nonprofit area in which the recommended accounting procedures are in conformity with those that were suggested as logically derived procedures in Chapter 1. In this section, we

1. observe more specifically some of the ways in which hospital accounting practices have responded to the institution's operating environment

2. show how the basis of accounting used for these institutions is consistent with their operating needs

3. describe cost-allocation procedures that have been developed in response to operating needs

---

1. *Chart of Accounts for Hospitals* (Chicago: American Hospital Association, 1976).
2. *Audits of Health Care Services* (New York: American Institute of Certified Public Accountants, 1990).

4. examine briefly the budgetary practices of hospitals
5. briefly discuss asset valuation practices
6. call attention to the accounting problems associated with malpractice litigation.

## Operating Environment

Most private (donor-supported) hospitals are expected to recover most or all of their operating costs from patient charges. As we observed before, such institutions can best be described as *quasi-nonprofit* entities. On the other hand, governmentally supported hospitals, such as those maintained for veterans, secure their operating resources from government allocations and therefore fall into the *pure nonprofit* category. For the most part, however, when we speak of hospitals, we are thinking of the institutions that provide health care services in exchange for fees related in some way to the costs of services rendered. It follows then that the need for matching costs with revenues has caused hospitals to adopt accounting procedures that closely resemble those followed for business enterprises.

Over the years, we have seen the responsibility for paying most hospital bills shifted to third parties, such as health care insurance companies and the federal government through its Medicare and Medicaid programs. Along with this change, hospital patients have, in effect, transferred not only the responsibility for payment but also the responsibility of monitoring hospital charges to third parties. This has forced hospitals to give special attention to cost-determination procedures as a means of justifying various patient service charges. Furthermore, rate approval agencies, the federal government, and insurance plans often impose their own requirements for determining the costs on which hospital charges are to be based. More recently (as we will explain later), we have seen Medicare payments tied to predetermined rates for different services rendered to patients. This method of reimbursement is called the Medicare Prospective Payment System. It appears likely that other third-party payors will move in that direction in determining the amounts to be paid for services to patients in the future. In the face of all of these demands, *accountability* and *full disclosure* have become key terms in identifying generally acceptable accounting practices for hospitals.

These externally imposed factors also require hospitals to give much attention to identifying the *cause and effect* relationships that exist between various types of expenses and the charges for services rendered. The need for more precisely matching costs against revenues has led hospitals to adopt the *full accrual basis of accounting*. Furthermore, the need for more precisely determined costs per units of services provided has caused hospitals to give much attention to developing highly sophisticated cost accumulation and allocation systems.

In some instances, there may be differences between the billed prices for services provided and the amounts paid by third parties as spelled out in third party reimbursement contracts with patients. If an account receivable has been recorded at the normally billed price, and the reimbursement contract provides for a smaller payment, the difference must be collected from the patient or absorbed by hospital operations. Because of that possibility, auditors of hospital financial statements should give particular attention to determining the amounts likely to be collected from third party payors, as accounts receivable are being examined.

Historically, Medicare and various other health insurance programs have paid hospitals for treatments of their clients on the basis of the costs of providing those treatments. Such health care costs, representing approximately 10 percent of the federal budget in 1980, have been increasing over several years at an annual rate of about 15 percent per year. Partly because of that experience, cost-based reimbursement has been criticized for encouraging inefficiency. Critics have reasoned that the greater the cost of hospital care, the more the hospitals received in payment from insurers. Also, wide variations in the costs of treating similar diagnoses from hospital to hospital and region to region have been cited as evidence of the inefficiency of cost-based reimbursement. From this historical background and these observations, Congress, as part of its Tax Equity and Fiscal Responsibility Act of 1982, developed a proposal for reimbursing hospitals for treatment of Medicare patients on the basis of a Medicare Prospective Payment Plan.[3] Within less than one year from the submission of that proposal, the Medicare program had evolved from using a cost-based, retrospective reimbursement system to a system that pays hospitals on the basis of predetermined prices for treating diagnosis-related groups (DRG) of patients. The new system, called Medicare Prospective Payment System, became effective with each hospital's first cost-recording period beginning on or after October 1, 1983.

The Medicare Prospective Payment System classifies patient illnesses into 467 diagnosis-related groups based on major diagnostic categories defined by the affected body system. The classification is further broken down by principal and secondary diagnoses requiring operating room procedures, age, sex, discharge disposition, and complications. The use of DRGs makes it necessary for hospitals to understand the nature of their "product lines" and to give special attention to measuring, monitoring, and controlling the costs of the services they provide.

The new system places a hospital financially at risk for the costs of the services it provides. Those institutions that incur costs less than the fixed payment rates will be permitted to keep the savings. Hospitals with costs in excess of the predetermined rates will have to absorb the difference or collect it directly from patients. This forces hospitals to manage available resources more effectively by controlling length of stay, use of ancillary services, and the mix of patients treated. To be successful in the new competitive environment, hospitals must be concerned with the *efficiency* as well as the *quality* of the services they provide.

With this radical change in the system of reimbursing hospitals for Medicare payments, we are likely to see other health care insurance programs adopt similar reimbursement practices. If hospitals are to continue to operate effectively in the new reimbursement environment, they are going to *have to give special attention to their accounting and financial reporting practices and the use of data derived from them.* Ultimately, hospitals will have to develop detailed profit and loss reports by DRGs to facilitate the identification and correction of inefficiencies. Their information systems

---

3. Material relating to Medicare Prospective Payment System summarized from *Medicare Prospective Payment System—Hospital Management Responses to Social Security Amendments of 1983.* Arthur Andersen & Co., 1983.

will need to be improved. For example, it may be necessary, as a result of operating information accumulated under the new reimbursement plan, for some hospitals to scale down from full-service institutions and to identify a particular market niche that is suitable for them. In the long run, hospitals may need to seek additional revenue sources through such things as the sale of services (either excess capacity or specialized services) to other hospitals. Promotion of such things as pharmacy services and sales to nonpatients and the expansion of fund-raising and auxiliary activities will also have to be considered as operating alternatives.

Implementation of the Prospective Payment System could well lead to the installation of standard cost systems by hospitals. This would involve the development of predetermined (standard) costs for the performance of each of the various functions associated with treating patients. Such an arrangement would allow hospital managers to control costs by giving attention to deviations from standards reflected in the form of unfavorable variances. We refer to this as "management by exception." A standard cost system could well provide the information that would be most useful to management in controlling costs.

Although the hospital is at risk for the costs of the services it provides under the new prospective payment system, *physicians make most of the decisions that affect hospital resource consumption,* particularly in terms of length of stay and use of ancillary services. Because of that fact, hospitals will need to involve physicians in the management and control of hospital resources. More emphasis will have to be given to improving productivity in the operations of hospitals.

Hospital operations require large investments in expensive facilities and equipment. As a result, the accounting practices for these organizations also place a strong emphasis on fixed-asset amortization practices. *Depreciation is recognized as an operating expense.* Also, price level changes and the need for recovering the equivalent current dollar costs of fixed assets consumed in rendering services have led hospitals to prefer basing depreciation on the current dollar values rather than on historical costs. (This is one of the significant points of difference between the accounting practices set out by the American Hospital Association and those approved by the American Institute of Certified Public Accountants through its Audits of Providers of Health Care Services.) Thus, it is clearly evident that accounting practices for hospitals are, in most respects, responsive to and consistent with the needs of their operating environment.

## Basis of Accounting

One of the most significant differences between the accounting practices followed by hospitals and those followed by governmental entities is that hospitals use the full *accrual basis of accounting,* which includes a distinction between capital and revenue items and the related recognition of depreciation as an operating expense. The hospital publication states that the accrual basis is used "to ensure completeness, accuracy, and meaningfulness in accounting data."[4]

The use of the full accrual basis of accounting suggests less emphasis on appropriation control of expenses and more emphasis on control through cost data than is

4. *Chart of Accounts for Hospitals,* p. 9.

commonly found in accounting for governmental units. Budgets, which are used extensively, fit into much the same place operationally as do budgets for profit entities. Planned operations are expressed in the form of a flexible budget that can be adjusted for changes in the level of operations.

Hospital accounting procedures nevertheless are similar to those used by other nonprofit enterprises in that they also follow fund-accounting practices. Thus, the accounting records for these organizations reflect the *unusual combination of the full accrual basis of accounting within the general framework of a fund accounting system.*

## Cost-Allocation Procedures

In an enterprise that depends on user- or buyer-based fees for a significant part of its revenue, it is important to be able to relate the costs of individual units of goods and/or services sold to the fees (revenues) realized from them. A manufacturing enterprise is concerned with matching the costs of producing each of its various products with the revenues realized from their sales. Therefore, their cost-allocation procedures are designed to allocate all manufacturing costs to the units being produced. Material and labor costs are charged directly to job orders or to processes out of which they are subsequently allocated to the units produced. Overhead costs are charged to the units of product by use of an overhead application rate related to some prime cost base, such as direct labor hours or direct labor dollars. Cost-allocation procedures, designed to allocate service department costs to producing departments on the basis of benefits received, are important elements in determining the overhead application rates for the various producing departments. The end result of these procedures is a total manufacturing cost per unit, which can then be matched against the sale price per unit to determine the margin realized on each of the various products or classes of products.

In service enterprises rendering different types of services, both direct and indirect costs should be allocated to the various services being performed in a manner similar to that described previously for the products of a manufacturing firm. The costs of providing a unit of service can then be compared to the prices billed for each unit of service provided to determine the margin realized from each type of service sold.

Hospitals depending on user-based charges fall into this category of resource conversion entities. Their cost-allocation procedures are similar to those found in profit-oriented service enterprises. As hospital services are used, the patient is charged for each of the various types of services provided on what is generally expected to be a cost-related basis. The *costs of operating the hospital therefore should be allocated to the revenue-producing centers recognized in patient billing.* The first step in the allocation process is to establish departmental cost centers. The cost of operating each department can include both direct and allocated charges. Direct costs, representing resources and services used entirely by the department, should be coded in such a way that they will be accumulated directly in the departmental expense control accounts. General expenses of the hospital should ultimately be allocated to the various revenue-producing departments, insofar as practicable, on the basis of the benefits each department receives from them. This requires the accountant to identify bases of allocation that are representative of the benefits realized by those departments. Building insurance, for example, might well be distributed to the various departments on the basis of square footage of floor space.

Within the conceptual arrangement calling for all operating costs to be allocated to revenue-producing departments, nonrevenue-producing departments, such as building maintenance, are designated as *supporting departments*. The costs of supporting departments should be allocated to revenue-producing departments on the basis of some measure of benefits received, thus allowing all operating costs to be accumulated in those cost centers.

After completing the cost-allocation process described earlier, managers can periodically compare the revenues realized from each of the various services with the costs of providing those services. This can be done on either an aggregate or unit basis. The cost-allocation process described earlier should be carried out for both budgeted and actual costs. This can best be done on a worksheet similar to the one shown in Exhibit 11–1, on which total budgeted costs for Hypothetical Hospital are allocated to its four revenue-producing departments.

## Budgetary Practices for Hospitals

We have observed that the hospital budgetary process must be responsive to the anticipated level of operations. To do this, it is generally desirable to develop a *flexible budget for each revenue-producing department*. This requires the separation of departmental costs into fixed and variable elements, after which they can be projected within a format similar to that shown for Hypothetical Hospital Department 1 in Exhibit 11–2. Such a budget allows us to project the cost of providing a unit of service at a number of possible levels of operations. Management must then make a judgment at the beginning of each period as to the probable level of operations for the period. After that judgment has been made, the operating plan, including operating-cost goals and service-billing prices, can be established for each department. As you relate the data in Exhibit 11–2 to those in Exhibit 11–1, you will observe that management is projecting an 80 percent level of operations for Department 1 during the next period.

Since the primary billing unit for many hospital services is a day of room occupancy, the overall level of operations in hospitals is typically expressed in terms of the rate of room occupancy. The flexible budgets setting out the anticipated operating costs at various room occupancy levels therefore are an important instrument in planning future operations and in establishing billing rates based on the anticipated costs of providing room-occupancy–related hospital services. Flexible budgets for other revenue-producing departments, such as X-ray services, should be prepared and related to various possible levels of operations for those respective departments.

Budgets obviously are developed and used in the plan phase of the plan-execute-evaluate-plan cycle. However, they should also be used to evaluate operations and as a guide for managerial action at the end of each reporting period. To illustrate that point, let's assume that Department 1 (see Exhibit 11–2) actually operates at an 85 percent level during the period when it was budgeted at an 80 percent level (see Exhibit 11–1). Expenses assumed to have been incurred during the period are shown in Exhibit 11–3, along with an analysis of the variances from the adjusted budget allowances for the period. Management should pursue the possible causes of unfavorable variances suggested in the notes at the bottom of the analysis.

**EXHIBIT 11–1.** Hypothetical Hospital—Allocation of Costs

| | Revenue-Producing Cost Centers | | | | Supporting Cost Centers | | | |
| | Dept 1 | Dept. 2 | Dept. 3 | Dept. 4 | Dept. 5 | Dept. 6 | Dept. 7 | Total |
|---|---|---|---|---|---|---|---|---|
| Direct expenses | $400,000 | $800,000 | $300,000 | $600,000 | $200,000 | $ 80,000 | $100,000 | $2,480,000 |
| Allocated expenses | 80,000 | 120,000 | 100,000 | 150,000 | 40,000 | 30,000 | 30,000 | 550,000 |
| Totals | $480,000 | $920,000 | $400,000 | $750,000 | $240,000 | $110,000 | $130,000 | $3,030,000 |
| Allocation of Dept. 6 costs (1) | 20,000 | 60,000 | 10,000 | 20,000 | | $110,000 | | |
| Allocation of Dept. 7 costs (2) | 60,000 | 30,000 | 25,000 | 15,000 | | | $130,000 | |
| Allocation of Dept. 5 costs (3) | 100,000 | 50,000 | 30,000 | 60,000 | $240,000 | | | |
| Totals | $660,000 | $1,060,000 | $465,000 | $845,000 | | | | $3,030,000 |
| Billing units | 66,000 | 10,600 | 93,000 | 42,250 | | | | |
| Cost per unit of service | $10 | $100 | $5 | $20 | | | | |

(1) Department 6 costs are building-related costs allocated on basis of square footage as follows: Dept 1–4,000; Dept. 2–12,000; Dept. 3–2,000; Dept. 4–4,000.

(2) Department 7 costs are employee-related costs allocated on basis of number of employees as follows: Dept. 1–60; Dept. 2–30; Dept. 3–25; Dept. 4–15.

(3) Department 5 costs are equipment-related costs allocated on basis of cost of equipment in each department as follows: Dept. 1–$1,000,000; Dept. 2–$500,000; Dept. 3–$300,000; Dept. 4–$600,000.

**EXHIBIT 11–2.**  Hypothetical Hospital—Flexible Budget for Department 1

| Level of Operations (related to capacity) | 70% | 80% | 90% | 100% |
|---|---|---|---|---|
| Direct expenses (variable) | $262,500 | $300,000 | $337,500 | $375,000 |
| Direct expenses (fixed) | 100,000 | 100,000 | 100,000 | 100,000 |
| Allocated general expenses (fixed) | 80,000 | 80,000 | 80,000 | 80,000 |
| Allocated service department expenses | | | | |
| Department 6 (fixed) | 20,000 | 20,000 | 20,000 | 20,000 |
| Department 7 (semifixed) | 55,000 | 60,000 | 65,000 | 70,000 |
| Department 5 (fixed) | 100,000 | 100,000 | 100,000 | 100,000 |
| Total expenses | $617,500 | $660,000 | $702,500 | $745,000 |
| Billing units | 57,750 | 66,000 | 74,250 | 82,500 |
| Cost per unit of service | $10.69 | $10.00 | $9.46 | $9.03 |

**EXHIBIT 11–3.**  Hypothetical Hospital—Budget Analysis Schedule for Department 1

| | Actual Expenses | Budget Allocation* | | Variances |
|---|---|---|---|---|
| Direct expenses (variable) | $320,000 | $318,750 | (1) | $1,250—Unfavorable |
| Direct expenses (fixed) | 101,000 | 100,000 | (2) | 1,000—Unfavorable |
| Allocated general expenses (fixed) | 78,000 | 80,000 | | 2,000—Favorable |
| Allocated service dept. expenses | | | | |
| Department 6 (fixed) | 20,500 | 20,000 | (3) | 500—Unfavorable |
| Department 7 (semifixed) | 65,000 | 62,500 | (4) | 2,500—Unfavorable |
| Department 5 (fixed) | 101,500 | 100,000 | (5) | 1,500—Unfavorable |
| Totals | $686,000 | $681,250 | | $4,750—Unfavorable |

*Based on operations at 85 percent level.

(1) This unfavorable variance should be explained by the Department 1 supervisor. It appears that he or she failed to properly control variable costs in relationship to the actual level of operations. Individual items of expense should be reviewed.
(2) This variance suggests that the departmental supervisor has "overspent" the allocation for fixed expenses.
(3) and (5) These variances have probably been caused by inadequate cost controls in service departments 6 and 5. Costs should be reviewed with departmental supervisors.
(4) This variance could have been caused either by Department 1 having too many employees or by inadequate cost controls in Department 7.

## Asset Valuation Practices

As we have observed, accounting practices for hospitals are essentially the same as those followed by businesses fitted into the framework of a fund accounting system. This includes asset valuation practices. However, the AICPA publication entitled *Audits of Providers of Health Care Services* gives special attention to the procedures that should be followed in accounting for donated assets, donated services, and investments.

Donated assets should be reported at fair market value as of the date of the gift. Recognition of the receipt of an unrestricted asset requires an offsetting credit to a revenue account in the unrestricted funds accounting entity. If the asset is used directly in operations, the credit should be to an operating revenue account. On the other hand, unrestricted bequests and gifts received in the form of cash or securities should be classified as nonoperating revenue. Externally restricted gifts should be recorded in the appropriate restricted fund as an increase to asset and fund balance accounts.

Donated services fall into two categories. First, there are those services that are significant, measurable, and controlled by the hospital. Such donated services are recognized as expenses and revenues at their fair market values. However, no values are recognized for the second category of donated services, such as those provided by "Candy Stripers" that do not meet all three of these requirements (significant, measurable, and controlled).

Investments are initially recorded at cost if purchased or at fair market values if received as donations. Subsequent adjustments to the initially recorded values are basically the same as those recognized by business entities. For example, marketable equity securities are valued at the lower of aggregate cost or market in accordance with the provisions of FASB 12. Long-term investments in debt securities are reported at amortized cost if they are intended to be held until maturity. If not intended to be held until maturity, such securities should be valued at the lower of cost or market. Significant influence investments in equity securities should be accounted for by use of the equity method in accordance with the provisions of APB 18.[5]

## Malpractice Litigation

Malpractice litigation has, during recent years, become an important element of hospital operations. Again we find the accounting practices followed in recognizing the contingent losses associated with such litigation to be the same as those followed by businesses. FASB 5 requires that the estimated losses be accrued (recognized as losses with credits to estimated liability accounts during the reporting period in which the alleged malpractice occurred) if they are *probable* and *measurable*. Other contingent losses from alleged malpractice activities should be disclosed in footnotes to the financial statements.[6]

# ■ Fund Entities Used in Hospital Accounting Systems

The use of fund-accounting techniques is recommended for hospitals, just as it is for governmental units and other nonprofit organizations. The major emphasis in this area, however, is on dividing all resources into unrestricted and restricted categories. *Unre-*

5. *Audits of Providers of Health Care Services* (New York: American Institute of Certified Public Accountants, 1990), pp. XIII–XIV.
6. Ibid, pp. 89–90.

*stricted funds* include all resources available to be used for operating purposes, at the discretion of management, including plant assets. It follows then that *all resources received, without external restrictions on their use, flow through the unrestricted funds accounting entity.*

Consistent with these general operating practices, we find that hospital accounting records typically show the following four major fund sections or groups of accounts:

1. unrestricted funds, sometimes characterized as the general fund or operating fund
2. specific purpose funds
3. plant replacement and expansion funds
4. endowment funds.

The last three funds in the list are included in the restricted funds category. This arrangement normally requires what is basically a *two-tier balance sheet—one for unrestricted funds and the second for restricted funds.* The restricted funds section then includes subdivisions for each of the last three types of funds. This type of balance sheet is shown in Exhibit 11–4.

## Unrestricted Funds

Unrestricted resources are accounted for through the medium of a general or operating fund. This fund entity serves the hospital in much the same way as the general fund serves a governmental entity. However, as you can observe in Exhibit 11–4, the balance sheet for unrestricted funds includes both current and noncurrent assets and liabilities. A fund balance account reflects the difference between total assets and total liabilities.

The statement of revenues and expenses (see Exhibit 11–5) includes revenue classifications for patient service revenue, other operating revenue, and nonoperating revenue. The six major functional or departmental categories recommended for operating expenses are

1. nursing services
2. other professional services
3. general services
4. fiscal services
5. administrative services
6. provision for depreciation.

These classifications are used in the statement of revenues and expenses for Sample Hospital shown in Exhibit 11–5.

The distinction between capital and revenue expenditures and the recognition of depreciation within a fund-accounting system requires some recordkeeping techniques that are different from those used by either businesses or governmental units. Because the property, plant, and equipment account is carried among the assets of unrestricted funds, we need to transfer resources from the plant replacement and expansion fund to

**EXHIBIT 11–4.** Sample Hospital Balance Sheet—December 31, 19B, with Comparative Figures for 19A

| Assets | Current Year | Prior Year | Liabilities and Fund Balances | Current Year | Prior Year |
|---|---|---|---|---|---|
| | | | *Unrestricted Funds* | | |
| Current: | | | Current: | | |
| Cash | $ 133,000 | $ 33,000 | Notes payable to banks | $ 227,000 | $ 300,000 |
| Receivables | 1,382,000 | 1,269,000 | Current installments of long-term debt | 90,000 | 90,000 |
| Less estimated uncollectibles and allowances | (160,000) | (105,000) | Accounts payable | 450,000 | 463,000 |
| | 1,222,000 | 1,164,000 | Accrued expenses | 150,000 | 147,000 |
| Due from restricted funds | 215,000 | 0 | Advances from third-party payors | 300,000 | 200,000 |
| Inventories (if material, state basis) | 176,000 | 183,000 | Deferred revenue | 10,000 | 10,000 |
| Prepaid expenses | 68,000 | 73,000 | Total current liabilities | 1,227,000 | 1,210,000 |
| Total current assets | 1,814,000 | 1,453,000 | Deferred revenue—third-party reimbursement | 200,000 | 90,000 |
| Other: | | | Long-term debt | | |
| Cash | 143,000 | 40,000 | Housing bonds | 500,000 | 520,000 |
| Investments | 1,427,000 | 1,740,000 | Mortgage note | 1,200,000 | 1,270,000 |
| Property, plant, and equipment | 11,028,000 | 10,375,000 | Total long-term debt | 1,900,000 | 1,880,000 |
| Less accumulated depreciation | (3,885,000) | (3,600,000) | Fund balance | 7,400,000 | 6,918,000 |
| Net property, plant, and equipment | 7,143,000 | 6,775,000 | | | |
| Total | $10,527,000 | $10,008,000 | Total | $10,527,000 | $10,008,000 |

*Restricted Funds*

**Assets**

Specific purpose funds

| | | |
|---|---:|---:|
| Cash | $ 1,260 | $ 1,000 |
| Investments | 200,000 | 70,000 |
| Grants receivable | 90,000 | 0 |
| Total specific purpose funds | $ 291,260 | $ 71,000 |

Plant replacement and expansion funds:

| | | |
|---|---:|---:|
| Cash | $ 10,000 | $ 450,000 |
| Investments | 800,000 | 290,000 |
| Pledges receivable, net of estimated uncollectibles | 20,000 | 360,000 |
| Total plant replacement and expansion funds | $ 830,000 | $1,100,000 |

Endowment funds:

| | | |
|---|---:|---:|
| Cash | $ 50,000 | $ 33,000 |
| Investments | 6,100,000 | 3,942,000 |
| Total endowment funds | $6,150,000 | $3,975,000 |

**Liabilities and Fund Balances**

Specific purpose funds:

| | | |
|---|---:|---:|
| Due to unrestricted funds | $ 215,000 | $ 0 |
| Fund balances: | | |
|   Research grants | 15,000 | 30,000 |
|   Other | 61,260 | 41,000 |
| | 76,260 | 71,000 |
| Total specific purpose funds | $ 291,260 | $ 71,000 |

Plant replacement and expansion funds:

| | | |
|---|---:|---:|
| Fund balances: | | |
|   Restricted by third-party payors | $ 380,000 | $ 150,000 |
|   Other | 450,000 | 950,000 |
| Total plant replacement and expansion funds | $ 830,000 | $1,100,000 |

Endowment funds:

| | | |
|---|---:|---:|
| Fund balances: | | |
|   Permanent endowment | $4,850,000 | $2,675,000 |
|   Term endowment | 1,300,000 | 1,300,000 |
| Total endowment funds | $6,150,000 | $3,975,000 |

**EXHIBIT 11–5.**  Sample Hospital Statement of Revenues and Expenses—Year Ended December 31, 19B, with Comparative Figures for 19A

| | Current Year | Prior Year |
|---|---|---|
| Patient service revenue | $ 8,500,000 | $ 8,000,000 |
| Allowances and uncollectible accounts (after deduction of related gifts, grants, subsidies, and other income—$55,000 and $40,000) | (1,777,000) | (1,700,000) |
| Net patient service revenue | 6,723,000 | 6,300,000 |
| Other operating revenue (including $100,000 and $80,000 from specific purpose funds) | 184,000 | 173,000 |
| Total operating revenue | 6,907,000 | 6,473,000 |
| Operating expenses: | | |
| Nursing services | 2,200,000 | 2,000,000 |
| Other professional services | 1,900,000 | 1,700,000 |
| General services | 2,100,000 | 2,000,000 |
| Fiscal services | 375,000 | 360,000 |
| Administrative services (including interest expense of $50,000 and $40,000) | 400,000 | 375,000 |
| Provision for depreciation | 300,000 | 250,000 |
| Total operating expenses | 7,275,000 | 6,685,000 |
| Loss from operations | (368,000) | (212,000) |
| Nonoperating revenue: | | |
| Unrestricted gifts and bequests | 228,000 | 205,000 |
| Unrestricted income from endowment funds | 170,000 | 80,000 |
| Income and gains from board-designated funds | 54,000 | 41,000 |
| Total nonoperating revenue | 452,000 | 326,000 |
| Excess of revenues over expenses | $    84,000 | $   114,000 |

unrestricted funds when they are used to acquire plant, property, and equipment. These transfers are illustrated in the statement of changes in fund balances for Sample Hospital (see Exhibit 11–6).

## Restricted Funds

Restricted fund resources fall into three categories:[7]

1.  specific purpose funds
2.  funds for plant replacement and expansion
3.  endowment funds.

7.  Ibid, pp. 17–20.

**EXHIBIT 11–6.** Sample Hospital Statement of Changes in Fund Balances—Year Ended December 31, 19B, with Comparative Figures for 19A

|  | Current Year | Prior Year |
|---|---|---|
| Unrestricted funds |  |  |
| Balance at beginning of year | $6,918,000 | $6,242,000 |
| Excess of revenues over expenses | 84,000 | 114,000 |
| Transferred from plant replacement and expansion funds to finance property, plant, and equipment expenditures | 628,000 | 762,000 |
| Transferred to plant replacement and expansion funds to reflect third-party payor revenue restricted to property, plant, and equipment replacement | (230,000) | (200,000) |
| Balance at end of year | $7,400,000 | $6,918,000 |
| Restricted funds |  |  |
| Specific purpose funds: |  |  |
| Balance at beginning of year | $    71,000 | $    50,000 |
| Restricted gifts and bequests | 35,000 | 20,000 |
| Research grants | 35,000 | 45,000 |
| Income from investments | 35,260 | 39,000 |
| Gain on sale of investments | 8,000 | 0 |
| Transferred to: |  |  |
| Other operating revenue | (100,000) | (80,000) |
| Allowance and uncollectible accounts | (8,000) | (3,000) |
| Balance at end of year | $    76,260 | $    71,000 |
| Plant replacement and expansion funds: |  |  |
| Balance at beginning of year | $1,100,000 | $1,494,000 |
| Restricted gifts and bequests | 113,000 | 150,000 |
| Income from investments | 15,000 | 18,000 |
| Transferred to unrestricted funds (described above) | (628,000) | (762,000) |
| Transferred from unrestricted funds (described above) | 230,000 | 200,000 |
| Balance at end of year | $  830,000 | $1,100,000 |
| Endowment funds: |  |  |
| Balance at beginning of year | $3,975,000 | $2,875,000 |
| Restricted gifts and bequests | 2,000,000 | 1,000,000 |
| Net gain on sale of investments | 175,000 | 100,000 |
| Balance at end of year | $6,150,000 | $3,975,000 |

These funds include only resources subject to *external restrictions,* such as endowment funds and funds designated for plant replacement or enlargement. *No resources may be transferred to these funds as a result of management action.* For example, if management decides to appropriate unrestricted resources for future plant construction, it can do so only by earmarking those resources within the unrestricted funds accounting entity. Thus, the resources included in the restricted funds are all there by virtue of *external restrictions.* In most instances, they flow directly into those funds as they are received from external sources. However, in some instances, the receipt of resources, subject to delayed external restrictions, may be initially recorded in unrestricted funds.

**Specific Purpose Funds.**    Assets of specific purpose funds consist of *donor-restricted resources* that are expected to be used for specific operating purposes. These funds are similar to "special revenue funds" for governmental units. Cash and investments are the assets most generally found in this type of fund. Investments held as part of specific purpose fund assets should be distinguished from the permanent investments held among the assets of endowment funds. These assets represent the temporary investment of funds to be used later for *specified operating purposes.* On the other hand, endowment fund investments are nonexpendable assets.

Expenditures of specific purpose fund assets usually appear in the accounting reports as amounts transferred to other operating revenue in the statement of revenues and expenses (see Exhibit 11–5). They are reflected as transfers in the statement of changes in fund balances for the specific purpose fund (see Exhibit 11–6). Expenses incurred in carrying out these activities are recorded as expenses in the operating fund. Therefore, when special purpose activities are carried out as part of the hospital's operations, the following entries are used to record that fact:

| | | |
|---|---|---|
| **Specific Purpose Funds** | | |
| Transfers to unrestricted funds | xxxx | |
|     Cash | | xxxx |
| **Unrestricted Funds** | | |
| Cash | xxxx | |
|     Other operating revenue | | xxxx |
| Expense | xxxx | |
|     Cash | | xxxx |

**Plant Replacement and Expansion Funds.**    Assets of these funds include resources *restricted by donors* to be used for replacements or additions to property, plant, and equipment. The resources of these funds often include, in addition to cash and investments, pledges receivable, which are shown as assets of the fund after providing for estimated losses in collecting them. As resources from this fund are used for plant replacement and expansion, the transfer is reflected in the statements of changes in fund balances of both funds (see Exhibit 11–6).

The following entries are used to record the acquisition of fixed assets from plant replacement and expansion fund assets:

**Plant Replacement and Expansion Fund**

| | | |
|---|---|---|
| Transfers to unrestricted funds | xxxx | |
|    Cash | | xxxx |

**Unrestricted Funds**

| | | |
|---|---|---|
| Cash | xxxx | |
|    Transfers from plant replacement and expansion fund | | xxxx |
| Fixed assets | xxxx | |
|    Cash | | xxxx |

If resources are received by unrestricted funds that are later restricted by the donor (externally restricted) to be used for plant replacement and expansion, the receipt and subsequent transfer of those resources would be recorded as follows:

**Unrestricted Funds**

| | | |
|---|---|---|
| Cash or other asset | xxxx | |
|    Fund balance | | xxxx |
| Fund balance (Transfers to plant replacement and expansion fund) | xxxx | |
|    Cash or other asset | | xxxx |

**Plant Replacement and Expansion Fund**

| | | |
|---|---|---|
| Cash or other asset | xxxx | |
|    Transfers from the unrestricted funds | | xxxx |

Plant replacement and expansion funds include cash and investments of unexpended funds. Revenues from such investments should be recorded only in that fund. The following entry should be used to record such revenues:

| | | |
|---|---|---|
| Cash | xxxx | |
|    Income from investments | | xxxx |

The balance in the income from investments account would then be reflected in the statement of changes in fund balances (see Exhibit 11–6). Gains on the sales of such investments would be handled in a similar manner. This fund may also be charged by unrestricted funds for services associated with handling its securities transactions.

**Endowment Funds.** Endowment funds for hospitals are similar to nonexpendable trust funds for governmental entities. The accounting practices are essentially the same for the elements of this fund in both areas.

Maintenance of the principal balance is an important aspect of endowment fund operations, and accounting records for these funds should be organized to show that this objective has been achieved. The assets of endowment funds typically include cash and investments. The fund balance account may include only permanent endowment, or it may include subdivisions for permanent endowment and term endowment. *Term endowment funds* are resources that may be expended upon the occurrence of a specified event or upon the passage of a stated period of time. Income from endowment may be restricted or unrestricted, depending on the endowment agreement.

The transfer of cash, represented by earnings from endowment fund assets, requires appropriate entries in the accounts of the funds involved. Unrestricted endowment fund earnings are transferred to unrestricted funds, where they are recognized in the statement of revenues and expenses as unrestricted income from endowment funds (see Exhibit 11–5). The earnings from restricted endowment funds may be transferred to specific purpose funds to be held until spent for the designated purpose. Small endowments to be used for different purposes may be pooled, with revenues allocated on the basis of market values determined as each new endowment is added.

# ■ Accounting Procedures Peculiar to Hospital Operations

Earlier in this chapter, we observed some of the characteristics associated with hospital accounting practices that can be directly related to the requirements of the hospital operating environment. For example, we noted the importance of allocating accrual-based costs to revenue-producing centers to facilitate the comparison between revenues generated and expenses incurred by each revenue-producing department. This allows operating performance to be more effectively planned, evaluated, and controlled. The chart of accounts suggested for use in hospitals by the American Hospital Association includes a carefully coded account numbering system that can be used in implementing the accumulation of those data.[8]

The Sample Hospital statement of revenues and expenses (Exhibit 11–5) shows another distinctive accounting practice generally followed by hospitals. This involves the disclosure, as a subtraction from gross patient-service revenue, of the amounts of allowances and uncollectible accounts (after deducting related gifts, grants, and subsidies), to arrive at net patient-service revenue. This element of the operating statement is important because it discloses the billing value of patient services that are in effect provided by the hospital as a charitable service to the community. A quick observation of those data as presented for Sample Hospital shows slightly more than 20 percent of patient-service revenue falling into this category of community service.

The recording process for transactions carried out by hospitals is essentially the same as that found in business enterprises, with the exception of transfers between funds. These were described briefly in a preceding section of this chapter. There we noted that transfers from specific purpose funds to unrestricted funds were reflected as part of other operating revenue (see Exhibit 11–5) in the unrestricted funds records. Other transactions between funds are reflected as "transfers to" and "transfers from" elements of the statement of changes in fund balances (see Exhibit 11–6). This statement is designed to explain the changes that have occurred between the beginning- and end-of-the-year fund balances. It also serves as a formal statement reconciling the balance sheet fund balance accounts for the beginning and end of the year.

---

8. *Chart of Accounts for Hospitals*, p. 10.

# ▪ Hospital Financial Statements

The annual financial report for a hospital includes four statements: a balance sheet, an operating statement, a statement of changes in fund balances, and a statement of cash flows. The use of a combined balance sheet with sections for unrestricted funds and restricted funds (subdivided into the three fund groups) discussed earlier is recommended. A balance sheet prepared in this manner is illustrated in Exhibit 11–4. The operating statement for a hospital is generally characterized as a statement of revenues and expenses and is presented within the general format shown in Exhibit 11–5. In addition to these two statements, a statement of changes in fund balances (see Exhibit 11–6) is prepared to account for the differences between the beginning-of-the-period and end-of-the-period fund balances for each fund.

Also consistent with the requirement for business enterprises, a statement of cash flows is prepared for the unrestricted fund, as shown in Exhibit 11–7. Each financial statement may be accompanied by appropriate footnotes describing certain elements of the statement in more detail.

**EXHIBIT 11–7.**  Sample Hospital Statement of Cash Flows for Current Year

| | | |
|---|---:|---:|
| Cash provided by operations | | |
| Loss from operations | | $(368,000) |
| Add provision for depreciation | $ 300,000 | |
| Increase in advances from third-party payors | 100,000 | |
| Increase in deferred revenue | 110,000 | |
| Increase in accrued expenses | 3,000 | |
| Decrease in prepaid expenses | 5,000 | |
| Decrease in inventories | 7,000 | 525,000 |
| | | $ 157,000 |
| Less increase in net receivables | $  58,000 | |
| Increase in amount due from restricted funds | 215,000 | |
| Decrease in accounts payable | 13,000 | 286,000 |
| | | $(129,000) |
| Nonoperating revenue | | 452,000 |
| | | $ 323,000 |
| Cash provided by financing activities | | |
| Decrease in long-term debt | (90,000) | |
| Decrease in notes payable to bank | (73,000) | $(163,000) |
| | | $ 160,000 |
| Cash provided by investing activities | | |
| Transfers from restricted funds | $ 398,000 | |
| Decrease in board designated funds | 210,000 | |
| Increase in plant and equipment | (668,000) | (60,000) |
| Increase to cash | | $ 100,000 |
| Cash balance at end of year | | $ 133,000 |
| Cash balance at beginning of year | | 33,000 |
| Increase in cash balance | | $ 100,000 |

# ■ Ethical Considerations Associated with Hospital Accounting Procedures

Clayton Crafty, chief administrative officer for Hillview Hospital, has just returned from a meeting of Hillview's Board of Trustees. Some members of the board have expressed concern about the declining percentage of gross patient revenue that has been charged to charity cases, discounts, losses in collecting accounts receivable, and so on over the last several months. Those board members call attention to the fact that these amounts reflect Hillview's contribution to community welfare and need to be maintained at an appropriate level for the hospital to maintain its image in the community. Crafty consults with the controller who suggests that the hospital has a number of past-due accounts that could be written off during the last month of the fiscal year to increase the amount shown as Hillview's contribution to the community. He feels that a large number of these accounts can and will be collected after the end of the year, but he points out that such action would increase the percentage of gross patient fees charged off in the current year operating statement. Consider the ethical issues associated with such action.

# ■ Summary

In this chapter, we have described and illustrated the more important elements of accounting practices for hospitals. We observed that the operating environment of hospitals causes a strong emphasis to be placed on the determination of accrual-based expenses and the allocation of those expenses to revenue-producing departments. At the same time we noted that the dependence on donors and/or governmental funds for long-term capital and special projects financing has also forced these institutions to follow fund-accounting practices.

We discussed the principles underlying accounting practices for hospitals and observed how a system developed within those guidelines would produce an operating statement disclosing operational accountability. That statement is designed to match operating expenses with revenues from patient services to disclose the extent to which those expenses have been recovered through user charges. A balance sheet disclosing dollar-accountability stewardship, as well as accrual-based assets and liabilities, is also included as part of the system.

Next, the fund entities used in hospital accounting systems were described. We noted that unrestricted resources are accounted for through the medium of an operating or general fund characterized as unrestricted funds. This fund includes both current and noncurrent resources available for discretionary use by management. Three types of restricted funds—special purpose funds, funds for plant replacement and expansion, and endowment funds—were also described. Some of the special problems of the interfund relationships that occur because of the dual need for an operating statement reflecting full operational accountability and the use of separate fund entities within the accounting system were also discussed.

In the last part of the chapter, we described selected accounting practices peculiar to hospitals and discussed some of the distinctive items included in the illustrated financial statements for Sample Hospital.

# ▪ Glossary

**DRG.**   Diagnosis-related group as defined in Medicare Prospective Payment System.

**Flexible Budget.**   A schedule of anticipated expenses or expenditures for more than one possible level of operations that recognizes the expected behavior of fixed and variable outlay items as the level of operations changes.

**Occupancy Percentage.**   In the analysis of hospital financial data, the relationship between actual room occupancy and the maximum possible room occupancy for a hospital over a period of time.

**Plant Replacement and Expansion Funds.**   A sub-entity of restricted funds used by hospital accounting systems to account for assets restricted by donors to be used for additions to property, plant, and equipment.

**Prospective Payment System.**   A pricing system that sets in advance the prices that will be paid by health insurance carriers for hospital treatment of diagnosis-related groups of patients. Initiated by Medicare in 1983.

**Restricted Funds.**   Fund entities or segments of fund entities that are subject to restrictions in the ways the resources included in them may be used. This term is also used in hospital accounting systems to describe all segments of resources that are externally restricted in any way, along with the obligations against those resources.

**Specific Purpose Funds.**   An accounting entity used in hospital accounting systems to account for resources that are donor restricted to use for specified purposes other than plant replacement and expansion and endowment.

**Unrestricted Funds.**   Generally, all expendable resources that are not restricted to specified uses either by external parties or by the management of the nonprofit organization. It is also used as a specific designation for all resources of hospitals that are not externally restricted and are therefore available for general operating purposes.

# ▪ Suggested Supplementary References

American Hospital Association. *Chart of Accounts for Hospitals,* 1976.

American Institute of Certified Public Accountants. *Audits of Providers of Health Care Services,* 1990.

Holder, William W., and Jan Williams. "Better Cost Control with Flexible Budgets and Variance Analysis." *Hospital Financial Management Accounting,* 30 (1976):12–20.

Jenkins, William L. "Nonprofit Hospital Accounting System," *Management Accounting,* 54 (1973):23–27.

Smalls, Isaac S. "Hospital Cost Controls." *Management Accounting,* 54 (1973):17–20.

## ■ Questions for Class Discussion

Q11-1.   It has been said that hospitals place less emphasis on fund-accounting techniques than do governmental units. Do you agree? Explain.

Q11-2.   Contrast the basis of accounting for hospitals with that for governmental units.

Q11-3.   Explain how the operating environment of hospitals has influenced their accounting practices.

Q11-4.   Explain how various hospital insurance programs coupled with Medicare and Medicaid programs have influenced the accounting practices of hospitals.

Q11-5.   Is the matching concept important in hospital accounting? Explain.

Q11-6.   The distinction between capital and revenue items, coupled with the use of fund entities in the hospital area, creates certain accounting problems. What are these problems? How are they solved?

Q11-7.   Why are cost-allocation procedures an important element of hospital accounting systems? Explain fully.

Q11-8.   Describe the considerations involved in establishing common cost-allocation procedures within a hospital accounting system.

Q11-9.   Explain how the budgetary practices of hospitals differ from those followed for governmental entities.

Q11-10.  What is meant by a flexible budget? How is it used within a hospital accounting system?

Q11-11.  Why are hospital administrators concerned with price level changes? Explain fully.

Q11-12.  Compare the accounting practices of hospitals with those followed by business enterprises.

Q11-13.  Compare and contrast the funds and fund groups recommended for hospitals with those suggested for governmental entities.

Q11-14.  What are specific purpose funds as used in hospital accounting?

Q11-15.  Explain the relationship between various health care insurance programs and the strong emphasis on development of cost data associated with hospital accounting procedures.

Q11-16.  Describe the two principal subdivisions normally found in a hospital balance sheet.

Q11-17.  What are the principal sources of revenue normally found in a hospital's statement of revenues and expenses?

Q11-18.  List the typical functional classifications normally found in the operating expenses section of a hospital statement of revenues and expenses.

Q11-19.  Describe the fund entities included in the restricted funds portion of a hospital balance sheet.

## ■ Exercises

E11-1.   The Good Turn Hospital enters into a building fund campaign. Funds amounting to $250,000 are received during the campaign and a building is constructed at a cost of $275,000. Unrestricted fund resources are used to meet the construction costs not covered by campaign contributions.

**Required:**
A. Journalize the preceding transactions.
B. Indicate the fund(s) in which each transaction is recorded.

**E11-2.** The new building (see Exercise E11-1) is depreciated at the rate of 5 percent per year. The management of the hospital initiates a policy requiring that cash equal to depreciation expense be earmarked for plant replacement as depreciation is recorded.

**Required:**
A. Record the recognition and earmarking of depreciation at the end of the first year.
B. Indicate the fund(s) in which the transactions are recorded.

**E11-3.** The Good Turn Hospital sells used equipment for $4,000. Proceeds from the sale are to be reserved for future equipment purchases. The accounting records show that the equipment originally cost $10,000 and currently has a book value of $3,800.

**Required:**
A. Make all journal entries required by the preceding transaction.
B. Indicate the fund(s) in which the entries are recorded.

**E11-4.** The following account balances appear in the unrestricted funds portion of the statement of changes in fund balances.

| | |
|---|---|
| Transferred from plant replacement and expansion fund | $8,000 |
| Transferred to plant replacement and expansion fund | 5,000 |

**Required:**
A. Describe transactions that could have caused these changes in the unrestricted fund balance.
B. What related items are likely to be found in the plant replacement and expansion fund segment of the statement of changes in fund balances?

**E11-5.** A hospital purchases $100,000 worth of equipment from unrestricted funds.

**Required:**
Record the transaction.

**E11-6.** General endowment funds for Community Hospital yield revenues in the amount of $25,000.

**Required:**
Record this fact in the appropriate fund(s).

**E11-7.** Central City Hospital estimates that the expense for a day of room occupancy at a 100 percent occupancy level for Department A is $25.75 of which $15.00 is fixed. Department A has 200 rooms.

**Required:**
A. Prepare a flexible budget showing the anticipated daily departmental costs for Department A at 70 percent, 80 percent, 90 percent, and 100 percent levels of occupancy.

    B.   Calculate the projected cost per day of room occupancy for Department A at each level of occupancy.

    C.   What causes the differences in the projected daily room occupancy costs at various levels of occupancy? Explain.

**E11-8.**    Central City Hospital (see Exercise E11-7) has actual expenses for Department A during the current year (365 days) of $1,850,000. These include fixed expenses of $1,095,000. The department had an occupancy rate of 92 percent for the year.

**Required:**

    A.   Prepare an analysis of the relationships between actual and budgeted expenses for Department A.

    B.   Comment on your findings in Requirement A.

**E11-9.**    Community Hospital purchased a specialized piece of equipment from plant replacement and expansion fund cash on January 1, 19XX, for an installed cost of $125,000. The equipment had an estimated useful life of ten years, with estimated salvage value at the end of that time of $35,000. At the close of the calendar year, the equipment had an estimated replacement cost new of $137,000 and a revised salvage value of $37,000.

**Required:**

    A.   Record the purchase of equipment.

    B.   Record depreciation of the equipment at the end of the year.

    C.   Comment on the implications of the end-of-year replacement cost for depreciation practices.

**E11-10.**    Mercy Hospital had a billing rate of $88 per day for a single-bed room in the maternity ward. The ward has 60 such beds and experiences a normal occupancy rate of 95 percent for year 19XX. The billing rate is set to cover user costs plus a share of the expected cost of social services rendered by the ward. An analysis of the accounts receivable attributable to the ward discloses the following reductions from operating revenues for the year:

| | |
|---|---|
| Charity services | $378,200 |
| Provision for uncollectible accounts | 106,000 |

A donation of $15,000, designated to cover charity cases, was also received.

**Required:**

    A.   Determine what the billing rate would be if no charity cases (including "bad" accounts) were accepted.

    B.   What amount is the average paying patient (average period of stay is three days) contributing to the coverage of charity cases? Explain.

**E11-11.**    Mercy Hospital (see Exercise E11-10) received a gift designated for the purchase of equipment.

**Required:**

    A.   Record this transaction.

    B.   Where would the purchase be shown in the statement of cash flows?

# Problems

P11-1. This is a comprehensive transactions and financial statements problem. A computer software package is available for solving this problem.

Hillview Hospital begins its year with the following account balances in its ledger:

**Unrestricted Funds**

| | |
|---|---:|
| Cash | $ 100,000 |
| Receivables | 1,000,000 |
| Allowance for uncollectible accounts | 120,000 |
| Inventories of supplies | 140,000 |
| Prepaid fiscal services expenses | 50,000 |
| Property, plant, and equipment | 8,000,000 |
| Accumulated depreciation | 3,000,000 |
| Accounts payable | 300,000 |
| Accrued general services expenses | 100,000 |
| Bonds payable | 1,200,000 |
| Fund balance | 4,570,000 |

**Restricted Funds**
**Specific Purpose Funds**

| | |
|---|---:|
| Cash | $ 1,000 |
| Grants receivable | 60,000 |
| Fund balance | 61,000 |

**Plant Replacement and Expansion Funds**

| | |
|---|---:|
| Cash | $ 8,000 |
| Investments | 600,000 |
| Pledges receivable | 50,000 |
| Allowance for uncollectible pledges | 10,000 |
| Fund balance—restricted | 248,000 |
| Fund balance—other | 400,000 |

**Endowment Funds**

| | |
|---|---:|
| Cash | $ 40,000 |
| Investments | 4,000,000 |
| Fund balance | 4,040,000 |

The following transactions occur during the year:
1. Patient services are billed in the amount of $6,000,000.
2. Allowances for losses on previously billed charity cases, $500,000.
3. Provided allowances for uncollectible accounts in the amount of $600,000.
4. Collected receivables in the amount of $4,600,000.
5. Receivables in the amount of $620,000 are written off as uncollectible.
6. Paid the following operating expenses:

| | |
|---|---:|
| Salaries to nurses | $1,600,000 |
| Salaries to other professionals | 1,400,000 |
| Salaries to administrators | 300,000 |

7.  Incurred other operating expenses as follows:

| | |
|---|---|
| General services | $1,300,000 |
| Fiscal services | 250,000 |
| Supplies | 125,000 |

8.  Paid accounts payable in amount of $1,500,000.
9.  Received unrestricted gifts available for general operations amounting to $225,000.
10. Realized income from endowment in amount of $120,000.
11. Received otherwise unrestricted pledges toward plant replacement and expansion in the amount of $120,000. It is anticipated that $15,000 of those pledges will be uncollectible.
12. Collected pledges for plant replacement and expansion in the amount of $130,000.
13. Sold fixed asset costing $40,000 and having a book value of $12,000 for $15,000.
14. Sold plant replacement and expansion fund investments with a book value of $100,000 for $105,000. Also received income from plant fund investments in the amount of $40,000.
15. Purchased fixed assets at a cost of $200,000.
16. Received securities for endowment valued at $500,000.
17. Depreciation for the year amounts to $250,000.
18. Special purpose fund grants outstanding at the beginning of the year are collected.
19. A new grant for a specified research project in the amount of $90,000 was received.
20. Special purpose projects are completed as part of unrestricted fund operations. These projects are charged at $48,000. The unrestricted fund is reimbursed by the specific purpose fund for these expenses.
21. Other end-of-period adjustments should be recognized as required by the following end-of-the-year balances:

| | |
|---|---|
| Supplies inventory | $120,000 |
| Prepaid fiscal services expenses | 70,000 |
| Accrued general services expenses | 75,000 |

**Required:**
A.  Enter the beginning-of-the-period account balances in the first two columns of a worksheet.
B.  Record the transactions for the period in the worksheet.
C.  Complete the worksheet and prepare appropriate financial statements for Hillview Hospital.

P11-2.  These problems refer to the accounts of a large nonprofit hospital that properly maintains four funds: unrestricted, special purpose, endowment, and plant replacement. Select the best answer for each of the following items:
1.  The endowment fund consists of several small endowments, each for a special purpose. The hospital treasurer has determined that it would be legally possible and more efficient to pool the assets and allocate the resultant revenue. The sound-

est basis on which to allocate revenue after assets are pooled and comply with the special purposes of each endowment would be to:
   a. determine market values of securities or other assets comprising each endowment at the time of transfer to the pool and credit revenue to each endowment on that pro rata basis.
   b. determine book value of each endowment at the time of transfer to the pool and credit revenue to each endowment on that pro rata basis.
   c. apportion future revenue in the moving-average ratio that the various endowments have earned revenue in the past.
   d. ask the trustee who administers the pooled assets to make the determination since she is in a position to know which assets are making the greatest contribution.

2. How should charity service, contractual adjustments, and bad debts be classified in the statement of revenues and expenses for a hospital?
   a. All three should be treated as expenses.
   b. All three should be treated as deductions from patient service revenues.
   c. Charity service and contractual adjustments should be treated as revenue deductions whereas bad debts should be treated as an expense.
   d. Charity service and bad debts should be treated as expenses whereas contractual adjustments should be treated as a revenue deduction.

3. Depreciation on some hospital fixed assets, referred to as "minor equipment," is not accounted for in the conventional manner. How is depreciation with respect to these assets accounted for?
   a. ignored on the basis of immateriality
   b. handled in essentially the same manner as would be the case if the assets were assigned to the activities of a city and were accounted for in its general fund
   c. determined periodically by inventorying minor equipment and writing the assets down to their value at the inventory date
   d. recognized only when minor equipment is replaced

4. To assure the availability of money for improvements, replacement, and expansion of plant, it would be most desirable for the hospital to:
   a. use accelerated depreciation to provide adequate funds for eventual replacement.
   b. use the retirement or replacement system of depreciation to provide adequate funds.
   c. sell assets at the earliest opportunity.
   d. earmark cash in the operating fund for plant replacement in amounts at least equal to the periodic depreciation charges.

5. Which of the following normally would be included in Other Operating Revenues of a hospital?

|  | Revenue from educational programs | Unrestricted gifts |
|---|---|---|
| a. | Yes | No |
| b. | Yes | Yes |
| c. | No | Yes |
| d. | No | No |

6. Revenue of a hospital from grants specified by the donor for research would normally be included in:
   a. other nonoperating revenue.
   b. other operating revenue.
   c. patient service revenue.
   d. ancillary service revenue.

7. Revenue from educational programs of a hospital normally would be included in:
   a. ancillary service revenue.
   b. patient service revenue.
   c. other nonoperating revenue.
   d. other operating revenue.

8. Proceeds from sale of cafeteria meals and guest trays to visitors operated by a hospital would normally be included in:
   a. patient service revenue.
   b. ancillary service revenue.
   c. other operating revenue.
   d. other nonoperating revenue.

**AICPA Adapted**

**P11-3.** Select the best answer for each of the following items.

1. An organization of high school seniors performs services for patients at Leer Hospital. These students are volunteers and perform services that the hospital would not otherwise provide, such as wheeling patients in the park and reading to patients. Leer has no employer–employee relationship with these volunteers, who donated 5,000 hours of service to Leer in 19X7. At the minimum wage rate, these services would amount to $18,750, while it is estimated that the fair value of these services was $25,000. In Leer's 19X7 statement of revenues and expenses, what amount should be reported as nonoperating revenue?
   a. $25,000
   b. $18,750
   c. $6,250
   d. $0

2. Under Cura Hospital's established rate structure, patient service revenues of $9,000,000 would have been earned for the year ended December 31, 19X7. However, only $6,750,000 was collected because of charity allowances of $1,500,000 and discounts of $750,000 to third-party payors. For the year ended December 31, 19X7, what amount should Cura record as patient service revenues?
   a. $6,750,000
   b. $7,500,000
   c. $8,250,000
   d. $9,000,000

3. In June 19X8, Park Hospital purchased medicines from Jove Pharmaceutical Co. at a cost of $2,000. However, Jove notified Park that the invoice was being canceled, and that the medicines were being donated to Park. Park should record this donation of medicines as:
   a. a memorandum entry only.
   b. other operating revenue of $2,000.

    c.  a $2,000 credit to operating expenses.

    d.  a $2,000 credit to nonoperating expenses.

4.  Cura Hospital's property, plant, and equipment, net of depreciation, amounted to $10,000,000, with related mortgage liabilities of $1,000,000. What amount should be included in the restricted fund grouping?

    a.  $0

    b.  $1,000,000

    c.  $9,000,000

    d.  $10,000,000

5.  Palma Hospital's patient service revenues for services provided in 19X6, at established rates, amounted to $8,000,000 on the accrual basis. For internal reporting, Palma uses the discharge method. Under this method, patient service revenues are recognized only when patients are discharged, with no recognition given to revenues accruing for services to patients not yet discharged. Patient service revenues at established rates using the discharge method amounted to $7,000,000 for 19X6. According to generally accepted accounting principles, Palma should report patient service revenues for 19X6 of:

    a.  either $8,000,000 or $7,000,000, at the option of the hospital.

    b.  $8,000,000.

    c.  $7,500,000.

    d.  $7,000,000.

6.  In 19X6, Pyle Hospital received a $250,000 pure endowment fund grant. Also in 19X6, Pyle's governing board designated, for special uses, $300,000, which had originated from unrestricted gifts. What amount of these resources should be accounted for as part of general (unrestricted) funds?

    a.  $0

    b.  $250,000

    c.  $300,000

    d.  $550,000

7.  Payne Hospital received an unrestricted bequest of $100,000 in 19X6. This bequest should be recorded as:

    a.  a memorandum entry only.

    b.  other operating revenue of $100,000.

    c.  nonoperating revenue of $100,000.

    d.  a direct credit of $100,000 to the fund balance.

8.  Ross Hospital's accounting records disclosed the following information:

| | |
|---|---:|
| Net resources invested in plant assets | $10,000,000 |
| Board-designated funds | 2,000,000 |

What amount should be included as part of unrestricted funds?

    a.  $12,000,000

    b.  $10,000,000

    c.  $2,000,000

    d.  $0

9.  Cedar Hospital has a marketable equity securities portfolio that is appropriately included in noncurrent assets in unrestricted funds. The portfolio has an aggregate cost of $300,000. It had an aggregate fair market value of $250,000 at the end of 19X7 and $290,000 at the end of 19X6. If the portfolio was properly reported in the balance sheet at the end of 19X6, the change in the valuation allowance at the end of 19X7 should be:
    a.  $0.
    b.  a decrease of $40,000.
    c.  an increase of $40,000.
    d.  an increase of $50,000.

Items 10 through 12 are based on the following information pertaining to Lori Hospital for the year ended May 31, 19X9:

In March 19X9, a $300,000 unrestricted bequest and a $500,000 pure endowment grant were received. In April 19X9, a bank notified Lori that the bank received $10,000 to be held in permanent trust by the bank. Lori is to receive the income from this donation.

10.  Lori should record the $300,000 unrestricted bequest as:
    a.  nonoperating revenue.
    b.  other operating revenue.
    c.  a direct credit to the fund balance.
    d.  a credit to operating expenses.

11.  The $500,000 pure endowment grant:
    a.  may be expended by the governing board only to the extent of the principal since the income from this fund must be accumulated.
    b.  should be reported as nonoperating revenue when the full amount of principal is expended.
    c.  should be recorded as a memorandum entry only.
    d.  should be accounted for as restricted funds upon receipt.

12.  The $10,000 donation being held by the bank in permanent trust should be:
    a.  recorded in Lori's restricted endowment fund.
    b.  recorded by Lori as nonoperating revenue.
    c.  recorded by Lori as other operating revenue.
    d.  disclosed in notes to Lori's financial statements.

Items 13 through 16 are based on the following information:

Metro General is a municipally owned and operated hospital and a component unit of Metro City. In 19X9, the hospital received $7,000 in unrestricted gifts and $4,000 in unrestricted bequests. The hospital has $800,000 in long-term debt and $1,200,000 in fixed assets.

The hospital has transferred certain resources to a hospital guild. Substantially all of the guild's resources are held for the benefit of the hospital. The hospital controls the guild through contracts that provide it with the authority to direct the guild's activities, management, and policies. The hospital has also assigned certain of its functions to a hospital auxiliary, which operates primarily for the benefit of the hospital. The hospital does *not* have control over the auxiliary. The financial statements of the guild and the auxiliary are *not* consolidated with the hospital's financial statements. The guild and the auxiliary have total assets of $20,000 and $30,000, respectively.

Before the hospital's financial statements were combined with those of the city, the city's statements included data on one special revenue fund and one enterprise fund. The city's statements showed $100,000 in enterprise fund long-term debt, $500,000 in enterprise fund fixed assets, $1,000,000 in general long-term debt, and $6,000,000 in general fixed assets.

13. What account or accounts should be credited for the $7,000 of unrestricted gifts and the $4,000 of unrestricted bequests?
   a. Operating revenue     $11,000
   b. Nonoperating revenue    $11,000
   c. Operating revenue     $ 7,000
      Nonoperating revenue    4,000
   d. Nonoperating revenue    $ 7,000
      Operating revenue     $ 4,000

14. The hospital's long-term debt should be reported in the city's combined balance sheet as:
   a. part of $900,000 enterprise fund type long-term debt in the enterprise-fund–type column.
   b. an $800,000 contra amount against fixed assets.
   c. part of the $1,800,000 general long-term debt account group.
   d. a separate "discrete presentation" of $800,000 in the hospital column.

15. In the hospital's notes to financial statements, total assets of hospital-related organizations required to be disclosed amount to:
   a. $0.
   b. $20,000.
   c. $30,000.
   d. $50,000.

16. The hospital's fixed assets should be reported in the city's combined balance sheet as:
   a. hospital fixed assets of $1,200,000 in a separate "discrete presentation" hospital column.
   b. special-revenue-fund–type fixed assets of $1,200,000 in the general fund assets account group column.
   c. part of $1,700,000 enterprise-fund–type fixed assets in the enterprise-fund–type column.
   d. part of $7,200,000 general fixed assets in the general fixed assets account group.
   —AICPA Adapted

P11-4. Esperanza Hospital's post-closing trial balance at December 31, 19X6, appears on the worksheet in Exhibit 11–8.

Esperanza, which is a nonprofit hospital, did *not* maintain its books in conformity with the principles of hospital fund accounting. Effective January 1, 19X7, Esperanza's board of trustees voted to adjust the December 31, 19X6, general ledger balances, and to establish separate funds for the general (unrestricted) funds, the endowment fund, and the plant replacement and expansion fund.

**EXHIBIT 11–8.** Esperanza Hospital—Worksheet to Adjust General Ledger Balances and to Establish Separate Funds, January 1, 19X7

| Account | Trial Balance December 31, 1986 | | Adjustments | | General (Unrestricted) Funds | | Endowment Fund | | Plant Replacement and Expansion Fund | |
|---|---|---|---|---|---|---|---|---|---|---|
| | Debit | Credit | Debit | Credit | Debit | Credit | Debit | Credit | Debit | Credit |
| Cash | 60,000 | | | | | | | | | |
| Investment in U.S. Treasury bills | 400,000 | | | | | | | | | |
| Investment in corporate bonds | 500,000 | | | | | | | | | |
| Interest receivable | 10,000 | | | | | | | | | |
| Accounts receivable | 50,000 | | | | | | | | | |
| Inventory | 30,000 | | | | | | | | | |
| Land | 100,000 | | | | | | | | | |
| Building | 800,000 | | | | | | | | | |
| Equipment | 170,000 | | | | | | | | | |
| Allowance for depreciation | | 410,000 | | | | | | | | |
| Accounts payable | | 20,000 | | | | | | | | |
| Notes payable | | 70,000 | | | | | | | | |
| Endowment fund balance | | 520,000 | | | | | | | | |
| Other fund balances | | 1,100,000 | | | | | | | | |

*Additional account information:*

1. *Investment in corporate bonds* pertains to the amount required to be accumulated under a board policy to invest cash equal to accumulated depreciation until the funds are needed for asset replacement. The $500,000 balance at December 31, 19X6, is less than the full amount required because of errors in computation of building depreciation for past years. Included in the allowance for depreciation is a correctly computed amount of $90,000 applicable to equipment.

2. *Endowment fund balance* has been credited with the following:

| | |
|---|---:|
| Donor's bequest of cash | $300,000 |
| Gains on sales of securities | 100,000 |
| Interest and dividends earned in 19X4, 19X5, | |
| and 19X6 | 120,000 |
| Total | $520,000 |

The terms of the bequest specify that the principal, plus all gains on sales of investments, are to remain fully invested in U.S. government or corporate securities. At December 31, 19X6, $400,000 was invested in U.S. Treasury bills. The bequest further specifies that interest and dividends earned on investments are to be used for payment of current operating expenses.

3. *Land* comprises the following:

| | |
|---|---:|
| Donation of land in 19X0, at appraised value | $ 40,000 |
| Appreciation in fair value of land as determined by | |
| independent appraiser in 19X0 | 60,000 |
| Total | $100,000 |

4. *Building* comprises the following:

| | |
|---|---:|
| Hospital building completed in January 19X7, when operations were started (estimated useful life 50 years), at cost | $720,000 |
| Installation of elevator in January 19X7 (estimated useful life 30 years), at cost | 80,000 |
| Total | $800,000 |

**Required:**
Prepare a worksheet like the one in Exhibit 11–8, and enter the adjustments necessary to restate the general ledger account balances properly. Distribute the adjusted balances to establish the separate fund accounts, and complete the worksheet. Formal journal entries are not required, but supporting computations should be referenced to the worksheet adjustments.

—**AICPA Adapted**

**P11-5.** The balance sheet for Dexter Hospital as of December 31, 19X1, is shown in Exhibit 11–9. During 19X2, the following transactions occurred:

**EXHIBIT 11–9.** Dexter Hospital Balance Sheet—December 31, 19X1

| Assets | | | Liabilities and Fund Balances | | |
|---|---|---|---|---|---|
| | | *Unrestricted Funds* | | | |
| Current | | | Current | | |
| Cash | | $   20,000 | Accounts payable | $   16,000 | |
| Accounts receivable | $   37,000 | | Accrued expenses | 6,000 | |
| Allowance for uncollectible | | | | | |
| accounts | 7,000 | 30,000 | | | |
| Supplies | | 14,000 | | | |
| Total current assets | | $   64,000 | Total current liabilities | $   22,000 | |
| Other | | | Long-term debt | | |
| Equipment | $  680,000 | | Mortgage bonds payable | $  150,000 | |
| Allowance for depreciation | 134,000 | 546,000 | Total liabilities | $  172,000 | |
| Buildings | $1,750,000 | | Fund balance | $2,158,000 | |
| Allowance for depreciation | 430,000 | 1,320,000 | | | |
| Land | | 400,000 | | | |
| Total plant and equipment | | $2,266,000 | | | |
| Total | | $2,330,000 | | $2,330,000 | |
| | | *Restricted Funds* | | | |
| | | *Plant Replacement and Expansion Fund* | | | |
| Cash | | $   53,800 | | | |
| Investments | | 71,200 | Fund balance | $  125,000 | |
| Total | | $  125,000 | Total | $  125,000 | |
| | | *Endowment Funds* | | | |
| Cash | | $    6,000 | | | |
| Investments | | 260,000 | Fund balance | $  266,000 | |
| Total | | $  266,000 | Total | $  266,000 | |

1. Gross charges for hospital services, all charged to accounts receivable, were as follow:

   | | |
   |---|---|
   | Room and board charges | $780,000 |
   | Charges for other professional services | 321,000 |

2. Deductions from gross earnings were as follow:

   | | |
   |---|---|
   | Provision for uncollectible receivables | $30,000 |
   | Charity service | 15,000 |

3. The operating fund paid $18,000 to retire mortgage bonds payable with an equivalent fair value. The operating fund will not be repaid.

4. During the year, the operating fund received general contributions of $50,000 and income from endowment fund investments of $6,500. The operating fund has been designated to receive income earned on endowment fund investments.

5. New equipment costing $26,000 was acquired through use of plant replacement and expansion fund cash. An X-ray machine that originally cost $24,000 and that had a depreciated cost of $2,400 was sold for $500.

6. Vouchers totaling $1,191,000 were issued for the following terms:

| | |
|---|---|
| Administrative service expenses | $120,000 |
| Fiscal service expense | 95,000 |
| General service expense | 225,000 |
| Nursing service expense | 520,000 |
| Other professional service expense | 165,000 |
| Supplies | 60,000 |
| Expenses accrued at December 31, 19X1 | 6,000 |

7. Collections on accounts receivable totaled $985,000. Accounts written off as uncollectible amounted to $11,000.

8. Cash payments on vouchers payable during the year were $825,000.

9. Supplies of $37,000 were issued to nursing services.

10. On December 31, 19X2, accrued interest income on plant fund investments was $800.

11. Depreciation of buildings and equipment was as follows:

| | |
|---|---|
| Buildings | $44,000 |
| Equipment | 73,000 |

12. On December 31, 19X2, an accrual of $6,100 was made for fiscal service expense on plant fund bonds.

**Required:**

A. Record the balance sheet as of December 31, 19X1, and the preceding transactions in a transactions worksheet.

B. Prepare financial statements for Dexter Hospital for the year ending December 31, 19X2.

—**AICPA Adapted**

P11-6. The administrator of Wright Hospital has presented you with a number of service projections for the year ending June 30, 19X2. Estimated room requirements for in-patients by type of service are:

| Type of Patient | Total No. Patients Expected | Average Number of Days in Hospital | | Percent of Regular Patients Selecting Types of Service | | |
|---|---|---|---|---|---|---|
| | | Regular | Medicare | Private | Semi-private | Ward |
| Medical | 2,100 | 7 | 17 | 10% | 60% | 30% |
| Surgical | 2,400 | 10 | 15 | 15 | 75 | 10 |

Of the patients served by the hospital, 10 percent are expected to be Medicare patients, all of whom are expected to select semiprivate rooms. Both the number and proportion of Medicare patients have increased over the past five years. Daily rentals per patient are $40 for a private room, $35 for a semiprivate room, and $25 for a ward.

Operating room charges are based on man-minutes (number of minutes the operating room is in use multiplied by number of personnel assisting in the operation). The per man-minute charges are $.13 for inpatients and $.22 for outpatients. Studies for the current year show that operations on inpatients are divided as follow:

| Type of Operation | Number of Operations | Average Number of Minutes per Operation | Average Number of Personnel Required |
|---|---|---|---|
| A | 800 | 30 | 4 |
| B | 700 | 45 | 5 |
| C | 300 | 90 | 6 |
| D | 200 | 120 | 8 |
| | 2,000 | | |

The same proportion of inpatient operations is expected for the next fiscal year and 180 outpatients are expected to use the operating room. Outpatient operations average 20 minutes and require the assistance of three persons.

The budget for the year ending June 30, 19X2, by department, is:

*General services:*
| | |
|---|---|
| Maintenance of plant | $    50,000 |
| Operation of plant | 27,500 |
| Administration | 97,500 |
| All others | 192,000 |

*Revenue-producing services:*
| | |
|---|---|
| Operating room | 68,440 |
| All others | 700,000 |
| | $1,135,440 |

The following information is provided for cost allocation purposes:

| | Square Feet | Salaries |
|---|---|---|
| *General services:* | | |
| Maintenance of plant | 12,000 | $  40,000 |
| Operation of plant | 28,000 | 25,000 |
| Administration | 10,000 | 55,000 |
| All others | 36,250 | 102,500 |

|  | Square Feet | Salaries |
|---|---|---|
| Revenue-producing services: | | |
| Operating room | 17,500 | 15,000 |
| All others | 86,250 | 302,500 |
|  | 190,000 | $540,000 |

Basis of allocations:
Maintenance of plant—salaries
Operation of plant—square feet
Administration—salaries
All others—8 percent to operating room

**Required:**
Prepare schedules showing the computation of:
A. The number of patient days (number of patients multiplied by average stay in hospital) expected by type of patients and service.
B. The total number of man-minutes expected for operating room services for inpatients and outpatients. For inpatients show the breakdown of total operating room man-minutes by type of operation.
C. Expected gross revenue from room charges.
D. Expected gross revenue from operating room services.
E. Cost per man-minute for operating room services, assuming that the total man-minutes computed in requirement B is 800,000 and that the step-down method of cost allocation is used (i.e., costs of the general services departments are allocated in sequence first to the general services departments that they serve and then finally to the revenue-producing departments). Allocations should be made in the order listed.

—**AICPA Adapted**

P11-7.  The following selected information was taken from the books and records of Glendora Hospital (a voluntary hospital) as of and for the year ended June 30, 19X2:
1. Patient service revenue totaled $16,000,000, with allowances and uncollectible accounts amounting to $3,400,000. Other operating revenue aggregated $346,000 and included $160,000 from specific purpose funds. Revenue of $6,000,000 recognized under cost reimbursement agreements is subject to audit and retroactive adjustment by third-party payors. Estimated retroactive adjustments under these agreements have been included in allowances.
2. Unrestricted gifts and bequests of $410,000 were received.
3. Unrestricted income from endowment funds totaled $160,000.
4. Income from board-designated funds aggregated $82,000.
5. Operating expenses totaled $13,370,000 and included $500,000 for depreciation computed on the straight-line basis. However, accelerated depreciation is used to determine reimbursable costs under certain third-party reimbursement agreements. Net cost reimbursement revenue amounting to $220,000, resulting from the difference in depreciation methods, was deferred to future years.

6. Also included in operating expenses are pension costs of $100,000, in connection with a noncontributory pension plan covering substantially all of Glendora's employees. Accrued pension costs are funded currently. Prior service cost is being amortized over a period of twenty years. The actuarially computed value of vested and nonvested benefits at year-end amounted to $3,000,000 and $350,000, respectively. The assumed rate of return used in determining the actuarial present value of accumulated plan benefits was 8 percent. The plan's net assets available for benefits at year-end was $3,050,000.

7. Gifts and bequests are recorded at fair market values when received.

8. Patient service revenue is accounted for at established rates on the accrual basis.

**Required:**

A. Prepare a formal statement of revenues and expenses for Glendora Hospital for the year ended June 30, 19X2.

B. Draft the appropriate disclosures in separate notes accompanying the statement of revenues and expenses, referencing each note to its respective item in the statement.

—**AICPA Adapted**

**P11-8.** Select the best answer for each of the following items:

1. A gift to a voluntary not-for-profit hospital that is not restricted by the donor should be credited directly to:
   a. fund balance.
   b. deferred revenue.
   c. operating revenue.
   d. nonoperating revenue.

2. Depreciation should be recognized in the financial statements of:
   a. proprietary (for-profit) hospitals only.
   b. both proprietary (for-profit) and not-for-profit hospitals.
   c. both proprietary (for-profit) and not-for-profit hospitals, only when they are affiliated with a college or university.
   d. all hospitals, as a memorandum entry not affecting the statement of revenues and expenses.

3. An unrestricted pledge from an annual contributor to a voluntary not-for-profit hospital made in December 19X1 and paid in cash in March 19X2 would generally be credited to:
   a. nonoperating revenue in 19X1.
   b. nonoperating revenue in 19X2.
   c. operating revenue in 19X1.
   d. operating revenue in 19X2.

4. Glenmore Hospital's property, plant, and equipment (net of depreciation) consists of the following:

| | |
|---|---|
| Land | $    500,000 |
| Buildings | 10,000,000 |
| Movable equipment | 2,000,000 |

What amount should be included in the restricted fund grouping?

a. $0
b. $2,000,000
c. $10,500,000
d. $12,500,000

5. On July 1, 19X1, Lilydale Hospital's Board of Trustees designated $200,000 for expansion of outpatient facilities. The $200,000 is expected to be expended in the fiscal year ending June 30, 19X4. In Lilydale's balance sheet at June 30, 19X2, this cash should be classified as a $200,000:

a. restricted current asset.
b. restricted noncurrent asset.
c. unrestricted current asset.
d. unrestricted noncurrent asset.

6. Donated medicines that normally would be purchased by a hospital should be recorded at fair market value and should be credited directly to:

a. other operating revenue.
b. other nonoperating revenue.
c. fund balance.
d. deferred revenue.

7. During the year ended December 31, 19X1, Melford Hospital received the following donations stated at their respective fair values:

| | |
|---|---|
| Employee services from members of a religious group | $100,000 |
| Medical supplies from an association of physicians. These supplies were restricted for indigent care and were used for such purposes in 19X1 | 30,000 |

How much revenue (both operating and nonoperating) from donations should Melford report in its 19X1 statement of revenues and expenses?

a. $0
b. $30,000
c. $100,000
d. $130,000

—AICPA Adapted

P11-9. Melford Hospital operates a general hospital but rents space and beds to separately owned entities rendering such specialized services as pediatrics and psychiatric care. Melford charges each separate entity for common services, such as patients' meals and laundry, and for administrative services, such as billings and collections. Space and bed rentals are fixed charges for the year, based on bed capacity rented to each entity.

Melford charged the following costs to pediatrics for the year ended June 30, 19X2:

|  | Patient Days (variable) | Bed Capacity (fixed) |
|---|---|---|
| Dietary | $ 600,000 | 0 |
| Janitorial | 0 | $ 70,000 |
| Laundry | 300,000 | 0 |
| Laboratory | 450,000 | 0 |
| Pharmacy | 350,000 | 0 |
| Repairs and maintenance | 0 | 30,000 |
| General and administrative | 0 | 1,300,000 |
| Rent | 0 | 1,500,000 |
| Billings and collections | 300,000 | 0 |
| Totals | $2,000,000 | $2,900,000 |

During the year ended June 30, 19X2, pediatrics charged each patient an average of $300 per day, had a capacity of 60 beds, and had revenue of $6,000,000 for 365 days.

In addition, pediatrics directly employed the following personnel:

|  | Annual Salaries |
|---|---|
| Supervising nurses | $25,000 |
| Nurses | 20,000 |
| Aides | 9,000 |

Melford has the following minimum departmental personnel requirements based on total annual patient days:

| Annual Patient Days | Aides | Nurses | Supervising Nurses |
|---|---|---|---|
| Up to 21,900 | 20 | 10 | 4 |
| 21,901 to 26,000 | 26 | 13 | 4 |
| 26,001 to 29,200 | 30 | 15 | 4 |

These staffing levels represent full-time equivalents. Pediatrics always employs only the minimum number of required full-time equivalent personnel. Salaries of supervising nurses, nurses, and aides are therefore fixed within ranges of annual patient days.

Pediatrics operated at 100 percent capacity on 90 days during the year ended June 30, 19X2. It is estimated that, during these 90 days, the demand exceeded 20 patients more than capacity. Melford has an additional 20 beds available for rent for the year ending June 30, 19X3. Such additional rental would increase pediatrics' fixed charges based on bed capacity.

**Required:**
A.  Calculate the minimum number of patient days required for pediatrics to break even for the year ending June 30, 19X3, if the additional 20 beds are not rented. Patient demand is unknown, but assume that revenue per patient day, cost per patient day, cost per bed, and salary rates will remain the same as for the year ended June 30, 19X2.
B.  Assume that patient demand, revenue per patient day, cost per patient day, cost per bed, and salary rates for the year ending June 30, 19X3, remain the same as for the year ended June 30, 19X2. Prepare a schedule of increase in revenue and increase in costs for the year ending June 30, 19X3, in order to determine the net increase or decrease in earnings from the additional 20 beds if pediatrics rents this extra capacity from Melford.

**—AICPA Adapted**

**P11-10.**  The accounting records for Central Hospital include the following four self-balancing accounting entities:
a.  unrestricted funds
b.  specific purpose funds
c.  funds for plant replacement and expansion
d.  endowment funds.

The following transactions occur during the fiscal period:
1.  Patient services are billed in the amount of $3,000,000.
2.  Receivables in the amount of $2,000,000 are collected.
3.  Operating expenses are paid in the amount of $1,500,000.
4.  Unrestricted gifts available for general operations are received amounting to $100,000.
5.  Securities designated as endowment valued at $300,000 are received.
6.  A grant is received for a specified research project in the amount of $50,000.
7.  Part of the special project (see transaction f) was completed as part of unrestricted fund operations at a cost of $25,000. The unrestricted fund is reimbursed by the specific purpose fund for these expenses.
8.  End-of-period adjustments include prepaid operating expenses in the amount of $35,000 and accrued operating expenses in the amount of $40,000.
9.  A contribution externally designated for plant replacement and expansion in the amount of $300,000 is received.
10.  Fixed assets to be used in operations are purchased from plant replacement and expansion fund cash at a cost of $150,000.

**Required:**
On a sheet of worksheet paper, label individual pairs of columns to show the types of fund entities included in the hospital accounting records. Then journalize the ten transactions listed by recording the accounts debited and credited to the left of the four columns and entering the money amounts as debits and credits in the appropriate fund(s) columns.

# Accounting for Colleges and Universities

## ■ Learning Objectives

When you have finished your study of this chapter, you should

1. Know the operating characteristics of colleges and universities.
2. Be aware of the funds that colleges and universities have conventionally used to record their financial activities.
3. Be able to record the routine transactions normally carried out by colleges and universities by (a) using conventional accounting practices, and (b) following accounting practices prescribed by FASB 93.
4. Be able to prepare financial statements from data accumulated from transactions recorded by following the provisions of both objectives 3a and 3b.

The organizational and operational characteristics of colleges and universities place them within our broad definition of nonprofit organizations. They provide educational services without the objective of realizing a profit from those activities. They are financed through contributions, taxes, and operating revenues. They have no equity interests that are capable of being sold or traded by individuals or profit-seeking entities. The internal managers of these organizations are directly accountable to a governing board representing the constituency of the institution.

In some respects, the operating characteristics of colleges and universities are similar to those of governmental units. Consequently, some of their accounting practices closely resemble those followed by such entities. However, since much of their operating revenue is realized from charges based on some measure of services rendered, we can more precisely characterize them as *quasi-nonprofit* rather than pure nonprofit enterprises. In this respect, their operations are much like those of hospitals.

In this chapter, we examine and illustrate the accounting and reporting practices followed by colleges and universities. As we do that, we shall

1. review briefly the operating characteristics of these organizations as they relate to their accounting practices

2. summarize the more important elements of the college and university statement of accounting principles

3. make certain observations relating to elements of the statement of principles

4. describe the fund entities used in accounting for college and university operations

5. present, for your review, the financial statements for Model College

6. illustrate how routine transactions for a college or university should be recorded based on the statement of principles

7. discuss and illustrate the accounting procedures that should be followed if an institution follows the provisions of FASB 93.

# ■ Operating Characteristics and Accounting Practices

Colleges and universities fall into two operational subcategories, private and state institutions. Private schools rely heavily on user-based charges, that is, tuition revenue, for a significant portion of their operating resources. The tuition charges are generally based on the number of credit hours of work taken by students and are received directly from students, their parents, or from scholarship funds. State schools also realize user-based revenue. However, the major portion of that revenue comes from state allocations rather than from the students themselves. It is, nevertheless, based on some measure of the level of enrollment and can therefore be characterized as user-based revenue. Also, most state schools collect some tuition directly from students.

The accounting system of any resource-converting entity should be responsive to the operating characteristics of that entity. When we developed the accounting practices for governmental general funds, we noted that these funds operate as pure nonprofit entities, and as a result, their accounting procedures are designed to place primary emphasis on disclosing information relating to the inflows and outflows of appropriable resources. We also noted that some of the other subentities of governmental units are self-sustaining and therefore follow accounting practices similar to those used for profit enterprises. Although the primary operating objective of a college or university is to convert resources into educational services, most of them will also have subentities that are expected to sustain themselves from prices and fees charged for their products or services. These are called *auxiliary activities*. Colleges and universities also have other self-sustaining subentities called *endowment funds*.

Because colleges and universities depend on user-based charges for a significant amount of their operating resources, there is a *theoretical need* for matching costs against those revenues to show the extent to which operations have been financed from that source. That same operating characteristic should logically cause the budgetary data of these organizations to be projected in relationship to the anticipated level of operations rather than in the form of rigid appropriation allocations. In spite of this logically derived need to match costs against revenues, we find that the conventionally followed accounting procedures for these organizations are more like those used by governmental-type fund entities than the ones followed by profit enterprises. They place strong emphasis on dollar-accountability, expenditure-based financial reports. They also use separate fund entities to account for the acquisitions and uses of resources restricted to specified uses.

As if in response to accounting and reporting needs that can be logically derived from an analysis of college and university operating practices, the FASB in 1987 issued its highly controversial Statement 93. That statement requires nonprofit financial reports to be presented on the *full accrual basis* including a distinction between capital and revenue expenditures and the recognition of depreciation on long-lived assets. Because of a controversy between the FASB and GASB about the application of this statement to state-operated institutions, its implementation was delayed until 1991.

This jurisdictional dispute was resolved in October 1989 when the Financial Accounting Foundation, the parent body of both the FASB and GASB, agreed that jurisdiction would continue to be based on ownership. Within this arrangement, the GASB would be responsible for all government-owned organizations while the FASB would be in charge of all others. That means that until a new pronouncement is issued by the GASB, state-owned institutions continue to follow the conventional accounting practices set out in the Statement of Principles, while private institutions follow full accrual-based accounting.

The National Association of College and University Business Officers (NACUBO) has expressed concern about the lack of uniformity of financial reporting by colleges and universities and has urged that all higher-education institutions be placed under a single board to ensure uniform standards. When NACUBO polled its members, the members overwhelmingly opted for the FASB procedures; yet a uniform standard has not been adopted. Therefore, we discuss and illustrate the procedures to be followed in recording transactions and preparing financial statements using both conventional *and* FASB 93-oriented systems.

## ■ College and University Statement of Accounting Principles

The most authoritative statement of conventional accounting principles for colleges and universities is found in the publication *College and University Business Administration*. The portion of that publication most pertinent to accounting procedures is the section dealing with the fundamental concepts of financial accounting and reporting for colleges and universities. The following key statements are taken from that publication.[1]

1. National Association of College and University Business Officers, *College and University Business Administration,* 4th ed. (Washington, D.C.: NACUBO, 1982), pp. 388–393 (selected sections). Used by permission.

## Fund Accounting

To satisfy the requirement to account properly for the diversity of resources and their use, the principles and practices of "fund accounting" are employed. Within this concept, there have evolved certain principles of classification and presentation of accounting data as well as standard terminology for institutions of higher education.

Fund accounting is the manner of organizing and managing the accounting by which resources for various purposes are classified for financial accounting and reporting purposes in accordance with activities or objectives as specified by donors, with regulations, restrictions, or limitations imposed by sources outside the institution, or with directions issued by the governing board. In this respect, a clear distinction between funds which are externally restricted and those which are internally designated by action of the governing board should be maintained in the accounts and disclosed in the financial reports.

A fund is an accounting entity with a self-balancing set of accounts consisting of assets, liabilities, and a fund balance. Separate accounts are maintained for each fund to insure observance of limitations and restrictions placed on use of resources. For reporting purposes, however, funds of similar characteristics are combined into fund groups. The fund groups generally found in an educational institution are as follows:

Current funds

Loan funds

Endowment and similar funds

Annuity and life income funds

Plant funds

Agency funds

In addition to the foregoing fund groups, there may be additional fund groups unique to particular institutions, such as self-administered employee retirement funds. If there are such fund groups, they should be accounted for separately and reported in the annual financial statements.

Since each fund group is considered as a separate entity, there are numerous transactions among the fund groups, which must recognize this entity concept. When the movement of funds from one fund group to another is intended to be permanent, it should be recorded as a transfer between the fund entities. However, when the movement is intended to be temporary, the transaction should be recorded as an interfund borrowing. To be considered temporary, and therefore an interfund borrowing, there should be a definite plan of repayment within a defined period of time. A further indication that a borrower–lender relationship exists would be if interest were being paid by the borrowing fund group to the lending fund group.

When the current funds group is divided into two or more parts, such as unrestricted, auxiliary enterprises, and restricted categories, the permanent or temporary movement of funds among these parts would follow the rule above. One example of this would be an auxiliary enterprise having a deficit that must be eliminated because of a provision in an agreement with bondholders. Another would be the lifting of a restriction by a donor, resulting in the movement of funds from a restricted to unrestricted category.

In some instances, legal provisions and government regulations pertaining to certain funds may require accounting and reporting practices that differ from generally accepted accounting principles. It is recognized that in these instances such legal and regulatory provisions must take precedence. However, such restrictions do not obviate the need for adhering to generally accepted accounting principles for the purpose of reporting financial position, changes in fund balances, and current funds revenues, expenditures, and other changes. An alternative that might be considered by an institution would be to prepare supplementary schedules that would disclose compliance with any restrictions while presenting the basic financial statements in accordance with generally accepted accounting principles. Such a presentation would make it unnecessary for the auditor to qualify the opinion on the basic financial statements absent other reservations concerning them. The auditor might be able to express a separate opinion on the supplementary schedules, for example, stating that they had been prepared in conformity with legal provisions, regulations, or other requirements.

### Basic Financial Statements

Colleges and universities generally use three basic statements: a balance sheet, a statement of changes in fund balances, and a statement of current funds revenues, expenditures, and other changes.

The balance sheet presents a series of fund groups, with each group having its own self-balancing assets, liabilities, and fund balances.

The statement of changes in fund balances portrays all the activity that changed the fund balances of the fund groups between the preceding and the current balance sheet dates. This statement includes all additions to, deductions from, and transfers among the fund groups.

The statement of current funds revenues, expenditures, and other changes supplements and presents in detail some of the information presented in summary form in the current funds section of the statement of changes in fund balances. It does not purport to match expenses with revenues to derive a net income—rather, it presents in detail the current funds revenues by source, the current funds expenditures by function, and other changes in current fund balances. Also, it does not report the total revenue and expenditure activity of the institution, but only that related to current funds. The reporting objectives achieved by this statement may be accomplished in other ways.

The emphasis in these basic financial statements is on the status of funds, the flow of resources through fund entities, and the financial operations of the institution. Consideration should be given to supplementary schedules that combine nonfinancial with financial information to assist in further evaluating the activity, achievements, and overall operations of the institution.

### Accrual Accounting

The accounts should be maintained and reports prepared on the accrual basis of accounting. Revenues should be reported when earned and expenditures when materials or services are received. Expenses incurred at the balance sheet date should be accrued and expenses applicable to future periods should be deferred. However, certain deferrals and accruals, such as investment income and interest on student loans, are often omitted. Nevertheless, the only basis for their omission should be that the omission does not have a material effect on the financial statements. Revenues and expenditures of an academic term, such as a summer session, which is conducted over a fiscal year end, should be reported totally within the fiscal year in which the program is predominantly conducted.

Encumbrances representing outstanding purchase orders and other commitments for materials or services not received as of the reporting date should not be reported as expenditures nor be included in liabilities in the balance sheet. Designations or allocations of fund balances or disclosure in the notes to the financial statements should be made where such commitments are material in amount. Failure to disclose the distinction between true liabilities and encumbrances that are not true liabilities could result in the presentation of misleading information to state authorities, regulatory bodies, budget commissions, and others.*

In the case of institutions that maintain their books on the cash basis, journal entries should be recorded, as necessary, to convert accounts to the accrual basis as of the end of a fiscal year.

## Accounting for Depreciation

Depreciation is an element of cost resulting from the service of long-lived assets in an economic organization. In business accounting, depreciation charges are recorded as an expense because they must be related to the revenue produced by the fixed assets in determining accurately the net profit or loss for a stated period of time. The correct determination of net profit or loss of a business operation is important for several reasons: (1) to gauge the value of the enterprise as a going concern; (2) to ascertain the value and earning power of its equity securities; (3) to provide a realistic basis for borrowing; (4) to determine earnings that may be available for distribution to owners in the form of dividends; and (5) to determine its tax liability under federal and state income tax laws.

Unlike businesses, colleges and universities are not faced with the same requirements for profit and loss determination. Rather, they exist to provide services, and the general expenditures incurred therefore have no causative relationship with and do not generate any general revenues. They do not pay taxes based on income; their fixed assets are not directly related to their general credit and debt-incurring capacity; they are not traded or sold as are businesses; and any excess of revenues over expenditures—for a single year or cumulatively—is not available for distribution in the manner that corporate profits are available for distribution to stockholders.

Under these operating characteristics, which are devoid of profitability considerations, any recording of depreciation on capital assets in the current operating accounts would not only fail to serve any essential informational purpose in the financial statements and reports, but could actually be misleading to the users of such statements and reports— misleading because the charging of current operations with depreciation indicates a matching of costs with directly related revenues in the generally accepted business accounting sense when, in fact, no causative relationship between revenues and expenditures exists for colleges and universities.

That depreciation is not recorded does not, of course, deny its existence as an economic fact of life. Nor does it preclude the calculation and recording of depreciation in certain specialized accounting and managerial operations. For certain activities that are susceptible of accurate and definitive measurement, it may be desirable for management to know the unit costs of providing such activities on a continuing basis. Full costs are sometimes required as a basis for charging using departments for goods and services. In such cases, depreciation is an essential element in the development of unit costs.

Thus, depreciation expense related to assets comprising the physical plant is reported neither in the statement of current funds revenues, expenditures, and other changes nor in the current funds section of the statement of changes in fund balances. Capital asset acquisitions financed from current funds are reported as expenditures of that group in the year of acquisition.

For purposes of statement presentation, depreciation allowance may be reported in the balance sheet and the provision for depreciation reported in the statement of changes

*American Institute of Certified Public Accountants, *Audits of Colleges and Universities* (New York: AICPA, 1975), p. 7.

in the balance of the Investment in Plant subgroup of the Plant Funds group. In the Endowment and Similar Funds group, depreciation should be provided on depreciable assets held as investments in order to maintain the distinction between principal and income in those funds.

Depreciation should not be confused with the provision of funds for maintenance and replacement of buildings and equipment.

## Accounting for Investments

Investment purchases usually are reported at cost and investments received as gifts usually are reported at the fair market or appraised value at the date of gift. As a permissible alternative, investments may be reported at current market or fair value, provided this basis is used for all investments in all funds. When using this alternative, unrealized gains and losses should be reported in the same manner as realized gains and losses under the cost basis.

Interfund sales of investments should be recorded by the purchasing fund at fair market or appraised value at date of sale. The differences between carrying value and fair market or appraised value should be accounted for in the selling fund as realized gains and losses.

Investments of the various funds may be pooled unless prohibited by statute or by terms of the gifts. Proper determination of equities and the basis of income distribution should be made by using current market values on a share or unit plan. This determination can be made through the use of memorandum records and does not require the recording of each investment at current market value in the accounts.

## Accounting for Institutions Operated by Religious Groups

Accounting and reporting records of an institution should be adequately segregated from the records of the sponsoring religious group so that the educational entity is in fact accounted for as a separate entity. Facilities made available to the educational entity by the religious group should be disclosed in the financial reports together with any related indebtedness.

The monetary value of services contributed by members of the religious group should be recorded in the accounts and reported in the financial statements. The gross value of such services should be determined by relating them to equivalent salaries and wages for similarly ranked personnel at the same or similar institutions, including the normal staff benefits such as group insurance and retirement provisions.

The amounts so determined should be recorded as expenditures by department or division, following the same classification as other expenditures, and a like amount should be recorded as gift revenue. The gift revenue should be reduced by the amount of maintenance, living costs, and personal expenses incurred, which are related to the contributing personnel and have no counterpart in a lay employee relationship.

In some cases, checks are drawn to the religious group and charged to expenditure accounts in the same manner as payroll checks. The religious group then makes a contribution to the institution, which records it as a gift. The determination of the contribution would rest with the religious group, since the latter is a separate entity.

In some cases, these institutions inform the reader of the financial report as to the relative value of such contributed services by comparison with the average return on the endowment fund investment. Such information should be limited to the notes to the financial statements, and the imputed capitalized value of such contributions should not be reflected in the balance sheet.

The accounting procedures discussed below are based on the provisions of this statement of principles as they have historically been interpreted by college and university accountants.

# ■ Observations

As you can see, the statement of principles for colleges and universities is similar in many respects to the one that is generally accepted as the guideline in accounting for operations of governmental units. Both cite the need for following fund accounting practices and both specifically indicate the funds or fund groups to be used. Both reject the practice of recognizing depreciation in the accounts except where it is funded or where the assets are associated with a self-sustaining activity. The statements do, however, display some differences that are significant and others that are more apparent than real. We now examine some of the differences and explore some of the similarities found within these statements with particular attention being given to:

1. legal provisions
2. budgetary practices
3. basis of accounting
4. accounting for depreciation
5. accounting for auxiliary enterprises.

After we examine these topics, we will also summarize some of the changes in accounting practices suggested by the AICPA publication entitled, *Audits of Colleges and Universities.*

## Legal Provisions

A comparison of the two statements of principles reveals an apparent difference regarding the emphasis on showing compliance with legal provisions. The statement for colleges and universities makes no mention of a need for organizing the system "to show that legal provisions have been complied with." Part of the explanation of fund accounting, however, suggests that "in some instances legal provisions and government regulations pertaining to certain funds may require accounting and reporting practices that differ from generally accepted accounting principles. It is recognized that, in these instances, such legal and regulatory provisions must take precedence."[2] State-supported institutions, no doubt, experience limitations of a legal nature, whereas limitations on the uses of resources by private schools are primarily imposed by their constituencies. In either case, the fiduciary responsibilities must be recognized and met; consequently, this difference in the statements of accounting principles seems more apparent than real and, therefore, has only a limited effect on the accounting practices followed. Both types of enterprises must *provide accounting data to show compliance with the regulations within which they operate.*

2.  *College and University Business Administration,* 4th ed., p. 390.

## Budgetary Practices

Governmental accounting principles require that the accounting system provide budgetary control of both revenues and expenditures. Although the college and university statement does not require such control, a rather complete system of operational budgeting is almost universally followed by these institutions.

While a number of the individual items included in the budget of a college or university are appropriation controlled, many are also formula controlled, with budget allowances being adjusted to compensate for changes in the level of operations achieved. In this respect, the budgetary practices of colleges and universities resemble those of profit enterprises. A significant amount of revenue, particularly among private schools, is earned by the provision of services rather than from an assessment based on a predetermined amount of proposed services. For example, if the enrollment is larger than expected, an appropriate increase in planned expenditures is often added to the originally budgeted amount to enable the institution to meet the requirements of an expanded program.

Under these circumstances, the college or university budget is a much more flexible instrument than the one typically used by governmental entities. As a result, budgetary data are typically given less formal recognition in the accounts of colleges and universities. If budgetary data are formally recorded in the financial records, they may be entered as credits in separate appropriation accounts, or they may be entered as credits in the expenditure accounts. Budgeted revenue is generally omitted from the formal accounting records.

## Basis of Accounting

Accounting principles for governmental units recommend use of the accrual basis to the extent that it is practicable to do so. This is interpreted to require the full accrual basis for proprietary funds and some modification of the pure accrual basis for governmental funds. Revenues for governmental funds are recognized when they become available and are objectively measurable. Expenditures, with limited exceptions, are recognized when obligations are incurred that are objectively measurable. Furthermore, no distinction is made between capital and revenue items and depreciation is not recognized in accounting for the activities of these funds.

The *college and university statement also recommends use of the accrual basis* in accounting for operations. This is interpreted to require the recognition of revenues when earned.[3] Expenditures are recognized when "materials or services are received."[4] Accrued and prepaid expenses, with some exceptions, are also recognized in the financial statements. Again, however, *the accrual basis as defined in this statement does not include a distinction between capital and revenue expenditures or the recognition of depreciation.* In summary, we can conclude that, except for proprietary funds of governmental entities, the accrual basis recommended for both types of organizations falls short of the pure accrual basis used in the profit area. The operating statements of both governmental-type funds and colleges and universities are *expenditure oriented.*

3. Ibid., p. 390.
4. Ibid.

## Accounting for Depreciation

Among governmental units, depreciation is recognized only on the assets of self-sustaining funds. Principle number 7 for governmental entities (see Chapter 3, page 77) states that "depreciation of general fixed assets should not be recorded in the accounts of governmental funds." Depreciation, however, is recognized in accounting for the assets of enterprise funds, internal service funds, and other self-sustaining funds.

The college and university statement indicates that, except for real property that are investments of endowment funds, "depreciation expense related to assets comprising the physical plant is reported neither in the statement of current funds, revenues, expenditures, and other changes nor in the current funds statement of fund balances."[5] This is not interpreted to preclude provisions for renewals and replacements as a substitute for depreciation in the accounting records of auxiliary enterprises. As we shall see in our analysis of the AICPA publication entitled *Audits of Colleges and Universities,* the position taken by the accounting profession regarding depreciation is one that would *permit* the reporting of depreciation in the plant fund section of the statement of changes in fund balances.[6] The statements of principles of both governmental units and colleges and universities suggest, however, that depreciation may be included in supplementary schedules for the purpose of computing unit costs when such costs are desired.

In general, as far as depreciation accounting relating to *general fixed assets* is concerned, there is little fundamental difference between the practices followed by these two kinds of nonprofit organizations.

## Auxiliary Enterprises

Auxiliary activities of colleges and universities—for example, intercollegiate athletics, residence halls, and cafeterias—are generally expected to be self-sustaining or to produce an excess of revenues over expenditures. Although one would logically expect their accounting records to be maintained in a manner similar to those of proprietary funds in the governmental area, they are significantly different in two respects.

The first difference is the practice of not recording depreciation on the facilities being used in the auxiliary activity. The college and university statement is permissive in saying that *provisions may be made for renewals and replacements* with these provisions being reported in the schedules of current expenditures. However, where this is done, cash or liquid assets are expected to be transferred from current funds to a plant fund, which is used to accumulate resources for renewals and replacements. As a result, the statement showing the operations of an auxiliary activity is in reality *a statement of revenues and expenditures* rather than an accrual-based operating statement.

The second difference centers on the fact that, as a general rule, no separate balance sheet is prepared for the individual auxiliary activity. Fixed assets used in auxiliary activities are shown as part of the plant fund accounting entity. Short-term assets and liabilities associated with these activities are generally included in the current funds balance sheet. This accounting practice is consistent with the exclusion of auxiliary activities from the fund groups listed on page 453.

5. Ibid., p. 392.
6. *Audits of Colleges and Universities,* 2nd ed., p. 10.

## Summary of Changes Suggested by AICPA Audit Guide

The original *AICPA Audit Guide for Colleges and Universities,* in many respects, clarified and expanded the accounting practices recommended by the statement of principles in the 1968 edition of *College and University Business Administration.* However, in 1974, that publication was revised, for the most part, to comply with the AICPA recommendations. Nevertheless, it is still desirable to point out major differences between the 1968 edition of *College and University Business Administration* and the audit guide requirements to highlight the more recent changes in college and university accounting practices. These differences may be summarized as follows:[7]

1. The audit guide permits the reporting of depreciation in the plant fund section of the statement of changes in fund balances.

2. It allows funds held in trust by others to be included in the financial statements under certain circumstances.

3. Endowment income stabilization reserves permitted by the 1968 college and university publication are indicated to be at variance with generally accepted accounting principles and therefore should be eliminated from the financial statements.

4. The audit guide requires that mandatory debt-service provisions relating to auxiliary enterprises be treated as transfers among the funds rather than as expenditures. This treatment is consistent with the requirement of the college and university publication regarding mandatory debt-service provisions relating to educational facilities.

5. Mandatory transfers from current funds should be *treated separately* from nonmandatory transfers. At the same time, the audit guide requires that the statement of current fund revenues, expenditures, and other changes include all current fund transfers both mandatory and nonmandatory.

6. The audit guide requires that the accounting procedures followed for encumbrances should be in accordance with the accrual basis of accounting. This requires that expenditures include only outlays and liabilities incurred in connection with goods and services received.

7. The audit guide states that agency funds *should not* be included in the statement of changes in fund balances.

8. The audit guide allows current market or fair value to be used as an alternative to cost in reporting the carrying value of investments.

9. In addition to the changes in accounting practices described above, the audit guide requires certain disclosures not specifically mentioned in the college and university publication. These include disclosure of the total performance of the investment portfolio and disclosure of pledges in the notes to the financial statements.

10. The audit guide requires that a clear distinction be maintained between the balances of funds that are externally restricted and those that are internally restricted.

7. Ibid., pp. 1–4.

11. The audit guide also permits recording the monetary value of services contributed by members of a religious group to an institution operated by that group.

# ■ Fund Entities

Both the governmental and college and university statements of principles require the use of fund accounting techniques. However, the fund entities recommended for colleges and universities show a number of significant differences from those used by governmental units. One difference is that the college and university statement refers to the accounting entities as fund groups rather than as funds. This practice clearly suggests that each group may have two or more subdivisions, each of which is equivalent to an individual fund.

As observed earlier, the college and university statement recommends use of the following *fund groups,* each of which is discussed in this section:[8]

1. current funds
2. loan funds
3. endowment and similar funds
4. annuity and life income funds
5. plant funds
6. agency funds.

## Current Funds

Current funds include resources available for general operating purposes, auxiliary activities, and current restricted operating purposes. The fund balance accounts for all of these funds is roughly equivalent to the general and special revenue fund balance accounts for a governmental unit. In the college and university balance sheet, however, the fund balance is subdivided into unrestricted and restricted categories. The unrestricted fund balance indicates the net amount of current fund resources available for discretional use by management of the institution within the limits of budgetary restrictions. On the other hand, the restricted fund balance reflects the net amount of current fund resources available for *specified operating purposes* only. It is somewhat similar to the special revenue fund for a governmental entity.

Generally, current fund accounting practices are similar to those followed in accounting for the general fund and special revenue fund activities of a municipal entity. The fund group includes separate subdivisions for current unrestricted assets and liabilities and current restricted assets and liabilities. Accounts used in these funds are illustrated later, in the balance sheet (see Exhibit 12–1) and in the statement of current fund revenues, expenditures, and other changes (see Exhibit 12–2).

---

8. National Association of College and University Business Offices, *College and University Business Administration* (Washington, D.C., pp. 388–389).

It is important to recognize that *inflows of restricted spendable resources are not recognized as revenues in the restricted fund until expenditures are made that meet the restrictions placed on their use.* Therefore, the revenues shown in the restricted current funds section of the statement of revenues, expenditures, and other changes will always be equal to the expenditures shown for those funds. Because of this fact, the initial inflows of resources into restricted current funds are generally recorded as credits to the fund balance. To illustrate that point, let's assume cash restricted to providing scholarships, equal to $50,000, is received. The receipt should be recorded as follows:

| | | |
|---|---|---|
| Cash | 50,000 | |
| Fund balance—restricted fund | | 50,000 |

If $35,000 worth of scholarships are then awarded from these funds, that fact would be recorded in the restricted current fund as follows:

| | | |
|---|---|---|
| Scholarship expenditures | | |
| Cash | 35,000 | 35,000 |
| Fund balance | 35,000 | |
| Revenue | | 35,000 |

## Loan Funds

Loan funds are used to account for resources that may be loaned to students, faculty, and staff. Assets of this fund include cash, investments, and accounts receivable from loans. Although there is no governmental fund exactly like it, the loan fund does have many of the characteristics of a self-sustaining fund that is maintained as a revolving loan fund. Thus, accounting practices for this fund entity are similar to those for governmental self-sustaining funds. The accrual basis is employed in determining interest earned by the fund unless the amount so earned is immaterial. Provisions are made for probable losses to be incurred in the collection of the loans. Loan fund assets are shown as part of the combined balance sheet (see Exhibit 12–1).

## Endowment Funds

Endowment funds are used to account for resources that donors or management have stipulated shall be held and invested to produce income, which may be expended or added to the principal. This funds group includes, in addition to pure endowment funds just described, term endowment and quasi-endowment funds.[9] *Pure endowment funds* are examples of self-sustaining entities operating as part of the institutional unit. *Term endowment funds* differ from pure endowment funds in that all or part of the principal may be used after a stated period of time. *Quasi-endowment funds* include resources that the governing board of an institution, rather than an outside donor, has designated to be retained and invested. Because these resources are internally designated, the governing board also has the right to use the principal if it so desires. In many respects,

9.  *College and University Business Administration,* p. 420.

endowment funds are similar to the principal segment of the agency fund discussed in Chapter 8.

Resources realized as earnings from the investment of endowment funds generally flow into current unrestricted or current restricted funds for general or a specifically designated operating use. As its name suggests, earnings from a *general endowment fund* may be used for general operations; consequently, resources realized from the investment of these funds flow into the current unrestricted fund. On the other hand, revenue earned by a *scholarship endowment fund,* characterized as restricted or designated endowment, flows into a current restricted fund (a segment of the current fund whose resources are restricted to specified uses).

Due to the differences in the designated uses of revenues, each endowment fund should theoretically be accounted for separately. This could be accomplished by setting up a separate fund for each endowment, but such a fragmentation of the investments and accounting records is often impractical. Instead, most institutions "pool" the assets of the various endowment funds, in which case each of the benefiting funds will simply hold a share of the "pool."

Even though investments are pooled, it is important to recognize that the claims of each of the separate funds must be maintained. Individual accounts, generally in the form of subsidiary records, should be originated to reflect the claims of each of the separate funds against the pooled investments. The claim of an individual participant in the pool is typically calculated by relating the market value of the assets contributed by the participant to the market value of all assets in the pool at the time of entry into the pool. Those claims are generally designated in terms of units carrying an arbitrary value, such as $100 per unit.

After the pool has been formed, the pooled assets are revalued at specific intervals (usually monthly or quarterly) for the purpose of arriving at a new value for each unit. New values per unit *must* be calculated each time a new fund is added to the pool. These values are also used to calculate the amount to be paid to a fund withdrawing from the pool.

In making distributions from the pool, the total investment earnings of the pool are divided by the average number of units held by all funds participating in the pool during the period, determining the amount per unit to be distributed. That amount, multiplied by the number of shares held by the individual fund, will then determine the amount of earnings to be distributed to that fund.

A controversy exists regarding the definition of income from endowment funds. These differences of opinion have centered on the question of whether gains realized from the sale of endowment investments or from an increase in market values of investments could be expended. Classically, these gains have been treated as additions to the principal of the endowment fund. This treatment adheres to the "trust fund theory" held to be legally binding in some states. In 1969, however, the Ford Foundation expressed a sharply contrasting view in saying that there is no authoritative support for treating gains as additions to principal.[10] People who advocate this point of view, an idea commonly called the *corporate law concept,* hold that the gains can be spent in much the same manner as are interest and dividends earned by endowment

---

10. *Audits of Colleges and Universities,* p. 38.

investments. As a result, some colleges and universities have adopted what is referred to as a *total return approach* to endowment fund management. Under this approach, the total investment return, including the traditional revenues, plus or minus gains and losses, have been made available for expenditures permitted under the endowment agreement. This approach generally calls for protection of the endowment principal from loss of purchasing power before appropriating gains. It appears, however, that conservative, prudent management of endowment resources would still call for retention of the gains on endowment fund resources as additions to endowment fund principal.

Transfers from endowment funds to current funds may be recorded in the records of the endowment fund by entering a debit to the endowment fund balance account and a credit to endowment fund cash. In the current fund, cash is debited and endowment fund income is credited. However, the cash realized as endowment income may flow directly into the appropriate segment of the current fund. When that occurs, the realization of endowment income will be recorded only in the current fund by debiting cash and crediting endowment income.

When endowment resources are received from outside donors, that fact is recorded in the endowment fund as follows:

| | | |
|---|---|---|
| Assets | xxxx | |
|    Fund balance | | xxxx |

The following entries are used to record the transfer of resources from current funds to an endowment fund (quasi endowment):

**Current Funds**

| | | |
|---|---|---|
| Nonmandatory transfers to endowment | xxxx | |
|    Cash or other assets | | xxxx |

**Endowment Fund**

| | | |
|---|---|---|
| Cash or other assets | xxxx | |
|    Fund balance—quasi endowment | | xxxx |

All such transfers should be authorized by the governing board of the institution.

## Annuity and Life Income Funds

Annuity and life income funds are used to account for resources held by a college or university that are subject to "annuity or living trust agreements." Funds in this category generally provide for payment of specified amounts per period (month, year, etc.) to the donor or someone designated by the donor for life or for a specified period. At the end of that period, resources left in the fund generally become the property of the institution and are then available for general use, additions to endowment funds, or for other specified uses. More specifically, an annuity fund is made up of resources that have been contributed to a college or university under an arrangement calling for the institution to pay the contributor or someone designated by the contributor an agreed amount per period (month or year) for either the life of the donor or a specified number of periods. The institution then becomes the residuary beneficiary and thus receives any assets left in the fund after the contractual obligation has been fulfilled.

A *life income agreement* is defined as one that calls for money or other property to be made available to an institution with a provision that the income earned by those resources be distributed to the donor during his or her lifetime. Upon the death of the donor, all rights to the property are transferred to the institution. Such property may then be used at the discretion of management, subject to any restrictions placed upon their use by the donor.

In some respects, annuity funds are similar to endowment funds. When they are relatively small in amount, they may be grouped in this category. Accounting practices for these funds are also similar to those followed in accounting for agency funds of governmental units.

In reflecting annuity fund data in the balance sheet, we must show the actuarily determined present value of the annuity obligation (see Model College balance sheet, page 468). The receipt of assets in exchange for an annuity agreement would then be recorded in the annuity fund as follows:

| | | |
|---|---|---|
| Assets | xxxx | |
|    Annuities payable | | xxxx |
|    Fund balance | | xxxx |

As payments are made to the annuitant, the annuities payable account will be reduced by an amount that will leave a balance in the account equal to the present value of projected future payments.

## Plant Funds

The plant funds of a college or university are similar in some respects to a combination of the governmental account groups for general fixed assets and general long-term debt. They are also different from these account groups in one important respect—resources designated for the acquisition of plant assets are also included in these fund entities. As a result, transactions recorded in plant funds typically include a mixture of memo account-group–type entries and governmental-type fund entries. Interestingly enough, a college or university will generally have a number of separate plant funds.

The asset side of the balance sheet for the plant fund group (Exhibit 12–1) typically includes subdivisions for unexpended plant funds, funds for renewal and replacement, funds for retirement of indebtedness, and investment in plant. The credit side of the balance sheet includes these fund balances plus notes and mortgages payable. The balance sheet in Exhibit 12–1 illustrates the presentation of these items.

Plant fund assets will typically include investments of unexpended funds. Revenues earned from such investments should be *recorded only in the plant fund*. The following entry would be used to record such revenues:

| | | |
|---|---|---|
| Cash | xxxx | |
|    Investment income–restricted | | xxxx |

Investment income would then be shown in the plant fund section of the statement of changes in fund balances (see Exhibit 12–3).

Spendable assets flow into a plant fund either from external contributions or by transfer from current funds. Contributions from external sources are recorded directly in the plant fund as follows:

| | | |
|---|---|---|
| Cash or other spendable assets | xxxx | |
|     Unexpended fund balance | | xxxx |

Resources transferred to a plant fund from current funds require the following entries:

**Current Funds**

| | | |
|---|---|---|
| Nonmandatory transfers to plant fund | xxxx | |
|     Cash or other spendable assets | | xxxx |

**Plant Fund**

| | | |
|---|---|---|
| Cash or other spendable assets | xxxx | |
|     Unexpended fund balance | | xxxx |

When plant assets are purchased from current fund resources, expenditures would be debited in the current fund. The following entry should be recorded in the plant fund:

| | | |
|---|---|---|
| Long-term asset | xxxx | |
|     Net investment in plant | | xxxx |

If plant fund resources are used to acquire a long-term asset, that fact should be recorded in the plant fund as follows:

| | | |
|---|---|---|
| Unexpended plant fund balance | xxxx | |
|     Cash | | xxxx |
| Long-term asset | xxxx | |
|     Investment in plant | | xxxx |

## Agency Funds

Agency funds are defined as funds in the custody of the institution but not belonging to it.[11] The implication of this definition is that the institution never expects to own the assets of such funds. The college or university serves only as a depository or fiscal agent to handle resources belonging to student organizations, faculty committees, or other groups connected with the institution.

# ■ Financial Statements

In this section, we illustrate and describe statements for Model College that include more of the accounts typically found in the annual financial report for colleges and universities. The report should include:

11.  *College and University Business Administration*, p. 426.

1. Balance sheets for each fund group included in the accounting records. These are generally combined into one balance sheet similar in form to the one shown in Exhibit 12–1.

2. A statement of current fund revenues, expenditures, and other changes showing revenues by sources and expenditures by functional classifications. This statement may be presented in a form similar to that shown in Exhibit 12–2.

3. Statements of changes in fund balances for each fund group. These statements can be presented in a combined statement similar to the one shown in Exhibit 12–3.

4. Various supporting schedules, including a separate statement of revenues and expenditures for each auxiliary activity. A condensed supporting schedule showing income and expenditures for intercollegiate athletics is shown later in Exhibit 12–5.

These statements show that although the accounting records of colleges and universities are generally maintained on a fund-entity basis similar to that discussed in Chapter 3 for governmental units, some of the accounting practices used by these institutions are significantly different from those used for governmental units. These differences can be summarized as follows:

1. Fund entities carry different names to accommodate the operational characteristics of educational institutions.

2. The accounting records of colleges and universities place greater emphasis than governmental units do on reports for endowment fund entities that include nonspendable resources.

3. The plant fund combines liquid resources designated for the acquisition of plant assets along with the elements included in the two account groups used for governmental entities.

4. Less emphasis is placed on strictly enforced appropriation control in budgeting, and budgetary data are less likely to be shown in the published financial reports of colleges and universities than in reports for governmental units.

5. Auxiliary activities, roughly comparable to self-sustaining funds for governmental units, are generally accounted for on a *departmental rather than a fund-entity* basis. This arrangement, while requiring separately designated nominal accounts, does not require separate self-balancing accounting entities for resources associated with auxiliary activities.

6. Logically, as a quasi-nonprofit enterprise relying on user-based charges, more emphasis is placed on the matching of revenues and expenditures in the financial reports for colleges and universities than is the case in the governmental area.

7. While fund-entity accounting practices underlie college and university accounting procedures, adherence to it is less complete than in the governmental area.

**EXHIBIT 12–1.  Model College Balance Sheet—End of Fiscal Period**

| Assets | Current Year | Prior Year | Liabilities and Fund Balances | Current Year | Prior Year |
|---|---|---|---|---|---|
| **Current funds:** | | | **Current funds:** | | |
| Unrestricted: | | | Unrestricted: | | |
| Cash | $ 210,000 | $ 110,000 | Accounts payable | $ 125,000 | $ 100,000 |
| Investments | 450,000 | 360,000 | Accrued liabilities | 20,000 | 15,000 |
| Accounts receivable, less allowance of $18,000 both years | 228,000 | 175,000 | Students' deposits | 30,000 | 35,000 |
| Inventories, at lower of cost (first-in, first-out basis) or market | 90,000 | 80,000 | Due to other funds | 158,000 | 120,000 |
| Prepaid expenses and deferred charges | 28,000 | 20,000 | Deferred revenue | 30,000 | 20,000 |
| | | | Fund balance | 643,000 | 455,000 |
| Total unrestricted | 1,006,000 | 745,000 | Total unrestricted | 1,006,000 | 745,000 |
| Restricted: | | | Restricted: | | |
| Cash | 145,000 | 101,000 | Accounts payable | 14,000 | 5,000 |
| Investments | 175,000 | 165,000 | Fund balances | 446,000 | 421,000 |
| Accounts receivable, less allowance of $8,000 both years | 68,000 | 160,000 | | | |
| Unbilled charges | 72,000 | 0 | | | |
| Total restricted | 460,000 | 426,000 | Total restricted | 460,000 | 426,000 |
| Total current funds | $1,466,000 | $1,171,000 | Total current funds | $1,466,000 | $1,171,000 |
| **Loan funds:** | | | **Loan funds:** | | |
| Cash | 30,000 | 20,000 | Fund balances: | | |
| Investments | 100,000 | 100,000 | U.S. Government grants refundable | 50,000 | 33,000 |
| Loans to students, faculty, and staff, less allowance of $10,000 current year, $9,000 prior year | 550,000 | 382,000 | University funds: | | |
| Due from unrestricted current funds | 3,000 | 0 | Restricted | 483,000 | 369,000 |
| | | | Unrestricted | 150,000 | 100,000 |
| Total loan funds | $ 683,000 | $ 502,000 | Total loan funds | $ 683,000 | $ 502,000 |

**Endowment and similar funds:**

| | | |
|---|---:|---:|
| Cash | 100,000 | 101,000 |
| Investments | 13,900,000 | 11,800,000 |
| Total endowment and similar funds | $14,000,000 | $11,901,000 |

**Annuity and life income funds:**

Annuity funds:

| | | |
|---|---:|---:|
| Cash | 55,000 | 45,000 |
| Investments | 3,260,000 | 3,010,000 |
| Total annuity funds | 3,315,000 | 3,055,000 |

Life income funds:

| | | |
|---|---:|---:|
| Cash | $ 15,000 | 15,000 |
| Investments | 2,045,000 | 1,740,000 |
| Total life income funds | 2,060,000 | 1,755,000 |
| Total annuity and life income funds | $ 5,375,000 | $ 4,810,000 |

**Plant funds:**

Unexpended:

| | | |
|---|---:|---:|
| Cash | 275,000 | 410,000 |
| Investments | 1,285,000 | 1,590,000 |
| Due from unrestricted current funds | 150,000 | 120,000 |
| Total unexpended | 1,710,000 | 2,120,000 |

**Endowment and similar funds:**

Fund balances:

| | | |
|---|---:|---:|
| Endowment | 7,800,000 | 6,740,000 |
| Term endowment | 3,840,000 | 3,420,000 |
| Quasi endowment—unrestricted | 2,360,000 | 1,741,000 |
| Total endowment and similar funds | $14,000,000 | $11,901,000 |

**Annuity and life income funds:**

Annuity funds:

| | | |
|---|---:|---:|
| Annuities payable | 2,150,000 | 2,300,000 |
| Fund balances | 1,165,000 | 755,000 |
| Total annuity funds | 3,315,000 | 3,055,000 |

Life income funds:

| | | |
|---|---:|---:|
| Income payable | $ 5,000 | 5,000 |
| Fund balances | 2,055,000 | 1,750,000 |
| Total life income funds | 2,060,000 | 1,755,000 |
| Total annuity and life income funds | $ 5,375,000 | $ 4,810,000 |

**Plant funds:**

Unexpended:

| | | |
|---|---:|---:|
| Accounts payable | 10,000 | 0 |
| Notes payable | 100,000 | 0 |
| Bonds payable | 400,000 | 0 |
| Fund balances: | | |
| Restricted | 1,000,000 | 1,860,000 |
| Unrestricted | 200,000 | 260,000 |
| Total unexpended | 1,710,000 | 2,120,000 |

*exhibit continues*

**EXHIBIT 12–1.** Continued

| Assets | Current Year | Prior Year |
|---|---|---|
| Renewal and replacement: | | |
| Cash | 5,000 | 4,000 |
| Investments | 150,000 | 286,000 |
| Deposits with trustees | 100,000 | 90,000 |
| Due from unrestricted current funds | 5,000 | 0 |
| Total renewal and replacement | 260,000 | 380,000 |
| Retirement of indebtedness: | | |
| Cash | 50,000 | 40,000 |
| Deposits with trustees | 250,000 | 253,000 |
| Total retirement of indebtedness | 300,000 | 293,000 |
| Investment in plant: | | |
| Land | 500,000 | 500,000 |
| Land improvements | 1,000,000 | 1,110,000 |
| Buildings | 25,000,000 | 24,060,000 |
| Equipment | 15,000,000 | 14,200,000 |
| Library books | 100,000 | 80,000 |
| Total investment in plant | 41,600,000 | 39,950,000 |
| Total plant funds | $43,870,000 | $42,743,000 |
| Agency funds: | | |
| Cash | 50,000 | 70,000 |
| Investments | 60,000 | 20,000 |
| Total agency funds | $ 110,000 | 90,000 |

| Liabilities and Fund Balances | Current Year | Prior Year |
|---|---|---|
| Renewal and replacement: | | |
| Fund balances: | | |
| Restricted | 25,000 | 180,000 |
| Unrestricted | 235,000 | 200,000 |
| Total renewal and replacement | 260,000 | 380,000 |
| Retirement of indebtedness: | | |
| Fund balances: | | |
| Restricted | 185,000 | 125,000 |
| Unrestricted | 115,000 | 168,000 |
| Total retirement of indebtedness | 300,000 | 293,000 |
| Investment in plant: | | |
| Notes payable | 790,000 | 810,000 |
| Bonds payable | 2,200,000 | 2,400,000 |
| Mortgages payable | 400,000 | 200,000 |
| Net investment in plant | 38,210,000 | 36,540,000 |
| Total investment in plant | 41,600,000 | 39,950,000 |
| Total plant funds | $43,870,000 | $42,743,000 |
| Agency funds: | | |
| Deposits held in custody for others | 110,000 | 90,000 |
| Total agency funds | $ 110,000 | 90,000 |

Copyright 1973 by the American Institute of Certified Public Accountants, Inc. Used with permission.

**EXHIBIT 12-2.** Model College Statement of Current Funds, Revenues, Expenditures, and Other Changes—For Fiscal Period

| | Unrestricted | Current Year Restricted | Total | Prior Year Total |
|---|---|---|---|---|
| **Revenues:** | | | | |
| Educational and general: | | | | |
| Student tuition and fees | $2,600,000 | | $2,600,000 | $2,300,000 |
| Governmental appropriations | 1,300,000 | | 1,300,000 | 1,300,000 |
| Governmental grants and contracts | 35,000 | $ 425,000 | 460,000 | 595,000 |
| Gifts and private grants | 850,000 | 380,000 | 1,230,000 | 1,190,000 |
| Endowment income | 325,000 | 209,000 | 534,000 | 500,000 |
| Sales and services of educational departments | 90,000 | | 90,000 | 95,000 |
| Organized activities related to educational departments | 100,000 | | 100,000 | 100,000 |
| Other sources (if any) | | | | |
| Total educational and general | 5,300,000 | 1,014,000 | 6,314,000 | 6,080,000 |
| Auxiliary enterprises | 2,200,000 | | 2,200,000 | 2,100,000 |
| Expired term endowment | 40,000 | | 40,000 | |
| Total revenues | 7,540,000 | 1,014,000 | 8,554,000 | 8,180,000 |
| **Expenditures and mandatory transfers:** | | | | |
| Educational and general: | | | | |
| Instruction and departmental research | 2,820,000 | 300,000 | 3,120,000 | 2,950,000 |
| Organized activities related to educational departments | 140,000 | 189,000 | 329,000 | 350,000 |
| Sponsored research | | 400,000 | 400,000 | 500,000 |
| Other separately budgeted research | 100,000 | | 100,000 | 150,000 |
| Other sponsored programs | | 25,000 | 25,000 | 50,000 |
| Extension and public service | 130,000 | | 130,000 | 125,000 |
| Libraries | 250,000 | | 250,000 | 225,000 |
| Student services | 200,000 | | 200,000 | 195,000 |
| Operation and maintenance of plant | 220,000 | | 220,000 | 200,000 |
| General administration | 200,000 | | 200,000 | 195,000 |
| General institutional expense | 250,000 | | 250,000 | 250,000 |
| Student aid | 90,000 | 100,000 | 190,000 | 180,000 |
| Educational and general expenditures | 4,400,000 | 1,014,000 | 5,414,000 | 5,370,000 |
| Mandatory transfers for: | | | | |
| Principal and interest | 90,000 | | 90,000 | 50,000 |
| Renewals and replacements | 100,000 | | 100,000 | 80,000 |
| Loan fund matching grant | 2,000 | | 2,000 | |
| Total educational and general | 4,592,000 | 1,014,000 | 5,606,000 | 5,500,000 |
| **Auxiliary enterprises:** | | | | |
| Expenditures | 1,830,000 | | 1,830,000 | 1,730,000 |
| Mandatory transfers for: | | | | |
| Principal and interest | 250,000 | | 250,000 | 250,000 |
| Renewals and replacements | 70,000 | | 70,000 | 70,000 |
| Total auxiliary enterprises | 2,150,000 | | 2,150,000 | 2,050,000 |
| Total expenditures and mandatory transfers | 6,742,000 | 1,014,000 | 7,756,000 | 7,550,000 |
| **Other transfers and additions/(deductions):** | | | | |
| Excess of restricted receipts over transfers to revenues | | 45,000 | 45,000 | 40,000 |
| Refunded to grantors | | (20,000) | (20,000) | |
| Unrestricted gifts allocated to other funds | (650,000) | | (650,000) | (510,000) |
| Portion of quasi-endowment gains appropriated | 40,000 | | 40,000 | |
| Net increase in fund balances | $ 188,000 | $ 25,000 | $ 213,000 | $ 160,000 |

**EXHIBIT 12–3.** Model College Statement of Changes in Fund Balances—for Fiscal Period

| | Current Funds | |
| --- | --- | --- |
| | Unrestricted | Restricted |
| Revenues and other additions: | | |
| Educational and general revenues | $ 5,300,000 | |
| Auxiliary enterprise revenues | 2,200,000 | |
| Expired term endowment revenues | 40,000 | |
| Expired term endowment—restricted | | |
| Gifts and bequests—restricted | | $ 370,000 |
| Grants and contracts—restricted | | 500,000 |
| Governmental appropriations—restricted | | |
| Investment income—restricted | | 224,000 |
| Realized gains on investments—unrestricted | | |
| Realized gains on investments—restricted | | |
| Interest on loans receivable | | |
| U.S. government advances | | |
| Expended for plant facilities (including $100,000 charged to current funds expenditures) | | |
| Retirement of indebtedness | | |
| Accrued interest on sale of bonds | | |
| Matured annuity and life income funds restricted to endowment | | |
| Total revenue & other additions | $ 7,540,000 | $1,094,000 |
| Expenditures and other deductions: | | |
| Educational and general expenditures | 4,400,000 | 1,014,000 |
| Auxiliary enterprises expenditures | 1,830,000 | |
| Indirect costs recovered | | 35,000 |
| Refunded to grantors | | 20,000 |
| Loan cancellations and write-offs | | |
| Administrative and collection costs | | |
| Adjustment of actuarial liability for annuities payable | | |
| Expended for plant facilities (including noncapitalized expenditures of $50,000) | | |
| Retirement of indebtedness | | |
| Interest on indebtedness | | |
| Disposal of plant facilities | | |
| Expired term endowments ($40,000 unrestricted, $50,000 restricted to plant) | | |
| Matured annuity and life income funds restricted to endowment | | |
| Total expenditures and other deductions | $ 6,230,000 | $1,069,000 |
| Transfers among funds—additions/(deductions): | | |
| Mandatory: | | |
| Principal and interest | (340,000) | |
| Renewals and replacements | (170,000) | |
| Loan fund matching grant | (2,000) | |
| Unrestricted gifts allocated | (650,000) | |
| Portion of unrestricted quasi-endowment funds investment gains appropriated | 40,000 | |
| Total transfers | (1,122,000) | |
| Net increase/(decrease) for the year | 188,000 | 25,000 |
| Fund balance at beginning of year | 455,000 | 421,000 |
| Fund balance at end of year | $ 643,000 | $ 446,000 |

| Loan Funds | Endowment and Similar Funds | Annuity and Life Income Funds | Plant Funds | | | |
|---|---|---|---|---|---|---|
| | | | Unexpended | Renewal and Replacement | Retirement of Indebtedness | Investment in Plant |
| 100,000 | 1,500,000 | 800,000 | 50,000 115,000 | | 65,000 | 15,000 |
| 12,000 | 10,000 | | 50,000 5,000 | 5,000 | 5,000 | |
| 4,000 | 109,000 50,000 | | 10,000 | 5,000 | 5,000 | |
| 7,000 | | | | | | |
| 18,000 | | | | | | |
| | | | | | | 1,550,000 |
| | | | | | | 220,000 |
| | | | | | 3,000 | |
| | 10,000 | | | | | |
| $141,000 | $ 1,679,000 | $ 800,000 | $ 230,000 | $ 10,000 | $ 78,000 | $ 1,785,000 |
| 10,000 | | | | | | |
| 1,000 | | | | | 1,000 | |
| 1,000 | | | | | | |
| | | 75,000 | | | | |
| | | | 1,200,000 | 300,000 | 220,000 | |
| | | | | | 190,000 | |
| | | | | | | 115,000 |
| | 90,000 | | | | | |
| | | 10,000 | | | | |
| $ 12,000 | $ 90,000 | $ 85,000 | $1,200,000 | $ 300,000 | $ 411,000 | $ 115,000 |
| | | | | | 340,000 | |
| | | | | 170,000 | | |
| 2,000 | | | | | | |
| 50,000 | 550,000 | | 50,000 | | | |
| | (40,000) | | | | | |
| $ 52,000 | $ 510,000 | | $ 50,000 | $ 170,000 | $ 340,000 | |
| 181,000 | 2,099,000 | 715,000 | (920,000) | (120,000) | 7,000 | 1,670,000 |
| 502,000 | 11,901,000 | 2,505,000 | 2,120,000 | 380,000 | 293,000 | 36,540,000 |
| $683,000 | $14,000,000 | $3,220,000 | $1,200,000 | $ 260,000 | $ 300,000 | $38,210,000 |

# ■ Typical Transactions Described and Recorded

The operating cycle for colleges and universities routinely includes the following types of transactions:

1. realization of current fund revenues
2. recognition of current fund expenditures
3. realization of other resource inflows
4. recognition of nonoperating expenditures
5. transfers between funds
6. auxiliary activity transactions.

In this section, we describe a series of assumed transactions for Illustration University. We shall then record those transactions in a transactions worksheet using conventional accounting procedures to show how they relate to the various funds and the financial statements.

## Realization of Current Fund Revenues

Cash and other resource receipts realized by a college or university fall into two general categories:

1. receipts available for operating purposes
2. nonoperating receipts.

Cash and other resources realized by a college or university to be used for direct operational outlays are subdivided into unrestricted and restricted revenues. Resources available for general operating purposes at the discretion of management are characterized as unrestricted revenues. As unrestricted current fund resources are received, the asset account is debited and the appropriate revenue account is credited. Resources available for operating purposes within *externally imposed* restrictions are credited to the restricted funds fund balance account. Typical educational and general revenue classifications include amounts received from[12]

1. student tuition and fees (gross amount charged less refunds for classes dropped)
2. governmental appropriations
3. governmental grants and contracts
4. gifts and private grants
5. endowment income
6. sales and services of educational departments
7. organized activities related to educational departments
8. other sources.

12. *Audits of Colleges and Universities,* pp. 20–23.

To illustrate the realization of current fund revenues, we assume that Illustration University (see transactions worksheet) realizes revenue from the following sources:

1. unrestricted revenues received from
   tuition and fees, $8,000,000
   governmental appropriations, $3,000,000
   gifts, $1,000,000
   other sources, $200,000

2. endowment income, $1,500,000, including $200,000 for specifically designated instruction and research

3. auxiliary enterprises, $2,000,000.

You will find the realization of these revenues reflected in journal entry numbers 1, 2, and 3 in the transactions worksheet for Illustration University (see Exhibit 12–4).

## Recognition of Current Fund Expenditures

As expenditures are made from general operating resources, the appropriate expenditure accounts are debited and the offsetting credits are recorded in the appropriate asset or liability accounts. Educational and general expenditures are normally subdivided into the following functional classifications:[13]

1. instruction and departmental research
2. organized activities related to educational departments
3. sponsored research
4. other separately budgeted research
5. other sponsored programs
6. extension and public service
7. libraries
8. student services
9. operation and maintenance of plant
10. general administration
11. general institutional expense
12. student aid.

In addition to the revenue and expenditure categories listed here, the unrestricted current fund normally includes revenues and expenditures for auxiliary enterprises, as well as transfers to and from other funds. The preceding classifications, including those for transfers among the funds, are included in Exhibit 12–2.

For the purpose of illustrating the accounting procedures followed in recording expenditures, we shall assume that Illustration University incurs expenditures as follows:

13. Ibid., pp. 27–29.

**EXHIBIT 12–4.** Illustration University Transactions Worksheet for Fiscal Period (Conventional Accounting Procedures)

| | Beginning Balances | |
|---|---:|---:|
| Unrestricted current funds | | |
| Cash | 100,000 | |
| Investments | 300,000 | |
| Accounts receivable | 50,000 | |
| Vouchers payable | | 50,000 |
| Fund balance | | 400,000 |
| Totals—unrestricted current funds | 450,000 | 450,000 |
| Restricted current funds | | |
| Cash | 60,000 | |
| Investments | 80,000 | |
| Vouchers payable | | 10,000 |
| Fund balance | | 130,000 |
| Totals—restricted current funds | 140,000 | 140,000 |
| Totals for current funds | 590,000 | 590,000 |
| *Loan Funds* | | |
| Cash | 20,000 | |
| Investments | 100,000 | |
| Loans to students | 300,000 | |
| Fund balance | | 420,000 |
| Totals for loan funds | 420,000 | 420,000 |
| *Endowment Funds* | | |
| Cash | 50,000 | |
| Investments | 15,000,000 | |
| Fund balances | | |
| Endowment | | 12,050,000 |
| Quasi endowment | | 3,000,000 |
| Available for distribution | | |
| Totals—endowment funds | 15,050,000 | 15,050,000 |
| *Annuity Funds* | | |
| Cash | 40,000 | |
| Investments | 4,000,000 | |
| Annuities payable | | 2,500,000 |
| Fund balance | | 1,540,000 |
| Totals—annuity fund | 4,040,000 | 4,040,000 |

| | | Transactions | | Statement of Revenues and Expenditures | Balance Sheet | |
|---|---|---|---|---|---|---|
| (1) | 12,200,000 | (4) | 12,850,000 | | 380,000 | |
| (2) | 1,300,000 | (9) | 70,000 | | | |
| (3) | 2,000,000 | (14) | 700,000 | | | |
| | | (15) | 1,600,000 | | | |
| | | | | | 300,000 | |
| | | | | | 50,000 | |
| | | | | | | 50,000 |
| | | (21) | 280,000 | | | 680,000 |
| | | | | | 730,000 | 730,000 |
| (16) | 107,000 | (17) | 300,000 | | 67,000 | |
| (2) | 200,000 | | | | | |
| | | | | | 80,000 | |
| (17) | 100,000 | (2) | 200,000 | | | 10,000 |
| (17) | 200,000 | (16) | 107,000 | | | 137,000 |
| | | | | | 147,000 | 147,000 |
| | | | | | 877,000 | 877,000 |

**Loan Funds**

| | | | | | |
|---|---|---|---|---|---|
| (5) | 400,000 | (18) | 390,000 | 30,000 | |
| (18) | 60,000 | | | 160,000 | |
| (18) | 330,000 | (5) | 275,000 | 355,000 | |
| | | (5) | 125,000 | | 545,000 |
| | | | | 545,000 | 545,000 |

**Endowment Funds**

| | | | | | |
|---|---|---|---|---|---|
| (2) | 1,500,000 | (2) | 1,500,000 | 100,000 | |
| (14) | 500,000 | (19) | 450,000 | | |
| (6) | 2,000,000 | | | 17,450,000 | |
| (19) | 450,000 | | | | |
| | | (6) | 2,000,000 | | 14,050,000 |
| | | (14) | 500,000 | | 3,500,000 |
| (2) | 1,500,000 | (2) | 1,500,000 | | |
| | | | | 17,550,000 | 17,550,000 |

**Annuity Funds**

| | | | | | |
|---|---|---|---|---|---|
| (7) | 320,000 | (11) | 250,000 | 110,000 | |
| | | | | 4,000,000 | |
| (11) | 250,000 | (7) | 200,000 | | 2,450,000 |
| | | (7) | 120,000 | | 1,660,000 |
| | | | | 4,110,000 | 4,110,000 |

*exhibit continues*

**EXHIBIT 12–4.**    Continued

| | | *Beginning Balances* |
|---|---:|---:|
| *Plant Funds* | | |
| Unexpended plant funds | | |
|   Cash | 150,000 | |
|   Investments | 2,000,000 | |
|   Notes payable | | 100,000 |
|   Bonds payable | | 500,000 |
|   Fund balance | | 1,550,000 |
| Total—unexpended plant funds | 2,150,000 | 2,150,000 |
| For retirement of indebtedness | | |
|   Cash | 50,000 | |
|   Deposits with trustees | 300,000 | |
|   Fund balance | | 350,000 |
| Totals for retirement of indebtedness | 350,000 | 350,000 |
| Investment in plant | | |
|   Land | 500,000 | |
|   Buildings | 20,000,000 | |
|   Equipment | 12,000,000 | |
|   Library books | 400,000 | |
|   Bonds payable | | 2,000,000 |
|   Net investment in plant | | 30,900,000 |
| Totals—investment in plant | 32,900,000 | 32,900,000 |
| Totals for plant funds | 35,400,000 | 35,400,000 |
| *Agency Funds* | | |
|   Cash | 40,000 | |
|   Investments | 80,000 | |
|   Deposits held for others | | 120,000 |
| Totals—agency funds | 120,000 | 120,000 |

*Unrestricted Current Funds—Nominal Accounts*

Educational and general revenues
  Tuition and fees
  Governmental appropriations
  Gifts
  Endowment income
  Other sources
Auxiliary activities

| Transactions | | | | Statement of Revenues and Expenditures | Balance Sheet | |
|---|---|---|---|---|---|---|

### Plant Funds

| | | | | | | |
|---|---|---|---|---|---|---|
| (8) | 1,000,000 | (12) | 1,100,000 | | 350,000 | |
| (9) | 100,000 | | | | | |
| (14) | 200,000 | | | | | |
| | | | | | 2,000,000 | |
| | | | | | | 100,000 |
| | | | | | | 500,000 |
| (12) | 1,100,000 | (8) | 1,000,000 | | | 1,750,000 |
| | | (9) | 100,000 | | | |
| | | (14) | 200,000 | | | |
| | | | | | 2,350,000 | 2,350,000 |
| | | | | | | |
| (9) | 70,000 | (20) | 100,000 | | 20,000 | |
| (20) | 100,000 | (13) | 150,000 | | 250,000 | |
| (13) | 150,000 | (9) | 70,000 | | | 270,000 |
| | | | | | 270,000 | 270,000 |
| | | | | | | |
| | | | | | 500,000 | |
| (12) | 800,000 | | | | 20,800,000 | |
| (12) | 300,000 | | | | 12,300,000 | |
| (4) | 300,000 | | | | 700,000 | |
| (13) | 100,000 | | | | | 1,900,000 |
| | | (12) | 1,100,000 | | | 32,400,000 |
| | | (13) | 100,000 | | | |
| | | (4) | 300,000 | | | |
| | | | | | 34,300,000 | 34,300,000 |
| | | | | | 36,920,000 | 36,920,000 |

### Agency Funds

| | | | | | | |
|---|---|---|---|---|---|---|
| (10) | 7,000 | | | | 47,000 | |
| | | | | | 80,000 | |
| | | (10) | 7,000 | | | 127,000 |
| | | | | | 127,000 | 127,000 |

### Unrestricted Current Funds—Nominal Accounts

| | | | | | |
|---|---|---|---|---|---|
| | | (1) | 8,000,000 | 8,000,000 | |
| | | (1) | 3,000,000 | 3,000,000 | |
| | | (1) | 1,000,000 | 1,000,000 | |
| | | (2) | 1,300,000 | 1,300,000 | |
| | | (1) | 200,000 | 200,000 | |
| | | (3) | 2,000,000 | 2,000,000 | |

*exhibit continues*

**EXHIBIT 12–4.** Continued

*Beginning Balances*

Educational and general expenditures
   Instruction and research
   Libraries
   Student services
   Plant operations
   General administration
   Other expenditures
Mandatory transfers
   Principal and interest
Auxiliary activities
Other transfers
   To plant fund
   To endowment fund
   To fund balance
Totals—revenues and expenditures
Excess of revenues over expenditures
Totals

*Restricted Current Funds—Nominal Accounts*

Educational and general revenue
   Endowment income
   Gifts and grants
   Other revenues
Educational and general expenditures
   Instruction and research
   Student aid
Transfer to fund balance
Totals

      Instruction and research, $11,000,000

      Libraries (for books), $300,000

      Student services, $200,000

      Plant operations, $1,000,000

      General administration, $300,000

      Other expenditures, $50,000.

You will find these expenditures recorded as journal entry number 4 in the transactions worksheet for Illustration University (see Exhibit 12–4). Although the expenditure transaction is recorded as a credit to cash in our illustration, in actual practice it would often go through a vouchers payable account.

| | Transactions | Statement of Revenues and Expenditures | | Balance Sheet |
|---|---|---|---|---|
| (4) | 11,000,000 | 11,000,000 | | |
| (4) | 300,000 | 300,000 | | |
| (4) | 200,000 | 200,000 | | |
| (4) | 1,000,000 | 1,000,000 | | |
| (4) | 300,000 | 300,000 | | |
| (4) | 50,000 | 50,000 | | |
| (9) | 70,000 | 70,000 | | |
| (15) | 1,600,000 | 1,600,000 | | |
| (14) | 200,000 | 200,000 | | |
| (14) | 500,000 | 500,000 | | |
| (21) | 280,000 | | | |
| | | 15,220,000 | 15,500,000 | |
| | | 280,000 | | |
| | | 15,500,000 | 15,500,000 | |

*Restricted Current Funds—Nominal Accounts*

| | | | | | |
|---|---|---|---|---|---|
| | | (17) | 200,000 | | 200,000 |
| | | (17) | 100,000 | | 100,000 |
| (17) | 200,000 | | | 200,000 | |
| (17) | 100,000 | | | 100,000 | |
| | | | | 300,000 | 300,000 |

Observe that the expenditures for long-term assets (libraries) are recorded as expenditures in the current fund and as additions to plant assets in the plant fund.

## Realization of Other Resource Inflows

Nonoperating receipts include cash and other property *externally designated* to be added to the fund balance accounts of nonoperating funds. The receipt of such resources, restricted by the donor or granting agency, is added to the fund balance of the designated fund. Receipts of this type are recorded directly in plant funds, endowment funds, or other nonoperating funds. The receipt of these resources is recorded by debiting the appropriate asset account and crediting the appropriate fund balance account.

To illustrate the accounting procedures followed in recognizing the realization of nonoperating inflows, we assume that Illustration University realizes the following resources designated for specified nonoperating purposes. These transactions are recorded in Exhibit 12–4 (see entry numbers with each transaction):

The loan fund receives $400,000 including loan repayments amounting to $275,000 and additional funds in the amount of $125,000 (see entry 5).

Securities having a fair value of $2,000,000 were received as endowment resources (see entry 6).

Annuity funds amounting to $320,000 were received. The annuity payable is calculated to be $200,000 (see entry 7).

Cash amounting to $1,000,000 designated to be used for plant construction was received (see entry 8).

Plant funds also received $170,000, composed of revenue on investments held in the fund in the amount of $100,000 and $70,000 as a mandatory transfer from the unrestricted current fund to cover principal and interest payments on plant fund indebtedness (see entry 9).

Agency funds realized additional cash from depositors in the amount of $7,000 (see entry 10).

## Recognition of Nonoperating Expenditures

In the preceding section, we dealt with the realization of nonoperating resource inflows. As these resources are received, they are recorded in their respective funds. As they are used, that fact must also be recorded in the appropriate funds. The following assumed transactions involving nonoperating expenditures are reflected in the transactions worksheet for Illustration University:

From annuity fund resources $250,000 was paid to meet the period obligations for annuities payable (see entry 11).

Construction was completed on buildings in the amount of $800,000, and equipment was purchased amounting to $300,000 from plant fund resources (see entry 12).

The university retired $100,000 worth of plant fund bonds and paid $50,000 in interest on bonds outstanding (see entry 13).

## Transfers Between Funds

Transfers between funds may be characterized as either mandatory or nonmandatory. *Mandatory transfers* are transfers required by contract or by external directive. In our illustration, we find mandatory transfers covering principal and interest on plant fund bonds ($70,000) and renewals and replacements ($100,000) recorded as part of entry 9.

Transfers made by the action of management rather than in response to external requirements are characterized as *nonmandatory transfers*. For example, within this classification fall resources designated to be transferred from unrestricted funds to specified nonoperating funds by the governing board of an institution. Because these allocations are not required by a donor or outside agency, they should be labeled as nonmandatory or other transfers. In our illustration, $700,000 of resources transferred from unrestricted funds to plant funds ($200,000) and endowment funds ($500,000) are reflected as other transfers in entry 14.

## Auxiliary Activity Transactions

Colleges and universities typically carry on a number of activities not directly related to their primary educational function. Dormitories, intercollegiate athletics, and bookstores are examples of such auxiliary activities.

Because it is important to know the extent to which these activities support themselves or how much they contribute to the educational function of the college or university, separate revenue and expenditure accounts are generally maintained for each of these activities. The long-term assets and long-term obligations associated with these activities may be recorded in a separate fund, but usually they are included in the plant fund accounts. Current assets and obligations may also be carried in a separate balance sheet for auxiliary funds, but they are generally included in the balance sheet for the current funds group.

A statement of assumed income and expenditures for intercollegiate athletics, one form of auxiliary activity, is shown in Exhibit 12–5. The revenue and expenditure totals in this statement reflect the revenue from auxiliary services (see entry 3) and expenditures (see entry 15) for auxiliary services shown in the worksheet.

Other entries included in the transactions worksheet but not described previously are as follow:

Entry 16 —Receipt of restricted educational and general revenue in the amount of $107,000. This included gifts and grants in the amount of $100,000.

Entry 17 —Payment of educational and general expenditures from restricted funds in the amount of $300,000 ($200,000 for instruction and research and $100,000 for student aid).

Entry 18 —Loan funds amounting to $60,000 are invested. Loans are also made to students from this fund in the amount of $330,000.

Entry 19 —Endowment cash amounting to $450,000 is invested.

Entry 20 —Plant fund cash, restricted to being used to retire debt of the fund amounting to $100,000, is deposited with the trustees.

Entry 21 —Excess of unrestricted revenues over expenditures amounting to $280,000 is transferred to unrestricted fund balance account.

After recording the described transactions as illustrated in Exhibit 12–4, formal financial statements can be prepared for Illustration University from data shown in the last four columns of the worksheet.

**EXHIBIT 12–5.** Model College Intercollegiate Athletics Statement of Income and Expenditures—For Fiscal Period

| | | |
|---|---:|---:|
| Income | | |
| Football | $xxx | |
| Basketball | xxx | |
| Etc. | xxx | $2,000,000 |
| Expenditures | | |
| Administration | xxx | |
| Publicity | xxx | |
| Maintenance of plant | xxx | |
| Football | xxx | |
| Basketball | xxx | |
| Etc. | xxx | 1,600,000 |
| Excess of income over expenditures | | $ 400,000 |

# ■ Provisions of FASB 93

As we explained earlier, implementation of the provisions of FASB 93 will significantly affect the accounting and reporting procedures followed by colleges and universities. Beginning in 1991, private institutions will be required to follow full accrual-based accounting procedures including the capitalization of long-lived assets and the recognition of depreciation of them. The NACUBO survey (see page 452) suggests that many state-owned institutions may also choose to follow those procedures. For that reason, we now illustrate how the preceding transactions should be recorded in a transactions worksheet (see Exhibit 12–6) when following FASB 93 accounting procedures.

FASB 93, while requiring use of the accrual basis of accounting, does not spell out the specific recording and reporting procedures to be used. Currently, two types of nonprofit organizations (hospitals and health and welfare organizations) have recording and reporting procedures that use the accrual basis of accounting within the framework of a fund accounting system. Because of operating similarities, the author favors use of an adaptation of the hospital system.[14] We use that system with the following assumptions relating to depreciation and asset lives.

Accumulated depreciation for assets held at the beginning of the period is assumed to be as follows:

| | |
|---|---:|
| Buildings | $8,000,000 |
| Equipment | 4,000,000 |
| Library books | 100,000 |

---

14. See Emerson O. Henke, and Lucian G. Conway, "A Recommended Reporting Format for College and University Financial Statements," *Accounting Horizons* (June 1989): 49–65.

**EXHIBIT 12–6.** Illustration University Transactions Worksheet—For Fiscal Period (FASB 93-Adapted Accounting Procedures)

| Unrestricted Current Funds | Beginning Balances | Transactions (debits) | | Transactions (credits) | | Balance Sheet |
|---|---|---|---|---|---|---|
| Cash | 100,000 | (1)<br>(2)<br>(3)<br>(17) | 12,200,000<br>1,300,000<br>2,000,000<br>300,000 | (17)<br>(4)<br>(9)<br>(13)<br>(15)<br>(14) | 300,000<br>12,850,000<br>70,000<br>150,000<br>1,600,000<br>700,000 | 230,000 |
| Investments | 3,300,000 | | | | | 3,300,000 |
| Accounts receivable | 50,000 | | | | | 50,000 |
| Vouchers payable | 50,000 | | | | | 50,000 |
| Land | 500,000 | | | | | 500,000 |
| Buildings | 20,000,000 | (12) | 800,000 | | | 20,800,000 |
| Accumulated depreciation | 8,000,000 | | | (12) | 832,000* | 8,832,000 |
| Equipment | 12,000,000 | (12) | 300,000 | | | 12,300,000 |
| Accumulated depreciation | 4,000,000 | | | (12) | 1,230,000* | 5,230,000 |
| Library books | 400,000 | (4) | 300,000 | | | 700,000 |
| Accumulated depreciation | 100,000 | | | (14) | 70,000* | 170,000 |
| Plant acquisition fund | | (14) | 200,000 | | | 200,000 |
| Quasi-endowment fund— cash | | (14) | 500,000 | (19) | 450,000 | 50,000 |
| Quasi-endowment fund investments | | (19) | 450,000 | | | 450,000 |
| Notes payable | 100,000 | (9) | 50,000 | | | 50,000 |
| Bonds payable | 2,500,000 | (13) | 100,000 | | | 2,400,000 |
| Fund balance | 21,600,000 | (21) | 852,000 | (12) | 1,100,000 | 21,848,000 |
| Total—unrestricted current fund | 36,350,000 | | 36,350,000 | | | 38,580,000 |
| | 36,350,000 | | | | | 38,580,000 |

*exhibit continues*

**EXHIBIT 12–6.** Continued

| | Beginning Balances | Transactions (Dr) | Transactions (Cr) | Balance Sheet |
|---|---|---|---|---|
| ***Restricted Current Funds*** | | | | |
| Cash | 60,000 | (2) 200,000   (16) 107,000 | (17) 300,000 | 67,000 |
| Investments | 80,000 | | | 80,000 |
| Vouchers payable | 10,000 | | | 10,000 |
| Fund balance | 130,000 | (17) 300,000 | (2) 200,000   107,000 | 137,000 |
| Totals—restricted current funds | 140,000 | | | 147,000   147,000 |
| ***Loan Funds*** | | | | |
| Cash | 20,000 | (5) 400,000 | (18) 390,000 | 30,000 |
| Investments | 100,000 | (18) 60,000 | | 160,000 |
| Loans to students | 300,000 | (18) 330,000 | (5) 275,000 | 355,000 |
| Fund balance | 420,000 | | (5) 125,000 | 545,000 |
| Totals for loan funds | 420,000 | | | 545,000   545,000 |
| ***Endowment Funds*** | | | | |
| Cash | 50,000 | | | 50,000 |
| Investments | 12,000,000 | (6) 2,000,000 | | 14,000,000 |
| Fund balance | 12,050,000 | | (6) 2,000,000 | 14,050,000 |
| Totals—endowment funds | 12,050,000 | | | 14,050,000   14,050,000 |
| ***Annuity Funds*** | | | | |
| Cash | 40,000 | (7) 320,000 | (11) 250,000 | 110,000 |
| Investments | 4,000,000 | (11) 250,000 | (7) 200,000 | 4,000,000 |
| Annuities payable | 2,500,000 | | (7) 120,000 | 2,450,000 |
| Fund balance | 1,540,000 | | | 1,660,000 |
| Totals—annuity fund | 4,040,000 | | | 4,110,000   4,110,000 |
| ***Plant Funds*** | | | | |
| Cash | 200,000 | (8) 1,000,000   (9) 100,000 | (12) 1,100,000   (20) 100,000 | 100,000 |
| Investments | 2,000,000 | | | 2,000,000 |
| Deposits with trustees | 300,000 | (20) 100,000 | | 400,000 |
| Fund balance | 2,500,000 | (12) 1,100,000 | (8) 1,000,000   (9) 100,000 | 2,500,000 |
| Totals for plant funds | 2,500,000 | | | 2,500,000   2,500,000 |

| | Beginning Balances | Transactions | | Balance Sheet |
|---|---|---|---|---|
| **Restricted Current Funds** | | | | |
| **Agency Funds** | | | | |
| Cash | 40,000 | (10) | 7,000 | 47,000 |
| Investments | 80,000 | | | 80,000 |
| Deposits held for others | 120,000 | (10) | 7,000 | 127,000 |
| Totals—agency funds | 120,000 | | | 127,000 |
| | | | | 127,000 |
| | | | | 127,000 |
| **Unrestricted Current Funds—Nominal Accounts** | | | | |
| Educational and general revenues | | | | |
| Tuition and fees | | (1) | 8,000,000 | |
| Governmental appropriations | | (1) | 3,000,000 | |
| Gifts | | (1) | 1,000,000 | |
| Endowment income | | (2) | 1,300,000 | |
| Other sources | | (1) | 200,000 | |
| Auxiliary activities | | (3) | 2,000,000 | |
| | | (15) | 1,600,000 | |
| Educational and general expenses | | | | |
| Instruction and research | | (17) | 200,000 | |
| | | (4) | 11,000,000 | |
| Student services | | (17) | 100,000 | |
| | | (4) | 200,000 | |
| Plant operations | | (4) | 1,000,000 | |
| | | | 2,062,000* | |
| General administration | | (4) | 300,000 | |
| Depreciation of library | | | 70,000* | |
| Interest expense | | (9) | 20,000 | |
| | | (13) | 50,000 | |
| | | (4) | 50,000 | |
| Other expenses | | | | |
| Excess of expenses over revenues | | (21) | 852,000 | |
| Revenue from restricted funds | | (17) | 300,000 | |

*Entry to record depreciation.

Depreciation for the reporting period is assumed to be as follows:

| | |
|---|---|
| Buildings | 4% |
| Equipment | 10% |
| Library books | 10% |

A full year's depreciation shall be recognized in the period of acquisition. We assume that the fiscal year is such that there are no accrued or prepaid revenues or expenses at the end of the period. We also assume that auxiliary activities have been accounted for on the full accrual basis. In Exhibit 12–6, transaction 9, the $70,000 mandatory transfer is assumed to be made up of $50,000 payment on notes payable and $20,000 interest expense. In transaction 19, the endowment funds invested are assumed to be those set aside for that purpose by management (see transaction 14).

The balance sheet and operating statement for Illustration University based on the two transactions worksheets (Exhibit 12–4 uses conventional accounting procedures; Exhibit 12–6 uses FASB 93-adapted accounting procedures) are shown in Exhibits 12–7, 12–8, 12–9, and 12–10. Observe that the operating statement prepared from the FASB 93-adapted worksheet includes a lower section (below data relating to continuing operations) that reflects restricted resource inflows, which have been conventionally reflected only in the statement of changes in fund balances.[15]

# ■ Ethical Considerations Associated with College and University Accounting Practices

Dr. Goodfellow, president of Waverly University, is discussing the school's end-of-period financial statements with Mr. Scheme, the university controller. Dr. Goodfellow has seen a projection of an anticipated excess of revenues over expenditures and transfers in the amount of $2,000,000. The president plans to recommend an increase in the tuition rate to the University Board of Trustees. He suggests to the controller that such an operating result is likely to create problems with some of the university's constituency who may feel that tuition charges are already too high. Mr. Scheme suggests that under conventional accounting procedures there are at least two ways to reduce the projected excess. One possibility is to purchase more long-term assets from current fund resources. Because such purchases would be charged to expenditures, the excess would be reduced. Another possibility is to ask the Board of Trustees to approve a nonmandatory transfer of $1,000,000 from current fund resources to quasi endowment. Consider the ethical issues associated with either action.

# ■ Summary

We began our discussion of accounting for colleges and universities by comparing their accounting practices with those followed by governmental entities. We observed that

15. For further discussion of the logic underlying this presentation, see "A Recommended Reporting Format for College and University Financial Statements," *Accounting Horizons* (June 1989): 49–65.

**EXHIBIT 12-7.** Illustration University Balance Sheet—End of Fiscal Period (Conventional Accounting Procedures)

| Assets | | Liabilities and Fund Balances | |
|---|---|---|---|
| **Current Funds—Unrestricted** | | | |
| Cash | $ 380,000 | Vouchers payable | $ 50,000 |
| Investments | 300,000 | | |
| Accounts receivable | 50,000 | Fund balance | 680,000 |
| Total | $ 730,000 | Total | $ 730,000 |
| **Current Funds—Restricted** | | | |
| Cash | $ 67,000 | Vouchers payable | $ 10,000 |
| Investments | 80,000 | Fund balance | 137,000 |
| Total | $ 147,000 | Total | $ 147,000 |
| Total current funds | $ 877,000 | Total current funds | $ 877,000 |
| **Loan Funds** | | | |
| Cash | $ 30,000 | | |
| Investments | 160,000 | | |
| Loans to students | 355,000 | Fund balance | $ 545,000 |
| Total | $ 545,000 | Total | $ 545,000 |
| **Endowment Funds** | | | |
| Cash | $ 100,000 | Fund balance—endowment | $14,050,000 |
| Investments | 17,450,000 | Fund balance—quasi endowment | 3,500,000 |
| Total | $17,550,000 | Total | $17,550,000 |
| **Annuity Funds** | | | |
| Cash | $ 110,000 | Annuity payable | $ 2,450,000 |
| Investments | 4,000,000 | Fund balance | 1,660,000 |
| Total | $ 4,110,000 | Total | $ 4,110,000 |
| **Plant Funds—Unexpended** | | | |
| Cash | $ 350,000 | Notes payable | $ 100,000 |
| Investments | 2,000,000 | Bonds payable | 500,000 |
| | | Fund balance | 1,750,000 |
| Total | $ 2,350,000 | Total | $ 2,350,000 |
| **For Retirement of Indebtedness** | | | |
| Cash | $ 20,000 | | |
| Deposit with trustees | 250,000 | Fund balance | $ 270,000 |
| Total | $ 270,000 | Total | $ 270,000 |
| **Investment in Plant** | | | |
| Land | $ 500,000 | | |
| Buildings | 20,800,000 | | |
| Equipment | 12,300,000 | Bonds payable | $ 1,900,000 |
| Library books | 700,000 | Fund balance | 32,400,000 |
| Total | $34,300,000 | Total | $34,300,000 |
| Total plant funds | $36,920,000 | Total plant funds | $36,920,000 |
| **Agency Funds** | | | |
| Cash | $ 47,000 | | |
| Investments | 80,000 | Deposits held for others | $ 127,000 |
| Total | $ 127,000 | Total | $ 127,000 |

**EXHIBIT 12–8.**   Illustration University Statement of Current Funds, Revenues, Expenditures, and Other Charges—For Fiscal Period (Conventional Accounting Procedures)

| | Unrestricted | Restricted | Total |
|---|---|---|---|
| Revenues | | | |
| Education and general | | | |
|   Tuition and fees | $ 8,000,000 | | $ 8,000,000 |
|   Governmental appropriations | 3,000,000 | | 3,000,000 |
|   Gifts | 1,000,000 | 100,000 | 1,100,000 |
|   Endowment income | 1,300,000 | 200,000 | 1,500,000 |
|   Other sources | 200,000 | | 200,000 |
|     Totals | $13,500,000 | $300,000 | $13,800,000 |
| Auxiliary activities | 2,000,000 | | 2,000,000 |
|   Total revenues | $15,500,000 | $300,000 | $15,800,000 |
| | | | |
| Expenditures | | | |
| Education and general | | | |
|   Instruction and research | $11,000,000 | $200,000 | $11,200,000 |
|   Libraries | 300,000 | | 300,000 |
|   Student services | 200,000 | 100,000 | 300,000 |
|   Plant operations | 1,000,000 | | 1,000,000 |
|   General administration | 300,000 | | 300,000 |
|   Other expenditures | 50,000 | | 50,000 |
|     Totals | $12,850,000 | $300,000 | $13,150,000 |
| Mandatory transfers | 70,000 | | 70,000 |
| Auxiliary activities | 1,600,000 | | 1,600,000 |
| Other transfers | | | |
|   To plant fund | 200,000 | | 200,000 |
|   To endowment fund | 500,000 | | 500,000 |
|     Total expenditures and transfers | $15,220,000 | $300,000 | $15,520,000 |
| | | | |
| Excess of revenues over expenditures and transfers | $ 280,000 | 0 | $ 280,000 |

both types of organizations conventionally follow fund accounting procedures designed primarily to reflect dollar accountability in reporting on the inflows and outflows of spendable resources. However, we also noted that as a quasi-nonprofit enterprise unit, a college or university logically places more emphasis on matching revenues and expenditures associated with operations than does a governmental entity.

Spendable resource inflows for colleges and universities fall into two general categories: operating and nonoperating. Operating resource inflows conventionally are reflected as revenues in the operating statement while nonoperating resource inflows are recorded as increases to the fund balance accounts of the appropriate funds. To be classified as nonoperating inflows, the uses of the resources must be externally restricted.

The fund entities for colleges and universities are labeled differently from those of governmental units to reflect their operating characteristics. The operating funds of

**EXHIBIT 12–9.** Illustration University Statement of Operations—For Fiscal Period (FASB 93-Imposed Accounting Procedures)

| | | |
|---|---:|---:|
| Operating revenues | | |
| Tuition and other user fees | | |
| Tuition and fees | $ 8,000,000 | |
| Government appropriations | 3,000,000 | |
| Revenues from restricted revenues | 300,000 | $11,300,000 |
| Auxiliary activities | | |
| Revenues | $ 2,000,000 | |
| Expenses (including depreciation) | 1,600,000 | 400,000 |
| Total operating revenues | | $11,700,000 |
| Operating expenses | | |
| General administrative expenses | $ 300,000 | |
| Instruction and research | 11,200,000 | |
| Student services | 300,000 | |
| Plant operations | 3,062,000 | |
| Depreciation of library books | 70,000 | |
| Interest expense | 70,000 | |
| Other expenses | 50,000 | 15,052,000 |
| Excess of operating revenues over operating expenses | | $ (3,352,000) |
| Nonoperating revenues | | |
| Endowment income | $ 1,300,000 | |
| Gifts | 1,000,000 | |
| Other income | 200,000 | 2,500,000 |
| Excess of revenues over expenses from continuing operations | | $ (852,000) |
| Restricted resource inflows—net | | |
| Current funds—restricted | $ 7,000 | |
| Loan funds | 125,000 | |
| Endowment funds | 2,000,000 | |
| Annuity funds | 120,000 | |
| Plant funds | 0 | |
| Agency funds | 7,000 | 2,259,000 |
| Excess of revenues and restricted resource inflows over expenses | | $ 1,407,000 |

Proofs

| | | |
|---|---:|---:|
| Unrestricted fund balance at beginning of fiscal period | | $21,600,000 |
| Excess of revenues over expenses from continuing operations | | (852,000) |
| Transfers from restricted funds | | 1,100,000 |
| Unrestricted fund balance at end of fiscal period | | $21,848,000 |
| Restricted fund balances at end of fiscal period | | |
| Current funds reported | $ 137,000 | |
| Loan funds | 545,000 | |
| Endowment funds | 14,050,000 | |
| Annuity funds | 1,660,000 | |
| Plant funds | 2,500,000 | |
| Agency fund (deposits held for others) | 127,000 | $19,019,000 |
| Restricted fund balances at beginning of fiscal period | | |
| Current funds restricted | $ 130,000 | |
| Loan funds | 420,000 | |
| Endowment funds | 12,050,000 | |
| Annuity funds | 1,540,000 | |
| Plant funds | 2,500,000 | |
| Agency funds (deposits held for others) | 120,000 | $16,760,000 |
| Net restricted resource inflows | | $ 2,259,000 |

**EXHIBIT 12–10.**  Illustration University Balance Sheet—End of Fiscal Period (FASB 93-Imposed Accounting Procedures)

### Unrestricted Funds

| Assets | | | Liabilities and Fund Balances | |
|---|---:|---:|---|---:|
| Cash | | $ 230,000 | Vouchers payable | $ 50,000 |
| Investments | | 3,300,000 | Notes payable | 50,000 |
| Accounts receivable | | 50,000 | Bonds payable | 2,400,000 |
| Land | | 500,000 | | |
| Buildings | $20,800,000 | | | |
| Accumulated depreciation | 8,832,000 | 11,968,000 | | |
| Equipment | $12,300,000 | | | |
| Accumulated depreciation | 5,230,000 | 7,070,000 | | |
| Library books | $ 700,000 | | | |
| Accumulated depreciation | 170,000 | 530,000 | | |
| Plant acquisition fund—cash | | 200,000 | | |
| Quasi-endowment fund | 0 | | | |
| Cash | $ 50,000 | | | |
| Investments | 450,000 | 500,000 | Fund balance | 21,848,000 |
| Total unrestricted | | $24,348,000 | Total unrestricted | $24,348,000 |

### Restricted Funds
#### Current Funds—Restricted

| | | | | |
|---|---:|---|---|---:|
| Cash | $ 67,000 | | Vouchers payable | $ 10,000 |
| Investments | 80,000 | | Fund balance | 137,000 |
| Total | $147,000 | | Total | $ 147,000 |

### Loan Funds

| | | | | |
|---|---:|---|---|---:|
| Cash | $ 30,000 | | | |
| Investments | 160,000 | | | |
| Loans to students | 355,000 | | Fund balance | $ 545,000 |
| Total | $545,000 | | Total | $ 545,000 |

### Endowment Funds

| | | | |
|---|---|---|---|
| Cash | $ 50,000 | Fund balance | $14,050,000 |
| Investments | 14,000,000 | | |
| Total | $14,050,000 | Total | $14,050,000 |

### Annuity Funds

| | | | |
|---|---|---|---|
| Cash | $ 110,000 | Annuities payable | $ 2,450,000 |
| Investments | 4,000,000 | Fund balance | 1,660,000 |
| Total | $ 4,110,000 | Total | $ 4,110,000 |

### Plant Funds

| | | | |
|---|---|---|---|
| Cash | $ 100,000 | | |
| Investments | 2,000,000 | | |
| Deposits with trustees | 400,000 | Fund balance | $ 2,500,000 |
| Total | $ 2,500,000 | Total | $ 2,500,000 |

### Agency Funds

| | | | |
|---|---|---|---|
| Cash | $ 47,000 | Deposits for others | $ 127,000 |
| Investments | 80,000 | | |
| Total | $ 127,000 | Total | $ 127,000 |

| | | | |
|---|---|---|---|
| Total restricted | $21,479,000 | Total restricted | $21,479,000 |
| Total assets | $45,827,000 | Total liabilities fund balances | $45,827,000 |

a college or university, for example, are accounted for in a current funds accounting entity. Also, colleges and universities typically hold large amounts of resources that are to be invested and held in perpetuity to produce income that can be used to cover general operating expenditures. The funds used to account for such resources are called endowment funds. In this section of the chapter, we also described each of the various types of funds used in accounting for the financial activities of colleges and universities.

In the last part of the chapter, we illustrated the entries to be made in recording a series of assumed transactions for Illustration University (and the allocation of the account balances to the financial statements in a transactions worksheet). We demonstrated how those transactions should be recorded using both conventional and FASB 93-oriented accounting procedures.

## ■ Glossary

**Agency Funds.** Accounting entities used in college and university accounting systems to account for resources held by the institution as custodian or fiscal agent for students, faculty, staff members, and organizations.

**Annuity Funds.** Accounting entities used in college and university accounting systems to account for resources held by the institution under agreements whereby money or other property is made available to the institution on condition that the institution bind itself to pay stipulated amounts periodically to the donors or other designated individuals with such payments to terminate at the time designated in the annuity agreement.

**Auxiliary Enterprises.** A segment of college and university operations that furnishes a service directly or indirectly to students, faculty, or staff and charges a fee related to, but not necessarily equal to, the cost of services.

**Current Funds.** The accounting entities used to record the inflows of operating resources for colleges and universities and health and welfare agencies. The net resources in these funds are divided into unrestricted and restricted subdivisions.

**Endowment Funds.** Accounting entities used to account for funds received from a donor with the restriction that the principal is not expendable but is to be held for the production of revenue for use by the organization.

**Loan Funds.** Accounting entities used in college and university accounting systems to account for resources available for loans to students, faculty, and staff.

**Mandatory Transfer.** In college and university accounting, transfers from the current fund group to other fund groups arising out of binding legal agreements relating to the financing of educational plant and grant agreements with agencies of the federal government, donors, and other organizations to match gifts and grants to loan and other funds; mandatory transfers may be required to be made from either unrestricted or restricted current funds.

**Nonmandatory Transfers.** In college and university accounting systems, transfers from the current fund group to other fund groups, which are made at the discretion of the governing board. Such transfers may include additions to loan funds, additions to quasi-endowment funds, general or specific plant additions, voluntary renewals and replacements of plant, and prepayments on debt principal.

**Plant Funds.** Accounting entities used in college and university accounting systems to account for unexpended funds to be used in the acquisition of long-lived assets for institutional purposes, funds set aside for renewal and replacement of institutional properties, funds set aside for debt-service charges and retirement of indebtedness on institutional plant, and the cost (or fair value at time of donation) of long-lived assets other than those of endowment and similar funds held by the college or university.

**Quasi-Endowment.** In college and university accounting systems, resources designated to be used as endowment by the institution's board of trustees.

# ▪ Suggested Supplementary References

American Institute of Certified Public Accountants. *Audits of Colleges and Universities*. Washington, D.C.: AICPA, 1975.

Azad, Ali N., and Ted D. Skekel. "Personal Attributes and Effective Operational Auditing: Perceptions of College and University Internal Auditors." *Government Accountants Journal* (Fall 1990).

Fountain, James R., and John Engstrom. "College and University Financial Reporting: A Survey of Important Financial Decision Makers." *Government Accountants Journal* (Summer 1989).

Henke, Emerson O., and Lucian G. Conway. "A Recommended Reporting Format for College and University Financial Statements." *Accounting Horizons* (June 1989): 49–65.

Larimore, L. Keith. "Break-Even Analysis for Higher Education." *Management Accounting, 56* (1974): 25–28.

National Association of College and University Business Officers. *College and University Business Administration*, 4th ed. New York: NACUBO, 1982.

Olson, Steven K., and Jacob R. Wambsganss. "Depreciation for Colleges and Universities: Is It Useful Information?" *Government Accountants Journal* (Winter 1987–88).

Patten, Dennis M. "Battle of the Boards: Identifying the Political Nature of the Standard-Setting Controversies." *Government Accountants Journal* (Fall 1989).

Price Waterhouse and Co. "Position Paper on College and University Accounting." From *Readings in Governmental and Nonprofit Accounting* by Richard J. Vargo. (Wadsworth Publishing Company), pp. 156–173.

Wambsganss, Jacob R., and Steven K. Olson. "How College and University Business Officers View Depreciation." *Government Accountants Journal* (Spring 1988).

# ▪ Questions for Class Discussion

**Q12-1.** Are colleges and universities pure nonprofit entities? Explain.

**Q12-2.** What is the primary operating objective of a college or university? How can we reconcile that objective with the auxiliary activities typically carried out by most colleges and universities?

Q12-3.    What effect does the fact that colleges and universities depend heavily on user-based charges to finance their operations have on the way their operating statements should be organized? Explain.

Q12-4.    Are conventional college and university financial statements logically consistent with the operating environment of those institutions? Explain.

Q12-5.    What is the difference between the current restricted and current unrestricted funds for a college or university? Explain.

Q12-6.    What is the difference between a pure endowment fund and a quasi-endowment fund? Explain.

Q12-7.    The plant fund for a college or university typically includes the items contained in the general fixed-assets account group of a governmental entity. If that is the case, why are such accounting entities called plant funds? Explain.

Q12-8.    Do conventional accounting procedures require colleges and universities to recognize depreciation of educational facilities as an element of operating costs? Explain.

Q12-9.    What basis of accounting would a college or university use if it followed the requirements of the College and University Statement of Accounting Principles presented in this chapter?

Q12-10.    Explain the difference between mandatory and nonmandatory transfers shown in a university operating statement.

Q12-11.    May a college or university use resources provided by increases in the values of general endowment assets for operating purposes? Discuss fully.

Q12-12.    What is an agency fund? Give an example of such a fund.

# ■ Exercises

E12-1.    A university has, among others, the following transactions during the current operating period:

1. Received tuition and fees in the amount of $4,000,000.
2. Received unrestricted gifts totaling $300,000.
3. A general endowment fund earned income in the amount of $500,000.
4. Instructional salaries amounting to $200,000 were paid.
5. Equipment costing $25,000 was purchased for the chemistry laboratory from current fund resources.
6. Library salary expenditures were incurred in the amount of $50,000.
7. General administrative expenses amounting to $60,000 were paid.
8. Securities designated by the donor to be used as endowment resources and valued at $200,000 were received.
9. An alumnus contributed $500,000 in cash, which he specified should be used for the construction of a classroom building.
10. One phase of the classroom building construction is completed and payment in the amount of $200,000 was made to cover that part of the contract.
11. A student organization deposited $5,000 with the university. These funds were left with the university for safekeeping and are subject to withdrawal by the student organization.

**Required:**

A. Journalize each of the preceding transactions using conventional accounting procedures.

B. Indicate the fund or funds in which each of the transactions would be recorded.

E12-2. The following account balances relating to the operations of a college bookstore are included in the current fund trial balance:

1. Book sales, $35,000
2. Inventory of books at beginning of period, $40,000
3. Book purchases, $25,000
4. Inventory of sundry items at beginning of period, $40,000
5. Sundry purchases, $20,000
6. Sundry sales, $30,000
7. Sales salaries, $20,000
8. Miscellaneous operating expenditures, $5,000.

End-of-the-period inventories for books and sundry items are $45,000 and $42,000, respectively.

**Required:**

A. Prepare an operating statement for the bookstore as an auxiliary activity of the university.

B. Where will the data reflected in the auxiliary activities operating statement appear in the university statement of revenues and expenditures?

C. Is the excess of revenues over expenditures the "real net income" from operating the bookstore? Explain.

E12-3. A prospective contributor is examining the published annual report for Alma Mater University. He discovers a quasi-endowment fund balance sheet showing a fund balance of $750,000 and a general endowment fund balance sheet showing a fund balance of $5,600,000. He does not understand the difference between these two funds.

**Required:**

A. Explain the fundamental difference between the ways in which the resources of a quasi-endowment fund and a general endowment fund may be used.

B. What are the probable sources of the assets in the two funds?

E12-4. Scholarship awards amounting to $30,000 are granted from current fund resources restricted to such usage.

**Required:**

Journalize the scholarship awards including an indication of the fund in which the entry is recorded. How will the results of the transaction be shown in the operating statements of the university? Explain.

E12-5. A current fund operating statement shows unrestricted revenues and expenditures of $4,200,000 and $4,150,000, respectively. Now assume the following supplementary data relating to various revenue and expenditure items:

1. Expenditures include outlays of $50,000 for fixed assets.
2. Depreciation of existing fixed assets calculated in accordance with generally accepted accounting practices amounts to $300,000.

**Required:**

A. Convert the current fund operating statement data to the full accrual basis.

B. What observations can you make regarding the differences in the operating picture portrayed by the two statements? Explain.

E12-6. A university accountant has asked you to help in the preparation of the university's current fund operating budget. Although capacity enrollment for the university is considered to be 10,000 students, the enrollment for the next year is expected to be in the vicinity of 9,000 students. The following operating data are considered appropriate for the university when operating at full capacity:

| | | |
|---|---:|---:|
| Tuition and fees | | $40,000,000 |
| Instructional salaries and other fixed | | |
| expenditures | $35,000,000 | |
| Variable expenditures | 4,000,000 | 39,000,000 |
| Excess of revenues over expenditures | | $ 1,000,000 |

**Required:**

A. Prepare a budget for the anticipated operating level of 9,000 students.

B. What actions do you feel the university should take in light of the projected budgetary data? Explain fully.

E12-7. A university borrowed $500,000 on a note to be used in the construction of a classroom building. They anticipate receiving future contributions to cover the cost of construction.

**Required:**

A. Journalize the borrowing transaction.

B. Identify the fund in which the transaction would be recorded. Explain.

E12-8. A university receives $200,000 that is externally restricted to be used for loans to students. During the year, loans are granted in the amount of $60,000, of which $20,000 are repaid prior to the end of the period. Interest received from loans amounts to $4,000.

**Required:**

A. Journalize the preceding transactions.

B. Identify the fund in which the transactions would be recorded.

C. Prepare a balance sheet for the fund at the end of the period.

E12-9. A university receives cash contributions in the amount of $300,000 that are designated to be used as general endowment resources. All cash in the fund is invested in securities. During the period, the university receives $15,000 as interest and dividend income from the securities. Cash equal to the income is made available to be used for general operations.

**Required:**

A. Journalize the preceding transactions.

B. Identify the fund or funds in which the transactions would be recorded.

C. Prepare a balance sheet for the endowment fund at the end of the period.

# ■ Problems

P12-1.  This is a comprehensive problem covering recording procedures for various transactions discussed and illustrated in Chapter 12. A computer software package is available for use in solving this problem. Alma Mater University begins its current-year operations with the following account balances:

| | |
|---|---:|
| **Unrestricted assets and liabilities** | |
| Cash | $ 200,000 |
| Investments | 600,000 |
| Accounts receivable | 50,000 |
| Payables | 100,000 |
| **Restricted assets and liabilities** | |
| Cash | 120,000 |
| Investments | 160,000 |
| Vouchers payable | 20,000 |
| **Loan funds** | |
| Cash | 40,000 |
| Investments | 200,000 |
| Loans to students | 600,000 |
| **Endowment funds** | |
| Cash | 100,000 |
| Investments (including $6,000,000 of quasi-endowment funds) | 30,000,000 |
| **Annuity funds** | |
| Cash | 80,000 |
| Investments | 8,000,000 |
| Annuities payable | 5,000,000 |
| **Plant funds** | |
| Unexpended | |
| Cash | 300,000 |
| Investments | 4,000,000 |
| Notes payable | 200,000 |
| Bonds payable | 1,000,000 |
| Retirement of indebtedness | |
| Cash | 100,000 |
| Deposits with trustees | 600,000 |
| Investment in plant | |
| Land | 1,000,000 |
| Buildings | 40,000,000 |
| Equipment | 24,000,000 |
| Library books | 800,000 |
| Bonds payable | 4,000,000 |
| **Agency funds** | |
| Cash | 80,000 |
| Investments | 160,000 |

During the year, the university has the following transactions:

1. Received unrestricted revenues as follows:

| | |
|---|---:|
| Tuition and fees | $16,000,000 |
| Governmental appropriations | 6,000,000 |
| Gifts | 2,000,000 |
| Other revenues | 400,000 |

2. Received endowment income amounting to $3,000,000, including $400,000 for specifically designated instruction and research.
3. Received revenue from auxiliary enterprises in the amount of $4,000,000.
4. Incurred expenditures of unrestricted resources as follows:

| | |
|---|---:|
| Instruction and research | $22,000,000 |
| Libraries (including $200,000 for books) | 600,000 |
| Student services | 400,000 |
| Plant operations | 2,000,000 |
| General administration | 600,000 |
| Other expenditures | 100,000 |

5. The loan fund received $800,000, including loans repayments in the amount of $550,000 and additional funds in the amount of $250,000.
6. Securities having a fair value of $4,000,000 were received as endowment funds.
7. Annuity fund revenues amounting to $640,000 were received.
8. Cash amounting to $2,000,000 designated to be used for plant construction was received.
9. Plant funds realized $340,000 was revenue from investments held by the fund. Of this amount, $140,000 was earmarked for retirement of indebtedness.
10. Agency funds realized cash from depositors in the amount of $14,000.
11. Obligations for annuities payable in the amount of $500,000 were paid from annuity fund resources.
12. Construction was completed on buildings in the amount of $1,600,000 and equipment was purchased at a cost of $600,000 from plant fund resources.
13. University retired $200,000 worth of plant funds (unexpended) bonds at par value and paid $100,000 in interest on bonds outstanding. Bond retirement was paid from deposits with trustees.
14. The university, by action of its trustees, transferred $1,400,000 of resources from unrestricted funds to plant funds and endowment funds. Of this amount, $400,000 went to the plant fund and $1,000,000 was transferred to endowment.
15. The university paid expenditures in the amount of $3,200,000 relating to auxiliary activities.
16. The university received $214,000 of restricted educational revenue. This included gifts and grants in the amount of $200,000 to be used for student aid.

17. Educational and general expenditures paid from restricted funds amounted to $600,000. This included $400,000 for instruction and research and $200,000 for student aid.
18. Loan funds in the amount of $120,000 were invested.
19. New loans to students from the loan fund amounted to $660,000.
20. Quasi-Endowment cash in the amount of $900,000 was invested in securities.
21. Plant fund cash restricted to being used to retire debt amounting to $200,000 is deposited with a trustee.
22. The excess of unrestricted revenues over expenditures and other changes is transferred to the unrestricted fund balance account.
23. The excess of restricted revenues over expenditures is transferred to the restricted fund balance account.

**Required:**
A. Prepare a transactions worksheet similar to the one illustrated in Exhibit 12−4 and record the preceding transactions in it.
B. Complete the worksheet and prepare financial statements for Alma Mater University. Use conventional accounting procedures.

**P12-2.** Refer to the data in P12-1 and add the following assumptions:
1. Accumulated depreciation:

| | |
|---|---|
| Buildings | $16,000,000 |
| Equipment | 8,000,000 |
| Library books | 200,000 |

2. Depreciation for the reporting period is assumed to be as follows:

| | |
|---|---|
| Buildings | 4% |
| Equipment | 10% |
| Library books | 10% |

A full year's depreciation is to be recognized in the year of an asset's requisition.
3. The fiscal period is such that there are no accrued or prepaid revenues or expenses at the end of the period.
4. Auxiliary activities have been recorded on the full accrual basis.

**Required:**
A. Prepare a transactions worksheet similar to the one illustrated in Exhibit 12−6 and record the transactions in it using FASB 93-oriented accounting procedures.
B. Complete the worksheet and prepare financial statements for Alma Mater University. Use the FASB 93-imposed accounting procedures illustrated in the chapter in preparing the financial statements.

**P12–3.**   The current funds trial balances for Apex University is shown below:

|  | Current Unrestricted Funds | | Current Restricted Funds | |
|---|---|---|---|---|
| Cash | $ 105,000 | | $ 60,000 | |
| Investments | 40,000 | | 30,000 | |
| Accounts payable | | $ 55,000 | | $ 12,000 |
| Tuition and fees | | 1,200,000 | | |
| Gifts | | 300,000 | | 150,000 |
| Auxiliary activities revenue | | 500,000 | | |
| Endowment income | | 200,000 | | 75,000 |
| Instructional expenditures | 1,300,000 | | | |
| Student aid | 75,000 | | 125,000 | |
| Research expenditures | | | 40,000 | |
| Operating expenditures | 600,000 | | | |
| Library expenditures | | | 10,000 | |
| Auxiliary activities expenditures | 480,000 | | | |
| Fund balance | | 345,000 | | 28,000 |
| Totals | $2,600,000 | $2,600,000 | $265,000 | $265,000 |

**Required:**

Prepare financial statements for the current funds. Follow conventional accounting procedures.

**P12-4.**   Select the best answer for each of the following items based on conventional accounting procedures:

1.  A university receives a cash gift in the amount of $500,000, which the donor specifies shall be used in constructing a classroom building. This gift should be recorded as:
    a.   gift revenue in the unrestricted current fund.
    b.   gift revenue in the restricted current fund.
    c.   an increase to cash and fund balance in the plant fund.
    d.   quasi-endowment in the endowment fund.

2.  The board of trustees of a college directs the controller to transfer $400,000 in cash from current funds unrestricted to endowment funds. This should be recorded as a nonmandatory transfer in current funds and:
    a.   as revenue in the endowment fund.
    b.   as quasi-endowment added to cash and fund balance in the endowment fund.
    c.   subtracted from expenditures in the statement of revenues and expenditures.
    d.   added to revenues in the statement of revenues and expenditures.

3.  A university borrows $1,000,000 to build a dormitory. This transaction should be recorded:
    a.   as a debit to cash in the current fund and a credit to mortgage note.

b. as a temporary addition to endowment fund so that it can be invested while the dormitory is being constructed.

c. as an addition to plant fund cash and a credit to mortgage payable in the plant fund.

d. in an agency fund until required in constructing the dormitory.

4. A university receives a government grant designated to be used in carrying out a specified research project. When received, this grant should be recorded:

a. as an increase to cash and fund balance in current funds—restricted.

b. as an addition to agency fund cash and the agency fund balance.

c. in a special purpose fund.

d. as revenue in the current funds—restricted statement of revenues and expenditures.

5. Funds that the governing board of an institution, rather than a donor or other outside agency, has determined are to be retained and invested for other than loan or plant purposes would be accounted for in the:

a. quasi-endowment fund

b. endowment fund

c. agency fund

d. current fund—restricted.

6. Which of the following funds are usually encountered in a not-for-profit private university?

|     | Current funds | Plant funds |
|-----|---------------|-------------|
| a.  | No            | Yes         |
| b.  | No            | No          |
| c.  | Yes           | No          |
| d.  | Yes           | Yes         |

7. Which of the following funds are usually encountered in a not-for-profit private university?

|     | Loan funds | Life income funds |
|-----|------------|-------------------|
| a.  | No         | Yes               |
| b.  | No         | No                |
| c.  | Yes        | No                |
| d.  | Yes        | Yes               |

8. Funds established at a college by donors who have stipulated that the principal is nonexpendable, but that the income generated may be expended by current operating funds would be accounted for in the:

a. quasi-endowment fund.

b. endowment fund.

c. term endowment fund.

d. agency fund.

9. Which of the following should be included in a university's current funds revenue?

| | Unrestricted gifts | Expended restricted current funds | Unexpended restricted current funds |
|---|---|---|---|
| a. | Yes | Yes | Yes |
| b. | Yes | Yes | No |
| c. | Yes | No | No |
| d. | No | No | Yes |

— AICPA Adapted

**P12-5.** Select the best answer for each of the following items based on conventional accounting procedures:

1. For the summer session of 19X7, Ariba University assessed its students $1,700,000 (net of refunds), covering tuition and fees for educational and general purposes. However, only $1,500,000 was expected to be realized because scholarships totaling $150,000 were granted to students, and tuition remissions of $50,000 were allowed to faculty members' children attending Ariba. What amount should Ariba include in the unrestricted current funds as revenues from student tuition and fees?
   a. $1,500,000
   b. $1,550,000
   c. $1,650,000
   d. $1,700,000

2. The following expenditures were among those incurred by Alma University during 19X7:

| | |
|---|---|
| Administrative data processing | $ 50,000 |
| Scholarships and fellowships | 100,000 |
| Operation and maintenance of physical plant | 200,000 |

   The amount to be included in the functional classification "Institutional Support" expenditures account is:
   a. $50,000.
   b. $150,000.
   c. $250,000.
   d. $350,000.

3. The following information was available from Forest College's accounting records for its current funds for the year ended March 31, 19X8:

| | |
|---|---|
| Restricted gifts received | |
| Expended | $100,000 |
| Not expended | 300,000 |
| Unrestricted gifts received | |
| Expended | 600,000 |
| Not expended | 75,000 |

What amount should be included in current funds revenues for the year ended March 31, 19X8?

   a.  $600,000
   b.  $700,000
   c.  $775,000
   d.  $1,000,000

4.  For the 19X7 summer session, Selva University assessed its students $300,000 for tuition and fees. However, the net amount realized was only $290,000 because of the following reductions:

| | |
|---|---:|
| Tuition remissions granted to faculty members' families | $3,000 |
| Class cancellation refunds | 7,000 |

How much unrestricted current funds revenues from tuition and fees should Selva report for the period?

   a.  $290,000
   b.  $293,000
   c.  $297,000
   d.  $300,000

5.  On July 31, 19X8, Sabio College showed the following amounts to be used for

| | |
|---|---:|
| Renewal and replacement of college properties | $200,000 |
| Retirement of indebtedness on college properties | 300,000 |
| Purchase of physical properties for college purposes, but unexpended at 7/31/X8 | 400,000 |

What total amount should be included in Sabio's plant funds at July 31, 19X8?

   a.  $900,000
   b.  $600,000
   c.  $400,000
   d.  $200,000

6.  For the 19X7 fall semester, Brook University assessed its students $4,000,000 (net of refunds), covering tuition and fees for educational and general purposes. However, only $3,700,000 was expected to be realized because tuition remissions of $80,000 were allowed to faculty members' children attending Brook and scholarships totaling $220,000 were granted to students. What amount should Brook include in educational and general current funds revenues from student tuition and fees?

   a.  $4,000,000
   b.  $3,920,000
   c.  $3,780,000
   d.  $3,700,000

7.  The following receipts were among those recorded by Kery College during 19X6:

| | |
|---|---:|
| Unrestricted gifts | $500,000 |
| Restricted current funds (expended for current operating purposes) | 200,000 |
| Restricted current funds (not yet expended) | 100,000 |

The amount that should be included in current funds revenues is:
a. $800,000.
b. $700,000.
c. $600,000.
d. $500,000.

8. Park College is sponsored by a religious group. Volunteers from this religious group regularly contribute their services to Park, and are paid nominal amounts to cover their commuting costs. During 19X6, the total amount paid to these volunteers aggregated $12,000. The gross value of services performed by them, determined by reference to lay-equivalent salaries, amounted to $300,000. What amount should Park record as expenditures in 19X6 for these volunteers' services?
a. $312,000
b. $300,000
c. $12,000
d. $0

9. Abbey University's unrestricted current funds comprised the following:

| | |
|---|---|
| Assets | $5,000,000 |
| Liabilities (including deferred revenues of $100,000) | 3,000,000 |

The fund balance of Abbey's unrestricted current funds was:
a. $1,900,000.
b. $2,000,000.
c. $2,100,000.
d. $5,000,000.

10. The following information pertains to interest received by Beech University from endowment fund investments for the year ended June 30, 19X8:

| | Received | Expended for Current Operations |
|---|---|---|
| Unrestricted | $300,000 | $100,000 |
| Restricted | 500,000 | 75,000 |

What amount should be credited to endowment income for the year ended June 30, 19X8?
a. $800,000
b. $375,000
c. $175,000
d. $100,000

Items 11 through 13 are based on the following information pertaining to Cabal University as of June 30, 19X9, and for the year then ended:

Unrestricted current funds comprised $7,500,000 of assets and $4,500,000 of liabilities (including deferred revenues of $150,000). Among the receipts recorded during the year were unrestricted gifts of $550,000 and restricted grants totaling $330,000, of which $220,000 was expended during the year for current operations and $110,000 remained unexpended at the close of the year.

Volunteers from the surrounding communities regularly contribute their services to Cabal and are paid nominal amounts to cover their travel costs. During the year, the total amount paid to these volunteers aggregated $18,000. The gross value of services performed by them, determined by reference to equivalent wages available in that area for similar services, amounted to $200,000.

11. At June 30, 19X9, the fund balance of Cabal's unrestricted current funds was
    a. $7,500,000.
    b. $3,150,000.
    c. $3,000,000.
    d. $2,850,000.

12. For the year ended June 30, 19X9, what amount should be included in Cabal's current funds revenues for the unrestricted gifts and restricted grants?
    a. $550,000
    b. $660,000
    c. $770,000
    d. $880,000

13. For the year ended June 30, 19X9, what amount should Cabal record as expenditures for the volunteers' services?
    a. $218,000
    b. $200,000
    c. $18,000
    d. $0

— AICPA Adapted

P12-6. DeMars College has asked your assistance in developing its revenue and expenditures budget for the coming 19X1–X2 academic year. You are supplied with the following data for the current year:

1.

| | Lower Division (Freshman–Sophomore) | Upper Division (Junior–Senior) |
|---|---|---|
| Average number of students per class | 25 | 20 |
| Average salary of faculty member | $20,000 | $20,000 |
| Average number of credit hours carried each year per student | 33 | 30 |
| Enrollment, including scholarship students | 2,500 | 1,700 |
| Average faculty teaching load in credit hours per year (10 classes of 3 credit hours) | 30 | 30 |

For 19X1–X2, lower division enrollment is expected to increase by 10 percent, while upper division enrollment is expected to remain stable. Faculty salaries will be increased by a standard 5 percent, and additional merit increases to be awarded to individual faculty members will be $90,750 for the lower division and $85,000 for the upper division.

2.  The current budget is $210,000 for operation and maintenance of plant and equipment; this incudes $90,000 for salaries and wages. Experience of the past three months suggests that the current budget is realistic, but that expected increases for 19X1–X2 are 5 percent in salaries and wages and $9,000 in other expenditures for operation and maintenance of plant and equipment.

3.  The budget for the remaining expenditures for 19X1–X2 is as follows:

| | |
|---|---:|
| Administrative and general | $240,000 |
| Library | 160,000 |
| Health and recreation | 75,000 |
| Athletics | 120,000 |
| Insurance and retirement | 265,000 |
| Interest | 48,000 |
| Capital outlay | 300,000 |

4.  The College expects to award twenty-five tuition-free scholarships to lower division students and fifteen to upper division students. Tuition is $45 per credit hour and no other fees are charged.

5.  Budgeted revenues for 19X1–X2 are as follows:

| | |
|---|---:|
| Endowments | $114,000 |
| Net income from auxiliary services | 235,000 |
| Athletics | 180,000 |

The College's remaining source of revenue is an annual support campaign held during the spring.

**Required:**
A.  Prepare a schedule computing for 19X1–X2 by division (1) the expected enrollment, (2) the total credit hours to be carried, and (3) the number of faculty members needed.
B.  Prepare a schedule computing the budget for faculty salaries by division for 19X1–X2.
C.  Prepare a schedule computing the tuition revenue budget by division for 19X1–X2.
D.  Assuming that the faculty salaries budget computed in requirement B was $2,400,000 and that the tuition revenue budget computed in requirement C was $3,000,000, prepare a schedule computing the amount that must be raised during the annual support campaign in order to cover the 19X1–X2 expenditures budget.

—AICPA Adapted

P12-7.  Presented next is the current funds balance sheet of Burnsville University as of the end of its fiscal year ended June 30, 19X0.

## Burnsville University Current Funds Balance Sheet June 30, 19X0

| Assets | | | Liabilities and Fund Balances | | |
|---|---|---|---|---|---|
| Current Funds: | | | Current Funds: | | |
| Unrestricted: | | | Unrestricted: | | |
| Cash | $210,000 | | Accounts payable | $ 45,000 | |
| Accounts receivable | | | Deferred revenues | 66,000 | |
| student tuition and | | | Fund balance | 515,000 | $626,000 |
| fees, less allowance | | | | | |
| for doubtful accounts | | | | | |
| of $9,000 | 341,000 | | | | |
| State appropriations | | | | | |
| receivable | 75,000 | $626,000 | | | |
| Restricted: | | | Restricted: | | |
| Cash | $ 7,000 | | Fund balance | | 67,000 |
| Investments | 60,000 | 67,000 | | | |
| Total current funds | | $693,000 | Total current funds | | $693,000 |

The following transactions occurred during the fiscal year ended June 30, 19X1:

1. On July 7, 19X0, a gift of $100,000 was received from an alumna. The alumna requested that one half of the gift be used for the purchase of books for the university library and the remainder be used for the establishment of a scholarship fund. The alumna further requested that the income generated by the scholarship fund be used annually to award a scholarship to a qualified disadvantaged student. On July 20, 19X0, the board of trustees resolved that the funds of the newly established scholarship fund would be invested in savings certificates. On July 21, 19X0, the savings certificates were purchased.

2. Revenue from student tuition and fees applicable to the year ended June 30, 19X1, amounted to $1,900,000. Of this amount, $66,000 was collected in the prior year and $1,686,000 was collected during the year ended June 30, 19X1. In addition, on June 30, 19X1, the university had received cash of $158,000 representing fees for the session beginning July 1, 19X1.

3. During the year ended June 30, 19X1, the university had collected $349,000 of the outstanding accounts receivable at the beginning of the year. The balance was determined to be uncollectible and was written off against the allowance account. On June 30, 19X1, the allowance account was increased by $3,000.

4. During the year, interest charges of $6,000 were earned and collected on late student fee payments.

5. During the year, the state appropriation was received. An additional unrestricted appropriation of $50,000 was made by the state but had not been paid to the university as of June 30, 19X1.

6. An unrestricted gift of $25,000 cash was received from alumni of the university.

7. During the year, investments in the current restricted fund of $21,000 were sold for $26,000. Investment income amounting to $1,900 was received.

8. During the year, unrestricted operating expenses of $1,777,000 were recorded. On June 30, 19X1, $59,000 of these expenses remained unpaid.
9. Restricted current funds of $13,000 were spent for authorized purposes during the year.
10. The accounts payable on June 30, 19X0, were paid during the year.
11. During the year, $7,000 interest was earned and received on the savings certificates purchased in accordance with the board of trustees resolution, as discussed in item 1.

**Required:**

A. Using conventional accounting procedures, prepare journal entries to record in summary the preceding transactions for the year ended June 30, 19X1. Each journal entry should be numbered to correspond with the transaction described. Your answer sheet should be organized as follows:

| | Current Funds | | | | Endowment Fund | |
| | Unrestricted | | Restricted | | | |
| Accounts | Dr. | Cr. | Dr. | Cr. | Dr. | Cr. |
| --- | --- | --- | --- | --- | --- | --- |

B. Prepare a statement of changes in fund balances for the year ended June 30, 19X1.

**—AICPA Adapted**

**P12-8.** Select the best answer to each of the following items based on conventional accounting procedures:
1. Which of the following should be used in accounting for not-for-profit colleges and universities?
   a. fund accounting and accrual accounting
   b. fund accounting but *not* accrual accounting
   c. accrual accounting but *not* fund accounting
   d. neither accrual accounting nor fund accounting
2. Which of the following is utilized for current expenditures by a not-for-profit university?

| | Unrestricted current funds | Restricted current funds |
| --- | --- | --- |
| a. | No | No |
| b. | No | Yes |
| c. | Yes | No |
| d. | Yes | Yes |

3. Tuition waivers for which there is *no* intention of collection from the student should be classified by a not-for-profit university as:

|   | Revenue | Expenditures |
|---|---------|--------------|
| a. | No | No |
| b. | No | Yes |
| c. | Yes | Yes |
| d. | Yes | No |

4. For the fall semester of 19X1, Cranbrook College assessed its students $2,300,000 for tuition and fees. The net amount realized was only $2,100,000 because of the following revenue reductions:

| | |
|---|---:|
| Refunds occasioned by class cancellations and student withdrawals | $ 50,000 |
| Tuition remissions granted to faculty members' families | 10,000 |
| Scholarships and fellowships | 140,000 |

How much should Cranbrook report for the period for unrestricted current funds revenues from tuition and fees?
a. $2,100,000
b. $2,150,000
c. $2,250,000
d. $2,300,000

5. During the years ended June 30, 19X1 and 19X2, Sonata University conducted a cancer research project financed by a $2,000,000 gift from an alumnus. This entire amount was pledged by the donor on July 10, 19X0, although he paid only $500,000 at that date. The gift was restricted to the financing of this particular research project. During the two-year research period, Sonata's related gift receipts and research expenditures were as follows:

| | Year Ended June 30 | |
|---|---|---|
| | 19X1 | 19X2 |
| Gift receipts | $1,200,000 | $ 800,000 |
| Cancer research expenditures | 900,000 | 1,100,000 |

How much gift revenue should Sonata report in the restricted column of its statement of current funds revenues, expenditures, and other changes for the year ended June 30, 19X2?

a.  $0
b.  $800,000
c.  $1,100,000
d.  $2,000,000

6.  On January 2, 19X2, John Reynolds established a $500,000 trust, the income from which is to be paid to Mansfield University for general operating purposes. The Wyndham National Bank was appointed by Reynolds as trustee of the fund. What journal entry is required on Mansfield's books?

|  |  | Dr. | Cr. |
|---|---|---|---|
| a. | Memorandum entry only | | |
| b. | Cash | $500,000 | |
|  | Endowment fund balance | | $500,000 |
| c. | Nonexpendable endowment fund | $500,000 | |
|  | Endowment fund balance | | $500,000 |
| d. | Expendable funds | $500,000 | |
|  | Endowment fund balance | | $500,000 |

—AICPA Adapted

**P12-9.**   The accounting system for State College includes the following funds:
a.  current funds unrestricted
b.  current funds restricted
c.  endowment and similar funds
d.  plant funds.

The accounting system also includes the following account titles for each of the various funds whose resources, obligations, or operations require them:
a.  cash
b.  other assets
c.  vouchers payable
d.  fund balance
e.  revenues
f.  expenditures
g.  transfers
h.  bonds payable.

**Transactions:**
1.  State University received tuition and fees in the amount of $6,000,000.
2.  The general endowment fund earned income in the amount of $300,000.
3.  Faculty salaries amounting to $400,000 were paid.
4.  The college received a contribution of $500,000 to be used in constructing a new building.
5.  The college transferred $500,000 of resources from unrestricted funds to endowment funds.
6.  The college received $200,000 of restricted revenue.

7. Education and general expenditures paid from restricted funds amounted to $100,000.
8. Securities having a fair value of $1,000,000 were received as endowment funds.
9. State College retired $100,000 worth of plant fund bonds from plant fund cash.
10. Depreciation of fixed assets is calculated to be $12,000.

**Required:**

A. On a worksheet, label the first four pairs of columns with the names of the four types of funds contained in State College's accounting records. Then label individual lines of the worksheet 1 through 9, with each line representing one of the transactions we have listed. Enter the letters reflecting the accounts to be debited and credited in each of the various funds as a result of each of the transactions (use conventional accounting procedures).

B. Repeat your work in Requirement A using FASB 93-imposed accounting procedures. Change item f. (expenditures) to expenses. Write in any accounts needed that are not listed.

# Accounting for Health and Welfare Agencies, Churches, and Other Similar Organizations

## ■ Learning Objectives

When you have finished your study of this chapter, you should

1. Know the funds used in accounting for health and welfare organization financial transactions.

2. Be able to record the routine transactions of a health and welfare organization and prepare financial statements from the accumulated data.

3. Know how to record the routine transactions of a church's general fund.

4. Be able to prepare financial statements from the trial balance of a church's general fund.

5. Be aware of recent AICPA pronouncements relating to other nonprofit organizations.

A number of other organizations such as school districts, health and welfare agencies, churches, and foundations are also classified as nonprofit organizations. The operational characteristics of these enterprise units are similar in many respects to those of the organizations already discussed. No authoritative statement of principles has been formulated for churches. School districts follow accounting practices similar to those found in the Summary Statement of Principles of the NCGA presented in Chapter 3. Accounting practices for health and welfare agencies are most authoritatively defined in two publications: *Standards of Accounting and Financial Reporting* for *Voluntary Health and Welfare Organizations* and *Audits of Voluntary Health and Welfare Organizations.*[1]

In this chapter, we primarily consider accounting practices followed by *health and welfare organizations and churches*. After we have described those practices, we illustrate the accounting procedures followed in recording a series of typical transactions, along with model financial statements for each type organization. In the closing pages of the chapter, we briefly consider some other developments relating to accounting procedures for *other nonprofit organizations*.

# ■ Accounting for Health and Welfare Organizations

Health and welfare agencies historically have exhibited less uniformity in their accounting practices than many other segments of the nonprofit area. They have usually followed fund-accounting practices to disclose dollar accountability for spendable resources received and used. However, the operations of some of these agencies are such that the accounting records contain no fund entities other than a general or operating fund. In such instances, fund-accounting techniques *were* often similar to the accounting procedures followed by businesses except for the emphasis on expenditure-based dollar-accountability rather than operational-accountability reporting.

The accounting practices for these organizations have *historically* involved use of the cash or modified cash basis rather than the full accrual basis of accounting. Financial reports were typically designed to show the flows of spendable resources and the financial position of the organization relative to appropriable assets only. As a result, their financial reports have been generally less comprehensive and complete than reports presented for business entities or other nonprofit organizations.

Although some health and welfare organizations are partially financed through user charges, they operate for the most part as *pure nonprofit enterprises*. They are primarily financed through contributions from constituents and provide services on the basis of need. This suggests a need for both dollar- and operational-accountability reporting. Nevertheless, the emphasis *historically* has been on presenting expenditure-oriented dollar-accountability financial statements. In addition, there was little uniformity in the detailed accounting and reporting practices of these organizations.

As more attention was focused on financial reporting by these organizations, the weaknesses described above have been corrected. We now turn our attention to the evolution of more appropriate accounting and reporting practices for these organizations. After that, we demonstrate how typical financial transactions of health and welfare organizations should be recorded and we describe and present illustrative financial statements.

---

1. *Standards of Accounting and Financial Reporting for Voluntary Health and Welfare Organizations* (New York: National Health Council, National Assembly of National Voluntary Health and Social Welfare Organizations, Inc., and United Way of America, 1975), and *Audits of Voluntary Health and Welfare Organizations* (New York: American Institute of Certified Public Accountants, 1988).

## Evolution of Accounting Practices

In an effort to alleviate the previously described inadequacies in financial reporting, the National Health Council and National Social Welfare Assembly jointly undertook a study of the accounting practices of health and welfare organizations in the early 1960s. The result was published in 1964.[2] For many years this was the most authoritative statement defining accounting practices in the health and welfare area. In general terms, this publication sought to promote more informative and uniform financial reporting for health and welfare organizations by establishing certain rules to govern the content and form of an entity's financial statements.

The rules cited in this publication are based on the recognition that the financial reports should reflect accountability of the organization to the public and other interested parties. They clearly imply that the reporting organization should recognize that it is accountable to its constituents for operational efficiency, as well as for dollars acquired and spent.

Working from that concept of accountability, the following significant rules were recommended:[3]

1.  The accrual basis of accounting should be used.

2.  Pledges receivable, properly adjusted for probable losses in collection, should be reflected in the balance sheet. They should be included as revenue "of the year for which they are pledged."

3.  All important assets (including fixed assets) for which management is responsible should be reported on the balance sheet.

4.  Depreciation should not normally be recorded as an expenditure unless it is funded. If nonfunded depreciation is recorded as a valuation account on the balance sheet, the offsetting debit should be to the investment fund balance account.

5.  The value of independently donated personal services should not be included in an organization's financial statements.

6.  Fund-accounting practices should be followed.

7.  The statement of revenues and expenditures should be organized to show revenues by sources and expenditures by functions performed.

8.  Expenditures incurred to support the organization should be carefully separated from those incurred in carrying out the programs of the organization.

Considerable attention was also given to the detailed implementation of these rules in the organization and presentation of accounting data. The various recommended financial statements are well illustrated in the last part of that book.

More recently, in 1974, the American Institute of Certified Public Accountants published its Industry Audit Guide, entitled *Audits of Voluntary Health and Welfare Organizations*. This publication sets out accounting practices that should significantly

2.  *Standards of Accounting and Financial Reporting for Voluntary Health and Welfare Organizations* (New York: National Health Council and National Social Welfare Assembly, 1964).

3.  Ibid. Comments from *Accounting Review* (October 1965) by permission of American Accounting Association.

improve health and welfare organization financial reports. Basically, it recommends an accounting system that is somewhat of a compromise between the system recommended for colleges and universities and that recommended for hospitals. Insofar as current or operating funds are concerned, the system closely follows the format prescribed for colleges and universities. It recognizes the need for using both a current unrestricted fund and a current restricted fund in accounting for current operating resources. The recommended procedures are also similar to those prescribed for colleges and universities in that it uses a land, building, and equipment fund (often referred to as a plant fund) to accumulate the investments in fixed assets along with resources contributed for the acquisitions of fixed assets. Mortgages and other liabilities relating to fixed assets are also reflected in this fund. The procedures set out in this publication are similar to those for hospitals in that it recommends the *accrual basis of accounting with full cost determination, including a provision for depreciation.* This publication was updated but not significantly changed in 1988.

Following the publication of the 1974 AICPA Audit Guide, the industry publication entitled *Standards of Accounting and Financial Reporting for Voluntary Health and Welfare Organizations* was revised. The significant changes from the 1964 publication are as follows:[4]

1. Depreciation is to be reported as an expense.

2. The term *expenses* should replace *expenditures* in the operating statement. Also, the title of the operating statement has been changed from summary of financial activities to statement of support, revenue and expenses, and changes in fund balances. "Funds functioning as endowment" has been replaced with "board-designated long-term investments."

3. The value of donated personal services are includable as an element of support where prescribed criteria are met.

4. Market value, as well as cost, is deemed to be an acceptable basis for reporting investments.

5. Gains on investment transactions in endowment funds are reported under the other revenue caption of the endowment fund in the "statement of support, revenue and expenses, and changes in fund balances" rather than directly in the fund balance as required in the 1964 statement. Resources equal to these gains may be transferred from the endowment fund to the current unrestricted fund by action of the agency's governing board where the laws of the state permit such transfer.

6. The number of funds has been reduced. The assets and liabilities of two former funds (unexpended plant funds and equity in lands, buildings, and equipment) are consolidated into a single fund for lands, buildings, and equipment. However, the balance sheet for that fund continues to show separate fund balances for expended and unexpended resources. Also, as observed before, current funds functioning as endowment have been eliminated

---

4. *Standards of Accounting and Financial Reporting for Voluntary Health and Welfare Organizations* (1975), pp. 2–3.

from the endowment fund. The new *Standards* publication requires that they be carried in the current fund as board-designated long-term investments.

7. Expense allocations, long considered important in reflecting accountability in the use of resources, now include a representative time test for determining staff time allocations to functions as an alternative to the daily time sheets required in the 1964 publication.

8. Columnar style is cited as the preferred format for the "statement of support, revenue and expenses, and changes in fund balances."

9. The agency is responsible for imposing appropriate internal controls on contributions from the time they are received, even though they have not yet been recorded.

10. Payments to affiliated organizations are reported as an expense on the "statement of support, revenue and expenses, and changes in fund balances," as was required before. However, the new *Standards* publication recognizes that there may be cases where it would be appropriate to report them as a deduction from total public support and revenue, provided certain criteria are met.

Another important change involves the recognition of certain donated materials and services in an agency's statement of support, revenue, and expense and changes in fund balances. Donated services must meet the following criteria to be included in that statement:

1. The services donated must be a normal part of the program or supporting services that would otherwise be performed by salaried personnel.

2. The organization must exercise control over the employment and duties of the persons donating the services.

3. The organization must have a clearly identifiable basis for measuring the values to be assigned to the donated services.[5]

Donated materials that are significant in amount should be recorded at their fair market values when received.

The accrual basis for recognizing revenues is interpreted to require recognition at the time a pledge or other asset is received unless the use of the resources received is deferred to future years. For example, if a pledge or other asset is received in 1991 with no stipulations as to when the resources are to be used, the amount received would be recognized as revenue in 1991. However, if half of the pledge or other resource is restricted to use in 1992, that part should be credited to deferred revenue in 1991 and converted to revenue in 1992. In all instances, an appropriate provision should be made for estimated uncollectible pledges as they are recorded.

Exhibit 13–1 shows that contributions to restricted funds (the building fund, for example) are reported as part of support revenue. Consistent with that treatment of externally restricted funds, health and welfare agencies recognize restricted current fund resource inflows as revenues when they are received rather than when they are used, as is the case for colleges and universities.

---

5. *Standards of Accounting and Financial Reporting for Voluntary Health and Welfare Organizations* (1975), p. 20.

To implement the concept of dollar accountability, the AICPA publication recommends use of the following funds in accounting for the resources of health and welfare agencies:

1. current unrestricted fund
2. current restricted funds
3. land, building, and equipment fund
4. endowment funds
5. custodian funds
6. loan and annuity funds.

The funds listed in the revised publication *Standards of Accounting and Financial Recording* are the same as those listed above.[6]

All of the funds listed here, except custodial funds, have been described in other sections of the text. Custodial funds are similar to agency funds in college and university accounting. They are established to account for assets received by an organization to be held or disbursed according to the instructions of the person or organization providing them. Generally, the revenue generated from investing custodial fund resources must also be used in accordance with the wishes of the contributor. Therefore, they are not normally included as part of the organization's revenue or support.

The land, buildings, and equipment fund, sometimes called "plant fund," is similar to the plant fund for colleges and universities. However, the fund balance is divided into only two categories, expended and unexpended, rather than the four used by colleges and universities (see Exhibit 13–3). The expended balance shows the net investment in fixed assets, while the unexpended balance is equal to the net spendable resources earmarked for the acquisition of additional plant assets.

Plant assets purchased by using spendable resources in the land, building 11 and equipment fund are recorded in that fund as follows:

| | | |
|---|---|---|
| Plant assets | xxxx | |
|   Cash | | xxxx |
| Fund balance—unexpended | xxxx | |
|   Fund balance—expended | | xxxx |

When plant assets are acquired by using unrestricted current fund resources, the acquisition should be recorded in both funds as follows:

**Current Fund—Unrestricted**

| | | |
|---|---|---|
| Property and equipment acquisitions from | | |
|     unrestricted funds (fund balance) | xxxx | |
|   Cash | | xxxx |

**Land Building and Equipment Fund**

| | | |
|---|---|---|
| Plant assets | xxxx | |
|   Property and equipment acquisitions from | | |
|     unrestricted funds (expended fund balance) | | xxxx |

6. *Audits of Voluntary Health and Welfare Organizations*, pp. 2–3.

The balance in the property and equipment acquisitions from the unrestricted funds account would then be shown as a subtraction from the unrestricted fund balance of the current fund and as an addition to the expended fund balance in the land building and equipment fund (see Exhibit 13–1).

**EXHIBIT 13–1.**   Model Voluntary Health and Welfare Service Statement of Support, Revenue, and Expenses and Changes in Fund Balances—Year Ended December 31, 19X2, with Comparative Totals of 19X1

| | 19X2 | | | | Total All funds | |
| --- | --- | --- | --- | --- | --- | --- |
| | Current Funds | | Land, Building, and Equipment Fund | Endowment Fund | | |
| | Unrestricted | Restricted | | | 19X2 | 19X1 |
| Public support and revenue: | | | | | | |
| Public support: | | | | | | |
| Contributions (net of estimated uncollectible pledges of $195,000 in 19X2 and $150,000 in 19X1) | $3,764,000 | $162,000 | — | $ 2,000 | $3,928,000 | $3,976,000 |
| Contributions to building fund | — | — | $72,000 | — | 72,000 | 150,000 |
| Special events (net of direct costs of $181,000 in 19X2 and $163,000 in 19X1) | 104,000 | — | — | — | 104,000 | 92,000 |
| Legacies and bequests | 92,000 | — | — | 4,000 | 96,000 | 129,000 |
| Received from federated and nonfederated campaigns (which incurred related fund-raising expenses of $38,000 in 19X2 and $29,000 in 19X1) | 275,000 | — | — | — | 275,000 | 308,000 |
| Total public support | $4,235,000 | $162,000 | $72,000 | $ 6,000 | $4,475,000 | $4,655,000 |
| Revenue: | | | | | | |
| Membership dues | $ 17,000 | — | — | — | $ 17,000 | $ 12,000 |
| Investment income | 98,000 | $ 10,000 | — | — | 108,000 | 94,000 |
| Realized gain on investment transactions | 200,000 | — | — | $25,000 | 225,000 | 275,000 |
| Miscellaneous | 42,000 | — | — | — | 42,000 | 47,000 |
| Total revenue | $ 357,000 | $ 10,000 | — | $25,000 | $ 392,000 | $ 428,000 |
| Total support and revenue | $4,592,000 | $172,000 | $72,000 | $31,000 | $4,867,000 | $5,083,000 |
| Expenses: | | | | | | |
| Program services: | | | | | | |
| Research | $1,257,000 | $155,000 | $ 2,000 | — | $1,414,000 | $1,365,000 |
| Public health education | 539,000 | — | 5,000 | — | 544,000 | 485,000 |
| Professional education and training | 612,000 | — | 6,000 | — | 618,000 | 516,000 |
| Community services | 568,000 | — | 10,000 | — | 578,000 | 486,000 |
| Total program services | $2,976,000 | $155,000 | $23,000 | — | $3,154,000 | $2,852,000 |

**EXHIBIT 13–1.** Continued

| | Current Funds | | Land, Building, and Equipment Fund | Endowment Fund | Total All Funds | |
|---|---|---|---|---|---|---|
| | | | *19X2* | | | |
| | *Unrestricted* | *Restricted* | *Fund* | *Fund* | *19X2* | *19X1* |
| Supporting services: | | | | | | |
| Management and general | $ 567,000 | — | $ 7,000 | — | $ 574,000 | $ 638,000 |
| Funding raising | 642,000 | — | 12,000 | — | 654,000 | 546,000 |
| Total supporting services | $1,209,000 | — | $ 19,000 | — | $1,228,000 | $1,184,000 |
| Total expenses | $4,185,000 | $155,000 | $ 42,000 | — | $4,382,000 | $4,036,000 |
| Excess (deficiency) of public support and revenue over expenses | $ 407,000 | $ 17,000 | $ 30,000 | $ 31,000 | | |
| Other changes in fund balances: | | | | | | |
| Property and equipment acquisitions from unrestricted funds | (17,000) | — | 17,000 | — | | |
| Transfer of realized endowment fund appreciation | 100,000 | — | — | (100,000) | | |
| Returned to donor | — | (8,000) | — | — | | |
| Fund balances, beginning of year | 5,361,000 | 123,000 | 649,000 | 2,017,000 | | |
| Fund balances, end of year | $5,851,000 | $132,000 | $696,000 | $1,948,000 | | |

## Financial Statements

The all-inclusive, multiple-column operating statement, entitled "statement of support, revenue and expenses, and changes in fund balances" (see Exhibit 13–1) reflects two principal categories of revenues. First and most significant is "revenue realized from public support." The second category is labeled "other revenue" and includes such things as membership dues, program service fees, sales of materials, investment income, and gains on investment transactions. The expense section of the statement is divided into two major categories. One is labeled "program expenses" and includes expenses incurred in implementing the services of the organization. The second, described as "supporting services," includes the costs of managing the organization and raising funds. A third category, sometimes included, is entitled "payments to national organization."[7]

One of the significant aspects of financial reporting in the health and welfare area is the need for distinguishing between the *sustentation costs,* shown as supporting services expenses in the illustrated operating statement, and *service implementation*

7. *Standards of Accounting and Financial Reporting for Voluntary Health and Welfare Organizations* (1975), Exhibit A.

**EXHIBIT 13-2.** Model Voluntary Health and Welfare Service Statement of Functional Expenses—For Fiscal Period

| | | | 19X2 | |
| --- | --- | --- | --- | --- |
| | | Program Services | | |
| | Research | Public Health Education | Professional Education and Training | Community Services |
| Salaries | $    45,000 | $291,000 | $251,000 | $269,000 |
| Employee health and retirement benefits | 4,000 | 14,000 | 14,000 | 14,000 |
| Payroll taxes, etc. | 2,000 | 16,000 | 13,000 | 14,000 |
| Total salaries and related expenses | $    51,000 | $321,000 | $278,000 | $297,000 |
| Professional fees and contract service payments | $      1,000 | $  10,000 | $    3,000 | $    8,000 |
| Supplies | 2,000 | 13,000 | 13,000 | 13,000 |
| Telephone and telegraph | 2,000 | 13,000 | 10,000 | 11,000 |
| Postage and shipping | 2,000 | 17,000 | 13,000 | 9,000 |
| Occupancy | 5,000 | 26,000 | 22,000 | 25,000 |
| Rental of equipment | 1,000 | 24,000 | 14,000 | 4,000 |
| Local transportation | 3,000 | 22,000 | 20,000 | 22,000 |
| Conferences, conventions, meetings | 8,000 | 19,000 | 71,000 | 20,000 |
| Printing and publications | 4,000 | 56,000 | 43,000 | 11,000 |
| Awards and grants | 1,332,000 | 14,000 | 119,000 | 144,000 |
| Miscellaneous | 1,000 | 4,000 | 6,000 | 4,000 |
| Total expenses before depreciation | $1,412,000 | $539,000 | $612,000 | $568,000 |
| Depreciation of buildings and equipment | 2,000 | 5,000 | 6,000 | 10,000 |
| Total expenses | $1,414,000 | $544,000 | $618,000 | $578,000 |

*costs,* also labeled "program service expenses" in the illustrated statement. We may think of sustentation costs as the *expenses incurred in keeping the organization in operation.* They include such things as fund-raising costs and administrative outlays that are not directly related to carrying out the services the entity was organized to provide. These can be thought of as overhead costs associated with sustaining the entity. On the other hand, service implementation costs include the outlays made to furnish the services the organization was created to provide. The third subdivision sometimes found in the expenses section—entitled "payments to national organizations"—indicates the extent to which local contributions are being used to finance the national operations of the agency.

Although the term *sustentation costs* can be defined with some degree of clarity, it is often much more difficult in actual practice to identify the costs that should be included in it. For example, one of the services expected of the American Cancer Society is that of educating the public concerning the detection of cancer symptoms. The cost of printing and distributing literature that contains this information and also invites the public to contribute to the organization is difficult to allocate between sustentation and service implementation costs except on an arbitrary basis. That is one of the reasons

| | | 19X2 | | | | |
|---|---|---|---|---|---|---|
| | | Supporting Services | | | Total Expenses | |
| Total | Management and General | Fund Raising | Total | 19X2 | 19X1 |
| $ 856,000 | $331,000 | $368,000 | $ 699,000 | $1,555,000 | $1,433,000 |
| 46,000 | 22,000 | 15,000 | 37,000 | 83,000 | 75,000 |
| 45,000 | 18,000 | 18,000 | 36,000 | 81,000 | 75,000 |
| $ 947,000 | $371,000 | $401,000 | $ 772,000 | $1,719,000 | $1,583,000 |
| $ 22,000 | $ 26,000 | $ 8,000 | $ 34,000 | $ 56,000 | $ 53,000 |
| 41,000 | 18,000 | 17,000 | 35,000 | 76,000 | 71,000 |
| 36,000 | 15,000 | 23,000 | 38,000 | 74,000 | 68,000 |
| 41,000 | 13,000 | 30,000 | 43,000 | 84,000 | 80,000 |
| 78,000 | 30,000 | 27,000 | 57,000 | 135,000 | 126,000 |
| 43,000 | 3,000 | 16,000 | 19,000 | 62,000 | 58,000 |
| 67,000 | 23,000 | 30,000 | 53,000 | 120,000 | 113,000 |
| 118,000 | 38,000 | 13,000 | 51,000 | 169,000 | 156,000 |
| 114,000 | 14,000 | 64,000 | 78,000 | 192,000 | 184,000 |
| 1,609,000 | — | — | — | 1,609,000 | 1,448,000 |
| 15,000 | 16,000 | 21,000 | 37,000 | 52,000 | 64,000 |
| $3,131,000 | $567,000 | $650,000 | $1,217,000 | $4,348,000 | $4,004,000 |
| 23,000 | 7,000 | 4,000 | 11,000 | 34,000 | 32,000 |
| $3,154,000 | $574,000 | $654,000 | $1,228,000 | $4,382,000 | $4,036,000 |

why the *Standards* publication gives considerable attention to these allocation procedures.[8] Nevertheless, discerning potential contributors are always interested in knowing how many cents out of each dollar of their contributions are actually being used to provide the intended services, and the accounting procedures for these organizations must be designed to meet that need.

The AICPA has issued Statement of Position 87-2, entitled *Accounting for Joint Costs of Informational Materials and Activities of Not-for-Profit Organizations That Include a Fund Raising Appeal,* to provide guidance in allocating such costs into sustentation and service implementation categories. The provisions of this statement as well as other suggestions relating to the allocation of expenses into these two categories are included in Chapter 6 of *Audits of Voluntary Health and Welfare Organizations.*[9]

One of the important changes reflected in the 1975 *Standards* publication is recognition of the need to record and report depreciation as an expense. This publication, as well as the AICPA publication, recommends separate disclosure of depreciation expense in the statement of functional expenses (see Exhibit 13–2).

8. Ibid., pp. 61–67.
9. *Audits of Voluntary Health and Welfare Organizations* (1988), pp. 24–31.

The balance sheet for voluntary health and welfare agencies is generally presented within a format similar to that conventionally used for colleges and universities (see Exhibit 13–3). However, the *Standards* publication also suggests the possibility of using an alternative columnar format listing the assets, liabilities, and fund balances of each fund in a separate column, with the totals accumulated in an extreme right column.[10] A statement of cash flows should also be included as part of the organization's financial statements.

## Typical Transactions Illustrated

We have noted that the accounting system for a health and welfare agency should be designed to disclose both dollar and operational accountability. It should combine fund-oriented records with the full accrual basis of accounting. We shall now illustrate how a series of typical health and welfare agency transactions should be recorded in a transactions worksheet (Exhibit 13–4). Assumed beginning-of-the-period balances are shown in the first two columns of the worksheet. A series of assumed transactions, described next, is recorded in the third and fourth columns. Transaction numbers are shown in the worksheet to identify the entries required to record each of them. Operating statement and balance sheet data, derived from those two pairs of columns, are recorded in the last four columns. Financial statements similar to those shown in Exhibits 13–1 and 13–3 can then be prepared from those data.

### Assumed Transactions

1. Contributions received:

| | | |
|---|---:|---|
| Unrestricted contributions | $3,000,000 | (in pledges) |
| Restricted contributions | 200,000 | (in cash) |
| For building fund | 70,000 | (in pledges) |
| For endowment fund | 5,000 | (in cash) |

2. Collected pledges as follows:

| | |
|---|---:|
| Unrestricted contributions | $2,900,000 |
| Building fund | 80,000 |

3. Other unrestricted revenues received in cash:

| | |
|---|---:|
| Special events (net of direct costs of $60,000) | $ 120,000 |
| Legacies and bequests | 80,000 |
| Membership dues | 20,000 |
| Investment income | 100,000 |
| Miscellaneous | 40,000 |

4. Program expenses incurred (handled through vouchers payable):

| | |
|---|---:|
| Research | $ 600,000 |
| Public education | 520,000 |
| Counseling services | 300,000 |
| Community services | 550,000 |

5. Program expenses paid from restricted resources:

| | |
|---|---:|
| Research | $ 150,000 |

6. Support and sustentation expenses (handled through vouchers payable):

| | |
|---|---:|
| General administration | $ 550,000 |
| Fund raising | 650,000 |

10. *Standards of Accounting and Financial Reporting for Voluntary Health and Welfare Organizations* (1975), Exhibit D.

**EXHIBIT 13–3.** Model Voluntary Health and Welfare Service Balance Sheets—December 31, 19X2 and 19X1

| Assets | 19X2 | 19X1 | Liabilities and Fund Balances | 19X2 | 19X1 |
|---|---|---|---|---|---|
| | | | **Current Funds** | | |
| | | | **Unrestricted** | | |
| Cash | $2,207,000 | $2,530,000 | Accounts payable | $ 148,000 | $ 139,000 |
| Investments | | | Research grants payable | 596,000 | 616,000 |
| For long-term purposes | 2,727,000 | 2,245,000 | Contributions designated for | | |
| Other | 1,075,000 | 950,000 | future periods | 245,000 | 219,000 |
| | | | Total liabilities and deferred revenues | $ 989,000 | $ 974,000 |
| Pledges receivable less allowance for uncollectibles of $105,000 and | | | | | |
| $92,000 | 475,000 | 363,000 | Fund balances: | | |
| Inventories of educational materials at cost | 70,000 | 61,000 | Designated by the governing board for: | | |
| Accrued interest, other receivables, and prepaid expenses | 286,000 | 186,000 | Long-term investments | $2,800,000 | $2,300,000 |
| | | | Purchases of new equipment | 100,000 | — |
| | | | Research purposes | 1,152,000 | 1,748,000 |
| | | | Undesignated, available for general activities | 1,799,000 | 1,313,000 |
| | | | Total fund balance | $5,851,000 | $5,361,000 |
| Total | $6,840,000 | $6,335,000 | Total | $6,840,000 | $6,335,000 |
| | | | **Restricted** | | |
| Cash | $ 3,000 | $ 5,000 | Fund balances: | | |
| Investments | 71,000 | 72,000 | Professional education | $ 84,000 | $ — |
| Grants receivable | 58,000 | 46,000 | Research grants | 48,000 | 123,000 |
| Total | $ 132,000 | $ 123,000 | Total | $ 132,000 | $ 123,000 |
| | | | **Land, Building, and Equipment Fund** | | |
| | | | Mortgage payable, 8% due | | |
| Cash | $ 3,000 | $ 2,000 | 19XX | $ 32,000 | $ 36,000 |
| Investments | 177,000 | 145,000 | | | |
| Pledges receivable less allowance for uncollectibles | | | Fund balances: | | |
| of $7,500 and $5,000 | 32,000 | 25,000 | Expended | $ 484,000 | $ 477,000 |
| Land, buildings, and equipment at cost less accumulated depreciation of | | | Unexpended–restricted | 212,000 | 172,000 |
| $296,000 and $262,000 | 516,000 | 513,000 | Total fund balance | $ 696,000 | $ 649,000 |
| Total | $ 728,000 | $ 685,000 | Total | $ 728,000 | $ 685,000 |
| | | | **Endowment Funds** | | |
| Cash | $ 4,000 | $ 10,000 | Fund balance | $1,948,000 | $2,017,000 |
| Investments | 1,944,000 | 2,007,000 | | | |
| Total | $1,948,000 | $2,017,000 | Total | $1,948,000 | $2,017,000 |

**EXHIBIT 13–4.**  Illustration Health and Welfare Agency Transactions Worksheet for Period

| | *Beginning-of-Period Balances* | |
|---|---:|---:|
| ***Current Funds*** | | |
| Unrestricted | | |
| Cash | 2,500,000 | |
| Pledges receivable net of allowances for uncollectibles | 300,000 | |
| Vouchers payable | | 150,000 |
| Fund balances | | |
| Designated by governing board for purchase of fixed assets | | 1,500,000 |
| Undesignated | | 1,150,000 |
| Totals | 2,800,000 | 2,800,000 |
| Restricted | | |
| Cash | 15,000 | |
| Fund balance | | 15,000 |
| Totals | 15,000 | 15,000 |
| Totals for current funds | 2,815,000 | 2,815,000 |
| ***Land, Building, and Equipment Fund*** | | |
| Cash | 3,000 | |
| Investments | 100,000 | |
| Pledges receivable net of allowances for uncollectibles | 20,000 | |
| Building and equipment | 650,000 | |
| Accumulated depreciation | | 250,000 |
| Land | 100,000 | |
| Mortgage payable | | 40,000 |
| Fund balances | | |
| Expended | | 460,000 |
| Unexpended | | 123,000 |
| Totals | 873,000 | 873,000 |
| ***Endowment Funds*** | | |
| Cash | 8,000 | |
| Investments | 2,010,000 | |
| Fund balance | | 2,018,000 |
| Totals | $2,018,000 | $2,018,000 |
| ***Operating Statement Accounts*** | | |
| Revenues | | |
| Contribution revenue—unrestricted | | |
| Contribution revenue—restricted | | |
| Special events revenue | | |
| Legacies and bequests | | |
| Membership dues | | |
| Investment (endowment) revenue | | |
| Miscellaneous revenue | | |

| Transactions and Adjustments | | | | Operating Statement Items | Balance Sheet | |
|---|---|---|---|---|---|---|

### Current Funds

| | | | | | | |
|---|---|---|---|---|---|---|
| (2) | 2,900,000 | (7) | 20,000 | | 2,790,000 | |
| (3) | 360,000 | (9) | 2,950,000 | | | |
| (1) | 3,000,000 | (2) | 2,900,000 | | 400,000 | |
| (9) | 2,950,000 | (4) | 1,970,000 | | | 370,000 |
| | | (6) | 1,200,000 | | | |
| (7) | 20,000 | | | | | 1,480,000 |
| | | (10) | 190,000 | | | 1,340,000 |
| | | | | | 3,190,000 | 3,190,000 |
| | | | | | | |
| (1) | 200,000 | (5) | 150,000 | | 65,000 | |
| | | (10) | 50,000 | | | 65,000 |
| | | | | | 65,000 | 65,000 |
| | | | | | 3,255,000 | 3,255,000 |

### Land, Building, and Equipment Fund

| | | | | | | |
|---|---|---|---|---|---|---|
| (2) | 80,000 | | | | 83,000 | |
| | | | | | 100,000 | |
| (1) | 70,000 | (2) | 80,000 | | 10,000 | |
| (7) | 20,000 | | | | 670,000 | |
| | | (8) | 35,000 | | | 285,000 |
| | | | | | 100,000 | |
| | | | | | | 40,000 |
| (10) | 35,000 | (7) | 20,000 | | | 445,000 |
| | | (10) | 70,000 | | | 193,000 |
| | | | | | 963,000 | 963,000 |

### Endowment Funds

| | | | | | | |
|---|---|---|---|---|---|---|
| (1) | 5,000 | | | | 13,000 | |
| | | | | | 2,010,000 | |
| | | (10) | 5,000 | | | 2,023,000 |
| | | | | | $2,023,000 | $2,023,000 |

### Operating Statement Accounts

| | | | | | | |
|---|---|---|---|---|---|---|
| | | (1) | 3,000,000 | 3,000,000 | | |
| | | (1) | 200,000 | 200,000 | | |
| | | (3) | 120,000 | 120,000 | | |
| | | (3) | 80,000 | 80,000 | | |
| | | (3) | 20,000 | 20,000 | | |
| | | (3) | 100,000 | 100,000 | | |
| | | (3) | 40,000 | 40,000 | | |

*exhibit continues*

**EXHIBIT 13–4.**   Continued

*Beginning-of-Period Balances*

Contributions to land building and equipment fund
Contributions to endowment fund
Expenses
　Research expenses—restricted
　Research expenses

　Public education expenses

　Counseling service expenses

　Community service expenses

　General education expenses

　Fund-raising expenses


　Excess of revenues over expenses
　　Unrestricted
　　Restricted
　　Land, building, and equipment fund
　　Endowment fund
Totals

| | | |
|---|---|---|
| 7. | Other changes in fund balances: | |
| | Fixed assets acquired by use of unrestricted funds | $    20,000 |
| 8. | Depreciation of fixed assets allocated as follows: | |
| | Program services: | |
| | 　Research | $     1,500 |
| | 　Public education | 6,000 |
| | 　Counseling services | 5,500 |
| | 　Community services | 11,000 |
| | Support and sustentation: | |
| | 　General administration | 6,000 |
| | 　Fund raising | 5,000 |
| 9. | Paid vouchers payable in amount of | $2,950,000 |
| 10. | Transferred excess of revenues over expenses to fund balance accounts. | |

# ▪ Accounting for Churches

Churches represent another segment of the nonprofit area whose operating environment requires a dollar-accountability–oriented accounting system. They operate as *pure non-*

| Transactions and Adjustments | | Operating Statement Items | Balance Sheet |
|---|---|---|---|
| | (1) 70,000 | 70,000 | |
| | (1) 5,000 | 5,000 | |
| (5) | 150,000 | 150,000 | |
| (4) | 600,000 | 601,500 | |
| (8) | 1,500 | | |
| (4) | 520,000 | 526,000 | |
| (8) | 6,000 | | |
| (4) | 300,000 | 305,500 | |
| (8) | 5,500 | | |
| (4) | 550,000 | 561,000 | |
| (8) | 11,000 | | |
| (6) | 550,000 | 556,000 | |
| (8) | 6,000 | | |
| (6) | 650,000 | 655,000 | |
| (8) | 5,000 | | |
| (10) | 190,000 | 190,000 | |
| (10) | 50,000 | 50,000 | |
| (10) | 35,000 | 35,000 | |
| (10) | 5,000 | 5,000 | |
| | | $3,635,000 | $3,635,000 |

profit organizations and follow fund-accounting procedures. Their resource conversion activities are almost exclusively controlled through budgetary appropriations. Typically, general or current fund expenditures are planned by the pastor and church officers to provide a specified program of services. The proposed service plan or budget is then generally presented to the congregation for acceptance, modification, or rejection. Once approved by the membership, the budget becomes the operating plan for the church during the ensuing fiscal period. Contributions are solicited to carry out the program, and expenditures are controlled within the limits of budgetary appropriations.

In 1978, the AICPA issued *Statement of Position on Accounting Principles and Reporting Practices for Certain Nonprofit Organizations*,[11] which was designed to promote greater uniformity in accounting and financial reporting for nonprofit organizations not governed by previously established industry audit guides. Although such statements do not establish standards that are enforceable under the AICPA's code of professional ethics, they do reflect the conclusions of at least a majority of the

11. American Institute of Certified Public Accountants, *Statement of Position on Accounting Principles and Reporting Practices for Certain Nonprofit Organizations* (New York: AICPA, 1978).

accounting standards executive committee. Therefore, it is interesting to observe that this statement of position would, if made effective, requires use of the full accrual basis of accounting, including the recognition of depreciation. This has now been made a required standard by FASB 93. However, because of the strong emphasis on appropriation control and dollar accountability in church operations, most churches still use the cash or modified-cash basis of accounting and financial reporting.

The Statement of Position described in the preceding paragraph along with other AICPA statements were later incorporated into a publication entitled *Audits of Certain Nonprofit Organizations*.[12] While churches are not included in the list of organizations covered by the publication, that list is clearly defined as "not all-inclusive."[13] Also, because this publication is designed to cover all nonprofit organizations not covered by the other audit guides[14] it is appropriate to conclude that its provisions apply to churches as well as the organizations specifically listed. Nevertheless, most churches still follow expenditure, dollar-accountability accounting procedures. Therefore, we shall demonstrate how those procedures are carried out.

Both revenues and expenditures of churches are related to a budget plan. Although budgetary data can be recorded in the accounts as illustrated for governmental entities, the more common practice is to relate actual and budgetary amounts to each other only in the periodic statements of revenues and expenditures. Exhibit 13–5 shows the form and some of the account titles that are typically used in reporting the revenues and expenditures for a church.

The relationship of benevolences to total budgeted expenditures is generally considered an important element to be disclosed in the operating statement. This is consistent with the basic operating philosophy of most churches, which calls for each church to seek to help others as well as to sustain its own program of ministering to its members.

The general or current fund balance sheet for a church typically discloses only appropriable assets and claims against those assets. If, as is often the case, the records are maintained on a cash basis, the only appropriable asset will be cash. The only liability likely to be shown on the balance sheet in that situation is payroll taxes payable. Fixed assets and long-term obligations may be disclosed in a separate plant fund balance sheet, but they are more often completely omitted from the financial reports.

The following illustration shows how two assumed transactions should be recorded in a transactions worksheet (Exhibit 13–6) and how financial statements (see Exhibits 13–7 and 13–8) may be prepared from the worksheet data. The statement of revenues and expenditures shows only control account balances in the expenditures section. In actual practice, these would be subdivided as shown in Exhibit 13–5.

---

12. The most recent edition of this book was published in 1987.
13. American Institute of Certified Public Accountants, *Audits of Certain Nonprofit Organizations* (New York: AICPA, 1987), p. 1.
14. Ibid.

**EXHIBIT 13–5.** Model Church Statement of Revenues and Expenditures—Last Month of 19X2

| | Actual Amount | | Budget | | Year to Date Over or (Under) |
|---|---|---|---|---|---|
| | This Month | Year to Date | This Month | Year to Date | |
| **Revenues** | | | | | |
| Sunday school offering | $ 300 | $ 2,950 | $ 350 | $ 3,000 | $ (50) |
| Plate offering | 400 | 3,000 | 300 | 2,800 | 200 |
| Pledges for 19X1 | 0 | 8,000 | 0 | 7,000 | 1,000 |
| Pledges for 19X2 | 18,000 | 180,000 | 18,500 | 188,000 | (8,000) |
| Miscellaneous | 100 | 1,000 | 150 | 1,700 | (700) |
| Total revenues | $18,800 | $194,950 | $19,300 | $202,500 | $(7,550) |
| **Expenditures** | | | | | |
| Benevolences | $ 5,000 | $ 58,000 | $ 6,000 | $ 60,000 | $(2,000) |
| Christian education | | | | | |
| Literature | $ 400 | $ 4,800 | $ 500 | $ 5,000 | $ (200) |
| Church school supplies | 300 | 4,000 | 250 | 4,500 | (500) |
| Conference and camp fund | 200 | 3,000 | 200 | 3,000 | 0 |
| Outside speakers and leaders | 0 | 100 | 100 | 400 | (300) |
| Parties and recreation | 250 | 1,000 | 300 | 1,300 | (300) |
| Miscellaneous | 100 | 1,100 | 150 | 1,500 | (400) |
| Subtotal (Christian education) | $ 1,250 | $ 14,000 | $ 1,500 | $ 15,700 | $(1,700) |
| Music | $ 250 | $ 3,000 | $ 200 | $ 3,300 | $ (300) |
| Staff | | | | | |
| Minister | $ 3,000 | $ 36,000 | $ 3,000 | $ 36,000 | $ 0 |
| Minister of education | 2,000 | 24,000 | 2,000 | 24,000 | 0 |
| Secretary | 1,500 | 18,000 | 1,500 | 18,000 | 0 |
| Janitor and maid | 1,200 | 14,400 | 1,200 | 14,400 | 0 |
| Subtotal (staff) | $ 7,700 | $ 92,400 | $ 7,700 | $ 92,400 | $ 0 |
| Current expenditures | | | | | |
| Printing and office supplies | $ 300 | $ 4,000 | $ 400 | $ 4,500 | $ (500) |
| Custodian supplies and services | 200 | 2,600 | 300 | 3,000 | (400) |
| Miscellaneous | 50 | 500 | 100 | 1,000 | (500) |
| Subtotal (current expenditures) | $ 550 | $ 7,100 | $ 800 | $ 8,500 | $(1,400) |
| Building | | | | | |
| Insurance (real estate and auto) | $ 400 | $ 4,800 | $ 400 | $ 4,800 | $ 0 |
| Utilities | 300 | 4,000 | 350 | 4,600 | (600) |
| Maintenance | 200 | 3,000 | 300 | 3,600 | (600) |
| Subtotal (building) | $ 900 | $ 11,800 | $ 1,050 | $ 13,000 | $(1,200) |
| Debt retirement | $ 800 | $ 9,600 | $ 800 | $ 9,600 | $ 0 |
| Total expenditures | $16,450 | $195,900 | $18,050 | $202,500 | $(6,600) |
| Revenues over (under) expenditures | $ 2,350 | $ (950) | $ 1,250 | $ 0 | $ (950) |

**EXHIBIT 13–6.   Illustration Church Transactions Worksheet—For Period**

| | Beginning-of-Period Balances | Transactions | | Operating Statement Items | Balance Sheet Items |
|---|---|---|---|---|---|
| | | (1) | (2) | | |
| Cash in bank | 11,800 | (1) 10,500 | (2) 8,000 | | 14,300 |
| Petty cash | 500 | | | | 500 |
| Payroll taxes payable | 100 | | (2) 100 | | 200 |
| Withholding taxes payable | 200 | | (2) 200 | | 400 |
| Fund balance | 12,000 | | | | 12,000 |
| Revenues from church school | | | (1) 100 | 100 | |
| Revenues from plate offering | | | (1) 200 | 200 | |
| Revenues from pledges | | | (1) 10,000 | 10,000 | |
| Miscellaneous revenues | | | (1) 200 | 200 | |
| Expenditures | | | | | |
| Benevolences | | (2) 1,500 | | 1,500 | |
| Christian education | | (2) 200 | | 200 | |
| Music program | | (2) 100 | | 100 | |
| Staff salaries | | (2) 4,000 | | 4,000 | |
| Current operations | | (2) 1,000 | | 1,000 | |
| Building costs | | (2) 1,500 | | 1,500 | |
| Totals | 12,300     12,300 | 18,800 | 18,800 | 8,300 | 12,600 |
| Excess of revenues over expenditures | | | | 2,200 | 2,200 |
| Totals | 12,300     12,300 | 18,800 | 18,800 | 10,500     10,500 | 14,800     14,800 |

**EXHIBIT 13−7.** Illustration Church Statement of Revenues and Expenditures— For Period

| | Actual Amounts | Budget Amounts | Actual Over or (Under) |
|---|---|---|---|
| Revenues | | | |
| Church school offering | $ 100 | $ 150 | $ (50) |
| Plate offering | 200 | 225 | (25) |
| Pledges | 10,000 | 9,800 | 200 |
| Miscellaneous | 200 | 300 | (100) |
| Total revenues | $10,500 | $10,475 | $ 25 |
| Expenditures | | | |
| Benevolences | $ 1,500 | $ 1,500 | $ 0 |
| Christian education | 200 | 250 | (50) |
| Music | 100 | 75 | 25 |
| Staff salaries | 4,000 | 4,000 | 0 |
| Current operations | 1,000 | 1,100 | (100) |
| Building costs | 1,500 | 1,500 | 0 |
| Total expenditures | $ 8,300 | $ 8,425 | $(125) |
| Excess of revenues over expenditures | $ 2,200 | $ 2,050 | $ 150 |

**EXHIBIT 13−8.** Illustration Church Balance Sheet—End of Period

### Assets

| | | |
|---|---|---|
| Cash in bank | | $14,300 |
| Petty cash | | 500 |
| Total assets | | $14,800 |

### Liabilities and Fund Balance

| | | |
|---|---|---|
| Payroll taxes payable | $ 200 | |
| Withholding taxes payable | 400 | $ 600 |
| Fund balance | | |
| Beginning-of-period balance | $12,000 | |
| Excess of revenues over expenditures for period | 2,200 | 14,200 |
| Total liabilities and fund balance | | $14,800 |

### Assumed Transactions

| | | |
|---|---|---|
| 1. | Receipts for period | |
| | Church school offering | $ 100 |
| | Plate offering | 200 |
| | Pledges | $10,000 |
| | Miscellaneous | 200 |

2.  Disbursements for period

| | |
|---|---:|
| Benevolences | $1,500 |
| Christian education | 200 |
| Music program | 100 |
| Staff salaries | 4,000 |
| Includes payroll taxes amounting to $100 and withholding taxes of $200 | |
| Current expenditures | 1,000 |
| Building expenditures | 1,500 |

# ■ Other Developments

As observed earlier, the AICPA issued a *Statement of Position on Accounting Principles and Reporting Practices for Certain Nonprofit Organizations*. This statement was intended to define accounting practices for nonprofit organizations other than those already covered by existing AICPA audit guides. By implication, it therefore prescribes accounting practices for *churches, schools, museums, and foundations*. Like the audit guides, it outlines procedures that must be followed if the organization is to have its financial statements recognized as being prepared in accordance with generally accepted accounting principles. In many instances, such recognition is not necessary for these organizations. As a result, churches and many of the other organizations mentioned previously will probably continue to use the dollar-accountability reporting practices we have already described.

The more significant requirements of the AICPA statement were as follows:

1.  The full accrual basis of accounting should be used.

2.  Separate funds should be used for financial reporting purposes only to disclose the nature and amounts of significant resources that are externally restricted.

3.  Financial reports should include a balance sheet, a statement of activity or operations, and a statement of changes in financial position (now statement of cash flows).

4.  Combined statements should be prepared for all financially interrelated segments of an organization.

5.  Pledges receivable should be recorded when they are received. Appropriate provision should be made for probable losses in collecting the pledges. Revenue from pledges should be recognized in the year that the donors intended the resources to be used. If that is not clear, they should be recognized as revenue in the year the donors indicate the pledges will be paid. That means that the credit offsetting the recognition of a pledge receivable can be either to deferred pledge income or pledge income, depending on the stipulations associated with the pledge.

6.  Current gifts with restricted uses should be recorded by crediting deferred income in the operating fund rather than by creating a separate restricted current funds accounting entity. Restricted grants should be handled in the same manner.

7.  The statement requires that certain specified criteria must be met before donated and contributed services may be recognized as revenue.

8.  Expenses should be reported according to functional or program classifications similar to the way they are reported for health and welfare agencies.

9.  Sustentation expenses (management and general expenses plus fund-raising expenses) should be separately disclosed.

10. Investments may be reflected in the financial statement at either market value or the lower of cost or market value. Valuation adjustments should be handled in accordance with FASB Statement 12.

11. Fixed assets should be capitalized and depreciation should be recognized periodically, except on structures used primarily as houses of worship or that are inexhaustible, such as landmarks, monuments, cathedrals, or historical treasures.

Most of these provisions have now been incorporated into the AICPA publication entitled *Audits of Certain Nonprofit Organizations*. FASB 93, discussed extensively in Chapter 12, also requires all nonprofit organizations to use the accrual basis of accounting including the distinction between capital and revenue expenditures and the recognition of depreciation.

Private foundations constitute a unique segment of the nonprofit area requiring specialized accounting procedures. In 1977, Price Waterhouse & Company carried out a survey of the financial reporting and accounting practices followed by these enterprise units.[15] That study showed that approximately two-thirds of the large foundations used the accrual basis of accounting while the other one-third reported on what is essentially the cash basis. Furthermore, of the fifty foundations surveyed, forty-seven presented a balance sheet or an equivalent statement of position. The financial report also generally included a statement of income, expenses, and changes in fund balance or an equivalent operating statement plus a statement of changes in fund balance.

# ■ Ethical Considerations Associated with Health and Welfare Organization Cost Allocation

Mortimer Manipulator is the CEO of Humanities, Inc., a national health and welfare organization. He has just returned from an extended business trip during which some of his time was spent implementing research projects. However, most of his time was spent in organizing fund-raising projects. When he turned in his expense report for the trip, he instructed the organization's accountant to charge the entire cost to research implementation expense. Consider the ethical issues associated with such a cost-allocation arrangement.

15. *A Survey of Financial Accounting and Reporting Practices of Private Foundations* (New York: Price Waterhouse & Co., 1977).

# ■ Summary

In the first part of this chapter, we described and illustrated the accounting procedures and financial statements for health and welfare agencies. We explained how those systems have evolved from cash-based dollar-accountability systems to full accrual-based systems reflecting both dollar and operational accountability. We then showed how a series of typical transactions should be recorded in a transactions worksheet to produce end-of-the-period financial statements from beginning-of-the-period data and the transactions.

After that, the accounting procedures and financial statements for Illustration Church were described and illustrated. We noted that church accounting systems are typically expenditure- and dollar-accountability oriented. Operations are controlled through budget appropriations established at the beginning of each period. The records are generally maintained on the cash or modified cash basis. Finally, we discussed some recent developments in accounting for miscellaneous nonprofit organizations having no officially recognized procedural publications.

# ■ Glossary

**Benevolences.**  The outflows of a church's resources used to support activities beyond the scope of the local church program.

**Custodian Fund.**  An accounting entity used to account for assets received by a health and welfare organization to be held or disbursed on instructions of the person or organization from whom the assets were received.

**Land, Building, and Equipment Fund.**  An accounting entity, often referred to as a plant fund, that is used to account for investments in fixed assets and the unexpended resources contributed specifically for the purpose of acquiring or replacing land, buildings, and equipment used by a health and welfare agency.

**Private Foundation.**  A nonprofit organization created by contributions from individuals or corporate entities for the purpose of carrying out projects and providing services considered to be socially beneficial. Such a foundation is in some respects an endowment fund. It is different, however, in that the specific projects or services to be provided by the foundation are determined (within the constraints of the foundation charter) by the foundation board or trustees.

**Public Support Revenue.**  Revenues realized from contributions of various kinds, special events, legacies and bequests, amounts received from federated and nonfederated federal campaigns, etc. It represents charitable giving by the public in support of a voluntary agency.

**Service Implementation Expenses.**  Also called *program service expenses*. All expenses that a health and welfare agency incurs in carrying out the services for which it was organized to provide.

**Supporting Services.**  One of the three expense categories used in the operating statements of health and welfare agencies to summarize the expenses associated with supporting the organization and its activities rather than with directly implementing the programs of the organization.

**Sustentation Expenses.**   Expenses incurred to sustain the organization. These include fund-raising expenses and some administrative expenses.

# ■ Suggested Supplementary References

American Institute of Certified Public Accountants. *Audits of Voluntary Health and Welfare Organizations*. New York: AICPA, 1988.

American Institute of Certified Public Accountants. *Statement of Position on Accounting Principles and Reporting Practices for Certain Nonprofit Organizations*. New York: AICPA, 1978.

Arndt, Terry L., and Richard W. Jones, "Closing the GAAP in Church Accounting." *Management Accounting* (August 1982): 26–31.

Carpenter, Vivian L. "Improving Accountability: Evaluating the Performance of Public Health Agencies." *Government Accountants Journal* (Fall 1990).

National Health Council, National Assembly of Voluntary Health and Welfare Organizations, Inc., and United Way of America. *Standards of Accounting and Financial Reporting for Voluntary Health and Welfare Organizations*, 1975.

Wolinsky, Daniel, and Arthur L. Breakstone. "Reporting for the Rehabilitation and Sheltered Workshop." *Journal of Accountancy* (1975): 56–62.

# ■ Questions for Class Discussion

**Q13-1.**   What is the purpose of a custodial fund? Are the earnings from the custodial fund resources restricted?

**Q13-2.**   What are sustentation expenses? Why is it important to reflect them separately in the operating statements of health and welfare agencies?

**Q13-3.**   What are service implementation expenses? How should they be reflected in the operating statement of a health and welfare organization?

**Q13-4.**   What is generally the primary source of funding for health and welfare agencies? How does this affect the financial reporting practices of these organizations?

**Q13-5.**   What important changes were recommended in health and welfare agency accounting by the 1974 AICPA Audit Guide? Have these changes been accepted by the industry?

**Q13-6.**   How are the financial operations of a church similar to and different from those of a college or university? Do the differences justify a greater emphasis on appropriation control practices in accounting for churches? Justify your position.

**Q13-7.**   Why is it important to distinguish between benevolences and local church expenditures in the statement of revenues and expenditures for a church? Explain.

**Q13-8.**   Describe the procedures generally followed in developing a budget for a church.

**Q13-9.**   Compare and contrast the accounting system recommended in *Audits of Voluntary Health and Welfare Organizations* with the system used for colleges and universities and for hospitals.

**Q13-10.**   The pastor of a church feels that his congregation should raise a budget of $200,000. A deacon, who also operates a large business establishment, states that the church should determine its needs before it begins to talk about the amount to be solicited for the budget. The pastor replies that an infinite amount of resources is needed to further the cause of Christianity. Therefore, he suggests that the congregation should first consider its giving potential and then apportion that among the various needs. Discuss the implications of these two points of view.

# ■ Exercises

**E13-1.** A health and welfare agency realizes revenues from its annual solicitation campaign in the amount of $50,000. The direct cost of the funds solicitation campaign was $8,000. Annual administration costs amount to $15,000. It is estimated that the administrative staff spends one-third of its time soliciting funds for the organization. All resources left after paying for the fund drive and administrative costs are used to directly implement services of the organization.

**Required:**
A.   Calculate the sustentation expenses for the organization.
B.   What portion of each dollar contributed is used for sustaining the organization?
C.   What portion of each dollar contributed is used for service-implementation purposes?

**E13-2.** Discuss the significance of the data developed in Exercise E13-1.

**E13-3.** A voluntary health and welfare organization solicits and receives pledges for construction of a new building in the amount of $80,000. It is estimated that 5 percent of the pledges will be uncollectible.

**Required:**
Record the preceding data in the accounts of the health and welfare agency.

**E13-4.** A health and welfare agency receives cash in the amount of $10,000 that is designated to be used in financing specified research.

**Required:**
Record the receipt of these funds.

**E13-5.** A church treasurer receives the morning offering of his church. The offering includes pledge envelopes containing checks and cash in the amount of $900 plus currency in the amount of $50.

**Required:**
Journalize the receipt of these revenues in the accounting records of the church.

**E13-6.** The church treasurer in Exercise E13-5 writes checks covering the following items:

| | |
|---|---:|
| Staff salaries | $ 500 |
| Church school literature | 80 |
| Printing and office supplies | 100 |
| Furnishings and equipment | 3,000 |

**Required:**
Journalize these disbursements.

E13-7. The budget for First Church shows estimated revenues of $7,000 from pledges, $350 from plate offerings, and $50 from miscellaneous contributions for the month of January 19XX. Actual revenues for the month were $6,500 from pledges, $375 from plate offerings, and $50 from miscellaneous sources. The budget also reflected planned expenditures for the month of $110 for music program, $4,000 for staff salaries, $1,500 for current operating expenditures, and $1,500 for building maintenance. Actual expenditures for January were:

| | |
|---|---:|
| Staff salaries | $4,000 |
| Current operations | 1,450 |
| Music program | 150 |
| Building maintenance costs | 1,500 |

**Required:**
Prepare a statement of revenues and expenditures for January 19XX to be presented to the board of deacons.

E13-8. The Activist Health Agency has a $200,000 building with an expected life of forty years. Estimated salvage value at the end of that time is expected to be $20,000. Depreciation is not to be funded.

**Required:**
Record the depreciation for the current year as recommended by the AICPA Audit Guide.

E13-9. The American Health Society has received contributions of $10,000. The Society spent $2,000 in soliciting the donations and $8,000 in service implementation costs.

**Required:**
A. Record the above transactions.
B. What observations can be made from these transactions regarding the operations of the society?

## ■ Problems

P13-1. This is a comprehensive problem illustrating the procedures for recording the various transactions of health and welfare organizations discussed and illustrated in this chapter. A computer software package is available for use in solving this problem.

    The Social Service Health and Welfare Agency shows the following balances in its accounting records at the beginning of the year:

| | |
|---|---:|
| Unrestricted current funds assets and liabilities: | |
|   Cash | $1,250,000 |
|   Pledges receivable (net of allowance for uncollectible | |
|     accounts) | 150,000 |
|   Vouchers payable | 75,000 |
|   (Note: Fund balance includes $750,000 designated by | |
|     the governing board for the purchase of fixed assets.) | |

Restricted current fund assets:

| | |
|---|---:|
| Cash | 7,500 |

Land, buildings, and equipment fund assets and liabilities:

| | |
|---|---:|
| Cash | 1,500 |
| Investments | 50,000 |
| Pledges receivable (net of allowance for uncollectible accounts) | 10,000 |
| Building and equipment | 325,000 |
| Allowance for depreciation | 125,000 |
| Land | 100,000 |
| Mortgage payable | 40,000 |

Endowment fund assets:

| | |
|---|---:|
| Cash | 4,000 |
| Investments | 1,005,000 |

## The agency had the following transactions during the year:

1. Received contributions as follows:

| | |
|---|---:|
| Unrestricted in the form of pledges (net of uncollectible amounts) | $1,500,000 |
| Restricted (in cash) | 100,000 |
| For building fund (in pledges) | 35,000 |
| For endowment fund (in cash) | 2,500 |

2. The following pledges were collected:

| | |
|---|---:|
| Unrestricted pledges | $1,450,000 |
| Building fund pledges | 40,000 |

3. Other unrestricted revenues were received in cash as follows:

| | |
|---|---:|
| Revenues from special events (net of direct costs) | $   60,000 |
| Legacies and bequests | 40,000 |
| Membership dues | 10,000 |
| Investment income | 50,000 |
| Miscellaneous revenues | 20,000 |

4. Program expenses incurred:

| | |
|---|---:|
| Research | $  300,000 |
| Public education | 260,000 |
| Medical services | 150,000 |
| Community information services | 75,000 |

5. Research expenses paid from restricted resources

| | |
|---|---:|
| amounted to | $   75,000 |

6. Support "sustentation" expenses incurred (handled through vouchers payable):

| | |
|---|---:|
| General administration | $  275,000 |
| Fund-raising expenses | 325,000 |

7. Fixed assets costing $10,000 were acquired by the use of unrestricted resources.

8. Depreciation of fixed assets was allocated as follows:

| | |
|---|---|
| Research | $ 750 |
| Public education | 3,000 |
| Medical services | 2,750 |
| Community information services | 5,500 |
| General administration | 3,000 |
| Fund raising | 2,500 |

9. Paid vouchers payable in the amount of $1,425,000.
10. Transferred excesses of revenues over expenses to fund balance accounts.

**Required:**

A. Prepare a transactions worksheet similar to the one illustrated in Exhibit 13–4 and record the preceding transactions in it.
B. Prepare the appropriate financial statements for Social Service Health and Welfare Agency.

**P13-2.** Hillcrest Blood Bank, a nonprofit organization handling all of its operations through one operating fund, shows the following balance sheets as of June 30, 19X1, and June 30, 19X2, and the statement of cash receipts and disbursements for the year ended June 30, 19X2.

Hillcrest Blood Bank Balance Sheet

| | June 30, 19X1 | June 30, 19X2 |
|---|---|---|
| **Assets** | | |
| Cash | $ 2,712 | $ 3,093 |
| U.S. treasury bonds | 15,000 | 16,000 |
| Accounts receivable—sales of blood: | | |
| Hospitals | 1,302 | 1,448 |
| Individuals | 425 | 550 |
| Inventories: | | |
| Blood | 480 | 640 |
| Supplies and serum | 250 | 315 |
| Furniture and equipment, less depreciation | 4,400 | 4,050 |
| Total assets | $24,569 | $26,096 |
| **Liabilities and Surplus** | | |
| Accounts payable—supplies | $ 325 | $ 275 |
| Fund balance | 24,244 | 25,821 |
| Total liabilities and fund balance | $24,569 | $26,096 |

Hillcrest Blood Bank Statement of Cash Receipts and Disbursements For the Year Ended June 30, 19X2

| | | | |
|---|---|---|---|
| Balance, July 1, 19X1 | | | |
| Cash in bank | | | $ 2,712 |
| | | | |
| Receipts: | | | |
| From hospitals: | | | |
| Hillcrest Hospital | $7,702 | | |
| Good Samaritan Hospital | 3,818 | $11,520 | |
| Individuals | | 6,675 | |
| From other blood banks | | 602 | |
| From sales of serum and supplies | | 2,260 | |
| Interest on bonds | | 525 | |
| Gifts and bequests | | 4,928 | |
| Total receipts | | | 26,510 |
| Total to be accounted for | | | $29,222 |
| | | | |
| Disbursements: | | | |
| Laboratory expense: | | | |
| Serum | $3,098 | | |
| Salaries | 3,392 | | |
| Supplies | 3,533 | | |
| Laundry and miscellaneous | 277 | $10,300 | |
| | | | |
| Other expenses and disbursements: | | | |
| Salaries | $5,774 | | |
| Dues and subscriptions | 204 | | |
| Rent and utilities | 1,404 | | |
| Blood testing | 2,378 | | |
| Payments to other blood banks for blood given to members away from home | 854 | | |
| Payments to professional blood donors | 2,410 | | |
| Other expenses | 1,805 | | |
| Purchase of U.S. treasury bond | 1,000 | 15,829 | |
| Total disbursements | | | 26,129 |
| Balance, June 30, 19X2 | | | $ 3,093 |

**Required:**
A.  Prepare a transactions worksheet for the Hillcrest Blood Bank that develops data for an accrual-based operating statement and end-of-period balance sheet.
B.  Prepare appropriate accrual-based financial statements.
C.  Assume now that the treasury bonds represent endowment funds and that Hillcrest follows accounting practices prescribed for health and welfare agencies. Prepare a balance sheet as of June 30, 19X2.

—**AICPA Adapted**

**P13-3.** First Church began its 19X1 operations with a cash balance of $5,000. It also had vouchers payable in the amount of $3,090 outstanding. (All vouchers payable are for current expense items.) During the year, the following actions and transactions occurred:

1. A budget calling for estimated revenues of $105,000 and anticipated expenditures of $105,000 was adopted by the congregation. Estimated revenues were subdivided into pledge revenues of $101,000 and other anticipated offerings and gifts in the amount of $4,000. Anticipated expenditures are subdivided into the following seven categories:

| | |
|---|---:|
| Benevolences | $ 15,000 |
| Christian education | 6,200 |
| Music | 600 |
| Staff | 48,800 |
| Current expenses | 8,700 |
| Building maintenance | 13,700 |
| Debt retirement | 12,000 |
| Total | $105,000 |

2. Cash receipts for the year were as follow:

| | |
|---|---:|
| Pledge offering | $ 98,000 |
| Other offerings and gifts | 5,000 |
| Total | $103,000 |

3. Cash disbursements for the year were as follow:

| | |
|---|---:|
| Benevolences | $ 12,000 |
| Christian education | 6,000 |
| Staff | 50,000 |
| Current expenses | 8,500 |
| Building maintenance | 14,000 |
| Debt retirement | 12,000 |
| Total | $102,500 |

4. Unpaid vouchers (all for current expenses) at the end of the year amount to $2,700.

**Required:**

A. Record the year's transactions in a transactions worksheet. It should be organized to develop a statement of revenues and expenditures for the year and an end-of-year balance sheet.

B. Prepare a statement of revenues and expenditures showing the relationship between the budgeted and actual operations.

C. Comment on the data shown in the statement prepared in B above.

**P13-4.** Service Health and Welfare Agency trial balance as of December 31, 19X1, is shown next:

## Service Health and Welfare Agency Trial Balance—December 31, 19X1

### Current Funds Unrestricted

| | | |
|---|---:|---:|
| Cash | $ 220,000 | |
| Investments | 270,000 | |
| Pledges receivable | 105,000 | |
| Prepaid expenses | 21,000 | |
| Accounts payable | | $ 15,000 |
| Fund balance—undesignated | | 567,000 |
| Contributions | | 375,000 |
| Legacies and bequests | | 10,000 |
| Investment income | | 9,000 |
| Fund-raising expense | 60,000 | |
| Management and general | 55,000 | |
| Research expenses | 125,000 | |
| Public health education expense | 65,000 | |
| Community services expense | 55,000 | |
| Totals | $ 976,000 | $ 976,000 |

### Restricted

| | | |
|---|---:|---:|
| Cash | $ 300 | |
| Pledges receivable | 15,700 | |
| Fund balance | | $ 15,000 |
| Contributions | | 16,000 |
| Designated research expense | 15,000 | |
| Totals | $ 31,000 | $ 31,000 |

### Land, Building, and Equipment Fund

| | | |
|---|---:|---:|
| Cash | $ 3,000 | |
| Investments | 18,000 | |
| Land, building, and equipment | 80,000 | |
| Allowance for depreciation | | $ 30,000 |
| Mortgage payable | | 3,000 |
| Fund balance—expended | | 47,000 |
| Fund balance—unexpended | | 20,700 |
| Depreciation expense | 8,000 | |
| Contributions | | 7,000 |
| Interest income | | 1,600 |
| Interest expense | 300 | |
| Totals | $ 109,300 | $ 109,300 |
| Grand totals | $1,116,300 | $1,116,300 |

**Required:**

A. Prepare appropriate financial statements for Service Health and Welfare Agency for the year ending December 31, 19X1. Building and equipment expenses should be distributed as follow:

| | |
|---|---|
| Fund raising | 10% |
| Management and general | 15% |
| Research | 20% |
| Public health education | 35% |
| Community services | 20% |

    B.  What portion of each dollar of public support and revenue has been spent for supporting services and for program services?

**P13-5.**  The characteristics of voluntary health and welfare organizations differ in certain respects from the characteristics of state or local governmental units. As an example, voluntary health and welfare organizations derive their revenues primarily from voluntary contributions from the general public, while governmental units derive their revenues from taxes and services provided to their jurisdictions.

**Required:**
    A.  Describe fund accounting and discuss whether its use is consistent with the concept that an accounting entity is an economic unit that has control over resources, accepts responsibilities for making and carrying out commitments, and conducts economic activity.
    B.  Distinguish between accrual accounting and modified accrual accounting and indicate which method should be used for a voluntary health and welfare organization.
    C.  Discuss how methods used to account for fixed assets differ between voluntary health and welfare organizations and governmental units.

                                                       —AICPA Adapted

**P13-6.**  Select the best answer for each of the following items:
    1.  A voluntary health and welfare organization received a pledge in 19X0 from a donor specifying that the amount pledged be used in 19X2. The donor paid the pledge in cash in 19X1. The pledge should be accounted for as:
        a.  a deferred credit in the balance sheet at the end of 19X0, and as support in 19X1.
        b.  a deferred credit in the balance sheet at the end of 19X0 and 19X1, and as support in 19X2.
        c.  support in 19X0.
        d.  support in 19X1, and *no* deferred credit in the balance sheet at the end of 19X0.
    2.  A reason for a voluntary health and welfare organization to adopt fund accounting is that:
        a.  restrictions have been placed on certain of its assets by donors.
        b.  it provides more than one type of program service.
        c.  fixed assets are significant.
        d.  donated services are significant.
    3.  In a statement of support, revenue, and expenses and changes in fund balances of a voluntary health and welfare organization, depreciation expense should:
        a.  be included as an element of expense.
        b.  be included as an element of other changes in fund balances.

c. be included as an element of support.

d. not be included.

4. Which of the following would appear in the plant fund of a voluntary health and welfare organization?

| | Land | Equipment |
|---|---|---|
| a. | Yes | No |
| b. | Yes | Yes |
| c. | No | Yes |
| d. | No | No |

5. In a statement of support, revenue, and expenses and changes in fund balances of a voluntary health and welfare organization, contributions to the building fund should:

a. be included as an element of support.

b. be included as an element of revenue.

c. be included as an element of other changes in fund balances.

d. not be included.

—AICPA Adapted

P13-7. Select the best answer for each of the following items:

1. Lema Fund, a voluntary welfare organization funded by contributions from the general public, received unrestricted pledges of $200,000 during 19X8. It was estimated that 10 percent of these pledges would be uncollectible. By the end of 19X8, $130,000 of the pledges had been collected. It was expected that $50,000 more would be collected in 19X9 and that the balance of $20,000 would be written off as uncollectible. What amount should Lema include under public support in 19X8 for net contributions?

a. $200,000

b. $180,000

c. $150,000

d. $130,000

2. Birdlovers, a community foundation, incurred $5,000 in management and general expenses during 19X9. In Birdlovers' statement of revenue, expense, and changes in fund balance for the year ended December 31, 19X9, the $5,000 should be reported as:

a. a contra account offsetting revenue and support.

b. part of program services.

c. part of supporting services.

d. a direct reduction of fund balance.

3. In 19X7, the Board of Trustees of Burr Foundation designated $100,000 from its current funds for college scholarships. Also in 19X7, the foundation received a bequest of $200,000 from an estate of a benefactor who specified that the bequest was to be used for hiring teachers to tutor handicapped students. What amount should be accounted for as current restricted funds?

a. $0

b. $100,000

c. $200,000

d. $300,000

4.  On January 2, 19X7, a nonprofit botanical society received a gift of an exhaustible fixed asset with an estimated useful life of 10 years and no salvage value. The donor's cost of this asset was $20,000, and its fair market value at the date of the gift was $30,000. What amount of depreciation of this asset should the society recognize in its 19X7 financial statements?
    a.  $3,000
    b.  $2,500
    c.  $2,000
    d.  $0

5.  Unity Fund is a voluntary welfare organization funded by contributions from the general public. During 19X7, unrestricted pledges of $100,000 were received, half of which were payable in 19X7, with the other half payable in 19X8 for use in 19X8. It was estimated that 20 percent of these pledges would be uncollectible. With respect to the pledges, the amount that should be reported for 19X7 as net contributions, under public support, is:
    a.  $100,000.
    b.  $ 80,000.
    c.  $ 50,000.
    d.  $ 40,000.

6.  Lane Foundation received a nonexpendable endowment of $500,000 in 19X6 from Gant Enterprises. The endowment assets were invested in publicly traded securities. Gant did not specify how gains and losses from dispositions of endowment assets were to be treated. No restrictions were placed on the use of dividends received and interest earned on fund resources. In 19X7, Lane realized gains of $50,000 on sales of fund investments, and received total interest and dividends of $40,000 on fund securities. The amount of these capital gains, interest, and dividends available for expenditure by Lane's unrestricted current fund is:
    a.  $0.
    b.  $40,000.
    c.  $50,000.
    d.  $90,000.

7.  In 19X7, a nonprofit trade association enrolled five new member companies, each of which was obligated to pay nonrefundable initiation fees of $1,000. These fees were receivable by the association in 19X7. Three of the new members paid the initiation fees in 19X7, and the other two new members paid their initiation fees in 19X8. Annual dues (excluding initiation fees) received by the association from all of its members have always covered the organization's costs of services provided to its members. It can be reasonably expected that future dues will cover all costs of the organization's future services to members. Average membership duration is 10 years because of mergers, attrition, and economic factors. What amount of initiation fees from these five new members should the association recognize as revenue in 19X7?
    a.  $5,000
    b.  $3,000
    c.  $500
    d.  $0

8. The following expenditures were among those incurred by a nonprofit botanical society during 19X7:

| | |
|---|---|
| Printing of annual report | $10,000 |
| Unsolicited merchandise sent to encourage contributions | 20,000 |

What amount should be classified as fund-raising costs in the society's activity statement?
   a. $0
   b. $10,000
   c. $20,000
   d. $30,000

9. In a statement of support, revenue, and expenses and changes in fund balances of a voluntary health and welfare organization, depreciation expense should:
   a. not be included.
   b. be included as an element of support.
   c. be included as an element of other changes in fund balances.
   d. be included as an element of expense.

Items 10 through 12 are based on the following information:

In 19W9, Community Helpers, a voluntary health and welfare organization, received a bequest of a $100,000 certificate of deposit maturing in 19X9. The testator's only stipulations were that this certificate be held until maturity and that the interest revenue be used to finance salaries for a preschool program. Interest revenue for 19X9 was $8,000. When the certificate was redeemed, the board of trustees adopted a formal resolution designating $20,000 of the proceeds for the future purchase of equipment for the preschool program.

10. In regard to the certificate of deposit. what should be reported in the endowment fund column of the 19X9 statement of support, revenue, and expenses and changes in fund balances?
   a. legacies and bequests, $100,000
   b. direct reduction in fund balance for transfer to current unrestricted fund, $100,000
   c. transfer to land, building, and equipment fund, $20,000
   d. revenues control, $100,000

11. What should be reported in the current unrestricted funds column of the 19X9 statement of support, revenue, and expenses and changes in fund balances?
   a. investment income, $8,000
   b. direct reduction of fund balance for transfer to land, building, and equipment fund, $20,000
   c. direct addition to fund balance for transfer from endowment fund, $100,000
   d. public support, $108,000

12. What should be reported in the 19X9 year-end current unrestricted funds balance sheet?

    a.   fund balance designated for preschool program, $28,000; undesignated fund balance, $80,000

    b.   fund balance designated for purchase of equipment, $20,000; undesignated fund balance, $80,000

    c.   fund balance designated for preschool program salaries, $8,000; undesignated fund balance, $80,000

    d.   undesignated fund balance, $72,000

13.   Aviary Haven, a voluntary welfare organization funded by contributions from the general public, received unrestricted pledges of $500,000 during 19X6. It was estimated that 12 percent of these pledges would be uncollectible. By the end of 1986, $400,000 of the pledges had been collected, and it was expected that $40,000 more would be collected in 19X7, with the balance of $60,000 to be written off as uncollectible. Donors did *not* specify any periods during which the donations were to be used. What amount should Aviary include under public support in 19X6 for net contributions?

    a.   $500,000

    b.   $452,000

    c.   $440,000

    d.   $400,000

Items 14 through 16 are based on the following information pertaining to Rega Foundation, a voluntary welfare organization funded by contributions from the general public:

    During 19X8, unrestricted pledges of $600,000 were received, of which it was estimated that $72,000 would be uncollectible. By the end of 19X8, $480,000 of the pledges had been collected, and it was expected that an additional $48,000 of these pledges would be collected in 19X9, with the balance to be written off as uncollectible. Donors did *not* specify any periods during which the donations were to be used.

    Also during 19X8, Rega sold a computer for $18,000. Its cost was $21,000 and its book value was $15,000. Rega made the correct entry to record the gain on sale.

14.   What amount should Rega include under public support in 19X8 for net contributions?

    a.   $480,000

    b.   $528,000

    c.   $531,000

    d.   $600,000

15.   In addition to the entry recording the gain on sale of the computer, the other accounts that Rega should debit and credit in connection with this sale are:

|  | *Debit* | *Credit* |
|---|---|---|
| a. | Current unrestricted funds | Fund balance—undesignated |
| b. | Excess revenues control | Sale of equipment |
| c. | Fund balance—unexpended | Fund balance—expended |
| d. | Fund balance—expended | Fund balance—unexpended |

16. The amount that should be debited and credited for the additional entry in connection with the sale of the computer is:
    a. $3,000.
    b. $15,000.
    c. $18,000.
    d. $21,000.

Items 17 and 18 are based on the following information pertaining to the sale of equipment by Nous Foundation, a voluntary health and welfare organization:

| | |
|---|---|
| Sales price | $12,000 |
| Cost | 14,000 |
| Carrying amount | 10,000 |

Nous made the correct entry to record the $2,000 gain on sale.

17. The additional entry that Nous should record in connection with this sale is:

| | Debit | Credit |
|---|---|---|
| a. | Fund balance—expended | Fund balance—unexpended |
| b. | Fund balance—unexpended | Fund balance—expended |
| c. | Excess revenues control | Sale of equipment |
| d. | Current unrestricted funds | Fund balance—undesignated |

18. The amount that should be debited and credited for the additional entry in connection with this sale is:
    a. $2,000.
    b. $10,000.
    c. $12,000.
    d. $14,000.

—AICPA Adapted

P13-8. The accounting records for a voluntary health and welfare agency include the following funds:
    a. current unrestricted funds
    b. current restricted funds
    c. land, building, and equipment funds
    d. endowment funds.
The following transactions occur during the fiscal period:
    1. Unrestricted contributions in the form of pledges in the amount of $750,000 are received.
    2. Building fund pledges in the amount of $70,000 are received.
    3. Revenues from special events in the amount of $30,000 are received.
    4. Support or sustentation expenses in the amount of $200,000 are incurred.
    5. Fixed assets costing $20,000 are acquired by the use of unrestricted resources.

6. Research expenses are paid from restricted resources in the amount of $35,000.
7. Externally restricted funds in the amount of $300,000 to be used for endowment purposes are received.
8. Cash restricted to use in the acquisition of building and equipment in the amount of $30,000 is spent to acquire a special piece of equipment to be used by the agency.
9. Service expenses paid from unrestricted funds during the period amount to $400,000.
10. Funds in the amount of $50,000 externally designated to be used for research activities are received.

**Required:**
On a sheet of worksheet paper, label individual pairs of columns to reflect the different fund entities included in the accounting records of the health and welfare agency. Then, record each of the ten transactions listed above to the left of the columns labeled by fund names and reflect the amounts in the debit and credit columns for the appropriate fund(s).

P13-9. Listed below are four independent transactions or events that relate to a local government and to a voluntary health and welfare organization:
1. $25,000 was disbursed from the general fund (or its equivalent) for the cash purchase of new equipment.
2. An unrestricted cash gift of $100,000 was received from a donor.
3. Listed common stocks with a total carrying value of $50,000, exclusive of any allowance, were sold by an endowment fund for $55,000, before any dividends were earned on these stocks. There are no restrictions on the gain.
4. $1,000,000 face amount of general obligation bonds payable were sold at par, with the proceeds required to be used solely for construction of a new building. This building was completed at a total cost of $1,000,000, and the total amount of bond issue proceeds was disbursed in connection therewith. Disregard interest capitalization.

**Required:**
A. For each of the above-listed transactions or events, prepare journal entries, without explanations, specifying the affected funds and account groups, and showing how these transactions or events should be recorded by a local government whose debt is serviced by general tax revenues.
B. For each of the above-listed transactions or events, prepare journal entries, without explanations, specifying the affected funds, and showing how these transactions or events should be recorded by a voluntary health and welfare organization that maintains a separate plant fund.

—AICPA Adapted

P13-10. Following are the adjusted current funds trial balances of Community Association for Handicapped Children, a voluntary health and welfare organization, at June 30, 19X4:

**Community Association for Handicapped Children Adjusted Current Funds Trial Balances—June 30, 19X4**

| | Unrestricted | | Restricted | |
|---|---|---|---|---|
| | Dr. | Cr. | Dr. | Cr. |
| Cash | $ 40,000 | | $ 9,000 | |
| Bequest receivable | | | 5,000 | |
| Pledges receivable | 12,000 | | | |
| Accrued interest receivable | 1,000 | | | |
| Investments (at cost, which approximates market) | 100,000 | | | |
| Accounts payable and accrued expenses | | $ 50,000 | | $ 1,000 |
| Deferred revenue | | 2,000 | | |
| Allowance for uncollectible pledges | | 3,000 | | |
| Fund balances, July 1, 19X3: | | | | |
| Designated | | 12,000 | | |
| Undesignated | | 26,000 | | |
| Restricted | | | | 3,000 |
| Transfers of endowment fund income | | 20,000 | | |
| Contributions | | 300,000 | | 15,000 |
| Membership dues | | 25,000 | | |
| Program service fees | | 30,000 | | |
| Investment income | | 10,000 | | |
| Deaf children's program | 120,000 | | | |
| Blind children's program | 150,000 | | | |
| Management and general services | 45,000 | | 4,000 | |
| Fund-raising services | 8,000 | | 1,000 | |
| Provision for uncollectible pledges | 2,000 | | | |
| | $478,000 | $478,000 | $19,000 | $19,000 |

**Required:**

A. Prepare a statement of support, revenue, and expenses and changes in fund balances, separately presenting each current fund, for the year ended June 30, 19X4.

B. Prepare a balance sheet separately presenting each current fund as of June 30, 19X4.

—**AICPA Adapted**

**P13-11.** Children's Agency, a voluntary health and welfare organization, conducts two programs: Medical Services Program and Community Information Services Program. It had the following transactions during the year ended June 30, 19X9:

1. Received the following contributions:

| | |
|---|---|
| Unrestricted pledges | $800,000 |
| Restricted cash | 95,000 |
| Building fund pledges | 50,000 |
| Endowment fund cash | 1,000 |

2. Collected the following pledges:

| | |
|---|---|
| Unrestricted | 450,000 |
| Building fund | 20,000 |

3. Received the following unrestricted cash revenues:

| | |
|---|---|
| From theater party (net of direct costs) | 12,000 |
| Bequests | 10,000 |
| Membership dues | 8,000 |
| Interest and dividends | 5,000 |

4. Program expenses incurred (processed through vouchers payable):

| | |
|---|---|
| Medical services | 60,000 |
| Community information services | 15,000 |

5. Services expenses incurred (processed through vouchers payable):

| | |
|---|---|
| General administration | 150,000 |
| Fund raising | 200,000 |

6. Fixed assets purchased with unrestricted cash   18,000
7. Depreciation of all buildings and equipment in the land, buildings, and equipment fund was allocated as follows:

| | |
|---|---|
| Medical services program | 4,000 |
| Community information services program | 3,000 |
| General administration | 6,000 |
| Fund raising | 2,000 |

8. Paid vouchers payable                                   330,000

### Required:
Set up a worksheet with column headings as labeled below and record the journal entries (without explanations) for the preceding transactions.

Children's Agency—Journal Entries for the Year Ended June 30, 19X9

| | Current Fund | | | | Land, Buildings, and Equipment Fund | | Endowment Fund | |
|---|---|---|---|---|---|---|---|---|
| | Unrestricted | | Restricted | | | | | |
| Account Title | Dr. | (Cr.) | Dr. | (Cr.) | Dr. | (Cr.) | Dr. | (Cr.) |

With credit amounts placed in parentheses, insert the amounts in the proper columns for each of the following funds:

Current fund—unrestricted

Current fund—restricted

Land, buildings, and equipment fund

Endowment fund

Number the journal entries to coincide with the transaction numbers indicated.

**P13-12.**   **Thought Projection Problem.** The June 30, 19X5 and 19X4, balance sheets of Dorn Foundation, a nonprofit research and scientific organization, are shown on page 555. Excerpts from Dorn Foundation's Notes to Financial Statements follow:

*Revenue recognition*—Substantially all of the organization's revenue is derived from restricted grants and cost-plus-fixed-fee contracts. Revenue is recognized based on the proportion of project expenses incurred to total anticipated project expenses (percentage-of-completion method). Losses on contracts are recognized when identified.

*Fund balances*—Of the $188,000 increase in fund balances from 19X4 to 19X5, $128,000 represents the results of current operating activities, and $60,000 represents capital additions from interest earned on endowment fund investments. The endowment fund, in the principal amount of $700,000, was received in 19X2. The donor of this fund specified that principal and accumulated interest not be expended until 19Y0, at which time the fund, including accumulated interest, will be used for environmental research projects. Net equity in property, plant, and equipment is the carrying value of all property, plant, and equipment less related noncurrent liabilities to finance their acquisition. There were no dispositions of property, plant, and equipment during the year.

*Lease commitments*—The organization uses scientific equipment under capital leases expiring in 19X1 which provide for the transfer of ownership of the equipment at the end of the lease term. The related future minimum lease payments as of June 30, 19X5, for subsequent fiscal years, are as follow:

| | |
|---|---:|
| 19X6 | $ 188,000 |
| 19X7 | 188,000 |
| 19X8 | 188,000 |
| 19X9 | 188,000 |
| 19Y0 | 188,000 |
| 19Y1 | 20,000 |
| Total | 960,000 |
| Less amount representing interest | (166,000) |
| Present value of minimum lease payments | $ 794,000 |

### Dorn Foundation Balance Sheets—June 30, 19X5, 19X4

|  | 19X5 | 19X4 |
|---|---|---|
| **Assets** | | |
| Current assets | | |
| Cash | $ 650,000 | $ 630,000 |
| Accounts receivable | 744,000 | 712,000 |
| Unbilled contract revenues and reimbursable | | |
| grant expenses | 976,000 | 780,000 |
| Prepaid expenses | 80,000 | 76,000 |
| Total current assets | 2,450,000 | 2,198,000 |
| Investments and endowment fund cash | 840,000 | 780,000 |
| Property, plant, and equipment | | |
| Land and building | 440,000 | 440,000 |
| Furniture and equipment | 334,000 | 312,000 |
| Leased property under capital leases | 958,000 | 958,000 |
| Total property, plant, and equipment | 1,732,000 | 1,710,000 |
| Less accumulated depreciation and amortization | 518,000 | 370,000 |
| Net property, plant, and equipment | 1,214,000 | 1,340,000 |
| Total Assets | $4,504,000 | $4,318,000 |
| **Liabilities and Fund Balances** | | |
| Current liabilities | | |
| Accounts payable | $ 836,000 | $ 776,000 |
| Restricted grant advances | 522,000 | 420,000 |
| Obligations under capital leases | 176,000 | 164,000 |
| Total current liabilities | 1,534,000 | 1,360,000 |
| Noncurrent capital lease obligations | 618,000 | 794,000 |
| Total liabilities | 2,152,000 | 2,154,000 |
| Fund balances | | |
| Unrestricted | 916,000 | 838,000 |
| Net equity in property, plant, and equipment | 596,000 | 546,000 |
| Endowment | 840,000 | 780,000 |
| Total fund balances | 2,352,000 | 2,164,000 |
| Total liabilities and fund balances | $4,504,000 | $4,318,000 |

**Required:**
Prepare the statement of cash flows.

—AICPA Adapted

# Using Nonprofit Organization Accounting Data

■ *CHAPTER 14*

**Cost-Accounting Procedures
for Nonprofit Organizations**

■ *CHAPTER 15*

**Internal Use of the Accounting System Data**

■ *CHAPTER 16*

**Use of Accounting Data
by Externally Interested Parties**

■ *CHAPTER 17*

**Operational-Accountability Reporting
for Nonprofit Organizations**

# Cost-Accounting
# Procedures
# for Nonprofit
# Organizations

---

## ■ Learning Objectives

When you have finished your study of this chapter, you should

1.  Recognize the need for appropriate cost data in managing nonprofit organizations.
2.  Understand the objectives of the cost-accumulation and -allocation process for service enterprises.
3.  Know the difference between direct and indirect costs and how that difference relates to planning and evaluating the operations of nonprofit enterprises.
4.  Know, in general, how costs should be accumulated and allocated to produce cost data useful in managing hospitals and colleges and universities.

---

Up to this point, we have been concerned with the accounting procedures followed in recording the financial activities of various types of nonprofit organizations and the preparation of financial statements from the accumulated data. In Part Four, we turn our attention to the ways in which those accounting data can be used by managers and externally interested parties. We begin, in Chapter 14, by developing cost-accumulation and -allocation procedures designed primarily to provide cost information for internal managerial use. The internal use of those and other data produced by the accounting system is expanded upon in Chapter 15. The use of accounting data by externally

Portions of this chapter are adapted from Emerson O. Henke and Charlene W. Spoede, *Cost Accounting: Managerial Use of Accounting Data* (Boston: PWS-KENT, 1991). Used with permission.

interested parties is discussed in Chapter 16. Finally, in Chapter 17, we consider some of the benefits that could be derived from operational-accountability reporting for nonprofit enterprises.

Managers cannot effectively discharge their responsibilities without some knowledge of the costs associated with carrying out the activities of the entity being managed. In manufacturing enterprises, for example, managers must have information about the cost of producing each of the firm's products. Therefore, the cost-accumulation and -allocation procedures for such firms are designed to allocate all production (resource-conversion) costs to the units of product being produced. That is typically done by use of either a job order or process costing system.

The development of such a cost system requires

1. identification of the ultimate cost-allocation targets
2. determination of preliminary cost-allocation devices to be used in the cost allocation process
3. classification of costs to be allocated at each step in the allocation process into direct and indirect categories
4. development of bases to be used in allocating indirect costs at each step in the allocation process.

The ultimate cost-allocation target for any cost system is the unit of product or service being produced or provided by the reporting entity. Preliminary allocation devices can include departmental cost-accumulation centers and job order sheets for individual lots of goods. *Direct costs* are those costs that can be directly associated with an allocation device or target. On the other hand, *indirect costs* are those costs that must be incurred to produce a product or service, but that cannot be directly related to it. The existence of such costs requires us to develop bases for allocation at each step in the allocation process. In doing that, we look for some directly associated measurement, such as direct labor hours, square footage of space occupied, or dollars invested in cost center equipment, *that most closely measures the benefits realized by the allocation devices or targets from the indirect expense.*

When using a job order system, costs are typically allocated to the ultimate allocation target through the use of both departmental cost centers and job order sheets as preliminary allocation devices (see Figure 14–1).

Production departments are those departments through which the goods flow as they are being produced. Service departments are those departments, such as maintenance and personnel, that exist for the purpose of providing services to producing departments.

When using a process costing system, all manufacturing costs flow through service and producing departments directly to the units of product or service, as shown in Figure 14–2.

Nonprofit organizations produce services, either for sale or to be distributed on the basis of need for them, rather than units of goods. It is just as important for such organizations to know the costs of providing those services as it is for manufacturing firms to know the unit costs of the products they produce. Such service-providing costs can be stated in terms of an aggregate amount per period. However, to be most useful, they should be expressed in terms of the amount per unit of service such as the cost per

**FIGURE 14–1.** Cost-Allocation in a Job Order Costing System

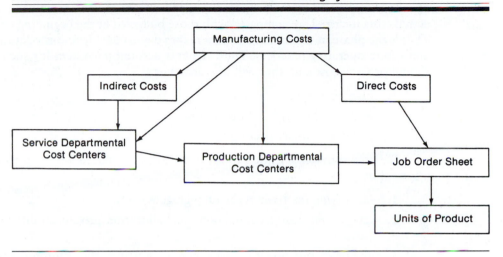

**FIGURE 14–2.** Cost-Allocation in a Process Costing System

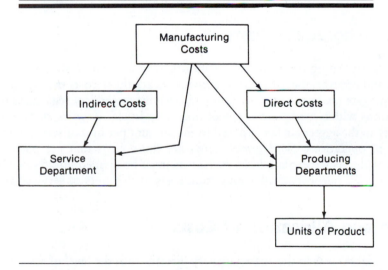

day of service, cost per unit of population, cost per project, or cost of some other unit of service.

Effectively managed enterprise units typically go through a plan-execute-evaluate-plan (PEEP) cycle each period. Managers should use cost data in both the plan and evaluate phases of this cycle. During the plan phase, the anticipated cost of carrying out projected service plans should be reflected in the form of a budget. Projected aggregate service costs can be developed as a product of the projected number of units of service multiplied by the projected cost per unit. In the evaluate phase of the cycle, actual costs incurred are compared with those budgeted at the beginning of the period. That is the phase in which management makes day-to-day decisions relating to current and future operating practices. Thus, the cost accounting system for such enterprises should provide cost data that will help managers

1. plan operations
2. evaluate the results of operations
3. make day-to-day decisions.

We now turn our attention to the procedures associated with implementing such a system by

1. identifying the basic types of aggregate costs
2. relating the cost-accumulation and -allocation process to different types of costs
3. demonstrating how the cost-accumulation and -allocation procedures can be used by hospitals
4. developing the framework of a cost-accumulation and -allocation system for colleges and universities.

## ■ Basic Types of Aggregate Costs

The various operating costs of a nonprofit organization can be subdivided into fixed, variable, and semivariable categories. *Fixed costs* are those costs that remain the same in the aggregate (as opposed to the amount per unit of service) regardless of the level of operations within a relevant range of operating levels. *Variable costs,* on the other hand, vary in the aggregate (as opposed to the amount per unit of service) directly with the level of operations. *Semivariable costs* are those costs that are partly fixed and partly variable. As we explain later, such costs must be divided into fixed and variable elements for the purpose of allocating total costs to the units of services provided.

## ■ Accumulation and Allocation of Costs

Because variable costs in the aggregate vary directly with the level of services rendered, we can allocate them directly to services being provided during each operating period. The variable cost per unit can be calculated by dividing aggregate costs by the units of service rendered. It then follows that we can project (plan) the variable cost of providing a certain number of units of service by multiplying the units by a projected variable cost per unit determined either by estimation or from historical data. When the actual variable cost of providing the services has been determined at the end of the reporting period, that amount can be compared with planned cost on a per-unit basis to evaluate the efficiency of operations insofar as variable costs are concerned. Because variable costs can be directly related to the units of service, we can characterize them as *direct costs* of providing services.

Fixed costs, on the other hand, are directly related to the passage of time, rather than to units of service provided. Therefore, the fixed cost per unit of service provided should *vary inversely* with the number of units of service provided. Because they cannot be directly attributed to the units of service provided, they are characterized as *indirect* or *support costs* and have to be allocated to the units of service provided on the basis of cause-and-effect relationships. In other words, we have to find some directly related attribute (such as directly attributed hours of service or square footage) to use as a basis for allocating such costs to the units of service rendered. This may be expressed as an amount per unit of the attribute or as a percentage of a dollar amount of the attribute. Such indirect costs are often characterized as *fixed overhead costs*. Predetermined allocation rates often are used in the accumulation and allocation process for indirect costs to facilitate cost of services determination.

Some costs (either fixed or variable) can be directly associated with departmental operations (either service or production departments). Figures 14−1 and 14−2 show that such costs should be allocated directly to those preliminary cost-allocation devices.

Semivariable costs must be divided into fixed and variable elements to facilitate the projection of probable amounts for a given level of services (planning) and to allow appropriate comparison of budgetary data with actual results (evaluation). The most common method of allocating semivariable costs into fixed and variable elements is the *high–low* method. As shown below, this method calls for listing historical or estimated data for both the units of service rendered and the total semivariable costs incurred or expected to be incurred at each of those levels over a series of reporting periods and then comparing the data for the highest and lowest levels of operations:

|  | *Units of Service* | *Aggregate Costs* |
|---|---|---|
| Highest | 6000 | $10,000 |
| Lowest | 3000 | 7,000 |
| Difference | 3000 | $ 3,000 |

The variable part of this semivariable cost can then be calculated as $1 per unit of service by dividing $3,000 by 3,000 units. The aggregate fixed part of this semivariable cost for each period can then be calculated by removing the variable element from either the $10,000 or the $7,000 as shown below:

| | | |
|---|---|---|
| Total cost | $10,000 | $7,000 |
| Variable element | | |
| 6000 × $1 = | 6,000 | |
| 3000 × $1 = | | 3,000 |
| Fixed element of semivariable cost | $ 4,000 | $4,000 |

This allows us to use the following equation to project the expected aggregate amount of this semivariable cost for any level of production:

$$\text{total projected cost} = \$4,000 + \$1 \text{ (units of service)}$$

*Quasi-nonprofit* enterprises exist for the purpose of providing socially desirable services to the general public in exchange for fees covering all or some part of the costs of providing those services. This category includes hospitals and colleges and universities, both of which provide services to clientele in exchange for fees that are established to cover part or all of the costs of providing the services but do not attempt to earn a profit for the benefit of nonclientele "owners." The cost-accounting systems for these enterprises need to include procedures for allocating operating costs to the individual types of services being provided on a user-fee basis. In the case of colleges and universities, for example, tuition charges generally are based on semester hours of services provided. Therefore, costs should be allocated to semester hours.

# ■ Cost-Accumulation and -Allocation Procedures for Hospitals

Hospitals bill patients for room service, drugs, operating room charges, X-ray services, and other services provided during their stays. These units of service then become the ultimate cost-allocation targets for such institutions.

Costs of services provided fall into two categories: costs that can be directly associated with a specific billable service being provided (such as rooms, surgery, and so on) and costs of operating supporting services (such as laundry, cleaning, building maintenance, and so on). The directly related costs should be charged directly to billable-service cost center accounts. However, supporting-service costs must be allocated to the billable-service cost centers on the basis of the best discernable cause-and-effect (cost–benefit) relationship. These allocation bases then are used to allocate those costs to the billable-service cost centers. We demonstrate those cost-allocation procedures for a Hypothetical Hospital in Exhibit 14–1.

The cost-allocation techniques shown in Exhibit 14–1 can be used for either projected or actual costs. The projection of costs requires the use of a flexible budget, such as the one shown in Exhibit 14–2. Observe from Exhibits 14–1 and 14–2 that management expects to operate Department 1 at 80 percent of capacity. Those projected cost data will be developed and used during the planning phase of the PEEP cycle.

In the evaluation phase of the PEEP cycle, planned costs can be compared with actual costs incurred by use of a budget analysis schedule such as the one shown in Exhibit 14–3. Observe that this exhibit shows assumed actual costs totaling $686,000, which are compared with *previously budgeted costs adjusted to the 85 percent level of operations actually achieved* by Department 1. The footnotes suggest actions management might take if the variances for the individual items are considered material.

In addition to the cost-accumulation and -allocation schedules described and illustrated above, actual costs as incurred should be accumulated and allocated to accounts for revenue-producing cost centers as shown below in the cost-of-services-provided accounts. Revenues realized from each service provided can be credited to

**EXHIBIT 14–1.** Hypothetical Hospital—Allocation of Costs

| | Revenue-Producing Cost Centers | | | | Supporting Cost Centers | | | Total |
|---|---|---|---|---|---|---|---|---|
| | Dept. 1 | Dept. 2 | Dept. 3 | Dept. 4 | Dept. 5 | Dept. 6 | Dept. 7 | |
| Direct costs | $400,000 | $ 800,000 | $300,000 | $600,000 | $200,000 | $ 80,000 | $100,000 | $2,480,000 |
| Allocated general costs | 80,000 | 120,000 | 100,000 | 150,000 | 40,000 | 30,000 | 30,000 | 550,000 |
| Totals | $480,000 | $ 920,000 | $400,000 | $750,000 | $240,000 | $110,000 | $130,000 | $3,030,000 |
| Allocation of Dept. 6 costs[a] | 20,000 | 60,000 | 10,000 | 20,000 | | $110,000 | | |
| Allocation of Dept. 7 costs[b] | 60,000 | 30,000 | 25,000 | 15,000 | | | $130,000 | |
| Allocation of Dept. 5 costs[c] | 100,000 | 50,000 | 30,000 | 60,000 | $240,000 | | | |
| Totals | $660,000 | $1,060,000 | $465,000 | $845,000 | | | | $3,030,000 |
| Billing units (quantity) | 66,000 | 10,600 | 93,000 | 42,250 | | | | |
| Cost per unit of service | $ 10 | $ 100 | $ 5 | $ 20 | | | | |

[a]Dept. 6 costs are building-related costs allocated on the basis of square footage as follows: Dept. 1, 4,000; Dept. 2, 12,000; Dept. 3, 2,000; Dept. 4, 4,000.
[b]Dept. 7 costs are employee-related costs allocated on the basis of number of employees as follows: Dept. 1, 60; Dept. 2, 30; Dept. 3, 25; Dept. 4, 15.
[c]Dept. 5 costs are equipment-related costs allocated on the basis of cost of equipment in each department as follows: Dept. 1, $1,000,000; Dept. 2, $500,000; Dept. 3, $300,000; Dept. 4, $600,000.

**EXHIBIT 14–2.**  Hypothetical Hospital—Flexible Budget for Department 1

| | Level of Operations (related to capacity) | | | |
|---|---|---|---|---|
| | 70% | 80% | 90% | 100% |
| Direct costs (variable) | $262,500 | $300,000 | $337,500 | $375,000 |
| Direct costs (fixed) | 100,000 | 100,000 | 100,000 | 100,000 |
| Total direct costs | $362,500 | $400,000 | $437,500 | $475,000 |
| Allocated general costs (fixed) | 80,000 | 80,000 | 80,000 | 80,000 |
| Allocated service dept. costs | | | | |
| Dept. 6 (fixed) | 20,000 | 20,000 | 20,000 | 20,000 |
| Dept. 7 (semifixed) | 55,000 | 60,000 | 65,000 | 70,000 |
| Dept. 5 (fixed) | 100,000 | 100,000 | 100,000 | 100,000 |
| Total costs | $617,500 | $660,000 | $702,500 | $745,000 |
| Billing units | 57,750 | 66,000 | 74,250 | 82,500 |
| Cost per unit of service | $ 10.69 | $ 10.00 | $ 9.46 | $ 9.03 |

**EXHIBIT 14–3.**  Hypothetical Hospital—Budget Analysis Schedule for Department 1 (Actually Operating at 85% of Capacity)

| | Actual Expenses | Budget Allocation | | Variances |
|---|---|---|---|---|
| Direct expenses (variable) | $320,000 | $318,750 | (1) | $1,250—Unfavorable |
| Direct expenses (fixed) | 101,000 | 100,000 | (2) | 1,000—Unfavorable |
| Allocated general expenses (fixed) | 78,000 | 80,000 | | 2,000—Favorable |
| Allocated service dept. expenses | | | | |
| Department 6 (fixed) | 20,500 | 20,000 | (3) | 500—Unfavorable |
| Department 7 (semifixed) | 65,000 | 62,500 | (4) | 2,500—Unfavorable |
| Department 5 (fixed) | 101,500 | 100,000 | (5) | 1,500—Unfavorable |
| Totals | $686,000 | $681,250 | | $4,750—Unfavorable |

(1) This unfavorable variance should be explained by the Department 1 supervisor. It appears that the supervisor failed to properly control variable costs in relation to the actual level of operations. Individual items of cost should be reviewed.

(2) This variance suggests that the departmental supervisor has "overspent" the allocation for fixed costs.

(3) and (5) These variances have probably been caused by inadequate cost controls in service departments 6 and 5. Costs should be reviewed with departmental supervisors.

(4) This variance could have been caused either by Department 1 having relatively more employees than were expected or by inadequate cost controls in Department 7.

these accounts or to separate departmental revenue accounts as services are charged to patients. If the first procedure is followed, the individual departmental accounts will reflect the difference between departmental revenues and departmental costs. If the second procedure is followed, the separate cost and revenue accumulation accounts will have to be closed against each other to arrive at those differences.

**Revenue-producing cost centers:**

| Rooms | |
|---|---|
| Direct costs<br>Allocated<br>  service<br>  depart-<br>  ment costs | Charges to pa-<br>tients* |

| Surgery | |
|---|---|
| Direct costs<br>Allocated<br>  service<br>  depart-<br>  ment costs | Charges to pa-<br>tients* |

| Emergency | |
|---|---|
| Direct costs<br>Allocated<br>  service<br>  depart-<br>  ment costs | Charges to pa-<br>tients* |

| Pharmacy | |
|---|---|
| Direct costs<br>Allocated<br>  service<br>  depart-<br>  ment costs | Charges to pa-<br>tients* |

| Laboratory | |
|---|---|
| Direct costs<br>Allocated<br>  service<br>  depart-<br>  ment costs | Charges to pa-<br>tients* |

| Pathology | |
|---|---|
| Direct costs<br>Allocated<br>  service<br>  depart-<br>  ment costs | Charges to pa-<br>tients* |

*These items may also be shown as revenues rather than credits to departmental cost accounts.

**Supporting-service cost centers:**

| Laundry | |
|---|---|
| Direct costs | Transfers to<br>  revenue-<br>  producing<br>  centers |

| Cleaning | |
|---|---|
| Direct costs | Transfers to<br>  revenue-<br>  producing<br>  centers |

| Food | |
|---|---|
| Direct costs | Transfers to<br>  revenue-<br>  producing<br>  centers |

| Building Maintenance | |
|---|---|
| Direct costs | Transfers to<br>  revenue-<br>  producing<br>  centers |

| Security | |
|---|---|
| Direct costs | Transfers to<br>  revenue-<br>  producing<br>  centers |

| Nursing | |
|---|---|
| Direct costs | Transfers to<br>  revenue-<br>  producing<br>  centers |

The differences between the costs charged to the revenue-producing cost centers and the amounts charged to patients are expected to cover general operating overhead and perhaps provide an operating profit. Another option, beyond the scope of this text, might call for the allocation of general operating overhead to the individual revenue-producing cost centers.

The costs and revenues discussed above should also be allocated to individual patient billings. This can be done by maintaining a separate subsidiary ledger that includes a separate job order sheet for each patient as shown on page 568.

| Charges for Services Provided | | Accounts Receivable | |
| --- | --- | --- | --- |
| Detailed patient charges (rooms, surgery, etc.) | Transfer to accounts receivable | Transfers from charges for services provided | |

**Subsidiary charges for services-provided account:**

| Patient 1 | | Patient 2 | | ... | Patient M | |
| --- | --- | --- | --- | --- | --- | --- |
| Detailed charges | Transfer to accounts receivable | Detailed charges | Transfer to accounts receivable | | Detailed charges | Transfer to accounts receivable |

# ■ Cost-Accumulation and -Allocation Procedures for Colleges and Universities

As observed earlier, the ultimate objective of any cost-accumulation and -allocation system is to associate costs with products being produced or services being provided. The operations of colleges and universities are typically directed toward providing *research* and *educational* services. Therefore, the general objective of a system designed to accumulate and allocate college or university operating costs should be to relate those costs to specific research and educational activities.

Research services are subdivided into projects. Therefore, the ultimate cost-allocation target for these costs should be the individual research projects. The system should be designed to meet that cost-allocation goal by requiring that the costs associated with each project be accumulated on a separate *project cost-accumulation sheet*. In that way, management will have appropriately supported cost data for each project that can be used as a basis for recovering costs from the government or other contracting agency. Furthermore, the historical data relating to past projects supplemented by analysis of new project requirements could also be used in estimating the probable costs of other similar research projects before they are accepted.

Educational services, on the other hand, are provided by the academic departments of a college or university over specified periods of time (quarters or semesters). The quantity (output) of services rendered typically is measured in credit hours. Logically, then, the costs of carrying out those activities should first be allocated to academic department cost-accumulation centers. However, the *ultimate cost-allocation target should be a credit hour of educational service*. That can best be reflected in terms of cost per credit hour, calculated by dividing the costs accumulated for each academic department by the number of credit hours of service provided by the department. Thus, the system should provide a departmental cost per credit hour of services rendered during each quarter or semester.

The system used to accumulate and allocate educational costs should call for ultimate allocation of those costs to various credit-hour targets ranging from a general (universitywide) credit hour of service down to, conceivably, a credit hour of service provided through each individual class. Such an arrangement would allow a college or university to determine, for example, the cost of providing a student credit hour of graduate educational service in accounting as well as the cost per credit hour for undergraduate educational services in accounting, and so forth. Such data would allow the management of a college or university to compare the tuition or appropriation revenue per student credit hour with the cost of providing a student credit hour of educational service by departmental disciplines or even by classes within each discipline.

To facilitate the cost-allocation process, the system should provide for the initial classification of operating costs into direct and indirect categories. Those costs that can be directly associated with specific services being rendered are characterized as *direct costs*. They should be assigned directly to the individual research projects and to educational services producing departments as they are incurred. The system should include the forms and procedures required to make those assignments of direct costs.

Other costs associated with providing facilities, internal services, and administrative oversight are characterized as *indirect operating costs*. These costs should be allocated to the individual research projects and academic departments on the basis of the best determinable cause-and-effect relationships. Costs are always incurred to provide benefits and the recipients of those benefits should be charged with the costs associated with providing them. One way of doing this is to measure such benefits in terms of the number of activity units of benefits received by each cost-allocation target (initially, research projects and educational departments). Such an allocation procedure has been characterized as *activity-based costing*. The procedure visualizes total operating costs of a college or university as first being classified into direct and indirect categories as shown in Figure 14–3.

The system the author proposes would require that the direct costs of providing educational services be allocated to the various academic departments based on each cost's direct association with the activities of each of those departments. These costs primarily would consist of instructional salaries (including fringe benefits). The amounts to be charged to each department would be determined by identifying the departmental affiliations of individual faculty members and coding payroll items to reflect those affiliations.

**FIGURE 14–3.**  Categories of Total Operating Costs

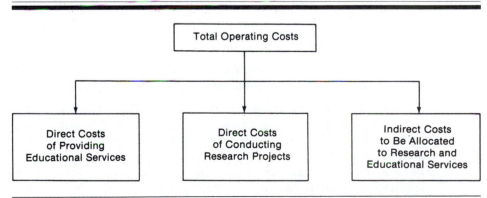

To facilitate the identification and use of cost–benefit relationships in allocating indirect costs to educational departments, we suggest that these costs first be subdivided into the categories of indirect instructional costs and other indirect costs. Indirect instructional costs would include such things as the costs of providing office space for instructors, classroom or laboratory space for classes, and perhaps certain educational equipment for use in the classrooms. The approximate amounts of these costs can best be allocated to departments by using a predetermined cost per square foot of space, which we may characterize as the activity unit of service provided by such space-providing costs. We may think of that as a *space cost-application rate* which can be used in the same manner as an overhead application rate is used by manufacturing firms. However, the allocation proposed above is more appropriately identified as a form of *activity-based costing*. Space is the "activity" or service provided by the incurrence of space-providing costs. Each department is thus charged with its share of those costs based on the amount of the service (space) units it uses. The space cost-application rate, for example, should include such items as depreciation, insurance, and maintenance costs for classroom buildings and so forth.

We suggest that similar procedures, using appropriate activity bases, be used in allocating other indirect operating costs to the cost-allocation targets. The general allocation process can be visualized as following a pattern similar to that shown in Figure 14–4. As you can see in that figure, all other indirect operating costs ultimately will be allocated to research projects and educational departments. The cost per credit hour of educational services rendered can then be calculated by dividing total educational department costs (both direct and allocated indirect) by the credit hours of services rendered.

We suggest that the indirect cost-allocation process be carried out through the following four steps. The step numbers correspond to the arrow numbers in Figure 14–4.

1. Subdivide other indirect operating costs into general administrative, service department, research projects, school, and educational departments based on the normal definitions of those terms.

2. Allocate service department costs to general administration, research projects, schools, and educational departments on the basis of some measure of the activity units of service provided for each of those cost accumulation centers.

3. Allocate general administrative costs, including allocated service department costs, to various research projects and to schools.

4. Allocate each school's costs, including amounts allocated in steps 2 and 3, to individual departments within each school.

We also suggest that predetermined (rather than actual) cost-allocation rates be used in allocating other indirect operating costs. When that procedure is followed, the allocations should be recorded by charges to the ultimate appropriate cost-accumulation site (research project or academic department) as the indirect costs are being allocated. The amounts so allocated should be credited to various indirect cost-application accounts (service department costs applied, general administrative costs applied, and school costs applied). At the same time, the actual costs incurred by each

**FIGURE 14–4.**    The General Allocation Process

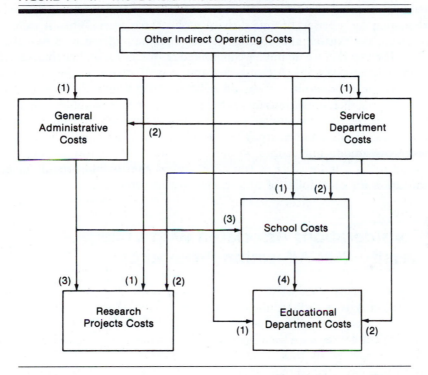

of those cost-accumulation centers should be recorded in cost-control accounts. At the end of each reporting period, the balances in the applied cost accounts should be closed against their respective actual cost-control accounts to arrive at the amounts of underapplied or overapplied costs.

To more specifically demonstrate how cost–benefit relationships should be identified and used in the cost-allocation process, let's briefly consider the ways in which some of the costs would logically be allocated. Service department costs, for example, might be allocated to the users of those services on the basis of some measure of activity units such as hours of services provided for each cost-accumulation center. It also seems appropriate to allocate the general administrative costs of a college or university to research projects and to the individual schools on the basis of the amounts of time (activity units) that chief administrative officers spend in supervising research projects and school activities. After those allocations have been made, school administrative costs will include the allocated general administrative costs and allocated service department costs plus the administrative costs directly associated with the school, such as the salary of the dean, the office space provided for the dean, and the clerical costs associated with the dean's office. The total of those costs should then be allocated to the individual academic departments within each school on the basis of the amount of the school administrator's time that is spent in dealing with the activities of the individual departments or on some other logical basis.

To avoid the clerical costs of repetitive accumulations of these activity units of services rendered, the data from a representative survey period may be used as bases for allocation for a period of time such as two or three years. When it seems appropriate to do so, the existing allocation bases may then be updated by a new survey.

The fact that we do not have unlimited resources for higher education is becoming more evident every day. A cost-accounting system similar to the one described above can provide information that should be helpful to college and university administrators in managing their operations more efficiently. Those data should be useful in budgeting, in pricing the various services provided, in fund-raising activities, and in allocating resources within a university. They could, perhaps, ultimately be used in allocating resources among universities within a specific political jurisdiction. That, in turn, would mean a more efficient education system that would provide more and better education for each dollar of educational cost incurred.

# ■ Ethical Considerations Associated with College and University Cost-Allocation Procedures

Sharp University is engaged in carrying out a research project for the Environmental Protection Agency of the United States government. Sharp is to be paid for the cost of the project plus a fixed fee upon completion of the project. Several of Sharp's administrative employees have been involved in this project. Although the actual accounts of services provided by these employees have been minimal, Mr. Crafty, the university controller, has directed that 50 percent of the salaries of these employees be allocated as indirect charges to the research project.

Consider the ethical issues associated with Crafty's cost allocation directive.

# ■ Summary

In this chapter, we have discussed cost-accumulation and -allocation procedures for nonprofit organizations with special emphasis on those that can be used by hospitals and colleges and universities. We began by observing that it is important for managers to have appropriate cost data to properly manage an enterprise unit. Such costs are useful especially in the planning and evaluation phases of the PEEP cycle.

The establishment of a cost system begins with the identification of the ultimate cost-allocation targets, which for service organizations will be the units of services rendered. As a general rule, the system will also involve the use of preliminary cost-accumulation and -allocation devices such as departmental cost centers and job order or project cost sheets. Finally, costs must be divided into direct and indirect categories with direct costs being charged directly to the service being provided and indirect costs being allocated on the basis of some directly attributable data that reflects the best discernible cause-and-effect (cost–benefit) relationship.

In the last sections of the chapter, we presented the general framework of cost systems that could be used for hospitals and colleges and universities.

# ■ Glossary

**Fixed Costs.** Costs that, in the aggregate, remain the same at different levels of operations within some relevant range of operating levels.

**Flexible Budget.** A budget showing the amounts of costs (and/or revenues) expected to be incurred or realized over a period of time at different levels of activity (measured in terms of some activity base such as direct labor hours, direct labor costs, or machine-hours). A *flexible manufacturing overhead budget* gives the projected costs of various manufacturing overhead items at different levels of activity.

**Functional-Unit Cost.** An amount equal to total costs allocated to each function performed divided by the number of functional activity units provided.

**PEEP Cycle.** The cycle of activities carried out during each period—plan, execute, evaluate, plan.

**Preliminary Cost-Allocation Devices.** Cost centers and job (project) cost sheets which are used to accumulate costs prior to their reallocation to ultimate cost-allocation targets.

**Project Cost-Accumulation Sheet.** A document used to accumulate the costs allocated to a specific project.

**Relevant Range.** A range of levels of operations over which aggregate fixed costs and aggregate variable costs can be projected to behave in a linear fashion.

**Revenue-Producing Cost Centers.** Cost-accumulation centers that provide billable services to an organization's clientele.

**Semivariable Costs.** Costs that include both variable and fixed components. Also called *semifixed costs*.

**Service Department.** A department within a business that exists for the purpose of providing services or assistance to other departments.

**Service Enterprises.** Enterprises engaged in converting resources into services rather than into finished goods.

**Service Implementation Costs.** Costs incurred by a business or nonprofit organization in providing services to the organization's clientele; comparable to cost of sales for a manufacturing or merchandising firm.

**Space Application Rate.** A predetermined amount per square foot used to allocate the approximate amounts of space occupancy costs to cost centers.

**Supporting-Service Cost Centers.** Cost-accumulation centers that provide services to revenue-producing cost centers; comparable to service department cost centers for a manufacturing firm.

**Sustentation Costs.** Costs incurred by a nonprofit organization in sustaining itself, primarily fund-raising costs and certain administrative costs.

**Ultimate Cost-Allocation Target.** The product or service unit to which all costs of producing products or providing services are to be allocated within the framework of a cost accounting system.

**Variable Costs.** Costs that, in the aggregate, vary directly with changes in the level of operations within a firm's relevant range. Within this range, the variable cost per unit will be constant.

# ■ Questions for Class Discussion

**Q14-1.** In what ways can a cost-accounting system be useful to the management of a service enterprise? Explain.

**Q14-2.** What would be the most important data a college or university cost-accounting system could provide for a manager of such an institution? Explain.

**Q14-3.** What is the primary objective in accumulating and allocating the operating costs of a hospital? Briefly explain how that allocation is achieved.

**Q14-4.** What procedures can be followed in evaluating the efficiency of a service-providing department in a hospital? Explain.

**Q14-5.** Define *variable costs, fixed costs,* and *semivariable costs.*

**Q14-6.** What is the relationship between aggregate fixed costs, the volume of services rendered, and fixed costs per unit of service?

**Q14-7.** What is the relationship between aggregate variable costs, the volume of services rendered, and variable costs per unit of service?

**Q14-8.** How are indirect costs allocated to the units of services rendered? Explain.

# ■ Exercises

**E14-1.** Human Services, Inc., provides counseling services to individuals experiencing emotional problems at a cost of $30 per hour. It's projected operating costs are as follows:

| | |
|---|---|
| Fixed costs | $80,000 per year |
| Variable costs | $25 per hour |

Semivariable costs are to be projected from the following historical data:

| | Counseling Hours | Aggregate Costs |
|---|---|---|
| Highest month | 1200 | $32,000 |
| Lowest month | 800 | 26,000 |

**Required:**
Determine the amount of contribution revenue that must be realized for next year if the agency expects to break even and to provide 12,000 hours of counseling service.

**E14-2.** Refer to the data provided in E14-1. Assume that the actual costs incurred in providing 13,000 hours of counseling services during the year are as follows:

| | |
|---|---:|
| Fixed cost | $ 82,000 |
| Variable costs | 310,000 |
| Semivariable costs | 390,000 |
| Total | $782,000 |

**Required:**
Evaluate the efficiency of the agency's operations for the year.

**E14-3.** The Ballroom Dance Club is an organization committed to the preservation and further-ance of ballroom dancing. Club officers and the board of directors serve without compen-sation. Membership fees of $125 per person per year entitle members to attend 10 dances each year. Average membership was 258 during the 19X5–19X8 period. The club began fiscal year 19X9 with $7,500 in surplus funds and the expectation that it would have 250 paid members during that year. The following costs were incurred during 19X9:

| | |
|---|---:|
| Orchestras | $25,300 |
| Room rentals | 4,550 |
| Postage and clerical costs | 1,950 |
| Miscellaneous expenses | 385 |

Paid members during 19X9 totaled 178, and the club netted $1,225 from the sale of drinks at the dances.

**Required:**
1. What would have been the cost incurred per member in 19X9 if the Ballroom Dance Club had enrolled a membership of 250?
2. What was the actual cost per member in 19X9?
3. What action would you recommend to the Ballroom Dance Club's board of di-rectors?

**E14-4.** Crestview Hospital allocates all costs to revenue-producing departments and uses past experience, adjusted for expected changes, to bill patients. Patients are assigned to departments based on space available and degree of care required. To evaluate the productivity (number of discharged patients) and efficiency (profitability) of each de-partment, Crestview calculates a ratio of departmental costs to revenues realized from services provided for patients.

Data for a recent period included the following:

| | Dept. 1 | Dept. 2 | Dept. 3 | Dept. 4 |
|---|---:|---:|---:|---:|
| Direct costs | $4,500 | $16,800 | $ 7,300 | $12,400 |
| Indirect costs | 4,725 | 17,640 | 7,665 | 13,020 |
| Patient revenues | 8,487 | 32,718 | 17,958 | 26,691 |
| Billing units | 100 | 500 | 1,000 | 50 |

**Required:**

1. Compute the ratio of costs to revenues for each of Crestview's revenue-producing departments.
2. Calculate the average billing price per unit of service.

E14-5.  Neighbors United is a nonprofit civic organization established to serve as a conduit between individuals and food merchants who are willing to donate surplus and damaged but usable food items to needy individuals in the community. With the exception of one paid employee, all labor is donated. Neighbors United received a $30,000 grant from the United Way and reported the following operating information for the fiscal year just ended:

| Expenses | |
|---|---|
| Salary | $29,700 |
| Rent and utilities | 6,600 |
| Truck | 1,950 |
| Postage | 390 |
| | |
| Number of meals served | 40,250 |

**Required:**

1. Compute the amount of funds Neighbors United had to raise from donations during the past fiscal year.
2. What was Neighbors United's cost per meal served?

# ■ Problems

P14-1.  The School of Music of Wright University, which occupies one of the oldest buildings on campus, is planning a campaign to raise funds to build a new music building and provide endowment for scholarships for music majors. Because music instruction requires very small classes or one-on-one instruction and individual practice rooms, the cost per student credit hour is assumed to be much higher for the School of Music than for the rest of Wright University. However, there are no hard data to support this assumption.

In order to have the necessary information to complete proposals to various foundations and to prepare solicitation letters to be used in the campaign, the dean of the School of Music has secured the following data from the university controller:

| | *Average Annual Amounts for Previous Three Years* | | | |
|---|---|---|---|---|
| | *School of Business* | *School of Education* | *Arts and Sciences* | *School of Music* |
| Direct operating costs | | | | |
| excluding depreciation | $6,240,000 | $2,496,000 | $11,024,000 | $1,040,000 |
| Facilities costs | $3,200,000 | $ 160,000 | $ 2,900,000 | $ 35,000 |
| Student hours enrolled | 49,800 | 21,248 | 106,000 | 3,320 |

University administration costs of $12,400,000 are allocated to the preceding university divisions on the basis of direct operating costs (to nearest thousand dollars).

**Required:**
1. Compute the average cost per student credit hour, excluding depreciation, for the School of Business, School of Education, Arts and Sciences, and School of Music.
2. Discuss the impact of facilities costs on the analysis.
3. As an outside consultant, what recommendation(s) would you make to the university administration concerning the allocation of general university costs?

**P14-2.** Maley Memorial Hospital has followed the procedure of matching revenues and expenses at the revenue-producing departmental level because reimbursement from insurance companies and the government (Medicare) has been tied to the billing rates for those departments. Maley is now in the process of refining its budgets for the year 19X6. It will use a variety of information, including the following actual data for the year ending December 31, 19X5:

|  | Revenue-Producing Cost Centers | | | Supporting Cost Centers | |
|---|---|---|---|---|---|
|  | Dept. 1 | Dept. 2 | Dept. 3 | Dept. 4 | Dept. 5 |
| Direct costs | $327,908 | $656,000 | $491,848 | $ 82,000 | $166,000 |
| Allocated general costs | 65,600 | 98,400 | 123,000 | 24,600 | 32,800 |
| Totals | $393,508 | $754,400 | $614,848 | $106,600 | $198,800 |
| Billing units | 54,120 | 8,692 | 34,645 |  |  |
| Charges (revenues) | $468,768 | $901,692 | $767,050 |  |  |

Department 4 costs are allocated to revenue-producing departments on the basis of number of employees. Department 5 costs are allocated on the basis of square footage. Relevant allocation data are:

|  | Dept. 1 | Dept. 2 | Dept. 3 | Dept. 4 | Dept. 5 |
|---|---|---|---|---|---|
| Employees | 50 | 30 | 10 | 15 | 10 |
| Square footage | 3,280 | 9,840 | 3,280 | 1,040 | 1,280 |

Using the method illustrated in the chapter, allocate supporting center costs to revenue-producing departments. Department 4 costs are to be allocated first. The level of operations for 19X6 is expected to be approximately the same as for 19X5 (approximately 83% of capacity).

**Required:**

1.  Prepare a schedule showing the total costs expected to be incurred by the three revenue-producing cost centers in 19X6.
2.  Based on your answers to requirement 1, compute for each revenue-producing department the
    a.  cost per unit of service
    b.  billing rate per unit of service
    c.  ratio of costs to charges (revenues).
3.  Which department(s) appear(s) to be most profitable?

**P14-3.**  The Golden Triangle Family Counseling Center is preparing budget requests for the coming year to be submitted to three municipalities and the state. Inasmuch as benefits of the Family Counseling Center to the community are impossible to measure objectively, the center has decided to analyze the cost of its various treatment programs to provide information to substantiate its request for funds for the coming year. The center engages in family counseling, substance abuse counseling, and psychological testing and evaluation of individuals referred by various governmental or educational units.

Total costs expected to be incurred in the coming year included the following:

| | |
|---|---:|
| Professional salaries | |
| Psychologists (2 full time) | $120,000 |
| Counselors (LPC)(10 full time) | 300,000 |
| Registered nurses (2 full time) | 50,000 |
| General and administrative salaries | |
| (1 director, 5 staff) | 150,000 |
| Rent, utilities, supplies | 98,000 |
| Test forms and grading | 49,000 |

Based on previous experience, the time of the professional staff is expected to be allocated to the three programs and administrative tasks as follows:

| | Family Counseling | Substance Abuse Counseling | Testing and Evaluation | Administration |
|---|---|---|---|---|
| Psychologists | 25% | 35% | 20% | 20% |
| Counselors | 28% | 42% | 25% | 5% |
| Nurses | 5% | 45% | 0% | 50% |

The Golden Triangle Family Counseling Center estimates it will treat 15,000 persons in the family counseling program, 6,100 in the substance abuse counseling program, and 7,500 in its testing and evaluation program. General and administrative costs are to be allocated to the three programs on the basis of number of persons going through the three programs.

**Required:**
Prepare a schedule showing costs expected to be allocated to the family counseling, substance abuse counseling, and testing and evaluation programs for the coming year. The projection for each program should show: (a) a listing of operating costs; (b) the percentage of total cost represented by each individual item of cost; and (c) the cost per person treated.

# Internal Use of the Accounting System Data

## ■ Learning Objectives

When you have finished your study of this chapter, you should

1. Recognize the need for budgets and know how the budgeting procedures are carried out.
2. Be familiar with measuring input–output relationships.
3. Know what is meant by *responsibility accounting* and the general procedures followed in implementing a responsibility accounting system.
4. Be aware of the general characteristics associated with effective controllership.
5. Have an understanding of the basic characteristics underlying an effective system of internal control.
6. Know what an internal auditor does within an organization.
7. Understand the difference between overhead and service implementation expenses and the importance of reporting them separately in the operating statement.
8. Have some understanding of the problems inherent in the politics and bureaucracy associated with nonprofit organizations.

In Chapter 14, we discussed and illustrated cost-accumulation and -allocation procedures designed to provide managers of nonprofit organizations (primarily hospitals and colleges and universities) with cost information that can be used in the PEEP cycle.

In this chapter, we consider *how internal managers use the accounting system and the data produced by it to help them operate the enterprise unit efficiently, effectively, and within externally imposed constraints.* Internal managers are concerned with segmental data reflecting performance of subordinates and with system procedures designed to force compliance with management policies and directives. They are accountable to their governing boards. Lower-level operating managers are then accountable to upper-level internal managers. The accounting system should be organized to disclose these accountability relationships within the financial structure of the enterprise unit.

In profit enterprises, internal accountability is typically disclosed through effort–achievement relationships such as divisional profits and unit cost data. In the nonprofit area, internal accountability must be built around cost data and other financial information designed to disclose the extent of adherence to externally imposed and budgetary constraints. As we saw in Chapter 14, in quasi-nonprofit organizations such as colleges, universities, and hospitals, departmental accountability can also involve a matching of costs against revenues for departmental services rendered. In many instances, both in the profit and quasi-nonprofit areas, it is important to determine and use *contribution margin data* in evaluating the performance of segments of the enterprise unit. Contribution margin is defined as the difference between incremental revenue and the additional costs incurred in earning that revenue.

Anthony and Herzlinger[1] suggest that a good management-control system will help internal managers make better plans and achieve greater assurance that subordinates will act effectively and efficiently toward the achievement of organizational objectives. They further suggest that such a control system should include an accounting system structured in terms of programs and also in terms of organizational responsibilities. The system should include

1. an effective set of budgetary procedures
2. procedures for measuring input–output relationships
3. financial performance reporting developed along authority-responsibility lines including cost-allocation procedures that will facilitate appropriate pricing of services to users.

After we have dealt with these topics, we shall discuss the problems an internal manager encounters in coping with the politics and bureaucracy often associated with nonprofit organizations. We shall then briefly summarize the characteristics of an effectively managed nonprofit organization.

## ■ Effective Budgeting Procedures

Appropriate planning is the first requisite for efficient and effective use of resources in resource conversion activities. As observed earlier, the budget for an organization is the expression financially of the plan phase of the plan-execute-evaluate-plan (PEEP) cycle. It is imperative that internal managers give attention to the budget development process if they are to effectively coordinate and control entity operations. In this section, we discuss elements of that planning process by giving special attention to

1. planning-programming-budgeting procedures
2. zero-base review of ongoing programs

---

1. Robert N. Anthony and Regina Herzlinger, *Management Control in Nonprofit Organizations* (Homewood, Ill.: Richard D. Irwin, 1980), pp. 77–184.

3.  cost–volume considerations

4.  use of program budgets and development of functional unit costs.

## Planning-Programming-Budgeting Procedures

A planning-programming-budgeting system, often referred to as PPB or PPBS, is a process for evaluating the probable efficiency and effectiveness of new programs. *It subjects those programs to systematic analysis before they are undertaken.* Ideally, it should relate an imputed value for services proposed to the costs of providing them. Viewed in that way, it is a procedure for *relating anticipated benefits to their costs.* It can be thought of as an application of the matching process, as it attempts to match projected outputs with planned inputs in the way we match revenues (output) and expenses (input) in the income statement for a business.

The problem in applying PPB, in the idealistic sense described here, is that, within the limits of our present level of knowledge, it is virtually impossible in most instances to develop an objective value for services rendered. Nevertheless, *the general conceptual framework of PPB should be used by both internal and external managers in evaluating proposed programs of service.* Service goals of the program should be described and quantified as far as possible, after which the costs of achieving those goals should be estimated. In this phase of the budgeting process, it is important for managers to recognize that the *organization is expected to provide an appropriate quality of service at minimum cost.* When the amount of resources available to provide the services has been determined, the organization should, within the qualitative constraint just cited, be expected to maximize the volume of services that can be provided with those resources.

Conceptually, PPB is a means of helping responsible officials systematically evaluate the benefits likely to result from a proposed program, along with its probable costs, as they make program-implementation decisions. In many respects, the application of PPB techniques in evaluating program possibilities is similar to capital budgeting techniques in the profit area. PPB is a system that seeks to relate anticipated benefits to the anticipated costs of providing those benefits. Therefore, with limited resources available, it can also be used in *establishing new program priorities,* so that the program appearing to provide the largest excess of benefits over costs would be implemented first. PPB can also help management choose among possible alternate courses of action in achieving a specified goal by indicating what course would be cheapest. Again, however, be reminded that output for the PPB analysis often cannot be evaluated in terms of dollars.

## Zero-Base Review

PPB techniques are used primarily in evaluating new programs. Historically, existing programs have generally been presumed to require continuance on the basis of past-period resource allocations adjusted upward to cover program enlargement and inflationary increases in costs. However, much attention has been focused on the apparent waste of resources caused by this practice, and efforts are being made to more critically review continuing programs.

In recent years, considerable attention has been given to the concept of zero-base budgeting as a technique for critically reviewing each ongoing program in a manner similar to the PPB preview of new programs. However, such a system of reevaluation can become quite burdensome and may be impractical because of that fact. Anthony and Herzlinger suggest as an alternative the use of zero-base review procedures. This system would require an organization to establish a *systematic plan for reviewing all of its programs over a period of years* rather than each time a budgetary plan is established. Zero-base review should raise the following four basic questions regarding all ongoing programs over a period of time:[2]

1. Should the function be performed?
2. What should be the quality level of the program?
3. If the function is justified, should it be carried out in the same manner as it is currently being performed?
4. How much should the program cost?

Zero-base review should, over a period of years, eliminate unneeded programs and scale down the level of services provided in other programs that have become less important to the general welfare of the constituent group.

## Cost–Volume Considerations

Effective budgetary procedures require that special attention be given to the relationship between individual cost items and the volume of operations. We generally begin by identifying the costs that vary directly with the level of operations. These are called *variable costs* and should be budgeted in direct relationship to the projected level of operations. For example, goods or services expected to cost $10,000 per period when the organization is operating at full capacity should be budgeted at $8,000 if the item is variable and the entity expects to operate at 80 percent of capacity during the budget period.

Next we should identify those costs that, in the aggregate, will remain the same within a relevant range of different levels of operations. These are characterized as *fixed costs* and should be budgeted at the same amount regardless of the anticipated level of operations. For example, a fixed cost expected to amount to $10,000 per period when operating at full capacity should be budgeted at $10,000 regardless of the anticipated level of operations.

As observed in Chapter 14, many costs will be excluded from the two classifications cited earlier because they are partially fixed and partially variable. It is important to divide such costs into fixed and variable elements to establish proper budgetary allowances for them. One way of doing that is to analyze the historical behavior of the cost item in relationship to the volume of operations. The change in the cost of the item should then be related to the change in level of operations to arrive at the variable element. Having identified that portion of the cost, we then assume that the remainder element is a fixed cost. The following illustration should help you understand the procedures involved. Assume the following historical data:

2. Anthony and Herzlinger, p. 213.

| Levels of operations | 80% | 100% |
|---|---|---|
| Historical cost | $9,500 | $10,000 |

From the assumed data we can conclude that for each 20 percent change in level of operations we have a variable cost change of $500. Therefore, at the 100 percent level we have $2,500 (5 × 500) of variable cost and $7,500 of fixed cost. Having established those facts, we can then properly budget the item at $9,750 for a 90 percent level of operations, as shown below:

| | |
|---|---|
| Fixed element | $7,500 |
| Variable element 90/20 × 500 | 2,250 |
| Total | $9,750 |

## Program Budgets and Functional Unit Costs

The expense or expenditure portion of operating budgets must often be organized by object of expense or expenditure to properly reflect budgetary-imposed constraints. For internal management purposes, however, it is important to have the budget organized so that it will place expenditure or expense control responsibilities on the shoulders of individual line managers. Since each of those managers will generally be assigned responsibilities relating to a specified program, we should allocate budgetary appropriations and charge expenditures to specified programs. This results in a program budget similar to the one illustrated in Chapter 4 for the City of Waco. Such a budget allows upper-level managers to place the responsibilities for controlling expenses or expenditures relating to specified programs on the shoulders of individual program managers.

Program budgeting also allows management to project *functional unit cost data*. This can be done by dividing individual program costs by either the units of service performed or the population served by the programs. For example, it helps a city manager to control costs if he or she has information about the budgeted police costs and other service costs per unit of population. In other areas, such as waste disposal services, it may be more beneficial to have unit cost data developed along output lines, such as the cost per ton of waste. Actual functional unit costs can be compared periodically with budgeted unit costs to help evaluate the efficiency with which the services are being performed. Also, it is often beneficial to compare those costs with the unit cost data for other similar-size cities.

## ◼ Measuring Input–Output Relationships

As we have observed, an ideal accounting arrangement for evaluating the efficiency of operations calls for matching the imputed values of services rendered against the costs of rendering those services. However, the impracticality of gathering such output data causes us to seek other methods of evaluating output. Managers may use input data as surrogates for output to gain some insight into the efficiency with which operations are being performed. As observed in the preceding paragraphs, this can take the form of program service classifications for expenses or expenditures supplemented by functional unit cost data. Such costs can, when compared to budgetary data, prior-periods data, and the cost data for other similar entities, be of significant assistance in controlling costs and promoting operating efficiency.

# ■ Financial Performance Reports

The internal manager of a nonprofit enterprise should insist on having an accounting system that will allow him or her to hold lower-level managers responsible for their particular parts of the resource conversion activities. We use the term *responsibility accounting* to describe the organization of the accounting records along those lines. In this section, we will

1. review the essential elements of a responsibility accounting system
2. describe interim performance reports
3. discuss procedures for motivating line managers toward efficient and effective resource conversion activities
4. describe the responsibilities of the effective controller
5. identify the functions of the internal auditor
6. recall the importance of using the accrual basis of accounting
7. briefly discuss the significance of the relationship between overhead and service-implementation costs.

## Responsibility Accounting System

As we observed in Chapter 14, the organizational structure of a nonprofit organization will typically have a specific lower-level manager charged with the responsibility of managing each of the major activities being performed. These can be subdivided into direct and supporting activities. Such functions as central administration, accounting, and property maintenance are *support programs* designed to help the direct service programs function more effectively. A municipality, for example, may well have *direct service programs* providing police protection, recreation and culture, waste disposal, and environmental protection services for its constituents. Both these and their supporting programs will usually have specified program managers in charge of them. *A responsibility accounting system should be organized so that the budgetary data and the accounting records in which actual operating data are accumulated will show the expense or expenditure responsibilities for each of those managers.* Such an arrangement allows the management of the enterprise unit to hold lower-level managers responsible for the efficient and effective use of resources made available to them for their respective segments of entity operations. Since budget allocations will also have been made along responsibility lines, the system can provide data showing the extent to which the various lower-level managers have complied with the budgetary constraints imposed on their respective activities. In summary, the allocation of appropriations and actual expenses or expenditures along the lines suggested earlier provides upper-level management with information that can be used in judging and controlling the activities of individual service center managers.

An accounting system organized along these lines should also provide for the allocation of supporting-activity costs to service implementation departments. We have illustrated the procedures used to allocate budgeted costs to the revenue-producing (service implementation) cost centers of Hypothetical Hospital in Exhibit 14–1. When we allocate costs in this manner, we help the enterprise manager to determine both total budget and actual costs per functional unit of services being provided. This in turn allows the managers of hospitals, colleges and universities, and other organizations, which sell their services with the intent of recovering all or a certain portion of the cost of providing those services, to deal more effectively with the service-pricing problem. In other instances where the services are distributed on the basis of need, such functional cost data provide the appropriate opening for discussing the affordability of various programs of service.

## Interim Performance Reports

If the responsibility accounting system described in the preceding paragraphs is to function effectively, cost center managers must have frequent interim performance reports. These reports should show actual costs incurred compared with budgetary allocations on an item-by-item basis. Variances from the budget should be analyzed to determine their causes so that management can act to correct those deviations in the future. We illustrated this analytical procedure for hospitals in Exhibit 14–3 (page 566). Similar schedules can be prepared to analyze the causes of deviations from budget data for most service-implementation departments of any nonprofit organization.

In using a system of accounting such as the one described above, it is always important to recognize that *program managers should be held accountable for only those expenses or expenditures that they can control.* Therefore, even though we should allocate the costs of various supporting services to revenue-producing service centers to arrive at a basis for billing such services, the manager of the revenue-producing service center should be held responsible for only the costs that he or she has the authority to control.

A key consideration in analyzing the differences between budget and actual data is an understanding of *cost–volume relationships.* This requires the division of operating costs into fixed and variable elements and the adjustment of budget allowances to conform to the actual level of operations. This was illustrated for hospitals in Chapter 14. Again, this concept can be applied to the analysis of service implementation department expenses for most nonprofit organizations.

If services are sold on a user-charge basis, it is also important to *match revenues realized from the sales of services against the costs of providing those services.* Referring again to our example of Hypothetical Hospital's flexible budget and the budget analysis schedule (Exhibits 14–2 and 14–3), we can observe that, if the services for Department 1 were priced to recover the cost per unit at an 80 percent level of activity, revenues at the actual level of activity would amount to $701,250 ($660,000 × 85/80). Comparing that figure with the $686,000 of actual expenses (see Exhibit 14–3), we get an excess of revenue over expenses of $15,250. Failure to develop the analysis shown in Exhibit 14–3 might lead the hospital manager to conclude that the manager of Department 1 had done an excellent job in controlling costs. A closer look, however, suggests that the margin should have been $20,000 ($15,250 plus the unfavorable variance of $4,750) rather than the $15,250 actually achieved by the department. Thus, instead of being complimented, the manager of Department 1 should be expected to explain why part of the unfavorable variance of $4,750 occurred.

The amount by which the revenues should have exceeded expenses can also be explained as follows:

| | |
|---|---:|
| Projected revenues at 85% level of operations | |
| 85/80(660,000) = | $701,250 |
| Projected expenses at 85% level of operations | |
| Direct variable expenses 85/80(300,000) | $318,750 |
| Direct expenses (fixed) | 100,000 |
| Allocated general expenses (fixed) | 80,000 |
| Allocated services department expenses | |
| Department 6 (fixed) | 20,000 |
| Department 7 (semifixed) | 62,500 |
| Department 8 (fixed) | 100,000 |
| Total projected expenses | $681,250 |
| Projected excess of revenues over expenses | $ 20,000 |

## Motivating Cost Center Managers

Although not directly related to the use of accounting data, we must recognize the importance of motivating cost center managers toward the efficient use of resources. In using the analytical procedures described earlier, *cost center managers should be held accountable only for those expenses that they have the capability of controlling.* Again referring to our analysis in Exhibit 14–3, we can observe that the items described in notes 1 and 2 are presumed to be controllable by the supervisor of Department 1. Therefore, management can appropriately hold him or her accountable for those portions of the unfavorable expense variance. On the other hand, variances reflected in notes 3 and 5 are probably controllable by the managers of Departments 5 and 6. These variances should be discussed with those departmental supervisors. As we observe in note 4, it is not possible from the information available to determine who may be responsible for the unfavorable variance in costs allocated from Department 7. Further analysis regarding the number of employees actually used by Department 1 would help determine who should be held accountable for this part of the variance.

As the preceding discussion suggests, one requirement for motivating managers to properly control their costs is a policy of holding each individual manager responsible only for those variances over which he or she has control. Furthermore, good performances in the control of costs should be recognized and rewarded.

Participation by lower-level managers in the budgetary process is another requirement for motivating those managers toward effectively controlling their costs. If they have a voice in establishing budget allowances, they will feel a stronger responsibility for operating within those allowances than would be the case with allocations imposed by upper-level management. Observe that this practice is followed by the City of Waco (see Chapter 4) in the preparation of the city budget.

It is also important to encourage the users of internal services to properly evaluate their needs for those services before using them. One of the best ways of doing this is to charge users, insofar as is practicable, for all or a portion of the costs of internal services provided for each cost center. Such an arrangement reduces the probability of departments using unnecessary services to avoid being charged for them. *Logically, therefore, a nonprofit organization should use as many self-sustaining internal service departments as is practicable.* For reasons similar to those cited earlier, a practice of charging outside users for a portion of the cost of providing services also causes those users to give greater consideration to whether or not the services are worth what they are being charged for them than they would if the services were provided without charge.

One of the most effective controls that can be placed on the use of goods or services is accomplished by exerting pressure on the "pocketbook nerve." This, incidentally, is one of the reasons why private colleges and universities, which cover a significant portion of their operating costs from tuition and fees rather than governmental allocations, are typically evaluated more critically by students and parents of students than are state-supported schools. Similar observations could be made for direct user charges for hospital and other services made available on a partial cost-recovery basis. Therefore, as an operating policy, *the manager of a nonprofit organization should organize the enterprise unit so that as few service users (both internal and external) as practicable receive services completely without charge.*

## Effective Controllership

So far we have emphasized internal management control through the lower-level operating managers of the enterprise unit. The controller of such an entity occupies a staff position and should be a key person in providing the accounting data needed to implement the control procedures discussed in the preceding sections of this chapter. However, if a controller is to discharge the responsibilities of that office effectively, he or she should be more than a chief accountant providing financial information. His or her responsibilities should extend to the point of advising management on all control matters and interpreting the data derived from the accounting system. A considerable portion of the controller's attention must be directed toward organizing the accounting system so that it meets the needs of management in controlling operations. This includes not only the authority-responsibility type of reporting arrangement described earlier, but also *appropriately organizing and monitoring the system of internal control.*

The system of internal control for any organization is designed to assure management that its policies are being followed and that resources are being appropriately used. We ordinarily think of appropriate use as involving protection against fraud and embezzlement, but it goes beyond that. The system should be designed to prevent waste or misuse of assets within the organization. We can briefly summarize the characteristics of a sound system of internal control as follows:

1.  The organization chart and procedures manual should provide for an *appropriate separation of duties* between persons charged with recordkeeping and

custodial responsibilities. This control characteristic is most important in connection with the handling of cash and securities. The chief custodial officer, generally characterized as the treasurer, and subordinates should be assigned all responsibilities associated with the handling and custody of cash and securities. The chief recordkeeping officer, generally characterized as the controller, should be in charge of all recordkeeping personnel. In that way, the organization is assured independently determined data showing the amounts of the assets that the custodial personnel are charged with. Custodial personnel know that the records exist and therefore will recognize that they cannot take the assets without the theft being detected. It also follows, then, that the system will not detect fraud if custodial and recordkeeping personnel collude in an embezzlement.

2. Those same documents (organization chart and procedures manual) should *place specific responsibilities on the shoulders of specific persons* within the organization.

3. An adequate system of records, authorization, and approval procedures should be established for all transactions. The system of *records should provide management with reliable financial data* for decision-making purposes. Initials or signatures of employees on supporting documents show that specific actions and checking procedures have been carried out and identify the persons responsible for each of them.

4. Employment procedures should be established to *assure that each employee is appropriately qualified for the tasks he or she is to perform.* In some respects, this item may well be the most important of these control characteristics. It has been said that with properly qualified employees, we can have appropriate internal control even with a poor system. However, even the best system cannot provide adequate control if it uses employees that are not properly qualified.

5. Actual *operating procedures should periodically be checked for compliance* with managerial policies and directives, including those listed in the procedures manual. This characteristic must be provided directly by management or by the internal audit arm of management.

6. *Physical assets should be appropriately protected* against theft, loss, improper use, and/or unreasonable damage from use and storage.

A control system incorporating these characteristics depends heavily on the provisions of the organization chart and procedures manual, the organization of the accounting system, proper employment procedures, and the appropriate use of internal auditors.

The six control characteristics cited here apply to the operations of both profit and nonprofit entities. However, nonprofit organizations typically have at least five operating characteristics that make them more likely to have control weaknesses and therefore require special attention.

The *governing body* (board of directors, board of trustees, or similar group) often is large and composed of volunteers who are relatively inactive in the day-to-day affairs of the organization. Furthermore, none of these people has ownership interests in the organization that they are trying to direct. Because of these characteristics, we typically find less emphasis on accountability and control by these groups than we would expect of a corporate board of directors.

There may be only a *limited amount of resources* that can be used to strengthen the system of internal control. Priorities in the operations of these organizations frequently place primary emphasis on implementing services and sustaining the organization rather than on improving internal control procedures.

The *accounting function* may receive little attention because of lack of staff or because the organization places most of its emphasis on its operating activities or programs.

The *staff of the organization* may be small, so that the desired segregation of duties is difficult to attain.

Nonprofit organizations receiving contributions *do not have the normal controls provided by customers in the profit area* because many resources are contributed without the expectation of receiving specific goods or services in exchange for them. For example, a person contributing cash to a nonprofit organization will typically receive only an acknowledging receipt from the solicitor. As a result, solicitors collecting contributions for a poorly controlled charitable organization may take the cash, provide no receipt for it, and simply not turn in the contribution to the organization.

Because of the last control weakness, nonprofit organizations should depend on the following *special control practices* to reduce the probability of fraud or embezzlement of charitable contribution receipts:

1. *Honesty and integrity of persons* charged with the responsibility of soliciting contributions is the most effective way of controlling door-to-door solicitations. Beyond that, however, contributors should be provided with a *duplicate receipt form* by the solicitor carrying a statement that the contribution will be independently acknowledged from the charitable organization office. The other copy of the receipt should be retained and turned in with the cash.

2. *Two volunteers or two employees* in the charitable organization's office should be involved in receiving contributions from solicitors and through the mail. Ideally, these persons should perform independent counts of contributions, which should then be reconciled with copies of receipts by a responsible official.

3. A *list of contributions received,* showing each of the contributor's names, should be prepared as soon as contributions are received in the office of the organization. At this time, the office should also acknowledge the receipt of each contribution directly to the contributor. This element of control can also be achieved, to some extent, by publishing the list of contributors.

4. The *list of prospects to be solicited* by each solicitor should be prepared in duplicate. The solicitor should then send one list with the money and pledges he or she has received to the soliciting team captain and the other directly to the charitable organization.

5. *Receipt forms* used in soliciting contributions should be prenumbered and an operating procedure requiring periodic accountability for all numbers should be established.

## Functions of the Internal Auditor

As enterprise units become larger and more complex, the relationship between top-level managers and employees becomes more remote. As that occurs, it becomes ever more important for an enterprise unit to use internal auditors. The internal auditor may be visualized as the arm of management charged with the responsibility of investigating various internal activities for compliance with management policies and for efficient execution of those policies. This is done by investigating the various phases of activities and reporting the findings back to management. Some of the investigations will be initiated by management directive, but most of them are made at the discretion of the internal auditing department.

The actions of internal auditors are designed to improve the efficiency of operations and to encourage compliance with managerial directives. These objectives are actually achieved in two ways. First, the internal auditor may discover inefficiencies or failures to comply with established directives and policies as he or she investigates the various activities of the organization. The reports rendered by the internal auditor therefore will often include recommendations for correcting such deficiencies. Management can then act to correct the problem. However, the greatest benefits are probably realized from the knowledge that the internal auditor functions within the organization and for that reason departmental managers will try to operate efficiently and to comply with the policies and directives simply because of the possibility of being investigated. Therefore, when an enterprise unit, either profit or nonprofit, becomes large enough to make it impractical for the top level manager to personally check on various phases of operations, the firm should employ an internal auditing staff to encourage efficiency and compliance with managerial directives.

## Use of the Accrual Basis of Accounting

We have previously observed that the basis of accounting for enterprise units may vary from the cash basis through the modified accrual basis to the full accrual basis. We also noted that the accrual basis is designed to recognize revenues as they are earned and expenses as resources and services are used. On the other hand, the cash basis emphasizes the points where cash is received and disbursed for the purpose of recognizing inflows and outflows.

In the author's judgment, it is important for an enterprise unit (either profit or nonprofit) to use the full accrual basis in accounting for resource inflows and outflows to obtain the most useful financial data. Only by doing so will the operating statement reflect the resources actually earned and used during the period. The accrual basis is more objective because the recognition of revenues and expenses is based on operational occurrences that cannot be deliberately shaped by discretional acts of management. Managers seeking to operate efficiently and effectively should insist on having an accounting system that tells the full objective story regarding operations of the period.

Only in that way can they have objectively determined full-revenue and full-cost data. This subject is treated more fully in Chapter 17.

## Overhead and Service-Implementation Costs

Contributors and taxpayers provide resources for nonprofit enterprises with the objective of having the enterprise provide specified, socially desirable services. *They are therefore justifiably concerned when the organization spends a large portion of its resources in sustaining itself.* We generally refer to some administrative and all fund-raising expenses as *support* or *sustentation expenses*. The internal managers of nonprofit organizations have to control these expenses within acceptable limits if they are to be judged to be using resources effectively and efficiently in carrying out the service objectives of the organization.

Because the compensation of managers in the nonprofit area is often based on the size of the organization and/or the size of the staff supervised by them, there may be an inclination to expand operations and staff beyond the optimum level. This is sometimes characterized as "pyramiding of staff" and should be avoided by the efficient manager. An expansion of staff should always be accompanied by an expansion of the quantity and/or improvement of the quality of services rendered.

It is important for managers to recognize that significant increases in fund-raising costs in relationship to contributions realized can be caused by a feeling within the constituency that excessive services are being provided by the organization. Should the ratio of fund-raising costs to contributions realized increase significantly, management should recognize that the constituency may not be sympathetic with the level or quality of services that the organization proposes to provide. In any event, it is important for the internal manager to give close attention to the relationship of sustentation to service-implementation costs at all times.

## ■ Coping with Politics and Bureaucracy

The elected managers of governmental entities hold their positions for limited terms, so many of their actions are politically motivated as they seek to preserve the support of voters. This can often cause them to *advocate providing a level of benefits and services that, in the long run, may be neither desirable nor affordable.* Failure to use the accrual basis for recognizing outflows can also encourage politicians to provide benefits in current periods that will be paid in the future without the costs being recognized in the current period operating statements. For example, they may grant pension benefits that, under presently accepted modified accrual basis accounting practices for governmental entities, may be recognized in the future when the benefits are paid rather than when the accrual-based obligations for the benefits are incurred. That action creates a favorable relationship with employees without the granting administration being held accountable for the full cost of providing the benefits. Use of the accrual basis would require recognition of the part of the pension benefit associated with current period employment in the current period.

This same political environment can persuade elected officials to support a colleague's program even though its desirability may be questionable, in order to obtain reciprocal support for programs benefiting their own constituencies. Because each person has one vote, politics can also influence elected managers to advocate programs that will provide certain benefits to large numbers of the constituency at the expense of a smaller taxpaying element of the constituency.

Salary and other employee compensation benefits of nonprofit organization managers generally tend to be lower than that of their counterparts in the business world. For that reason, fewer of the more capable people are generally attracted to those positions. Also, Civil Service regulations tend to inhibit rather than to facilitate good management control. For the most part, they prevent the use of both the motivation and penalty devices normally required for effective control.

We can only suggest that in coping with the problems of politics, governmental managers should attempt to be public servants rather than selfishly oriented politicians. This requires, among other things, a long-term look at the costs of programs and employee benefits to the point of questioning their affordability. Insofar as the accounting profession is concerned, it should insist on accrual-based determination of costs so that the obligations incurred by a political manager during his or her administration will be appropriately charged to the period of that administration.

Bureaucracy is a way of life in governmental and some other nonprofit organizations. The bureaucratic process tends to emphasize routinized work tasks and rules approved by supervisors. It is a system "that operates by complicated rules and routines."[3] The environment of the bureaucracy therefore tends to dehumanize the individual and breeds inflexibility and lack of creativity.

The effective manager of any organization must recognize that bureaucracy is probably a necessary condition in large and complex organizations. In spite of our observations in the preceding paragraphs, its characteristics are not all bad. However, the effective manager of a nonprofit organization, in particular, must be aware of some of the *dysfunctional actions* that may be proposed within a bureaucratic environment simply because of the nature of that environment. Appropriate reactions to such proposals can then minimize the dysfunctional characteristics of the system.

## ■ The Effectively Managed Nonprofit Organization

Anthony and Herzlinger suggest that an effectively managed nonprofit organization should include the following characteristics:[4]

1.  a governing board with an active interest in seeing the organization function efficiently and effectively

2.  top management that is involved in programming, in performance evaluation, and in systems improvement

3.  well-compensated senior managers

3.  Anthony and Herzlinger, p. 450.
4.  Ibid., pp. 590–591.

4. adequate rewards for good managers accompanied by refusal to tolerate poor managers

5. use of an accrual-based accounting system that is consistent with program and responsibility budgets

6. internal reports structured so that they are consistent with budget data

7. evaluations of operations on a regular basis

8. evaluations of effectiveness of all elements of the overall program on a regular basis

9. operation through a carefully designed program structure

10. use of benefit–cost analysis where it is practical to do so

11. operation through profit centers (self-sustaining units) with well-designed transfer prices insofar as is possible

12. special attention to pricing policy in the sales of services to outside clients

13. emphasis on the development of output measures whenever practicable to measure performance

14. development and use of unit cost data

15. use of variance analysis in evaluating effectiveness of lower-level managers.

## ■ Ethical Considerations Associated with the Political Process

Congressman Sly plans to introduce legislation that would provide subsidy payments for a crop produced in his state. One of Sly's colleagues, Congressman Patronage, is concerned about the possibility of a military base in his state being closed as part of a program to reduce military expenditures. Although Sly is convinced that the base should be closed because of reduced need for military strength, he approaches his colleague with an offer to vote against closing the military base provided that Patronage will support the bill creating subsidy payments for the crop produced in his state.

Consider the ethical issues associated with such a political arrangement.

## ■ Summary

In this chapter, we have focused our attention on how the accounting data and the system that produces those data can be used by the internal managers of nonprofit organizations.

First, we described how the accounting system can be organized along authority-responsibility lines to allow the managers of an organization to measure the effectiveness of departmental or cost center supervisors. This requires us to relate efforts to achievements by matching departmental costs with revenues and/or developing cost–volume relationships including analysis of variances from budget allowances. We also explained how budgetary data should be developed along responsibility lines to facilitate such evaluations.

Next, attention was given to the problem of motivating lower-level managers to operate in an efficient and effective manner. We touched upon the importance of an effective system of internal control and ways in which the internal auditor can help promote operating effectiveness and compliance with managerial directives.

Later in the chapter, attention was given to some of the special problems created by the basic environment surrounding nonprofit organizations. More specifically, we examined the bias toward the pyramiding of staff and the dysfunctional aspects of politics and bureaucracy. Fifteen characteristics that one should expect to find in an effectively managed nonprofit organization were listed in the final section of the chapter.

## ■ Glossary

**Contribution Margin.**   An amount equal to the difference between sales revenue and variable costs.

**Direct Service Programs.**   Elements (cost centers) of a program budget used to accumulate the costs associated with the specific services provided for the citizens of a governmental unit.

**Interim Performance Reports.**   Reports reflecting the performance of individual cost centers over segments of a fiscal period.

**Internal Auditor.**   An employee whose primary responsibilities involve verification of compliance with internal profitability goals and with directives and policies of management relating to internal control.

**Internal Control.**   A plan of organization under which employees' duties are so arranged and records and procedures so designed as to make it possible to exercise effective accounting control over assets, liabilities, revenues, and expenditures. Under such a system, the work of employees is subdivided so that no single employee performs a complete cycle of operations. Thus, for example, an employee handling cash would not post the accounts receivable records. Moreover, under such a system, the procedures to be followed are definitely laid down and require proper authorizations by designated officials for all actions to be taken.

**Responsibility Accounting.**   A system of accounting under which individual employees are held responsible for particular segments of activities occurring within an enterprise unit. Accounting reports are prepared for each of these segments to reflect the effectiveness with which each of the activities has been carried out. Such reports are often referred to as performance reports.

**Support Programs.**   Elements (cost centers) of an organization's budgeting system used to accumulate the costs of supporting direct service activities such as maintenance, administration, accounting, and so forth.

**Zero-Base Review.**   An alternative to the use of zero-base budgeting. This procedure requires an organization to establish a systematic plan for reviewing all of its operations over a period of years rather than each time a budgetary plan is established.

# ■ Suggested Supplementary References

*Atkisson, Robert M., and Edward P. Chaitt. "The Case for the Internal Auditor in Local Government: The Eyes and Ears of Public Officials and the People." *Governmental Finance* (August 1978).

Caldwell, Charles W., and Judith K. Welch. "Applications of Cost–Volume–Profit Analysis in the Governmental Environment." *Government Accountants Journal* (Summer 1989).

*Caldwell, Kenneth S. "Operational Auditing in State and Local Government." *Governmental Finance* (November 1975).

Clark, Stephen A. "Linking Employee Salary Adjustments to Performance: Is It Worth the Effort?" *Governmental Finance* (December 1982): 15–18.

Drucker, Meyer. "Importance of Internal Review for Local Governments." *Governmental Finance,* 2 (1973): 25–28.

Glisson, Patrick C., and Stephen H. Holley. "Developing Local Government User Charges: Technical and Policy Considerations." *Governmental Finance* (March 1982): 3–7.

Harrill, E. Reece, Thomas E. Richardo, and Jonathan M. Wallman. "FAMIS—A Financial Accounting and Management Information System for Local Government." *Management Controls,* 21 (1974): 85–94.

Hickey, James A. "A Comprehensive Approach to Management." *Government Accountants Journal* (Fall 1981): 31–37.

Holder, William W., and Jan Williams. "Better Cost Control with Flexible Budgets and Variance Analysis." *Hospital Financial Management,* 30 (1976): 12–20.

Kent, Calvin A. "Users' Fees for Municipalities." *Governmental Finance,* 1 (1972): 2–7.

Kory, Ross C. "Costing Municipal Services." *Governmental Finance* (March 1982): 21–26.

Larimore, L. Keith. "Break-Even Analysis for Higher Education." *Management Accounting,* 56 (1974): 25–28.

McRae, Robert D. "The Cost Burden Study: A Method for Recovering Costs from Non-Residents." *Governmental Finance* (March 1982): 9–11.

Mendel, Colleen Bell, Jack O. Hall, Jr., and C. Richard Aldridge. "Cost Analysis in Project Headstart." *Government Accountants Journal* (Fall 1988).

Morris, Russell D. "Government Financial Management: Fix It or Find It?" *Government Accountants Journal* (Summer 1986).

Mushkin, Selma J., and Charles L. Vehorn. "User Fees and Charges." *Governmental Finance* (November 1977): 42–48.

Oatman, Donald. "It's Time for Productivity Accounting in Government." *Governmental Finance* (November 1979): 9–14.

Price Waterhouse & Co. "Effective Internal Accounting Control for Nonprofit Organizations." (Price Waterhouse & Co., 1980).

Rea, Patrick, and Maynard Brandon. "Applying Cash Management Techniques." *Government Accountants Journal* (Spring 1983): 45–49.

Scantleberry, Donald L., and Ronell B. Raaum. "Future Directions in Government Accounting." *Federal Accountant,* 24 (1975): 2–9.

Shenkir, William G. "A Paradigm for Operational Auditing." *Federal Accountant,* 20 (1971): 106–111.

Steinberg, Harold I., and Donald Tashner. "Cash Management for Local Government." *Management Controls,* 23 (Peat, Marwick, Mitchell & Co., 1976): 22–28.

*Also available in *Accounting in the Public Sector: The Changing Environment—A Book of Readings* by Robert W. Ingram (Salt Lake City: Brighton Publishing Company, 1980).

Weisenbach, Paul E. "Vulnerability Assessment and Internal Control Studies: What Are They and How Do You Do Them?" *Government Accountants Journal* (Spring 1983): 1–11.

Wesberry, James P., Jr. "The Importance of Control over Cash." *International Journal of Government Auditing,* 3 (1976): 2–6.

Wolinsky, Daniel, and Arthur L. Breakstone. "Reporting for the Rehabilitation and Sheltered Workshop." *Journal of Accountancy,* 140 (1975): 56–62.

Woodridge, Blue. "Toward the Development of an Integrated Financial Management System." *Government Accountants Journal* (Fall 1982): 37–44.

# ▪ Questions for Class Discussion

**Q15-1.** What is meant by the term *internal accountability* as it is used by internal managers in controlling the operations of an enterprise unit?

**Q15-2.** How does an effective set of budgetary procedures help internal managers in controlling the operations of an enterprise unit? Explain fully.

**Q15-3.** Why is it important to develop financial performance reporting along the lines of an entity's authority-responsibility relationships?

**Q15-4.** What is meant by *planning-programming-budgeting system?*

**Q15-5.** What is the primary problem in applying PPB in the nonprofit area? Does that mean that the PPB technique is of no value? Explain fully.

**Q15-6.** What is meant by the term *cost–volume relationships?* How are they used in the budgeting process?

**Q15-7.** What is meant by a *program budget?* How is it different from an *object-of-expenditure budget?* Explain the relationship between these two types of budgets for a particular governmental entity.

**Q15-8.** What is meant by a *responsibility accounting system?* How is such a system used?

**Q15-9.** What is meant by a *flexible budget?* How is it used in controlling a segment of operations?

**Q15-10.** Discuss the relationship between motivating cost center managers and the control of departmental costs.

**Q15-11.** Why is it important to provide as many internal services as is possible on a self-sustaining basis? Explain fully.

**Q15-12.** Describe the general responsibilities of the controller in a nonprofit enterprise.

**Q15-13.** Why is it important to have a sound system of internal control within an enterprise unit?

**Q15-14.** Describe the functions of an internal auditor. What is his or her relationship to top-level management?

**Q15-15.** Is it more difficult to have a sound system of internal control in a nonprofit enterprise than in a profit enterprise? Explain.

**Q15-16.** Explain the difference between overhead and service implementation costs in the nonprofit area. What is the significance of this distinction? Explain.

**Q15-17.** What is meant by "pyramiding of staff" in the nonprofit area?

Q15-18.    How does the fact that governmental officials are elected for a limited term logically affect their attitude toward the use of accrual-based accounting practices in the governmental area? Discuss.

# ■ Exercises

E15-1.    A senator proposes to establish a governmental agency to exterminate a rodent that consumes grain crops and also serves as a carrier of certain disease germs. The projected cost of the program is $800,000,000. The proposal cites the following data in support of the proposed expenditures: Elimination of the rodent would result in a saving of grain crops with an estimated value of $1 billion. The senator also estimates that the disease generally attributed to the rodent could be eliminated with savings in medical costs of $500,000. Elimination of the disease would also reduce the number of work days lost by 25,000. Each work day recovered is estimated to be worth $20.

**Required:**
A.    Complete a PPB analysis of the proposal.
B.    What arguments can you advance in support of the senator's proposal?
C.    Assume now that you are a member of the opposition party. What questions would you ask and what arguments would you advance in your effort to defeat the proposal?

E15-2.    A governmental agency is preparing its budget for the next year. The accountant for the agency wishes to divide total agency expenditures into fixed and variable elements before he develops a budget. The level of operations of the agency this year was approximately 110 percent of the level for last year. As a result of taxpayer discontent, the governmental unit has decided to reduce agency operations for next year to 85 percent of its current level. Expenditures for last year amounted to $850,000. Current year expenditures have increased from that figure to $900,000. The increase has been caused entirely by the change in level of operations.

**Required:**
A.    Calculate the approximate fixed and variable elements of total expenditures for last year and the current year.
B.    Prepare a budget that should be appropriate for next year if the level of operations are to be reduced by 15 percent.

E15-3.    A college has prepared its budget based on the assumption that 10,000 students would be enrolled. When registration was completed, the actual enrollment was 11,000 students. The supervisor of a department of the college whose activities are directly related to the overall level of enrollment has requested that his budget for expenditures be adjusted to compensate for the expected increase in enrollment. His present budget allows the department to spend $65,000, of which $40,000 are fixed expenditures.

**Required:**
Calculate the amount that should be added to the department's budgeted expenditures.

E15-4.    A hospital has a revenue-producing department that was budgeted to operate at 80 percent of capacity (6,000 units of service). Charges for services were established to recover costs of $600,000 at that operating level. During the year, actual operating costs amounted to $650,000 and 6,600 units of service were sold. Further analysis reveals that $350,000 of the budgeted operating costs are fixed.

**Required:**
A. Calculate the extent to which costs were recovered by the department.
B. Evaluate the efficiency of the department in controlling its costs. Show computations in good form.

E15-5. A small health and welfare agency has an office staff of two persons who are charged with the responsibilities of handling cash receipts, maintaining the accounting records, paying bills, and serving as receptionist for persons seeking the services of the agency or contributing funds to it. One person has had experience both as a cashier and bookkeeper. As a result that person has been assigned the responsibilities of handling cash receipts and maintaining the accounting records. However, when that person is out of the office, the other person handles the cash receipts, many of which are cash contributions from donors.

**Required:**
A. Discuss the primary internal control weaknesses present in this situation.
B. How could the system of control be improved?

E15-6. The operating procedures for a governmental agency include a salary policy that allows a supervisor's salary to be increased by 5 percent each time the staff working under that person's direction increases by three people.

**Required:**
As a member of the oversight board for the agency, what concern would you have about the agency's salary policy? Explain.

# ▪ Problems

P15-1. Select the best answer for each of the following items:
1. Which of the following best describes proper internal control over payroll?
   a. The preparation of the payroll must be under the control of the personnel department.
   b. The confidentiality of employee payroll data should be carefully protected to prevent fraud.
   c. The duties of hiring, payroll computation, and payment to employees should be segregated.
   d. The payment of cash to employees should be replaced with payment by checks.
2. Internal control over cash receipts is weakened when an employee who receives customer mail receipts also:
   a. prepares initial cash receipts records.
   b. records credits to individual accounts receivable.
   c. prepares bank deposit slips for all mail receipts.
   d. maintains a petty cash fund.

3. A nonprofit organization published a monthly magazine that had 15,000 sub-scribers on January 1, 19X6. The number of subscribers increased steadily throughout the year and at December 31, 19X6, there were 16,200 subscribers. The annual magazine subscription cost was $10 on January 1, 19X6, and was increased to $12 for new members on April 1, 19X6. An auditor would expect that the receipts from subscriptions for the year ended December 31, 19X6, would be approximately:
   a. $179,400.
   b. $171,600.
   c. $164,400.
   d. $163,800.

4. To strengthen the system of internal accounting control over the purchase of merchandise, a company's receiving department should:
   a. accept merchandise only if a purchase order or approval granted by the purchasing department is on hand.
   b. accept and count all merchandise received from the usual company vendors.
   c. rely on shipping documents for the preparation of receiving reports.
   d. be responsible for the physical handling of merchandise but not the prepa-ration of receiving reports.

5. Operating control over the check signature plate normally should be the respon-sibility of the:
   a. secretary.
   b. chief accountant.
   c. vice president of finance.
   d. treasurer.

6. Which of the following is an *invalid* concept of internal control?
   a. A person may be made responsible for all phases of a transaction, as long as there is a clear designation of that person's responsibility.
   b. The recorded accountability for assets should be compared with the existing assets at reasonable intervals and appropriate action should be taken if there are differences.
   c. Accounting control procedures may appropriately be applied on a test basis in some circumstances.
   d. Procedures designed to detect errors and irregularities should be performed by persons other than those who are in a position to perpetrate them.

7. A well-designed system of internal control that is functioning effectively is most likely to detect an irregularity arising from:
   a. the fraudulent action of several employees.
   b. the fraudulent action of an individual employee.
   c. informal deviations from the official organization chart.
   d. management fraud.

8. The financial management of a company should take steps to see that company investment securities are protected. Which of the following is *not* a step that is designed to protect investment securities?
   a. Custody of securities should be assigned to persons who have the accounting responsibility for securities.

b.  Securities should be properly controlled physically in order to prevent unau-
thorized usage.

c.  Access to securities should be vested in more than one person.

d.  Securities should be registered in the name of the owner.

9.  An example of an internal control weakness is to assign to a department supervisor the responsibility for:

a.  reviewing and approving time reports for subordinate employees.

b.  initiating requests for salary adjustments for subordinate employees.

c.  authorizing payroll checks for terminated employees.

d.  distributing payroll checks to subordinate employees.

10.  When used for performance evaluation, periodic internal reports based on a
responsibility accounting system should *not:*

a.  be related to the organization chart.

b.  include allocated fixed overhead.

c.  include variances between actual and budgeted controllable costs.

d.  distinguish between controllable and noncontrollable costs.

—**AICPA Adapted**

**P15-2.**  The following flexible operating expense budget has been established for the service
center internal service fund:

| Types of Expenses | Levels of Operations | | | |
|---|---|---|---|---|
| | 70% | 80% | 90% | 100% |
| Variable expenses | $ 7,000 | $ 8,000 | $ 9,000 | $10,000 |
| Fixed expenses | 12,000 | 12,000 | 12,000 | 12,000 |
| Mixed expenses (fixed and variable) | 7,000 | 7,500 | 8,000 | 8,500 |
| Totals | $26,000 | $27,500 | $29,000 | $30,500 |

The level of operations is measured by the number of hours of services provided by the
service center. At the 100 percent level, the service center provides 5,000 hours of service.

**Required:**

A.  Calculate the budgeted variable expense rate and total fixed expense included in
mixed expenses.

B.  Assume that the service center is expected to provide 4,100 hours of service during
the next period. Prepare an operating expense budget for the service center including the rate per hour that should be charged for services to provide for recovery of
operating expenses.

C.  Assume actual operations show the following data:

| | |
|---|---|
| Hours of service provided | 4,400 |
| Actual variable expenses | $ 8,600 |
| Actual fixed expenses | $12,100 |
| Actual mixed expenses | $7,800 |

Analyze the operations of the service center in relationship to the budget and hourly charge developed in Requirement B.

**P15-3.** Refer to the data in Problem P15-2. Assume now that the service charge rate was based on an anticipated 80 percent level of operations.

**Required:**

A. Calculate the rate per hour to be charged for service center work.
B. Assume further that the service center actually performs 3,600 hours of work and incurs the following costs:

| | |
|---|---|
| Variable expenses | $ 7,100 |
| Fixed expenses | $12,000 |
| Mixed expenses | $ 7,000 |

Calculate the difference between revenues and expenses for the department. Has the department been effectively managed? Explain.

**P15-4.** A nonprofit organization shows the following operating data over a three-year period:

| | 19X1 | 19X2 | 19X3 |
|---|---|---|---|
| Revenues | | | |
| Contribution revenue | $80,000 | $90,000 | $100,000 |
| User charges | 10,000 | 9,000 | 8,000 |
| Total revenues | $90,000 | $99,000 | $108,000 |
| Expenses | | | |
| Fund raising | $10,000 | $12,000 | $ 15,000 |
| Administrative | 12,000 | 16,000 | 22,000 |
| Service implementation | 66,000 | 68,000 | 70,000 |
| Total expenses | $88,000 | $96,000 | $107,000 |
| Excess of revenues over expenses | $ 2,000 | $ 3,000 | $ 1,000 |

**Required:**

Evaluate the operations of the organization. Support your comments with specific calculations.

**P15-5.** A private college has prepared the following budget on the assumption that it would enroll 10,000 students:

| | |
|---|---|
| Revenues | |
| Tuition revenue 10,000 @ $1,500 each | $15,000,000 |
| Endowment income | 4,000,000 |
| Gifts and other income | 1,000,000 |
| Total revenues | $20,000,000 |

Expenditures
   Educational and general

| | |
|---|---:|
|      Instructional salaries | $10,000,000 |
|      Library expenditures | 1,200,000 |
|      Student services | 1,500,000 |
|      Plant operations and maintenance | 2,000,000 |
|      Student aid | 1,300,000 |
|      Mandatory transfers | 700,000 |
|      General administration | 1,000,000 |
|      General instructional expenditures | 1,200,000 |
|      Other miscellaneous expenditures | 800,000 |
|        Total expenditures | $19,700,000 |
|   Excess of revenues over expenditures | $   300,000 |

In developing the budgetary data, the following cost–volume relationships have been observed for the various expenditure items:

1. Instructional salaries are contracted on an annual basis. Also, $7,000,000 of the total salaries are paid to tenured faculty and therefore cannot be eliminated. Other instructional salaries can be adjusted to meet the projected level of revenue before the beginning of each year.

2. The board of trustees for the college has established a policy requiring the college to operate, insofar as is possible, within the revenue available to it each year. Any deficiency in meeting this goal for any single year is to be made up in the following year.

3. The college plans to spend $50 per student in library acquisitions. Other library expenditures are for salaries and may be considered fixed.

4. Student services expenditures include fixed expenditures amounting to $600,000. Other elements of this expenditure should vary directly with enrollment.

5. Plant operations and maintenance expenditures should be the same within a relevant range of 6,000 to 12,000 students enrolled. However, maintenance expenditures amounting to $600,000 could be postponed if necessary.

6. Student aid expenditures are committed for the current year. This item is budgeted at $130 per student based on anticipated enrollment.

7. Mandatory transfers is a fixed dollar amount, regardless of level of operations.

8. General administration includes $400,000 of expenditures that are necessary to keep the college in operation. Other costs are expected to vary with the level of enrollment.

9. General instructional expenditures is always expected to be equal to 12 percent of instructional salaries.

10. Other miscellaneous expenditures include approximately $300,000 that is fixed. The remainder of this should vary directly with the level of enrollment.

**Required:**

A. Actual enrollment at the beginning of the fall term is 9,000 students. You are asked to prepare a revised budget based on that level of enrollment.

B. The administration feels that the level of enrollment may decline even further next year. Furthermore, a 5 percent increase in the general price level over the current year is anticipated. In the light of those observations, you are asked to develop a budget for next year based on a projected enrollment of 8,000 students. Revenues other than tuition should remain the same as they were during the current year. The college will endeavor to provide an average 8 percent increase in instructors' salaries.

P15-6.   A city is currently operating with a balanced budget calling for the following expenditures by service categories:

| | |
|---|---:|
| Administration | $ 4,000,000 |
| Police services | 3,500,000 |
| Sanitation services | 2,500,000 |
| Recreation services | 3,000,000 |
| Social services | 2,000,000 |
| Environmental protection services | 5,000,000 |
| Total budgeted expenditures | $20,000,000 |

1. Population is expected to increase by 5 percent. This is expected to produce a 2 percent increase in tax revenue at the current tax rate.
2. The general price level is expected to rise by 6 percent over the current year on all expenditures except salaries. Union demands will probably require an 8 percent increase in those items. Salaries included in each service category are as follows:

| | |
|---|---:|
| Administration | $ 2,500,000 |
| Police services | 2,500,000 |
| Sanitation services | 1,500,000 |
| Recreation services | 1,500,000 |
| Social services | 1,500,000 |
| Environmental protection services | 3,000,000 |
| Total | $12,500,000 |

3. All expenditures other than salaries are expected to remain the same except for inflationary changes. The present number of employees is adequate to meet the present level of service needs for a population level up to 15 percent above the current level.

**Required:**
A. Prepare a budget for the next year based on the assumption that the city will maintain its present level of services. Will such a budget require an increase in the property tax rate? Explain.
B. The city council anticipates a taxpayer revolt against any proposed increase in the tax rate. In anticipation of that possibility, you are asked to adjust the budget developed in Requirement A to allow the city to operate within available revenues. No service category budgeted expenditures are to be reduced more than 7 percent. Police and sanitation services are to be maintained at the levels established in Requirement A.

# Use of Accounting Data by Externally Interested Parties

## ■ Learning Objectives

When you have finished your study of this chapter, you should

1. Be aware of the things that externally interested parties need to know to evaluate the extent to which the internal managers of a nonprofit organization have met their fiduciary responsibilities to constituents.

2. Recognize the three basic concerns of externally interested parties as they evaluate the operations of a nonprofit organization.

3. Understand the difference between measurement of efficiency and measurement of effectiveness.

4. Be aware of the general procedures followed in analyzing the financial statements of both pure profit and pure nonprofit enterprise units.

5. Be able to calculate and use analytical data derived from the financial statements of colleges and universities, hospitals, health and welfare agencies, and churches.

The accounting systems we have described and illustrated in Part Two and Part Three are designed to *record, classify,* and *accumulate* financial data that can be used by those interested in the operations of various nonprofit enterprises. The interested parties fall into two general groups: internal managers who use the financial data to make day-to-day operating decisions, and those outside the organization who have a constituency, regulatory, or credit interest in the organization. In Chapters 14 and 15, we explained how those data are used by internal managers. In this chapter, we turn our attention to the ways in which externally interested parties use the data in published financial reports. Such reports are made available to external users (primarily constituents and creditors) to be used in making various support and credit decisions. In this chapter, *we explain how the accounting data may be analyzed and used by those externally interested parties.*

Externally interested parties play an important role in promoting operating efficiency and effectiveness of nonprofit organizations. They do so by oversight of internal managers and by providing or withdrawing their support of the enterprise on the basis of their judgments regarding the efficiency and effectiveness of its operations. Most nonprofit organizations have a board of trustees or a legislative body elected by constituents that monitors the activities of the internal managers. The *constituents* may also become directly involved to the point of challenging the actions taken by the elected boards or by withholding financial support from the organization. The voter support of "Proposition 13" in California in 1978 and taxpayer revolt activities in other parts of the United States are examples of direct constituency reaction to the operations of governmental units. *Creditors* of nonprofit organizations are concerned with the same things (perceived ability to meet interest and principal payments) in the nonprofit area as they are in the profit area. These and other externally interested parties must be prepared to analyze and use the published financial data of these organizations in making decisions regarding their relationships with them.

We begin our discussion by explaining how the published financial data may be used by externally interested parties *in monitoring the fiduciary responsibility of internal managers*. After that, we turn to a more specific consideration of the *general procedures to be followed in analyzing and interpreting the financial data for externally interested parties*. In the last portion of the chapter, we *describe and illustrate specific analytical procedures* followed in evaluating the operations of different types of nonprofit entities and cite some of the actions that externally interested parties might take in response to those data.

## ■ Evaluating the Fiduciary Responsibility of Internal Managers

Internal managers are expected to carry out the resource conversion activities of an enterprise in accordance with the perceived desires of the owners in the case of profit entities or of the contributing constituency in the case of nonprofit organizations. Those resource conversion activities are expected to be carried out in an efficient and effective manner. In addition, all enterprise units operate within certain socially imposed constraints, and internal managers are also expected to operate in compliance with those constraints. External boards, in discharging their responsibilities to their constituencies, are thus concerned with evaluating *efficiency* and *effectiveness* of operations and the *extent of compliance* with externally imposed constraints. They use the financial data in making those evaluations.

Both the efficiency and effectiveness of a profit enterprise can be evaluated by judging the extent to which the long-term profit objective has been achieved. Past profit achievements, along with calculations reflecting the probable liquidity and stability of the enterprise, are used to judge the extent to which that objective is being achieved. Compliance in this area largely involves adherence to legally imposed constraints on operations. The recent emphasis on the elimination of corrupt practices in international corporate activities, the protection of the environment, and the establishment of safety requirements for the products of domestic companies represent extensions of the concept of compliance beyond those specifically prescribed by regulatory agencies. Thus, to an increasing degree, we find managers (both internal and external) of profit enterprises being held accountable for *ethical operations* and *proper treatment of customers* in addition to their responsibility for operational efficiency and effectiveness.

The internal managers of nonprofit enterprises are expected to carry out the resource conversion activities efficiently and effectively just as are managers of profit enterprises. However, because nonprofit organizations have a service objective rather than a profit objective, it is much more difficult to judge whether resource conversion activities have been carried out efficiently. In most instances, it is impossible to objectively measure the benefits produced by the services rendered so as to allow efforts to be matched against achievements as we do in the profit area. Nevertheless, the governing boards and constituencies of nonprofit organizations are expected to evaluate the efficiency and effectiveness of internal managers' resource conversion activities and to react appropriately to their findings. That requires a *critical evaluation of cost data in relationship to services rendered.*

Compliance in the nonprofit area is partially determinable by relating the acquisitions and uses of resources to externally imposed constraints and to budgetary plans for resource flows. The accounting system, using separate funds for externally restricted resources and appropriation control techniques within funds, provides the required information for that evaluation. The other fiduciary responsibilities of the internal managers of nonprofit organizations to their governing boards and constituencies are essentially the same as those of the internal managements of profit enterprises to their boards of directors and owners. However, we shall observe in the following pages that the devices used in evaluating their efforts are significantly different.

# ■ Analysis and Interpretation of Financial Data

We begin our description of the analysis and interpretation of financial data by exploring the implications for the analytical process of the three basic concerns—*efficiency, effectiveness,* and *compliance*—discussed in the preceding section. After that, we describe how the financial data of profit enterprises may be analyzed and interpreted to show the extent to which those basic concerns have been met. In the last part of this section, we develop general analytical techniques that can be applied in interpreting the financial statements of nonprofit entities.

## Basic Concerns

The efficiency with which resource conversion activities are carried out can best be measured by *relating efforts to achievements.* In the profit area, we do this in the income statement by relating revenues earned to expenses incurred in earning those revenues in order to determine the net income from operations. To supplement this, we also divide the costs of producing goods or services by the output achieved to determine the effort–achievement relationship in the production segments of operations. Other things being equal, a lower cost per unit of output represents a better effort–achievement relationship and is therefore more efficient than a higher cost per unit. We also relate effort to achievement when we compute the relationship between net income and invested capital. Therefore, in evaluating the efficiency of operations, we must strive to develop data showing effort–achievement relationships that can be compared with standards or with past period data.

Enterprise units *operate effectively when they achieve their operating objectives.* An enterprise unit may operate effectively, that is, achieve its operating objectives, without operating efficiently. For example, in killing a fly, we might use a sledge hammer to very thoroughly meet that operating objective. However, this would not be an efficient way of accomplishing it. So, effectiveness should be evaluated separately from efficiency. The analytical process should be designed to produce data that will help externally interested parties in evaluating both the extent to which operating objectives have been achieved and how efficiently that achievement has been carried out.

The third basic concern of externally interested parties involves determining whether an enterprise unit has complied with legal and/or other externally imposed requirements. Among profit enterprises this means operating within the constraints of the law and the charter under which the entity was created. Breaches of compliance will often result in legal action against the enterprise unit. Boards of directors, creditors, and other constituents of profit enterprises are always vitally concerned with contingent obligations evidenced by lawsuits and other information indicating possible conflict with the law or regulatory agencies. Nonprofit organizations must adhere to these legal constraints and must also comply with specific limitations on resource use imposed by external constraints and budgetary actions. This is sometimes referred to as *fiscal accountability.* As we have observed, the records of these organizations must be organized to disclose the extent to which internal managers have complied with those constraints.

## Analysis of Profit Enterprise Financial Statements

In Chapter 1, we explained how the universe of enterprise units could be beneficially classified into pure profit, quasi-profit, quasi-nonprofit, and pure nonprofit entities for the purpose of determining how their financial statements should be organized. The analytical procedures associated with the interpretation of certain quasi-nonprofit enterprises will include some elements of profit enterprise analytical procedures along with elements of pure nonprofit analysis. So, it is important for you to understand the basic procedures for analyzing pure profit enterprise financial statement data as well as the techniques used in analyzing the financial statements of pure nonprofit entities.

The *operational efficiency and effectiveness* of profit enterprises is basically measured through an evaluation of effort–achievement relationships. In analyzing the published financial statements, we begin by observing the relationship between revenues (achievements) and the expenses (efforts) incurred in realizing them. From that we get the net income figure (an achievement), which can be related to efforts expended in the form of invested resources. This key measurement can be reflected in terms of *earnings per share or in terms of a percentage return on equity capital.* Also, in measuring the effectiveness with which assets of the firm have been used, we can calculate the rate of return on total assets by dividing net income by total assets. Another indication of overall efficiency and effectiveness of operations can be secured by measuring relationships among various elements of the income statement. The gross margin percentage is important in evaluating the competitiveness of the environment in which the firm operates, and the percentage relationship between net operating income and sales is important in evaluating operating effectiveness. The latter tells us what portion of the sales dollar the company is able to keep to cover income taxes and to increase equity capital.

If a profit enterprise is to continue to operate effectively and efficiently, it must also be able to meet its current obligations as they mature. Furthermore, the working-capital position of the firm must provide adequate operational flexibility. The current ratio, calculated by dividing current assets by current liabilities, is generally used as the starting point in measuring *current liquidity*. That ratio should, however, be supplemented by other ratios measuring the liquidity of current assets. These include the acid-test or quick-asset ratio, the turnover of receivables, and the turnover of inventory. The acid-test ratio is calculated by dividing cash plus near-cash assets, such as marketable securities and receivables, by current liabilities. Receivables turnover is calculated by dividing sales on account by average accounts receivable, and inventory turnover is determined by dividing cost of sales by average inventory. High ratios or turnovers point toward greater liquidity, while lower figures indicate a less satisfactory current liquidity position. In making an overall judgment regarding current liquidity, however, it is important to observe that a lower-than-normal current ratio can be compensated for by high acid-test and high turnover ratios. The analyst has to look at these ratios as a group to evaluate the overall current liquidity of the firm.

The constituents of a business entity, who are considering long-term ownership or credit commitments, are also concerned with the firm's long-term outlook for overcoming economic adversity. We generally refer to this as a firm's prospects for *long-term stability and liquidity*. To meet this test, a firm must show a capability for absorbing reasonable financial reverses without becoming insolvent. One of the key ratios in measuring probable long-term stability and liquidity is the debt-to-equity capital ratio. A profit enterprise using debt capital is said to be *trading on its equity*. Other things being equal, a firm relying heavily on debt capital would have more risk of insolvency in a situation of economic adversity than would a firm that was financed entirely through equity capital. Another way of measuring the extent of trading on the equity is to calculate the ratio of equity capital to total assets. Again, other things being equal, a high ratio would suggest a greater probability of the firm being able to weather economic adversity. To supplement the equity-capital-to-total-assets ratio, we frequently calculate the number of times fixed interest has been earned by dividing the net income before income taxes and interest expense by the amount of annual interest charges. Here, too, other things being equal, a larger number indicates a greater margin of safety. Another calculation that will help evaluate the effectiveness of trading on the equity is the comparison of the average interest rate on debt capital with the rate of return on total assets. We have already observed that the rate of return on total assets can be calculated by dividing net income by total assets. If that percentage is significantly higher than the average interest rate being paid on debt capital, we have a clear indication that the firm has been successful in its efforts to trade on the equity. This type of relationship justifies, to some extent, the use of debt capital because it is directly beneficial to those holding owner equity interests in the firm.

As we have previously observed, externally interested parties are always concerned with the extent to which enterprise units have complied with legal or other externally imposed requirements. In the profit area, failure to comply would normally be evidenced by legal proceedings against the firm or possibly by questions being raised by regulatory agencies such as the Securities and Exchange Commission. Externally interested parties are therefore concerned with identifying any such evidence of non-compliance.

## Analysis of Nonprofit Organization Statements

In analyzing the financial statements of pure nonprofit organizations, externally interested parties are concerned with evaluating the same basic characteristics that they are concerned with in the profit area. They want to evaluate the efficiency and effectiveness of operations and to determine the extent to which fiscal and other compliance responsibilities have been met. However, due to differences in operating objectives and organizational characteristics, the relationships and ratios used for analytical purposes are significantly different.

Because of the direct relationship between ownership and control in the profit area, we can expect the board of directors to act in the best interests of stockholder constituents. But this relationship does not necessarily prevail in the nonprofit area. The natural bias of legislative bodies and boards controlling nonprofit enterprises is typically in the direction of *enlargement and expansion of organizational activities without appropriate regard for the affordability of programs proposed.* Furthermore, nonprofit organizations have no externally imposed "self-cleansing" force similar to the need for earning a profit in the profit area. No profit enterprise can continue to exist indefinitely without meeting its operating objective of earning a profit. A nonprofit enterprise, on the other hand, can continue to operate as long as the constituency can be prevailed upon to support it. These characteristics can cause nonprofit organizations to enlarge their services beyond a reasonable level of social need.

There is also a natural inclination for internal managers to enlarge the operations of the enterprise to justify greater salary benefits. That inclination coupled with the tendency for the governing boards of these organizations to often have the same bias means that constituents must be prepared to give more attention to entity operations than is necessary in the profit area. This is particularly true when boards tend to become rubber-stamp oversight bodies ready to approve any actions proposed by internal managers.

Even though we recognize these external control weaknesses, we begin our analysis by developing the data that a constituency-oriented board ought to use. However, we recognize that these data should also be of value to the constituents as they make decisions regarding initiation or continuance of support.

The basic technique for measuring the efficiency of any organization is to relate its outputs to its inputs. In the profit area, we do this by matching revenues and expenses and by relating net income to equity investments. The primary problem in measuring this relationship for a pure nonprofit entity is that we seldom have an objective quantitative measurement of the values of outputs. If we could objectively determine the values associated with the services provided by such an organization, we could develop a ratio of those values to the cost of providing the services, or we could quantitatively match those two sets of data to arrive at efficiency indicators. Inputs can be easily measured as the accrual-based costs of providing the services. Therefore, if objective values were available for the service output, it would be relatively easy to develop cost–benefit analyses that would allow analysts to evaluate the efficiency of operations.

In actual practice, we seldom have an objective determination of the values of services rendered by a pure nonprofit organization. Therefore, it is important that externally interested parties have available to them at least a description of the services provided by the organization over the operating period being evaluated. This can take the form of tonnage of waste processed by the waste disposal department of a city, or the number of degrees granted by a college or university. These data can be used as *surrogates for the value of output.* By using such data along with the accrual-based cost data as input information, interested parties can calculate the *unit functional costs of services rendered.* Those costs can then be compared with past period data, similar costs for other entities, or predetermined standards to gain some insight into operating efficiency.

The type of measurements cited in the preceding paragraph gives no consideration to the quality of services rendered. Although this may be relatively unimportant in evaluating a waste disposal service, it can be extremely important in evaluating the output of a college or university. Because of this need, *selected input data are sometimes used as surrogates for measuring the quality of output.* Accrediting agencies for colleges and universities, for example, evaluate the qualitative aspects of a school's operations by looking at such things as the amounts spent on instructional costs per student and the faculty–student ratio, with the implicit assumption that a higher cost of input per student should produce a higher quality program.

Further insight into operating efficiency can sometimes be achieved by *relating overhead costs to total expenses or expenditures.* Overhead costs in this case are defined to include general administrative and fund-raising costs. While an increase in the ratio of these costs to total costs is not always an indicator of less efficient operations, it does show that the organization is spending a larger amount to sustain itself in relationship to the implementation of services. Input changes in that direction should always be critically evaluated.

As we have observed, efficiency should ideally be evaluated by relating outputs to inputs. Effectiveness, on the other hand, can best be evaluated by *relating outputs to the objectives of the organization.* This suggests that a clear statement, of not only the general objectives of reporting but also of the specific goals that were expected to be achieved during the operating period, be disclosed along with the financial statement data. *The measurement of effectiveness is not cost oriented.* It simply *measures results against intentions.* However, externally interested parties should be concerned with the *affordability of the stated goals* as well as whether the goals have been achieved. Ideally, the external board should strive for a balance between the satisfaction of perceived needs and the capability of the constituency to bear the costs of meeting those needs.

Total accrual-based costs should also be related to total revenues and other operating inflows for the period to help judge the extent of *capital maintenance or erosion* and whether reasonable *intergenerational equity* is being preserved with the present level of services. The incurrence of expenses in excess of revenues earned during the period erodes capital and shifts the tax or contribution burden for current services to future generations.

In recent years, the proposed services of governmental units have mushroomed with the apparent objective of achieving the "perfect society." Until 1980, little attention was given to the capability of our economy to support those services or to the question of intergenerational equity in providing them. Even less attention was given to the psychological effects of providing too many services on the basis of perceived need rather than requiring recipients to earn the right to have them. In recent decades, we have seen the inclination to provide services beyond what can be financed from current taxes. The federal government has secured funds through debt financing and as a result has created a generational inequity which forces future generations to pay for services being currently provided. Legislative bodies and governing boards in general ought to consider the responsibility of maintaining intergenerational equity as they evaluate the overall effectiveness of nonprofit operations. They should be aware that these enterprise units have no external "self-cleansing" pressure similar to that found in the profit area.

The inclination of the government and other nonprofit organizations to provide an ever-increasing amount of services has often been accompanied by budgetary practices involving percentage additions to prior-period budgets without considering whether any of the services provided in the past could be discontinued. Partly in response to this budgetary deficiency, some attention has been given to *zero-base budgeting*. This budgetary technique requires that the budget requests be developed from a zero base each year. That in effect requires that the need for all services provided by the entity be critically evaluated each year. One publication has suggested that, while zero-base budgeting may be impractical, zero-base review of ongoing programs is highly desirable in establishing future operating objectives.[1] Zero-base review requires that all programs be evaluated on a rotating basis over a period of three to five years rather than each year.

Externally interested parties should also evaluate the extent to which internal management has complied with specified operating plans. Insofar as the financial data are concerned, this is most directly determined by observing the use of appropriate fund entities and by relating actual to budgetary financial data. Since nonprofit organizations are usually controlled by specifying how resources may be used, it is important that the inflows and outflows of individual fund entities be related to their stated objectives and that general or operating fund inflows and outflows be compared with the budgetary plan. It is especially important for external boards to determine that expenses or expenditures have been properly controlled within appropriation limits. This is done by comparing actual expenses or expenditures with those established when the budget was approved.

Because nonprofit organizations have no equity capital in the sense of ownership shares outstanding, they must often depend on debt financing for a large portion of their long-term resources. In Chapter 3, we cited eight elements of information in addition to the financial statement data that Standard & Poor's requires as they evaluate municipal general obligation bonds.[2] Because these enterprise units are often

---

1. Robert N. Anthony and Regina Herzlinger, *Management Control in Nonprofit Organizations* (Homewood, Ill.: Richard D. Irwin, 1980), p. 589.
2. Hugh C. Sherwood, *How Corporate Municipal Debt Is Rated* (New York: John Wiley & Sons, 1976), pp. 115–116.

unable to continue to exist without debt financing, these eight items of information are recalled again as important elements to be considered as operations are evaluated by externally interested parties. The oversight board, as well as potential creditors, should be particularly interested in these characteristics because of the importance of "borrowing capability" to the enterprise unit's continuity. It is therefore important for those groups to critically review the organization's overall debt position, the total valuation of property in relationship to the tax levies, the statement of tax collections, and the population being served by the entity. It is also important for them to know who the largest taxpayers are and be aware of the nature of the area's economy. Internal managers should be expected to provide a statement of borrowing plans for a reasonable period in the future, as well as a statement setting out the proposed capital improvement program and plans for the next few years.

## ■ Application of Analytical Techniques

We have observed that many of the resource conversion units that fall within our broad definition of nonprofit organizations are more realistically quasi-nonprofit enterprises realizing a significant amount of resource inflows from user-based charges. Therefore, when we analyze and interpret the financial statements of these organizations, we must selectively employ analytical procedures from both the profit and nonprofit areas. To illustrate that point, we now briefly explore the procedures that should be followed in analyzing the financial statements of:

1. governmental units
2. colleges and universities
3. hospitals
4. health and welfare agencies
5. churches.

### Analysis of Governmental Financial Statements

In analyzing published financial statements, we must always recognize the limitations inherent in those data. When we analyze governmental financial statements, we must be aware that they are conventionally prepared on the modified accrual rather than the full accrual basis of accounting and that we will not have an objectively determined value for their output. The first of these two shortcomings can be overcome by converting the expenditure-based financial data to the full accrual basis as illustrated in the appendix to Chapter 9. Also, we can partially compensate for the lack of an objectively determined value for output by using nondollar quantitative data relating to the services provided. Primary attention will be focused on the general or operating fund data as we carry out the analytical process.

In recognition of the weaknesses cited in the preceding paragraph, the external users of the financial data will want to begin their analyses by *calculating the amount of expenditures or expenses per service unit*. These data should be compared with the budgeted amount per unit, prior period amount per unit, and/or amount per unit for similar operating entities to help judge how efficiently resources were used as they were converted to services.

In evaluating the effectiveness of operations, it is important to begin by *comparing some measure of the actual services provided with the operating goals established at the beginning of the period*. From that comparison, we can learn the extent to which period operating objectives have been met. It is also important to give some attention to the quality of services provided by the entity. As observed earlier in this chapter, accrediting and regulatory agencies, with the benefit of exposure to the operations of many similar entities, typically evaluate the quality of service by analyzing input data.

The legislative body or governing board should be concerned with providing an *optimum* level and quality of service that *properly balances needs and affordability*. The level of need is generally determinable from the voices of the electorate. An objective analysis of the relationships between taxes and the bases on which the taxes are assessed can provide some insight in judging affordability. The legislative board is expected to consider these factors as they establish service objectives. Failure to properly react to them can cause constituency action to overrule them. Quite obviously, the property owners in California, in their so-called taxpayer revolt through "Proposition 13," said that they could not afford the current level of services unless they could be provided more efficiently. Other actions also suggest that legislative bodies may have failed to give adequate attention to the question of affordability. Total service expenses or expenditures for the period should also be compared with revenues realized during the period to help decide whether the appropriate level of services is being provided for the present generation of taxpayers.

As observed earlier, governmental units are legally bound to control operating expenditures within budgetary appropriations. Legislative bodies and governing boards are therefore responsible for ascertaining from the financial reports or by certification from the auditors that the internal management of the governmental unit has adhered to budgetary constraints imposed upon its spending.

Since governmental units depend heavily on debt financing in carrying out many of their activities, it is also important for externally interested parties—in particular, governing boards—to be concerned with the capability of the entity to meet interest-payment and debt-retirement obligations. This is determined primarily by the entity's capability of realizing sufficient tax inflows to meet those obligations. In decisions to incur long-term debt, therefore, it is important to realize that interest and principal obligations will have to be met through increased taxes unless the expenditure of borrowed funds or other increases in values will increase the tax base.

Externally interested parties should also be aware that the modified accrual statements for these organizations will often fail to disclose significant amounts of liabilities incurred but not due to be paid until a later period. For example, future pension benefits incurred during the work lives of employees are generally not recorded in governmental financial statements, even though the productive efforts of the employees' services have already been realized. Long-term creditors must be aware of these future obligations as they judge whether credit should be extended and the terms under which it should be granted. Full accrual-based cost data can beneficially be used in making these and other analytical judgments. We will illustrate the calculation of the various analytical ratios and percentages in Chapter 17 when we consider the effect of using the accrual basis of accounting in the governmental area.

## Analyzing Financial Statements of Colleges and Universities

Colleges and universities are quasi-nonprofit organizations. They have the basic equity financing characteristics of nonprofit entities but also realize a significant amount of their resource inflows from *user-based charges* in the form of tuition and fees. There-fore, in analyzing the financial statements of these institutions, we use some procedures from profit entity analysis along with other procedures used in evaluating the financial data of pure nonprofit enterprise units.

In judging the operational efficiency of a college or university, the analyst should begin by observing the relationship between operating revenues and operating out-flows. Conventionally prepared financial statements will show most revenues as they are earned. Outflows, however, are reflected on an expenditure basis. We shall use the expenditure-based outflow data for analytical purposes. It is important, however, for you to be aware of that limitation in our analysis.

Although a college or university may be justified in operating with an excess of expenditures over revenues for a certain year or a certain short span of years, it cannot operate that way and continue as a going concern over a long period of time. Since a college or university is a quasi-nonprofit organization, it is imperative that operating revenues, including contributions for that purpose, cover operating expenditures over a period of several years. Any annual excess of revenues over expenditures should also not be excessive, because that would represent a *student generational inequity bias* against presently enrolled students. In summary, we expect an efficiently operated institution to meet its operating expenditures from current operating revenues, but at the same time to decrease user charges or increase the quality of its services by increas-ing expenditures when revenues significantly exceed expenditures.

In analyzing expenditures, it is important to determine the *percentages of expen-ditures associated with general administration and overhead,* distinguished from such things as instruction and research. It is also important to relate instruction and other student-oriented expenditures to tuition and fees to determine the portion of total student costs being covered by user-based charges. We often use a common-size oper-ating statement to disclose these and some of the other relationships described. These data can also be presented in the form of "pie charts" similar to those shown in Figure 16–1. Total educational expenditures per credit hour and per degree granted are other data that are helpful in evaluating the quality of service and operating efficiency.

In evaluating the effectiveness of operations in the college and university area, it is important to know such nondollar quantitative data as the number of degrees granted, number of student credit hours provided, and the number of fulltime-equivalent faculty members employed, including their degree qualifications. These data help us to evaluate both the extent and quality of educational services being rendered. Volumes of *College Blue Book,*[3] and the publication entitled *American Universities and*

---

3.  See various volumes of *College Blue Book,* 19th ed. (New York: Macmillan Information, 1983).

**FIGURE 16-1.**   Pie Chart Analysis of Revenues and
Expenditures

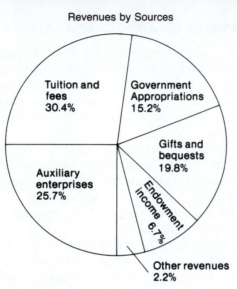

Revenues by Sources

Tuition and fees 30.4%

Government Appropriations 15.2%

Gifts and bequests 19.8%

Auxiliary enterprises 25.7%

Endowment income 6.7%

Other revenues 2.2%

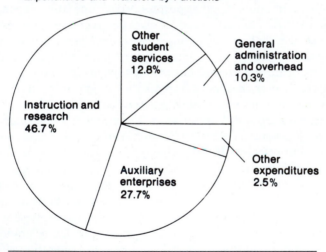

Expenditures and Transfers by Functions

Other student services 12.8%

General administration and overhead 10.3%

Instruction and research 46.7%

Auxiliary enterprises 27.7%

Other expenditures 2.5%

*Colleges,*[4] published to inform potential students of the general operating characteristics of various colleges and universities, include many of these data for most schools. We include ratios and percentages developed from such data in the illustrated analysis later in this chapter.

4.  *American Universities and Colleges,* 12th ed. (Washington, D.C.: American Council on Education, 1983).

Operational effectiveness is also contingent upon the capability of the institution to continue to exist in the foreseeable future. The current ratio for unrestricted funds can be calculated to help evaluate current liquidity. The analyst will also be concerned with measures of the demand for the services of the institution. The *relationship between admissions and applications* can be quite important in evaluating that aspect of operations. A school that has significantly more qualified applicants than it is able to admit clearly shows a heavy demand for its educational services that should help sustain it in the event of economic adversity.

The *amount and nature of nonoperating inflows* of a college or university are also important factors in judging probability of continuance. An institution that consistently realizes significant resource inflows into endowment funds and plant funds shows a constituency committed to improving and enlarging its program. On the other hand, failure to realize such resource inflows can cast a shadow on the probability of an institution continuing into the foreseeable future as a going concern.

One of the most important features in judging effectiveness of college or university operations is reflected in the form of the *accreditations and other recognitions* granted to the institution. Various disciplines and schools of a typical college or university are periodically subjected to accreditation evaluations. Agencies performing these evaluations use much of the data described in the preceding paragraphs to arrive at an overall judgment regarding operating effectiveness.

Compliance is evaluated in the college and university area primarily by determining that externally imposed restrictions on the uses of resources have been properly honored. In some instances, it may also be important to prove budgetary compliance, but this responsibility is generally delegated to internal managers.

To illustrate the analytical procedures described in the preceding pages, we now show how the financial statements of Model College presented in Chapter 12 (with certain assumptions added) should be analyzed by external users. Assumptions regarding nondollar quantitative data for the current year:

Enrollment— 2,000 fulltime-equivalent students

Faculty— 100 fulltime-equivalent teachers

Doctorally qualified faculty— 60

Student credit hours— 60,000

Degrees granted— 400

Applications for admission— 1,500

New students admitted— 500.

Analytical Data:

1.  Relationship between operating revenues and operating expenditures (excess of operating revenues over operating expenditures):
    ($8,554,000 − $7,756,000)         $798,000
    Ratio of operating revenue to operating expenditures:
    (8,554,000 ÷ 7,756,000)         1.103

2. Structure of operating revenues:

| Items | Percent |
|---|---|
| Educational and general | |
|     Student tuition and fees | 30.4 |
|     Government appropriations | 15.2 |
|     Gifts and grants | 19.8 |
|     Endowment income | 6.7 |
|     Other revenues | 2.2 |
| Auxiliary enterprises | 25.7 |
| Total | 100.0 |

3. Structure of operating expenditures:

| Items | Percent |
|---|---|
| Educational and general | |
|     Instruction and research | 46.7 |
|     Other student services | 12.8 |
|     General administration and overhead | 10.3 |
|     Other expenditures | 2.5 |
| Auxiliary enterprises | 27.7 |
| Total | 100.0 |

4. Student-oriented expenditures related to tuition and fees:
($3,760,000 ÷ 2,600,000)        1.446

5. Educational expenditures per degree granted:
(5,414,000 ÷ 400)        $13,535

6. Educational expenditures per student credit hour:
(5,414,000 ÷ 60,000)        $90.23

7. Student faculty ratio:
(2,000 ÷ 100)        20 to 1

8. Doctorally qualified to fulltime-equivalent faculty members:
(60 ÷ 100)        60%

9. Current ratio:
(1,006,000 ÷ 363,000)        2.77 to 1

10. Ratio of applications for admissions to new students admitted:
(1,500 ÷ 500)        3 to 1

11. Nonoperating inflows (totals):

| Fund | Amount | Percent Increase |
|---|---|---|
| Loan funds | 141,000 | 26.1 |
| Endowment funds | 1,679,000 | 14.1 |
| Annuity funds | 800,000 | 31.9 |
| Plant funds | 2,103,000 | 5.3 |
| Total | 4,723,000 | 8.7 |

This structure of operating revenues and operating expenditures can also be displayed graphically in "pie charts," as shown in Figure 16–1. Although analytical observations relating to Model College would be made primarily through comparison of the ratios and other data calculated above, with similar data for past years or for other institutions, we can gain some insight into the operations of this institution from the preceding data. For example, our first calculation shows that Model College realized slightly more operating revenues than it incurred in the way of operating expenditures. As we look at the common size data relating to the operating revenues and operating expenditures, we find that the student tuition and fees plus governmental appropriations represented about the same percentage of gross revenues as instruction and research expenditures in relationship to total expenditures. The institution may be somewhat concerned that expenditures on auxiliary enterprises represented a larger percentage of total expenditures than did the revenues realized from those activities in relationship to total revenues. Items 5 and 6 suggest that the quality of educational services is reasonably good, based on the expenditures for them. The student–faculty ratio suggests a relationship that allows students to become acquainted with faculty members and to use them as counselors. The current ratio indicates good current liquidity, and the extent of nonoperating inflows suggests a stable constituency dedicated to enlarging the resource base of the college. The fact that only one of three applicants for admissions could be admitted shows a high level of demand for the type of education program provided by Model College.

## Analysis of Hospital Financial Statements

The analytical procedures applicable to the financial statements of hospitals are similar in many respects to both those used for colleges and universities and those used for business entities. In developing common-size data for hospitals, however, it is important to emphasize the extent of allowances and uncollectible accounts deducted from patient revenue. That shows the amount of patient services provided without remuneration as a gratuitous service to the community. In analyzing hospital statements, we are working with accrual-based (expense-oriented) rather than expenditure-oriented data. In this section, we illustrate (with certain assumptions added) the calculation of selected ratios and percentages for Sample Hospital financial statements shown in Chapter 11. Assumptions regarding nondollar quantitative data for current year are:[5]

| | |
|---|---|
| Rooms | 150 |
| Admissions | 6,000 |
| Average occupancy | 120 |
| Employees | 450 |

Analytical Data:

1. Relationships between operating revenues and operating expenses (excess of operating revenues over operating expenses):

---

5.  Data for most hospitals available in *Guide to the Health Care Field* (Chicago, Ill.: American Hospital Association, 1983).

($6,907,000 − 7,275,000) =                                    ($368,000) loss

Ratio of operating revenues to operating expenses:
(6,907,000 ÷ 7,275,000) =                                               .949

Nonoperating revenue:                                               $452,000

2.  Structure of operating revenues:

| Items | Percent |
|---|---|
| Patient service revenue | 123.0 |
| Allowances and uncollectible accounts | (25.7) |
| Other operating revenue | 2.7 |
| Net operating revenue | 100.0 |

3.  Structure of operating expenses:

| Items | Percent |
|---|---|
| Nursing services | 30.2 |
| Other professional services | 26.1 |
| General services | 28.9 |
| Administrative and fiscal services | 10.7 |
| Depreciation expense | 4.1 |
| Total | 100.0 |

4.  Net patient service revenue:

a.  Per available room ($6,723,000 ÷ 150)                        $44,820
b.  Per average occupancy ($6,723,000 ÷ 120)                     $56,025
c.  Per admission ($6,723,000 ÷ 6,000)                           $ 1,121

5.  Percentage occupancy:
(120 ÷ 150)                                                          80%

6.  Operating revenue per employee:
($6,907,000 ÷ 450)                                              $15,349

7.  Operating expenses:

a.  Per available room ($7,275,000 ÷ 150)                        $48,500
b.  Per average occupancy ($7,275,000 ÷ 120)                     $60,625
c.  Per admission ($7,275,000 ÷ 6,000)                           $ 1,213

8.  Current ratio:
($1,814,000 ÷ $1,227,000)                                        1.5 to 1

9.  Nonoperating inflows (totals):

| Fund | Amount | Percent Increase |
|------|--------|------------------|
| Specific purpose funds | 113,260 | 159.5 |
| Plant replacement funds | 128,000 | 11.6 |
| Endowment funds | 2,175,000 | 54.7 |
| Total | 2,416,260 | 47.0 |

As observed in connection with the analysis of Model College financial data, the preceding percentages and ratios can be used most effectively by comparing them with prior-year data and/or with data derived from other hospital financial statements. Nevertheless, we can observe that the relationship between operating revenues and operating expenses shows a slight operating loss. However, that loss was more than covered by nonoperating revenue in the amount of $452,000. The structure of operating revenues shows a reasonable proportion of patients' service revenue being committed to covering the allowances and uncollectible accounts, representing services provided without remuneration to the community. The structure of operating expenses shows the highest percentage of expenses being incurred in providing nursing services. Administrative and fiscal services reflected the smallest percentage of the four functional categories. In looking at patient service revenue, we can observe that the average revenue per room for the year was $44,820. This is also reflected as an average of $1,121 per admission. The occupancy percentage may be lower than would normally be expected in hospital operations. Also, in view of the liquidity of current assets, the current ratio seems to suggest that an appropriate level of current liquidity is being maintained. Increases in nonoperating inflows, particularly the additions to endowment funds, suggest a constituency dedicated to the continued support of the hospital.

## Analysis of Financial Statements for Health and Welfare Agencies

Since health and welfare agencies are pure nonprofit organizations, we follow many of the same analytical procedures for those organizations that are used in analyzing governmental financial statements (see page 613). These organizations typically provide a number of related services that are distributed on the basis of need. Therefore, externally interested parties will be concerned with having a *profile of those services along with the sources of support for the organization*. This can be provided by indicating the portion of each dollar spent in implementing the different types of services. A common-size operating statement can be prepared to provide a revenue and expense profile (see Exhibit 16–1). Functional cost data can be calculated as shown in Exhibit 16–2.

The amount spent for administrative and fund-raising activities is also of critical importance to the constituents of health and welfare agencies. For that reason, it is important to show, as part of the common-size data already mentioned, the portion of each contribution dollar that is spent in sustaining the organization.

In measuring the effectiveness of an entity's operations, it is important to have nondollar quantitative data summarizing the services performed by the agency over a

**EXHIBIT 16–1.**   Model Voluntary Health and Welfare Service
Common-Size Operating Statement—19X2

| | | |
|---|---:|---:|
| Revenues by sources: | | |
| Public support | | 91.9% |
| Revenues earned | | 8.1 |
| Total | | 100.0% |
| Expenses: | | |
| Sustentation | | 28.0% |
| Service implementation | | |
| Research | 32.3% | |
| Public health education | 12.4 | |
| Professional education and training | 14.1 | |
| Community services | 13.2 | 72.0 |
| Total | | 100.0% |

**EXHIBIT 16–2.**   Model Voluntary Health and Welfare Service Functional Cost
Data—19X2

| | |
|---|---:|
| Assumptions regarding services rendered: | |
| Research projects | 100 |
| Public health education (persons served) | 10,000 |
| Professional education and training (persons served) | 600 |
| Community services (population of community) | 100,000 |
| Service implementation services: | Functional Cost Per Unit |
| Research | $ 14,140.00 |
| Public health education | 54.40 |
| Professional education and training | 1,030.00 |
| Community services | 5.78 |

period of time. Effectiveness can then be evaluated by relating actual achievements to the goals of the organization for the period.

Health and welfare agencies generally operate under an object-of-expense appropriation-controlled budget. They can also have resources that are restricted to specified uses. Therefore, in evaluating the extent of compliance, it is important to determine whether the agency has operated within budgetary and externally imposed restrictions on the uses of funds.

To illustrate the most important elements of health and welfare agency financial statement analysis, we present a common-size operating statement (Exhibit 16–1), along with functional unit cost data for Model Voluntary Health and Welfare Service financial statements shown in Chapter 13. Functional cost data are shown in Exhibit 16–2.

As we review the analytical data for Model Voluntary Health and Welfare Service, we see a typical relationship among sources of revenue. A very large part of revenues comes from contributions by the public. We can also observe that 28¢ out of every dollar of expenses was used to sustain the organization. This may be a bit high, as it tells contributors that only 72¢ out of every dollar contributed will be spent in implementing the services of the organization. Also, as we observe the functional unit cost data, we find that this agency is spending slightly more than $14,000 per research project undertaken. It is also spending $54.40 per person served through public health education. Professional education and training have required $1,030 per person served. The agency has spent $5.78 per person in the community on community services.

## Analysis of Financial Statements for Churches

Churches operate as pure nonprofit entities. Because of the nature of their mission, the analyst is primarily concerned with proving that expenditures have been controlled within budgetary allocations. Beyond that, it is important to know whether revenues are being realized in accordance with budgetary projections. These data are typically analyzed by preparation of a common size financial statement similar to the one shown in Exhibit 13−7.

Since a primary operating objective of a church is to extend its influence beyond its own congregation and to share its resources with others, the relationship of expenditures for benevolences to total expenditures is always an important ratio to use in judging effectiveness of operations. It is also helpful to know the proportions of the expenditures budget that are being used for religious education, building maintenance, and so on.

We illustrate most of the analytical techniques described earlier by presenting a common-size operating statement for Illustration Church (see Exhibit 13−7) in Exhibit 16−3. On the revenue side, it is also useful to know the average contribution per member or per family unit. We can calculate that by dividing contribution revenue by the number of members or family units in the congregation.

As we observe the common-size operating statement data for Illustration Church in Exhibit 16−3, we find that this church realizes slightly more than 95 percent of its revenue from pledges. Also, 18¢ out of every dollar of expenditures has been devoted to benevolences. Since churches will generally establish goals for such expenditures, this figure should be evaluated in relationship to that goal for this church. Furthermore, slightly more than 48¢ of every dollar of expenditures has gone to staff salaries, with only slightly more than 2 percent going to Christian education. The governing board of the church may well want to reevaluate the low priority being given to this aspect of the church's activities.

## Actions in Response to Financial Statements Analysis

Externally interested parties provide resources for enterprise units either by purchasing ownership shares, paying taxes, making contributions, or extending credit to the enterprise. In the profit area, favorable impressions from the analytical data cause externally interested parties to seek to invest in the enterprise unit or loan money to it.

**EXHIBIT 16–3.**  Illustration Church Common-Size
Operating Statement—For Period

| Revenues: | | |
|---|---|---|
| Church school offering | | 1.0% |
| Plate offering | | 1.9 |
| Pledges | | 95.2 |
| Miscellaneous | | 1.9 |
| Total | | 100.0% |
| Expenditures: | | |
| Benevolences | | 18.1% |
| Local church services | | |
| Christian education | 2.4% | |
| Music | 1.2 | |
| Staff salaries | 48.2 | |
| Current operations | 12.0 | |
| Building costs | 18.1 | 81.9 |
| Total | | 100.0% |

Unfavorable impressions cause those parties to withdraw financial support by selling stock interests or by refusing to loan additional resources to the enterprise unit.

In the nonprofit area, the noncreditor constituents are trying to decide whether they should provide support to the entity in the form of taxes or contributions. Favorable impressions regarding efficiency, effectiveness, and compliance encourage such support, while unfavorable observations regarding these characteristics lead to decreased support, which can manifest itself in reduced contributions or taxpayer revolts. Creditors and potential creditors of nonprofit organizations look to the operating history and environmental characteristics to help them determine whether credit should be extended and, if so, the terms under which it should be granted.

# ■ Ethical Considerations Associated with the Operations of a Voluntary Health and Welfare Organization

The manager of Aggressive Health and Welfare, Inc., proposes to the organization's Board of Trustees that special efforts must be exerted to realize a larger amount of contributions so that services to the community may be expanded. His projected operating plan calls for expansion of the organization's staff to help provide the additional services. One member of the Board notes that the organization is already spending $.40 of each dollar contributed to realize its present level of contributions.

Consider the ethical issues associated with the manager's proposal.

# ■ Summary

In this chapter, we explored the ways in which the published financial report data of nonprofit enterprises are used by externally interested parties. We began by reviewing the analytical procedures normally followed in evaluating the operations and financial positions of pure profit and pure nonprofit enterprises. We then described the analytical process and illustrated how some of those techniques can be applied in analyzing the financial statements of colleges and universities, hospitals, health and welfare agencies, and churches.

We explained that externally interested parties are primarily concerned with evaluating the activities of internal managers. Basically, they want to know whether operations have been carried out efficiently and effectively and whether resources have been used in compliance with externally imposed constraints. Creditors are primarily concerned with whether or not interest and principal obligations can be met as they come due.

# ■ Glossary

**Current Liquidity.**  An entity's ability to meet current obligations as those obligations come due.

**Effective.**  Accomplishment of the task an entity is expected to perform.

**Efficiency.**  Maximizing the objectives of the organization in relation to the resources consumed in accomplishing that goal. Also, maximizing achievements in relationship to efforts expended.

**Fiduciary Responsibility.**  The responsibility that the management of a nonprofit organization has to its constituency to carry out the operations of the organization efficiently.

**Long-Term Stability.**  The ability of an enterprise unit to exist through periods of economic adversity.

**Nonoperating Inflows.**  Resources received by a nonprofit organization that are not immediately available to be used to cover operating outlays.

**Surrogates for Value of Output.**  A substitute for use of output as an element in evaluating efficiency of operations.

# ■ Suggested Supplementary References

*Caldwell, Kenneth S. "Operational Auditing in State and Local Government." *Governmental Finance* (November 1975).

*Fountain, James R., and Robert Lockridge. "Implementation and Management of a Performance Auditing System." *Governmental Finance* (November 1976).

*Also available in *Accounting in the Public Sector: The Changing Environment—A Book of Readings* by Robert W. Ingram (Salt Lake City: Brighton Publishing Company, 1980).

Freeman, Robert J. "Governmental Auditing of Variable Scope." *International Journal of Auditing,* 2 (1975): 7–11.

Granof, Michael H. "Operational Auditing Standards for Audits of Government Services." *CPA Journal* (New York), 43 (1973): 1079–1085, 1088.

*Hara, Lloyd F. "Performance Auditing: Where Do We Begin?" *Governmental Finance* (November 1976).

Henke, Emerson O. "Performance Evaluation for Not-for-Profit Organizations." *Journal of Accountancy* (June 1972): 51–55.

Knighton, Lennis M. "Information Preconditions for Performance Auditing." *Governmental Finance,* 5 (1976): 22–27.

Morse, Ellsworth H., Jr. "Performance and Operational Auditing." *Journal of Accountancy* (June 1971): 41–46.

Peterson, Thomas. "Cost–Benefit Analysis for Evaluating Transportation Proposals: Los Angeles Cash Study." *Land Economics,* 51 (1975): 72–79.

## ■ Questions for Class Discussion

**Q16-1.** Compare the way consumable resources are distributed within a capitalistic economic system with the way they are distributed within a socialistic system.

**Q16-2.** How does profit motivation promote the efficient use of resources? Discuss.

**Q16-3.** How do externally interested parties help promote operating efficiency and effectiveness in the profit area? In the nonprofit area?

**Q16-4.** Explain why it is more difficult to evaluate the efficiency of enterprise unit operations in the nonprofit area than in the profit area.

**Q16-5.** What are three basic concerns of governing boards and constituencies as they seek to evaluate the activities of an enterprise unit?

**Q16-6.** Explain the difference between *efficiency* and *effectiveness* as these terms are used in characterizing the operations of an enterprise unit. How are these terms related to the fundamental evaluation of effort–achievement relationships?

**Q16-7.** How do we evaluate the current liquidity of a profit-type enterprise unit?

**Q16-8.** What are some of the relationships that are generally considered in evaluating the operational effectiveness of a profit enterprise? Is it appropriate to use these in evaluating the operational effectiveness of a nonprofit enterprise? Explain.

**Q16-9.** Compare and contrast the relationship between the board of directors of a corporate business entity and the business entity with the relationship between a legislative body or board and the governmental entity that it serves.

**Q16-10.** Explain how the need for earning a profit in the profit area constitutes a "self-cleansing" force in that area. Does such a force exist in the nonprofit area? Explain.

**Q16-11.** Can we always count on the governing board of a nonprofit entity to act in the best interests of the constituents? Discuss fully.

**Q16-12.** The basic technique for measuring the operating efficiency of any enterprise unit is to relate its outputs to its inputs. How can that be done in the profit area? In the nonprofit area?

*Also available in *Accounting in the Public Sector: The Changing Environment—A Book of Readings* by Robert W. Ingram (Salt Lake City: Brighton Publishing Company, 1980).

Q16-13.   Explain how functional cost data can be used as surrogates for output data in the nonprofit area.

Q16-14.   Explain the conceptual difference between zero-base review and zero-base budgeting. What are these techniques intended to do when they are applied in the management of a nonprofit entity?

Q16-15.   Discuss the concerns of long-term creditors and potential long-term creditors as they consider loans to nonprofit enterprises.

Q16-16.   Why is it important to specifically define the operating goals of a nonprofit enterprise?

Q16-17.   What does the accountant do to reflect the extent of compliance with legal requirements as he or she prepares the financial reports for a governmental entity?

Q16-18.   Compare and contrast the techniques used to evaluate the operational efficiency of a governmental unit with those used to evaluate the operational efficiency of a college or university.

Q16-19.   Discuss the importance of nondollar quantitative data in evaluating the operational effectiveness of a college or university. How is that related to accreditation practices?

Q16-20.   How does the amount and nature of nonoperating inflows of a college or university relate to the probability of long-term continuance or existence of the school? Discuss.

Q16-21.   What is the significance of the percentage of room occupancy in evaluating the operations of a hospital?

Q16-22.   Explain why it is important to disclose separately the amounts spent for administrative and fund-raising activities in reporting the operations of health and welfare agencies.

Q16-23.   How can a common-size operating statement be used in evaluating the operations of a health and welfare agency?

Q16-24.   Why is it important to emphasize the extent of expenditures for benevolencies in the operating statement of a church?

# ■ Exercises

E16-1.   The balance sheets for an enterprise fund include the following items for the ends of years A and B:

|                             | Year A     | Year B     |
|-----------------------------|-----------|-----------|
| Current assets              | $250,000  | $275,000  |
| Current liabilities         | 110,000   | 190,000   |
| Utility plant and equipment | 600,000   | 750,000   |
| Bonds payable               | 650,000   | 625,000   |
| Bond debt-service fund      | 35,000    | 45,000    |
| Contribution from city      | 100,000   | 200,000   |
| Retained earnings           | 25,000    | 55,000    |

**Required:**
A.   Compute the current ratio for the fund at the end of each year.

B.  Compute the change in net working capital during Year B.
C.  Calculate the ratio of equity capital to long-term debt capital at the end of each year.
D.  What was the net income of the enterprise fund for Year B?
E.  Comment on your findings in A, B, C, and D.

**E16-2.**  The revenues and expenditures statement for a nonprofit entity includes the following items for the current and preceding years:

|  | Preceding Year | Current Year |
|---|---|---|
| Revenues | $1,000,000 | $1,200,000 |
| Expenditures |  |  |
| Fund raising | 200,000 | 270,000 |
| Administration | 150,000 | 225,000 |
| Service implementation | 625,000 | 675,000 |
| Excess of revenues over expenditures | 25,000 | 30,000 |

**Required:**
A.  Calculate the percentage of revenues used to cover overhead expenditures. Comment on your findings.
B.  Revenues for the current year were larger than they were last year. Show how the added revenue was used. Comment on your findings.
C.  Prepare common-size statements of revenues and expenditures for each of the two years. What observations can be made from those statements?

**E16-3.**  A governmental entity shows revenues and expenditures for the current year of $1,425,000 and $1,410,000, respectively. When these data are converted to the full accrual basis the entity shows revenues of $1,415,000 and expenses of $1,450,000.

**Required:**
A.  Has the present generation of taxpayers paid for all the services they have provided for themselves during the current year? Explain.
B.  Relate your findings to the concept of intergenerational equity.
C.  Has the entity maintained its "capital resources" during the current year? Explain.
D.  What are some of the ways in which the tax burden for services may be shifted to future generations? Explain.

**E16-4.**  The following data are available for the same year relating to two universities (labeled A and B) providing similar educational services:

|  | University A | University B |
|---|---|---|
| Enrollment (fulltime equivalent) | 10,000 | 15,000 |
| Student credit hours | 300,000 | 400,000 |
| Faculty (fulltime equivalent) | 500 | 600 |
| Doctorally qualified faculty | 400 | 300 |
| Applications for admission | 5,000 | 4,000 |
| New students admitted | 2,500 | 4,000 |

**Required:**

A. Develop appropriate analytical ratios for each school.

B. Comment on your findings regarding the similarities and differences in the operating characteristics of the two schools.

E16-5. The operating statements for Schools A and B (see Exercise E16−4) show the following educational revenue data expressed on a common-size basis:

|  | School A | School B |
|---|---|---|
| Student tuition and fees | 60.0% | 10.0% |
| Governmental appropriations | 0 | 80.0 |
| Gifts and grants | 20.0 | 5.0 |
| Endowment income | 20.0 | 5.0 |
| Total | 100.0% | 100.0% |

**Required:**

Describe the nature of each school's operations as disclosed by the preceding data.

E16-6. The operating statements for Schools A and B (see Exercises E16-4 and E16-5) also contain the following educational expenditure data expressed on a common-size basis:

|  | School A | School B |
|---|---|---|
| Instruction and research | 60.0% | 70.0% |
| Other student services | 20.0 | 5.0 |
| General administration | 10.0 | 15.0 |
| Other educational expenditures | 10.0 | 10.0 |
| Total | 100.0% | 100.0% |

**Required:**

What further insight into the general operations of the two schools is provided by these data?

E16-7. The operating statements for Schools A and B (see Exercises E16-4 through E16-6) also show the following educational revenue and expenditure data:

|  | School A | School B |
|---|---|---|
| Educational revenues | $40,000,000 | $42,000,000 |
| Educational expenditures | 39,500,000 | 41,900,000 |
| Excess of revenues over expenditures | $ 500,000 | $ 100,000 |

**Required:**
A. Calculate the ratio of educational revenues to educational expenditures for each school.
B. Calculate the amount of educational expenditures per fulltime student and per student credit hour for each school.
C. Calculate the amounts being spent for instruction and research by each school.
D. Calculate the amount of endowment income being realized by each school.
E. Comment on your findings.

**E16-8.** The condensed operating statements and other quantitative data for a hospital for the current year and preceding year are shown below:

| | Preceding Year | Current Year |
|---|---|---|
| Patient service revenue | $6,000,000 | $7,000,000 |
| Allowances and uncollectible accounts (net of gifts covering these services) | 1,200,000 | 1,500,000 |
| Net patient revenue | $4,800,000 | $5,500,000 |
| Operating expenses | 5,000,000 | 6,000,000 |
| Loss from operations | $ (200,000) | $ (500,000) |
| Nonoperating revenues | 250,000 | 475,000 |
| Excess or (deficiency) of revenues over expenses | $ 50,000 | $ (25,000) |
| Other quantitative data | | |
|   Rooms | 250 | 250 |
|   Average occupancy | 225 | 235 |
|   Admissions | 10,000 | 11,000 |
|   Employees | 600 | 625 |

**Required:**
A. Calculate the following ratios and percentages for each year:
  1. ratio of operating revenues to operating expenses
  2. percentage of patient revenue representing direct community service provided by the hospital each year
  3. percentage occupancy
  4. patient service revenue and operating expenses per available room, per average occupancy, and per admission
  5. operating revenue per employee.
B. Comment on your findings.

**E16-9.** The condensed operating statements for a health and welfare agency for the current year and preceding year are shown on the following page.

**Required:**
A. Prepare common-size operating statements for both years.
B. Calculate the functional cost per unit for each type of service rendered by the agency.
C. Comment on your findings.

| | Preceding Year | Current Year |
|---|---|---|
| **Revenues** | | |
| Public support | $ 85,000 | $100,000 |
| Revenues earned | 5,000 | 8,000 |
| Total | $ 90,000 | $108,000 |
| **Expenses** | | |
| Sustentation | 20,000 | 25,000 |
| Service implementation | | |
| Public health education | 30,000 | 35,000 |
| Research | 14,000 | 18,000 |
| Medical services | $ 25,000 | 30,500 |
| Total expenses | $ 89,000 | $108,500 |
| Excess (deficiency) of revenues over expenses | $ 1,000 | $ (500) |
| **Other data** | | |
| Community served | 100,000 | 105,000 |
| Persons served by public health education | 10,000 | 11,000 |
| Research projects | 200 | 225 |

**E16-10.** A church estimates that it will receive revenues in the form of pledges from its members amounting to $100,000 for the year. The operating policy of the church calls for it to contribute 20 percent of its revenues to benevolent causes. Projected local service costs are budgeted to cost $85,000.

**Required:**
What alternate courses of action may the congregation follow?

# ■ Problems

**P16-1.** The balance sheet and statement of revenues and expenditures for a well-known, private, church-related university are shown on pages 633 and 634.

The following nondollar quantitative data are also included in the annual report for the university:

| | 19X2 | 19X1 |
|---|---|---|
| Enrollment | 8,400 | 8,000 |
| Faculty employed | 400 | 380 |
| Doctorally qualified faculty | 300 | 250 |
| Student credit hours | 250,000 | 240,000 |
| Degrees granted | 1,800 | 1,700 |
| Applications for admission | 3,300 | 3,000 |
| New students admitted | 2,100 | 2,000 |

**Required:**

A. Develop analytical ratios and other data that can be used in evaluating the operations of the university.

B. Comment on your findings.

P16-2. The New Hospital balance sheets and statements of revenues and expenses for 19X1 and 19X2 are shown below and on page 635.

## New Hospital Balance Sheets 12/31/19X1 and 12/31/19X2 (all dollar amounts in thousands)

| Assets | 19X2 | 19X1 | Liabilities and Fund Balances | 19X2 | 19X1 |
|---|---|---|---|---|---|
| **Unrestricted Funds** | | | | | |
| Current | | | Current | | |
| Cash | $ 65 | $ 30 | Accounts payable | $ 225 | $ 230 |
| Receivables | 690 | 630 | Notes payable | 150 | 200 |
| Inventories | 85 | 90 | Accrued expenses | 200 | 175 |
| Prepaid expenses | 35 | 36 | | | |
| Total current assets | $ 875 | $ 786 | Total current liabilities | $ 575 | $ 605 |
| Other | | | Long-term debt | $ 900 | $1,000 |
| Property, plant, and equipment | $ 5,500 | $ 5,000 | Fund balances | 3,100 | 2,681 |
| Accumulated depreciation | (1,800) | (1,500) | | | |
| Totals | $ 4,575 | $ 4,286 | Totals | $4,575 | $4,286 |
| **Restricted Funds** | | | | | |
| **Specific Purpose Funds** | | | | | |
| Cash | $ 1 | $ 1 | | | |
| Investments | 100 | 35 | | | |
| Grants receivable | 45 | 0 | Fund balances | $ 146 | $ 36 |
| Totals | $ 146 | $ 36 | Totals | $ 146 | $ 36 |
| **Plant Replacement and Expansion Funds** | | | | | |
| Cash | $ 10 | $ 225 | | | |
| Investments | 400 | 145 | | | |
| Pledges receivable | 10 | 180 | Fund balances | $ 420 | 550 |
| Totals | $ 420 | $ 550 | Totals | $ 420 | $ 550 |
| **Endowment Funds** | | | | | |
| Cash | $ 25 | $ 17 | | | |
| Investments | 3,100 | 2,000 | Fund balances | $3,125 | $2,017 |
| Totals | $ 3,125 | $ 2,017 | Totals | $3,125 | $2,017 |

# Balance Sheets—May 31, 19X2 and 19X1 (all dollar amounts in thousands)

| Assets | 19X2 | 19X1 | Liabilities and Fund Balances | 19X2 | 19X1 |
|---|---|---|---|---|---|
| **Current Funds—Unrestricted** | | | **Current Funds—Unrestricted** | | |
| Cash | $ 900 | $ 500 | Accounts payable | $ 700 | $ 350 |
| Investments | 2,200 | 2,400 | Other liabilities | 3,600 | 3,670 |
| Other assets | 1,400 | 1,300 | Fund balances | 200 | 180 |
| Totals | $ 4,500 | $ 4,200 | Totals | $ 4,500 | $ 4,200 |
| **Current Funds—Restricted** | | | **Current Funds—Restricted** | | |
| Miscellaneous assets | $ 1,400 | $ 1,200 | Fund balances | $ 1,400 | $ 1,200 |
| Totals | $ 5,900 | $ 5,400 | Totals | $ 5,900 | $ 5,400 |
| **Loan Funds** | | | **Loan Funds** | | |
| Notes receivable | $ 4,700 | $ 4,700 | Fund balances | $ 6,100 | $ 5,900 |
| Other assets | 1,400 | 1,200 | | | |
| Totals | $ 6,100 | $ 5,900 | Totals | $ 6,100 | $ 5,900 |
| **Endowment Funds** | | | **Endowment Funds** | | |
| Investments—endowment | $28,000 | $27,000 | Fund balances—endowment | $28,000 | $27,000 |
| Investments—quasi-endowment | 8,000 | 7,000 | Fund balances—quasi-endowment | 8,000 | 7,000 |
| Totals | $36,000 | $34,000 | Totals | $36,000 | $34,000 |
| **Annuity and Life Income Funds** | | | **Annuity and Life Income Funds** | | |
| Annuity funds invested | $ 4,200 | $ 3,700 | Annuities payable | $ 1,600 | $ 1,300 |
| Life income funds invested | 2,400 | 2,500 | Fund balances—annuities | 2,600 | 2,400 |
| | | | Fund balances—life income funds | 2,400 | 2,500 |
| Totals | $ 6,600 | $ 6,200 | Totals | $ 6,600 | $ 6,200 |
| **Plant Funds** | | | **Plant Funds** | | |
| Cash | $ 600 | $ 600 | Notes and bonds payable | $ 4,500 | $ 4,400 |
| Investments | 3,900 | 3,400 | Advances from quasi-endowment | 3,000 | 0 |
| Land, buildings, and improvements | 43,000 | 36,000 | Other obligations | 500 | 200 |
| Equipment | 9,500 | 8,000 | Fund balances unexpended | (3,500) | (600) |
| | | | Fund balances—investment in plant | 52,500 | 44,000 |
| Totals | $57,000 | $48,000 | Totals | $57,000 | $48,000 |

## Statement of Revenues and Expenditures (all dollar amounts in thousands)

| | Year Ending May 31, 19X2 | | | Year Ending May 31, 19X1 | | |
|---|---|---|---|---|---|---|
| | Total | Unrestricted | Restricted | Total | Unrestricted | Restricted |
| **Revenues** | | | | | | |
| Tuition and fees | $11,000 | $11,000 | 0 | $ 9,700 | $ 9,700 | 0 |
| Church-affiliated contributions | 1,300 | 1,300 | 0 | 1,100 | 1,100 | 0 |
| Endowment income | 2,500 | 2,300 | $ 200 | 1,900 | 1,600 | $ 300 |
| Government grants and contracts | 900 | 100 | 800 | 1,000 | 100 | 900 |
| Gifts | 800 | 600 | 200 | 400 | 100 | 300 |
| Other educational and general income | 1,700 | 1,200 | 500 | 1,400 | 1,300 | 100 |
| Total educational and general | 18,200 | 16,500 | 1,700 | 15,500 | 13,900 | 1,600 |
| Auxiliary enterprises | 8,000 | 7,700 | 300 | 7,200 | 6,900 | 300 |
| Total revenues | $26,200 | $24,200 | $2,000 | $22,700 | $20,800 | $1,900 |
| **Expenditures** | | | | | | |
| Instruction and research | $ 8,500 | $ 8,300 | $ 200 | $ 7,500 | $ 7,200 | $ 300 |
| Library | 1,200 | 1,100 | 100 | 1,100 | 1,000 | 100 |
| Student services | 1,300 | 1,000 | 300 | 1,000 | 900 | 100 |
| Plant operations | 1,700 | 1,700 | 0 | 1,300 | 1,300 | 0 |
| General institutional expense | 2,000 | 1,900 | 100 | 1,700 | 1,600 | 100 |
| Student aid | 1,100 | 400 | 700 | 1,100 | 400 | 700 |
| Other educational and general expenditures | 1,200 | 800 | 400 | 1,000 | 700 | 300 |
| Total educational and general expenditures | $17,000 | $15,200 | $1,800 | $14,700 | $13,100 | $1,600 |
| Auxiliary activities | $ 8,000 | $ 7,800 | $ 200 | $ 7,000 | $ 6,700 | $ 300 |
| Total expenditures | $25,000 | $23,000 | $2,000 | $21,700 | $19,800 | $1,900 |
| Excess of revenues over expenditures | $ 1,200 | $ 1,200 | 0 | $ 1,000 | $ 1,000 | 0 |
| Transfers to endowment funds | $ 400 | $ 400 | | $ 300 | $ 300 | |
| Transfers to plant fund | 400 | 400 | | 200 | 200 | |
| Excess of revenues over expenditures and transfers | $ 400 | $ 400 | | $ 500 | $ 500 | |

New Hospital Statement of Revenues and Expenses Years Ending
12/31/19X1 and 19X2 (all dollar amounts in thousands)

|  | 19X2 | 19X1 |
|---|---|---|
| Patient service revenue | $4,250 | $4,000 |
| Allowances and uncollectible accounts | (900) | (800) |
| Net patient service revenue | $3,350 | $3,200 |
| Other operating revenue | 90 | 80 |
| Total operating revenue | $3,440 | $3,280 |
| Operating expenses |  |  |
| Nursing services | $1,100 | $1,000 |
| Other professional services | 900 | 800 |
| General services | 1,100 | 1,000 |
| Provision for depreciation | 150 | 125 |
| Other operating expenses | 300 | 400 |
| Total operating expenses | $3,550 | $3,325 |
| Loss from operations | $ (110) | $ (45) |
| Nonoperating revenue |  |  |
| Unrestricted gifts and bequests | $ 114 | $ 100 |
| Endowment income | 85 | 40 |
| Total nonoperating revenue | $ 199 | $ 140 |
| Excess of revenues over expenses | $ 89 | $ 95 |

You are also given the following nondollar quantitative data for the two years of operation:

|  | 19X2 | 19X1 |
|---|---|---|
| Rooms | 75 | 75 |
| Admissions | 3,000 | 2,400 |
| Average occupancy | 60 | 50 |
| Employees | 225 | 225 |

**Required:**
A.  Develop analytical ratios and other data that can be used in evaluating the operations of New Hospital over the two-year period.
B.  Comment on your findings.

P16-3.  The statement of support, revenues, and expenses for a health and welfare agency shows the following data relating to the agency's operations for 19X1 and 19X2:

**Required:**
A.  Develop appropriate analytical data to be used in evaluating the operations of the health and welfare agency.
B.  Comment on your findings.

Health and Welfare Agency Statement of Support Revenues and Expenses Years Ending 12/31/19X1 and 19X2 (all dollar amounts in thousands)

|  | 19X2 | 19X1 |
|---|---|---|
| Public support and revenue |  |  |
| Contributions | $ 2,200 | $ 2,300 |
| Revenues earned | 145 | 215 |
| Total revenues | $ 2,345 | $ 2,515 |
| Expenses |  |  |
| Management and general | $     300 | $     325 |
| Fund raising | 325 | 270 |
| Program expenses |  |  |
| Service No. 1 | 700 | 690 |
| Service No. 2 | 275 | 240 |
| Service No. 3 | 300 | 260 |
| Service No. 4 | 290 | 245 |
| Total expenses | $ 2,190 | $ 2,030 |
| Excess of public support and revenues over expenses | $     155 | $     485 |
| Additional nondollar quantitative data: |  |  |
|  | 19X2 | 19X1 |
| Units of Service No. 1 | 50 | 40 |
| Units of Service No. 2 | 5,000 | 4,500 |
| Units of Service No. 3 | 300 | 260 |
| Units of Service No. 4 | 50,000 | 40,000 |

# Operational-Accountability Reporting for Nonprofit Organizations

---

## ■ Learning Objectives

When you have finished your study of this chapter, you should

1. Understand the full meaning of operational-accountability reporting and how the statements required for it differ from dollar-accountability–oriented financial statements.

2. Be aware of the reasons for insisting on operational-accountability reporting.

3. Recognize the relationship between operational accountability and the full accrual basis of accounting including the recognition of depreciation.

4. Know that the accrual basis of accounting can be implemented within a fund accounting system.

5. Understand the difference between an expense- and an expenditure-oriented operating statement.

---

Throughout the preceding portions of this text, we have observed how the generally accepted accounting practices of some nonprofit organizations deviate from those judged by the author to be logically desirable in meeting user needs. In those situations, we noted that accountants have been satisfied with dollar-accountability rather than insisting on operational-accountability reporting. This causes all spendable resource outflows, regardless of whether they represent the cost of resources consumed during the reporting period or the cost of long-term assets, to be reflected as outflows in the operating statement. No depreciation is recognized in that statement to show the cost of long-term assets consumed. Also, all spendable resource inflows, including those acquired by the incurrence of long-term debt, are reflected as revenues. For that reason, as we have developed analytical data in the last two chapters, we have been careful to call attention to the limitations associated with the expenditure-based data provided in governmental and college and university financial statements.

Having observed the difference between logically desirable data and the data actually available, it is appropriate that we should further explore the topic of operational-accountability reporting for nonprofit organizations in this closing chapter. In doing that, we begin by recalling and more specifically defining *operational-accountability reporting and show how it relates to financial analysis.* After that, *analytical data from the dollar-accountability and operational-accountability financial statements for Model City* presented in Chapter 9 are calculated. We then consider how use of the operational-accountability data can affect our evaluation of Model City operating efficiency and effectiveness. In the last section of the chapter, *our case for accrual-based, operational-accountability financial reporting for nonprofit organizations is developed more completely.*

## ■ Operational Accountability Defined

The term *operational-accountability reporting* has been used throughout this text to mean disclosure of operating data showing the extent to which an organization has succeeded in *efficiently* and *effectively* meeting its operating objectives. Pure profit enterprises operate primarily to realize profits. Therefore, their operating statements are organized to match revenues against the costs of realizing those revenues to arrive at net income. That shows the extent to which the profit objective has been met. Pure nonprofit organizations operate to render socially desirable services. Logically, then, operational-accountability financial statements for those enterprises should disclose the extent to which the rendering of the entity's service objective has been met. Ideally, this would call for their operating reports to be organized to match the imputed values of services rendered against the costs of rendering those services. In that way, the operating statement would disclose operational accountability by showing how efficiently and effectively the service objective had been met.

However, as we have observed before, it is virtually impossible to arrive at an objective, quantitative measure of the values associated with the services rendered by a nonprofit organization. As a result, accountants in some segments of the nonprofit area have accepted spendable resource inflow–outflow operating reports designed primarily to disclose dollar accountability. Those who feel that operational accountability is important will argue that even though we cannot get an objective measure of the value of output so as to produce the ideal operational-accountability financial report, we should nevertheless *disclose, to the extent that our present level of knowledge permits, operating data regarding the "service story" of the enterprise.* As was observed elsewhere in this text, such an operating statement can be presented by disclosing full accrual-based cost data relating to the various service functions performed by the organization. Such a statement opens the way for the development of functional unit cost data that can be compared with budgeted functional unit costs for the current period, as well as with actual functional unit costs for other periods and for other similar enterprise units.

In the profit area, accountants have interpreted operational-accountability reporting to include the presentation of a statement of financial position consistent with the accrual-based profit-oriented operating statement. Such a reporting arrangement helps the analyst in evaluating the effort–achievement relationship existing between the resources available to the enterprise unit and the net income earned by the enterprise unit. This is consistent with the general expectation that, other things being the same, an enterprise unit with a larger amount of net resources available to it should be expected to produce a larger amount of net income than one with less resources available to it. It seems to follow, then, that operational-accountability financial position statements for nonprofit organizations should also disclose the accrual-based value of the net resources available to the enterprise for the purpose of carrying out its service objectives. Other things being the same, an organization with more resources available to it should provide more and/or better services than one with a smaller resource base. In summary, the author concludes that operational-accountability financial reports for nonprofit organizations should include an accrual-based operating statement disclosing expenses by service functions performed, along with a financial position statement reflecting the resources and obligations of the organization determined by use of the accrual basis of accounting.

# ■ Operational Accountability and Financial Analysis

In Chapter 9, we demonstrated how the generally accepted dollar-accountability financial statements for Model City could be converted to accrual-based statements reflecting operational accountability. Now we calculate the various ratios, identified in Chapter 16 as being helpful in our analytical process, for both the dollar-accountability and operational-accountability statements. We assume for purposes of our analysis that Model City has a population of 20,000 persons with incomes approximating the national average. The property tax rate has been based on an assessed value of $36,250,000 (see Chapter 6), which we shall assume is approximately 40 percent of fair market value. We also recall that general fund expenditures and transfers were subclassified as follows in Chapter 6 (see Exhibit 6–2, page 185):

| | |
|---|---:|
| General fund expenditures | |
| General government | $ 348,000 |
| Police services | 249,000 |
| Sanitation services | 160,000 |
| Recreation services | 75,000 |
| Street maintenance services | 393,000 |
| School services | 375,000 |
| Total direct functional expenditures | 1,600,000 |
| Transfers and miscellaneous | 284,000 |
| Total general fund expenditures and transfers | $1,884,000 |

In Chapters 7 and 8, we showed the following expenditures from other funds:

| | |
|---|---:|
| Capital projects expenditures | $402,000 |
| Special assessment fund expenditures | 251,050 |
| Trust fund expenditures | 2,000 |
| Total expenditures | $655,050 |

These expenditures added to general fund expenditures and transfers give us total expenditures and transfers of $2,539,050. For purposes of our analysis, we shall allocate expenditures not carrying functional labels as follows:

transfers and miscellaneous items on basis of direct functional expenditures

capital projects and special assessment project expenditures to street maintenance services

trust fund expenditures to recreational services.

After making those allocations, total expenditures and transfers are classified by functions as follows (rounded to $50):

| | |
|---|---:|
| General government | $ 409,800 |
| Police services | 293,200 |
| Sanitation services | 188,400 |
| Recreation services | 90,300 |
| Street maintenance services | 1,115,800 |
| School services | 441,550 |
| Total expenditures | $2,539,050 |

In arriving at the total expense balance of $1,603,400 shown in Exhibit 9–6 (1,466,500 + 6,050 + 130,850), we began by eliminating capital expenditures from the expenditures balance. Our major adjustments reflect the removal of capital expenditures and investments in other funds and the recording of depreciation. For purposes of our illustration, we now remove capital expenditures from their respective functional service categories. Because of the complexities involved in allocating other adjustments to functional categories, we allocate them on the basis of the ratio of each direct service expenditure to total direct service expenditures. These adjustments are reflected in the following schedule:

| Items | Expenditure Balances | Capital Items Removed | Allocated Balances Removed | Expense by Service Function |
|---|---:|---:|---:|---:|
| General government | $ 409,800 | $ 0 | $14,150 | $ 395,650 |
| Police services | 293,200 | 0 | 10,100 | 283,100 |
| Sanitation services | 188,400 | 0 | 6,500 | 181,900 |
| Recreation services | 90,300 | 25,000 | 3,100 | 62,200 |
| Street maintenance services | 1,115,800 | 798,050 | 38,500 | 279,250 |
| School services | 441,550 | 25,000 | 15,250 | 401,300 |
| Totals | $2,539,050 | $848,050 | $87,600 | $1,603,400 |

## ■ Analysis of Model City Operating Data

We begin our analysis of the operating data developed in the preceding pages by applying the analytical techniques described in Chapter 16 to the expenditure-based data. Then we apply the same analytical techniques to the full accrual- (expense-) based data for the purpose of showing how external users of the financial data can be misled by relying on expenditure-based data when capital expenditures are significantly more or less than the long-term assets consumed (depreciation).

## Analysis of Expenditure-Based Data

| Items | Expenditures | Percent | Expenditure per Capita |
|---|---|---|---|
| General administration | $ 409,800 | 16.2 | $ 20.49 |
| Police services | 293,200 | 11.6 | 14.66 |
| Sanitation services | 188,400 | 7.3 | 9.42 |
| Recreation services | 90,300 | 3.6 | 4.51 |
| Street maintenance services | 1,115,800 | 43.9 | 55.79 |
| School services | 441,550 | 17.4 | 22.08 |
| Total expenditures | $2,539,050 | 100.0 | $126.95 |

### Relationship Between Revenues and Expenditures

| | |
|---|---|
| Excess of revenues over expenditures | $81,875 |
| Ratio of revenues to expenditures ($2,620,925 ÷ $2,539,050) | 1.032 |
| General long-term debt per capita ($500,000 ÷ 20,000) | $ 25 |
| Tax assessment to market value of property ($1,460,000 ÷ $90,625,000) | 1.6% |
| Expenditures per person ($2,539,050 ÷ 20,000) | $126.95 |

## Analysis of Expense-Based Data

### Common-Size and Functional-Expense Data

| Items | Expenses | Percent | Expense per Capita |
|---|---|---|---|
| General administration | $ 395,650 | 24.7 | $19.78 |
| Police services | 283,100 | 17.7 | 14.16 |
| Sanitation services | 181,900 | 11.3 | 9.10 |
| Recreation services | 62,200 | 3.9 | 3.11 |
| Street maintenance services | 279,250 | 17.4 | 13.96 |
| School services | 401,300 | 25.0 | 20.06 |
| Total expenditures | $1,603,400 | 100.0 | $80.17 |

## Relationship Between Revenues and Expenses

| | |
|---|---:|
| Excess of revenues over expenses | $494,575 |
| Ratio of revenues to expenses ($2,097,975 ÷ 1,603,400) | 1.308 |
| General long-term debt per capita ($500,000 ÷ 20,000) | $ 25 |
| Tax assessment to market value of property ($1,460,000 ÷ $90,625,000) | 1.6% |
| Expenses per person (1,603,400 ÷ 20,000) | $ 80.17 |

## Interpretations of the Analytical Data

The analytical ratios and percentages developed in the preceding section can be used by externally interested parties in determining whether, in their judgment, the organization has operated efficiently and effectively. Compliance with externally imposed constraints must be evaluated primarily by reference to the financial statements of individual funds. In this section, we examine the ratios and percentages calculated earlier for the purpose of judging *whether the constituents would be likely to react differently to the operational-accountability data than they would to the conventionally presented dollar-accountability data.*

As we review the analytical data presented in the preceding pages, we find that they reflect a significantly different picture of operations when calculated from expenditures than when developed from the accrual-based expense data. For example, the common-size percentages show a larger portion of resources consumed being devoted to overhead or general administration when those percentages are based on expense data than when they are based on expenditure data. Also, due to the significant amount of expenditures for street improvement and street maintenance equipment, the percentage of each resource dollar used for street maintenance service is significantly larger when we use the expenditure data than when it is calculated from the expense-based data. Although these are the two common-size items that are different enough to stand out, others are also significantly different. Obviously, one must raise the question as to which set of common-size data most realistically discloses the resource allocation (service) story. Since accrual-based expense data reflect resource usage rather than spendable resource outlays, it appears that they more appropriately disclose the service story.

As we examine the functional expenditures or expense per capita, we can also observe significant differences between the results shown by expenditure- and expense-based data. Perhaps the most obvious difference is in the total amount spent per person. The expenditure-based data shows $126.95 in contrast to the expense-based figure of $80.17. You will also observe some significant differences in the per capita amounts spent for each of the various services provided. Again, we can conclude that the data shown in the expense-based analysis are probably the more realistic of the two.

It is also interesting to observe that both sets of analytical data show the current generation of taxpayers more than "paying its own way." However, as we examine the relationships between total inflows and outflows, we find that the extent of this *generational inequity* is much greater when we use the expense data than it is when we reflect the outlays in the form of expenditures. The excess of revenues over expenses quite obviously could constitute a justification for constituent pressure to reduce taxes during the next year.

Taxes assessed amount to 1.6 percent of the market value of property in both situations. Considering that Proposition 13 calls for taxes to be limited to 1 percent of fair market value, this may be considered a bit high for the citizens of an average income community.

Since the data used for purposes of our analysis are fictitious and are also based on certain assumptions regarding the length of life of assets and other factors, it is appropriate to raise the question as to whether similar differences between expenditure- and expense-based data would, in fact, actually exist in the real world. This analysis does not answer that question. It simply shows that *when capital expenditures are significantly different from the cost of fixed assets consumed, as reflected in the depreciation figure, the financial and analytical data will be different when we use the full accrual basis of accounting than when we use the modified accrual basis.* Those differences can be significant enough to cause constituents to react differently to politically oriented tax and spending issues. Therefore, throughout the remainder of this chapter, we shall give attention to the arguments for and against accrual-based, operational-accountability financial reporting.

# ■ The Case for Operational-Accountability Reporting

We have identified the characteristics of operational-accountability reporting in the nonprofit area and have shown how the data in operational-accountability financial statements can differ significantly from the more conventionally prepared dollar-accountability reports. We have shown that some of the judgments and evaluations made from the two sets of data could be significantly different if they were based on the operational-accountability rather than the dollar-accountability inflow–outflow data. Stated another way, the operational-accountability financial statements can provide a *significantly different picture of the service story* than we would get from the dollar-accountability data. The next question to be raised concerns which set of data presents the more realistic picture of what has actually happened.

To deal with that question, we shall:

1. explore more completely the implications associated with the basis of accounting used

2. observe the relationship between intergenerational equity and objective, consistent financial reporting

3. examine briefly the relationship between the service story and the disclosures coming from accrual-based cost data

4. explain why it is important to use community resources efficiently

5. cite the need for consolidated financial statements in emphasizing the organization as a reporting unit within the constraints of fund accounting procedures

6. examine the pros and cons associated with the depreciation question

7. summarize our concluding remarks relating to the need for operational accountability reporting.

## Implications of the Basis of Accounting Used

The basis of accounting determines the points at which resource inflows and outflows will be recognized as revenues and expenditures or expenses. The cash basis establishes recognition at the times when cash is received and disbursed. The modified accrual basis recognizes inflows as revenues when they become available and are objectively measurable. Outflows, characterized as expenditures, are recognized in the period in which obligations for goods and services are incurred and are objectively measurable. Both inflows and outflows are measured in terms of appropriable resources without regard for the period in which inflows are earned or the period(s) benefited by outflows.

With the accrual basis, the measurement of revenues and expenses is determined by the points in time when resources and/or services are earned and used, respectively. An outflow is recognized as creating an asset when the goods or services resulting from it will benefit future periods. Also, the expiration of a long-lived asset is recognized as an expense as its future service potential declines. A liability is recognized when an organization becomes obligated for goods or services that it has received. Inflows of spendable resources that must be repaid are recognized as liabilities.

*The need for measuring and comparing financial data for specified reporting periods makes the basis of accounting important.* Revenues and expenses reflecting effort–achievement relationships must, with period-oriented financial reporting, be related to specific intervals of time. If beneficial comparisons are to be made, the points of recognition should be determined by *objectively measurable occurrences* rather than by acts of management designed to shift the inflows and outflows reported as revenues and expenditures to the period(s) where they desire them to be shown. This can be accomplished by intentional or accidental variations in the movements of appropriable resources into and out of the entity. Furthermore, if we are to measure inflows and outflows appropriately for the purpose of evaluating intergenerational equity, it appears that the points of earning and using are more meaningful in determining the extent to which a particular term of office or generation of people is paying for the services it uses.

Dollar-accountability–oriented financial statements currently published by some nonprofit entities are useful for limited purposes, but *they do not report all that is practical and feasible concerning financial position and results of operations.* More informative disclosure could be achieved through use of the accrual basis and the preparation of statements naturally evolving from its use. Revenues and costs of operations can be assigned more appropriately to reporting periods than is possible with the modified accrual basis. Appropriately determined costs are of critical importance; and the accrual basis makes cost calculations sharper and more meaningful.

Both profit and nonprofit organizations operate within the same legal and economic framework. The power to hold claims against others and to be obligated to others is essentially the same in both areas. Within limits, each has the same power to hold title, to sue, and to be sued. Accordingly, the points in time when rights and obligations become associated with a particular organization are the same, whether its efforts are directed toward realizing a profit or providing a service for society.

An adequate disclosure of operating results requires that the acquisitions and uses of all resources over a reporting period be shown and that they be measured at the times of earning and using. This practice is necessary to provide interested groups with an adequate basis for evaluating the operational stewardship of management and the real accomplishment of the organization within a particular period. Thus, an emphasis on the concepts of earning and using resources is important to an adequate and complete presentation of the operating results and to the disclosure of the net resources available to the organization.

Disclosure of operational accountability requires an accurate measurement of the net resources available to a nonprofit organization and of the changes in these resources over each operating period. The preceding analysis points out that the accrual basis provides such a measurement more objectively and precisely than does the cash or modified accrual bases, which are sometimes used in accounting for nonprofit organizations. The need for disclosure of the balance of resources available to the organization in readily appropriable form can be met by the use of proper account classifications within the framework of the accrual basis. Therefore, the author concludes that the full accrual basis is superior to either the cash or modified accrual bases in accounting for the activities of any nonprofit organization engaged in the management and conversion of economic resources and at the same time does not preclude disclosure of fiscal accountability. The accrual basis is desirable because it provides the capability of reflecting operational accountability as well as dollar accountability in the financial statements. It allows the operating statement to disclose full cost and revenue data for each reporting period as well as a consistent and objective measurement of the resources and obligations of the entity at the end of each period.

A number of publications evaluating the accounting procedures followed in the governmental, college and university, hospital, and health and welfare areas all include statements supporting the use of the accrual basis.[1] However, as observed earlier, the amplifications of these statements also show that the conventional accounting procedures for organizations other than hospitals and health and welfare agencies still fall short of using the full accrual basis as it is conventionally defined in the profit area. Nevertheless, there is a trend toward greater use of the accrual basis of accounting in the nonprofit area. The most recent actions reflecting this trend are the issuance of FASB 93 and GASB 11. Both of these pronouncements were discussed at some length earlier in the text.

## The Need for Objectivity and Consistency

To be of greatest use to all interested groups, financial statement data should be both *objectively established* and *consistently measured* from period to period. If the data are biased in the direction desired by any one group such as, for example, the internal managers, they become less useful to all others. For this reason, it is important that recognition of inflows and outflows be based on objectively determined criteria rather than on what management wishes to show in the way of inflows and outflows. The

1. See, for example: Sidney Davison, David O. Green, Walter Hellerstein, Albert Madansky, and Roman L. Weil, *Financial Reporting by State and Local Government Units* (Chicago, Ill.: University of Chicago, 1977); Robert N. Anthony and Regina Herzlinger, *Management Control in Nonprofit Organizations* (Homewood, Ill.: Richard D. Irwin, 1975); Accounting Advisory Committee, *Report to the Commission on Private Philanthropy and Public Needs* (Washington, D.C.: The Commission on Private Philanthropy and Public Needs, 1974); Touche Ross & Co., *Issues and a Viewpoint, Public Financial Reporting by Local Government* (New York: Touche Ross & Co., 1977); and AICPA *Industry Audit Guides*.

accrual basis provides a more objective and consistent measurement of these items than does either the cash or modified accrual basis.

Comparison in one form or another is the greatest single analytical device for evaluating the operating and financial position data of an organization. But if this comparison is to be reliable, financial information must be developed and presented in a consistent manner from period to period. Consistency in the presentation of financial data is at least as important for nonprofit organizations as it is for commercial enterprises. Consistency of measurement can best be achieved by use of the accrual basis of accounting.

## Full-Cost Data and the Service Story

When we analyzed the financial statements for Model City using first the modified accrual basis and then the accrual-basis data, we observed a significant difference both in the amounts of individual service function outflows and in their relationships to each other. Since our present level of knowledge does not permit us to impute a value for services rendered to be matched against the resources consumed in rendering them, we must depend largely upon the functional or program distribution of outflows to convey the service story of the organization.

Since the accrual (expense-oriented) data are based on the points of resource use rather than when appropriable resources are surrendered, they appear to be better measures of the true costs of services provided by the organization during a reporting period. Thus, we can conclude that *the service story is disclosed more appropriately by expense-based rather than the expenditure-based data included in the conventional dollar-accountability statements.*

## Effective Use of Community Resources

Because the amount of resources available to any community will always be less than the amount of resources that the community desires to use, it is important that the financial reports emphasize the actual uses of resources as a partial measure of organizational efficiency. Although nonprofit organizations are not concerned with the distribution of dividends or the payment of income taxes, the financial reports for these organizations are no less important to their constituents in evaluating efficiency and effectiveness than are the financial reports of businesses are to their stockholders. In at least one respect, they are much more important. In the profit area, an inefficient organization will eventually be forced out of business because of its inability to make a profit. Its very existence depends upon its ability to operate in a competitively efficient manner. Thus, barring governmental subsidies or some other outside support, less efficient enterprises automatically go out of existence as their segment of the economy becomes more competitive. This situation is considered desirable, within limits, because it promotes efficiency in the use of resources and helps the public enjoy a better standard of living.

This natural process of elimination does not always occur in the nonprofit area. Actually, when revenues are geared only to proposed expenditures, an organization providing less service per dollar of expenditures can fare just as well or better than a more efficient one. As we have observed, an appropriately informed constituency and public can help prevent this situation from occurring. Some measure of the efficiency with which an organization uses resources in performing its services is important to these groups. This can take the form of appropriately prepared financial statements that disclose information about *operating stewardship as well as dollar accountability*. These operational-accountability statements can be used by the public as they judge the efficiency with which a nonprofit organization has converted its resources into services. That judgment in turn becomes the basis for deciding whether or not the organization merits continued public support.

## Operational-Accountability Reporting and Fund Accounting

Throughout the text, we have pointed out that the fiduciary nature of nonprofit organizations requires that their accounting systems be built along fund entity lines. Externally imposed restrictions on the uses of resources must be recognized in the accounting records. This practice often results in the presentation of numerous fund entity statements with less-than-adequate disclosure of financial information about the organization as an operating entity. If constituents and other externally interested parties are to make the types of decisions described in this text, they have to be primarily concerned with the operation of the organizational unit rather than the fund subentities. They should be provided with *an operating statement disclosing full cost and revenue data* for the organization as a unit.

It is also important that a balance sheet showing all resources available to the organization be included as one of the financial statements. Because management will have different rights in the uses of different groups of resources, it is important that this statement distinguish between those resources available for discretional use and those that can be used only for specified purposes. This objective can be accomplished by dividing the balance sheet items into two major classifications. One category, characterized as *unrestricted items,* should include all operating resources available for discretionary use by management. The other, characterized as *restricted resources,* should include assets whose uses are *externally restricted* along with the obligations against them. This would result in a balance sheet similar to the one shown for Model City in Exhibit 9–7 on page 358. The unrestricted category could advantageously be subdivided to show uncommitted assets, assets committed to general operations, assets committed to auxiliary enterprises, and miscellaneous assets. Subdivisions could be used in the restricted section to show the nature of restrictions placed on the uses of those resources. Fund balances, in all instances, could be subdivided to show expendable and nonexpendable balances.

The reporting arrangement described above makes the fund entity reports essentially supporting schedules for the statements showing the financial data for the organization as a unit. This plan of reporting requires the following statements for the organization as an operating entity:

1. A *balance sheet* showing all resources available and obligations owed by the organization. The resources and related obligations should be classified to show the nature of restrictions placed upon their use.

2. An *operating statement,* such as the one described in the preceding paragraphs, that would show the full accrual-based revenue and expense data for the organization as an operating unit.

3. A statement showing the sources and uses of appropriable resources. This statement is essentially a *statement of revenues and expenditures.*

4. A statement of *changes in fund balances* subdivided by funds.

This general proposal for a reporting framework was supported by an American Accounting Association Committee on accounting practices for nonprofit organizations as early as 1971. In that report, the committee called for financial statements showing total operational accountability over time to supplement the traditional not-for-profit accounting reports. More specifically, the committee recommended that[2]

> statements of financial position and operations for not-for-profit organizations as a whole be prepared in consolidated or consolidating form in addition to the usual separate fund statements.

These conclusions led to a consideration of the modifications required in nonprofit accounting practices to facilitate preparation of the additional recommended financial statements. The American Accounting Association Committee, in its 1971 report, described procedures that could be used in developing "crosswalks" between the conventional revenue–expenditure related data and the functionally oriented operational-accountability data.[3] This clearly shows that we have the technical capabilities to meet both the dollar-accountability and operational-accountability reporting requirements suggested by the preceding recommendations within the framework of one accounting system.

## The Depreciation Question

The full accrual basis of accounting followed by business enterprises requires a distinction between capital and revenue expenditures and a related recognition of depreciation. However, because the question of recognizing depreciation for nonprofit organizations has been debated strenuously in accounting literature, a separate consideration of depreciation accounting is appropriate. Conventionally accepted practice in the governmental and university areas limits the recognition of depreciation to assets for which depreciation is funded and to assets of self-sustaining activities. Hospitals and health and welfare agencies, on the other hand, record depreciation in much the same manner as do businesses. As explained earlier in the text, FASB 93, when implemented, will require the recognition of depreciation in college and university financial reports.

The basic objective of depreciation accounting is to provide a *systematic allocation* of the cost of plant and equipment over the period of estimated use, in order that the full cost of carrying out the activities of the enterprise can be determined and disclosed. If accounting reports are based on a stable measuring unit or if an appropriate adjustment is made for the instability of the measuring unit, depreciation data can also be used to provide other meaningful information. For example, within these conditions accumulated depreciation discloses the cumulative current dollar cost of

---

2. *Report of the Committee on Accounting for Not-for-Profit Organizations* (Evanston, Ill.: American Accounting Association, 1971). *Accounting Review Supplement* to Vol. XLVI, pp. 93–94.
3. Ibid., pp. 142–143.

fixed-asset service units consumed to date and book value discloses the current dollar cost of unexpired service units.

Our further discussion of the depreciation question includes a

1. summary of the reasons for opposing the recognition of depreciation
2. summary of reasons for favoring the recognition of depreciation
3. concluding statement regarding the recognition of depreciation.

**Reasons for Opposing Depreciation Recognition.** Some who insist that depreciation should not be recorded argue that nonprofit organizations typically operate under an appropriation type of budgetary control as a basic premise for their reasoning. They point out that because legal requirements specify that budgets (particularly for tax-supported organizations) show proposed realization and disposal plans for appropriable resources, accounting records must disclose these data. They therefore hold that, unless depreciation is being funded, it should not be recorded. Furthermore, they contend that the outflows section of the operating statement must conform to the actual appropriable funds given up. In effect, proponents of this view contend that this primary objective of showing the inflows and outflows of appropriable resources is so important that it eliminates the need for reporting appropriately determined costs or providing objectively determined cost data in the operating statement. They suggest, however, that cost data may be computed separately and included as supplementary information.

There is no doubt that a budget showing the plan for realizing and spending appropriable resources should be presented as a basis for approval of appropriation requests. The legal requirements at this point must be met. However, does not every operating entity do part of its planning in this way? This basic requirement does not seem to preclude capitalizing fixed assets and recognizing depreciation of them. For many years, it was a common practice in accounting for business enterprises to prepare a "statement of changes in financial position" by using a relatively simple set of adjustments to convert the accrual-basis data to figures that showed the inflows and outflows of net working capital or cash. The same practice could be followed for nonprofit entities.

Because expenditures (the outflows of appropriable funds) are generally more closely controlled against appropriations in nonprofit organizations, an alternate procedure could be used. Initially, the formal records could be organized to disclose all inflows and outflows of appropriable resources. These accounts could then be analyzed periodically to classify outflows benefiting future periods as assets and those relating to operations of the current period as expenses. The mechanics of carrying out this type of presentation are not difficult and have been demonstrated in Chapter 9 and by groups studying the depreciation question.[4] In light of this alternate procedure, the fact that budgetary data must be based on the acquisitions and disposals of appropriable resources does not preclude the capitalization of fixed assets and the subsequent recording of depreciation on them.

---

4. *Report of the Committee on Accounting for Not-for-Profit Organizations* (Evanston, Ill.: American Accounting Association, 1971). *Accounting Review Supplement* to Vol. XLVI, pp. 156–157.

It has also been suggested that depreciation can become a factor leading to excessive charges in nonprofit organizations that charge fees for their services. This argument has been advanced, particularly in connection with hospitals, where solicitations for the replacement of fixed assets have been conducted even though depreciation had ostensibly been included in the fees charged. When such campaigns are really for replacement and not for expansion, they can often be justified as resulting from a failure to include depreciation based on current replacement cost as an element of the fees charged. However, when such campaigns lead to a "double recovery," this is not caused by the recording of depreciation. Two completely separate decisions are involved here. One relates to *costing policy,* the other to *pricing policy.* The recording of depreciation as an element of costs *per se* does not cause excessive charges. Excessive charges can result, however, from the decision to recover depreciation as an element of fees while, at the same time, soliciting funds for replacing fixed assets.

A few other arguments are sometimes advanced in support of present practices. For example, some suggest that it is not practical to record depreciation because expenditures, rather than expired costs, constitute the basis for the development of the budget. This technique for controlling expenditures, however, does not change the fact that operating efficiency cannot most appropriately be evaluated without full cost data which in turn requires a careful distinction between capital and revenue items and the recognition of depreciation.

The practice of basing budget requests on past expenditures can also lead to inefficiencies in the uses of resources. Under this arrangement, for example, department heads are often placed in a position of trying to find ways to spend funds to justify future appropriation requests, rather than trying to get the most service for a given amount of outlay. Consequently, it seems preferable to use functional cost data to support budgetary requests rather than to base those requests on past-period expenditures. Incidentally, *zero-base budgeting* is another attempt to get away from the inclination to "spend to justify future expenditures." Nevertheless, it is probably safe to conclude that under currently existing accounting practices, appropriations for many nonprofit organizations are too often based almost exclusively on past-period expenditures, some of which may have been made in an attempt to use up the appropriations of that period. This operating characteristic can, as observed previously, contribute to inefficient operations in these organizations.

The need for standards of measurement is obvious. Indeed, the fact that contribution toward a profit is not present as a control device in the nonprofit area suggests that appropriately determined cost data may be even more important for that area than it is for the profit area. These data are needed to establish an appropriate check on the requested appropriations.

**Reasons for Favoring Depreciation Recognition.**   The preceding discussion shows that the major reasons advanced for excluding depreciation from the operating costs of nonprofit organizations can be refuted. Thus, as we further examine this issue, we can conclude that the justification for recognizing depreciation must be based on the positive benefits that can arise from distinguishing between capital and revenue expenditures and recognizing depreciation. This section considers some of the arguments generally advanced in favor of that practice.

The basic premise for favoring the recognition of depreciation as an element of cost is the contention that *the responsibility of operational stewardship in nonprofit organizations extends through the acquisitions and uses of all assets*. If this premise is accepted, it follows that the financial statements should disclose (1) the consumption of all assets used in the operation of the entity and (2) the changes in the net equity balances. Furthermore, when fees are charged for services rendered or when (for some other reason) expenses are related to the realization of income, all costs for the period (including depreciation) should be matched against the revenues for the period. Present accounting knowledge offers no better method of reflecting the amounts of fixed assets used than application of the depreciation device.

Fixed assets are, in effect, nothing more than unexpired units of service. As these units expire through usage, they should be accounted for as part of the full costs of services rendered by the organization. This practice can best be accomplished through the recording of depreciation.

Another argument cites the responsibility of managements of nonprofit organizations to provide for maintenance of capital in accordance with the established policies of the organization. This responsibility probably exists, to some degree, in almost any operating entity. It is impossible to evaluate the extent to which management has met this responsibility without disclosing the extent of capital additions and erosions. Even when it is the policy of the organization to dissipate capital rather than maintain it, the rate of erosion should be disclosed to help evaluate the extent of adherence to this policy.

Accountants also suggest that the recording of depreciation would increase the usefulness of functionally allocated cost data particularly in situations involving a significant amount of multipurpose fixed assets. Another reason sometimes advanced is the belief that accounting for depreciation would probably promote a better system of accountability for fixed assets. The recording of depreciation could also provide a sounder basis for solicitation of funds to cover an operating deficit.

It is especially important to distinguish between capital and revenue items to objectively reflect the properly determined operating revenues and costs for a specified period of time. Quite logically, this distinction cannot be made without a commitment to recognize depreciation of capital expenditures as the assets represented by them are consumed. Therefore, the *decision to recognize depreciation as an element of cost is also one that requires the entity to distinguish between capital and revenue expenditures in reporting the financial results of operations*.

More recently, measurement of the extent to which intergenerational equity has been maintained has become an objective of financial reporting for governmental entities.[5] This cannot be most appropriately done without the recognition of depreciation.[6] The concept of resource base reporting, developed by the author and Dr. Lucian Conway, also requires the distinction between capital and revenue expenditures and the recognition of depreciation.[7]

5. Governmental Accounting Standards Board, "GASB Concepts Statement No. 1 Objectives of Financial Reporting" (Governmental Accounting Standards Board, 1987).
6. Emerson O. Henke, "Generational Equity Reporting," *Government Accountants Journal* (Spring 1987).
7. Emerson O. Henke, and Lucian G. Conway, "Governmental Resource Base Reporting," *Government Accountants Journal* (Fall 1990).

**Procedures for Depreciation Recognition.**   The reasons cited in the preceding pages show that in order to have statements that reflect full operational accountability, it is desirable to use the accrual basis of accounting, including a distinction between capital and revenue expenditures and the recognition of depreciation. The preceding discussion points out the weaknesses associated with arguments in support of conventional dollar-accountability reporting practices and the advantages that could result from recording and reporting depreciation. This line of reasoning shows that presently accepted accounting practices for nonprofit organizations should be modified to require all such organizations to capitalize fixed assets and to account for the depreciation of those assets, where these items are material.

Depreciation procedures for nonprofit organizations may not, however, follow exactly the same pattern as is followed for businesses. Because of the close trustee relationship of a nonprofit organization with its constituency and the public and its resultant use of fund-accounting techniques, the accounting practices for nonprofit organizations recognizing depreciation may well require an expansion or extension of those followed for businesses.

When fund-accounting practices are used, plant assets *may* be recorded in a separate fund designed to disclose the original value of fixed assets held. As we observed earlier, this accounting entity is called a *fixed-asset account group* in the governmental area and a *plant fund* in the college and university area. The exact nature of the transaction between the plant fund and the operating fund when depreciation is recorded depends on whether depreciation is funded. Specifically, when management elects to fund depreciation partially or completely, its accounting reports should disclose the extent to which the funding responsibility has been met. This objective can probably best be accomplished by the use of reciprocal accounts in the plant and operating fund sections of the combined balance sheet. The following entries illustrate the use of these accounts:

> **Operating Fund**
> Depreciation expense
> ⸱ Due to plant fund
> To record the depreciation of fixed assets.

> Due to plant fund
> ⸱ Cash
> To record the transfer of cash to the plant fund.

> **Plant Fund**
> Due from operating fund
> ⸱ Accumulated depreciation
> To record depreciation accumulation.

> Cash for replacement of assets
> ⸱ Due from operating fund
> To record the receipt of cash from the operating fund.

The absence of funding indicates a contribution of "the use of plant" from the plant fund to general operations. Entries to record this fact follow.

Operating Fund
Depreciation expense
   Use of plant (an element of the fund balance account section)
To record depreciation.

Plant Fund
Contribution to operations (a contra account in the fund balance account section)
   Allowance for depreciation
To record depreciation.

Within this arrangement, when capital expenditures are made from operating fund resources, the following entries could be recorded to close the expenditure accounts:

Operating Fund
Contribution to plant (a contra account in the fund balance account section)
   Expenditures
To close capital expenditures.

Plant Fund
Fixed assets
   Contribution from operating fund (an element of the fund balance account section)
To record operating fund purchase of fixed assets.

Another solution to the problem of recognizing depreciation within the framework of fund-accounting practices is to pattern financial statements after those currently presented by hospitals. As you will observe by reference to Exhibit 11–4 (page 420), the *fixed assets committed to operations are included in the unrestricted funds section of the balance sheet.* Such an arrangement was also suggested as one result of a research project conducted by the author for the American Institute of Certified Public Accountants and published in "Accounting for Nonprofit Organizations: An Exploratory Study" in 1965.[8] It seems that such an arrangement would simplify the accounting procedures for many nonprofit organizations such as colleges and universities and health and welfare agencies within their presently followed fund-accounting framework.

**Concluding Comments.**   The preceding analysis and discussion strongly support the need for operational-accountability financial reports emphasizing the use of operating performance and accrual-basis financial position statements for each nonprofit orga-

8.   Emerson O. Henke, "Accounting for Nonprofit Organizations: An Exploratory Study," *Indiana Business Information Bulletin No. 53* (Bloomington, Ind.: Bureau of Business Research, Graduate School of Business, Indiana Univ., 1965), p. 73.

nization as a unit. These statements should be presented within the overall constraints of the full accrual basis of accounting, including the recognition of depreciation. Since it is also important to disclose the flows of appropriable resources, the full financial report should include the four statements described on pages 647–648.

A number of other studies tend to support this position, and it is gratifying to see the accounting profession moving in the direction of demanding operational-accountability reporting for all nonprofit organizations. Technically, these financial reports can be prepared by using cross-over worksheets similar to those illustrated in Chapter 9. Such an arrangement allows the organization to meet the externally imposed dollar-accountability reporting requirements and at the same time present statements reflecting accrual-based operational-accountability data for the organization as an enterprise unit.

# Ethical Considerations Associated with Reporting an Operational Efficiency

For a number of years, the City Council of Ordinary City has heard citizens raise questions regarding the efficiency with which the operations of the city were carried out. Finally, a member of the Council was appointed to discuss disclosures that might be provided relating to this issue with the City Controller. The Controller suggested that one possibility would be to disclose the cost per capita of providing services over a series of reporting periods. He then provided the following data relating to the last three years of operations. Population has remained at approximately 20,000 over all of those years.

| Years | 19X1 | 19X2 | 19X3 |
|---|---|---|---|
| Expenditures | $1,800,000 | $1,850,000 | $1,700,000 |
| Expenditures per capita | $    90.00 | $    92.50 | $    85.00 |

The Council released the preceding data to the news media along with comments pointing out the efficiency with which 19X3 operations were carried out. Mr. Curious, a public accountant in the city, questioned the reliability of the expenditure-per-capita data as a measure of operating efficiency. He pointed out that the published financial statement for the city showed expenditures for long-lived assets for the three years to be as follows:

| 19X1 | $150,000 |
|---|---|
| 19X2 | $190,000 |
| 19X3 | $ 20,000 |

Consider the ethical issues associated with the use of such expenditure-per-capita data as a measure of operational efficiency.

# ■ Summary

In this chapter, we first gave attention to the characteristics of and the general need for operational-accountability reporting. We then demonstrated the difference between the service story reflected by the dollar-accountability and operational-accountability financial statements for Model City. We identified the differences that manifested themselves as we analyzed both the conventionally available data and the accrual-based operational-accountability statements.

Next, the implications of the basis of accounting for both operating and financial position statements were explored in some depth. We cited the importance of basing inflows and outflows of net resources on the points of earning and using those resources for the purpose of providing objective and consistently derived financial data.

We also developed logical support for presenting organizationally oriented financial reports in disclosing operational accountability. We suggested that four financial statements be prepared for each nonprofit organization as an operating entity.

Because the depreciation question has been debated over the years and because of its significance in operational-accountability reporting, special attention was given to the arguments that may be advanced in favor of and against the recognition of depreciation. We showed that the recognition of depreciation can be reconciled with fund-accounting practices. This discussion led to the conclusion that nonprofit organizations should prepare operational-accountability organization-oriented financial statements for external users. We also observed that this can be done through the use of cross-over worksheets similar to those illustrated in Chapter 9.

# ■ Glossary

**Capital Expenditures.**   Outflows of spendable resources for the acquisitions of long-term assets.

**Expenditure-Based Data.**   Operating data in which operating outflows are expressed in terms of expenditures.

**Expense-Based Data.**   Operating data in which the operating outflows are expressed in terms of expenses.

**Operational-Accountability Reporting.**   Disclosure of operating data showing the extent to which an organization has succeeded in efficiently and effectively meeting its operating objectives.

# ■ Suggested Supplementary References

Attmore, Robert H., John R. Miller, and James R. Fountain. "Governmental Capital Assets: The Challenge to Report Decision-Useful Information." *Government Finance Review* (August 1989).

Bagley, Larry W., Del D. Borgsdorf, and William H. Hudnut, III. "A View from the Top: What Mayors and City Managers Want from Their Financial Staff." *Governmental Finance* (December 1982): 3–6.

*Baron, C. David. "Obtaining Information for Government Program Evaluation." *Federal Accountant* (June 1973).

*Bastable, C. W. "Collegiate Accounting Needs Re-Evaluation." *Journal of Accountancy* (December 1973).

Bowlin, William F. "Evaluating Performance in Governmental Organizations." *Government Accountants Journal* (Summer 1986).

Canary, Hal. "Timely Financial Reporting." *Government Finance Review* (August 1988).

Copeland, Ronald M., and Robert W. Ingram. "Municipal Financial Reporting Deficiencies: Causes and Solutions." *Governmental Finance* (November 1979): 21–24.

Drebin, Allan R. "Governmental vs. Commercial Accounting: The Issues." *Governmental Finance* (November 1979): 3–8.

Enke, Ernest I., "The Accrual Concept in Federal Accounting." *Federal Accountant,* 22 (1973): 4–9.

Flaherty, Mel. "Financial Data for Cost Comparison and Control: Who Needs It?" *Government Accountants Journal* (Spring 1982): 45–48.

Francis, Charles D., and Allan J. Borwick. "The Equivalency Factor: Municipal Budgeting by the Household." *Government Finance Review* (August 1990).

Gross, Malvern J. "Report on Nonprofit Accounting." *Journal of Accountancy* (1975): 55–59.

Gross, Malvern J. "Nonprofit Accounting: A Revolution in Process." *Price Waterhouse Review,* 18 (1973): 43–50.

Gustafson, George A. "Depreciation in Governmental Accounting." *Federal Accountant,* 21 (1972): 47–59.

Howard, Thomas P. "The Role of Financial Statements in the Predictions of Interest Rates for Municipal Bonds." *Government Accountants Journal* (Winter 1979–80): 58–62.

Ingram, Robert W. "Evaluating Efficiency in the Public Sector." *Government Accountants Journal* (Winter 1981–82): 20–25.

Price Waterhouse & Co. "Enhancing Government Accountability—A Program for Evaluating Accounting Controls and Improving Public Reporting." Price Waterhouse & Co. (1979).

Robertson, Wyndham. "Going Broke the New York Way." *Fortune,* 92 (1975): 144–149; 212–214.

Shalala, Donna E. "Using Financial Management to Avert Financial Crisis." *Governmental Finance* (December 1979): 17–21.

*Sorensen, James F., and Hugh D. Grove. "Cost Outcome and Cost–Effectiveness Analysis: Emerging Nonprofit Performance Evaluation Techniques." *Accounting Review* (July 1977): 658–675.

Wrege, W. T., and Relmond P. Van Daniker. "Accounting Information Needed by State Legislators and Fiscal Officers." *Government Accountants Journal* (Spring 1986).

Wyson, Earl M., Jr. "Accounting Systems in the Civil Agencies—Could They Serve Management Better?" *GAO Review* (Winter 1973): 52–58.

## ■ Questions for Class Discussion

**Q17-1.** Describe what is involved in operational-accountability reporting for nonprofit organizations.

**Q17-2.** How does the statement of financial position for a profit enterprise help disclose the operational-accountability (effort–achievement) relationship?

*Also available in *Accounting in the Public Sector: The Changing Environment—A Book of Readings* by Robert W. Ingram (Salt Lake City: Brighton Publishing Company, 1980).

Q17-3.    How can functional expenditure or expense-per-capita data be used in evaluating the operational effectiveness of a nonprofit organization?

Q17-4.    Explain how common-size functional expense data can help in disclosing the service story of a nonprofit organization.

Q17-5.    What is meant by the term *intergenerational equity?* How does it relate to the operating (inflow–outflow) data of a governmental unit?

Q17-6.    Explain why it is important to use the full accrual basis of accounting in evaluating the intergenerational equity of a particular tax and service program.

Q17-7.    We have identified regulatory agencies as one of the groups interested in the financial statements of nonprofit organizations. List the reasons for having regulatory agencies monitor the operations of such organizations.

Q17-8.    Why is it important to identify the overhead costs associated with operating a nonprofit organization? Explain fully.

Q17-9.    How do potential long-term creditors of a municipality evaluate the repayment capability of such an entity?

Q17-10.   Explain how bond rating agencies serve nonprofit organizations and the investing public.

Q17-11.   Why is it inefficient to rely on the natural process of elimination to determine which nonprofit organizations will continue to exist and which ones will go out of existence?

Q17-12.   Explain the relationship between nonprofit organization financial statements and the efficient use of community resources.

Q17-13.   The accrual basis of accounting allows a more objective presentation of the operating data for nonprofit organizations. Is the preceding statement true or false? Discuss.

Q17-14.   Some accountants say that it is highly impractical to try to maintain a system of appropriation control and still use the full accrual basis of accounting. Do you agree? Discuss.

Q17-15.   Briefly discuss the arguments typically cited for not recognizing depreciation as an element of expense in the operations of nonprofit organizations.

Q17-16.   Cite arguments that might be advanced in opposition to the reasons cited in Question Q17-15.

Q17-17.   Discuss briefly the reasons favoring the recording of depreciation as an expense in the operations of nonprofit organizations.

# ■ Problems

P17-1.    Over a period of several years, Fantasy City has consistently increased the level of services to its citizens through increased expenditures and compensating increases in its tax rates. However, during the current year a taxpayer uprising has convinced the city council that the tax rate for next year should not be increased. They therefore direct you, as the chief accounting officer, to prepare an expenditures budget that can be financed with the current year's tax rate. There are certain built-in increases and inflationary pressures that will make it necessary to increase total budgeted expenditures above those of the current year. The council insists, however, that the city must not engage in deficit financing because by so doing the current generation would receive services that would have to be paid for by future generations of taxpayers.

As a result of those instructions you proceed to develop a budget calling for total budgeted expenditures in the amount of $30,000,000, the same as was budgeted last year. Revenues at the current tax rate should also equal $30,000,000. In developing the budget, you have reduced proposed expenditures for fixed assets from $800,000 (amount spent last year) to $200,000 and certain other outlays such as some for normal maintenance have been postponed. Salaries and other expenditures subject to price level increases have been increased to again reflect total budgeted expenditures of $30,000,000. The city council enthusiastically approved the budget with a published statement that the level of services will be maintained and that no deficit will be incurred.

As you examine this situation, you ascertain the following additional facts relating to the operations of the city:

1. If depreciation were calculated on existing fixed assets, it would amount to approximately $1,000,000.
2. City employees have a pension plan on which the cost for the current year (calculated in accordance with FASB requirements for profit enterprises) would amount to $300,000. Only $75,000 was included in budgeted expenditures to cover pension payments to presently retired employees.
3. Normal maintenance estimated to cost $200,000 is being postponed to achieve a balanced budget.
4. Accrued expenses at the beginning and end of the year are estimated to be $15,000 and $25,000, respectively.
5. Prepaid expenses are expected to amount to $20,000 and $5,000 at the beginning and end of the year, respectively.

**Required:**

A. Convert the $30,000,000 expenditure-based budget to an accrual- (expense-oriented) budget.
B. Has the city council achieved intergenerational equity with its balanced budget? Explain fully.
C. Which items described above can cause the expenditure-based budget to be a less objective projection of real operations than the expense-based budget? List and explain.
D. How could your answer in Requirement C relate to the operating philosophy of limited-term elected officers?
E. Discuss implications of this situation for future years' operations.

P17-2.  The various elements of the statements of expenditures and transfers for Freemanville, a city of 50,000 persons, for 19X1 and 19X2 are shown on page 659. The population has remained relatively stable over the two-year period. The primary source of general fund revenue is property taxes. The assessed valuation of property was $200,000,000 each year, which is approximately 50 percent of market value.

| General Fund Expenditures | 19X1 | 19X2 |
|---|---|---|
| General government | $ 1,800,000 | $ 1,900,000 |
| Police services | 1,200,000 | 2,500,000 |
| Sanitation services | 700,000 | 1,000,000 |
| Recreation services | 1,100,000 | 2,000,000 |
| Street maintenance services | 2,000,000 | 2,500,000 |
| School services | 2,500,000 | 3,500,000 |
| Transfers and miscellaneous expenditures | 900,000 | 1,200,000 |
| Total | $10,200,000 | $14,600,000 |
| | | |
| Other expenditures | | |
| Capital project expenditures | $ 900,000 | $ 500,000 |
| Special assessment expenditures | 500,000 | 300,000 |
| Trust fund expenditures | 10,000 | 10,000 |
| Total expenditures and transfers | $11,610,000 | $15,410,000 |

General fund revenues amounted to $11,000,000 for 19X1 and $15,000,000 for 19X2. Revenues of other funds were equal to expenditures.

For purposes of this problem, you should allocate transfers and miscellaneous expenditures equally to each of the six service areas. Capital projects expenditures are for a new city administration building. Special assessment expenditures were incurred to improve the streets of a new subdivision. Trust fund expenditures were for the improvement of city recreational facilities.

**Required:**
A.  Analyze the city's revenues and functional expenditure data as illustrated in the chapter.
B.  Comment on your findings.

**P17-3.**   Assume the same expenditure data as in Problem P17-2. Assume also that those data require adjustments for the following significant items to convert them to the full accrual basis:

| | 19X1 | 19X2 |
|---|---|---|
| Expenditures for fixed assets | | |
| General government | $1,200,000 | $ 800,000 |
| Police services | 100,000 | 800,000 |
| Sanitation services | 50,000 | 300,000 |
| Recreation services | 100,000 | 600,000 |
| Street maintenance services | 500,000 | 800,000 |
| School services | 400,000 | 900,000 |
| Totals | $2,350,000 | $4,200,000 |

*continues*

| | 19X1 | 19X2 |
|---|---|---|
| Depreciation on fixed assets | | |
| General government | $1,000,000 | $1,200,000 |
| Police services | 400,000 | 500,000 |
| Sanitation services | 250,000 | 250,000 |
| Recreation services | 400,000 | 500,000 |
| Street maintenance services | 200,000 | 250,000 |
| School services | 600,000 | 700,000 |
| Totals | $2,850,000 | $3,400,000 |

**Required:**

A. Convert the expenditure-based data from Problem P17-2 to accrual- (expense-) based data.

B. Analyze the expense-based data as illustrated in this chapter.

C. Comment on your findings, including any differences in impressions gained from analysis of the expense-based and expenditure-based data.

# Thought Projection Cases for Chapters 14, 15, 16, and 17

■ **Case 1: Slippery Handle Mental Health Center, Treacherous Waters, USA**

### Introduction

The Slippery Handle Mental Health Center (hereinafter referred to as SHMHC) is a private, not-for-profit corporation, offering comprehensive services in mental health and alcohol and drug abuse.

Recently, the executive director has become concerned over certain operational characteristics of SHMHC, namely,

Staff productivity
  Service-delivery levels
  Caseloads

Client treatment patterns

Quality of services

Scheduling reliability (appointments)

Adherence to standard fees

Propriety of ability-to-pay discounts

Effectiveness of billing and collection efforts

Cases developed by Professors James Sorensen and Glyn Hanbery, School of Accountancy, University of Denver. Used with permission.

To initiate the investigation, the executive director first focused on the outpatient service and obtained the following information from the program evaluator, accountant, and statistician.

## Outpatient Services

The Outpatient Service is staffed by 16 full-time therapists (assume an 8-hour day and 22 working days per month). All 16 therapists provide both group and individual therapy.

Clients are assigned exclusively to either group or individual therapy. SHMHC has been attempting to increase, within appropriate bounds, the utilization of its group therapy. More specifically, approximately 66 percent of SHMHC's clients are believed appropriate for group therapy. Each outpatient group is scheduled to convene twice monthly for two-hour sessions and is intended to accommodate five clients.

The historical pattern for individual therapy has been three one-hour contacts per month for each client.

## Statistics

For the past three months (the base period for the executive director's investigation), the statisticians reported the following service-delivery data:

|                          | *Group* | *Individual* |
|--------------------------|---------|--------------|
| Outpatient services      |         |              |
| Direct service hours     | 648     | 2,309        |
| Number of sessions       | 324     | 3,078        |
| Number of groups         | 54      |              |
| Total client contacts    | 972     | 3,078        |
| Clients enrolled         | 162     | 342          |

Additional data relative to outpatient-individual treatment were provided as follows:

| | |
|---|---|
| Scheduled appointments | 3,224 |
| No-shows | (36) |
| Cancellations | (158) |
| Scheduled appointments realized | 3,030 |
| Unscheduled contacts* | 48 |
| Total contacts | 3,078 |

*Not emergency contacts (ignore emergency services)

**EXHIBIT C1–1.** Slippery Handle Mental Health Center Actual and Standard Service Delivery Levels—Outpatient Services, (Recent) Three-Month Period

| | % of Hours Available | Direct Service Hours | Direct Service % | Number of Sessions | Average Session Duration | Number of Groups | Total Client Contacts | Clients Per Unit | Clients Enrolled | Number of Therapists | Caseload |
|---|---|---|---|---|---|---|---|---|---|---|---|
| **Actual production** | | | | | | | | | | | |
| Group | 8 | 648 | 22 | 324 | 2 hrs. | 54 | 972 | 3[1] | 162 | 16 | 10 |
| Individual | 27 | 2,309 | 78 | 3,078 | ¾ hr. | | 3,078 | 1 | 342 | 16 | 21 |
| | 35 | 2,957 | 100 | | | | | | 504 | 16 | 31 |
| **Standard production** | | | | | | | | | | | |
| Group | 15 | 1,272 | 30 | 636 | 2 hrs. | 106[2] | 3,180 | 5 | 630 | 16 | 39 |
| Individual | 35 | 2,952 | 70 | 2,952 | 1 hr. | | 2,952 | 1 | 328 | 16 | 21 |
| | 50 | 4,224 | 100 | | | | | | 958 | 16 | 60 |

[1] Clients per unit is a function of total client contacts ÷ number of sessions, i.e., 972 ÷ 324 = 3.

[2] Each group meets twice monthly for 2 hours each session; thus, each group meets 6 times within a quarter. The number of groups should be 106 (636 sessions ÷ 6 sessions per group).

**EXHIBIT C1–2.** Slippery Handle Mental Health Center Comparison of Budgeted with Actual Revenues and Expenses—Outpatient Services, (Recent) Three-Month Period

|  | Budget | Actual | Variance Favorable (Unfavorable) |
|---|---|---|---|
| **Revenues** |  |  |  |
| State | $ 56,100 | $ 56,100 |  |
| County | 8,200 | 10,200 | $ 2,000 |
| Third-party | 37,200 | 25,890 | (11,310) |
| First-party | 72,400 | 49,703 | (22,697) |
| Other | 2,000 | 3,500 | 1,500 |
| Total | $175,900 | $145,393 | $(30,507) |
| **Expenses** |  |  |  |
| Staff compensation | $111,200 | $111,200 |  |
| Other direct | 33,700 | 30,300 | $ 3,400 |
| Allocated | 23,600 | 23,900 | (300) |
| Total | $168,500 | $165,400 | $ (3,100) |
| Excess (deficiency) of revenues over expenses | $ 7,400 | $ (20,007) | $(27,407) |

Further, 845 outpatient-individual appointments are scheduled for the next month.

## Fees, Discounts, and Uncollectibles

The rates for individual and group outpatient therapy are $40 and $16 per client contact, respectively. The latter rate is derived as follows:

2 therapist's hours at $40 each, spread among 5 clients (i.e. $(2 \times \$40)/5$).

Approximately 22 percent of all outpatient clients have qualified for third-party reimbursement programs. Of third-party billings (all at standard rates), usually 10 percent are not collectible because of differences between SHMHC's rates and those paid by third parties. Clients who qualify for third-party programs, but for whom no such payments are received because of minimum deductible provisions, are themselves billed according to ability to pay.

Customarily, standard fees for services rendered either to clients not eligible for third-party payments or to clients who are eligible for third-party reimbursements, but who have not satisfied minimum deductible provisions are discounted 45 percent (in accordance with ability-to-pay schedules). Of the amounts actually billed to such clients, 30 percent are expected to be uncollectible according to past patterns.

**EXHIBIT C1–3.** Slippery Handle Mental Health Center Third- and First-Party Fees and Discounts—Outpatient Services, (Recent) Three-Month Period

|  | Revenues | Discounts | Billings |
|---|---|---|---|
| Third-party |  |  |  |
| Group | $ 3,110 |  | $ 3,110 |
| Individual | 22,780 |  | 22,780 |
| Total | $ 25,890 |  | $25,890 |
|  |  |  |  |
| First-party |  |  |  |
| Group | $ 12,442 | $ 6,470 | $ 5,972 |
| Individual | 91,106 | 47,375 | 43,731 |
| Total | $103,548 | $53,845 | $49,703 |
|  |  |  |  |
| Totals |  |  |  |
| Group | $ 15,552 | $ 6,470 | $ 9,082 |
| Individual | 113,886 | 47,375 | 66,511 |
|  | $129,438 | $53,845 | $75,593 |

**EXHIBIT C1–4.** Slippery Handle Mental Health Center Third- and First-Party Billings and Collections—Outpatient Services, (Recent) Three-Month Period

|  | Third-Party | First-Party | Total |
|---|---|---|---|
| Billings | $25,890 | $49,703 | $75,593 |
| Collections | 23,820 | 38,768 | 62,588 |
| Write-offs (uncollectible) | $ 2,070 | $10,935 | $13,005 |
|  |  |  |  |
| Percentage of collections | 92% | 78% | 83% |
| Percentage of write-offs | 8% | 22% | 17% |

The reports relating to delivery levels, revenues and expenses, fees and discounts, and billings and collections for the past three months were prepared by SHMHC's statistician and accountant.

**Required:**
Based on the data reflected in the preceding pages, discuss each of the operational characteristics that are of concern to the executive director.

**EXHIBIT C1–5.** Slippery Handle Mental Health Center Actual and Standard Fees and Discounts—Outpatient Services, (Recent) Three-Month Period

| | Units of Service | Fee Per Unit | Total Fees | Third Party | First Party Total | First Party Discount | First Party Billings | Memo: Average Discount Per Unit of Service |
|---|---|---|---|---|---|---|---|---|
| **Actual fees and discounts** | | | | | | | | |
| Group | 972 | $16 | $ 15,552 | $ 3,110 | $ 12,442 | $ 6,470 | $ 5,972 | $ 6.65 |
| Individual | 3,078 | $37[1] | 113,886 | 22,780 | 91,106 | 47,375 | 43,731 | $15.39 |
| | 4,050 | | $129,438 | $25,890 | $103,548 | $53,845 | $49,703 | |
| **Standard fees and discounts** | | | | | | | | |
| Group | 3,180 | $16 | $ 50,900[2] | $11,200[3] | $ 39,700 | $17,900[4] | $21,800 | $ 5.63 |
| Individual | 2,952 | $40 | 118,000[2] | 26,000[3] | 92,000 | 41,400[4] | 50,600 | $14.02 |
| | 6,132 | | $168,900 | $37,200 | $131,700 | $59,300 | $72,400 | |

[1] Derivation: total fees $113,886 ÷ units of service 3,078 = $37
[2] Rounded to nearest $100
[3] Typically, 22 percent of total fees
[4] Typically, 45 percent of first-party fees

# Case 2: Break-Even Community Mental Health Center*

After several discussions in the executive committee, the executive director of Break-Even CMHC summarized several of the key intermediate term objectives formulated by the committee. Each objective was to be reflected in the next three-year budget and the budget would lead the way toward achieving the stated objectives. The objectives for the next year to allow for program enrichment, merit raises, and inflation were

1. increase first- and third-party revenues per unit of service by something in the neighborhood of 10 percent to allow for program enrichment

2. increase the level of the outpatient service (viz., hours of direct service) by 2 percent per year.

Dr. Rose E. Bud suggested that a review of projected service levels, variable costs, and fixed costs would be helpful in determining the amount of expansion in total expense the center could expect if its objectives are achieved. "If we use up all of the gains in program enrichment and merit raises and if inflation takes its 5 percent, do we have anything left over for program expansion?" asked Dr. Bud.

Ms. G. Ledger, financial director at Break-Even CMHC, responded with the following analysis of last year's cost and revenue structure of the center:

| | Outpatient | | Partial | | Total | |
|---|---|---|---|---|---|---|
| Percent of revenues | 50% | | 50% | | 100% | |
| Service revenues | | | | | $ 300,000 | |
|   1st and 3rd parties | $ 100,000+ | | $ 200,000 | | | |
|   Grants | 400,000 | | 300,000 | | 700,000 | (100%) |
|     Total | $ 500,000 | (100%) | $ 500,000 | (100%) | $1,000,000 | |
| Variable costs | (100,000) | (20%) | (300,000) | (60%) | (400,000) | (40%) |
| Contribution margin | $ 400,000 | (80%) | $ 200,000 | (40%) | $ 600,000 | (60%) |
| | | | | | | |
| Common fixed costs++ | - | | - | | 600,000 | |
| Other recovery | | | | | $ 0 | |
|   Number of staff | 15 | | 5 | | | |
|   Units of service | 12,000 (Client Hours) | | 8,000 (Client Days) | | | |

+Represents 4,000 client hours of service or an average of $25 per hour.
++Includes costs for consultation and education, administration, a small fixed fee for contracted inpatient services ($25,000), and staff for all services.

Grant revenue is expected to remain stable but the increase in productivity would probably influence first and third party payments in proportion to the increase in productivity.

*Prepared for the Staff College, National Institute of Mental Health, 1980.

**Required:**

A.  Develop a projection of the amount of revenue that should be realized by Break-Even if its objectives are to be achieved.

B.  Determine the amount of net revenue that should be available for program enrichment, merit raises, and expansion of program.

# ■ Case 3: Seek-a-Client (SAC) Community Mental Health Center

The SAC Community Mental Health Center in Downpour, USA, currently operates two direct mental health services and contracts with various agencies for the balance of its services. The board of directors wants to make a cost study to determine whether the center is economically justified in continuing to directly manage the day care services or if the day care services should be contracted. Exhibit C3–1 was obtained from the center's cost-accounting records for the preceding fiscal year.

Prior to the board meeting, Mr. Livid, chairman of the board and president of Bonbon Industries, received a contractual offer from Mor Growth Services, Inc., to take over the day care services. Mor Growth Services, Inc., would assume the current volume of services for $550,000 per year and would like to contract for a five-year period with changes in volume of services and inflation adjustments to be negotiated on a yearly basis.

**EXHIBIT C3–1.**    19X9 Cost-Finding Report

| | | Services | | |
|---|---|---|---|---|
| Expense | Total | Administration* | Outpatient | Day Care |
| Salaries & wages | $   550,000 | $ 125,000 | $275,000 | $150,000 |
| Telephone & telegraph | 16,000 | 300 | 12,000 | 3,700 |
| Materials & supplies | 310,000 | 10,000 | 50,000 | 250,000 |
| Occupancy costs | 165,000 | 10,000 | 75,000 | 80,000 |
| Other general & admin. | 114,000 | 44,000[0] | 40,000 | 30,000 |
| Depreciation | 50,000 | 5,000 | 5,000 | 40,000 |
| | $1,205,000 | $ 194,300 | $457,000 | $553,700 |
| Allocation of admin.[+] | | (194,300) | +87,855 | +106,445 |
| Total cost | $1,205,000 | | $544,855 | $660,145 |
| Units of service | | | 13,621 visits | 11,002 days |
| Cost per unit | | | $40 | $60 |

*Including executive director and related staff
[0]Includes mortgage interest payment
[+]$457,000/$1,010,700 = 45.216%; 553,700/1,010,700 = 54.783%

"You know, Liv," commented Curley Letgo, "that deal sounds good to me. According to our own cost reports our day care is costing $660,145. I think we ought to take it. Besides we're going to have trouble with our labor negotiations and I'd just as soon let Mor Growth have all of those headaches. Is a motion in order?"

"Well, Curley," said Livid, "you make a lot of sense, but I'm not sure we've got all the right facts. Let's ask our business manager, Ralph Flimflam, to check out our questions. OK?"

"OK, then I'll expect to see his analysis by the next board meeting," replied Letgo.

At the next board meeting, Mr. Flimflam began his presentation by stating that an incremental rather than average costing analysis was the most appropriate type of analysis. "In rate setting, we make a number of allocations of common-joint costs that will not be eliminated if we discontinue a service, and not all costs will be eliminated," observed Flimflam. "For example, if day care is discontinued, the outpatient service will need one additional clerk at $4,000 per year to handle correspondence with the contractor. Three staff will be required, at an aggregate annual cost of $17,000; all other personnel in the day care service can be released. One clerk, at $8,000 will be retained. Employees whose employment was being terminated would immediately receive, on the average, three months' termination pay. The termination pay would be amortized over a five-year period for accounting purposes."

Several other key items were reviewed by Flimflam if day care were contracted out:

1. Long-distance telephone and telegraph charges are identified and distributed to the responsible service. The remainder of the telephone bill, representing basic service at a cost of $4,000, is allocated in the ratio of 10 to outpatient, 5 to day care, and 1 to administrative. The discontinuance of day care is not expected to have a material effect on the basic service cost.

2. The estimated cost of materials and supplies would be $5,000 per year; all other day care general and administrative costs will be eliminated.

3. The center would retain its present building but would sublet a portion of the space to the new contractor at an annual rental of $50,000. Taxes, insurance, heat, light, and other occupancy costs would not be significantly affected.

4. One administrative clerk would *not* be required ($5,000 per year) if day care was discontinued. Other administrative personnel would be retained.

5. Included in administrative expenses is interest expense on a 5 percent mortgage loan of $500,000.

6. Existing day care equipment having a net book value of $50,000 can be sold without gain or loss. These funds in excess of termination pay would be invested in marketable securities earning 5 percent.

7. Volume, prices, and revenues will continue at last year's level.

After reviewing these major points, Flimflam presented Exhibit C3–2, "The punch line is real simple: If we contract for day care our costs will increase by over

**EXHIBIT C3–2.**   Comparison of Last Year *with* Day Care to Last Year *without* Day Care

| Revenue or Expense | Day | | | Outpatient | | | Administration | | |
|---|---|---|---|---|---|---|---|---|---|
| | Last Year | Change | W/O Day | Last Year | Change | W/O Day | Last Year | Change | W/O Day |
| Salaries & wages | $150,000 | −125,000 | $ 25,000 | $275,000 | +4,000 | $279,000 | $125,000 | −5,000 | $120,000 |
| Telephone & telegraph | 3,700 | −2,450 | 1,250[a] | 12,000 | | 12,000 | 300 | | 300 |
| Materials & supplies | 250,000 | −245,000 | 5,000 | 50,000 | | 50,000 | 10,000 | | 10,000 |
| Occupancy cost (Rental) | 80,000 | | 80,000 | 75,000 | | 75,000 | 10,000 | | 10,000 |
| | 0 | +50,000 | (50,000) | | | | | | |
| G & A | 30,000 | −30,000 | 0 | 40,000 | | 40,000 | 44,000 | | 44,000 |
| [Depreciation][b] | [40,000] | [?] | [?] | [5,000] | | [5,000] | [5,000] | | [5,000] |
| Contract | 0 | +550,000 | 550,000 | | | | | | |
| (Interest) | 0 | −875 | (875)[c] | | | | | | |
| Totals[d] | $513,700 | | $610,375 | $452,000 | | $456,000 | $189,300 | | $184,300 |

| Summary: | With Day Care | Without Day Care | Change (Excess) |
|---|---|---|---|
| Day | $ 513,700 | $ 610,375 | $(96,675) |
| Outpatient | 452,000 | 456,000 | (4,000) |
| Administration | 189,300 | 184,300 | 5,000 |
| Totals[d] | $1,155,000 | $1,250,675 | $(95,675) |

[a] If $4,000 is a fixed committed but allocated cost, then each phone receives a $250 allocation (viz., $4,000 ÷ 16 = $250). Since 5 phones are in day care, $1,250 will still remain after day care is contracted out (viz., $250 × 5 = $1,250).

[b] Not included in any totals; shown for information only.

[c] $125,000 + $5,000 = $130,000; $130,000 · ¼ = $32,500; ($50,000 − $32,500).05 = $875.

[d] If the depreciation of $50,000 is added, then the total cost of last year is reproduced. ($513,700 + $452,000 + $189,300 + $50,000 = $1,205,000)

$95,000 . . . or $95,675 more precisely," concluded Flimflam. "Based on this analysis, I recommend we keep our day care service."

**Required:**
1. Whose analysis do you accept: Letgo or Flimflam?
2. What is your recommendation? Why?

# ■ Case 4: Albatross CMHC*

Albatross CMHC is located in medium-sized Gotham City, USA, and is affiliated with the Loch Ness Hospital. When the center first began operations in July five years ago, it offered the five basic services (viz., inpatient, partial hospitalization, outpatient, consultation and education, and emergency) and was staffed by 56 full-time-equivalent staff at a direct cost of $1,000,000. Now Albatross is beginning its sixth year. During the past year, four additional services were added (viz., drug and alcohol, early intervention, children's, and aftercare services) and staff has grown to 82 full-time-equivalents at a direct cost of $1,500,000. In its first five years, the center saw 8,200 primary patients or about 5 percent of the area population.

Currently, the center is operating at an identified deficit of $300,000 per year, which will grow by another $400,000 when the federal operations grant reaches the end of its final fiscal year in June of 19X2 or in three fiscal years from now.

Dr. Croding, Director, expressed his concern: "What measures should be taken to prepare for this loss of funds without losing valuable community services? If we have to make some adjustments, what should they be?"

Dr. D. Scent, Director of Outpatient Services, offered a suggestion. "Before we can plan where we're going and figure out how we're going to get there, we need to know where we are. Exactly what is our current financial status?"

Mr. Stan True, Associate Director for Administration, offered Exhibit C4–1 as a thumbnail sketch of the center's financial situation, assuming services and costs remained the same. "We have a short-run problem that will grow into an even bigger long-run problem," observed True. "The hospital may be able to help with the $300,000 by absorbing some of our indirect costs since our allocated costs from the hospital are about $400,000. But, there is no way they can do more than that and I'm

**EXHIBIT C4–1.**   Fiscal Status of Albatross CMHC

|  | FY 19W9–X0 | FY 19X2–X3 |
|---|---|---|
| Revenues (all sources) | $1,900,000 | $1,500,000 |
| Expenses | 2,200,000 | 2,200,000 |
| Deficit | $ (300,000) | $ (700,000) |

*Prepared for Staff College of the National Institute of Mental Health. A special note of thanks goes to Barbara Burwell for the approach used in this case.

**FIGURE C4–1.** Percent of Center Cost by Department (19W9–X0)

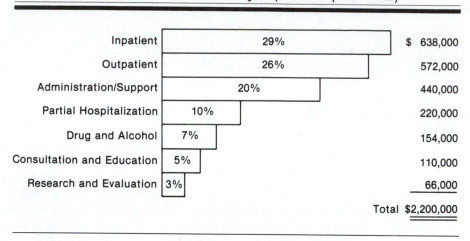

| Inpatient | 29% | $ 638,000 |
| Outpatient | 26% | 572,000 |
| Administration/Support | 20% | 440,000 |
| Partial Hospitalization | 10% | 220,000 |
| Drug and Alcohol | 7% | 154,000 |
| Consultation and Education | 5% | 110,000 |
| Research and Evaluation | 3% | 66,000 |
| | | Total $2,200,000 |

**FIGURE C4–2.** Percent of Center Cost by Major Cost Category (19W9–X0)

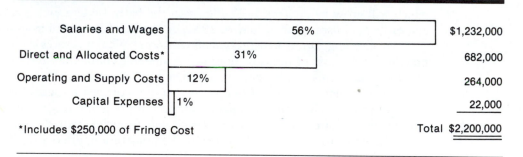

| Salaries and Wages | 56% | $1,232,000 |
| Direct and Allocated Costs* | 31% | 682,000 |
| Operating and Supply Costs | 12% | 264,000 |
| Capital Expenses | 1% | 22,000 |
| *Includes $250,000 of Fringe Cost | | Total $2,200,000 |

not sure they can pick up the $300,000. We need to do something today and to plan for tomorrow. I've prepared some information that I thought we would find helpful to our group and responsive to Dr. Scent's question. (See Figures C4–1 through C4–3.)

Mr. True observed, "Indirect costs are alluded to but not clearly understood by most of our staff. These costs represent the costs of nonrevenue producing departments (that provide a portion of their services to support the CMHC) and are allocated to the CMHC on a percentage basis. These include personnel, administration, payroll, budget, accounting, housekeeping, and so forth. This figure also includes fringe benefits (at $250,000), presently estimated to be about 11 percent of the total cost (or 20 percent of salary costs). Our direct costs are about 69 percent (or $1,518,000) and indirect including fringe is 31 percent (or $682,000)."

Dr. Falacy, who joined the meeting late, said, "Sorry I'm late folks; we had an emergency that delayed my arrival. Mental health is such a crazy business! You know, Stanley, I find your financial exhibits fascinating, but, as an outpatient clinician, I have a hard time relating to them. For me it's a lot easier if you can tell me what I've done with my time. Do you have such a breakdown?"

**FIGURE C4–3.**   Sources of Income for 19W9–X0

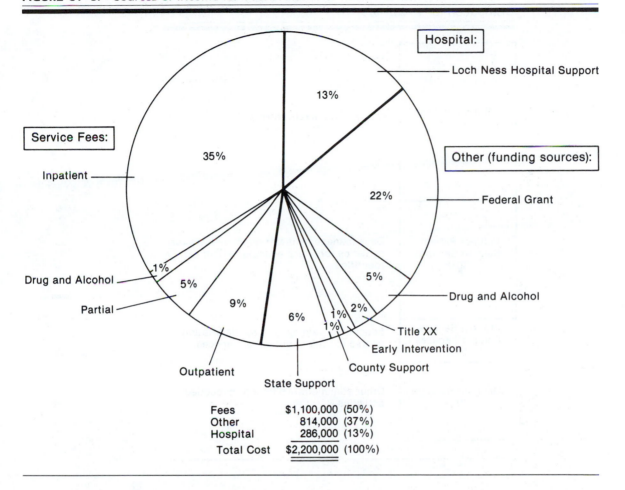

| Fees | $1,100,000 | (50%) |
| Other | 814,000 | (37%) |
| Hospital | 286,000 | (13%) |
| **Total Cost** | **$2,200,000** | **(100%)** |

"Dr. Falacy," replied Stan True, "you must be telepathic. That's my very next exhibit." (See Figure C4–4.)

Dr. Croding observed that one of the unique features of center management was the capability to identify clinician's time by activity. "We are mandated by federal/state/county licensing, accreditation, and funding requirements to commit clinician's time to activities which are nonreimbursable. Specifically, we have:

|  | Quality Assurance | Case Related: |
|  | Case Management | (Individual patient can be |
|  | Case Consultation | identified) |
| Service Related: | Supervision | |
| (groups of patients or | Consultation and Education | |
| services can be identified) | Administration | |

**FIGURE C4–4.** Mental Health Outpatient Clinicians, Time Distribution for 19W8–W9

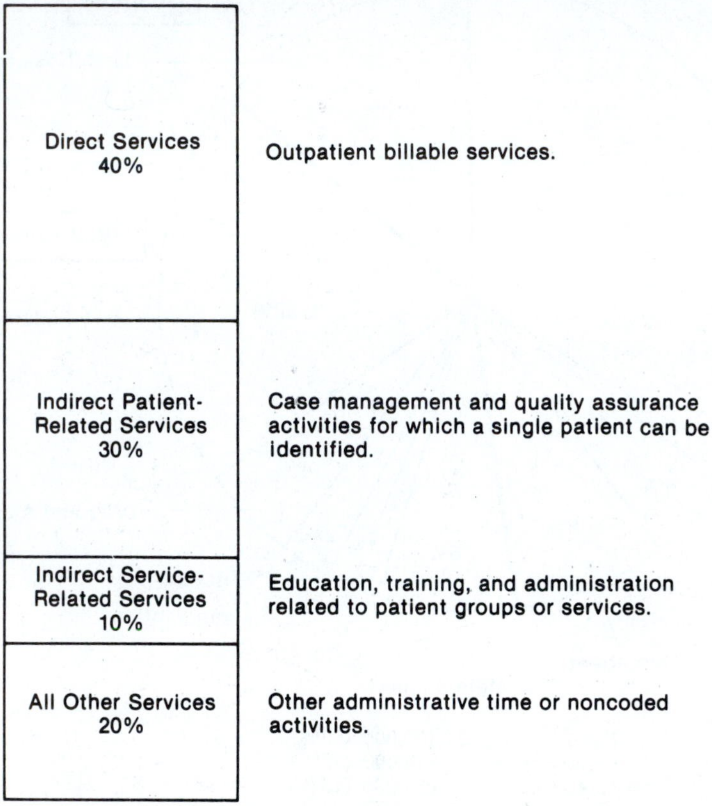

| | |
|---|---|
| **Direct Services**<br>**40%** | Outpatient billable services. |
| **Indirect Patient-Related Services**<br>**30%** | Case management and quality assurance activities for which a single patient can be identified. |
| **Indirect Service-Related Services**<br>**10%** | Education, training, and administration related to patient groups or services. |
| **All Other Services**<br>**20%** | Other administrative time or noncoded activities. |

"We also provide information and referral to hospital departments, as well as crisis intervention and supportive services to hospital employees, all free of charge. Our overall cost picture looked pretty good because we held our 19W9 costs to 19W8 levels despite inflation. Our unit costs didn't do so bad either." (See Exhibit C4–2.)

"If you examine the composition of the unit cost, especially outpatient, you see some interesting results. The $64 *per hour cost* contains:"

$15 clinical salary and fringe

$25 clinical staff time not billable ("overhead")

$15 other operating and support costs including CMHC administration

$ 9 allocated costs from the hospital

$64

**EXHIBIT C4–2.**   Unit Costs for 19W8 and 19W9

| Service | Unit | Cost | Change from 19W8 |
|---|---|---|---|
| Outpatient | Visit | $ 62 | No change |
| | Hour | $ 64 | No change |
| Partial hospitalization | Day | $ 47 | 2% increase |
| | Hour | $ 10 | 2% increase |
| Inpatient | Day | $133 | 1% decrease |

**EXHIBIT C4–3.**   Comparison with Regional Median

| Variable | Regional Median | Our Center |
|---|---|---|
| Percent of budget for administration | 15% | 21% |
| Clinical salaries | | |
| OP | $18,000 | $30,000 |
| PH | 13,000 | 16,000 |
| IP | 14,000 | 12,000 |
| Clinical Productivity per FTE per day | | |
| OP (Hours) | 3.0 | 3.2 |
| PH (Client) | 4.0 | 4.2 |
| IP (Patients) | 3.0 | 2.9 |
| Cost per unit of service | | |
| OP | $45 | $64 |
| PH | 30 | 47 |
| IP | 115 | 133 |
| Clients per clinician (per year) | | |
| OP | 129 | 128 |
| PH | 24 | No data |
| IP | 19 | 14 |
| Admissions and discharges per clinician | 54 | 37 |
| Fiscal support | | |
| Fees | 25% | 50% |
| State and local | 40% | 8% |

"We've also seen shifts in the patterns of use," commented Dr. Smug, Director of R & E. Children (ages 0–18) admissions have risen by 30 percent between 19W8 and 19W9 while adults (ages 19–64) have decreased by 22 percent. There is a decrease in geriatrics, but the numbers are so small they are deceptive.

"We look pretty good when compared to other centers in our region. I've prepared an excerpt from our annual evaluation report (Exhibit C4–3) to show how well we're doing."

"On second thought, those unit cost rates are not so good, but I know there are lots of centers who have higher costs than we do," continued Dr. Smug. "But just look at how well we're doing with fees (first- and third-party and contracts)."

**Required:**
A.  Given the foregoing analysis, what general suggestions would you give in response to Dr. Croding's question?
B.  Using the data offered by Stan True, will Albatross be financially viable in 19X2–X3? Document your response.
C.  What steps would you suggest be taken in light of your answers to Requirements A and B?

# Appendix: Audits of Nonprofit Organizations

The financial statements of nonprofit organizations are used by many parties who depend on them to fairly reflect the operating results and financial positions of the entities. Because internal personnel may be inclined to introduce biases into the data, the external users of those data generally want them to be examined by an independent third party. That examination is referred to as an *audit of the financial statements*. Such audits may be performed by independent accountants, called *public accountants,* or, in the case of governmental entities, by the "auditing arm" of another governmental entity.

If the audit is performed by an independent public accounting firm, the findings of the audit are expressed in the form of an *opinion* on the fairness of presentation of the statement data when evaluated against generally accepted accounting principles (GAAP). Included with that opinion is a *scope paragraph* stating whether the examination was performed in accordance with generally accepted auditing standards (GAAS). A typical, unqualified, short-form audit report for a business is shown in Exhibit A–1.

Audit reports for various nonprofit organizations include essentially the same information as shown in Exhibit A–1 appropriately adapted to the organization that was audited. In each case, the term *generally accepted accounting principles* refers to the principles applying to the organization being audited. Observe that the illustrated audit report includes key phrases that relate the work and findings to specific standards. First, the scope paragraph states that the examination was made "in accordance with generally accepted auditing standards" (GAAS). Then, the opinion paragraph states that the statements "present fairly . . . in conformity with generally accepted accounting principles" (GAAP).

Generally accepted auditing standards have been established by the AICPA. They are divided into three categories as shown on page 678.

---

*Portions of this appendix are adapted from C. William Thomas, Bart H. Ward, and Emerson O. Henke, *Auditing: Theory and Practice,* 3rd ed. (Boston: PWS-KENT, 1991). Used with permission.

## EXHIBIT A–1. Independent Auditor's Report

We have audited the accompanying balance sheets of X Company as of December 31, 19X2 and X1, and the related statements of income, retained earnings, and cash flows for the years then ended. These financial statements are the responsibility of the Company's management. Our responsibility is to express an opinion on these financial statements based on our audits.

We conducted our audits in accordance with generally accepted auditing standards. Those standards require that we plan and perform the audit to obtain reasonable assurance about whether the financial statements are free of material misstatement. An audit includes examining, on a test basis, evidence supporting the amounts and disclosures in the financial statements. An audit also includes assessing the accounting principles used and the significant estimates made by management, as well as evaluating the overall financial statement presentation. We believe that our audits provide a reasonable basis for our opinion.

In our opinion, the financial statements referred to above present fairly, in all material respects, the financial position of X Company at December 31, 19X2 and 19X1, and the results of its operations and its cash flows for the years then ended in conformity with generally accepted accounting principles.

Best and Company
Certified Public Accountants
March 21, 19X3

1. *General standards.* General standards relate to the personal qualifications and attributes of the auditor and to the quality of audit work performed. The auditor must in effect decide whether these standards can be met in performing an audit before he or she can accept the engagement. The general standards are as follows:

   a. The examination is to be performed by a person or persons having adequate technical training and proficiency as an auditor.

   b. In all matters relating to the assignment, an independence of mental attitude is to be maintained by the auditor or auditors.

   c. Due professional care is to be exercised in performance of the examination and the preparation of the report.

2. *Field work standards.* The field work standards set forth the guidelines for the actual evidence-gathering segment of the audit. Three standards govern the field work of independent auditors:

   a. The work is to be adequately planned, and assistants, if any, are to be properly supervised.

   b. There is to be a proper study and evaluation of the existing system of internal control as a basis for judging its reliability and for determining the extent of the tests to which auditing procedures are to be restricted.

   c. Sufficient competent evidential matter is to be obtained through inspection, observation, inquiries, and confirmation to afford a reasonable basis for an opinion regarding the financial statements under examination.

3.  *Reporting standards.* The audit report is the primary tangible product of the audit. It is the only communication that most users receive from the auditor. It is very important, therefore, that this report be as informative as possible. However, it must also be clear and concise; in addition, it must conform to a style that is uniform throughout the auditing profession. The following AICPA reporting standards, which govern independent audits, are intended to provide audit reports that meet these objectives:

    a.  The report shall state whether the financial statements are presented in accordance with generally accepted accounting principles.

    b.  The report shall state whether such principles have been consistently observed in the current period in relation to the preceding period.

    c.  Informative disclosures in the financial statements are to be regarded as reasonably adequate unless otherwise stated in the report.

    d.  The report shall either contain an expression of opinion regarding the financial statements, taken as a whole, or an assertion to the effect that an opinion cannot be expressed. When an overall opinion cannot be expressed, the reasons therefor should be stated. In all cases where an auditor's name is associated with financial statements, the report should contain a clear-cut indication of the character of the auditor's examination, if any, and the degree of responsibility he is taking.

Note that the second field work standard requires that the system of internal control be studied and evaluated for reliability. This is necessary because it is impractical for the auditor to examine in detail all of the transactions of the auditee. The opinion regarding fairness must therefore be based on tests of the transactions and balances. That in turn means that the auditor must rely on the system of internal control to cause the unaudited transactions and balances to be consistent with the findings from those tested.

As we have observed throughout the text, generally accepted accounting practices for nonprofit organizations can differ significantly from those followed by businesses. That, in turn, means that some auditing practices associated with the examination of the statements of these organizations will also differ from those followed in auditing business financial statements. In this appendix, we identify some of the audit practices that are unique to the nonprofit area and discuss those differences and the effects that they have on the performance of the audit. Our discussion covers the following major topics:

1.  major differences between generally accepted accounting practices of nonprofit organizations and those of business enterprises
2.  internal control problems peculiar to many nonprofit organizations
3.  special problems that may be encountered in auditing the financial statements of a nonprofit organization
4.  the single audit.

Just as with profit-based organizations, the accountant may perform both audit and nonaudit services for nonprofit entities. Among the nonaudit services are *reviews* or *compilations* of financial statements and issuances of *special reports*. The latter may be provided in connection with any of the following situations: financial statements prepared in accordance with a comprehensive basis of accounting other than generally accepted accounting principles; specified elements, accounts, or items in financial statements; compliance with aspects of contractual agreements or regulatory requirements related to audited financial statements; or financial information presented in prescribed forms or schedules that require a prescribed form of audit report. Statement on Auditing Standards (SAS) 14 provides the primary source of guidance on the wording of the special reports for these entities. Just as is the case with profit organizations, if the data associated with the special report are to be audited, generally accepted auditing standards apply. If they are not to be audited, the statements on standards for accounting and review services (SSARSs) apply.

# ■ Generally Accepted Accounting Practices

Because the operating objectives of nonprofit organizations are different from those of profit entities, their generally accepted accounting practices are, in some respects, also different. The primary operating objective for profit enterprises is to earn income for their owners. In contrast, nonprofit entities operate for the purpose of providing a service with no intention of realizing a profit from rendering those services. Also, nonprofit organizations have no stockholders to whom resources may be distributed. Therefore, any excess of revenues over expenses or expenditures is simply added to the resource base of the organization to enlarge its service-rendering capability. These organizations have *no personally held ownership interests* that can be sold, transferred, or redeemed.

Because nonprofit organizations are characterized by these differences in operating objectives and ownership characteristics, their accounting practices, too, logically should be organized to tell the "service story" rather than the profit story. Instead of emphasizing the distinction between capital and revenue items for the purpose of determining net income, some of these organizations *control operations by monitoring the inflows and outflows of spendable resources*. Consequently, they use appropriation control techniques and fund accounting practices in controlling operations, accounting practices that have led some of these organizations to use a *cash* or *modified accrual basis* of accounting rather than the pure accrual basis for financial reporting purposes.

In this section, we will first observe how these operational characteristics affect the performance of an audit. Then we will list the various publications that most directly define GAAP for these organizations and the AICPA industry audit guides that most directly relate those accounting practices to the performance of an audit.

## Appropriation Control

Business entities control their operations through accounting practices designed primarily to disclose the extent to which the profit objective has been achieved. Because the service objective is substituted for the profit objective in the nonprofit area, the operations of a nonprofit organization may be controlled by monitoring the ways in which resources are used. Within individual fund entities, this is accomplished through a technique called *appropriation control,* which requires management to use resources within budget constraints established for each of the different types of expenditures (outflows of spendable resources).

Appropriations are reflected as budgeted outflows approved by an appropriate representative body. Governmental entities, for example, begin their operating cycle by establishing a *line-item budget* showing the amounts proposed to be spent for each of the various items required to carry out the entity's operations. The budget must be approved by a body of citizens (for example, the city council in the case of a city) before management is authorized to spend against it. When the budgetary provisions are approved, they are referred to as *appropriations.* Management can then spend against the appropriations but *must confine its spending to the amounts provided for each of the individual items.* As we shall see later, in those instances the auditor must evaluate management's compliance with budgetary provisions before expressing an opinion on the operating statement.

## Fund Accounting Practices

While some resources received by nonprofit entities are available for discretionary use (within appropriation-imposed controls) by the managements of those organizations, other resources carry externally imposed restrictions as to ways in which they may be used. For example, a governmental unit may, with proper approval by its voting constituency, sell bonds to secure resources for the construction of a municipal building. The accounting system of the governmental unit must then be designed to provide assurance that such funds will be used only for the intended purposes. This can best be achieved by organizing the accounting records of nonprofit organizations to maintain separate accountability, or *separate funds,* for each body of resources contractually or externally restricted to a specified use.

It is important to recognize that the transactions of each fund are accounted for in a separate, self-balancing accounting entity. Because of that fact, we also have *interfund transactions,* which require accounting recognition in each of the funds involved. The records of each account group are also maintained in a separate self-balancing accounting entity. During the course of the audit engagement, the auditor must determine whether the management of a nonprofit entity has properly complied with restrictions placed on the uses of resources by using appropriate fund accounting procedures before rendering an opinion on its financial statements.

## Bases of Accounting

Generally accepted accounting practices require that business accounting records be maintained on the accrual basis. This requires recognition of accrued and prepaid items, a distinction between capital and revenue items, and the recognition of depreciation of fixed assets. Because of the emphasis on controlling operations through appropriation control and fund accounting techniques, governmental fund entities are accounted for on the *modified accrual basis.* In using this method of accounting, no distinction is made between capital and revenue items and there is no accounting recognition of depreciation. Furthermore, there is typically no recognition of accrued or prepaid items. Governmental entities, for example, use the modified accrual basis in accounting for the transactions in all their governmental funds. The accrual basis, however, is used in accounting for the transactions of proprietary funds.

Colleges and universities have conventionally used expenditure-based accounting practices that do not distinguish between capital and revenue items.[1] Also, no depreciation is recognized under that system. However, with the implementation of FASB 93, at least the private colleges and universities will account for their financial activities on the full accrual basis including the recognition of depreciation.

The official publications defining hospital[2] and health and welfare accounting practices[3] prescribe the *full accrual basis of accounting,* including the distinction between capital and revenue items and the recognition of depreciation. Therefore, the auditor should expect the same basis of accounting to be used by these entities as is used by businesses.

In December 1978, the AICPA issued its Statement of Position (SOP) 78-10, setting out accounting principles and reporting practices for certain nonprofit organizations. This statement is intended to apply to *all categories of nonprofit organizations except those that are already covered by the existing AICPA audit guides* (governmental units, colleges and universities, hospitals, and voluntary health and welfare organizations). This SOP requires that the accrual basis of accounting should be used in preparing the financial statements of these organizations to comply with GAAP. However, it does recognize the possibility that cash-basis financial statements may, in some instances, not be materially different from those prepared on the accrual basis and may therefore be acceptable. In 1987, the FASB issued Statement 93 requiring all nonprofit organizations to recognize depreciation. In 1988, the AICPA published the most recent edition of *Audits of Certain Nonprofit Organizations,* which includes the data from the various SOPs relating to such nonprofit organizations.

## Special Accounts

The accounting records of nonprofit organization funds will include many of the same types of balance sheet accounts as those found in the records of business entities. However, the differences between assets and liabilities will be reflected in *fund balance accounts* rather than in capital accounts. Furthermore, funds using the modified accrual basis of accounting will use the term *revenues* to describe all spendable resource inflows (capital and revenue) and the term *expenditures* to reflect all outflows (capital and

1. National Association of College and University Business Officers, *College and University Business Administration,* 3rd ed. (Washington, D.C.: National Association of College and University Business Officers, 1982).
2. American Hospital Association, *Chart of Accounts for Hospitals* (Chicago: American Hospital Association, 1976).
3. National Health Council, National Assembly of National Voluntary Health and Social Welfare Organizations, Inc., and United Way of America, *Standards of Accounting and Financial Reporting for Voluntary Health and Welfare Organizations* (New York: National Health Council, National Assembly of National Voluntary Health and Social Welfare Organizations, Inc., and United Way of America, 1975).

revenue) of those resources. As a result, the term *expense* will not appear in those records. Also, because the separate fund entities can have transactions with each other, we find accounts labeled *transfers from other funds, transfers to other funds, due to other funds,* and *due from other funds.* Because of the strong emphasis on appropriation control, governmental funds use *encumbrance* and *reserve for encumbrance* accounts to earmark appropriated resources committed to be used to meet specified future obligations. These accounts are designed to reduce the probability of managers "overspending" their line-item appropriations. The amount still available to be spent for a particular category of expenditure can be determined by subtracting the sum of expenditures and encumbrances for the item from the appropriation for it.

## Official Literature

For many years the accounting profession depended on each of the individual industries within the nonprofit segment of our economy to prescribe its own generally accepted accounting practices. These were reflected in the following *industry publications:*

Governmental Entities—*Governmental Accounting, Auditing, and Financial Reporting (GAAFR).* The most recent edition of this volume was published in 1988.

Colleges and Universities—*College and University Business Administration.* The most recent edition of this volume was published in 1982.

Hospitals—*Chart of Accounts for Hospitals.* The most recent edition of this volume was published in 1976.

Voluntary Health and Welfare Organizations—*Standards of Accounting and Financial Reporting for Voluntary Health and Welfare Organizations.* The most recent edition of this volume was published in 1975.

Now, the AICPA has published *audit guides* describing generally accepted accounting practices in each of the above four segments of the nonprofit organization universe. They include the following publications:

*Audits of State and Local Governmental Units* (1989)

*Audits of Colleges and Universities* (1975)

*Audits of Providers of Health Care Services* (1990)

*Audits of Voluntary Health and Welfare Organizations* (1988).

Also as stated earlier the AICPA has also issued *Audits of Certain Nonprofit Organizations* (1987) to cover audits of other nonprofit organizations.

These guides should be used by the auditor in determining whether financial statements have been presented in accordance with GAAP.

## ■ Internal Controls

The auditor may find, for a number of reasons, that the internal controls for a nonprofit organization may be relatively weak compared with those found for most business enterprises. This observation may be particularly true for some charitable organizations.

The *weaknesses* in internal control can often be linked to the following operational characteristics:

1. The *governing body* (board of directors, board of trustees, or similar group) is often large and composed of volunteers who are relatively inactive in the day-to-day affairs of the organization. Furthermore, none of these people have ownership interests in the organization that they are trying to protect. Because of these characteristics, the auditor typically finds less emphasis on accountability and control by these groups than he or she would typically expect of a corporate board of directors.

2. There may be only a *limited amount of resources* that can be used to strengthen the system of internal control. Priorities in the operations of these organizations frequently place primary emphasis on implementing services and sustaining the organization rather than on improving internal control procedures.

3. The *accounting function* may receive relatively little attention because of a lack of staff or because the organization places most of its emphasis on its operating activities or programs.

4. The *staff of the organization* may be small, so that the desired segregation of duties is difficult to attain.

5. Nonprofit organizations *do not have the normal controls provided by customers in the profit area* because many resources are contributed without the expectation of receiving specific goods or services in exchange for them. For example, a person contributing cash to a nonprofit organization typically will receive only an acknowledging receipt from the solicitor. As a result, solicitors collecting contributions for a poorly controlled charitable organization may take the cash and simply not turn in the contribution.

The auditor should look for the following *control practices* to be used to reduce the probability of fraud or embezzlement of charitable contribution receipts:

1. *Honesty and integrity of persons* charged with the responsibility of soliciting contributions is the most effective way of controlling door-to-door solicitations. Beyond that, however, contributors should be provided with a *duplicate receipt form* by the solicitor carrying a statement that the contribution will be independently acknowledged from the charitable organization office. The other copy of the receipt should be retained and turned in with the cash.

2. *Two volunteers or two employees* in the charitable organization's office should be involved in receiving contributions from solicitors and through the mail. Ideally, these persons should perform independent counts of contributions, which should then be reconciled with copies of receipts by a responsible official.

3. A *list of contributions received,* showing each contributor's name, should be prepared as soon as contributions are received in the office of the organization. At this time, the office should also acknowledge the receipt of each contribution directly to its contributor. This element of control can also be achieved, to some extent, by publishing the list of contributors.

4.  The *list of prospects to be solicited* by each solicitor should be prepared in duplicate. The solicitor should then send one list with the money and pledges he or she has received to the soliciting team captain and the other directly to the charitable organization.

5.  *Acknowledgment forms* should be prenumbered, and an operating procedure requiring periodic accountability for all numbers should be established.

In addition to looking for the controls cited above, the auditor evaluating the system of internal control for a nonprofit organization should be concerned with the same characteristics of good internal control described earlier in the text: proper segregation of duties; clearly defined lines of authority and responsibility; adequately trained employees; appropriate records, authorization, and approval procedures; appropriate provision for protection of assets; and provisions for monitoring compliance with established operating policies. Furthermore, because of the characteristic weaknesses (described above), the auditor should exercise special care *not to depend as much on the system of internal control in auditing nonprofit organizations as he or she would in auditing business entities*. It is also desirable for the auditor to make some general judgments regarding the apparent honesty of employees and the general attitude toward establishing individual accountabilities within the organization.

## ◼ Special Audit Considerations

In presenting the financial statements for a nonprofit organization, the management of the organization is, in effect, making these assertions:

1.  Resources and obligations reflected in the statements exist.

2.  Recorded changes in those items (transactions) are valid and complete.

3.  Restrictions relating to the rights and obligations associated with resources have been met and are appropriately reflected in the statements.

4.  Resources, obligations, revenues, and expenses (or expenditures) have been valued at the appropriate amounts in the financial statements and have been allocated to the appropriate periods.

5.  Various financial statement components have been properly disclosed and presented in conformity with generally accepted accounting practices reflected in the entity's industry publication.

Notice that many of the financial statement assertions described in the preceding list for nonprofit entities are essentially the same as those for profit-seeking entities. Audit objectives for nonprofit entities are, therefore, also similar to those for profit-seeking entities and include: (1) verification of appropriate statement presentation; (2) verification of transaction validity; (3) verification of ownership; (4) verification of proper cutoff; (5) verification of proper valuation techniques; and (6) verification of existence.

However, as we have observed, the generally accepted accounting practices for many subentities (funds) in the nonprofit area are different from those for business enterprises. Therefore, it is important for the auditor to recognize those differences in deciding which auditing procedures will best meet the various audit objectives. Because of the natural inclination of nonprofit organizations to have less reliable systems of internal control than those found in business enterprises, *expansion of the substantive tests* of various asset and liability accounts is advisable in order to provide an appropriate level of confidence that the financial statements have been fairly presented. In addition, certain unique accounting practices for nonprofit entities may require special types of disclosures. In meeting the statement presentation objective, the auditor must be familiar with the statement formats and disclosures set forth by the various industry publications cited earlier. He or she should then take steps to see that the financial statements of the nonprofit client are organized along those lines.

Another very important difference in auditing nonprofit organization financial statements hinges on the necessity for the auditor to determine the extent to which management has adhered to the *various spending constraints* imposed on it. In this respect, we must recognize that the auditor providing an unqualified opinion on a nonprofit organization's financial statements is, in effect, saying that management has adhered to the spending constraints imposed by the governing board or constituency of the organization.

## The Evidence-Gathering Process

The special considerations just described and the operating characteristics of nonprofit organizations require the auditor to give special recognition to the following items in the evidence-gathering process and in meeting the reporting requirements associated with the audit of a nonprofit organization:

1. For many nonprofit organizations, the *budget* is a key element controlling the ways in which resources may be used. Therefore, in determining whether the management of the organization has effectively discharged its responsibilities to the governing board and the constituency, the auditor should review the actual results of operations and should question deviations from budgetary provisions.

2. It is important for the auditor to identify the specific body to whom the audit report should be rendered. Many nonprofit organizations will have *audit committees* made up of board members not involved in the day-to-day activities of the organization. When this arrangement exists, the auditor should meet with that committee prior to the audit for the purpose of defining the audit scope and discussing internal control problems and other particular areas or activities that the committee believes should be stressed during the audit. After the audit has been completed, the auditor should again meet with the audit committee to discuss the results of the audit, including areas where internal controls or operating procedures might be improved.

3. Special attention should be given to the system of control over the handling of cash receipts. Although, as we have observed earlier, the control over cash contributions may not be complete, it should be sufficient to provide reasonable assurance that contributions are not materially misstated.

4. The organization may receive *grants from outside organizations,* such as the federal government, which must be used in accordance with specified grant provisions. The auditor must be concerned with determining that the grant provisions have been met in the uses of such resources. Often, for example, the grant contract will include a stipulation that in the event funds are used improperly, the organization will be required to make refunds to the grantor equal to the misused resources. Thus, an improper use of grant funds could require the recognition of a liability to the grantor. Also, the auditor should be concerned with the distinction between revenue and deferred revenue in the receipt of grant funds. Often such funds should not be treated as revenues until they are committed to use for their intended purpose. This matter is discussed further later in this Appendix under "The Single Audit."

5. *Documents relating to restricted gifts* must be examined to determine that such resources are being used in accordance with the wishes of the donors. Often this requires the organization to carefully distinguish between spendable and nonspendable resources. Again, it may be necessary to evaluate the distinctions that have been made between revenues and deferred revenues. Because it is sometimes difficult to determine that funds have been used in accordance with donor restrictions, in some cases, the auditor may need to obtain the opinion of legal counsel in resolving this matter.

6. A major audit concern with organizations holding *pledges* is whether the pledges are, in fact, contingent assets that are not to be recognized until actual receipt or whether they should be shown as receivables. The industry audit guides and SOP 78-10 are not all in agreement on the appropriate accounting treatment for such items. Therefore, the auditor will need to refer to the pertinent publication for guidance in evaluating the client's treatment of pledges. If they are properly classified as assets, the auditor should apply the same auditing procedures to them as are applied to accounts receivable in the profit area.

7. Many nonprofit organizations receive *donated services.* If these are significant, certain key ratios, such as the relationship of supporting services to total contributions, can be significantly different if costs are imputed for those services than they would be if costs are not imputed for them. Generally speaking, the industry pronouncements restrict the circumstances under which the value of these service contributions should be recorded to those situations where they can be evaluated against the costs of professional personnel and are actually used to replace such personnel.

8. Some nonprofit organizations, particularly hospitals, receive *payments from third parties* for services provided. The auditor must be familiar with the contractual arrangements with such third-party payers. In evaluating receivables from Medicare, for example, the auditor should be familiar with the provisions of the Prospective Payment Plan. In the audit of receivables based on cash reimbursements contracts, the auditor must critically evaluate the practices followed in determining such costs to determine whether they conform to the requirements of the contract.

9.  Many nonprofit organizations solicit *members who agree to pay dues,* generally on an annual basis. Different membership levels are also provided by some organizations. The resources received in the form of membership dues would, by implication, be available for use during the membership year, which might be different from the fiscal period of the organization. Therefore, the auditor must give special attention to the possible need for deferring portions of such revenue. It is also desirable to provide an overall analysis of such dues in relationship to the recognized membership of the organization as a partial proof of cash inflows.

10. We have already observed that some nonprofit organizations use the *modified accrual basis of accounting,* which does not call for the capitalization or depreciation of fixed assets. Where this is the case, the records in support of fixed assets may be inadequate. The auditor, particularly during an initial audit, may need to conduct a physical inventory of and establish values for such assets. If historical costs are not known, a specialist may be needed to appraise such assets.

11. As we observed earlier, fund accounting practices carry with them the possibilities of *interfund transactions.* Borrowing between funds, for example, is not uncommon. However, when an operating fund borrows from a restricted fund, the auditor must be particularly concerned as to whether it violates the contractual constraints associated with restricted fund resources. Furthermore, the auditor must make sure that all interfund borrowings are disclosed and have been approved by the governing board. Sometimes the collectibility of interfund loans may be in doubt. In such a situation, the auditor must make a judgment as to whether a due-from (receivable) account in a particular fund would be more appropriately listed as a transfer.

12. The audit guides and SOP 78-10 generally require or encourage the *presentation of expenditures or expenses on a functional basis.* The auditor in these situations must be satisfied that the organization's cost allocation techniques adhere to GAAP.

13. If a nonprofit organization being audited *controls another financially interrelated organization,* the financial statements of the two organizations should be either combined or consolidated. The key word in this provision is *control.* It is defined in SOP 78-10 as "the direct or indirect ability to determine the direction of management and policies through ownership, by contract, or otherwise." When there is professed or readily apparent control of one organization over another, the auditor may need to insist upon access to the records of the legally separate organization in order to reach a satisfactory judgment regarding the possible need for consolidated or combined statements.

14. Generally speaking, nonprofit organizations are not subject to income taxes. However, because of a recent emphasis by the Internal Revenue Service on *taxing nonrelated net income* of these organizations, the auditor must give

special attention to these income sources. For example, pharmacy sales to nonpatients in a hospital can be construed to be subject to income taxes. Furthermore, the auditor should examine the information tax returns filed by the nonprofit organization to see that such reporting obligations have been properly met.[4]

## Reporting Requirements

If the evidence-gathering process supports the hypothesis that the financial statements of a nonprofit organization are fairly presented in accordance with the generally accepted accounting principles described in the pertinent industry audit guide, the auditor will use the standard short-form audit report in rendering an opinion on those statements. Qualified or adverse opinions would also be rendered because of deviations from industry GAAP or a violation of the principle of consistency. For most nonprofit organizations, this opinion will relate to the financial statements of the entity as a unit. However, in the governmental area, the Government Finance Officers Association (GFOA) has recommended that the scope of the annual audit should "also encompass the combining and individual financial statements of the funds and account groups."[5] This logically suggests that the opinion should make references to the fairness of these statements in relation to the combined financial statements for the governmental unit.

Some nonprofit organizations may use the cash basis of accounting, or modifications thereof, and in that way depart from GAAP. Still other nonprofit entities may use comprehensive bases of accounting to comply with the requirements of financial reporting provisions of a governmental regulatory agency to whose jurisdiction the entity is subject. When a comprehensive basis of accounting other than GAAP is used, the special reporting provisions of SAS 14 apply and essentially allow the auditor to express an unqualified audit opinion as long as the entity complies with a comprehensive basis of accounting (other than GAAP) having substantial support. In such cases, it is important for the auditor to recognize that financial statements developed from comprehensive bases of accounting other than GAAP should be properly labelled. The terms *balance sheet* and *income statement* are appropriate only for financial statements prepared in accordance with GAAP. In contrast, financial statements prepared on the cash basis of accounting might be described as statements of cash receipts and disbursements and statements of assets and liabilities arising from cash transactions. Also, since such statements do not reflect the financial condition or results of operations, the basis of accounting used should be described in the footnotes to the statements. The opinion paragraph of the audit report should be worded somewhat like this:

> In our opinion, the aforementioned statements present fairly the assets and liabilities of ABC Company at 12/31/X2, arising from cash transactions and the revenues collected and expenditures made by it during the year then ended, on the basis of accounting described in Note X, which basis is consistent with that of the preceding year.

4. Summarized from professional development materials provided by Texas Society of CPAs.
5. *Governmental Accounting, Auditing, and Financial Reporting* (Chicago: Government Finance Officers Association, 1988), p. 33.

The financial statements for the proprietary funds of governmental entities are organized and presented within essentially the same format as are the statements of business enterprises. The financial data for governmental funds, however, are typically presented in two statements, labelled as follows:

1. statement of revenues, expenditures, and changes in fund balances
2. balance sheet.

These statements are illustrated in Chapters 6 and 7.

Although colleges and universities place strong emphasis on fund accounting, the financial data will conventionally be presented through the medium of the following three financial statements, which show the combined data from various fund entity accounting records:

1. balance sheet
2. statement of changes in fund balances
3. statement of current funds revenues, expenditures, and other changes.

These statements are illustrated in Chapter 12.

As we have suggested earlier in the text, hospitals operate more like business enterprises than do any other nonprofit organizations. It follows logically, then, that their financial data should be presented within a format similar to that used for business entities. This includes four statements:

1. balance sheet
2. statement of revenues and expenses
3. statement of changes in fund balances
4. statement of cash flows.

These statements are illustrated in Chapter 11.

Voluntary health and welfare organizations use the accrual basis of accounting but also give much emphasis to fund accounting techniques. Their financial data reflect those influences as they are presented through the medium of three statements for the organization as a unit:

1. statement of support revenue and expenses and changes in fund balances
2. statement of functional expenses
3. balance sheet.

These statements are illustrated in Chapter 13.

# ■ The Single Audit

Grants from various agencies of the federal government frequently provide significant sources of financing for state and local government operations. Each of these grants is likely to have its own specific accountability and reporting requirements, which therefore may differ from program to program. Because each federal agency making a grant has the right to an onsight audit of the recipient of its grant, a state or local government with ten grants, for example, could be subject to ten different audits, as each individual agency determines whether the accountability and reporting requirements associated with its particular grant have been met. Obviously, this type of verification is inefficient and counterproductive. As a result, governmental entities have for some time sought a less cumbersome verification process.

The first efforts to standardize accountability reporting and auditing requirements occurred in 1979 when the Office of Management and Budget (OMB) issued Attachment P, *Audit Requirements to OMB Circular A-102* (Uniform Administrative Requirements for Grants in Aid Made to State and Local Governments). This document *directed that audits be made on an organization-wide basis rather than on a grant-by-grant basis*. This was the first official movement towards use of the single audit.

Essentially, the single audit was to have the following characteristics:

conducted on an organization-wide basis rather than on a grant-by-grant basis

includes financial and compliance audits, but not efficiency or effectiveness audits

satisfies the audit needs of all levels of government

performed by independent grantee or grantee-designated auditors

conducted at least once every two years

monitored by designated federal "cognizant" audit agency

follows standard guidelines

issues audit reports using standard requirements.[6]

Later, the OMB began assigning cognizant audit agencies to state and larger local governmental entities. In 1981, *Cognizant Audit Agency Guidelines* under OMB Circular A-102 was developed and approved by the Federal Inspectors General and issued by the Joint Financial Improvement Program.[7] These actions ultimately led to the Single Audit Act of 1984, which was designed to

1.  improve the financial management of state and local governments with respect to federal financial assistance programs

2.  establish uniform requirements for audits of federal financial assistance grants provided to state and local governments

3.  promote the efficient and effective use of audit resources

4.  ensure that federal departments and agencies, to the maximum extent practicable, rely on and use audit work pursuant to this Act.[8]

The Act requires any state or local government receiving a total of $100,000 or more of federal assistance grants per fiscal year to have an audit made in accordance with the provisions of the Single Audit Act. This minimum amount, incidentally, in-

6.  Chuck Hamilton, "SIS10: The Uniform Single Financial Audit Bill," *Government Accountants Journal,* 32(3):1 (1983).
7.  D. Scott Showalter and John R. Miller, "A Report Card on the Single Audit Concept," *Government Accountants Journal* (Spring 1984), p. 45.
8.  W. Broadus, Jr. and Joseph D. Comtois, "The Single Audit Act: A Needed Reform," *Journal of Accountancy* (April 1985), p. 63.

cludes "pass through" grants, which in effect, require most state and local governments to have such an annual audit performed.

The act further provides that state and local governmental units receiving only $25,000–$100,000 in federal assistance grants have the option of having an organization-wide audit performed or simply complying with the reporting statutes of the individual governmental programs. Those entities receiving less than $25,000 are exempt but must maintain records that are accessible to the comptroller general or the federal agencies.

These audits are *required to be conducted in accordance with generally accepted governmental auditing standards applying to financial and compliance audits.* However, they do not require economy and efficiency audits or program evaluations unless those are required under the laws applying to the grants. The single audit can be performed by any independent auditor, which is defined to include external state or local governmental auditors that meet the independence standards or public accountants who meet those standards.

Thus, independent auditors making audits of governmental entities receiving federal funds will have to comply with the AICPA auditing standards listed on pages 677–679 plus government standards for auditing governmental organizations, programs, activities, and functions (otherwise known as the "yellow book"). As is evident in Figure A–1, these standards govern not only financial audits but also performance audits. The single audit requires adherence only to the general standards and financial audits standards.

In this context, financial auditing includes the traditional function of providing an independent opinion as to whether an entity's financial statements present fairly the results of financial operations and whether other financial information is presented in conformity with GAAP or other stated criteria. In the case of a governmental entity, GAAP includes financial reporting requirements of the Governmental Accounting Standards Board (GASB), the FASB, and the GAO. Some state and local governments and regulatory bodies also have established specific accounting principles. However, besides providing reasonable assurance regarding fair presentation of financial statements, the financial audit prescribed by the GAO also encompasses procedures designed to determine whether the entity has adhered to specific *financial compliance requirements,* such as those prescribed by grant contracts.

The Single Audit Act requires that reports showing the findings of the audits of federal grants be transmitted to the appropriate federal officials within thirty days after completion of the audit. If the audit finds noncompliance, the auditee is required to submit a plan for corrective action to the appropriate federal officials. That plan must be consistent with the internal control standards established by the comptroller general under 31 U.S.C. 3511, the *Federal Financial Managers' Integrity Act* referred to in Chapter 10 (see page 384).

The act also requires oversight and monitoring by federal agencies. The OMB is charged with the responsibility of designating the cognizant agency, which is then held responsible for implementing the requirements of the act with respect to particular state or local governmental entities. Those responsibilities include:

1.   seeing that audits are performed in a timely manner and in accordance with the requirements of the act

**FIGURE A–1.** Generally Accepted Government Auditing Standards (GAGAS)

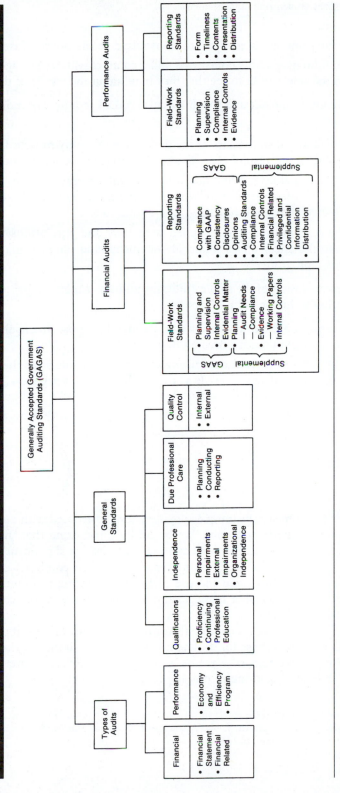

*Source: Washington, D.C.-General Accounting Office, 1988.*

2.  seeing that audit reports are transmitted to the appropriate federal officials

3.  coordinating audits done by or under contract with federal agencies in addition to the single audit to see that they build upon the results of the single audit.[9]

The Single Audit Act and OMB Circular A-124 require the auditor to determine whether:

1.  the financial statements of the governmental entity present fairly its financial position and results of its financial operations in accordance with GAAP

2.  the internal accounting and other control systems provide reasonable assurance that federal financial assistance programs have been carried out in compliance with applicable laws and regulations

3.  the organization has complied with laws and regulations that may have a material effect on its financial statements and on each major federal assistance program.[10]

At the conclusion of the single audit, the auditor is required to issue the following reports relating to his or her findings:

1.  a report on the examination of the general purpose financial statement of the governmental entity covered by the audit

2.  a report on internal accounting control based solely on the study and evaluation of that system made as part of the audit of the general purpose or basic financial statements

3.  a report on compliance with laws and regulations that may have a material effect on the financial statements.[11]

## ■ Summary

In this appendix, some of the unique considerations associated with audits of nonprofit organizations have been explained. We began by recognizing that, for some of these organizations, generally accepted accounting practices are significantly different from the GAAP for profit entities. This difference extends to emphasis on appropriation controls over expenditures and the use of fund accounting techniques. The auditor, therefore, must judge whether management has complied with the constraints associated with those controls.

We also observed that the internal control systems for nonprofit organizations are often less effective than those for profit entities. Thus, the auditor normally must extend his or her substantive tests of account balances and must rely more heavily on those procedures in rendering an audit opinion.

9.  Broadus and Comtois, p. 65.
10. American Institute of Certified Public Accountants, *Audits of State and Local Governmental Units* (New York: AICPA, 1986), p. 135.
11. Ibid., p. 136.

Next, fourteen special audit considerations associated with the evidence-gathering process in auditing nonprofit organizations were listed and described. We also described the special financial-reporting formats followed for governmental funds, colleges and universities, hospitals, and health and welfare agencies.

In the last section of the appendix, we briefly described the single audit as a technique designed to overcome the inefficiencies associated with the performance of separate audits of each of the individual grants received by a state or local governmental unit.

## ■ Suggested Supplementary References

Casabona, Patrick A., and Anthony T. Barbera. "Survey of Procedures for Selection of External Auditors by Public Sector Entities." *Government Accountants Journal* (Summer 1987).

DeStefano, David. "Using Computer-Assisted Audit Techniques in Public Sector Audits." *Government Accountants Journal* (Fall 1989).

Dittenhofer, Mortimer A. "State and Local Government Audit Committees." *Government Accountants Journal* (Summer 1988).

Dumil, James, and Peter Millspaugh. "Government Auditing and Legal Liability." *Government Accountants Journal* (Fall 1988).

Eckert, Harvey, Edward M. Klasny, and Dennis D. Moody. "Joint Audits for Governments—The Pennsylvania Experience." *Government Accountants Journal* (Winter 1986–87).

Foltz, Roland P., and Gilbert W. Crain. "Auditing Internal Administrative Controls for Federal Financing Assistance Programs." *Government Accountants Journal* (Winter 1987–88).

Hanley, Thomas R., and Frank S. Synowiec, Jr. "Look What's New with the Single Audit Guide." *Government Accountants Journal* (Spring 1986).

Heins, Stephen, Sharon R. Parrish, and Relmond P. Van Daniker. "Quality Assurance at the State Audit Level." *Government Accountants Journal* (Fall 1987).

Kraft, William H., Jr. "Audit Management—A Practical Perspective." *Government Accountants Journal* (Winter 1987–88).

Kusserow, Richard B. "Audit Financial Statements: The Social Security Administration Experience." *Government Accountants Journal* (Summer 1988).

McBride, Peggy. "Preparing for the Single Audit." *Government Accountants Journal* (Fall 1986).

Raaum, Ronell B. "Precise Objective—Prerequisite to a Quality Audit." *Government Accountants Journal* (Summer 1988).

Rothschild, Joseph. "Evaluating Internal Controls: Are the Auditors as Good as the Audit Standards?" *Government Accountants Journal* (Summer 1986).

Stelzer, Patrick T., and Robert A. Gray. "Training Adults to Use Micro-Computers: A Technical and Psychological Approach." *Government Accountants Journal* (Fall 1988).

Stepnick, Edward W. "The Nitty-Gritty and Hurly-Burly of Government Auditing: It's All in My Working Papers." *Government Accountants Journal* (Winter 1987–88).

Swafford, James. "Communications in an 'Auditor's World.'" *Government Accountants Journal* (Summer 1986).

Tracy, Richard C. "Performance Auditing: Catalyst for Change in Portland, Oregon." *Government Finance Review* (February 1988).

Van Beverhoudt, Arnold E., Jr. "The Tools of the Electronic Auditor." *Government Accountants Journal* (Fall 1987).

Wilder, Michael C. "Good Internal Audits Don't Just Happen." *Government Accountants Journal* (Summer 1987).

# ■ Questions for Class Discussion

QA-1.   What are four different types of nonprofit entities?

QA-2.   What operating characteristics distinguish nonprofit entities from business-type entities?

QA-3.   What are the primary differences between generally accepted accounting practices for business entities and generally accepted accounting practices for governmental entities? Justify the difference.

QA-4.   What do we mean by the term *appropriation control*? Why is it used in the nonprofit area?

QA-5.   How are fund accounting practices different from the accounting practices of business entities? Why are fund accounting practices followed by nonprofit entities?

QA-6.   What is the difference between governmental and proprietary funds?

QA-7.   What is the difference between the terms *expenditures* and *expenses*?

QA-8.   How do the transactions typically associated with a capital projects fund compare with those carried out through the general fund?

QA-9.   How does a special assessment capital projects fund differ from a capital projects fund?

QA-10.  How do the operations of enterprise funds differ from the operations of internal service funds?

QA-11.  What is meant by the *modified accrual basis of accounting*? Explain. In what situations is that basis of accounting in accordance with generally accepted accounting principles?

QA-12.  How do expenditure accounts differ from encumbrance accounts? Under what circumstances would the encumbrance and reserve for encumbrance accounts be used?

QA-13.  Which operating characteristics often contribute to weaknesses in the systems of internal control for nonprofit organizations?

QA-14.  What control practices should normally be associated with handling and recording the receipts of charitable contributions to reduce the probability of fraud or embezzlement? Indicate the type of fraud or embezzlement that each practice is designed to prevent.

QA-15.  How do the formats of financial statements for governmental entities compare with those of business entities?

QA-16.  How do the statement formats for college and university financial statements compare with those of business entities?

QA-17.  Of what significance is the emphasis on appropriation control by governmental units in the audits of such units?

QA-18.  Is the auditor concerned with examining the budgetary data for a governmental unit in connection with the audit of such an entity? Explain.

QA-19.  Many nonprofit organizations receive restricted gifts; what are the auditor's special responsibilities in verifying restricted gifts transactions?

QA-20.  Should pledges solicited by a nonprofit organization be shown as an asset in the organization's balance sheet? Discuss.

QA-21.  What is the significance of donated services in the audit of nonprofit organization financial statements?

QA-22.  What special concerns does an auditor have in verifying claims against third-party payers in auditing the financial statements of a hospital?

QA-23. What is the key consideration in determining whether the financial statements of two or more financially interrelated nonprofit organizations should be combined or consolidated?

QA-24. What wording should be used in the opinion portion of an audit report for a nonprofit organization that used the cash basis of accounting rather than the generally acceptable basis? Justify each of the different phrases used.

QA-25. How does the financial statement format followed for hospitals compare with that used for business entities? Justify the differences.

QA-26. What is the significance of supporting services in presenting the operating results for a health and welfare agency? Discuss.

# ■ Exercises

EA-1. A friend of yours who has been operating a business for some years is commenting on the problems of preventing fraud and embezzlement. Another member of the group discussing the problem is Edgar Fallows, the chief executive officer for a large health and welfare agency. Fallows responds with a statement that the resources of his organization are even more vulnerable to fraud and embezzlement than are those of a business enterprise.

**Required:**
Discuss the justification for Fallows's remark.

EA-2. Laura Canavan shows you a statement of revenues and expenditures for the general fund of the city in which she lives. She, too, is an accounting student but does not understand why the city has used the term *expenditures* rather than *expenses* to describe its outflows of resources.

**Required:**
Explain the difference between the two terms; justify the use of the term *expenditures* in the governmental statements.

EA-3. You are working as a staff accountant on the audit of River City's financial statements. You have been assigned to review the transactions of a capital projects fund. During the course of your examination, you discover a disbursement of capital project fund resources for municipal employee salaries.

**Required:**
Explain the concern that you, as an auditor, would have about such a transaction.

EA-4. In examining the engagement letter for the audit of Millersville's financial statements, you discover that the senior in charge has requested the city manager to provide the audit staff with a copy of the city budget. Another staff accountant working with you states that he does not understand why the audit team would be concerned with budgetary data since the primary objective of the audit is to determine whether the financial statements are fairly presented.

**Required:**
Explain to your co-worker why the senior has requested a copy of the city budget.

EA-5.    In the audit of a governmental entity, you discover a significant balance in an account called Revenues from Grants.

**Required:**
What special auditing procedures should be applied in the verification of this account and the resources received in connection with it?

EA-6.    You are auditing the financial statements of a university. During the audit you find that the university has received a significant number of gifts from its constituency.

**Required:**
Explain your special concerns in verifying the transactions giving recognition to those gifts.

EA-7.    In auditing the financial statements of a health and welfare agency, Carol Campanelli discovers an account entitled Pledge Revenue.

**Required:**
Describe the special concerns that Campanelli would have as an auditor in verifying that account and its related assets accounts.

EA-8.    In auditing the financial statements of a hospital, you discover a large balance in an account entitled Receivable from Medical Insurance Claims.

**Required:**
Explain the special concerns you would have in the examination of that account and its related nominal accounts.

EA-9.    In auditing the financial statements of a university, Gunther Schmidt, CPA, discovers that a number of fixed assets have been purchased by use of current fund resources during the period under audit. All of these have been debited to expenditure accounts rather than to the specific fixed-assets accounts.

**Required:**
Comment on this procedure, and suggest a reasonable course of action for Schmidt to undertake in verifying these items.

EA-10.    During the audit of the city of Hillsboro, you have been assigned the responsibility of examining interfund transactions. Some of these involve loans from certain restricted funds to the Hillsboro general fund.

**Required:**
Discuss any concerns you might have relating to such transactions.

# ◼ Problems

PA-1.    Select the best answer for each of the following items:
1.    Governmental auditing often extends beyond examinations leading to the expression of opinion on the fairness of financial presentation and includes audits of efficiency, economy, effectiveness, and also:

    a.  accuracy.

    b.  evaluation.

    c.  compliance.

    d.  internal control.

2.  A nonprofit organization published a monthly magazine that had 15,000 subscribers on January 1, 19X6. The number of subscribers increased steadily throughout the year, and at December 31, 19X6, there were 16,200 subscribers. The annual magazine subscription cost was $10 on January 1, 19X6, and was increased to $12 for new members on April 1, 19X6. An auditor would expect that the receipts from subscriptions for the year ended December 31, 19X6, would be approximately:

    a.  $179,400.

    b.  $171,600.

    c.  $164,400.

    d.  $163,800.

3.  How should charity service, contractual adjustments, and bad debts be classified in the statement of revenues and expenses for a hospital?

    a.  All three should be treated as expenses.

    b.  All three should be treated as deductions from patient service revenues.

    c.  Charity service and contractual adjustments should be treated as revenue deductions, whereas bad debts should be treated as an expense.

    d.  Charity service and bad debts should be treated as expenses, whereas contractual adjustments should be treated as a revenue deduction.

4.  A university receives a cash gift in the amount of $500,000, which the donor specifies shall be used in constructing a classroom building. This gift should be recorded as:

    a.  gift revenue in the unrestricted current fund.

    b.  gift revenue in the restricted current fund.

    c.  an increase to cash and fund balance in the plant fund.

    d.  a quasi endowment in the endowment fund.

5.  What would be the effect on the general fund balance in the current fiscal year of recording a $15,000 purchase for a new fire truck out of general fund resources, for which a $14,600 encumbrance had been recorded in the general fund in the previous fiscal year?

    a.  a reduction in the general fund balance of $15,000

    b.  a reduction in the general fund balance of $14,600

    c.  a reduction in the general fund balance of $400

    d.  It would have no effect on the general fund balance.

6.  Brockton City's debt-service fund (for term bonds) recorded required additions and required earnings for the current fiscal year of $15,000 and $7,000, respectively. The actual revenues and interest earnings were $16,000 and $6,500, respectively. What are the necessary entries to record the year's actual additions and earnings in the debt-service fund and in the general long-term debt group, respectively?

   a.  $22,500 and $22,000
   b.  $22,000 and $22,000
   c.  $22,500 and $22,500
   d.  $22,500 and no entry

**—AICPA Adapted**

PA-2.  At the beginning of your examination of the accounts of the City of Waterford, you discovered that the bookkeeper failed to keep the accounts by funds. The trial balance of the general fund for the year ended December 31, 19X2, shown below, was available.
Your examination disclosed that:

   a.  The budget for the year 19X2, not recorded on the books, reflected estimated revenues and expenditures as follows: revenues $815,000, expenditures $775,000.
   b.  Outstanding purchase orders at December 31, 19X2, for operating expenses not recorded on the books totalled $2,500.
   c.  Included in the revenues account is a credit of $190,000, representing the value of land donated by the state as a grant-in-aid for construction of the River Bridge.
   d.  Interest payable in future years totals $60,000 on River Bridge bonds sold at par for $200,000.
   e.  Examination of the subledger containing the details of the appropriation expenditures account revealed the following items included therein:

| | |
|---|---:|
| Current operating expenses | $472,000 |
| Additions to structures and improvements | 210,000 |
| Equipment purchases | 10,000 |
| General obligation bonds paid | 50,000 |
| Interest paid on general obligation bonds | 18,000 |

### City of Waterford General Fund Trial Balance for December 31, 19X2

| | Debit | Credit |
|---|---:|---:|
| Cash | $ 207,500 | |
| Taxes receivable—current | 148,500 | |
| Allowance for uncollectible taxes—current | | $ 6,000 |
| Appropriation expenditures | 760,000 | |
| Revenues | | 992,500 |
| Donated land | 190,000 | |
| River Bridge bonds authorized—unissued | 100,000 | |
| Work in process—River Bridge | 130,000 | |
| River Bridge bonds payable | | 200,000 |
| Contracts payable—River Bridge | | 25,000 |
| Retained percentage—River Bridge contracts | | 5,000 |
| Vouchers payable | | 7,500 |
| Fund balance | | 300,000 |
| Total | $1,536,000 | $1,536,000 |

**Required:**
Prepare a worksheet showing the given general fund trial balance, adjusting entries, and distributions to the proper funds or groups of accounts. The following column headings are recommended:

> General fund trial balance—debit
>
> General fund trial balance—credit
>
> Adjustments—debit
>
> Adjustments—credit
>
> General fund—debit
>
> General fund—credit
>
> Capital projects fund
>
> General fixed assets
>
> General long-term debt.

Number all adjusting and transaction entries. Formal journal entries are not required.

**—AICPA Adapted**

PA-3.   The current funds trial balances for Apex University are shown below.

| | Current Unrestricted Funds | | Current Restricted Funds | |
|---|---|---|---|---|
| Cash | $ 105,000 | | $ 60,000 | |
| Investments | 40,000 | | 30,000 | |
| Accounts payable | | $ 55,000 | | $ 12,000 |
| Tuition and fees | | 1,200,000 | | |
| Gifts | | 300,000 | | 150,000 |
| Auxiliary activities revenue | | 500,000 | | |
| Endowment income | | 200,000 | | 75,000 |
| Instructional expenditures | 1,300,000 | | | |
| Student aid | 75,000 | | 125,000 | |
| Research expenditures | | | 40,000 | |
| Operating expenditures | 600,000 | | | |
| Library expenditures | | | 10,000 | |
| Auxiliary activities expenditures | 480,000 | | | |
| Fund balance | | 345,000 | | 28,000 |
| Totals | $2,600,000 | $2,600,000 | $265,000 | $265,000 |

**Required:**
Prepare financial statements for the current funds.

PA-4.   Hillcrest Blood Bank is a nonprofit organization handling all its operations through one operating fund. Its statement of cash receipts and disbursements for the year ended June 30, 19X2, is shown on page 702, and its balance sheets as of June 30, 19X1, and June 30, 19X2, follow.

### Hillcrest Blood Bank Statement of Cash Receipts and Disbursements for the Year Ending June 30, 19X2

| | | | |
|---|---|---:|---:|
| Balance, July 1, 19X1 | | | |
| Cash in bank | | | $ 2,712 |
| Receipts | | | |
| From hospitals: | | | |
| Hillcrest Hospital | $7,702 | | |
| Good Samaritan Hospital | 3,818 | $11,520 | |
| Individuals | | 6,675 | |
| From other blood banks | | 602 | |
| From sales of serum and supplies | | 2,260 | |
| Interest on bonds | | 525 | |
| Gifts and bequests | | 4,928 | |
| Total receipts | | | 26,510 |
| Total to be accounted for | | | 29,222 |
| | | | |
| Disbursements: | | | |
| Laboratory expense: | | | |
| Serum | $3,098 | | |
| Salaries | 3,392 | | |
| Supplies | 3,533 | | |
| Laundry and miscellaneous | 277 | 10,300 | |
| | | | |
| Other expenses and disbursements: | | | |
| Salaries | 5,774 | | |
| Dues and subscriptions | 204 | | |
| Rent and utilities | 1,404 | | |
| Blood testing | 2,378 | | |
| Payments to other blood banks for blood given to members away from home | 854 | | |
| Payments to professional blood donors | 2,410 | | |
| Other expenses | 1,805 | | |
| Purchase of U.S. Treasury bond | 1,000 | 15,829 | |
| Total disbursements | | | 26,129 |
| | | | |
| Balance, June 30, 19X2 | | | $ 3,093 |

## Hillcrest Blood Bank Balance Sheets

| | June 30, 19X1 | June 30, 19X2 |
|---|---|---|
| **Assets** | | |
| Cash | $ 2,712 | $ 3,093 |
| U.S. Treasury bonds | 15,000 | 16,000 |
| Accounts receivable—sales of blood: | | |
| Hospitals | 1,302 | 1,448 |
| Individuals | 425 | 550 |
| Inventories: | | |
| Blood | 480 | 640 |
| Supplies and serum | 250 | 315 |
| Furniture and equipment, less depreciation | 4,400 | 4,050 |
| Total assets | $24,569 | $26,096 |
| **Liabilities and Surplus** | | |
| Accounts payable—supplies | $ 325 | $ 275 |
| Fund balance | 24,244 | 25,821 |
| Total liabilities and fund balance | $24,569 | $26,096 |

**Required:**
A. Prepare a transactions worksheet for the Hillcrest Blood Bank that develops data for an accrual-based operating statement and end-of-period balance sheet.
B. Prepare appropriate accrual-based financial statements.

**—AICPA Adapted**

PA-5. Assume that you are a CPA who has recently acquired a large local church as an audit client. Since this is the first audit client of its type for your firm, you feel it is necessary to instruct the audit staff as to particular problem areas often associated with the audit of charitable organizations before proceeding with the engagement. You have arranged for a conference with the audit senior to discuss the upcoming engagement.

**Required:**
Outline the agenda of the upcoming meeting, giving particular attention to:
A. potential internal control problems to look for and attributes of the church's system of internal controls that might prevent, detect, or correct the problems
B. areas of special emphasis, if any, during the substantive testing phase of the audit
C. the audit report to be issued on financial statements of the church at the conclusion of the audit.

# Master Glossary

**Accounting System.** The total structure of records and procedures that discover, record, classify, summarize, and report information on the financial position and results of operations of any entity including a government or any of its funds, fund types, balanced account groups, or organizational components.

**Accrual Basis.** The basis of accounting under which inflows of resources are recognized as revenues when the rights to them have been earned, and resource outflows are recognized as expenses when resources and services are used.

**Adjusting Entries.** Nontransaction changes in assets and liabilities and the offsetting changes in revenue and expense items required to meet the earning and use criteria established under the accrual basis of accounting.

**Agency Fund.** A fund used to account for assets held by a government as an agent for individuals, private organizations, other governments, and/or other funds; for example, taxes collected and held by a municipality for a school district.

**Agency Funds.** Accounting entities used in college and university accounting systems to account for resources held by the institution as custodian or fiscal agent for students, faculty, staff members, and organizations.

**Allocated Appropriations.** Previously appropriated amount distributed between periods or to different segments of a fiscal period.

**Amount Available in Debt-Service Funds.** An "other debit" account in the general long-term debt account group that designates the amount of assets available in debt-service funds for the retirement of general obligation debt.

**Amount to Be Provided.** An "other debit" account in the general long-term debt account group that represents the amount to be provided from taxes or other general revenues to retire outstanding general long-term debt.

Approximately 60 percent of the items included in this glossary are taken or adapted, with permission, from the glossary contained in *Governmental Accounting, Auditing and Financial Reporting,* published by the Municipal Finance Officers Association—now Government Finance Officers Association—in 1988.

**Annuity Funds.**   Accounting entities used in college and university accounting systems to account for resources held by the institution under agreements whereby money or other property is made available to the institution on condition that the institution bind itself to pay stipulated amounts periodically to the donors or other designated individuals with such payments to terminate at the time designated in the annuity agreement.

**Appropriable Resources.**   Spendable resources available for use in carrying out general operations.

**Appropriation.**   A legal authorization granted by a legislative body to make expenditures and to incur obligations for specific purposes. An appropriation is usually limited in amount and as to the time when it may be expended.

**Appropriation Account.**   A budgetary account set up to record specific authorizations to spend. The account is credited with original and any supplemental appropriations and is charged with expenditures and encumbrances.

**Appropriation Bill, Ordinance, Resolution, or Order.**   A bill, ordinance, resolution, or order by means of which appropriations are given legal effect. It is the method by which the expenditure side of the annual operating budget is enacted into law by the legislative body. In many governmental jurisdictions, appropriations cannot be enacted into law by resolution but only by a bill, ordinance, or order.

**Appropriation Control.**   The control placed on the incurrence of expenditures by virtue of legal authorizations granted by a legislative or other controlling body.

**Appropriation Expenditure.**   An expenditure chargeable to an appropriation. Since virtually all expenditures of governments are chargeable to appropriations, the term *expenditures* by itself is widely and properly used.

**Appropriation Ledger.**   A subsidiary ledger containing an account for each appropriation. Each account usually shows the amount originally appropriated, transfers to or from the appropriation, amounts charged against the appropriation, the net balance, and other related information.

**Assess.**   To value property officially for the purpose of taxation.

**Assessed Valuation.**   A valuation set upon real estate or other property by a government as a basis for levying taxes.

**Assessment.**   (1) The process of making the official valuation of property for purposes of taxation. (2) The valuation placed upon property as a result of this process.

**Auxiliary Enterprises.**   A segment of college and university operations that furnishes a service directly or indirectly to students, faculty, or staff and charges a fee related to but not necessarily equal to the cost of services.

**Balance Sheet.**   The basic financial statement that discloses the assets, liabilities, and equities of an entity at a specified date in conformity with GAAP.

**Basic Financial Statements.**   Those financial statements, including notes thereto, that are necessary for a fair presentation of the financial position and results of operations of an entity in conformity with GAAP. Under Statement 1, basic financial statements include a balance sheet, an "all inclusive" operating statement, and (for proprietary funds, pension trust funds, and nonexpendable trust funds) a statement of changes in financial position (now statement of cash flows). See *Financial Reporting Pyramid*; *Combined Statements—Overview*; *Combining Statements—By Fund Type*; *General Purpose Financial Statements (GPFS)*; and *Generally Accepted Accounting Principles (GAAP)*.

**Benevolences.**   The outflows of a church's resources used to support activities beyond the scope of the local church program.

**Bond.**   A written promise to pay a specified sum of money, called the *face value* or *principal amount,* at a specified date or dates in the future, called the *maturity date(s),* together with periodic interest at a specified rate. The difference between a note and a bond is that the latter runs for a longer period of time and requires greater legal formality.

**Bond Discount.**   The excess of the face value of a bond over the price for which it is acquired or sold. The price does not include accrued interest at the date of acquisition or sale.

**Bond Fund.**   A fund formerly used to account for the proceeds of general obligation bond issues. Such proceeds are now accounted for in a capital projects fund.

**Bond Ordinance or Resolution.**   An ordinance or resolution authorizing a bond issue.

**Bond Premium.**   The excess of the price at which a bond is acquired or sold over its face value. The price does not include accrued interest at the date of acquisition or sale.

**Bonds Authorized and Unissued.**   Bonds that have been legally authorized but not issued and that can be issued and sold without further authorization. This term must not be confused with the term *margin of borrowing power* or *legal debt margin,* either one of which represents the difference between the legal debt limit of a government and the debt outstanding against it.

**Bonds Issued.**   Bonds sold.

**Bonds Payable.**   The face value of bonds issued and unpaid.

**Budget.**   A plan of financial operation embodying an estimate of proposed expenditures for a given period and the proposed means of financing them. Used without any modifier, the term usually indicates a financial plan for a single fiscal year. The term *budget* is used in two senses in practice. Sometimes it designates the financial plan presented to the appropriating body for adoption and sometimes the plan finally approved by that body. It is usually necessary to specify whether the budget under consideration is preliminary and tentative or whether it has been approved by the appropriating body.

**Budgetary Accounts.**   Accounts used to enter the formally adopted annual operating budget into the general ledger as part of the management control technique of formal budgetary integration.

**Budgetary Comparisons.**   Governmental GAAP financial reports must include comparisons of approved budgeted amounts with actual results of operations. Such reports should be subjected to an independent audit, so that all parties involved in the annual operating budget/legal appropriation process are provided with assurances that government monies are spent in accordance with the mutually agreed-upon budgetary plan.

**Budgetary Control.** The control or management of a government or enterprise in accordance with an approved budget for the purpose of keeping expenditures within the limitations of available appropriations and available revenues.

**Bureau of the Budget (BOB).** A department of the executive branch of the U.S. government charged with assembling the budgeting data submitted by the various departments of the government and presenting the composite budget to Congress.

**CAFR.** See *Comprehensive Annual Financial Report.*

**Capital Expenditures.** Outflows of spendable resources for the acquisitions of long-term assets.

**Capital Outlays.** Expenditures that result in the acquisition of or addition to fixed assets.

**Capital Program.** A plan for capital expenditures to be incurred each year over a fixed period of years to meet capital needs arising from the long-term work program or otherwise. It sets forth each project or other contemplated expenditure in which the government is to have a part and specifies the full resources estimated to be available to finance the projected expenditures.

**Capital Projects Fund.** A fund created to account for financial resources to be used for acquisition or construction of major capital facilities (other than those financed by proprietary funds, special assessments, and trust funds).

**Cash Basis.** A basis of accounting under which transactions are recognized only when cash changes hands.

**Central Financial Management System (CFMS).** A system designed by the Treasury Department to augment its reporting capability and to facilitate its supervision over agency operations.

**Closing Entries.** Entries recorded at the end of each fiscal period to transfer the balances in the various revenue and expense or expenditure accounts to the permanent equity accounts of an accounting entity.

**Combined Statements—Overview.** The five basic financial statements comprising the first of the financial reporting pyramid's three reporting levels containing GAAP basic financial statements. They include: (1) combined balance sheet—all fund types and account groups; (2) combined statement of revenues, expenditures, and changes in fund balances—all governmental fund types; (3) combined statement of revenues, expenditures, and changes in fund balances—budget and actual—general and special revenue fund types (and similar governmental fund types for which annual budgets have been legally adopted); (4) combined statement of revenues, expenses, and changes in retained earnings (or equity)—all proprietary fund types; (5) combined statement of changes in financial position (now statement of cash flows)—all proprietary fund types; and (6) notes to the financial statements. Trust fund operations may be reported in (2), (4), and (5) above, as appropriate, or separately. The combined statements—overview are also referred to as the "liftable" general purpose financial statements (GPFS).

**Combining Statements—By Fund Type.** The second of the financial reporting pyramid's three reporting levels containing GAAP basic financial statements. Such statements are presented for each fund type for which the government maintains more than one fund. They include GAAP basic financial statements for each fund of a particular fund type in separate adjacent columns and a total column that duplicates the column for that fund type in the combined statements—overview.

**Comprehensive Annual Financial Report (CAFR).** The official annual report of a government. It includes five combined statements—overview (the "liftable" GPFS) and basic financial statements for each individual fund and account group prepared in conformity with GAAP and organized into a financial reporting pyramid. It also includes supporting schedules necessary to demonstrate compliance with finance-related legal and contractual provisions, extensive introductory material, and a detailed statistical section. Every government should prepare and publish a CAFR as a matter of public record.

**Comptroller General.** The head of the General Accounting Office.

**Congressional Budget Office.** Office, operating under supervision of Congress, charged with responsibility relating to the development and analysis of the federal budget.

**Conservatism.** The interpretation of accounting valuations and classifications so as to reflect the less or least optimistic disclosure of equally acceptable alternatives.

**Consistency.** The use of the same generally accepted accounting practice for a particular reporting entity in each succeeding period.

**Constituency.** All those who directly support an organization; in the case of a nonprofit enterprise, this group includes those contributing time or resources without receiving equivalent tangible benefits in exchange for those contributions.

**Contracts Payable—Retained Percentage.** A liability account reflecting amounts due on construction contracts that have been completed but on which part of the liability has not been paid pending final inspection or the lapse of a specified time period, or both. The unpaid amount is usually a stated percentage of the contract price.

**Contribution Margin.** An amount equal to the difference between sales revenue and variable costs.

**Control Account.** An account in the general ledger in which are recorded the aggregate of debit and credit postings to a number of identical or related accounts called *subsidiary accounts*. For example, taxes receivable is a control account supported by the aggregate of balances in individual property taxpayers' accounts. See *Subsidiary Account*.

**Cost.** The amount of money or other consideration exchanged for property or services. Costs may be incurred even before money is paid; that is, as soon as a liability is incurred. Ultimately, however, money or other consideration must be given in exchange. Again, the cost of some property or service may, in turn, become a part of the cost of another property or service. For example, the cost of part or all of the materials purchased at a certain time will be reflected in the cost of articles made from such materials or in the cost of those services in the rendering of which the materials were used.

**Cost–Volume Relationships.** The identifiable relationship between the aggregate amount of a cost and the volume of operations.

**Council of Economic Advisors.** A group of economists, operating under the supervision of the president, charged with the responsibility of economic forecasting and projections.

**Cumulative Results of Operations.** An account used to reflect the accumulated net difference between total expenses and losses of a governmental agency and the total financing sources and gains of the agency since its inception (comparable to retained earnings for a business entity).

**Current Funds.** The accounting entities used to record the inflows and outflows of operating resources for colleges and universities and health and welfare agencies. The net resources in these funds are divided into unrestricted and restricted subdivisions.

**Current Liquidity.** An entity's ability to meet current obligations as those obligations come due.

**Current Special Assessments.** Special assessments levied and becoming due within one year.

**Current Taxes.** Taxes levied and becoming due within one year.

**Custodian Fund.** An accounting entity used to account for assets received by a health and welfare organization to be held or disbursed on instructions of the person or organization from whom the assets were received.

**Customer Deposits.** A liability account used in an enterprise fund to reflect deposits made by customers as a prerequisite to receiving services and/or goods provided by the fund.

**Debt-Service Fund.** A fund established to account for the accumulation of resources for, and the payment of, general long-term debt principal and interest. Formerly called a *Sinking Fund*.

**Deficit.** (1) The excess of the liabilities of a fund over its assets. (2) The excess of expenditures over revenues during an accounting period; or, in the case of proprietary funds, the accumulated excess of expenses over income over the life of the fund.

**Delinquent Taxes.** Taxes remaining unpaid on and after the date on which a penalty for nonpayment is attached. Even though the penalty may be subsequently waived and a portion of the taxes may be abated or cancelled, the unpaid balances continue to be delinquent taxes until abated, cancelled, paid, or converted into tax liens.

**Department of Treasury.** A department of the executive branch of the federal government charged with the responsibility of handling government finances. As the chief custodial office of the federal government, it can be thought of as the bank for the federal government.

**Depreciation.** (1) Expiration in the service life of fixed assets, other than wasting assets attributable to wear and tear, deterioration, action of the physical elements, inadequacy, and obsolescence. (2) The portion of the cost of a fixed asset other than a wasting asset that is charged as an expense during a particular period. In accounting for depreciation, the cost of a fixed asset, less any estimated salvage value, is prorated over the estimated service life of such an asset, and each period is charged with a portion of such cost. Through this process, the entire difference between the cost and salavage value of the asset is ultimately charged off as an expense.

**Direct Service Programs.**  Elements (cost centers) of a program budget used to accumulate the costs associated with the specific services provided for the citizens of a governmental unit.

**Dollar-Accountability Reporting.**  A system of reporting that shows the flows of spendable resources into and out of the reporting entity. The emphasis in this type of reporting is on the sources from which dollars were realized and the ways in which those dollars were used.

**DRG.**  Diagnosis-related group as defined in Medicare Prospective Payment System.

**Due from _____ Fund.**  An asset account used to indicate amounts receivable from another fund in the same government for goods sold or services rendered. This account includes only short-term obligations on open account and not noncurrent portions of long-term loans.

**Due to _____ Fund.**  A liability account reflecting amounts owed by a particular fund to another fund in the same government for goods sold or services rendered. These amounts include only short-term obligations on open account and not noncurrent portions of long-term loans.

**Effective.**  Accomplishing the task an entity is expected to perform.

**Efficiency.**  Maximizing the objectives of an organization in relation to the resources consumed in accomplishing those objectives. Also, maximizing achievements in relationship to efforts expended.

**Encumbrances.**  Commitments related to unperformed (executory) contracts for goods or services.

**Endowment Funds.**  Accounting entities used to account for funds received from a donor with the restriction that the principal is not expendable but is to be held for the production of revenue for use by the organization.

**Enterprise Fund.**  A fund established to account for operations (a) that are financed and operated in a manner similar to private business enterprises—where the intent of the governing body is that the costs (expenses, including depreciation) of providing goods or services to the general public on a continuing basis be financed or recovered primarily through user charges; or (b) where the governing body has decided that periodic determination of revenues earned, expenses incurred, and/or net income is appropriate for capital maintenance, public policy, management control, accountability, or other purposes. Examples of enterprise funds are those for water, gas, and electric utilities; swimming pools; airports; parking garages; and transit systems.

**Enterprise Units.**  A pool of productive resources and talents contributed by two or more parties for the purpose of carrying out coordinated resource-conversion activities.

**Entitlement.** A payment that an individual or other entity is entitled to receive under some statute such as social security payments.

**Entity.** The basic unit upon which accounting and/or financial reporting activities focus. The basic governmental legal and *accounting entity* is the individual fund and account group. Under NCGA Statement 1, governmental GAAP *reporting entities* include (1) the combined statements—overview (the "liftable" GPFS) and (2) financial statements of individual funds (which may be presented as columns on combining statements—by fund type, on physically separate individual fund statements, or both). The term *entity* is also sometimes used to describe the composition of "the government as a whole" (whether the library is part of the city or a separate government, whether the school system is part of the county or an independent special district, etc.).

**Entity Convention.** A practice followed by accountants that requires that accounting reports shall be presented for each individual economic unit, defined as any body of resources being used toward the achievement of a common operating goal.

**Estimated Revenues.** The amount of spendable resource inflows expected to be realized during a budgetary period.

**Expendable Trust Fund.** A trust fund whose resources, including both principal and earnings, may be expended. Expendable trust funds are accounted for in essentially the same manner as governmental funds.

**Expended Appropriation.** An appropriation that has been used to cover the costs of goods or services.

**Expenditure-Based Data.** Operating data in which operating outflows are expressed in terms of expenditures.

**Expenditures.** Decreases in net spendable resources; these include current operating expenses that require current or future use of net current assets, payments toward the retirement of general long-term debt, and outlays for long-term assets.

**Expense-Based Data.** Operating data in which the operating outflows are expressed in terms of expenses.

**Fiduciary Responsibility.** The responsibility that the management of a nonprofit organization has to its constituency to carry out the operations of the organization efficiently.

**Financial Reporting Pyramid.** NCGA Statement 1 organization plan for the Financial Section of the CAFR. The pyramid presents GAAP basic financial statements on three distinct and progressively more detailed reporting levels: (1) combined statements—overview (the "liftable" GPFS); (2) combining statements—by fund type; and (3) where necessary or appropriate individual fund statements.

**Financing Sources.** A nominal account used in federal government accounting to reflect the inflow of spendable resources equal to depreciation.

**Fiscal Period.** The period of time lapsing between the dates on which the accounting records of a reporting entity are closed.

**Fixed Costs.** Costs that in the aggregate remain the same at different levels of operations within some relevant range.

**Flexible Budget.**   A budget showing the amounts of costs (and/or revenues) expected to be incurred or realized over a period of time at different levels of activity (measured in terms of some activity base such as direct labor hours, direct labor costs, or machine-hours). A *flexible manufacturing overhead budget* gives the projected costs of various manufacturing overhead items at different levels of activity.

**Formula-Related Basis.**   Calculable relationships between budgetary items.

**Full Disclosure.**   A principle followed by accountants that requires them to accept responsibility of seeing that all significant financial facts are appropriately disclosed either within the body of the financial statements or in the footnotes and parenthetical statements accompanying those statements.

**Functional Classification.**   Expenditure classification according to the principal purposes for which expenditures are made. Examples are public safety, public health, public welfare, etc.

**Functional-Unit Cost.**   An amount equal to total costs allocated to each function performed divided by the number of functional activity units provided.

**Fund.**   A fiscal and accounting entity with a self-balancing set of accounts recording cash and other financial resources, together with all related liabilities and residual equities or balances, and changes therein, which are segregated for the purpose of carrying on specific activities or attaining certain objectives in accordance with special regulations, restrictions, or limitations.

**Fund Balance.**   The fund equity of governmental funds and trust funds.

**Fund Balance Reserved for Encumbrances.**   The part of the total fund balance that has been reserved to cover encumbrances outstanding at the end of a reporting period.

**Fund Balance with U.S. Treasury.**   An account used by federal governmental agencies to reflect the amount of cash appropriated for agency operations.

**Funds Appropriated.**   The amount of resources earmarked for use by a federal agency in the approved federal budget.

**General Accounting Office (GAO).**   An arm of the legislative branch of the federal government, reporting to Congress on the financial position, operating results, and accounting systems of government agencies. It functions mainly as an internal auditor of the federal government.

**General Fixed Assets Account Group.**   A self-balancing group of accounts set up to account for the general fixed assets of a government.

**General Fund.**   The fund used to account for all financial resources of a governmental entity except those required to be accounted for in another fund.

**General Fund Accounts.**   Accounts used by federal agencies to record the financial transactions associated with congressional appropriations and other authorizations to spend those resources.

**General Long-Term Debt.**   Long-term debt (other than special assessment bonds) expected to be repaid from governmental funds.

**General Long-Term Debt Account Group.**   A self-balancing group of accounts set up to account for the unmatured general long-term debt of a government.

**Generally Accepted Accounting Principles (GAAP).**   Uniform minimum standards of and guidelines to financial accounting and reporting. They govern the form and content of the basic financial statements of an entity. GAAP encompass the conventions, rules, and procedures necessary to define accepted accounting practice at a particular time. They include not only broad guidelines of general application, but also detailed practices and procedures. GAAP provide a standard by which to measure financial presentations. The primary authoritative statement on the application of GAAP to state and local governments is NCGA Statement 1. Every government should prepare and publish financial statements in conformity with GAAP. The objectives of governmental GAAP financial reports are different from, and much broader than, the objectives of business enterprise GAAP financial reports.

**Generally Accepted Auditing Standards (GAAS).**   Measures of the quality of the performance of auditing procedures and the objectives to be attained through their use. They are concerned with the auditor's professional qualities and with the judgment exercised in the performance of an audit. Generally accepted auditing standards have been prescribed by (1) the American Institute of Certified Public Accountants (AICPA) and (2) the U.S. General Accounting Office (GAO) in *Standards for Audit of Governmental Organizations, Programs, Activities, & Functions* (the "yellow book").

**General Obligation Bonds.**   Bonds for the payment of which the full faith and credit of the issuing government are pledged.

**General Obligation Special Assessment Bonds.**   See *Special Assessment Bonds.*

**General Purpose Financial Statements (GPFS).**   Those basic financial statements that comprise the minimum acceptable fair presentation in conformity with GAAP. As such, they constitute the minimum acceptable scope of independent annual GAAP audits. Under 1968 GAAFR, the GPFS included financial statements for each individual fund and account group maintained by a government. In Statement 1, the NCGA redefined governmental GPFS to consist of financial statements for each of the eight fund types in use and for both account groups presented in separate adjacent columns on the financial reporting pyramid's five Combined Statements— Overview. See *Basic Financial Statements, Combined Statements—Overview,* and *Financial Reporting Pyramid.*

**General Services Administration (GSA).**   A department of the executive branch of the federal government charged with the responsibility of providing an effective system, including data processing and communications systems, for the management of governmental properties and records associated with those properties.

**Generational Equity.**   A measurement of the extent to which the taxpayers of a particular reporting period are paying for the services which the governmental entity is providing during that period. (See also *Intergenerational Equity.*)

**Going Concern Convention.**   An accounting practice that requires accountants to present financial data with the assumption that the enterprise unit will continue to operate during the foreseeable future unless there is reason to doubt the continuity of existence.

**Government Equity.**   The owners' equity section of a federal agency balance sheet, including subcategories for invested capital, cumulative results of operations, and unexpended appropriations.

**Interfund Accounts.**   Accounts in which transfers between funds are reflected.

**Intergenerational Equity.**   A measurement of the extent to which the taxpayers of a particular reporting period are paying for the services which the governmental entity is providing during that period.

**Interim Financial Statement.**   Financial statements prepared for a reporting entity covering less than a full fiscal period.

**Interim Performance Reports.**   Reports reflecting the performance of individual cost centers over segments of a fiscal period.

**Internal Auditor.**   An employee whose primary responsibilities involve verification of compliance with internal profitability goals and with directives and policies of management relating to internal control.

**Internal Control.**   A plan of organization under which employees' duties are so arranged and records and procedures so designed as to make it possible to exercise effective accounting control over assets, liabilities, revenues, and expenditures. Under such a system, the work of employees is subdivided so that no single employee performs a complete cycle of operations. Thus, for example, an employee handling cash would not post the accounts receivable records. Moreover, under such a system, the procedures to be followed are definitely laid down and require proper authorizations by designated officials for all actions to be taken.

**Internal Service Fund.**   A fund used to account for the financing of goods or services provided by one department or agency to other departments or agencies of a government, or to other governments, on a cost-reimbursement basis.

**Invested Capital.**   The part of a federal agency's governmental equity represented by the book value of fixed assets.

**Investment in General Fixed Assets.**   An account in the general fixed-assets account group that represents the government's equity in general fixed assets. The balance of this account is generally subdivided according to the source of the monies that financed the asset acquisition, such as general fund revenues, special assessments, etc.

**Land, Building, and Equipment Fund.**   An accounting entity, often referred to as the plant fund, that is used to account for investments in fixed assets and the unexpended resources contributed specifically for the purpose of acquiring or replacing land, buildings, and equipment used in the operations of a health and welfare agency.

**Lease–Purchase Agreements.**   Contractual agreements that are termed "leases," but which in substance amount to purchase contracts.

**Loan Funds.**   Accounting entities used in college and university accounting systems to account for resources available for loans to students, faculty, and staff.

**Long-Term Stability.**   The ability of an enterprise unit to exist through periods of economic adversity.

**Management Fund Accounts.**   Federal agency receipt and expenditure accounts established by law to facilitate accounting for and administration of the intragovernmental operations of a federal agency.

**Mandatory Transfer.**   In college and university accounting, transfers from the current fund group to other fund groups arising out of binding legal agreements relating to the financing of educational plant and grant agreements with agencies of the federal government, donors, and other organizations to match gifts and grants to loan and other funds; mandatory transfers may be required to be made from either unrestricted or restricted current funds.

**Master Budget.**   A document that consolidates all budgets of an entity into an overall plan of operations for a budgetary period.

**Matching Convention.**   An accounting practice adopted by accountants that requires that expenses incurred in the realization of revenues should be matched against those revenues for financial reporting purposes.

**Materiality.**   A principle or concept followed by accountants that in effect says that, in making decisions relating to the accounting process, the accountant should be concerned only with those things and amounts that have a significant effect on the financial statement data.

**Matured Bonds Payable.**   A liability account reflecting unpaid bonds that have reached or passed their maturity date.

**Modified Accrual Basis.**   The accrual basis of accounting adapted to the governmental fund type, spending measurement focus. Under it, revenues are recognized when they become both "measurable" and "available to finance expenditures of the current period." Expenditures are recognized when the related fund liability is incurred, except for: (1) inventories of materials and supplies that may be considered expenditures either when purchased or when used; (2) prepaid insurance and similar items that need not be reported; (3) accumulated unpaid vacation, sick pay, and other employee benefit amounts that need not be recognized in the current period, but for which larger-than-normal accumulations must be disclosed in the notes to the financial statements; (4) interest on special assessment indebtedness that may be recorded when due rather than accrued, if approximately offset by interest earnings on special assessment levies; and (5) principal and interest on long-term debt that are generally recognized when due. All governmental funds and expendable trust funds are accounted for using the modified accrual basis of accounting.

**Nonexpendable Trust Fund.**   A trust fund, the principal of which may not be expended. Nonexpendable trust funds are accounted for in essentially the same manner as proprietary funds.

**Nonmandatory Transfers.**   In college and university accounting systems, transfers from the current fund group to other fund groups, which are made at the discretion of the governing board. Such transfers may include additions to loan funds, additions to quasi-endowment funds, general or specific plant additions, voluntary renewals and replacements of plant, and prepayments on debt principal.

**Nonoperating Inflows.**   Resources received by a nonprofit organization that are not immediately available to be used to cover operating outlays.

**Nonprofit Entity.**　An organization created for the purpose of providing socially desirable services without the intention of realizing a profit and having no ownership shares that can be sold or traded. Any excess of revenues over expenses or expenditures realized by these organizations is used to enlarge the service capability of the organization. These organizations must be financed at least partially by taxes and/or contributions based on some measure of ability to pay, and some or all of the services must be distributed on the basis of need rather than effective demand for them.

**Nonspendable Resources.**　Assets that cannot be spent either because of their nature (for example, buildings) or because they are restricted from being spent (for example, endowment assets).

**Notes to the Financial Statements.**　The summary of significant accounting policies and other disclosures required for a fair presentation of the basic financial statements of an entity in conformity with GAAP which are not included on the face of the basic financial statements themselves. The notes to the financial statements are an integral part of the basic financial statements.

**Objectivity.**　A principle or concept of accounting that requires that the items and amounts recorded in the financial statement should, insofar as is practical, be those that are most clearly verifiable to supporting documents or other evidence originating outside the business.

**Occupancy Percentage.**　In the analysis of hospital financial data, the relationship between actual room occupancy and the maximum possible room occupancy for a hospital over a period of time.

**Office of Management and Budget (OMB).**　Office, operating under the supervision of the president, charged with various responsibilities relating to the continued improvement of governmental organization, information, management systems, governmental budgeting, and accounting procedures.

**Operating Expenses.**　Proprietary fund expenses that are directly related to the fund's primary service activities.

**Operating Income.**　The excess of proprietary fund operating revenues over operating expenses.

**Operating Revenues.**　Proprietary fund revenues that are directly related to the fund's primary service activities. They consist primarily of user charges for services.

**Operating Statement.**　The basic financial statement that discloses the financial results of operations of an entity during an accounting period in conformity with GAAP. Under NCGA Statement 1, operating statements and statements of changes in fund equity are combined into "all-inclusive" operating statement formats.

**Operational Accountability.**　The state of being held accountable for the efficiency and effectiveness of an entity's resource conversion activities when measured against its operating objectives.

**Operational Accountability Reporting.**　A system of financial reporting that discloses the extent to which an organization has efficiently and effectively met its operating objectives.

**Other Financing Sources.**  Governmental fund spendable resource inflows from long-term debt, transfers, and material amounts received from fixed-asset dispositions. A revenue-type account.

**PEEP Cycle.**  The cycle of activities carried out during each period—plan, execute, evaluate, plan.

**Pension Trust Fund.**  A trust fund used to account for public employee retirement systems. Pension trust funds are accounted for in essentially the same manner as proprietary funds, but with an important expanded emphasis on required fund balance reserves.

**Performance Budget.**  A budget emphasizing the relationships between outputs of services and the costs of providing those services.

**Planning-Programming-Budgeting Systems.**  See *PPBS.*

**Plant Funds.**  Accounting entities used in college and university accounting systems to account for unexpended funds to be used in the acquisition of long-lived assets for institutional purposes, funds set aside for renewal and replacement of institutional properties, funds set aside for debt-service charges and retirement of indebtedness on institutional plant, and the cost (or fair value at time of donation) of long-lived assets other than those of endowment and similar funds held by a college or university.

**Plant Replacement and Expansion Funds.**  A subentity of restricted funds used in hospital accounting systems to account for assets restricted by donors to be used for additions to property, plant, and equipment.

**PPBS.**  Acronym for planning-programming-budgeting systems. Such systems include procedures for evaluating the probable efficiency and effectiveness of new programs by relating the anticipated values of proposed services to the costs of providing those services.

**Preliminary Cost-Allocation Devices.**  Cost centers or job (project) cost sheets which are used to accumulate costs prior to their reallocation to ultimate cost-allocation targets.

**Private Foundation.**  A nonprofit organization created by contributions from individuals or corporate entities for the purpose of carrying out projects and providing services considered to be socially beneficial. Such a foundation is in some respects an endowment fund. It is different, however, in that the specific projects or services to be provided by the foundation are determined (within the constraints of the foundation charter) by the foundation board or trustees.

**Program Budget.**  A budget wherein expenditures are based primarily on programs of work and secondarily on character and object class. A program budget is a transitional type of budget between the traditional character and object class budget, on the one hand, and the performance budget, on the other.

**Project Cost-Accumulation Sheet.**  A document used to accumulate the costs allocated to a specific project.

**Proprietary Funds.**  Funds, within a governmental accounting system, that operate like business entities. These funds are characterized as either enterprise or internal service funds.

**Prospective Payment System.**   A pricing system that sets in advance the prices that will be paid by health insurance carriers for hospital treatment of diagnosis-related groups of patients. Initiated by Medicare in 1983.

**Public Support Revenue.**   Revenues realized from contributions of various kinds, special events, legacies and bequests, amounts received from federated and nonfederated federal campaigns, etc. It represents charitable giving by the public in support of a voluntary agency.

**Pure Nonprofit Entity.**   An enterprise unit that provides socially beneficial services to the community based entirely on the need for services. Revenues for such an organization are realized from taxes and contributions based on some measure of ability to pay. Also, the organization has no equity shares that are capable of being sold or traded.

**Pure Profit Entity.**   An enterprise unit organized for the purpose of realizing financial benefits for its owners.

**Quasi Endowment.**   In college and university accounting systems, resources designated to be used as endowment by the institution's board of trustees.

**Quasi-External Transactions.**   Interfund transactions that would be treated as revenues, expenditures, or expenses if they involved organizations *external* to the governmental unit—for example, payments in lieu of taxes from an enterprise fund to the general fund; internal service fund billings to departments; routine employer contributions from the general fund to a pension trust fund; and routine service charges for inspection engineering, utilities, or similar services provided by a department financed from one fund to a department financed from another fund— should be accounted for as revenues, expenditures, or expenses in the funds involved.

**Quasi-nonprofit entities.**   A nonprofit organization that provides services with partial cost recovery through user charges.

**Quasi-profit entity.**   An enterprise unit that is financed by member contributions and provides service benefits for its members. A country club is an example of a quasi-profit entity.

**Realization Convention.**   The primary guideline that the accountant uses in determining when inflows of resources should be recognized as revenues. The point of recognition under this convention is the point where the earning process has been completed and a legally enforceable claim to cash has been received in exchange for the goods delivered or services rendered.

**Registered Bond.**   A bond whose owner is registered with the issuing government and which cannot be sold or exchanged without a change of registration. Such a bond may be registered as to principal and interest or as to principal only.

**Relevance.**   The financial information that is appropriate for its intended use.

**Relevant Range.**   A range of levels of operations over which aggregate fixed costs and aggregate variable costs can be projected to behave in a linear fashion.

**Reliability.**   In accounting theory, the requirement that accounting information be verifiable and representationally faithful.

**Reserve.** (1) An account used to earmark a portion of fund balance to indicate that it is not available to meet new expenditures; and (2) an account used to earmark a portion of fund equity as legally segregated for a specific future use.

**Reserve for Encumbrances.** An account used to segregate a portion of fund balance for expenditure upon vendor performance. (Delivery of goods or services.)

**Reserve for Inventory of Supplies.** An account used to segregate a portion of fund balance to indicate that, using the purchase method, inventories of supplies do not represent "available spendable resources" even though they are a component of net current assets.

**Residual Equity Transfers.** Nonrecurring or nonroutine transfers of equity between funds, for example, contribution of enterprise fund or internal service fund capital by the general fund, subsequent return of all or part of such contribution to the general fund, and transfers of residual balances of discontinued funds to the general fund or a debt-service fund.

**Responsibility Accounting.** A system of accounting under which individual employees are held responsible for particular segments of activities occurring within an enterprise unit. Accounting reports are prepared for each of these segments to reflect the effectiveness with which each of the activities has been carried out. Such reports are often referred to as performance reports.

**Restricted Funds.** Fund entities or segments of fund entities that are subject to restrictions in the ways the resources included in them may be used. This term is also used in hospital accounting systems to describe all segments of resources that are externally restricted in any way, along with the obligations against those resources.

**Retained Earnings.** An equity account reflecting the accumulated earnings of an enterprise or internal service fund.

**Revenue Goal.** The targeted amount of revenue needed to meet projected expenditures within the constraints of a planned change in the unreserved fund balance during the budgetary period.

**Revenue-Producing Cost Centers.** Cost-accumulation centers that provide billable services to an organization's clientele.

**Revenues (Dollar Accountability).** Spendable resource inflows.

**Revolving Fund Accounts.** Receipt and expenditure accounts established by law to facilitate accounting for a continuing cycle of operations with receipts from such operations usually available for use by the fund without further action by Congress.

**Semivariable Costs.** Costs that include both variable and fixed components. Also called *semifixed costs*.

**Serial Bonds.** Bonds included in an issue that mature in series (parts of the issue mature each year over a period of time).

**Service Department.** A department within a business that exists for the purpose of providing services or assistance to other departments.

**Service Enterprises.** Enterprises engaged in converting resources into services rather than into finished goods.

**Service Implementation Costs.** Costs incurred by a business or nonprofit organization in providing services to the organization's clientele; comparable to cost of sales for a manufacturing or merchandising firm.

**Space Application Rate.** A predetermined amount per square foot used to allocate the approximate amounts of space-occupancy costs to cost centers.

**Special Assessment.** A compulsory levy made against certain properties to defray part or all of the cost of a specific improvement or service deemed to primarily benefit those properties.

**Special Assessment Bonds.** Bonds payable from the proceeds of special assessments. If the bonds are payable only from the collections of special assessments, they are known as special assessment bonds. If, in addition to the assessments, the full faith and credit of the government are pledged, they are known as general obligation special assessment bonds.

**Special Assessments Receivable—Current.** Uncollected special assessments that a government has levied and are due within one year.

**Special Assessments Receivable—Deferred.** Uncollected special assessments that a government has levied but that are not due within one year.

**Special Fund Accounts.** Federal government receipt and expenditure accounts for receipts that are earmarked by law for a specific purpose but not generated by a cycle of operations for which there is continuing authority to reuse the receipts.

**Specific Purpose Funds.** An accounting entity used in hospital accounting systems to account for resources that are donor restricted to use for specified purposes other than plant replacement and expansion and endowment.

**Statement of Cash Flows.** A statement showing the sources of cash inflows and how cash was used during a reporting period. The net difference between inflows and outflows is reconciled to the change in the cash balance during the period.

**Statement of Changes in Financial Position.** The basic financial statement that (for proprietary funds, nonexpendable trust funds, and pension trust funds) formerly was used to present information on the amount (but not necessarily the nature) of the sources and uses of an entity's cash or working capital during an accounting period in conformity with GAAP. The statement of changes in financial position may be presented in any of the following four ways: (1) as a statement of revenues and expenditures *detailing all revenues,* other financing sources, expenditures, and other financing uses; (2) as a statement beginning with reported net income, adjusting it for items not requiring (providing) working capital, and *detailing only* nonoperating financing sources and uses; (3) as a statement of cash receipts and disbursements *detailing all* cash receipts and disbursements; (4) as a statement beginning with reported net income, adjusting it for items not requiring (providing) cash, and *detailing only* nonoperating cash receipts and disbursements.

**Statement of Changes in Fund Equity.** The basic financial statement that reconciles the equity balances of an entity at the beginning and end of an accounting period in conformity with GAAP. It explains the relationship between the operating statement and the balance sheet. Under NCGA Statement 1, statements of changes in fund equity are combined with operating statements into "all-inclusive" operating statement formats.

**Statement of Revenues and Expenditures.**   The basic financial statement that is the governmental fund and expendable trust fund GAAP operating statement. It presents increases (revenue and other financing sources) and decreases (expenditures and other financing uses) in an entity's net current assets.

**Statement of Revenues and Expenses.**   The basic financial statement which is the proprietary fund, nonexpendable trust fund, and pension trust fund GAAP operating statement. It presents increases (revenues) and decreases (expenses) in an entity's net total assets resulting from operations.

**Subsidiary Account.**   One of a group of related accounts that support in detail the debit and credit summaries recorded in a control account. An example is the individual property taxpayers' accounts for the taxes receivable control account in the general ledger. See *Control Account* and *Subsidiary Ledger.*

**Subsidiary Ledger.**   A group of subsidiary accounts, the sum of the balances of which is equal to the balance of the related control account. See *Subsidiary Account.*

**Substance Over Form.**   Used to express the fact that in presenting financial statement data, the economic substance of the transaction originating the data should be used in reflecting those data, even though it may be different from the legal form describing the transaction.

**Supporting-Service Cost Centers.**   Cost-accumulation centers that provide services to revenue-producing cost centers; comparable to service department cost centers for a manufacturing firm.

**Supporting Services.**   One of the three expense categories used in the operating statements of health and welfare agencies to summarize the expenses associated with supporting the organization and its activities rather than with directly implementing the programs of the organization.

**Support Programs.**   Elements (cost centers) of a city's budgeting system used to accumulate the costs of supporting direct service activities such as maintenance, administration, accounting, etc.

**Surrogates for Value of Output.**   Substitute for use of output as an element in evaluation of efficiency of operations.

**Sustentation Costs.**   Costs incurred by a nonprofit organization in sustaining itself, primarily fund-raising costs and certain administrative costs.

**Sustentation Expenses.**   Expenses incurred to sustain the organization. These include fund-raising expenses and some administrative expenses.

**Taxes Receivable—Current.**   The uncollected portion of taxes that a government has levied, which are due within one year and which are not considered delinquent.

**Taxes Receivable—Delinquent.**   Taxes remaining unpaid on and after the date on which a penalty for nonpayment attaches. Delinquent taxes receivable are classified as such until paid, abated, cancelled, or converted into tax liens.

**Term Bonds.**   Bonds of which the entire principal matures on one date.

**Trial Balance.**   A list of the balances of the accounts in a ledger kept by double entry, with the debit and credit balances shown in separate columns. If the totals of the debit and credit columns are equal or their net balance agrees with a control account, the ledger from which the figures are taken is said to be "in balance."

**Trust and Agency Fund.**   One of the eight generic fund types in governmental accounting.

**Trust Funds.**   Funds used to account for assets held by a government in a trustee capacity for individuals, private organizations, other governments, and/or other funds. See *Pension Trust Fund*.

**Ultimate Cost-Allocation Target.**   The product or service unit to which all costs of producing products or providing services are to be allocated within the framework of a cost-accounting system.

**Unallocated Appropriations.**   Appropriations that have not been apportioned to specific periods within the fiscal year.

**Unapportioned Appropriation.**   The amount appropriated for an agency's operation in the approved federal budget.

**Unencumbered Appropriation.**   That portion of an appropriation not yet expended or encumbered.

**Unexpended Appropriation.**   The amount of an agency's appropriation that has not been used at the end of a reporting period. Part of governmental equity that may include unallocated appropriations, unobligated allotments, and unliquidated obligations.

**Uniformity.**   Use of the same accounting practices by different accounting entities carrying out essentially the same activities. This is not presently a generally accepted accounting practice.

**Unobligated Allotments.**   The part of unexpended appropriations that has been apportioned to a period of time but has not yet been committed to use.

**Unrestricted Funds.**   Generally, all expendable resources that are not restricted to specified uses either by external parties or by the management of the nonprofit organization. It is also used as a specific designation for all resources of hospitals that are not externally restricted and are therefore available for general operating purposes.

**Variable Costs.**   Costs that in the aggregate vary directly with changes in the level of operations within a firm's relevant range. Within this range, the variable cost per unit will be constant.

**Vouchers Payable.**   Liabilities for goods and services evidenced by vouchers that have been preaudited and approved for payment but that have not been paid.

**Warrant.**   An order drawn by the legislative body or an officer of a government upon its treasurer directing the latter to pay a specified amount to the person named or to the bearer. It may be payable upon demand, in which case it usually circulates the same as a bank check; or it may be payable only out of certain revenues when and if received, in which case it does not circulate as freely.

**Zero-Base Budgeting.**   A budgeting program that requires a complete review and annual justification on the basis of that review prior to the approval of budgeted expenditures for the accounting entity.

**Zero-Base Review.**   An alternative to the use of zero-base budgeting. This procedure requires an organization to establish a systematic plan for reviewing all of its operations over a period of years rather than each time a budgetary plan is established.

# Bibliography

Accounting Advisory Committee. *Report to the Commission on Private Philanthropy and Public Needs.* Washington, D.C.: The Commission on Private Philanthropy and Public Needs, 1974.

Adams, Bert K., Quentin M. Hill, Joseph A. Perkins, Jr., and Philip S. Shaw. *Principles of Public School Accounting.* State Educational Records and Reports Series, Handbook II B. Washington, D.C.: National Center for Educational Statistics, Department of Health, Education and Welfare, U.S. Government Printing Office, 1967.

Adams, Paul A. "Combating Fraud in the FHA Insurance Program." *Government Accountants Journal* (Fall 1989).

AGA. "AGA Comments on the Report of the AGA's Committee to Review Structure for Governmental Accounting Standards." *Government Accountants Journal* (Summer 1989).

Ailshie, Stephen A. "An Integrated FMIS: BPA's Experience." *Government Accountants Journal* (Summer 1987).

Allen, Phillip C., Peter Foye, and Thomas M. Henderson. "Recycling and Incineration: Not Mutually Exclusive in Broward County, Florida." *Government Finance Review* (October 1990).

Alley, Lee R., and Stephen D. Willits. "In-Office Microcomputing: The Return of Users' Abdicated Responsibilities." *Government Accountants Journal* (Summer 1986).

American Council on Education. *College and University Business Administration.* 4th ed. Washington, D.C.: American Council on Education, 1982.

———. *American Universities and Colleges.* 12th ed. Washington, D.C.: American Council on Education, 1983.

American Hospital Association. *Chart of Accounts for Hospitals.* Chicago: American Hospital Association, 1976.

———. *Guide to the Health Care Field.* Chicago: American Hospital Association, 1977.

American Institute of Certified Public Accountants. Accounting Standards Executive Committee. Exposure Draft. "Proposed Statement of Position on Accounting Principles and Reporting Practices for Nonprofit Organizations Not Covered by Existing AICPA Audit Guides." New York: AICPA, 1978.

———. APB Statement 4, *Basic Concepts and Accounting Principles Underlying Financial Statements of Business Enterprises.* New York: AICPA, 1970.

———. *Accounting and Financial Reporting by State and Local Governments: An Experiment.* New York: AICPA, 1981.

———. *Audits of Certain Nonprofit Organizations.* New York: AICPA, 1987.

_____ . *Audits of Colleges and Universities.* 2nd ed. New York: AICPA, 1975.

_____ . *Audits of Providers of Health Care Services.* New York: AICPA, 1990.

_____ . *Audits of State and Local Governmental Units.* New York: AICPA, 1986.

_____ . Committee on Health Care Institutions. *Medicare Audit Guide.* New York: AICPA, 1969.

_____ . Committee on Voluntary Health and Welfare Organizations. *Audits of Voluntary Health and Welfare Organizations.* New York: AICPA, 1988.

_____ . *Local Governmental Accounting Trends and Techniques.* New York: AICPA, 1988.

_____ . *Planning Considerations for an Audit of a Federally Assisted Program.* New York: AICPA, 1981.

_____ . Report of the Study Group on the Objectives of Financial Statements. *Objectives of Financial Statements.* New York: AICPA, 1973.

_____ . Statement of Position 74-8, *Financial Accounting and Reporting by Colleges and Universities.* New York: AICPA, 1974.

_____ . Statement of Position 78-1, *Accounting by Hospitals for Certain Marketable Equity Securities.* New York: AICPA, 1978.

_____ . Statement of Position 78-7, *Financial Accounting and Reporting by Hospitals Operated by a Governmental Unit.* New York: AICPA, 1978.

_____ . Statement of Position 78-10, *Accounting Principles and Reporting Practices for Certain Nonprofit Organizations.* New York: AICPA, 1978.

_____ . Statement of Position 80-2, *Accounting and Financial Reporting by Governmental Units.* New York: AICPA, 1980.

Andrews, F. Emerson. *Attitudes Toward Giving.* New York: Russell Sage Foundation, 1953.

Anthony, Robert N. *Financial Accounting in Nonbusiness Organizations: An Exploratory Study of Conceptual Issues.* Stamford, Conn.: Financial Accounting Standards Board, 1978.

Anthony, Robert N., and Regina Herzlinger. *Management Control in Nonprofit Organizations.* Homewood, Ill.: Richard D. Irwin, 1985.

Armstrong, Mary Beth, and Steven M. Mintz. "Professional Ethics Department." *Government Accountants Journal* (Summer 1989).

Attmore, Robert H., John R. Miller, and James R. Fountain. "Governmental Capital Assets: The Challenge to Report Decision-Useful Information." *Government Finance Review* (August 1989).

Azad, Ali N., and Ted D. Skekel. "Personal Attributes and Effective Operational Auditing: Perceptions of College and University Internal Auditors." *Government Accountants Journal* (Fall 1990).

Babunakis, Michael. *Budgets: An Analytical and Procedural Handbook for Government and Nonprofit Organizations.* Westport, Conn.: Greenwood Press, 1976.

Barzel, Dari. "Financing Programs for Local Government Agencies: A Regional Approach." *Government Finance Review* (August 1988).

Belkaoui, Ahmed. *Socio-Economic Accounting.* Westport, Conn.: Greenwood Press, 1984.

Beuley, Robert W. "Strengthening Controllership: A Study of Existing Functions." *Government Accountants Journal* (Spring 1988).

Bogard, Allen. "Impact Fees in a Small Texas City." *Government Finance Review* (June 1990).

Bowlin, William F. "Evaluating Performance in Governmental Organizations." *Government Accountants Journal* (Summer 1986).

Bowsher, Charles A. "Government Finances: A New Structure Needed." *Government Accountants Journal* (Fall 1986).

Boyett, Arthur S., and Gary A. Giroux. "The Relevance of Municipal Financial Statements for Investor Decisions: An Empirical Study." Paper presented at American Accounting Association Southwest Regional Meeting, New Orleans, March 24, 1977.

Brown, Ray L. "The Line Item Veto: How Well Does It Work?" *Government Accountants Journal* (Winter 1987–88).

Brown, Ray L., and John C. Corless. "Government Auditor Job Satisfaction." *Government Accountants Journal* (Spring 1990).

Bruce, Paul K., Robert Elkin, Daniel D. Robinson, and Harold I. Steinberg. *Reporting of Service Efforts and Accomplishments*. Stamford, Conn.: Financial Accounting Standards Board, 1980.

Caldwell, Charles W., and Judith K. Welch. "Applications of Cost–Volume–Profit Analysis in the Governmental Environment." *Government Accountants Journal* (Summer 1989).

Calvelli, Alfred M. "The Junkyard Dogs Versus the Federal Deficit." *Government Accountants Journal* (Fall 1987).

Campfield, William L. "Practitioner Vis-à-Vis Educator: A 50-Year Career Retrospective." *Government Accountants Journal* (Fall 1990).

Canadian Institute of Chartered Accountants. *Financial Reporting for Non-Profit Organizations*. Toronto: Canadian Institute of Chartered Accountants, 1980.

Canary, Hal. "Timely Financial Reporting." *Government Finance Review* (August 1988).
Carpenter, Vivian L. "Improving Accountability: Evaluating the Performance of Public Health Agencies." *Government Accountants Journal* (Fall 1990).

Cary, Thurman, and G. Stevenson Smith. The U.S. Standard General Ledger: What It Means for Equity and Budgetary Accounting in the Federal Government." *Government Accountants Journal* (Fall 1988).

Casabona, Patrick A., and Anthony T. Barbera. "Survey of Procedures for Selection of External Auditors by Public Sector Entities." *Government Accountants Journal* (Summer 1987).

Chan, James L., ed. *Research in Governmental and Non-Profit Accounting*. Greenwich, Conn.: Jai Press, Inc., 1985.

Club Managers Association of America. *Uniform System of Accounts for Clubs*. 2nd rev. ed. Washington, D.C.: Club Managers Association of America, 1967.

*College Blue Book*. 19th ed. New York: Macmillan Information, 1983.

Committee on Accounting in the Public Sector, 1974–76. "Report of the Committee on Accounting in the Public Sector." *Accounting Review,* 52, Supplement, pp. 33–52.

Committee on Concepts of Accounting Applicable to the Public Sector, 1970–71. "Report of the Committee on Concepts of Accounting Applicable to the Public Sector." *Accounting Review,* 47, Supplement, pp. 77–108.

Committee on Nonprofit Organizations. "Report of the Committee on Accounting Practice for Not-for-Profit Organizations." *Accounting Review,* 46, Supplement, pp. 81–163.

_____ . "Report of the Committee on Not-for-Profit Organizations, 1972–73." *Accounting Review,* 49, Supplement, pp. 225–49.

_____ . "Report of the Committee on Not-for-Profit Organizations, 1973–74." *Accounting Review,* 50, Supplement, pp. 1–39.

Comptroller General of the United States. *Standards for Audit of Governmental Organizations, Programs, Activities and Functions*. Washington, D.C.: U.S. General Accounting Office, 1972.

_____ . "Accounting Principles and Standards for Federal Agencies." Title 2 to the *Government Accounting Office Manual for Guidance of Federal Agencies*. Washington, D.C.: U.S. General Accounting Office, 1986.

Cooley, John W., and Michael E. Simon. "The Case for a Standard Government-Wide Chart of General Ledger Accounts." *Government Accountants Journal* (Summer 1987).

Copeland, Ronald M., and Robert W. Ingram. *Municipal Financial Reporting and Disclosure Quality*. Reading, Mass.: Addison-Wesley, 1983.

Dasent, Andre C., and George J. Whelan. "Government-Owned Utilities: A Rationale for Payments Made to Government Owners." *Government Finance Review* (February 1988).

David, Irvin T., C. Eugene Sturgeon, and Eula L. Adams. *How to Evaluate and Improve Internal Controls in Governmental Units.* Chicago: Municipal Finance Officers Association, 1981.

Davidson, Sidney, David O. Green, Walter Hellerstein, Albert Madansky, and Roman L. Weil. *Financial Reporting by State and Local Government Units.* Chicago: The Center for Management of Public and Nonprofit Enterprise of the Graduate School of Business, The University of Chicago, 1977.

DeStefano, David. "Using Computer-Assisted Audit Techniques in Public Sector Audits." *Government Accountants Journal* (Fall 1989).

Dickson, Elizabeth L., and George D. Friedlander. "The Impact of Tax and Expenditure Limitations on the Quality of Municipal Bonded Debt." *Government Finance Review* (February 1988).

Dittenhofer, Mortimer A. "State and Local Government Audit Committees." *Government Accountants Journal* (Summer 1988).

Doczy, Edward F. "Linking a Strategic Plan to the Budgetary Process." *Government Finance Review* (December 1987).

Donnelly, W. F., and Gary Miller. "Financial Officers' Opinions to GASB's Proposed Statement on Measurement Focus and Basis of Accounting—Government Funds." *Government Accountants Journal* (Fall 1989).

Doost, Roger K. "The Importance of Budget Execution in Governments." *Government Accountants Journal* (Spring 1986).

Douglas, Patricia P. "GASB's Proposed Statement on Objectives of Financial Reporting." *Government Accountants Journal* (Summer 1986).

Drebin, Allan R., James L. Chan, and Lorna C. Ferguson. *Objectives of Accounting and Financial Reporting for Governmental Units: A Research Study,* Vols. 1 and 2. Chicago: National Council on Governmental Accounting, 1981.

Dumil, James, and Peter Millspaugh. "Government Auditing and Legal Liability." *Government Accountants Journal* (Fall 1988).

Eckert, Harvey, Edward M. Klasny, and Dennis D. Moody. "Joint Audits for Governments—The Pennsylvania Experience." *Government Accountants Journal* (Winter 1986–87).

Edwards, Kimberly K. "Reporting for Tax Expenditures and Tax Abatement." *Government Finance Review* (August 1988).

Egenolf, Robert V., and Fred Nordhauser. "Status of Governmental and Nonprofit Accounting Education in Master of PAIA Programs." *Government Accountants Journal* (Spring 1990).

Engstrom, John H., John Simon, and Louis Karrison. "Property Tax Revenue Recognition Under NCGA Interpretation 3." *Government Accountants Journal* (Spring 1986).

Ernst & Young. *Introduction to Governmental Accounting.* Washington, D.C.: Ernst & Young, 1989.

Foltz, Roland P., and Gilbert W. Crain. "Auditing Internal Administrative Controls for Federal Financing Assistance Programs." *Government Accountants Journal* (Winter 1987–88).

Ford Foundation Advisory Committee on Endowment Management. *Managing Educational Endowments.* New York: Ford Foundation, 1969.

Forman, Steven D. "The Federal Government Operations Accountant—A Need for Upgrading." *Government Accountants Journal* (Summer 1989).

Fort, Debra B. "From Reactive to Proactive Fiscal Planning: The Results of Strategic Planing in McKinney, Texas." *Government Finance Review* (August 1989).

Fountain, James R., and John Engstrom. "College and University Financial Reporting: A Survey of Important Financial Decision Makers." *Government Accountants Journal* (Summer 1989).

Francis, Charles D., and Allan J. Borwick. "The Equivalency Factor: Municipal Budgeting by the Household." *Government Finance Review* (August 1990).

Freeman, Robert J., and Craig D. Shoulders. "Evaluating the Revised GASB Measurement Focus and Basis of Accounting Proposals." *Government Accountants Journal* (Fall 1989).

Furman, William T. "Higher Professional Standards—A Different View." *Government Accountants Journal* (Summer 1988).

Gaffney, Mary Anne, and Susan A. Lynn. "The Expectations GAP and Municipal Auditing." *Government Accountants Journal* (Summer 1989).

Gauthier, Stephen J., and Warren Shawn. *GAAFR Study Guide.* Chicago, Ill.: Government Finance Officers Association, 1990.

Governmental Accounting Standards Board. *Governmental Accounting and Financial Reporting Standards.* Stamford, Conn.: GASB, 1987.

_____ . *Objectives of Financial Reporting.* Stamford, Conn.: GASB, 1987.

_____ . *The Needs of Users of Governmental Financial Reports.* Stamford, Conn.: GASB, 1985.

Graff, Stuart L. "Online Inquiry: Vital Information Directly from a County's General Ledger." *Government Accountants Journal* (Fall 1989).

Grosshans, Werner. "High Ethical Standards—Essential to Success." *Government Accountants Journal* (Fall 1989).

Haller, Edward J. "Fluffard Stuff and Their Influence on Federal Financial Management." *Government Accountants Journal* (Summer 1988).

Hanley, Thomas R., and Frank S. Synowiec, Jr. "Look What's New with the Single Audit Guide." *Government Accountants Journal* (Spring 1986).

Harr, David J. "Productive Unit Resourcing: A Business Perspective in Governmental Financial Management." *Government Accountants Journal* (Summer 1989).

Helmi, Medhat A. "Deciding on Cuts in Social Programs: An Accounting Framework." *Government Accountants Journal* (Summer 1987).

Henke, Emerson O. "Accounting for Nonprofit Organizations: An Exploratory Study." *Indiana Business Information Bulletin No. 53.* Bloomington, Ind.: Bureau of Business Resarch, Graduate School of Business, Indiana University, 1965.

_____ . "Generational Equity Reporting." *Government Accountants Journal* (Spring 1987).

_____ . "Government Financial Reports: A Creative Response to User Needs." *Government Accountants Journal* (Summer 1986).

Henke, Emerson O., and Lucian G. Conway. "Governmental Resource Base Reporting." *Government Accountants Journal* (Fall 1990).

_____ . "Recommended Format for College and University Financial Statements." *Accounting Horizons* (June 1989), pp 49–65.

Herbert, Leo, Larry N. Killough, and Alan Walter Steiss. *Accounting and Control for Governmental and Other Nonbusiness Organizations.* New York: McGraw-Hill, 1987.

Holder, William W. *A Study of Selected Concepts for Government Financial Accounting and Reporting.* Chicago: National Council on Governmental Accounting, 1980.

Huang, Juinn C., Thomas F. Monohan, and James M. Emig. "Responsibility Accounting in Mass Transit: Its Time Has Come." *Government Accountants Journal* (Winter 1986–87).

Icerman, Rhoda C., and William Hillison. "Risk and Materiality in Governmental Audits." *Government Accountants Journal* (Fall 1989).

Ingram, Robert W., Walter A. Robbins, and Mary S. Stone. "Financial Reporting Practices of Local Governments: An Overview." *Government Finance Review* (April 1988).

Ives, Martin. "Pension Accounting—The Controversy Continues." *Government Finance Review* (December 1988).

Jeffcoat, Clyde E. "Improving Army's Financial Management." *Government Accountants Journal* (Fall 1989).

Kamnikar, Judith A., and Edward C. Kamnikar. "The Professional Recognition of Governmental Accounting and Auditing." *Government Accountants Journal* (Fall 1987).

Kee, Robert, Walter Robbins, and Nicholas Apostolou. "Capital Budgeting Practices of U.S. Cities: A Survey." *Government Accountants Journal* (Summer 1987).

Kendig, William L. "Solving Federal Accounting System Problems." *Government Accountants Journal* (Fall 1988).

Kerns, Dennis W., Vic Tomlinson, and Rodney E. Gordon. "Automating the Budget Process." *Government Finance Review* (April 1988).

Kidd, Stephen. "Experience with Packaged Financial Software in Federal Agencies." *Government Accountants Journal* (Summer 1990).

Kirkendall, Donald. "Can Auditors Polish Their Sometimes Tarnished Image?" *Government Accountants Journal* (Summer 1990).

Kraft, William H., Jr. "Audit Management—A Practical Perspective." *Government Accountants Journal* (Winter 1987–88).

Kusserow, Richard B. "Audit Financial Statements: The Social Security Administration Experience." *Government Accountants Journal* (Summer 1988).

Lazenby, Scott D., Donald E. Siggelkow, and Robert R. Drake. "Priority on Policies: How Glendale, Arizona, Streamlined the Budget Process." *Government Finance Review* (February 1990).

Lehan, Edward A. *Simplified Governmental Budgeting*. Chicago: Municipal Finance Officers Association, 1981.

Lewin, Arie Y., and James H. Scheiner. *Requiring Municipal Performance Reporting: An Analysis Based Upon Users' Information Needs*. Durham, N.C.: Graduate School of Business Administration, Duke University, 1977.

Loeb, Stephen E., ed.—Professional Ethics Department. Bedingfield, James P., and A. J. Stagliano. "A Developing Picture of Business Ethics and Accountability: The Defense Industry Initiative." *Government Accountants Journal* (Spring 1990).

Luter, J. Thomas. "GAO Title Six Revision." *Government Accountants Journal* (Spring 1990).

Lynn, Edward S., and Robert J. Freeman. *Fund Accounting: Theory and Practice*. 2nd ed. Englewood Cliffs, N.J.: Prentice-Hall, 1983.

McBride, Peggy. "Preparing for the Single Audit." *Government Accountants Journal* (Fall 1986).

McCann, James A., and Michael J. Daun. "Strategic Fiscal Planning in the City of Milwaukee: A Description and Assessment." *Government Finance Review* (June 1989).

Mangano, Michael F., and Brian M. Rawdon. "Issuing Reports Not Covered by Government Auditing Standards: What Are They? What Is Required?" *Government Accountants Journal* (Summer 1990).

Maher, John J. "CSRS or FERS: How to Compare?" *Government Accountants Journal* (Summer 1987).

Matzer, John, Jr., ed. *Practical Financial Management: New Techniques for Local Government*. Washington, D.C.: International City Management Association, 1984.

Mendel, Colleen Bell, Jack O. Hall, Jr., and C. Richard Aldridge. "Cost Analysis in Project Headstart." *Government Accountants Journal* (Fall 1988).

Miller, William D. "Multi-Stage Program Auditing—The VA's Home Loan Guaranty Program." *Government Accountants Journal* (Spring 1988).

Morris, Russell D. "Government Financial Management: Fix It or Find It?" *Government Accountants Journal* (Summer 1986).

Mosk, Lennox L. *Municipal Bonds-Planning Sale and Administration*. Chicago: Municipal Finance Officers Association, 1982.

Municipal Finance Officers Association—now Government Finance Officers Association. *Guidelines for Preparation of a Public Employee Retirement System: Illustrations of Notes to the Financial Statements of State and Local Governments*. Financial Reporting Series 1. Chicago: Municipal Finance Officers Association, 1983.

_____ . *Guidelines for Preparation of a Public Employee Retirement System: Guide to Municipal Leasing,* edited by A. John Vogt and Lisa Cole. Chicago: Municipal Finance Officers Association, 1983.

_____ . *Guidelines for Preparation of a Public Employee Retirement System: Disclosure Guidelines for State and Local Governments.* Chicago: Municipal Finance Officers Association, 1979.

_____ . *Guidelines for Preparation of a Public Employee Retirement System: Fiscal Almanac.* Chicago: Municipal Finance Officers Association, 1982.

_____ . *Guidelines for Preparation of a Public Employee Retirement System: Developing a Financial Management Information System for Local Government.* Chicago: Municipal Finance Officers Association, 1980.

_____ . *Guidelines for Preparation of a Public Employee Retirement System. Directory of Financial Services for State and Local Government.* Chicago: Municipal Finance Officers Association, 1982.

_____ . *Disclosure Guidelines for Offerings of Securities by State and Local Governments.* Chicago: Municipal Finance Officers Association, 1976.

National Association of College and University Business Officers. *Planning, Budgeting and Accounting: Section II of a College Operating Manual.* Prepared by Peat, Marwick, Mitchell & Co. Washington, D.C.: National Association of College and University Business Officers, 1970.

_____ . *College and University Business Administration.* 4th ed. Washington, D.C.: National Association of College and University Business Officers, 1982.

National Association of Independent Schools. *Accounting for Independent Schools.* 2nd ed. Boston: National Association of Independent Schools, 1977.

National Committee on Governmental Accounting. *Governmental Accounting, Auditing, and Financial Reporting.* Chicago: Municipal Finance Officers Association, 1980.

National Council on Governmental Accounting. *GAAFR Restatement Principles: Exposure Draft.* Chicago: Municipal Finance Officers Association, 1978.

National Health Council, National Assembly of National Voluntary Health and Social Welfare Organizations, Inc., and United Way of America. *Standards of Accounting and Financial Reporting for Voluntary Health and Welfare Organizations.* New York: National Health Council, National Assembly of National Voluntary Health and Social Welfare Organizations, Inc., and United Way of America, 1975.

O'Keefe, Herbert A., and Pete Rose. "Overview of the Issues Involved in Measurement Focus and Basis of Accounting for Governmental Funds." *Government Accountants Journal* (Summer 1987).

Olson, Stevan K., and Jacob R. Wambsganss. "Depreciation for Colleges and Universities: Is It Useful Information?" *Government Accountants Journal* (Winter 1987–88).

O'Toole, Daniel E., and James Marshall. "Budgeting Practices in Local Government: The State of the Art." *Government Finance Review* (October 1987).

Page, Marcus. "Two Centuries in Financial Management." *Government Accountants Journal* (Fall 1989).

Patten, Dennis M. "Battle of the Boards: Identifying the Political Nature of the Standard-Setting Controversies." *Government Accountants Journal* (Fall 1989).

Payne, Richard D., William C. Lathen, and Craig E. Bain. "Possible Methodology for Determining Revenue from the Taxation of Services." *Government Accountants Journal* (Summer 1990).

Peterson, John E., and Wesley C. Hough. *Creative Capital Financing for State and Local Governments.* Chicago: Municipal Finance Officers Association, 1983.

Peterson, Tracy E. "Seattle Metro: Regional Solutions to Local Problems." *Government Finance Review* (June 1990).

Phillips, Thomas E. "Impact Fees: Addressing Growth by Calculating Estimated Usage." *Government Accountants Journal* (Summer 1990).

Pitsvada, Bernard T., and James A. Howard, "The Theory and Practice of Budget Execution." *Government Accountants Journal* (Summer 1986).

Polivka, Jirina S. "Relational Approach to Problem Solving." *Government Accountants Journal* (Winter 1986–87).

Premchand, A. *Governmental Budgeting and Expenditure Controls: Theory and Practice*. Washington, D.C.: International Monetary Fund, 1983.

_____ . "International Problems in Governmental Accounting: Role and Efforts of the IMF." *Government Accountants Journal* (Fall 1987).

Price Waterhouse & Co. *A Survey of Financial Reporting and Accounting Practices of Private Foundations*. New York: Price Waterhouse & Co., 1977.

_____ . *Accounting Principles and Reporting Practices for Certain Nonprofit Organizations*. New York: Price Waterhouse & Co., 1978.

_____ . *Understanding Local Government Financial Statements: A Citizen's Guide*. New York: Price Waterhouse & Co., 1976.

Pumphrey, Lela D., and J. Dwight Hadley. "Measurement Focus and Basis of Accounting—Governmental Fund Operating Statement." *Government Accountants Journal* (Summer 1990).

Raaum, Ronell B. "Precise Objective—Prerequisite to a Quality Audit." *Government Accountants Journal* (Summer 1988).

Raymond, Peter R., James M. Fremgen, and Benjamin Roberts. "Postaudit of Government Capital Investment Projects." *Government Accountants Journal* (Summer 1988).

Reed, William. "Managing the Cost of Audit Quality." *Government Accountants Journal* (Fall 1989).

Riemer, David R. "Milwaukee's Successful Effort to Control Employee Health Care Costs." *Government Finance Review* (February 1990).

Roehm, Harper A., Joseph F. Castellano, and David A. Karns. "Contracting Services to the Private Sector: A Survey of Management Practices." *Government Finance Review* (February 1989).

Rothschild, Joseph. "Evaluating Internal Controls: Are the Auditors as Good as the Audit Standards?" *Government Accountants Journal* (Summer 1986).

Sadowski, Thomas J. "AGA Testimony at GASB Hearing on Agenda and General Progress to Date." *Government Accountants Journal* (Fall 1988).

Schoen, David, Mark Olsen, and William Jaeger. "Establishing a Fixed-Asset System for the State of New York: A Multi-Step Process." *Government Finance Review* (February 1989).

Seguiti, Maria Laura, and Bernard T. Pitsvada. "Comparative Reforms in the Provision of Public Goods in the U.S. and Europe." *Government Accountants Journal* (Spring 1988).

Sharp, Florence C. "Factors Affecting Asset Acquisition Decisions of Municipalities." *Government Accountants Journal* (Summer 1986).

Shear, Jeffrey. "New York City Unearths the Underground Economy." *Government Finance Review* (June 1990).

Sherwood, Hugh C. *How Corporate and Municipal Debt Is Rated*. New York: John Wiley & Sons, 1976.

Shonick, William, and Ruth Roemer. *Public Hospitals Under Private Management*. Berkeley, Cal.: Institute of Governmental Studies, 1983.

Short, Thomas W. "Financial Reporting—Treasury's Report on Operations." *Government Accountants Journal* (Spring 1986).

Shoulders, Craig, Walter L. Johnson, and W. T. Wrege. "The Rise and Near Demise of the Governmental Accounting Standards Board." *Government Accountants Journal* (Spring 1990).

Skousen, K. Fred, Jay M. Smith, and Leon W. Woodfield. *User Needs: An Empirical Study of College and University Financial Reporting*. Washington, D.C.: National Association of College and University Business Officers, 1975.

Sourwine, Darrel A. "Are Organizations Improving Themselves out of Business?" *Government Accountants Journal* (Fall 1986).

Stelzer, Patrick T., and Robert A. Gray. "Training Adults to Use Micro-Computers: A Technical and Psychological Approach." *Government Accountants Journal* (Fall 1988).

Stepnick, Edward W. "The Nitty-Gritty and Hurly-Burly of Government Auditing: It's All in My Working Papers." *Government Accountants Journal* (Winter 1987–88).

Stout, Larry D. "A Vision of Federal Financial Management: Can We Create a Bottom Line?" *Government Accountants Journal* (Summer 1987).

Stroud, J. B. "Prioritization of Municipal Financial Statement Users." *Government Accountants Journal* (Fall 1988).

Sunner, Michael W. "Financing and Managing Our Public Debt." *Government Accountants Journal* (Fall 1990).

Swafford, James. "Communications in an 'Auditor's World.' " *Government Accountants Journal* (Summer 1986).

Tierney, Comelius E. "Accounting for Government: Sense, Not Nonsense." *Government Accountants Journal* (Spring 1990).

Tierney, Cornelius E., and Phillip T. Calder. *Financial Reporting for American Cities and Counties*. New York: Elsevier Science, 1986.

Tierney, Cornelius E., and Chuck Hamilton. "Strengthening Controllership in the Federal Government—A Proposal Revisited." *Government Accountants Journal* (Fall 1987).

Tracy, Richard C. "Performance Auditing: Catalyst for Change in Portland, Oregon." *Government Finance Review* (February 1988).

United Way of America. *Accounting and Financial Reporting: A Guide for United Ways and Not-for-Profit Human Service Organizations*. Alexandria, Va.: United Way of America, 1974.

Uyeda, Susuma. "Federal Financial Management Reorganization—Points to Ponder." *Government Accountants Journal* (Winter 1986–87).

Vinter, Robert D., and Rhea K. Kish. *Budgeting for Not-for-Profit Organizations*. New York: The Free Press, 1984.

Wallick, Ruth M. "A Survey of State Finance Officers Associations: Organizational Profiles and Association Activities in State-Level Policy Making." *Government Finance Review* (December 1988).

Wambsganss, Jacob R., and Stevan K. Olson. "How College and University Business Officers View Depreciation." *Government Accountants Journal* (Spring 1988).

Webster, John D. "Reform of the Federal Employee Health Benefits Program." *Government Accountants Journal* (Fall 1990).

Weirich, Thomas R., and Alan Reinstein. "Implementing the Disclosure Requirements of GASB Statement No. 3." *Government Accountants Journal* (Fall 1990).

Wesberry, James P., Jr., ed.—International Affairs Department. Almaguer, Frank. "Honesty and Integrity in the Management of Public Resources." *Government Accountants Journal* (Spring 1990).

Wesberry, James P., Jr. "The United States Constitution and International Accounting and Auditing Standards." *Government Accountants Journal* (Winter 1987–88).

Wilder, Michael C. "Good Internal Audits Don't Just Happen." *Government Accountants Journal* (Summer 1987).

Willits, Stephen D., and Mark S. Bettner. "Arguments and Evidence Regarding Cash Basis Accounting and Small Municipalities." *Government Accountants Journal* (Summer 1988).

Witsman, F. Tim, and Jerome A. Lonergan. "Economic Development and Tax Structure: Kansas Analyzes Its Competitive Position." *Government Finance Review* (August 1988).

Wolfe, Harry B., Judith D. Bentkover, Helen H. Schauffler, and Ann Venable. *Health Cost Containment: Challenge to Industry.* New York: Financial Executives Research Foundation, 1980.

Worthington, Margaret M. "Government and Industry." *Government Accountants Journal* (Summer 1989).

Wrege, W. T., and Relmond P. Van Daniker. "Accounting Information Needed by State Legislators and Fiscal Officers." *Government Accountants Journal* (Spring 1986).

Young, Ronald S. "GAO's Efforts to Establish Federal Government Accounting Standards." *Government Accountants Journal* (Fall 1989).

Zlatkovich, Charles P., and Karl B. Putnam. "State and Local Government Tax Trends." *Government Accountants Journal* (Summer 1989).

# Index

## A

Account groups, 84, 270–280
  accounting procedures, 270–276
  defined, 270
  general fixed asset, 31, 270
    accounting equation, 271
    accounting procedures illustrated, 271–273
    illustrative transactions, 271
    statements, 273
  general long-term debt, 32, 274
    accounting equation, 274
    accounting procedures illustrated, 275
    statements, 276
  NCGA Statements relating to, 276–280
    capital leases, 279, 280
    others, 276–279
Accountability
  dollar, 16, 24
  operational, 6, 10
Accounting, evolution of, 4
Accounting conventions, 43–46, 79–82
  entity, 45, 82
  going concern, 44, 81
  matching, 45, 81
  realization, 44, 81
  transaction, 44
Accounting cycles, 9, 30
  businesses, 9
  dollar-accountability, 30
Accounting entities
  account groups, 84
  fiduciary-type funds, 84
  governmental-type funds, 82
  proprietary-type funds, 83
  types of, 82
Accounting equations
  dollar-accountability, 25–27

general fixed-assets account group, 271
general long-term debt account group, 274
pure nonprofit entities, 27
Accounting for Colleges and Universities, 450–494 See
    also Colleges and Universities
Accounting for Health and Welfare Agencies, Churches
    and Other Similar Organizations, 514–536
Accounting for other funds and account groups,
    252–292
Accounting practices,
  sources of, 37, 48
Accounting principles
  conservatism, 42
  consistency, 43
  defined, 42
  full disclosure, 43
  materiality, 42
  objectivity, 42
Accounting principles, statements of
  colleges and universities, 452–457
  governmental entities, 75–79
Accounting Principles Board (APB), 38
Accounting procedures
  and actions by professional organizations, 37
  conceptual foundation underlying, 35–37
  and governmental agencies, 39
  and pronouncements of official bodies, 38
  and Statements of Financial Accounting Concepts, 38, 39
  underlying assumptions, principles and conventions,
    41–46
Accounting standards setting structure, 40
Accrual basis,
  for colleges, 458, 484
  for combined financial statements, 335–363
  defined, 46
  and governmental accounting, 77
  for health and welfare organizations, 517, 518

for hospitals, 413, 414
  implications of, 644, 645
  objectivity and, 645, 646
Accrued expenses, 9
Accrued revenues, 9
Actions in response to financial statement analysis, 623, 624
Adjusting entries, 9, 10
Agency funds, 265–470, 466
  colleges and universities, 466
  governmental, 265–270
*AICPA Audit Guide for Colleges and Universities,* 457
*AICPA Audit Guide for Health and Welfare Organizations,* 516
*AICPA Statement of Position on Accounting Principles and Reporting Practices for Certain Nonprofit Organizations,* 534
American Accounting Association (AAA), 37
American Institute of Certified Public Accountants (AICPA), 37
*American Universities and Colleges,* 615
Amortization of fixed assets, 9
Analysis of financial statement data, 607
  application of analytical techniques, 613–625
  basic concerns, 607
  church financial statements, 623
  college and university financial statements, 615–619
  evaluating fiduciary responsibility of internal managers, 606
  expenditure-data, 641, 642
  expense and expenditure per unit data, 641, 642
  expense-based data, 641, 642
  governmental financial statements, 613–615
  health and welfare organization statements, 621–623
  hospital financial statements, 619–621
  input-output relationships, 584
  interpretation of analytical data, 607–625, 642, 643
  Model City operating data, 640–642
    analysis of expenditure-based data, 641, 642
    analysis of expense-based data, 642–643
    interpretation of analytical data, 642
  needs and affordability, 614
  nonprofit organization statements, 610
  overhead and service-implementation costs, 592
  profit enterprise financial statements, 602
  related to operating objectives, 606, 607
  response to analysis data, 623, 624
  surrogates for value of output, 611
Analysis of governmental financial statements, 613–615, 640–642
Analysis of hospital financial statements, 619–621
Analysis and interpretation of financial data, 613–625
Analysis of nonprofit organization statements, 610
Analysis of profit enterprise financial statements, 608
Analysis of statements for health and welfare agencies, 621–623

Analyzing financial statements for colleges and universities, 615–619
Annuity funds, *See* Colleges and universities, 466
Anthony, Robert N., 581, 593
Appropriation control, 33, 35
  for churches, 529
  for colleges and universities, 458
  constraints, 33, 35
  defined, 33
Audits of Colleges and Universities, 457
Audits of nonprofit organizations, 677–695
  and appropriation control, 680
  audit reports, 678
  audit standards, 677–679
    field work, 678
    general, 677–678
    reporting, 679
  and bases of accounting, 681
  evidence gathering process, 686–689
  and fund accounting practices, 681
  internal control, 683
  internal control weaknesses, 684, 685
  official literature, 683
  and reporting requirements, 689–690
  reports, audit, 678, 689, 690
  single audit, 690–694
  special accounts, 682
  special audit considerations, 685, 686
*Audits of State and Local Governmental Units,* 93
*Audits of Voluntary Health and Welfare Organizations,* 516
Auxiliary activities, 459

**B**

Balance sheet
  business, 11
  capital projects fund, 219
  church, 533
  college and university, 468–470, 491–492
  combined (Model City), 348–352
  consolidated (Model City), 358–360
  debt-service fund, 225
  general fund, 186
  health and welfare organization, 525, 526
  hospitals, 420, 421
  proprietary funds, 264
    enterprise fund, 259, 264
    internal service fund, 256
  special assessment agency fund, 233
  special assessment capital projects fund, 230
Basic principles and conventions, 79–82
  application of, 79
  conservatism, 81
  entity, 82

Basic principles and conventions, *(continued)*
  going concern, 81
  matching, 81
  materiality, 81
  realization, 81
Basis of accounting, 46–48
  accrual basis, 46
  cash basis, 47
  implications for analysis, 644
  modified accrual basis, 47
  nonprofit enterprises, 47
  profit enterprises, 46
Bibliography, 724–733
Bonds, general obligation, 215–218, 274
Bonds, revenue, 258
Bonds, special assessment, 230, 231
Budget as control device, 121
Budgetary accounts, 121
Budgetary controls, expenditures, 108–110, 112, 121,
    122
Budgetary practices
  capital projects fund, 127
  churches, 530, 531
  closing entries, 123
  colleges and universities, 458
  debt-service funds, 127
  development and use of cost data, 128
  ethical considerations situation, 129
  general fund, 108–126
  governmental funds, 108–129
    planning for acquisitions and uses of resources,
      103–107
    PPB and zero-base budgeting, 111
    underlying philosophy, 108–110
  hospitals, 415–417
  proprietary funds, 103
    applying formula relationships, 104
    changes due to managerial decisions, 105
    projecting resource inflows, 103
    summarizing the budgetary data, 105
  PPBS, 111
  program budgeting, 124
  zero-base, 111
Budgeting
  based on prior operations, 108
  calendar, 120
  capital projects funds, 127
  for churches, 530, 531
  control accounts, 121
  and cost data, 128
  cost-volume considerations, 104, 583
  debt-service funds, 127
  ethical issues relating to, 129
  formula relationships, 104
  and functional unit costs, 125, 126
  general fund, 108–126

  inflation considerations, 105, 106
  and interim performance reports, 186–188
  planning-programming-budgeting system (PPBS), 111
  program budgeting, 124
    illustrated, 124
    and responsibility accounting system, 584, 586
    zero-base, 111
    zero-base review, 582
  projecting resource inflows, 103
Bureaucracy, coping with, 592, 593

## C

Calendar for budget preparation, 120
Capital improvements, 214
  general, 214
  special-assessment-type, 226
Capital projects funds, 214–220
  assumed transactions, 215
  authorization, 216
  balance sheet, 219
  budgeting, 127
  closing entries, 217, 218
  defined, 214
  encumbrances, 217
  ethical considerations situation, 233–234
  financial statements, 219, 220
  journalizing transactions, 215–217
  posting transactions, 218, 219
  statement of revenues, other financing sources,
    expenditures, and changes in fund balance, 220
  transactions, 215–217
Cases, thought projection, 661–676
  Albatross CMHC, 671–676
  Break-Even Community Mental Health Center, 667–668
  Seek-a-Client (SAC) Community Mental Health Center,
    668–671
  Slippery Handle Mental Health Center, 661–666
Cash basis of accounting defined, 47
Charity services for hospitals, 426
*Chart of Accounts for Hospitals,* 413, 418
Churches, 528–534
  accounting for, 528–534
  analysis of financial statements, 623
  appropriation control, 529
  balance sheet, 533
  benevolences in budget, 530
  budget, 530, 531
  common-size operating statement, 624
  dollar-accountability, 528
  statement of revenues and expenditures, 531, 533
  transactions worksheet, 532
Closing entries
  budgetary accounts general fund, 101, 102
  capital projects fund, 217, 218
  debt-service fund, 223

enterprise fund, 262
internal-service-fund, 255
special assessment agency fund, 232
special assessment capital projects fund, 229
trust and agency fund, 267
*College and University Business Administration,* 452
*College Blue Book,* 615
Colleges and universities, 450–494
accounting for, 450–494
accounting principles, 452–457
accounting for depreciation, 455
accounting for institutions operated by religious
groups, 456
accounting for investments, 456
accrual accounting, 454
basic financial statements, 454
fund accounting, 453
statement of, 452–457
agency funds, 466
*AICPA Audit Guide for,* 457
analysis of financial statements, 615–619
annuity and life income funds, 464
appropriation controls for, 458
auxiliary enterprises, 459
balance sheet, 468–470, 491–492
basis of accounting, 458, 484
budgetary practices, 458
*College and University Business Administration,* 452
current funds, 461
depreciation accounting, 459
dollar-accountability, 452
endowment funds, 462
ethical considerations situation, 488
expenditures, 475, 476, 482
current funds, 475
nonoperating, 482
FASB 93 and college and university accounting, 484–493
accounting procedures illustrated, 485–487
financial statements, 489–493
financial statements, 466–473
balance sheet, 468–470
plant funds, 465
statement of changes in fund balances, 472, 473
statement of current funds revenues, expenditures,
and other changes, 471
fixed assets, 465
fund accounting, 453
fund entities, 461
agency funds, 466
annuity and life income funds, 464
current funds, unrestricted and restricted, 461
endowment funds, 462
loan funds, 462
plant funds, 465
investments, accounting for, 456
legal provisions and operations, 457

loan funds, 462
mandatory transfers, 482
NACUBO, 452
nonmandatory transfers, 482
nonoperating inflows, 482
observations regarding accounting practices, 457
accounting for auxiliary enterprises, 459
accounting for depreciation, 459
basis of accounting, 458
budgetary practices, 458
legal provisions, 457
summary of changes suggested by AICPA Audit
Guide, 460
operating characteristics and accounting practices, 451
plant funds, 465, 466
nonoperating inflows and, 482
provisions of FASB 93, 482 *See also* FASB and college
and university accounting, 484
revenues, 474, 475
current fund, 474
nonoperating, 474
suggested accounting and reporting procedures to
comply with FASB 93, 484–493
financial statements, 491–493
system, 484–488
summary of accounting principles, 452–457
summary of changes suggested by AICPA Audit Guide,
460
transactions worksheet, 476–481, 485–487
transfers between funds, 482
mandatory, 482
nonmandatory, 482
typical transactions described and recorded, 474–484
auxiliary activity transactions, 474, 483
realization of current fund revenues, 474
realization of other resource inflows, 481
recognition of current fund expenditures, 475
recognition of nonoperating expenditures, 482
transfers between funds, 482
Committee on Accounting Procedures, 38
Comparability, 43
Comprehensive annual financial report (CAFR), 337, 338
Conceptual foundation, 35–46
accounting conventions, 43–46
accounting principles, 41–43
basic assumption underlying, 41
principles, 41–43
underlying assumptions principles and conventions,
41–46
Congressional Budget Office, 368
Conservatism, 42
Consistency, 43
Constituents
decisions, 73
defined, 7
special reporting needs, 7

Constraints on uses of resources
  appropriations control and, 26, 27
  fund accounting and, 33–35
Coping with politics and bureaucracy, 592, 593
  ethical considerations situation, 594
Corporate law concept for endowment funds, 463
Cost-Accounting Procedures for Nonprofit Organizations,
      559–572
  accumulation and allocation of costs, 562
    cost-allocation devices, 560
    cost-allocation targets, 560
    fixed costs, 563
    quasi-nonprofit enterprise costs, 564
    semi-variable costs, 563, 564
    variable costs, 562, 563
  basic types of aggregate costs, 562
  cost-accumulation and -allocation procedures for
      colleges and universities, 568–572
    activity based costing, 570
    categories of operating costs, 569
    cost per credit hour, 568
    ethical considerations situation, 572
  cost-accumulation and -allocation procedures for
      hospitals, 564–568
    cost per unit of service billing, 565
    flexible budget, 564–566
  flexible budget, 564–566
  high-low method, 563
  job order costing system, 560, 561
  need for cost data, 559, 560
  process costing system, 560, 561
Cost-volume relationships, 562–564, 583
Creditors
  decisions by, 74
  and governmental accounting, 74
Cross-over worksheets, 354–357
Current funds, 461, 519
  colleges and universities, 461
  health and welfare organizations, 519
Custodian funds, 519

D

Debt financing, governmental entities, 220, 221
  use of fiscal agent to service, 225
Debt-service fund, 220–226
  budgeting, 127
  closing entries, 223
  complementing entries, 234
  defined, 220
  disposal of resources, 224
  establishment of, 220
  financial statements, 224
    balance sheet, 225
    statement of revenues, other financing sources,
        expenditures, and change in fund balance, 225

    illustrated transactions, 221–223
    investment of assets, 221
    journalizing transactions, 221–223
    posting transactions, 223
    reciprocal entries, 234
    use of fiscal agent to service debt, 225
Decision making and financial data, 73
  constituency, 73
  creditors, 74
  managerial, 73
Depreciation of general fixed assets, 648–654
  arguments against recognizing, 649, 650
  arguments for recognizing, 650, 651
  college and university assets, 459, 484–493
  and full accrual basis, 353, 648, 649
  health and welfare organization assets, 517
  hospital assets, 413
  and operational accountability, 647, 648
  procedures for recognizing, 563, 652
Development and use of cost data, 128
Disclosure See Full disclosure
Dollar-accountability accounting system, 24–48
  and account groups, 31, 32
  accounting cycle, 30
  accounting equation, 25, 26
  accounting procedures, 24–48
  accounting system, 24–48
  actions and transactions, 29, 30
  budgetary data, 26
  for churches, 528, 529
  closing entries, 30, 31
  for colleges and universities, 452
  defined, 16
  financial statements, 29, 30
  and fund accounting, 33–35
  for governmental funds, 71
  and operational accountability, 638, 639
  reporting, 16
  specialized procedures for, 26–28
  system illustrated, 28

E

Earnings as measure of achievement, 46
Earnings per share, 608
Effective controllership, 588
Effectively managed nonprofit organization, 593
Effectiveness, evaluation of, 607, 608
Effort-achievement relationships, 73, 607
Encumbrances
  capital projects fund, 217
  defined, 153
  elimination of, 30, 31
  entries, 31
  general fund accounting, 153, 159
  recognition of, 27, 123

Endowment, 425, 426, 462–464, 519
  pure, 462
  quasi-, 462
  term, 462
Endowment funds, 425, 426, 462–464, 519
  accounting for, 425, 426
  college and university, 462–464
  health and welfare organizations, 519
  hospitals, 425, 426
  pooling of, 463
  pure, 462
  quasi-, 462
  term, 462
Endowment income, 463–465
Enterprise fund, 256–265
  accounting procedures, 256–265
  budgets for, 106, 107
  ethical consideration situations, 292
  financial statements, 264, 265
  journalizing transactions, 260
  master budget for, 107
  posting transactions, 263
  transactions, 260
Enterprise units, 12, 13
  types, 13, 14
Entity convention, 45
Entity definition criteria, governmental, 344–347
Erosion of capital and depreciation, 650, 651
Ethical consideration situations associated with
  awarding a capital projects contract, 233
  budgetary process, 129
  college and university accounting procedures, 488
  college and university cost-allocation procedures, 572
  deficit reduction actions, 398
  establishing billing prices for enterprise fund services, 292
  governmental fund accounting, 94
  health and welfare organization cost-allocation, 535
  hospital accounting procedures, 427
  interfund transfers of spendable resources, 190
  operations of health and welfare organization, 624
  the political process, 594
  publicizing a city's financial statements, 351
  reporting on operating efficiency, 654
  use of data produced by use of the modified accrual basis of accounting, 161
Evaluation of managerial performance, 70, 606
Expenditure-based data, analysis of, 641
Expenditures
  budgeting, 112
  colleges and universities, 475
  defined, 26
Expense-based data, analysis of, 641, 642
Expenses
  accrued, 9
  defined, 10

  per unit, 125, 126, 641
  prepaid, 10
External management group, 7, 8
Externally interested parties, 7, 8
Externally restricted resources, 33

**F**

FASB Statements
  Statement *5*, 277
  Statement *13*, 89, 278, 279
  Statement *35*, 89, 268
  Statement *93*, 484–493
  Statement *95*, 268
Federal government accounting, 382–399
  basis of accounting, 391
  Bureau of Budget (BOB), 383
  comptroller general, 384
  Central Financial Management System (CFMS), 384
  Congressional Budget Office, 368
  federal agency accounting illustrated, 392–398
    authorization actions, 392
    closing entries, 395
    elimination of encumbrances (obligations), 394
    expenditure transactions, 393
    financial statements, 397–398
    interfund transactions, 393
    other actions and transactions, 394
    realization of revenues, 393
    recognition of encumbrances, 393
    transactions worksheet, 396
  fund structure, 390
  General Accounting Office, 383, 385
  General Services Administration, 383, 388
  historical background, 383
  Office of Management and Budget (OMB), 383, 387
  resources derived from general taxation and revenue powers, 390
    general fund accounts, 390
    management fund accounts, 390, 391
    revolving fund accounts, 390
    special fund accounts, 390
  resources held by government in capacity of custodian or trustee, 391
    deposit fund accounts, 391
    trust fund accounts, 391
    statutorily assigned responsibilities, 385
    terminology, 388
    Treasury Department, 383, 387
Fiduciary funds, 265–270
  accounting procedures illustrated, 267, 268
  expendable trust fund, 265, 266
  hybrid-type trust fund, 266
  nonexpendable trust fund, 266
  pension funds, 268–270
  statement of cash flows for, 268

Financial Accounting Standards Board, 38
Financial data for decision-making purposes, 73–75
  constituency decisions, 73
  decisions by creditors, 74
  managerial operating decisions, 73
Financial performance reports, 585
  effective controllership, 588
  functions of internal auditor, 591
  interim performance reports, 586
  managerial performance evaluation, 7, 8
  motivating cost center managers, 587
  overhead and service implementation costs, 592
  responsibility accounting system, 585
  use of accrual basis of accounting, 591
Financial reporting needs, 7–12
  constituents and, 7, 8
  ethical considerations associated with, 351
  nonprofit organizations, 7
  profit entities, 7
  related to operating objectives, 8, 9
Financial reporting pyramid, 337, 339
Financial statements
  annual, 78
  annual governmental, 335–363
  business enterprises, 10, 11
  colleges and universities, 466–473
  combined governmental, 337–351
  ethical considerations situation, 351–352
  general fund, 183–186
  governmental, annual, 339–363
  health and welfare organizations, 520–524
  hospitals, 420–422, 427, 428
  interim, 78
  interpreting, 607–624
  nonprofit enterprises, 14, 15, 29, 30
  profit enterprises, 11, 12
  proprietary funds, 256, 257, 264–266
  qualitative factors, 35–37
  underlying assumption, 41
Fiscal compliance, 75
Fixed assets
  accounting for, 76
  colleges and universities, 465
  depreciation of, 77
  governmental, 77
  health and welfare organizations, 519
  hospitals, 413, 424
  valuation of, 77
Foundations, 534, 535
Freeman, Robert J., 68
Full accrual basis *See* Accrual basis
Full-cost data and the service story, 646
Full disclosure, principle of, 43
Functional unit costs, 72, 125
  controls, 126
Functions of internal auditor, 591

Fund accounting
  and colleges and universities, 453
  and depreciation, 652, 653
  and dollar-accountability, 33–35
  and governmental accounting, 75
  and health and welfare organizations, 519
  and hospitals, 418–426
  systems, 75
  types of funds, 35
Fund balances, statement of changes in
  capital projects fund, 220
  colleges and universities, 472, 473
  debt-service fund, 225
  general fund, 185
  health and welfare agencies, 520, 521
  hospitals, 423
  special assessment agency fund, 234
  special assessment capital projects fund, 231
Fund-raising costs, health and welfare organizations, 521, 522
Funds
  defined, 75
  fiduciary, 76
  governmental, 76
  proprietary, 76
  types of, 76

## G

GASB, 40, 89
  conceptual projects, 93
  *Objectives of Financial Reporting*, 94
  Statement *1*, 90
  Statement *2*, 90, 268
  Statement *3*, 90, 91
  Statement *4*, 91, 269
  Statement *5*, 91
  Statement *6*, 83, 91
  Statement *7*, 91
  Statement *8*, 91
  Statement *9*, 92, 268
  Statement *10*, 92
  Statement *11*, 92
  Statement *12*, 93, 269
  Statement *13*, 93
  user Needs Study, 89
General Accounting Office, 383, 385
General fixed-asset account group, 270–273
  accounting equation, 271
  financial statement, 273
  illustrated transactions, 272
  journalizing transactions, 272
  posting transactions, 273
General fund, 144–212
  accounting equation, 153
  accounting procedures illustrated, 173

accounts, 147
  control, 149, 150, 151
    functional classifications, 150
    revenue, 149
    subclassifications, 149
    subsidiary, 147, 150, 151
appropriation account, 121
balance sheet, 186
budget as control device, 121
budget development cycle, 110
budget for, 108–126
budgetary accounts, 121, 152
budgetary entry, 152
budgetary process, 110
capital items, 156, 157
cash receipts and disbursements statement, 187
cashflow forecast, 187
closing entries, 181
complementing entries, 155, 188
controls over expenditures, 122
delinquent taxes, 161
encumbrances, 153, 159
  end of period, 159
  recognition of, 153
ethical considerations situation, 190
expenditure accounts, 147, 149
  control accounts, 151
  subclassifications, 150, 151
  subsidiary accounts, 151
expenditures, recognition of, 152, 153
expenditures budget, 112
  implementing controls, 121
financial statements, 183–186
  balance sheet, 186
  interim reporting, 186–188
  interpreting operating statements, 184
  objectives, 183
  statement of revenues, expenditures, and changes in
    fund balances, 183, 185
functional classification of expenditures, 125, 126, 151
functional unit costs, 126
illustrated transactions, 173–175
interfund resource transfers, 154
interim financial reports, 186–188
interpreting operating statement, 184
journalizing transactions, 175–180
nominal accounts, 181, 182
objectives of financial statements, 183
operational characteristics, 145
posting transactions, 180
practical accounting deviations, 156
probable losses in collection of taxes, 160
program budgeting, 124
quasi-external transactions, 154
realization of revenues, 152
reciprocal entries, 155, 188

recognition of expenditures, 152, 153
revenue accounts, 147–149
  control accounts, 150
  subclassifications, 149, 150
  subsidiary accounts, 150
sale of assets, revenue from, 156
short-term borrowing, 158
special accounting procedures problems, 154
  capital items, 156, 157
  encumbrances at end of period, 159
  practical accounting deviations, 156
  probable losses in collecting taxes, 160
  short-term borrowing, 158
  supplies inventories, 157
statement of revenues and expenditures, 183, 185
subsidiary ledgers, 177
  appropriations, 177
  expenditures, 177
  revenues, 177
supplies inventories, 157, 158
tax rate, determination of, 174
transactions, 173–175
transactions involving other funds and account groups,
  154, 155
transactions worksheet, 188–190
types of accounts, 147–189
typical activities requiring accounting recognition, 152,
  173–175
General long-term debt account group, 274–276
  accounting equation, 274
  financial statement, 276
  illustrated transactions, 275
  journalizing transactions, 275
  posting transactions, 276
General purpose financial statements (GPFS), 337
  illustrated, 347–352
General Services Administration, 383, 388
Generally accepted accounting practices, 680
Generally accepted accounting principles (GAAP), 35–48
Generational equity See Intergenerational equity
Going-concern convention, 44
Governmental Accounting
  account groups, 270–280
  accounting information, users of, 70
  accrual based financial statements, 353–360
    consolidated balance sheet, 358–359
    conversion of modified accrual based statements,
      353–357
    statement of financial performance, 360
  accrual basis of accounting, 77
  annual financial reports, 335–360
  basic principles of, 75–79
  basis of accounting, 77
  budgeting, 102–129
  entity definition criteria, 45, 344–347
  general capital improvements, 214–220

Governmental Accounting, *(continued)*
  financial data for decision making purposes, 73–75
  funds
    capital projects, 214–220
    debt-service, 220–226
    enterprise, 256–265
    fiduciary, 265–270
    general, 144–212
    governmental, 76, 82, 144–233
    internal service, 253–256
    number of, 76
    special assessment agency, 230–233
    special assessment capital projects, 226–230
    special revenue, 76, 144–212
    trust and agency, 265–270
  interfund relationships, 234, 280–291
  measurement of entity achievement, 71, 72
  modified accrual basis of accounting, 77
  objectives of, 69
  governmental, 144–233
  proprietary, 253–265
  Summary Statement of Principles, 75–79
  users of accounting information, 70
Governmental accounting information, 70
  use of, 70
Governmental Accounting Standards Board, *See also*
    GASB, 40, 89
Governmental (dollar-accountability) funds, 82
  accounting cycle, 30
  accounting practices, 82, 83
  budgetary practices, 108–129
  capital projects, 214–220
  closing entries, 31
  debt-service, 220–226
  defined, 76, 82, 83
  and dollar-accountability, 71
  ethical considerations, 94
  financial statements, 29
  general, 144–212
  other, 213–235
  special assessment project, 226–233
  typical transactions, 28, 30
  Zero-base budgeting, 111
*Government Accounting, Auditing and Financial
    Reporting* (GAAFR), 40
Government Finance Officers Association, 40, 75

# H

Health and welfare organizations, 515–528
  accounting for, 515
  accrual basis of accounting, 517, 518
  analysis of financial statements, 621–623
  Audits of voluntary Health and Welfare Organizations,
    516
  balance sheet, 525, 526

common-size operating statement, 624
current restricted funds, 519
current unrestricted funds, 519
custodian funds, 519
depreciation recognition, 517
donated materials, 518
donated services, 518
endowment funds, 519
ethical considerations situation, 535, 624
evolution of accounting practices, 516
financial statements, 520–524
functional cost data, 622
fund entities, 519
  current restricted funds, 519
  current unrestricted funds, 519
  custodian funds, 519
  endowment funds, 519
  land, building, and equipment fund, 519
  loan and annuity fund, 519
fund-raising costs, 521, 522
illustrated transactions   *See* typical transactions
    illustrated
land, buildings, and equipment fund, 519
loan and annuity funds, 519
pledges receivable, accounting for, 518
program expenses, 521
service implementation costs, 521, 522
*Standards of Accounting and Financial Reporting for
    Voluntary Health and Welfare Organizations,* 514,
    515
statement of functional expenses, 522, 523
statement of support, revenue, and expenses, 520, 521
support revenue, 521
sustentation costs, 522
transactions worksheet, 526–529
typical transactions illustrated, 524–529
Herzlinger, Regina, 593
Hospitals, accounting for, 409–429
  accounting practices and operating environment, 410
  accounting procedures peculiar to hospital operations, 426
  accrual basis of accounting, 413, 414
  analysis of financial statements, 619–621
  asset valuation practices, 417, 418
  Audits of Providers of Health Care Services, 418
  balance sheet, 420, 421
  basis of accounting, 413
  billing rates and budgeting, 414, 415
  budget analysis schedule, 417
  budgetary practices, 415–417
  capital and revenue items, 413, 419
  charity services and uncollectible amounts, 426
  *Chart of Accounts for Hospitals,* 413, 418
  cost-allocation procedures, 414, 415
  depreciation, accounting for, 413
  endowment funds, 425, 426
  donated assets, 418

donated services, 418
ethical considerations situation, 427
financial statements, 420–422, 427, 428
fixed assets, 413, 424
flexible budgets for, 415, 417
fund entities, 418–426
malpractice litigation, accounting for, 418
operating environment, 411
patient charges and cost-allocation, 415
patient service revenue, 422, 426
plant replacement and expansion funds, 424, 425
pledges receivable, 421, 424
Prospective Payment Plan, 411
restricted funds, 422, 424–426
revenue-producing departments, 414
special accounting procedures, 426, 427
specific purpose funds, 424
statement of changes in fund balances, 423
statement of revenues and expenses, 419, 422
supporting services departments, 415
unrestricted funds, 419–422

**I**

Income statement, 11
Inflation and budgeting, 105, 106
Input-output relationships, 584
Interfund payables and receivables, 154
Interfund relationships summarized, 280–291
Intergenerational equity, 45, 46
Interim performance reports, 186–188
Internal auditors, functions of, 591
Internal control for nonprofit organizations, 588–591
Internal-service-funds, 253–257
accounting procedures, 253–256
budgets for, 105, 106
financial statements, 256, 257
journalizing transactions, 254
posting transactions, 255
specialized accounting procedures, 253
Internal use of accounting data, 580–595
cost-volume considerations, 583
effective budgeting procedures, 581
functional unit costs, 584
measuring input-output relationships, 584
planning-programming-budgeting procedures, 582
program budgets and functional unit costs, 584
zero-base review, 582
Inventories in general fund accounting, 157, 158

**L**

Leased assets, accounting for, 278–280
Legal requirements
colleges and universities, 457
and depreciation recognition, 459
vs. generally accepted accounting principles, 68

governmental entities, 49, 68
Loan funds, 462
Long-term liabilities, accounting for, 77
Lower-level managers and responsibility accounting, 585–588

**M**

Management, and
budgetary decisions, 104, 105
governmental accounting, 70–74
operating decisions, 73
Management by objectives, 3, 7
Managerial operating decisions, 73
Managerial operating objectives, 73
Managers
evaluation of, 606, 607
and governmental accounting, 70–75
motivation of, 587, 588
and overhead costs, 592
Matching convention, 45
college and university accounting, 451, 452
and governmental accounting, 45, 46
and intergenerational equity, 45, 46
Materiality, 42
Measuring governmental entity achievement, 71, 72
Measuring input-output relationships, 584
Medicare, 409, 411–413
Memo account groups, 31, 32, 270–274
accounting procedures, 272, 273, 275
general fixed assets, 270–273
general long-term debt, 274–276
and governmental accounting, 76, 77, 270–276
Modified accrual basis, 77
defined, 47
ethical considerations associated with, 161
Motivation of managers, 587, 588
Multiple funds accounting, 82–85
Municipal Finance Officers Association. *See* Government Finance Officers Association, 40, 75

**N**

National Assembly of National Voluntary Health and Social Welfare Organizations, 41
National Association of College and University Business Officers (NACUBO), 452
National Council on Governmental Accounting (NCGA), 40
National Health Council, 41
NCGA Interpretations of Statement *1*, 85–87
NCGA Statements
Interpretations, 85–88
Statement *1*, 68, 79, 276, 277, 336–347
Statement *2*, 88
Statement *3*, 89
Statement *4*, 89, 277

NCGA Statements, *(continued)*
  Statement *5*, 89, 278
  Statement 6, 89
  Statement *7*, 346, 347
Needs and affordability, balancing of, 614
Needs of Users of Governmental Financial Reports, 81
Nonprofit organizations
  categories, 6
  defined, *5*
  objectives of, *5*
  private, 6
  public, 6
  reporting procedures, 10
Nonspendable resources, and fund accounting, 34, 35

## O

Objectives of
  general fund budgeting, 108
  governmental accounting, 69
  nonprofit organizations, *5*
Objectivity and financial statement data, 35, 42, 43
Office of Management and Budget, 383, 387
Operating characteristics, 12–15
  analysis of, 12–15
Operating statements, 14
  pure nonprofit entities, 13, 15
  pure profit entities, 13, 14
  quasi-nonprofit entities, 13, 15
  quasi-profit entities, 13, 14
Operational accountability and financial analysis,
      639–643
  analysis Model City operating data, 640–642
  interpretations of analytical data, 642
Operational-accountability reporting, 6, 10, 637–655
  and accrual basis of accounting, 10
  case for, 643
  consistency, 43
  defined, 10, 638
  and depreciation, 648–654
    concluding comments, 653, 654
    procedures for depreciation recognition, 652
    reasons for favoring depreciation recognition,
      650–651
    reasons for opposing depreciation recognition,
      649–650
  disclosure of, 13
  effective use of community resources, 646
  ethical considerations situation, 654
  and financial analysis, 639
  full cost data and service story, 646
  and fund accounting, 647
  and governmental accounting, 641–654
  implications of basis of accounting used, 644
  and Model City operating data, 640–642
  objectivity and consistency need for, 645

Operational-accountability reporting and fund
      accounting, 647
Operational-Accountability Reporting for Nonprofit
      Organizations, 637–655
Organization chart for city, 113
Overhead and service implementation costs, 592

## P

Patient service revenue, accounting for, 422, 426
Pensions, 87
Periodic summary of financial data, 10, 11, 29, 30
Planning acquisitions of other governmental fund
      resources, 126
Planning-programming-budgeting system, 111
Plan-operate-evaluate-plan cycle, 7
Plant fund, 32, 33
Plant funds, colleges *See also* Colleges and universities,
      465, 466
Plant replacement and expansion funds *See* Hospitals,
      424, 425
Pledges receivable, accounting for
  health and welfare organizations, 518
  hospitals, 421, 424
Politics, coping with, 592, 593
PPBS, 111
Prepaid expenses, 10
Prepaid revenues, 10
Price Waterhouse & Company, 535
Price-level changes, 41
Principles of accounting, 41–43
  conservatism, 42
  consistency, 43
  full disclosure, 43
  materiality, 42
  objectivity, 42
Principles, summary statement of, 75–79, 452–457
  colleges and universities, 452–457
  governmental, 75–79
Private nonprofit organizations, *5*
Professional organizations actions by, 37–41
Profit enterprises
  analysis of financial statements, 608–610
  evaluating efficiency, 608
  and operational accountability, 638, 639
Program budgeting, 124
  functional unit costs and, 125
  illustrated, 124
Pronouncements of official bodies, 38–41
Proposition *13*, 108, 606
Proprietary fund budgets
  budgetary practices, 103
  changes due to managerial decisions, 105
  formula relationships in budgeting, 104
  projecting resource inflows, 103
  summarizing budgetary data, 105

Proprietary funds, 253–265
    accounting cycle, 9
    adjusting entries, 9
    budgetary practices, 103
    closing entries, 255, 262
    defined, 257–258
    enterprise funds, 104
        accounting procedures illustrated, 256–265
        ethical considerations, 292
        financial statements, 264–266
Public nonprofit organizations, 5
Pure nonprofit enterprises, 13, 14
    defined, 14
Pure profit enterprises, 13, 14
    defined, 14
Pyramiding of staff, 592

Q

Quasi-endowment funds, 462
Quasi-external transactions, 154
Quasi-nonprofit entities, 13, 15
    defined, 15
Quasi-profit entities, 13, 14
    defined, 14

R

Realization convention, 44
Recognition of encumbrances, 27, 123
Relevance in financial reporting, 35
Reliability in financial reporting, 35
Reporting needs, 7
Resource-obligation position statement, 15
Resources, stewardship of, 71
Response to financial statement analysis, 623, 624
Responsibility accounting system, 585–587
Restricted current funds. See Colleges and universities,
        Health and welfare organizations, 461, 519
Restricted funds. See Hospitals, 422, 424–426
Restricted resources, 34, 35
    and fund accounting, 34, 35
Revenue bonds, 258
Revenue-producing centers for hospitals, 414

S

Securities and Exchange Commission (SEC), 39
Service implementation costs, 521, 522
Single audit, 690–694
Sherwood, Hugh C., 75, 612
Short-term borrowing, governmental, 158
Special assessment agency fund, 230–233
    assumed transactions, 226, 227
    balance sheet, 233
    closing entry, 232
    financial statements, 233, 234
    journalizing transactions, 231
    posting transactions, 232
    reciprocal and complementing entries, 234
    statement of revenues and expenditures, 234
Special assessment capital projects funds, 227–231
    accounting objectives, 227
    assumed transactions, 226, 227
    balance sheet, 230
    budgeting, 227
    closing entries, 229
    defined, 227
    financial statements, 230, 231
    journalizing transactions, 228
    origination of, 226
    posting transactions, 229
    statement of revenues and expenditures, 231
Special assessment projects, 226–234
    assumed transactions, 226–227
    closing entries, 229, 232
    debt-related transactions, 230
    defined, 226
    ethical considerations, 233
    financing and construction transactions, 227, 228
    posting transactions, 229, 232, 233
    reciprocal and complementing entries, 233, 234
    special assessment agency fund, 230–233
        financial statements, 230, 231
    special assessment capital projects fund, 227–230
        financial statements, 230, 231
Special revenue funds, 144–212
Specific purpose funds. See Hospitals, 424
Spendable resources, 26
Standard & Poor's evaluation of municipal bonds, 75
Standards of Accounting and Financial Reporting for
        Voluntary Health and Welfare Organizations, 514,
        515
Statement of cash flows, 12, 257, 266, 268
Statement of financial performance for Model City, 360
Statements of financial accounting concepts (SFAC),
        38–39
Statements of Principles, 75–79, 452–457
    colleges and universities, 452–457
    governmental entities, 75–79
Statement of revenues, expenditures, and changes in fund
        balances (combined), 350
Stewardship of resources, 71
Substance over form, 36, 51
Summary statement of principles, governmental, 75–79
Sustentation costs, 521

T

Taxes
    and budgeting for government, 109
    and general fund accounting, 174, 176
    probable losses in collecting, 160–161

Taxpayer revolts, 108, 606
Tax rate calculation, 108
Term endowment, 462
Thought projection cases, 661–676   *See also* Cases,
    thought projection
Total return approach to endowment income, 464
Transaction convention, 44
Transfers in governmental accounting, 78, 159
Treasury Department, 383, 387
Trust and agency funds, 265–270
    financial statements, 268
    illustrated transactions, 267
    journalizing transactions, 267
    posting transactions, 267
Trust funds, 265–270

## U

Underlying assumptions, principles, and conventions,
    41–46
    basic assumption, 41
    conservatism, 42
    consistency, 43
    full disclosure, 43
    materiality, 42
    objectivity, 42
    principles, 41–46
Uniformity distinguished from consistency, 43
United Way, 41
Unrestricted current funds. *See* Colleges and universities,
    Health and welfare organizations, 461, 519
Unrestricted funds. *See* Hospitals, 419–422
Unrestricted resources, 34
  and fund accounting, 34, 35

Use of Accounting Data by Externally Interested Parties,
    605–625
  analysis and interpretation of financial data, 607
    analysis of nonprofit organization statements, 610
    analysis of profit enterprise financial statements, 608
    basic concerns, 607
    efficiency and effectiveness, 608
  evaluating the fiduciary responsibility of internal
    managers, 606
Use of fiscal agent to service debt, 225

## V

Values, assignment of, 44
Variable costs, 562
Verifiability, 36, 43
Voluntary health and welfare organizations *See* Health
    and welfare organizations
Voting rights of constituents, 7, 8

## W

Waco, Texas, budgeting for, 112–121
Worksheets, transaction for
  churches, 532
  colleges and universities, 476–481, 485–487
  consolidating governmental financial statements,
    354–357
  general fund, 188–189
  health and welfare organizations, 526–529

## Z

Zero-base budgeting, 111
Zero-base review, 582